HANDBOOK ON THE SCIENCE OF EARLY LITERACY

Also Available

Handbook of Early Literacy Research, Volume 1
edited by Susan B. Neuman and David K. Dickinson

Handbook of Early Literacy Research, Volume 2
edited by David K. Dickinson and Susan B. Neuman

Handbook of Early Literacy Research, Volume 3
edited by Susan B. Neuman and David K. Dickinson

Knowledge Development in Early Childhood:
Sources of Learning and Classroom Implications
*edited by Ashley M. Pinkham, Tanya Kaefer,
and Susan B. Neuman*

Handbook on THE SCIENCE OF EARLY LITERACY

edited by
Sonia Q. Cabell
Susan B. Neuman
Nicole Patton Terry

Foreword by David K. Dickinson

THE GUILFORD PRESS
New York   London

Copyright © 2023 The Guilford Press
A Division of Guilford Publications, Inc.
370 Seventh Avenue, Suite 1200, New York, NY 10001
www.guilford.com

Printed in the United States of America

This book is printed on acid-free paper.

Last digit is print number: 9 8 7 6 5 4 3 2 1

Library of Congress Cataloging-in-Publication data
Names: Cabell, Sonia Q., editor. | Neuman, Susan B., editor. | Terry,
    Nicole Patton, editor. | Dickinson, David K., writer of foreword.
Title: Handbook on the science of early literacy / edited by Sonia Q.
    Cabell, Susan B. Neuman, Nicole Patton Terry ; foreword by David K.
    Dickinson.
Description: New York : The Guilford Press, [2023] | Includes
    bibliographical references and index. |
Identifiers: LCCN 2023002949 | ISBN 9781462551545 (cloth)
Subjects: LCSH: Language arts (Early childhood) | Early childhood
    education—Research. | BISAC: EDUCATION / Research | EDUCATION /
    Educational Psychology
Classification: LCC LB1139.5.L35 H38 2023 | DDC 372.6—dc23/eng/20230224
LC record available at *https://lccn.loc.gov/2023002949*

For my sister, Salma, who has always inspired me to strive for greater heights.
—SQC

For all the families who contributed to our research.
You have enriched not only the science of literacy but also the researchers' lives.
—SBN

For my children, Nia, Tyson, and Jadon. You bring me joy.
—NPT

About the Editors

Sonia Q. Cabell, PhD, is Associate Professor in the School of Teacher Education and the Florida Center for Reading Research at Florida State University. Her research focuses on early language and literacy instruction, with a particular interest in the prevention of reading difficulties. Dr. Cabell has authored approximately 80 publications, including peer-reviewed articles, books, book chapters, and early childhood language and literacy curricula. She has served as Principal Investigator or co-Principal Investigator on numerous federally funded grant projects. Dr. Cabell has been an advisor or consultant for a variety of national organizations and state departments of education. She is a recipient of the International Literacy Association's Diane Lapp & James Flood Professional Collaborator Award (with Tricia Zucker). Previously, Dr. Cabell worked as a second-grade teacher and literacy coach in Oklahoma and Virginia.

Susan B. Neuman, EdD, is Professor of Teaching and Learning at New York University. Previously, she was Professor at the University of Michigan and served as the U.S. Assistant Secretary for Elementary and Secondary Education, in which role she established the Early Reading First program and the Early Childhood Educator Professional Development Program, and was responsible for all activities in Title I of the Elementary and Secondary Education Act. Dr. Neuman has served on the Board of Directors of the International Literacy Association and as coeditor of *Reading Research Quarterly*. She has received two lifetime achievement awards for research in literacy development and is a member of the Reading Hall of Fame and a Fellow of the American Educational Research Association. Dr. Neuman has published over 100 articles and numerous books.

Nicole Patton Terry, PhD, is the Olive and Manuel Bordas Professor of Education in the School of Teacher Education, Director of the Florida Center for Reading Research (FCRR), and Director of the Regional Education Lab–Southeast at Florida State University. Prior to joining FCRR, she was Associate Professor of Special Education at Georgia State University (GSU). Dr. Patton Terry is the founding director of two university-based research entities where researchers collaborate with diverse school and community stakeholders to promote student success: the Urban Child Study Center at GSU and The Village at FCRR. Her work focuses on young learners vulnerable to experiencing difficulty with language and literacy achievement in school, in particular, Black children, children growing up in poverty, and children with disabilities. Previously, Dr. Patton Terry worked as a special education teacher in Illinois.

Contributors

Stephanie Al Otaiba, PhD, Department of Teaching and Learning, Southern Methodist University, Dallas, Texas

Anita Faust Berryman, PhD, program evaluator, Alpharetta, Georgia

Gary E. Bingham, PhD, Department of Early Childhood and Elementary Education, Georgia State University, Atlanta, Georgia

Seyma Birinci, MA, Department of Educational Psychology, University of Minnesota, Minneapolis, Minnesota

Karalynn E. Brown, MEd, Department of Educational Psychology, University of Nebraska–Lincoln, Lincoln, Nebraska

Adriana G. Bus, PhD, Faculty of Arts and Education, Norwegian Reading Centre, University of Stavanger, Stavanger, Norway

Sonia Q. Cabell, PhD, School of Teacher Education, Florida State University, Tallahassee, Florida

Judith J. Carta, PhD, Juniper Gardens Children's Project, Institute for Life Span Studies, University of Kansas, Kansas City, Kansas

Kate Caton, MPA, College of Education and Human Development, Georgia State University, Atlanta, Georgia

Janelle Clay, MS, College of Education, Georgia State University, Atlanta, Georgia

Donald L. Compton, PhD, Department of Psychology, Florida State University, Tallahassee, Florida

Anne E. Cunningham, PhD, School of Education, University of California, Berkeley, Berkeley, California

Maura Curran, PhD, School of Health and Rehabilitation Sciences, Massachusetts General Hospital Institute of Health Professions, Boston, Massachusetts

Nell K. Duke, EdD, School of Education, University of Michigan, Ann Arbor, Michigan

Tonia R. Durden, PhD, Department of Early Childhood and Elementary Education, Georgia State University, Atlanta, Georgia

Ashley A. Edwards, PhD, Department of Psychology, Florida State University, Tallahassee, Florida

Allison R. Firestone, PhD, School of Education, University of California, Berkeley, Berkeley, California

Veronica P. Fleury, PhD, School of Teacher Education, Florida State University, Tallahassee, Florida

Barbara R. Foorman, PhD, School of Teacher Education, Florida State University, Tallahassee, Florida

Nicole Gardner-Neblett, PhD, Department of Psychology, University of Michigan, Ann Arbor, Michigan

Jorge E. Gonzalez, PhD, Department of Psychological, Health, and Learning Sciences, University of Houston, Houston, Texas

Amelia Wenk Gotwals, PhD, Department of Teacher Education, Michigan State University, Lansing, Michigan

Hope K. Gerde, PhD, Department of Teaching, Learning, and Culture, Texas A&M University, College Station, Texas

Charles R. Greenwood, PhD, Juniper Gardens Children's Project, Institute for Life Span Studies, University of Kansas, Kansas City, Kansas

Nuria Gutiérrez, PhD, Department of Psychology, Florida State University, Tallahassee, Florida

Annemarie H. Hindman, PhD, Department of Teaching and Learning, Temple University, Philadelphia, Pennsylvania

Trude Hoel, PhD, Faculty of Arts and Education, Norwegian Reading Centre, University of Stavanger, Stavanger, Norway

Tiffany Hogan, PhD, School of Health and Rehabilitation Sciences, Massachusetts General Hospital, Institute of Health Professions, Boston, Massachusetts

HyeJin Hwang, PhD, Department of Educational Psychology, University of Minnesota, Minneapolis, Minnesota

Nneka Ibekwe-Okafor, PhD, Wheelock College of Education and Human Development, Boston University, Boston, Massachusetts

Iheoma U. Iruka, PhD, Department of Public Policy, University of North Carolina at Chapel Hill, Chapel Hill, North Carolina

Hui Jiang, PhD, Crane Center for Early Childhood Research and Policy, The Ohio State University, Columbus, Ohio

Victoria Johnson, MA, Department of Educational Psychology, University of Minnesota, Minneapolis, Minnesota

Laura M. Justice, PhD, Crane Center for Early Childhood Research and Policy, The Ohio State University, Columbus, Ohio

Nenagh Kemp, DPhil, School of Psychological Sciences, University of Tasmania, Hobart, Tasmania, Australia

Panayiota Kendeou, PhD, Department of Educational Psychology, University of Minnesota, Minneapolis, Minnesota

James S. Kim, EdD, Graduate School of Education, Harvard University, Cambridge, Massachusetts

Young-Suk Grace Kim, EdD, School of Education, University of California, Irvine, Irvine, California

Ofra Korat, PhD, School of Education, Bar-Ilan University, Ramat-Gan, Israel

Susan H. Landry, PhD, Department of Pediatrics, University of Texas Health Science Center at Houston, Houston, Texas

Kathryn A. Leech, PhD, School of Education, University of North Carolina at Chapel Hill, Chapel Hill, North Carolina

Erica Lembke, PhD, Department of Special Education, University of Missouri, Columbia, Missouri

Nonie K. Lesaux, PhD, Graduate School of Education, Harvard University, Cambridge, Massachusetts

Julia B. Lindsey, PhD, Advanced Education Research Development Fund, Reading Reimagined, Oakland, California

Jeannette Mancilla-Martinez, EdD, Department of Special Education, Vanderbilt University, Nashville, Tennessee

Nancy C. Marencin, MEd, School of Teacher Education, Florida State, Tallahassee, Florida

Kristen L. McMaster, PhD, Department of Educational Psychology, University of Minnesota, Minneapolis, Minnesota

Douglas M. Mosher, EdM, Graduate School of Education, Harvard University, Cambridge, Massachusetts

Susan B. Neuman, EdD, Department of Teaching and Learning, New York University, New York, New York

H. N. Lam Nguyen, BSc, Department of Psychology, Carleton University, Ottawa, Ontario, Canada

Ellen Orcutt, MA, Department of Educational Psychology, University of Minnesota, Minneapolis, Minnesota

Gene Ouellette, PhD, Department of Psychology, Mount Allison University, Sackville, New Brunswick, Canada

Nicole Patton Terry, PhD, School of Teacher Education, Florida State University, Tallahassee, Florida

Beth M. Phillips, PhD, Department of Educational Psychology and Learning Systems, Florida State University, Tallahassee, Florida

Emily Phillips Galloway, EdD, Department of Teaching and Learning, Vanderbilt University, Nashville, Tennessee

Shayne B. Piasta, PhD, Department of Teaching and Learning, The Ohio State University, Columbus, Ohio

Sharolyn D. Pollard-Durodola, EdD, Department of Early Childhood, Multilingual, and Special Education, University of Nevada, Las Vegas, Las Vegas, Nevada

Valeria M. Rigobon, MS, Department of Psychology, Florida State University, Tallahassee, Florida

Rachel R. Romeo, PhD, Department of Human Development and Quantitative Methodology, University of Maryland, College Park, Maryland

Meredith L. Rowe, EdD, Graduate School of Education, Harvard University, Cambridge, Massachusetts

Dayna Russell Freudenthal, MEd, Department of Teaching and Learning, Southern Methodist University, Dallas, Texas

Amber B. Sansbury, MEd, College of Education and Human Development, George Mason University, Fairfax, Virginia

Ora Segal-Drori, PhD, Education and Early Childhood Department, Levinsky College of Education, Tel-Aviv, Israel

Monique Sénéchal, PhD, Department of Psychology, Carleton University, Ottawa, Ontario, Canada

Emma Shanahan, MEd, Department of Educational Psychology, University of Minnesota, Minneapolis, Minnesota

Susan M. Sheridan, PhD, Department of Educational Psychology, University of Nebraska–Lincoln, Lincoln, Nebraska

Laura M. Steacy, PhD, School of Teacher Education, Florida State University, Tallahassee, Florida

Sarah Surrain, PhD, Department of Pediatrics, University of Texas Health Science Center at Houston, Houston, Texas

Nicole A. Telfer, MA, Department of Psychology, University of Maryland, Baltimore County, Baltimore, Maryland

Rebecca Treiman, PhD, Department of Psychological and Brain Sciences, Washington University in St. Louis, St. Louis, Missouri

Barbara A. Wasik, PhD, Department of Teaching and Learning, Temple University, Philadelphia, Pennsylvania

Kelly Whalon, PhD, School of Teacher Education, Florida State University, Tallahassee, Florida

Crystal N. Wise, PhD, Department of Curriculum and Instruction, University of Illinois Chicago, Chicago, Illinois

Tanya S. Wright, PhD, Department of Teacher Education, Michigan State University, Lansing, Michigan

Gloria Yeomans-Maldonado, PhD, Department of Pediatrics, University of Texas Health Science Center at Houston, Houston, Texas

Mai W. Zaru, MEd, Department of Teaching and Learning, Southern Methodist University, Dallas, Texas

Mónica Zegers, MA, School of Education, University of California, Berkeley, Berkeley, California

Tricia A. Zucker, PhD, Department of Pediatrics, University of Texas Health Science Center at Houston, Houston, Texas

Foreword

This volume marks a watershed moment in the convergence of diverse fields of research around the study of early development. Until the 1970s, early literacy was studied by scholars who were primarily interested in reading instruction. Their chief goal was to determine how best to teach children to read. They made several assumptions: Children learn to read as a result of formal instruction in school; oral language plays no role in early reading; writing, while an important type of literate behavior, is of secondary importance; and teachers can successfully teach children if provided the correct instructional materials. Research focused on typically developing, monolingual speakers of English from the dominant culture in the United States. These fundamental assumptions began to be challenged in the 1980s, and over the ensuing 40 years the result has been an explosion of research that has yielded a vastly broader, deeper, and more nuanced understanding of early literacy presented in this volume.

In the 1980s, research, mostly taking the form of small scale qualitative studies, began to challenge the dominant approach to literacy, viewing it as a fascinating capacity that develops in the years before school as a result of adult support, biological maturation, and children's efforts to construct an understanding of printed language. The hallmarks of literacy were noticed in prosody and word choices as children pretended to read (Sulzby, 1985) and in nonstandard but predictable ways children began writing (Richgels, 2002; Teale & Sulzby, 1986). Careful observation of parents as they conversed with very young children during book reading (Snow, 1983) suggested that the origins of literacy can be traced back into the toddler years, and that the home also might be a place where early literacy is fostered (Tabors, Snow, & Dickinson, 2001). Preschools began to be viewed as potentially playing a role in supporting both literacy-related language and early print knowledge (Dickinson & Smith, 1994), and with that understanding came realization of the need for professional development to help teachers understand and foster literacy development (Dickinson & Caswell, 2007). As the origins of literacy were traced back into the early childhood years, the impact of broad societal factors began to be more apparent, with issues of income becoming salient. Near the turn of the century, an authoritative review of research (Whitehurst & Lonigan, 1998) marked the coming of age of this new and expanded view of the origins of literacy. During the first decades of the 20th century, research reported in this volume built on and expanded our understanding of the emergence of literacy. Research has moved beyond only studying typically developing, monolingual children to examining the literacy and language development of children who speak languages other than English, are racially diverse, come from many cultures, and have developmental disabilities. Over the past 20 years, a multitude of studies has revealed how literacy emerges from a confluence of capacities that are fostered by early and lasting environmental supports, that have bidirectional effects on each other, and that contribute to later reading comprehension (reviewed in Dickinson & Morse, 2019). These include language (Dickinson & Porche, 2011; Rowe, 2008, 2012; Storch & Whitehurst, 2002), executive function (Blair & Raver,

2015; Kuhn et al., 2014), and theory of mind (Muller, Liebermann-Finestone, Carpendale, Hammond, & Bibok, 2012).

Chapters in this volume describe the latest advances in our understanding of the capacities children are acquiring and how families support literacy from infancy through the early school years. Writing development, now viewed as part of the constellation of literacy-related capacities that begin flourishing in the preschool years and continue developing in the early school years, also is discussed from multiple perspectives. Novel strategies for enhancing children's opportunities to become fluent readers by providing teachers with professional development at scale, by including content-rich material as part of the curriculum, and by taking advantage of the affordances of digital tools also are addressed. In summary, in this volume, the leading scholars from multiple disciplines report the sophisticated approaches they employ to study how early literacy develops and promising strategies for fostering its development among all children.

DAVID K. DICKINSON, EdD
Vanderbilt University

References

Blair, C., & Raver, C. C. (2015). School readiness and self-regulation: A developmental psychobiological approach. *Annual Review of Psychology, 66,* 711–731.

Dickinson, D. K., & Caswell, L. (2007). Building support for language and early literacy in preschool classrooms through in-service professional development: Effects of the Literacy Environment Enrichment Program (LEEP). *Early Childhood Research Quarterly, 22*(2), 243–260.

Dickinson, D. K., & Morse, A. B. (2019). *Connecting through talk: Nurturing children's development with language.* Brookes.

Dickinson, D. K., & Porche, M. V. (2011). Relation between language experiences in preschool classrooms and children's kindergarten and fourth-grade language and reading abilities. *Child Development, 82*(3), 870–886.

Dickinson, D. K., & Smith, M. W. (1994). Long-term effects of preschool teachers' book readings on low-income children's vocabulary and story comprehension. *Reading Research Quarterly, 29*(2), 105–122.

Kuhn, L. J., Willoughby, M. T., Wilbourn, M. P., Vernon-Feagans, L., Blair, C. B., & the Family Life Project Key Developers. (2014). Early communicative gestures prospectively predict language development and executive function in early childhood. *Child Development, 85*(5), 1898–1914.

Muller, U., Liebermann-Finestone, D. P., Carpendale, J. I. M., Hammond, S. I., & Bibok, M. B. (2012). Knowing minds, controlling actions: The developmental relations between theory of mind and executive function from 2 to 4 years of age. *Journal of Experimental Child Psychology, 111*(2), 331–348.

Richgels, D. J. (2002). Invented spelling, phonemic awareness, and reading and writing instruction. In S. B. Neuman & D. K. Dickinson (Eds.), *Handbook of early literacy research* (Vol. 1, pp. 142–158). Guilford Press.

Rowe, M. L. (2008). Child-directed speech: Relation to socioeconomic status, knowledge of child development and child vocabulary skill. *Journal of Child Language, 35*(1), 185–205.

Rowe, M. L. (2012). A longitudinal investigation of the role of quantity and quality of child-directed speech in vocabulary development. *Child Development, 83*(5), 1762–1774.

Snow, C. E. (1983). Literacy and language: Relationships during the preschool years. *Harvard Educational Review, 53*(2), 165–189.

Storch, S. A., & Whitehurst, G. J. (2002). Oral language and code-related precursors to reading: Evidence from a longitudinal structural model. *Developmental Psychology, 38*(6), 934–947.

Sulzby, E. (1985). Children's emergent reading of favorite storybooks. *Reading Research Quarterly, 20*(4), 458–481.

Tabors, P. O., Snow, C. E., & Dickinson, D. K. (2001). Homes and schools together: Supporting language and literacy development. In D. K. Dickinson & P. O. Tabors (Eds.), *Beginning literacy with language: Young children learning at home and school* (pp. 313–334). Brookes.

Teale, W., & Sulzby, E. (1986). *Emergent literacy: Reading and writing.* Ablex.

Whitehurst, G. J., & Lonigan, C. J. (1998). Child development and emergent literacy. *Child Development, 69*(3), 848–872.

Acknowledgments

We would like to express gratitude to the following editorial assistants, who are doctoral students in Reading Education in the School of Teacher Education and in the Florida Center for Reading Research at Florida State University: Sen Wang (lead), Jenny Passalacqua, Debbie Slik, and Rhonda Raines. Their excitement for this volume was contagious, and their tireless work was much appreciated. In addition to carefully reviewing individual chapters, they also helped to write the chapter summaries that appear in the Introduction.

Contents

PART III. DEVELOPMENT AND INSTRUCTION
OF MEANING-RELATED LITERACY SKILLS

PART IV. USING THE SCIENCE OF EARLY LITERACY
IN PROFESSIONAL DEVELOPMENT AND FAMILY ENGAGEMENT

PART V. USING THE SCIENCE OF EARLY LITERACY TO SUPPORT EQUITY

PART VI. USING THE SCIENCE OF EARLY LITERACY
TO LEARN ACROSS BOUNDARIES

Introduction

Sonia Q. Cabell, Susan B. Neuman, and Nicole Patton Terry

The science of reading has been thrust into the national spotlight in recent years, with the media calling attention to the troubling lack of knowledge teachers have about how early literacy develops and how to provide effective instruction. This is particularly concerning for children who are vulnerable to experiencing poor school readiness and early achievement outcomes in U.S. schools, including children growing up in poverty and low-income households, children in race- and ethnic-minority groups, children who are dual language learners or who are multilingual, and children with disabilities. Although the COVID-19 global pandemic has only amplified long-standing educational disparities, it is likely that the long-term consequence for student achievement will be substantial. Now more than ever, it is essential that those who are training to be researchers, professors, administrators, teacher leaders, and instructional coaches have informative, research-based sources that codify the accumulated science.

This volume, *Handbook on the Science of Early Literacy*, presents accumulated scientific knowledge about early literacy development and instruction (preschool through grade 2) from experts in the field who have conducted cutting-edge and transformative research.

As part of the handbook's design, we purposefully embraced the following:

- Interdisciplinary perspectives
- A range of populations and topics
- Both reading *and* writing research, along with the early skills that underpin both areas (e.g., oral language, alphabet knowledge)
- Broad views on the science of early literacy
- Bridging the preschool and primary grades research literatures

Although it is impossible to comprehensively include all topic areas and perspectives, this volume provides a solid base for those seeking to develop the next generation of scholars in the field of early literacy research across multiple disciplines. It is our hope that it also provides foundational knowledge on the science of early literacy that will be essential for district leaders and organizations seeking to make change.

The handbook is divided into six parts that cover conceptualization, development and instruction (of both code- and meaning-related literacy skills), professional development and family engagement, supporting equity across populations, and learning across boundaries. Where applicable, we provide cross-references to relevant chapters in the handbook.

Contents of This Handbook

Part I: Conceptualizing the Science of Early Literacy

Part I of the volume presents theories and frameworks that provide a basis for how to think about children's early literacy development, including environmental influences and instructional processes.

In Chapter 1, Y.-S. Kim reviews the simple view of reading (SVR) and its associated empirical evidence, and presents an expanded theoretical model called the *direct and indirect effects model of reading* (DIER). She discusses several compelling hypotheses that stem from the hierarchical, interactive, and dynamic relations among skills delineated by the DIER.

In Chapter 2, Rowe, Romeo, and Leech examine environmental influences on children's oral language development from birth through the preschool period, to include vocabulary, syntactic, and pragmatic skills development. They emphasize the importance of social interactions in language development, explain neural mechanisms, and examine causal intervention effects that elucidate the importance of environmental influences on children's language development.

In Chapter 3, Mancilla-Martinez points out the diversity within the population of dual language learners (DLLs) and challenges the "at-risk" label often associated with DLLs. She argues for prioritizing the assessment of language comprehension in the earliest grades to allow children to use their full linguistic repertoires and conceptual knowledge.

In Chapter 4, Russell Freudenthal, Zaru, and Al Otaiba describe promising early literacy interventions that can be used within response to intervention (RTI) and multi-tiered systems of support (MTSS) approaches in kindergarten through third grade. Drawing on the SVR and data-based decision making, the authors describe their theoretical and empirical framework, followed by an overview of the effects reported in recent studies of early literacy interventions.

Romeo, in Chapter 5, explains early literacy development through the perspective of neuroscience. She introduces the neuroanatomy of the reading brain and how the brain develops during literacy acquisition. She then discusses individual differences in the neural architecture that supports reading, concluding that a better understanding of these differences can potentially reduce existing disparities in literacy development.

Part II: Development and Instruction of Code-Related Literacy Skills

Part II provides insight into the development and instruction code-related literacy skills, including how children learn to decode and the role of spelling in both reading and writing.

Foorman, in Chapter 6, discusses how children learn to encode and decode an alphabetic orthography. She first describes the characteristics of the English alphabetic orthography. She then explains how children learn to identify and recognize words and discusses both the SVR and the reading systems framework. She concludes with an examination of evidence-based instructional practices and challenges to implementation.

In Chapter 7, Piasta focuses on one important aspect of learning the code—alphabet knowledge. She discusses ways to support young children's alphabet knowledge, thoroughly reviews the extant research base on instruction, and outlines promising practices such as combining letter-name and letter-sound instruction, including explicit instruction and embedded mnemonics, and utilizing quicker pacing.

In Chapter 8, Sénéchal, Ouellette, and Nguyen provide a comprehensive review of invented spelling. They first provide thorough descriptions of children's early spelling attempts, then synthesize correlational studies that examine the associations among invented spelling, other important early literacy skills, reading, and conventional spelling. Finally, they extensively review intervention research that collectively demonstrates that invented spelling can play a causal role in the acquisition of more advanced literacy skills.

Likewise, Kemp and Treiman, in Chapter 9, take a deep dive into children's spelling development. They highlight the concept of statistical learning and inner and outer visual forms of writing, noting differences with existing stage or phase models of spelling. These differences have significant implications for spelling instruction.

In Chapter 10, McMaster, Birinci, Shanahan, and Lembke describe early writing assessment and intervention research in grades 1–3 using a data-based instruction (DBI) approach. They frame their chapter in the context of the SVR, followed by an overview of DBI, then detail a program of research in which they applied these frameworks to support teachers' individualization of writing instruction, including a discussion of assessment and professional development tools.

Part III: Development and Instruction of Meaning-Related Literacy Skills

Part III focuses on the development and instruction of meaning-related literacy skills, emphasizing the language basis of comprehension and examining language interventions in the early childhood period. In addition, several chapters advocate for integrated instruction to support comprehension, with particular attention paid to the integration of oral language and content knowledge.

In Chapter 11, Justice and Jiang outline the connection between early language development and later reading comprehension. They argue that language is the basis for skilled reading, highlighting the work of the Language and Reading Research Consortium (LARRC). This body of work examined the dimensionality of language skills and the positive impact of a language-focused curricular supplement, focusing on explicit instruction of both lower- and higher-level skills, on children's language skills and reading comprehension.

In a similar vein, Phillips, in Chapter 12, summarizes an ongoing program of research on small-group, supplemental language-focused interventions for children in preschool and kindergarten. Specifically, she discusses the development and testing of three interventions that target language broadly, including semantics, syntax, and narrative text structure and listening comprehension. The interventions are built on a theoretical framework that emphasizes the child as an active language learner and include an emphasis on eliciting increasingly complex language from children. Phillips reports both proximal and distal impacts of these interventions on children's language skills, along with the modular nature of these impacts.

In Chapter 13, Pollard-Durodola and Gonzalez highlight the project Words of Oral Reading and Language Development (WORLD), a content-enriched, interactive, shared book-reading intervention for young children that focuses on social studies themes. Through scaffolded textual and extratextual conversations that simultaneously support children's language and knowledge, WORLD demonstrates a positive impact on monolingual English and DLL children's learning.

Wright and Gotwals, in Chapter 14, outline their research focusing on the integration of science and literacy in the early elementary grades as a way to promote learning across both domains. Taking a disciplinary literacy perspective, they describe the development and key components of the SOLID Start curriculum, including the five instructional strategies of Ask, Explore, Read, Write, and Synthesize. They also discuss professional development to support teachers in their science talk.

Taking a complementary perspective of integrating content-rich instruction into English language arts (ELA), Cabell and Hwang (Chapter 15) discuss how this type of instruction can be leveraged to improve children's language comprehension. They review the extant literature on the impact of integrated approaches on children's vocabulary and comprehension, followed by an examination of the effects of content-rich ELA instruction more specifically.

Integration of literacy instruction, however, goes beyond language and knowledge, and Duke, Lindsey, and Wise (Chapter 16) introduce *instructional simultaneity*, in which instruction addresses multiple targets at once. In addition to literacy and content-area knowledge integration, research demonstrates that multiple reading foundational skills and language arts processes can be addressed simultaneously, along with the development of literacy bridging processes.

Orcutt, Johnson, and Kendeou, in Chapter 17, discuss comprehension as a generalized cognitive process and learning product. Because comprehension is an important cognitive outcome across many contexts and media formats, it can be developed early on through nonreading contexts and transferred to reading comprehension later. The authors discuss the inferential language comprehension (iLC) framework serving as a theoretical guide for designing curricula. They describe Inference Galaxy—a suite of instructional tools using the iLC framework—and the evidence for its usability, feasibility, and promise.

Part IV: Using the Science of Early Literacy in Professional Development and Family Engagement

Improving teacher knowledge and practice are important targets of professional development. Moreover, teachers need guidance on promoting family engagement through school and home partnerships. Part IV examines the extant research on professional development and family engagement.

In Chapter 18, Cunningham, Firestone, and Zegers articulate the need for teachers to have both early literacy subject-matter content knowledge and pedagogical content knowledge, synthesizing the existing literature on the topic. They discuss the importance of conducting professional development in small groups over extended periods of time and the need for both well-designed, relationship-based professional learning opportunities and precise measures that can evaluate their effectiveness.

Hindman and Wasik, in Chapter 19, point out that professional development is a "linchpin" in the translation of the science of early literacy to classroom instruction. Their research is designed to bolster language development by supporting teachers in refining their linguistic interactions with young children by providing teachers with professional development to improve both their conceptual and procedural knowledge. The authors describe the development of their efficacious professional development model, refined through multiple iterations over time and across varied contexts.

In addition to the importance of professional development in language instructional practices, teachers also benefit from professional development in early writing practices. Gerde and Bingham, in Chapter 20, detail a fully online professional learning program designed to promote early language and literacy skills through high-quality writing instruction in preschool classrooms. The authors also examine what the science reveals about promoting early writing development, then describe how it was used to design professional learning, followed by the outcomes of engagement in professional learning for teachers and children.

Although professional development research has demonstrated efficacy across multiple areas of early literacy, scaling up interventions in a way that can have a broader impact has been an ongoing challenge. In Chapter 21, Kim and Mosher argue that the concept of *structured adaptations* should play a more central role in models for scaling up evidence-based literacy interventions. Specifically, they recommend that teachers receive guidance on how to make productive adaptations that maintain implementation fidelity and build teachers' motivation. Using four proof-of-concept case studies, they demonstrate that using structured adaptations is a feasible and effective approach, yielding principles that may generalize across different types of interventions.

Shifting from professional development efforts to family engagement, Zucker, Yeomans-Maldonado, Surrain, and Landry (Chapter 22) argue for aligned school and home intervention efforts to improve children's learning. They first describe a framework for early childhood MTSS, including the unique affordances of this over tradi-

tional family engagement approaches. They then explain the initial tests of this model that demonstrate the promise of doing more with teachers and parents together, rather than with interventions in the school or the home setting alone. The authors end with a call for other researchers to examine school-home MTSS that will further elucidate the potential of this approach.

Similarly, in Chapter 23, Brown and Sheridan review the links between family engagement and early literacy, describing two evidence-based family–school partnership approaches. They argue for a partnership model that is distinct from a parent involvement paradigm, characterized by reciprocal relationships and complementary roles among school and home systems.

Part V: Using the Science of Early Literacy to Support Equity

In addition to the science informing professional development and family engagement efforts, in this section authors argue that the science of early literacy can be used to support equitable opportunities for all children.

In Chapter 24, Phillips Galloway and Lesaux synthesize research focused on early literacy skills, both code- and meaning-related, among multilingual learners (MLLs) and describe contexts of literacy learning and teaching for MLLs. Importantly, the authors attend to the ways educational inequities shape literacy learning opportunities for MLLs and argue for a careful design of *literacy architectures* in schools, which are blueprints that create settings and systems of learning and teaching to propel MLLs' literacy development. They illustrate this idea using the advanced literacy leadership framework, which has been adopted in large urban districts in the United States.

In Chapter 25, Compton, Steacy, Gutiérrez, Rigobon, Edwards, and Marencin discuss *lexical asymmetry* among children with dyslexia, which refers to an uneven pattern of growth in the subsystems that comprise the orthographic lexicon. The authors hypothesize that lexical asymmetry results in a reduction of successful self-teaching opportunities because of limited knowledge of sublexical orthographic-to-phonological connections. Lexical asymmetry may also lead to processing only partial information from words and a dependence on more global orthographic processing, which limits the ability of children with dyslexia to develop advanced word reading and spelling skills. The results of both computational and behavioral modeling that support these hypotheses is discussed, along a few suggestions for targeted instruction.

Curran and Hogan (Chapter 26) discuss a common learning disability, developmental language disorder (DLD), its key characteristics, comorbidities, and impact on children's short- and long-term outcomes. They outline a call to action for both researchers and educators to best support children with DLD in the early years.

In Chapter 27, Whalon and Fleury review the state of the science of early literacy for children with autism spectrum disorder (ASD), with particular attention to the preschool period. Acknowledging that the extant literature base is still in its infancy, they describe findings from two independent research teams, both focused on interactive shared reading, which converge in the conclusion that to offset later reading comprehension difficulties, quality early language and literacy interventions are necessary for children with ASD.

Carta and Greenwood, in Chapter 28, address how MTSS in preschool can reduce disparities in early literacy outcomes and increase equity in learning opportunities for young children. Acknowledging the challenges that early education programs face in addressing the individual needs and strengths of children, the authors outline issues around access to quality Tier 1 instruction, culturally responsive measures to identify children in need of additional support, and Tier 2 interventions to address these needs.

In Chapter 29, Iruka, Sansbury, Telfer, Ibekwe-Okafor, Gardner-Neblett, and Durden challenge researchers to center an anti-racist and equity lens when considering young Black children's development. They implore others not to look at ways to "fix" Black children and their families, but rather to fix the racist systems and institutions that continue to oppress and deny equitable opportunities that promote and support Black children's development and learning.

Part VI: Using the Science of Early Literacy to Learn across Boundaries

The final section of the handbook examines how the science of early literacy can be used to help children learn beyond traditional boundaries, with chapters focusing on learning: out of school, within digital contexts, and within the context of research–practice partnerships.

Neuman, in Chapter 30, discusses how literacy learning can effectively take place outside of school contexts in hybrid spaces that foster language and content-rich learning through everyday interactions. Using a learning ecology framework, she provides several examples of how modest transformations in public spaces (e.g., laundromats, grocery stores, salons) can shape novel learning opportunities for young children. Neuman also highlights how literacy learning can be distributed across time and resources in these multiple settings, contributing to a young child's overall learning ecology.

Bus and Hoel, in Chapter 31, discuss the promise of digital picture books by presenting evidence-based insights into which digital enhancements are beneficial for children's meaning making and incidental word learning. They then review research regarding digital books' potential impact on book-reading routines in families with a particular focus on MLLs. The chapter ends with a set of recommendations for enhancing and investigating the utility of digital books in the early years.

Relatedly, Korat and Segal-Drori (Chapter 32) discuss how ebooks with digital dictionaries can promote word learning. They examine how these dictionaries can impact children's vocabulary development, including discussion on dictionary design, children's independent ebook reading compared to adult–child printed book reading, ebook reading with a dictionary together with an adult, and use of the ebook with a dictionary by children with learning difficulties.

In Chapter 33, Terry, Bingham, Berryman, Clay, and Caton discuss how robust research–practice partnerships can help to overcome systems-level obstacles for children who are vulnerable to experiencing difficulty in school, through the use of research and evidence to create change. In the context of Atlanta 323, a research–practice partnership focused on creating a cohesive preschool to third-grade early learning system, the authors describe lessons learned, delineating both challenges and opportunities.

PART I

CONCEPTUALIZING THE SCIENCE OF EARLY LITERACY

CHAPTER 1

Simplicity Meets Complexity

Expanding the Simple View of Reading
with the Direct and Indirect Effects Model of Reading

Young-Suk Grace Kim

Reading comprehension—understanding, interpreting, and evaluating written texts—is a highly complex construct that involves "the process of simultaneously constructing and extracting meaning through interaction and engagement with print" (Snow, 2002, p. 413) and requires "the most intricate workings of the human mind" (Huey, 1968, p. 6). Given the ubiquitous demand of reading in contemporary information-driven society, it is critical to understand the skills that contribute to reading comprehension. One of the theories of reading comprehension that has garnered tremendous attention in the last three decades is the simple view of reading (SVR; Gough & Tunmer, 1986). In this chapter, I review the SVR and associated empirical evidence. I then present a recent theoretical model called the direct and indirect effects model of reading (DIER; Kim, 2017, 2020a, 2020b), which builds on and critically expands and integrates the SVR and other theories and lines of work.

The SVR

The central argument of the SVR is that reading comprehension involves word reading and linguistic comprehension processes; therefore, decoding or word reading (D) and linguistic comprehension (C) are two essential skills that contribute to reading comprehension (R = D × C), and neither of them is sufficient alone (Gough & Tunmer, 1986; Hoover & Gough, 1990). Decoding (called word reading hereafter) is the skill to "read isolated words quickly, accurately, and silently," and linguistic comprehension is the "process by which given lexical (i.e., word) information, sentences and discourses are interpreted" (Gough & Tunmer, 1986, p. 7; see revised definitions of these in Hoover & Tunmer, 2018).

The SVR is robustly supported across languages and writing systems, and first and second language (L1 and L2) learners (e.g., for review of evidence, see Florit & Cain, 2011; Kim, 2022). Indeed, word reading and linguistic comprehension are two powerful predictors of reading comprehension, explaining the vast majority of variance in reading comprehension when constructs are measured with little measurement error (i.e., using latent variables). For example, Kim (2017) found that word reading and listening comprehension (comprehension of oral passages) explained 100% of the variance in reading comprehension for English-speaking students in second grade. Similar findings were reported for

Korean-speaking children (Kim, 2015a), Norwegian-speaking children (Hjetland et al., 2019), and Romanian-speaking children (Dolean, Lervag, Visu-Petra, & Melby-Lervag, 2021).

The product term (D × C) indicates that both word reading and linguistic comprehension are necessary, because 0 in either word reading or linguistic comprehension leads to 0 in reading comprehension—lack of either skill leads to unsuccessful reading comprehension (Gough & Tunmer, 1986; Kirby & Savage, 2008). The product term also indicates moderation: The contribution of word reading to reading comprehension differs for individuals with low versus high linguistic comprehension, and the contribution of linguistic comprehension to reading comprehension differs for individuals with high versus low word reading (see Hoover & Gough, 1990). Although this hypothesis was not supported in cross-sectional studies (e.g., Joshi & Aaron, 2000; Lee & Wheldall, 2009), longitudinal studies and cross-sectional studies with children in different developmental stages of reading showed differential importance of word reading versus linguistic comprehension as a function of reading development: Word reading skill dominates reading comprehension during the beginning phase of reading development, whereas linguistic comprehension makes increasingly greater contributions as word-reading skill develops (Adlof, Catts, & Little, 2006; Hoover & Gough, 1990; Kim & Wagner, 2015).

The power of the SVR is its intuitive simplicity: Intra- and interindividual differences in reading comprehension are explained by only two skills, word reading and linguistic comprehension. This is a powerful way of thinking about reading comprehension and a crucial way by which the SVR has contributed to the field. This has a straightforward implication that is of high utility: If success or difficulties with reading comprehension arise from word reading and linguistic comprehension (Catts, Adlof, & Ellis Weismer, 2006; Hoover & Gough, 1990), both need to be assessed and taught. One way in which the SVR is operationalized is through identifying individuals' strengths and needs according to their skills in word reading and linguistic comprehension (Castles, Rastle, & Nation, 2018; Catts et al., 2006): (1) high in word reading and high in linguistic comprehension (high–high), (2) high in word reading and low in linguistic comprehension (high–low), (3) low in word reading and high in linguistic comprehension (low–high),

and (4) low in word reading and low in linguistic comprehension (low–low). This information then informs instruction. For example, students with the high–low profile—high word reading and low linguistic comprehension—would need more intensive instruction on linguistic comprehension than word reading, whereas students with the low–high profile—low word reading and high linguistic comprehension—would have the opposite need. Students with the low–low profile—low word reading and low linguistic comprehension—would need intensive instruction on both word reading and linguistic comprehension.

Expanding the SVR

Simplicity for a complex construct comes at a cost, however, and there are several important limitations of the SVR. First and foremost, the SVR does not present a full picture about reading comprehension, as it does not specify sources and mechanisms for the development of word reading and linguistic comprehension (Castles et al., 2018). Word reading and linguistic comprehension are the "proximal" causes of reading comprehension (Gough & Tunmer, 1986, p. 8); that is, word reading and linguistic comprehension are two necessary skills for reading comprehension from a 20,000-foot or bird's-eye view (Kim, 2020c). A 20,000-foot view helps describe reading comprehension in simple terms, but it presents a considerable challenge, as it does not fully address the *what* question (what skills contribute to word reading and linguistic comprehension), nor does it address the *why* and *how* questions (why and how skills relate to reading comprehension). No articulation on mechanisms entails no information about how to improve word reading and linguistic comprehension. The SVR noted the importance of phoneme–grapheme correspondence knowledge for word reading but was silent about other factors such as morphological awareness, factors that influence linguistic comprehension, and the relation between word reading and linguistic comprehension. The simplicity of the SVR has been subject to many criticisms (e.g., Barrs, Pradl, Hall, & Dombey, 2008; Castles et al., 2018; Cervetti et al., 2020; Duke & Cartwright, 2021; Kirby & Savage, 2008; Pressley et al., 2009).

Second, a large body of research in the past three decades has revealed that numerous language and cognitive skills and knowledge beyond word reading and linguistic comprehension contribute to reading comprehension, including text reading fluency, text structure knowledge, content/topic knowledge, inference, perspective taking, comprehension monitoring, morphological awareness, working memory, and attentional control. An outstanding question is whether and how these numerous constructs fit together coherently with word reading and linguistic comprehension. If word reading and linguistic comprehension explain the vast majority of variance in reading comprehension, are the other skills and knowledge reported in the literature superfluous? Are they related to word reading and linguistic comprehension and if so, how?

Last, the SVR was ambiguous about the constructs of decoding and linguistic comprehension, which led to various interpretations and approaches to measuring them (see Castles et al., 2018; Kirby & Savage, 2008). Particularly relevant to this point is the construct of linguistic comprehension—the earlier definition did not provide a clear picture about how to operationalize it, nor did it recognize its complexity. Not surprisingly, linguistic comprehension has been operationalized in multiple divergent ways, including as vocabulary (e.g., Ouellette & Beers, 2010), syntactic knowledge or sentence skills (e.g., Yeung, Ho, Chan, & Chung, 2016), passage or story comprehension (e.g., Kim, 2015a, 2017, 2020a, 2020b; Mancilla-Martinez, Kieffer, Biancarosa, Christodoulou, & Snow, 2011), story retell (e.g., Shapiro, Fritschmann, Thomas, Hughes, & McDougal, 2014), or various combinations of these (e.g., Adlof et al., 2006; Braze et al., 2016; Catts et al., 2006; Foorman, Koon, Petscher, Mitchell, & Truckenmiller, 2015; Ho et al., 2017; Lonigan, Burgess, & Schatschneider, 2018; Tunmer & Chapman, 2012). Together, this rich body of literature revealed that oral language skills broadly contribute to reading comprehension. However, inconsistency in measurement has hindered development of a coherent picture about the construct of linguistic comprehension, the relations among different aspects of oral language skills, and the nature of their roles in reading comprehension.

The DIER

The DIER (Kim, 2020a, 2020b) is an integrative theoretical model that builds on and integrates influential theoretical models and lines of work

such as the SVR, the triangle model (Harm & Seidenberg, 2004), construction–integration model (Kintsch, 1988), reading systems framework (Perfetti & Stafura, 2014), and automaticity theory (LaBerge & Samuels, 1974) into a single unifying model. The DIER is a component skills model that specifies individuals' skills and knowledge (called component skills hereafter) that contribute to reading comprehension, *and* the relations among skills. The skills develop via interactions between individual characteristics and multiple layers of environmental influences (e.g., home language and literacy environment, formal instruction, policy; van Bergen, van der Leiji, & de Jong, 2014). The DIER explicitly specifies the interactions between individual skills and the immediate activity and task environment (including assessment features and text characteristics) in which reading is embedded (see the dynamic relations hypothesis below). Theories that focus on reading comprehension processes have been well articulated before (e.g., Kintsch, 1988; McNamara & Magliano, 2009; van den Broek, Rapp, & Kendeou, 2005), and the DIER articulates the skills that are involved in and contribute to the comprehension processes.

Component Skills of Reading Comprehension

The skills that contribute to reading comprehension according to the DIER (see Figure 1.1) are word reading; knowledge and awareness of phonology, orthography, and morphology; listening comprehension; vocabulary; grammatical knowledge (morphosyntactic and syntactic knowledge); higher-order cognitions and regulations (e.g., reasoning, inference, perspective taking, goal setting, comprehension monitoring, and metacognitive strategies); background knowledge (content/topic knowledge, world knowledge, and discourse and genre knowledge such as text structure and genre-associated linguistic features); text reading fluency, social–emotional factors[1] (e.g., reading motivation, attitude and interest, efficacy, anxiety); and domain-general cognitions or executive functions (e.g., working memory, inhibitory and attentional control). See Kim (2020b) for a review of empirical evidence.

Architecture of Relations among Skills

The DIER does not simply catalogue skills. Instead, it specifies hierarchical, interactive, and dynamic relations among skills.

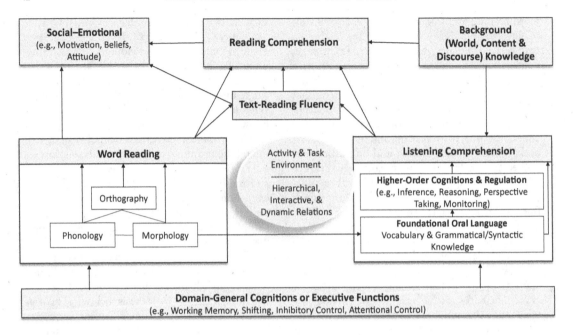

FIGURE 1.1. The direct and indirect effects model of reading (DIER; Kim, 2020a, 2020b). The majority of paths are shown as unidirectional, but they develop interactively (see text). Copyright © 2020 American Psychological Association. Reprinted by permission.

The *hierarchical relations hypothesis* states that lower-order skills support higher-order skills in a cascading manner. The skills in DIER are not a series of independent or disconnected constructs; instead, they are connected systematically in a chain of relations. Proximal predictors of reading comprehension are text reading fluency, word reading, and listening comprehension, and these skills mediate the contributions of other skills to reading comprehension. Text reading fluency, widely known as *oral reading fluency*, is one's skill in reading connected texts with accuracy, speed, and expression (reading prosody; see National Institute of Child Health and Human Development, 2000) and is built on automaticity theory[2] (Jenkins, Fuchs, van den Broek, Espin, & Deno, 2003; Kim, 2015b; LaBerge & Samuels, 1974; Wolf & Katzir-Cohen, 2001). Although extensive research has shown its strong relation to reading comprehension (see Kim et al., 2021, for a review), text reading fluency has not been explicitly accounted for in previous theoretical models of reading comprehension. In the DIER, text reading fluency is specified as a mediator in the relation of word reading and listening comprehension to reading comprehension (Kim, 2015b; Kim, Quinn, & Petscher, 2021; Kim &

Wagner, 2015; see Figure 1.1). Text reading fluency is a text-level reading skill that emerges and develops from word reading skill, but it is a dissociable construct from word reading skill because it involves postlexical processing that is inherent in connected text reading (or reading in context), but not in context-free word reading (or reading a list of words; Jenkins et al., 2003; Kim, 2015b; Wolf & Katzir-Cohen, 2001). The postlexical semantic processing implies that text reading fluency draws on language comprehension over and above word reading (Kim, 2015b; Kim & Wagner, 2015).

The nature of mediation varies for word reading versus listening comprehension and depends on the developmental phase of reading skill. In the beginning phase of reading development (e.g., beginning of grade 1 for English-speaking children), word-reading and text-reading fluency are very strongly related and largely overlap. With reading development, text-reading fluency increasingly mediates the contribution of word reading to reading comprehension, leading to a complete mediation of text-reading fluency at a later phase of reading development (e.g., grade 2 for English-speaking children; Kim & Wagner, 2015). In contrast, listening comprehension does not contribute to text-reading fluency in the beginning phase of reading development over and above word reading due to the large constraining role of word-reading skills. As word-reading skills develop, the constraining role of word reading decreases, and individuals' listening comprehension begins to contribute to text-reading fluency (Kim, 2015b). However, unlike word reading, text-reading fluency never completely mediates the relation of listening comprehension to reading comprehension (Kim & Wagner, 2015) because postlexical comprehension processes captured in text-reading fluency tap shallow comprehension, not deep comprehension (Kim, 2015b). This is a theoretically vital point, as this is precisely why text-reading fluency is a dissociable construct from reading comprehension (Kim, 2015b). Previous theoretical accounts acknowledged that text-reading fluency taps comprehension processes (Jenkins et al., 2003; Wolf & Katzir-Cohen, 2001), but they did not articulate how text-reading fluency is different from reading comprehension.

A crucial part of the hierarchical relations hypothesis is the specification of the skills that contribute to word reading and listening comprehension. Causal factors for word-reading skill are phonological, orthographic, and morphological awareness in line with the triangle model (Adams, 1990; Harm & Seidenberg, 2004), and their relative importance varies depending on the orthographic depth and linguistic and orthographic features of a focal language (see Kim, 2020a, 2020b). Importantly, the DIER also unpacks listening comprehension. Note that the term *listening comprehension,* not linguistic comprehension, is used in the DIER for theoretical precision and clarity of measurement. Listening comprehension refers to comprehension of oral texts such as sentences and texts including multiutterance conversations, stories, and informational texts (Kim, 2015a, 2016, 2020a, 2020b). Listening comprehension is a discourse skill that is equivalent to reading comprehension (Hoover & Gough, 1990; Kim, 2015a)—the only difference between listening and reading comprehension is whether texts are oral or written. This implies that listening comprehension involves the same complex construction and integration processes as reading comprehension except for word-reading processes involved in reading comprehension. This also means that listening comprehension, like reading comprehension, draws on background knowledge, higher-order cogni-

tions and regulations, vocabulary, grammatical knowledge, and domain-general cognitions (Figure 1.1; see Kim, 2016, for a theoretical model and a review of empirical evidence, and the mapping of these skills with different mental representations during comprehension processes). Clear and precise definition of listening comprehension has an important implication for measurement. Strictly speaking, operationalizing linguistic comprehension as vocabulary or syntactic knowledge without discourse comprehension of oral texts does not fully test the SVR, because listening and reading comprehension should be measured in an *equivalent* manner according to the SVR. Because reading comprehension is generally conceptualized and measured as comprehension of connected texts (sentences and passages; i.e., discourse), measurement of listening comprehension should be of connected texts, not of vocabulary or syntax. Listening comprehension, vocabulary, and syntactic knowledge are all oral language skills, but they are different in hierarchy, and vocabulary and syntactic knowledge contribute to listening comprehension (Kim, 2020a, 2020b).

The recognition of listening comprehension as a discourse skill is a crucial point that allows unification of the SVR with other large bodies of work that revealed the contributions of many skills (e.g., working memory, morphological awareness, inference) to reading comprehension. According to the DIER, these skills are not superfluous, but instead, they are necessary for the two powerful predictors according to the SVR, word reading and listening comprehension. Phonological awareness, orthographic awareness, and morphological awareness contribute to word reading; vocabulary, grammatical knowledge, higher-order cognitions and regulations, and background knowledge contribute to listening comprehension; and domain-general cognitive skills or executive functions contribute to all. A heuristic that illustrates this idea is found in Figure 1.2. The structure of the building is sustained by word reading and listening comprehension, while text-reading fluency bridges word reading and listening comprehension to reading comprehension. Word reading is built on the foundation of phonological, orthographic, and morphological awareness, while listening comprehension is built on the foundation of higher-order cognitions and regulations, vocabulary, and grammatical knowledge. At the very foundation are domain-general cognitions or executive functions. Background (world, content and discourse) knowledge closely interacts with comprehension and associated skills, and social–emotional factors closely interact with reading skills (word reading, text reading such as text-reading fluency and reading comprehension).

A corollary of the hierarchical relations hypothesis is a cascade or chains of relations; that is, not all the skills are directly related to reading comprehension, and instead, they have direct and indirect relations via a series of interconnections. For example, phonological awareness is important to word reading, which in turn is important to text-reading fluency and reading comprehension. Therefore, the effect of phonological awareness on reading comprehension is channeled through word reading and text-reading fluency (i.e., phonological awareness → word reading → text-reading fluency → reading comprehension). The chains of connections for domain-general cognitions/executive functions are via listening comprehension (domain-general cognitions → vocabulary and grammatical knowledge → higher-order cognitions → listening comprehension → text-reading fluency → reading comprehension) and via word reading

(domain-general cognitions → phonological, orthographic, and morphological awareness → word reading → text-reading fluency → reading comprehension). Many more pathways can be specified when considering separately phonological, orthographic, and morphological awareness; vocabulary and grammatical knowledge; and the higher-order cognitions and regulations (e.g., inference, perspective taking, monitoring), and when considering partial mediation pathways (e.g., listening comprehension → reading comprehension over and above text-reading fluency; working memory → higher-order cognitions over and above vocabulary and grammatical knowledge).

Decomposing component skills and specifying chains of relations reveal the nature of relations and mechanisms, making the invisible visible. The hierarchical relations hypothesis implies that once higher-order skills are accounted for, lower-order skills do not have direct relations or have reduced relations to reading comprehension, because their relations to reading comprehension are completely or partially mediated by higher-order skills. For example, phonological awareness, orthographic awareness, and mor-

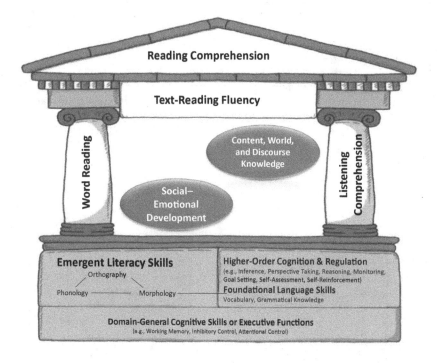

FIGURE 1.2. A heuristic illustration of the DIER, which shows component skills and their hierarchical relations. Interrelations among these skills are not fully shown.

phological awareness (Kim & Petscher, 2016) or rapid automatized naming (Ho et al., 2017) are not independently or directly related to reading comprehension once word reading has been accounted for. Another example is the role of working memory in reading comprehension. Theoretically, the role of working memory in reading comprehension is robust (Daneman & Carpenter, 1980; Kintsch, 1988). However, previous studies reported inconsistent findings about a direct relation of working memory to reading comprehension. According to the DIER, this inconsistency is explained by whether higher-order skills are accounted for, and this is exactly what was found: When higher-order skills were accounted for, there was no longer a direct relation between working memory and reading comprehension (Freed, Hamilton, & Long, 2017; Kim, 2015a, 2017; Van Dyke, Johns, & Kukona, 2014).

Another illustration for the importance of specifying structural relations is a recent study on the relation between word reading and listening comprehension. Research on the SVR consistently found that word-reading and listening-comprehension skills are not independent, but they are moderately to strongly related (e.g., Foorman et al., 2015; Hoover & Gough, 1990; Kim & Wagner, 2015; Lonigan et al., 2018; Tunmer & Chapman, 2012). For example, a longitudinal study with English-speaking students found the correlation from .43 in grade 1 to .53 in grade 4 (Kim & Wagner, 2015). Similar or stronger magnitudes were reported for Greek-speaking students (Protopapas, Simos, Sideridis, & Mouzaki, 2012), Malay-speaking students (Lee & Wheldall, 2009), Korean-speaking students (Kim, 2020b), and Chinese-speaking students (Ho et al., 2017; Joshi, Tao, Aaron, & Quiroz, 2012). According to the DIER, the relation between word reading and listening comprehension is largely explained by their shared reliance on domain-general cognitions/executive functions, and the connection of morphological awareness with vocabulary and grammatical knowledge (see Figure 1.1). Therefore, domain-general cognitions and morphological awareness should explain the relation between word reading and listening comprehension. This is exactly what was found: The relation disappeared once domain-general cognitions and morphological awareness were accounted for (Kim, 2022).

The *interactive relations hypothesis* states that the language, cognitive, and reading systems interact during reading processes (Perfetti & Stafura, 2014; Stanovich, 1984), and that language, cognitive, and reading skills develop interacting with one another via experience and learning. Although the majority of arrows in Figure 1.1 show one-way causal paths for clarity of hierarchical chains of relations, according to the interactive relations hypothesis, comprehension processes are not either bottom-up or top-down processes; instead, both bottom-up and top-down processes interact during reading (Stanovich, 1984). Moreover, the skills in Figure 1.1 have interactive or reciprocal developmental relations via experience and learning (including both implicit and formal learning via instruction). For example, background knowledge, vocabulary, and grammatical/syntactic knowledge influence listening and reading comprehension, while exposure to texts (via either listening or reading mode) helps develop background knowledge, vocabulary, and grammatical/syntactic knowledge, which, in turn, support comprehension (e.g., better comprehenders likely engage in more reading, and the more they read, the more topic knowledge and genre knowledge they gain, which contributes to better comprehension; e.g., Quinn et al., 2020). Similarly, children with advanced word reading generally experience better reading comprehension, which leads to a greater amount of reading, which leads to more exposure to and practice of reading words, which improves word-reading and text reading fluency, which in turn contributes to reading comprehension. Experience- and learning-mediated interactive relations also apply to the relations between higher-order cognitions (e.g., perspective taking) and comprehension (e.g., Kim, 2016); between attentional control and learning (e.g., Masek et al., 2021); between phonological, orthographic, and morphological awareness, and word reading (e.g., Bentin & Leshem, 1993; Chow, McBride-Chang, & Burgess, 2005); between morphological awareness and vocabulary (e.g., Kieffer & Lesaux, 2012; McBride-Chang et al., 2008); and between reading and social–emotional aspects (e.g., Lepola, Salonen, & Vauras, 2000).

The *dynamic relations hypothesis* states that the nature of relations is not static, but changes as a function of two factors: (1) development and (2) activity and task environment (including assessment and text characteristics). The dynamic relations as a function of development are primarily due to the development of word-reading skill. Word reading has a large constraining influence on reading comprehension in the beginning phase of reading development, but as word reading develops, its constraining role decreases, and listening comprehension and associated skills play greater roles in reading comprehension (see the D × C idea of SVR; also see the dual-stream model of reading, Pugh et al., 2001). In other words, determinants of reading comprehension performance varies as a function of developmental phase of reading skill.

The dynamic relations hypothesis as a function of activity and task environment states that the nature of relations varies depending on factors such as reading activities (e.g., reading a novel for leisure vs. reading for learning), assessment features, and text characteristics. Although this hypothesis is more about ontological considerations than epistemological or conceptual considerations, ontological considerations are explicitly stated in the DIER because of their critical bearing on theory and literature. Reading does not occur in a vacuum; depending on the goal or nature of an activity, the component skills are differentially utilized or tapped. For example, reading for the purpose of learning requires setting a high level of standards of coherence and likely draws on attentional control, monitoring, and perspective taking to a greater extent than reading for leisure. The construct of reading comprehension is complex and multidimensional, and demands required by activities and tasks (including assessment and text features) vary in the multidimensional space of language, cognition, and knowledge. Successful reading comprehension requires dynamic use of resources depending on the nature of tasks.

With regard to the dynamic relations as a function of assessment features, particularly notable is measurement of comprehension (both reading and listening; see Francis, Fletcher, Catts, & Tomblin, 2005; Keenan, Betjemann, & Olson, 2008). Comprehension is measured in multiple formats, such as open-ended, multiple choice, cloze, sentence verification, and retell or free recall. If these different methods vary in the extent to which they draw on comprehension processes and associated skills, then the relations of component skills to comprehension would differ. For example, evidence suggests that the maze task, where a word is missing every nth place, and the free recall or retell task rely more on decoding skills than language comprehension (Cao & Kim, 2021; Muijselaar, Kendeou, de Jong, & van den Broke, 2017). Then, the relation of higher-order cognitive skills to comprehension

would not be as strong when comprehension is measured by a maze task or a free-recall task compared to when comprehension is measured by a task that taps inferences and evaluations (e.g., asking questions that require inferences and evaluations). Open-ended comprehension tasks may also place higher demands on oral language skills than tasks that do not require oral production in response (Collins, Compton, Lindstrom, & Gilbert, 2020).

Another important aspect in the dynamic relations hypothesis is text characteristics. Texts vary widely in their goals, content, and organizational and linguistic features (Kim, 2020a; Mesmer, Hiebert, Cunningham, & Kapania, 2021); therefore, text features would place differential demands on one's language, cognitive, and decoding skills. Texts with a high proportion of uncommon vocabulary would place a greater demand on vocabulary knowledge than texts with high-frequency vocabulary. Texts in a specific field would require field-specific vocabulary and topic knowledge. Texts with many multimorphemic words would place greater demands on morphological awareness for decoding and inferring meaning. One way to capture differences in text characteristics broadly is to categorize them as narrative versus informational genres. Narrative texts are typically about social or interpersonal relationships involving a series of events; therefore, processes related to creating a coherent mental representation in thematic and causal structure involving events and characters are important in narrative comprehension (Graesser, Singer, & Trabasso, 1994; Trabasso & Magliano, 1996). In contrast, informational texts are about concepts and ideas and logical relations among them; therefore, creating a mental representation of the text content, including connections and causal structure of ideas is more important in comprehension of informational texts (Kim, Dore, Cho, Golinkoff, & Amendum, 2021). Thus, narrative texts in general would place a greater demand on understanding perspectives as an interpretive mechanism than expository texts, which was indeed what was found in prior research (Kim et al., 2021).

Variation in text features, in addition to assessment format, is likely one reason that reading comprehension tasks vary in the extent to which they draw on word reading, vocabulary, and syntactic knowledge (Cutting & Scarborough, 2006; Keenan et al., 2008). In addition, the relations of component skills to reading comprehension vary depending on the equivalence of texts or lack thereof in listening and reading comprehension tasks. Let us take an example of the relation of vocabulary to reading comprehension in the presence of listening comprehension. If vocabulary demands of texts in listening comprehension and reading comprehension tasks are not substantially discrepant, vocabulary would not make an independent contribution to reading comprehension over and above listening comprehension because the effect of vocabulary on reading comprehension is captured in listening comprehension (i.e., listening comprehension completely mediates the relation of vocabulary to reading comprehension). In contrast, if reading comprehension texts place considerably greater demands on vocabulary than do listening comprehension texts, vocabulary would be directly related to reading comprehension over and above listening comprehension (see, e.g., Kim, Guo, Liu, Peng, & Yang, 2020, and Metsala, Sparks, David, Conrad, & Deacon, 2021). Another important aspect of the dynamic relations hypothesis is differential contributions of component skills to reading as a function of orthographic depth and linguistic characteristics (see Kim, 2020a, 2020b, for more details). For example, in orthographically shallow orthographies, orthographic awareness and phonological awareness play dominant roles in word reading. In orthographies with morphophonological (e.g., English, Arabic, Hebrew, Korean) or morphosyllabic (e.g., Chinese) writing systems, morphological awareness additionally plays an important role in word reading (e.g., McBride-Chang et al., 2005).

Implications of the DIER

Theoretical models, including the DIER, have important implications for instruction and assessment (see Kim, 2020b, for greater details about implications). The first implication is that in order to develop reading comprehension, students need opportunities to develop all the skills specified in the DIER. It is important to recognize that students' strengths and needs are not uniform and differ across and within individuals. Then part and parcel of maximally effective teaching is accurate assessment of students' needs and instruction that is tailored to identified needs (i.e., differentiated instruction). The hierarchical relations hypothesis of the DIER informs a systematic approach to assessment and instruction. Broadly speaking, assessments should start with skills that are higher in the hierarchy and go down the hierarchy. For example, screening assessments for readers beyond the beginning reading phase would include reading comprehension; for beginning readers, proximal predictors of reading comprehension such as word reading, text-reading fluency, and listening comprehension should be included; and for prereaders, key predictors of word reading such as phonological awareness, orthographic awareness (e.g., letter knowledge), and morphological awareness, as well as listening comprehension should be assessed. The hierarchical relations also inform diagnostic assessments to identify the sources of difficulties for students who need additional attention. For those with word-reading difficulties, diagnostic assessments should include phonological awareness, orthographic awareness (e.g., letter knowledge), and morphological awareness, as well as domain-general cognitions/executive functions. Diagnostic assessments for listening comprehension difficulties should include higher-order cognitions, vocabulary, grammatical knowledge, and background knowledge, as well as domain-general cognitive skills.

The hierarchical and interactive relations hypotheses indicate that the skills in the DIER are interconnected with one another. This implies that for a maximal effect, instruction should address the multiple skills in a concerted manner because they bootstrap each other in development (Duke, Lindsey, & Wise, Chapter 16, this volume). However, targeting instruction on specific skills identified through systematic assessment does not imply teaching skills in isolation. For example, teaching phonological awareness with alphabet letters is more effective in improving word reading than teaching phonological awareness alone. Instruction of grapheme–phoneme correspondences would be also reinforced with opportunities to read decodable and authentic texts. Comprehension instruction should also systematically address vocabulary, sentence structures, higher-order cognitions, and background knowledge in a carefully integrated manner, in addition to devoted time to teach each.

The hierarchical and interactive relations also indicate the importance of establishing foundational skills and sustained support for development of skills to promote virtuous cycle and prevent vicious cycle (e.g., see the Mathew effect; Stanovich, 1986). In practice, this means that teaching of foundational skills of word reading and comprehension should be not be delayed, and one-time inoculation does not warrant success in reading skills. Although formal reading instruction may not start until kindergarten or later, the foundational skills that support word-reading development (e.g., phonological, morphological, and orthographic awareness) should be taught explicitly and systematically earlier. The same principle applies to comprehension skill. Listening comprehension as an equivalent skill to reading comprehension (except word-reading skill) implies that comprehension is a continuum that develops in oral language contexts (listening comprehension) and continues to develop in written language contexts (reading comprehension). In fact, comprehension skill of complex multiple texts with multiple viewpoints continues to develop into adulthood (Chall, 1983). The language and cognitive skills that contribute to comprehension are unconstrained, large-domain skills that take a prolonged time to develop (e.g., vocabulary, understanding multiple viewpoints). Therefore, comprehension instruction should be an integral part of reading instruction in all grades, including primary grades and preschool years (see Orcutt, Johnson, & Kendeou, Chapter 17, this volume). For prereaders and beginning readers, it is crucial that foundational skills for word reading *and* comprehension, not those for *either* word reading *or* comprehension, are taught concurrently in an explicit and systematic manner.

The dynamic relations as a function of text features suggest the importance of attending to text features in instruction and assessment. For example, even texts with the same readability values result in different number of words read per minute (i.e., text-reading efficiency; Francis et al., 2008); therefore, it is important to use equated texts, not simply following grade-level texts and readability values, for progress-monitoring assessment (e.g., Toyoma, Hiebert, & Pearson, 2017). Decoding, linguistic, content, and cognitive demands should also be carefully considered in planning and implementing teaching (e.g., Hiebert, Toyoma, & Irey, 2020). The dynamic relations as a function of assessment format also have implications. For example, maze tasks and free recall/retell are widely used as measures of reading comprehension in U.S. school settings (e.g., Dynamic Indicators of Basic Early Literacy Skills [DIBELS] and informal inventory). However, these tasks are limited in

tapping deep inferential and evaluative comprehension (Francis et al., 2005; Shanahan, Kamil, & Tobin, 1982). Therefore, although results from these tasks provide valuable information regarding a general picture about reading comprehension, reliance on these tasks *alone* would not paint a precise picture of students' reading comprehension (e.g., Cao & Kim, 2021).

Conclusion

Reading is a complex phenomenon and thus requires multiple theories to describe it. SVR offers a bird's-eye view of the reading phenomenon and has an important place in the field. However, it is insufficient to explain the complex nature of reading. DIER critically extends SVR, putting flesh on SVR, and integrates other theories and bodies of work to describe the landscape and details of skills that contribute to reading comprehension, and the nature of their structural relations. It is important for a theoretical model to describe and specify the forest and trees. Future work across languages and developmental phases is needed to test the propositions presented in DIER.

Acknowledgments

This work was supported by grants from the Institute of Education Sciences, U.S. Department of Education (R305A130131; R305A180055; R305A200312) and the Eunice Kennedy Shriver National Institute of Child Health and Human Development (National Institute of Child Health and Human Development [NICHD]; P50HD052120). The content is solely the responsibility of the author and does not necessarily represent the official views of the funding agency.

Notes

1. Individuals' experiences of reading success and difficulties is provisionally hypothesized to start the interactive, bidirectional relations between social–emotional attitudes toward reading and reading skills (e.g., Chapman & Tunmer, 2003; see the interactive relations hypothesis).

2. Although not explicitly represented in Figure 1.1, the DIER recognizes the importance of developing automaticity and overlearning—effortless and efficient access and retrieval of information—beyond text-reading fluency. The impor-

tance of automaticity, in addition to accuracy, applies to all the skills, including word reading (see Ehri, 2005), text reading (text-reading fluency), sublexical skills (e.g., phonological awareness, letter knowledge, morphological awareness), language skills (e.g., vocabulary, syntactic knowledge), higher-order cognitions and regulations, and background knowledge. For example, automaticity of letter-sound knowledge facilitates accessing and retrieving sounds associated with each letter or grapheme, and blending them to read words without placing high demands on working memory and attentional resources.

References

Adams, M. J. (1990). *Beginning to read: Thinking and learning about print*. MIT Press.

Adlof, S. M., Catts, H. W., & Little, T. D. (2006). Should the simple view of reading include a fluency component? *Reading and Writing, 19*, 933–958.

Barrs, M., Pradl, G., Hall, K., & Dombey, H. (2008). Literacy: Whose complex activity? *Literacy, 42*(2), 55–58.

Bentin, S., & Leshem, H. (1993). On the interaction between phonological awareness and reading acquisition: It's a two-way street. *Annals of Dyslexia, 43*, 125–148.

Braze, D., Katz, L., Magnuson, J. S., Mencl, W. E., Tabor, W., Van Dyke, J. A., . . . Shankweiler, D. P. (2016). Vocabulary does not complicate the simple view of reading. *Reading and Writing, 29*, 435–451.

Cao, Y., & Kim, Y.-S. G. (2021). Is retell a valid measure of reading comprehension? *Educational Research Review, 32*.

Castles, A., Rastle, K., & Nation, K. (2018). Ending the reading wars: Reading acquisition from novice to expert. *Psychological Science in the Public Interest, 19*, 5–51.

Catts, H., Adlof, S., & Ellis Weismer, S. (2006). Language deficits in poor comprehenders: A case for the simple view of reading. *Journal of Speech, Language, and Hearing Research, 49*, 278–293.

Cervetti, G. N., Pearson, P. D., Palincsar, A. S., Afflerbach, P., Kendeou, P., Biancarosa, G., . . . Berman, A. I. (2020). How the reading for understanding initiative's research complicates the simple view of reading invoked in the science of reading. *Reading Research Quarterly, 55*(Suppl. 1), S161–S172.

Chall, J. S. (1983). *Stages of reading development*. McGraw-Hill.

Chapman, J. W., & Tunmer, W. E. (2003). Reading difficulties, reading-related self-perceptions, and strategies for overcoming negative self-beliefs. *Reading and Writing Quarterly, 19*, 5–24.

Chow, B. W., McBride-Chang, C., & Burgess, S. (2005). Phonological processing skills and early reading abilities in Hong Kong Chinese kindergartners learning to read English as a second language. *Journal of Educational Psychology, 97*(1), 81–87.

Collins, A. A., Compton, D. L., Lindstrom, E. R., & Gilbert, J. K. (2020). Performance variations across reading comprehension assessments: Examining the unique contributions of text, activity, and reader. *Reading and Writing, 33*, 605–634.

Cutting, L. E., & Scarborough, H. S. (2006). Prediction of reading comprehension: Relative contributions of word recognition, language proficiency, and other cognitive skills can depend on how comprehension is measured. *Scientific Studies of Reading, 10*, 277–299.

Daneman, M., & Carpenter, P. A. (1980). Individual differences in working memory and reading. *Journal of Verbal Learning and Verbal Behavior, 19*, 450–466.

Dolean, D. D., Lervag, A., Visu-Petra, L., & Melby-Lervag, M. (2021). Language skills, not executive functions, predict the development of reading comprehension of early readers: Evidence from an orthographically transparent language. *Reading and Writing, 34*, 1491–1512.

Duke, N. K., & Cartwright, K. B. (2021). The science of reading progresses: Communicating advances beyond the simple view of reading. *Reading Research Quarterly, 56*(Suppl. 1), S25–S44.

Ehri, L. C. (2005). Development of sight word reading: Phases and findings. In M. J. Snowling & C. Hulme (Eds.), *Blackwell handbooks of developmental psychology. The science of reading: A handbook* (pp. 135–154). Blackwell.

Florit, E., & Cain, K. (2011). The simple view of reading: Is it valid for different types of alphabetic orthographies? *Educational Psychology Review, 23*, 553–576.

Foorman, B. R., Koon, S., Petscher, Y., Mitchell, A., & Truckenmiller, A. (2015). Examining general and specific factors in the dimensionality of oral language and reading in 4th–10th grades. *Journal of Educational Psychology, 107*, 884–899.

Francis, D. J., Fletcher, J. M., Catts, H. W., & Tomblin, J. B. (2005). Dimensions affecting the assessment of reading comprehension. In S. G. Paris & S. A. Stahl (Eds.), *Children's reading comprehension and assessment* (pp. 369–394). Erlbaum.

Francis, D. J., Santi, K. L., Barr, C., Fletcher, J. M., Varisco, A., & Foorman, B. R. (2008). Form effects on the estimation of students' oral reading fluency using DIBELS. *Journal of School Psychology, 46*(3), 315–342.

Freed, E. M., Hamilton, S. T., & Long, D. L. (2017).

Comprehension in proficient readers: The nature of individual variation. *Journal of Memory and Language, 97,* 135–153.

Gough, P. B., & Tunmer, W. E. (1986). Decoding, reading, and reading disability. *Remedial and Special Education, 7,* 6–10.

Graesser, A. C., Singer, M., & Trabasso, T. (1994). Constructing inferences during narrative text comprehension. *Psychological Review, 101,* 371–395.

Harm, M. W., & Seidenberg, M. S. (2004). Computing the meanings of words in reading: Cooperative division of labor between visual and phonological processes. *Psychological Review, 111,* 662–720.

Hiebert, E. H., Toyoma, Y., & Irey, R. (2020). Features of known and unknown words for first graders of different proficiency levels in winter and spring. *Education Sciences, 10,* Article 389.

Hjetland, H. N., Lervag, A., Lyster, S. H., Hagtvet, B. E., Hulme, C., & Melby-Lervag, M. (2019). Pathways to reading comprehension: A longitudinal study from 4 to 9 years of age. *Journal of Educational Psychology, 111,* 751–763.

Ho, C. S., Zheng, M., McBride, C., Hsu, L. S. J., Waye, M. M. Y., & Kwok, J. C. (2017). Examining an extended simple view of reading in Chinese: The role of naming efficiency for reading comprehension. *Contemporary Educational Psychology, 51,* 293–302.

Hoover, W. A., & Gough, P. B. (1990). The simple view of reading. *Reading and Writing, 2,* 127–160.

Hoover, W. A., & Tunmer, W. E. (2018). The simple view of reading: Three assessments of its adequacy. *Remedial and Special Education, 39*(5), 304–312.

Huey, E. (1968). *The psychology and pedagogy of reading.* MIT Press.

Jenkins, J. R., Fuchs, L. S., van den Broek, P., Espin, C., & Deno, S. L. (2003). Sources of individual differences in reading comprehension and reading fluency. *Journal of Educational Psychology, 95*(4), 719–729.

Joshi, R. M., & Aaron, P. G. (2000). The component model of reading: Simple view of reading made a little more complex. *Reading Psychology, 21,* 85–97.

Joshi, R. M., Tao, S., Aaron, P. G., & Quiroz, B. (2012). Cognitive component of componential model of reading applied to different orthographies. *Journal of Learning Disabilities, 45*(5), 480–486.

Keenan, J. M., Betjemann, R. S., & Olson, R. K. (2008). Reading comprehension tests vary in the skills they assess: Differential dependence on decoding and oral comprehension. *Scientific Studies of Reading, 12,* 281–300.

Kieffer, M. J., & Lesaux, N. K. (2012). Develop-ment of morphological awareness and vocabulary in Spanish-speaking language minority learners: A parallel process latent growth curve model. *Applied Psycholinguistics, 33,* 23–54.

Kim, Y.-S. (2015a). Language and cognitive predictors of text comprehension: Evidence from multivariate analysis. *Child Development, 86,* 128–144.

Kim, Y.-S. G. (2015b). Developmental, component-based model of reading fluency: An investigation of word-reading fluency, text-reading fluency, and reading comprehension. *Reading Research Quarterly, 50,* 459–481.

Kim, Y.-S. G. (2016). Direct and mediated effects of language and cognitive skills on comprehension of oral narrative texts (listening comprehension) for children. *Journal of Experimental Child Psychology, 141,* 101–120.

Kim, Y.-S. G. (2017). Why the simple view of reading is not simplistic: Unpacking the simple view of reading using a direct and indirect effect model of reading (DIER). *Scientific Studies of Reading, 21*(4), 310–333.

Kim, Y.-S. G. (2020a). Hierarchical and dynamic relations of language and cognitive skills to reading comprehension: Testing the direct and indirect effects model of reading (DIER). *Journal of Educational Psychology, 112*(4), 667–684.

Kim, Y.-S. G. (2020b). Toward integrative reading science: The direct and indirect effects model of reading (DIER). *Journal of Learning Disabilities, 53*(6), 469–491.

Kim, Y.-S. G. (2020c, May/June). The simple view of reading unpacked and expanded: The direct and indirect effects model of reading. *The Reading League,* pp. 15–22.

Kim, Y.-S. G. (2022). *Executive functions and morphological awareness explain the relation between word reading and listening comprehension.* Manuscript submitted for publication.

Kim, Y.-S. G., Dore, R. A., Cho, M., Golinkoff, R., & Amendum, S. (2021). Theory of mind, mental state talk, and discourse comprehension: Theory of mind process is more important for narrative comprehension than for informational text comprehension. *Journal of Experimental Child Psychology, 209,* Article 105181.

Kim, Y.-S. G., Guo, Q., Liu, Y., Peng, Y., & Yang, L. (2020). Multiple pathways by which compounding morphological awareness is related to reading comprehension: Evidence from Chinese second graders. *Reading Research Quarterly, 55*(2), 193–212.

Kim, Y.-S. G., & Petscher, Y. (2016). Prosodic sensitivity and reading: An investigation of pathways of relations using a latent variable approach. *Journal of Educational Psychology, 108,* 630–645.

Kim, Y.-S. G., Quinn, J., & Petscher, Y. (2021).

What is reading fluency and how is it related to reading comprehension?: A longitudinal investigation. *Developmental Psychology, 57*(5), 718–732.

Kim, Y.-S. G., & Wagner, R. K. (2015). Text (oral) reading fluency as a construct in reading development: An investigation of its mediating role for children from grades 1 to 4. *Scientific Studies of Reading, 19*, 224–242.

Kintsch, W. (1988). The use of knowledge in discourse processing: A construction–integration model. *Psychological Review, 95*, 163–182.

Kirby, R. K., & Savage, R. S. (2008). Can the simple view deal with the complexities of reading? *Literacy, 42*(2), 75–82.

LaBerge, D., & Samuels, S. J. (1974). Toward a theory of automatic information processing in reading. *Cognitive Psychology, 6*(2), 293–323.

Lee, L. W., & Wheldall, K. (2009). An examination of the simple view of reading among beginning readers in Malay. *Reading Psychology, 30*, 250–264.

Lepola, J., Salonen, P., & Vauras, M. (2000). The development of motivational orientations as a function of divergent reading careers from pre-school to the second grade. *Learning and Instruction, 10*(2), 153–177.

Lonigan, C. J., Burgess, S. R., & Schatschneider, C. (2018). Examining the simple view of reading with elementary school children: Still simple after all these years. *Remedial and Special Education, 39*, 260–273.

Mancilla-Martinez, J., Kieffer, M. J., Biancarosa, G., Christodoulou, J. A., & Snow, C. E. (2011). Investigating English reading comprehension growth in adolescent language minority learners: Some insights from the simple view. *Reading and Writing, 24*, 339–354.

Masek, L. R., McMillan, B. T. M., Paterson, S. J., Tamis-LeMonda, C. S., Gonlinkoff, R. M., & Hirsh-Pasek, K. (2021). Where language meets attention: How contingent interactions promote learning. *Developmental Review, 60*, Article 100961.

McBride-Chang, C., Cho, J.-R., Liu, H., Wagner, R. K., Shu, H., Zhou, A., Cheuk, C. S.-M., & Muse, A. (2005). Changing models across cultures: Associations of phonological awareness and morphological structure awareness with vocabulary and word recognition in second graders from Beijing, Hong Kong, Korea, and the United States. *Journal of Experimental Child Psychology, 92*, 140–160.

McBride-Chang, C., Tardif, T., Cho, J.-R., Shu, H., Fletcher, P., Strokes, S. F., . . . Leung, K. (2008). What's in a word?: Morphological awareness and vocabulary knowledge in three languages. *Applied Psycholinguistics, 29*, 437–462.

McNamara, D. S., & Magliano, J. (2009). Toward a comprehensive model for comprehension. In B. Ross (Ed.), *The psychology of learning and motivation* (pp. 297–384). Elsevier.

Mesmer, H. A. E., Hiebert, E. H., Cunningham, J. W., & Kapania, M. (2021). Does one size fit all?: Exploring the contribution of text features, text content, and grade of use on comprehension. *Reading Psychology, 41*(1), 42–72.

Metsala, J. L., Sparks, E., David, M., Conrad, N., & Deacon, S. H. (2021). What is the best way to characterize the contributions of oral language to reading comprehension: Listening comprehension or individual oral language skills? *Journal of Research in Reading, 44*, 675–694.

Muijselaar, M. M. L., Kendeou, P., de Jong, P. F., & van den Broke, P. W. (2017). What does the CBM-Maze test measure? *Scientific Studies of Reading, 21*(2), 120–132.

National Institute of Child Health and Human Development. (2000). *Report of the National Reading Panel. Teaching children to read: An evidence-based assessment of the scientific research literature on reading and its implications for reading instruction* (NIH Publication No. 00–4769). U.S. Government Printing Office.

Ouellette, G., & Beers, A. (2010). A not-so-simple view of reading: How oral vocabulary and visual-word recognition complicate the story. *Reading and Writing, 23*(2), 189–208.

Perfetti, C., & Stafura, J. (2014). Word knowledge in a theory of reading comprehension. *Scientific Studies of Reading, 18*, 22–37.

Pressley, M., Duke, N. K., Gaskins, I. W., Fingeret, L., Halladay, J., Hilden, K., . . ., Solic, K. L. (2009). Working with struggling readers: Why we must get beyond the simple view of reading and visions of how it might be done. In T. B. Gutkin & C. R. Reynolds (Eds.), *The handbook of school psychology* (4th ed., pp. 522–546). Wiley.

Protopapas, A., Simos, P., Sideridis, G. D., & Mouzaki, A. (2012). The components of the simple view of reading: A confirmatory factor analysis. *Reading Psychology, 33*, 217–240.

Pugh, K. R., Mencl, W. E., Jenner, A. R., Katz, L., Frost, S. J., Lee, J. R., . . . Shaywitz, B. A. (2001). Neurobiological studies of reading and reading disability. *Journal of Communication Disorders, 34*(6), 479–492.

Quinn, J. M., Wagner, R. K., Petscher, Y., Roberts, G., Menzel, A. J., & Schatschneider, C. (2020). Differential codevelopment of vocabulary knowledge and reading comprehension for students with and without learning disabilities. *Journal of Educational Psychology, 112*(3), 608–627.

Shanahan, T., Kamil, M. L., & Tobin, A. B. (1982). Cloze as a measure of intersentential comprehension. *Reading Research Quarterly, 17*(2), 229–255.

Shapiro, E. S., Fritschmann, N. S., Thomas, L. B.,

Hughes, C. L., & McDougal, J. (2014). Concurrent and predictive validity of reading retell as a brief measure of reading comprehension for narrative text. *Reading Psychology, 35,* 644–665.

Snow, C. E. (2002). Reading for understanding: Toward an R&D program in reading comprehension. RAND. Retrieved from *www.videnomlaesning.dk/media/2526/reading-for-understanding.pdf.*

Stanovich, K. E. (1984). The interactive–compensatory model of reading: A confluence of developmental, experimental, and educational psychology. *Remedial and Special Education, 5*(3), 11–19.

Stanovich, K. E. (1986). Matthew effects in reading: Some consequences of individual differences in the acquisition of literacy. *Reading Research Quarterly, 21*(4), 360–407.

Toyoma, Y., Hiebert, E. H., & Pearson, P. D. (2017). An analysis of the text complexity of leveled passages in four popular classroom reading assessments. *Educational Assessment, 22*(3), 139–170.

Trabasso, T., & Magliano, J. P. (1996). Conscious understanding during comprehension. *Discourse Processes, 21*(3), 255–287.

Tunmer, W. E., & Chapman, J. W. (2012). The simple view of reading redux: Vocabulary knowledge and the independent components hypothesis. *Journal of Learning Disabilities, 45,* 453–466.

van Bergen, E., van der Leij, A., & de Jong, P. F. (2014). The intergenerational multiple deficit model and the case of dyslexia. *Frontiers in Human Neuroscience, 8*(346), 1–13.

van den Broek, P., Rapp, D. N., & Kendeou, P. (2005). Integrating memory-based and constructionist processes in accounts of reading comprehension. *Discourse Processes, 39,* 299–316.

Van Dyke, J. A., Johns, C. L., & Kukona, A. (2014). Low working memory capacity is only spuriously related to poor reading comprehension. *Cognition, 131,* 373–403.

Wolf, M., & Katzir-Cohen, T. (2001). Reading fluency and its intervention. *Scientific Studies of Reading, 5,* 211–239.

Yeung, P., Ho, C. S., Chan, D. W., & Chung, K. K. (2016). A componential model of reading in Chinese. *Learning and Individual Differences, 45,* 11–24.

CHAPTER 2

Early Environmental Influences on Language

Meredith L. Rowe, Rachel R. Romeo, and Kathryn A. Leech

The science of early literacy begins with language. A large body of literature documents clear associations between young children's oral language skills and their literacy development (Justice & Jiang, Chapter 11, this volume). Decoding skills are also essential for literacy but need to be explicitly taught starting in the preschool years. Oral language skills, on the other hand, develop from birth, and are highly influenced by environmental experiences. We use the term *oral language skills* broadly to refer to the various components of language that children acquire over the first 5 years, including phonology, vocabulary, syntax, and pragmatic skills. In this chapter we provide a brief overview of the research on environmental influences on oral language development, with a specific focus on the important role of language input during social interactions. Our review is limited primarily to typically developing children learning a first language. After summarizing the literature, we highlight some of our recent work in this area and suggest directions for future research and implications for intervention and instruction.

Background

Infants Need Social Interaction to Learn a Language

Infants need to be exposed to language used around them to learn language, and it is essential that this input is social. The *social gating* hypothesis (e.g., Kuhl, 2007) highlights how the infant brain benefits from contingent social interaction early in life for language learning. As an example, one study revealed that American infants who were exposed to Mandarin in a series of book-reading sessions with a live Mandarin-speaking woman reading the books with them were able to learn how to discriminate different phonemes in Mandarin. However, a separate group of American infants who were exposed to only a video of the same woman reading the same books in Mandarin did not learn to discriminate the sounds. Thus, it is not just the input that is necessary for phonological development in infancy, but the contingent social interaction that comes along with the input (Kuhl, 2010). Research with toddlers found similar results in which children were able to learn new verbs when interacting with a live experimenter or an experimenter in a contingent interaction over Skype; however, when watching and listening to the same input on a yoked video, they did not learn the new verbs (Roseberry, Hirsh-Pasek, & Golinkoff, 2014). However, beginning later in the second year of life, once children's cognitive and language skills increase, they become able to learn from nonsocial input, such as video, and from overheard speech spoken to others (e.g., Akhtar, 2005). Yet despite these increasing skills, research suggests that toddlers continue to benefit most from speech used in contingent back-and-forth social interactions (Hirsh-Pasek et al., 2015).

Input and Vocabulary Development

Young, preliterate children need to hear words to learn those words. While there is experimental evidence that children can pick up words relatively quickly from single exposures (e.g., Carey & Bartlett, 1978), research on everyday parent–child interactions shows a developmental progression where in infancy there is a positive association between repetition in the input and later vocabulary size (Newman, Rowe, & Ratner, 2016), yet in toddlerhood it is diversity in the input that is associated with vocabulary growth (e.g., Rowe, 2012). In infancy, children are also more likely to learn words if they are used to label objects in the child's line of attention (Yu & Smith, 2012), for example, labeling the "shoe" while the child is looking at the shoe. Relatedly, toddlers learn more when language is used during episodes of joint attention in which caregiver and child are jointly interacting around a shared focus than from language used outside of joint attention episodes (Tomasello & Farrar, 1986), echoing the importance of contingent social interaction discussed earlier. Preschoolers, with their more advanced cognitive and language skills, benefit from contingent conversations that are more challenging, in that they have an abstract focus (talking about future plans or why dinosaurs are extinct) than those that are more grounded in there here-and-now (e.g., Rowe, 2012). Indeed, experience with these types of decontextualized conversations in early childhood is associated with kindergarten vocabulary, syntax, and narrative skills, as well as academic language skills in adolescence (e.g., Demir, Rowe, Heller, Goldin-Meadow, & Levine, 2015; Uccelli, Demir-Lira, Rowe, Levine, & Goldin-Meadow, 2019). Thus, across early development, children of all ages benefit from contingent back-and-forth interactions, yet the complexity of the linguistic input should increase with age, as well as the abstractness of the topic of conversation (e.g., Rowe & Snow, 2020).

Syntactic Exposure and Development

While syntactic development follows a relatively predictable course in early childhood, children do vary widely in their syntactic skills at any given age (e.g., Fenson et al., 1994) and language exposure still plays an important role. For example, exposure to verbs used in diverse sentence frames is found to support learning of those verbs (e.g., Naigles & Hoff-Ginsberg, 1995). More generally, children who are exposed to input that is more syntactically complex and contains more diverse syntactic structures have faster growth over time in their own productive syntax as measured by the mean length of utterances (MLU) produced (Huttenlocher, Waterfall, Vasilyeva, Vevea, & Hedges, 2010). Parents who use a larger proportion of complex sentences when interacting with their preschool-age children have children who use a larger proportion of complex sentences in those same interactions and perform better on a separate syntax comprehension assessment (Huttenlocher, Vasilyeva, Cymerman, & Levine, 2002). In addition, preschool children in classrooms with teachers who use a larger proportion of complex sentences have greater increases over the course of the school year in their syntactic comprehension (Huttenlocher et al., 2002). This finding is important, because it rules out any potential genetic confounds, as the teachers are not related to the children. Thus, exposure to a variety of syntactic structures in the input is positively associated with children's understanding of and use of those structures.

There is some evidence from short-term interventions that the relationship is causal. For example, use of passive sentences is relatively rare in day-to-day input in English speaking families (e.g., Maratsos, Fox, Becker, & Chalkley, 1985), and passives prove challenging for children to comprehend. To test out whether increased exposure to the passive voice in the input would promote syntactic development, Vasilyeva, Huttenlocher, and Waterfall (2006) developed a book-reading intervention in which they inserted passive sentences into books, then tested whether regular exposure to the passive stories (compared to the active stories) over a short period of time would influence children's comprehension of passive sentences on a separate assessment. Indeed, they found significant positive increases in passive understanding for the children in the passive book condition, suggesting that increasing exposure to certain syntactic constructions can cause an increase in understanding of those constructions (Vasilyeva et al., 2006).

Environmental Influences on Pragmatic Development

Pragmatic development includes the ability to use language socially to convey different intents, such as to pose a question or issue a command, and to use language appropriately given the situation, which often requires understanding the perspective of a conversational partner. Children as young as 9 months of age are found to understand the communicative intentions of others (Stephens & Matthews, 2014), and beginning in infancy, through their uses of gesture, children produce different intents such as "to give" or "to direct attention" or "to provide information" (Bates, Camaioni, & Volterra, 1975; Liszkowski, Carpenter, & Tomasello, 2008). Across early childhood there is large variation in children's pragmatic development that is associated with, but distinct from, variation in other facets of language development such as vocabulary and syntax (O'Neill, 2007). Studies looking at caregiver uses of communicative intents with children suggest that parents use a limited range of intents with infants (i.e., directing attention, discussing joint focus of attention), and similar to lexical and syntactic input, they increase in the diversity and sophistication of communicative intents produced as children age and increase in language ability (Pan, Imbens-Baily, Winner, & Snow, 1996). However, we do not have much literature on the environmental factors that contribute to variation in pragmatic development or on the specific pragmatic skills that are most relevant for later outcomes (e.g., Matthews, Biney, & Abbott-Smith, 2018). Nonetheless, there are studies showing that engaging in certain types of communicative acts/interchanges with children promotes language development more broadly. For example, positive associations are found between parents' use of conversation-eliciting utterances, such as wh-questions, and toddler's language (e.g., Rowe, Leech, & Cabrera, 2017), whereas negative associations are noted between parents' use of utterances to direct their child's behavior and language learning (e.g., Rowe, Coker, & Pan, 2004; Tomasello & Todd, 1983). Taken together, the findings are consistent with the notion that using language in a way that helps to engage children in extended back-and-forth conversations on more and more abstract topics as they age is beneficial for developing conversational skill and language development more broadly (Rowe & Snow, 2020; Tomasello, 1988).

Why Do Home Language Environments Vary So Much?

In line with sociocultural theory (e.g., Bruner, 1983; Vygotsky, 1978), the previous review demonstrates how social interaction is at the core of language development and that variation in children's language exposure predicts variation in language development. This leads to an important follow-up question: What factors contribute to this variation in language environments? Indeed, myriad factors play a role, including socioeconomic status (SES; often measured as parental income and/or education level), literacy skills, and knowledge of child development, each of which positively relates to the amount and diversity of parent communication with children (e.g., Hart & Risley, 1995; Leung & Suskind, 2020; Rowe, 2008; Rowe, Pan, & Ayoub, 2005). On the other hand, factors such as maternal stress, depression, financial hardship, and household chaos are typically negatively associated with features of parent input found to promote language learning (e.g., Ellwood-Lowe, Foushee, & Srinivasan, 2022; Evans, Maxwell, & Hart, 1999; Kaplan, Danko, & Diaz, 2010; Rowe et al., 2005). Furthermore, whether the parents are bilingual and their beliefs about bilingualism affect the extent to which children are exposed to one or more languages at home and school (Surrain, 2021). For more on language exposure and bilingual development, a topic beyond the scope of this chapter, see Hoff (2018) for a review. (For more on language and literacy development in dual language learners, see Mancilla-Martinez, Chapter 3, and Phillips Galloway & Lesaux, Chapter 24, this volume.)

Summary

In summary, the research on parent input and child language development highlights the importance of frequently engaging children in back-and-forth extended conversations on topics of interest to them. Given these findings, our recent work has focused on (1) trying to better understand the mechanisms underlying the relationship between language exposure and language development, and (2) determining whether parent input is malleable through intervention, and if so, whether changes in input cause changes in children's language development. We present some of our recent findings in each of these areas in the following section.

Building on the Research to Understand Neural Mechanisms and Causal Intervention Effects

Neurodevelopmental Mechanisms

Children's observable language development is supported by the development of a complex neurobiological network that spans all four lobes of the cerebral cortex (for review, see Friederici, 2006). Current evidence overwhelmingly supports a gene × environment theory of brain development, whereby a child's genetics provide the blueprint for neural development, yet the child's early experiences shape individual differences in neural development (Boyce, Sokolowski, & Robinson, 2020). Indeed, the developing brain is remarkably plastic, and children's early experiences—both favorable and adverse—influence developmental trajectories of both brain structure and function, through a process called "biological embedding" (Gabard-Durnam & McLaughlin, 2020). A core topic of neurodevelopmental investigation is how early experiences become biologically embedded, and how these brain changes in turn influence cognitive and behavioral development. Specifically, for children's language exposure to influence their language development, presumably this must be mediated by one or more neurodevelopmental mechanisms (Noble, Houston, Kan, & Sowell, 2012; Perkins, Finegood, & Swain, 2013). Guided by theories of biological embedding, we recently investigated these mechanisms in a series of magnetic resonance imaging (MRI) studies aimed at understanding relationships between SES, language exposure, and cognitive and brain development.

While most early studies of language exposure relied on hand-coding of videotaped parent–child interactions, typically, in a laboratory setting or in short home recordings, an increasing number of studies utilize LENA (Language ENvironment Analysis)—a small, 2-ounce recorder worn in a child's shirt pocket that records full days of the child's firsthand auditory experience (Gilkerson et al., 2017). LENA software analyzes children's auditory environments, segments the speech, and estimates how many words the child heard spoken by an adult within earshot ("adult word count"), how many utterances were spoken by the child wearing the recorder ("child vocalization count"), and how many back-and-forth conversational turns occurred between the child and any adult with no more than 5 seconds pause ("conversational turn count"). A SES-diverse sample of families with children ages 4–6 years completed 2 days of LENA recordings, as well as lab-based measures of language skills and brain development.

Higher parental education and family income were associated with greater numbers of adult words and conversational turns (Romeo, Leonard, et al., 2018; Romeo, Segaran et al., 2018), consistent with several earlier studies of SES and language experience (e.g., Rowe, 2018). SES was also positively correlated with children's language skills (a composite of receptive and expressive vocabulary and morphosyntax). However, after controlling for SES, conversational turns continued to predict unique variance in children's verbal scores, and significantly mediated the relationship between SES and children's verbal scores (Romeo, Leonard, et al., 2018; Romeo, Segaran, et al., 2018). No such relationships were found with adult word count, suggesting that after accounting for socioeconomic variance, conversational experience is more strongly linked to language development than the sheer number of words heard.

Turn-taking experience was also associated with measures of children's brain function and structure. Using functional MRI (fMRI), children's brain activation was measured during a story-listening task that indexes language comprehension (Romeo, Leonard, et al., 2018). Higher conversational turn experience was correlated with greater activation in Broca's area, a region of the left inferior frontal gyrus known to be involved in speech and language processing. Additionally, diffusion-weighted imaging (DWI) indexed the structural connectivity of white-matter tracts between brain regions. Children who experienced more conversational turns also exhibited greater fractional anisotropy—a measure of white-matter integrity and maturity—in the left arcuate and superior longitudinal fasciculi, which connect Broca's area to other language regions in the brain development (Romeo, Segaran, et al., 2018). Each of these neural measures independently mediated the relationship between conversational turns and language scores, indicating both a functional and structural mechanism linking language experience to language skill.

A partially overlapping sample of children from the cross-sectional study also participated in a longitudinal examination of neural plasticity in response to modifications to the language environment. Families were randomly assigned either to a control group or to attend a 9-week family-based intervention designed to increase parent–child communication through "meaningFULL," responsive, and balanced language use (Neville et al., 2013). On average, families who completed the intervention showed greater increases in conversational turns but no changes in the overall number of adult words or child vocalizations (Romeo et al., 2021). Furthermore, the magnitude of change in conversational turns was positively correlated with longitudinal cortical thickening in two regions: a large part of left inferior frontal gyrus, including Broca's area, as well as prefrontal regions known to be involved in executive functioning (Diamond, 2013; Miller & Cohen, 2001), and the left supramarginal gyrus, a part of the parietal lobe that is known to subserve language comprehension, phonological processing, and social cognition (Tremblay & Dick, 2016; Oberhuber et al., 2016; Adolphs, 2009). Finally, growth the in the supramarginal region mediated the relationships between changes in turn taking and children's language development (Romeo et al., 2021). This indicates that conversational turns support language development through cortical growth in language and social processing regions, and suggests that socially motivated verbal interaction, rather than passive language exposure, best supports brain and language growth.

Parent-Focused Interventions

Intervention designs are especially important in language research for theoretical and practical reasons. From a theoretical perspective, such designs help to establish causal effects of caregiver input, because one can test whether the intervention—focused on only parents—leads to improved child outcomes. From a practical standpoint, conversational interventions hold promise for large-scale implementation because they do not involve expensive materials, rather revolving around enhancing existing conversation practices in the home. Recently we have developed several light-touch interventions of this sort to improve child language by intervening around socially contingent caregiver–child interactions (Leech, Wei, Harring, & Rowe, 2018; Leech & Rowe, 2020; Rowe & Leech, 2019). In these studies, parents receive information about the importance of conversations for oral language skills and strategies for how to engage in these conversations. The theory of change associated with these interventions is that increasing parent knowledge may change the home language environment and in turn improve children's developing oral language capacities. This theory of change is based on work showing that parents who are more knowledgeable about child devel-

opment and developmental milestones engage in parenting practices that are more promotive of children's language and cognitive development (Garrett-Peters et al., 2008; Leung & Suskind, 2020; Miller, 1998; Rowe, 2008).

In one intervention study (Leech et al., 2018), we sought to increase abstract conversations between parents and preschoolers. As discussed earlier, preschoolers' oral language skills benefit from caregiver input, which challenges them to think and discuss abstract, nonpresent concepts. We refer to these conversations as *decontextualized language* (Snow, 1991), which may include discussions about the past or future, explanations and definitions of new words, or engagement in pretense. Decontextualized language is a particularly appealing focus for intervention, because parents already use this type of language with their children and it can be embedded in many routines such as play or mealtimes, the latter of which was the focus of this study (Beals, 1993, 2001).

Because asking parents to increase their decontextualized talk is a rather opaque message to communicate, we devised an acronym called READY Talk to provide parents with examples of decontextualized talk in an accessible framework. Each letter of READY stood for a different type of decontextualized language (Recall past events, Explain new words and concepts, Ask lots of questions, Discuss the future), and a message to increase parents' motivation and efficacy (You can make a difference in your child's academic success). To test the effectiveness of the READY Talk program, 36 higher-SES parents of 4-year-old children were randomly assigned to receive the program or to a control condition. Parents assigned to the intervention condition watched a 15-minute video, which consisted of an introduction to READY Talk and video models of dyads using each type of READY Talk. All parents then recorded one mealtime conversation per week for the following month (four recordings in total), which we transcribed and coded for decontextualized language.

Findings indicated that parents who received the intervention used more than twice as much decontextualized language during home mealtimes than parents in the control condition. Intervention effects were maintained across the study; at the final recording intervention parents' decontextualized talk comprised 49.1% of their total utterances versus 18.9% in the control condition. Parents who received the intervention also increased other forms of decontextualized language not covered in the READY Talk program (e.g., scripts, connections between the present and nonpresent), suggesting that parents understood READY Talk as a broad style of conversation. Critically, children of intervention parents used significantly more decontextualized language than children of control parents (42.1 vs. 13.9% of utterances). This is especially important, because preschoolers' own use of decontextualized language is predictive of future academic language abilities (Uccelli et al., 2019).

In a follow-up analysis with the same sample of families, we investigated whether the READY Talk intervention also increased the quantity and quality of conversational turn taking (Leech & Rowe, 2020). We hypothesized that the abstract focus of decontextualized conversation would require extended utterances to ensure the message is clear to conversational partners (Curenton & Justice, 2004; Demir et al., 2015; Snow & Uccelli, 2009; Westby, 1991). Transcripts were processed manually to yield the number of conversational turns ("turn-taking quantity") and measures of "turn-taking quality": whether the turn contained decontextualized language, and each turn's mean length of utterance, vocabulary diversity, and total number of words. Consistent with our predictions, intervention parents increased the quantity of their turn taking compared to control parents. Importantly, there were also effects on the quality of turn taking such that conversational turns in the intervention condition contained more decontextualized references and greater vocabulary diversity. These findings illustrate that encouraging parents to incorporate decontextualized language into their everyday conversation leads to an increase in the types of socially contingent interactions that support preschoolers' oral language and school readiness skills.

Future Directions

Based on our current knowledge of environmental effects on language, we suggest that future empirical research dig deeper in three areas. First, a continued effort to uncover the specific features of caregiver communication and social situations that optimize learning across early development is helpful, as we can build on this work in later design of parent or classroom interventions. Second, additional research on

mechanisms, both neural and behavioral, that contribute to young children's language learning will also help inform our understanding of the language-learning process and efforts to maximize environments for learning. Finally, we know that context plays a large role in shaping children's language environments and language learning (e.g., Rowe & Weisleder, 2020). Thus, it is increasingly important to gain a greater understanding of the cultural-, societal-, and individual-level factors that lead to variation in young children's language environments, and to determine the extent to which children in different populations benefit from similar or different environmental factors.

In terms of implications for intervention, we encourage further testing of programs designed to promote contingent conversations between caregivers and young children. The majority of parent-focused intervention research has been with parents of children at risk for language impairment. In this population, several meta-analyses show general positive effects of parent-focused interventions on children's language development (e.g., Roberts, Curtis, Sone, & Hampton, 2019; Roberts & Kaiser, 2011). Interventions with low-SES families in which children may be at risk for slower language development due to environmental factors have also recently shown positive effects on parent input and child vocabulary growth (Heidlage et al., 2020; Leung, Hernandez, & Suskind, 2020), yet we have less research in this area and more evidence is needed. Furthermore, now that technological advances are providing opportunities to reach parents via different modalities, a greater understanding of the role of technology in delivering parent interventions would be useful. Finally, we know that intervention effects can differ for different families (e.g., Rowe & Leech, 2019). Thus, further understanding of what types of parent-focused interventions work or don't work for parents with different characteristics (i.e., growth mindsets, depression) will help in adapting intervention delivery.

Finally, while much of the research reviewed in this chapter is from parent–child interactions at home, there are parallel implications for instruction. First and foremost, teachers should understand that children are going to arrive in their classrooms with diverse home language experiences and language skills. Maximizing opportunities for children to engage in extended conversations in classrooms is just as important as it is in home environments. Indeed, one study of the language use in a single classroom of 2- to 3-year-olds from low-SES backgrounds found that those children who engaged in more conversational turns in the classroom over the course of the year increased the most in their language development (Perry et al., 2018). Teachers can take advantage of this literature on caregiver input to optimize the language environments of their classrooms by exposing children to diverse vocabulary, complex syntax, and opportunities to engage in extended and abstract conversations.

References

Adolphs, R. (2009). The social brain: Neural basis of social knowledge. *Annual Review of Psychology, 60*(1), 693–716.

Akhtar, N. (2005). The robustness of learning through overhearing. *Developmental Science, 8*(2), 199–209.

Bates, E., Camaioni, L., & Volterra, V. (1975). The acquisition of performatives prior to speech. *Merrill-Palmer Quarterly of Behavior and Development, 21*(3), 205–226.

Beals, D. (1993). Explanatory talk in low-income families' mealtime conversations. *Applied Psycholinguistics, 14*, 489–513.

Beals, D. (2001). Eating and reading: Links between family conversations with preschoolers and later langauge and literacy. In D. K. Dickinson & P. O. Tabors (Eds.), *Beginning literacy with language* (pp. 75–92). Brookes.

Boyce, W. T., Sokolowski, M. B., & Robinson, G. E. (2020). Genes and environments, development and time. *Proceedings of the National Academy of Sciences USA, 117*(38), 23235–23241.

Bruner, J. (1983). *Child's talk: Learning to use language*. Norton.

Carey, S., & Bartlett, E. (1978). Acquiring a single new word. *Papers and Reports on Child Language Development (Stanford University Department of Linguistics), 15*, 17–29.

Curenton, S. M., & Justice, L. M. (2004). African American and Caucasian preschoolers' use of decontextualized language: Literate language features in oral narratives. *Language, Speech, and Hearing Services in Schools, 35*(3), 240–253.

Demir, Ö. E., Rowe, M. L., Heller, G., Goldin-Meadow, S., & Levine, S. C. (2015). Vocabulary, syntax, and narrative development in typically developing children and children with early unilateral brain injury: Early parental talk about the "there-and-then" matters. *Developmental Psychology, 51*(2), 161–175.

Diamond, A. (2013). Executive functions. *Annual Review of Psychology, 64*(1), 135–168.

Ellwood-Lowe, M. E., Foushee, R., & Srinivasan, M. (2022). What causes the word gap?: Financial concerns may systematically suppress child-directed speech. *Developmental Science, 25*, Article e1351.

Evans, G. W., Maxwell, L. E., & Hart, B. (1999). Parental language and verbal responsiveness to children in crowded homes. *Developmental Psychology, 35*(4), 1020–1023.

Fenson, L., Dale, P. S., Reznick, J. S., Bates, E., Thal, D. J., Pethick, S. J., . . . Stiles, J. (1994). Variability in early communicative development. *Monographs of the Society for Research in Child Development, 59*, 1–185.

Friederici, A. D. (2006). The neural basis of language development and its impairment. *Neuron, 52*(6), 941–952.

Gabard-Durnam, L., & McLaughlin, K. A. (2020). Sensitive periods in human development: Charting a course for the future. *Current Opinion in Behavioral Sciences, 36*, 120–128.

Garrett-Peters, P., Mills-Koonce, R., Adkins, D., Vernon-Feagans, L., Cox, M., & the Family Life Project Key Investigators. (2008). Early environmental correlates of maternal emotion talk. *Parenting: Science and Practice, 8*, 117–152.

Gilkerson, J., Richards, J. A., Warren, S. F., Montgomery, J. K., Greenwood, C. R., Kimbrough Oller, D., . . . Paul, T. D. (2017). Mapping the early language environment using all-day recordings and automated analysis. *American Journal of Speech–Language Pathology, 26*(2), 248–265.

Hart, B., & Risley, T. R. (1995). *Meaningful differences in the everyday experience of young American children*. Brookes.

Heidlage, J. K., Cunningham, J. E., Kaiser, A. P., Trivette, C. M., Barton, E. E., Frey, J. R., & Roberts, M. Y. (2020). The effects of parent-implemented language interventions on child linguistic outcomes: A meta-analysis. *Early Childhood Research Quarterly, 50*, 6–23.

Hirsh-Pasek, K., Adamson, L. B., Bakeman, R., Owen, M. T., Golinkoff, R. M., Pace, A., . . . Suma, K. (2015). The contribution of early communication quality to low-income children's language success. *Psychological Science, 26*(7), 1071–1083.

Hoff, E. (2018). Bilingual development in children of immigrant families. *Child Development Perspectives, 12*(2), 80–86.

Huttenlocher, J., Vasilyeva, M., Cymerman, E., & Levine, S. (2002). Language input and child syntax. *Cognitive Psychology, 45*(3), 337–374.

Huttenlocher, J., Waterfall, H., Vasilyeva, M., Vevea, J., & Hedges, L. V. (2010). Sources of variability in children's language growth. *Cognitive Psychology, 61*(4), 343–365.

Kaplan, P. S., Danko, C. M., & Diaz, A. (2010). A privileged status for male infant-directed speech in infants of depressed mothers?: Role of father involvement. *Infancy, 15*(2), 151–175.

Kuhl, P. K. (2007). Is speech learning "gated" by the social brain? *Developmental Science, 10*(1), 110–120.

Kuhl, P. K. (2010). Brain mechanisms in early language acquisition. *Neuron, 67*(5), 713–727.

Leech, K. A., & Rowe, M. L. (2020). An intervention to increase conversational turns between parents and young children. *Journal of Child Language, 48*(2), 339–412.

Leech, K., Wei, R., Harring, J. R., & Rowe, M. L. (2018). A brief parent-focused intervention to improve preschoolers' conversational skills and school readiness. *Developmental Psychology, 54*(1), 15–28.

Leung, C. Y., Hernandez, M. W., & Suskind, D. L. (2020). Enriching home language environment among families from low-SES backgrounds: A randomized controlled trial of a home visiting curriculum. *Early Childhood Research Quarterly, 50*, 24–35.

Leung, C. Y., & Suskind, D. L. (2020). What parents know matters: Parental knowledge at birth predicts caregiving behaviors at 9 months. *Journal of Pediatrics, 221*, 72–80.

Liszkowski, U., Carpenter, M., & Tomasello, M. (2008). Twelve-month-olds communicate helpfully and appropriately for knowledgeable and ignorant partners. *Cognition, 108*(3), 732–739.

Maratsos, M., Fox, D. E., Becker, J. A., & Chalkley, M. A. (1985). Semantic restrictions on children's passives. *Cognition, 19*(2), 167–191.

Matthews, D., Biney, H., & Abbot-Smith, K. (2018). Individual differences in children's pragmatic ability: A review of associations with formal language, social cognition, and executive functions. *Language Learning and Development, 14*(3), 186–223.

Miller, S. A. (1998). Parents' beliefs about their children's cognitive development. *Child Development, 59*, 259–285.

Miller, E. K., & Cohen, J. D. (2001). An integrative theory of prefrontal cortex function. *Annual Review of Neuroscience, 24*(1), 167–202.

Naigles, L. R., & Hoff-Ginsberg, E. (1995). Input to verb learning: Evidence for the plausibility of syntactic bootstrapping. *Developmental Psychology, 31*(5), 827–837.

Neville, H. J., Stevens, C., Pakulak, E., Bell, T. A., Fanning, J., Klein, S., & Isbell, E. (2013). Family-based training program improves brain function, cognition, and behavior in lower socioeconomic status preschoolers. *Proceedings of the National Academy of Sciences USA, 110*(29), 12138–12143.

Newman, R. S., Rowe, M. L., & Ratner, N. B. (2016). Input and uptake at 7 months predicts toddler vocabulary: The role of child-directed speech and infant processing skills in language development. *Journal of Child Language, 43*(5), 1158–1173.

Noble, K. G., Houston, S. M., Kan, E., & Sowell, E. R. (2012). Neural correlates of socioeconomic status in the developing human brain. *Developmental Science, 15*(4), 516–527.

Oberhuber, M., Hope, T. M. H., Seghier, M. L., Parker Jones, O., Prejawa, S., Green, D. W., & Price, C. J. (2016). Four functionally distinct regions in the left supramarginal gyrus support word processing. *Cerebral Cortex, 26*(11), 4212–4226.

O'Neill, D. K. (2007). The language use inventory for young children: A parent-report measure of pragmatic language development for 18- to 47-month-old children. *Journal of Speech, Language, and Hearing Research, 50*(1), 214–228.

Pan, B. A., Imbens-Bailey, A., Winner, K., & Snow, C. (1996). Communicative intents expressed by parents in interaction with young children. *Merrill-Palmer Quarterly, 42*(2), 248–266.

Perkins, S. C., Finegood, E. D., & Swain, J. E. (2013). Poverty and language development: Roles of parenting and stress. *Innovations in Clinical Neuroscience, 10*(4), 10–19.

Perry, L. K., Prince, E. B., Valtierra, A. M., Rivero-Fernandez, C., Ullery, M. A., Katz, L. F., . . . Messinger, D. S. (2018). A year in words: The dynamics and consequences of language experiences in an intervention classroom. *PLoS ONE, 13*(7), Article e0199893.

Roberts, M. Y., Curtis, P. R., Sone, B. J., & Hampton, L. H. (2019). Association of parent training with child language development: A systematic review and meta-analysis. *JAMA Pediatrics, 173*(7), 671–680.

Roberts, M. Y., & Kaiser, A. P. (2011). The effectiveness of parent-implemented language interventions: A meta-analysis. *American Journal of Speech–Language Pathology, 20*(3), 180–199.

Romeo, R. R., Leonard, J. A., Grotzinger, H. M., Robinson, S. T., Takada, M. E., Mackey, A. P., . . . Gabrieli, J. (2021). Neuroplasticity associated with changes in conversational turn-taking following a family-based intervention. *Developmental Cognitive Neuroscience, 49*, Article 100967.

Romeo, R. R., Leonard, J. A., Robinson, S. T., West, M. R., Mackey, A. P., Rowe, M. L., & Gabrieli, J. D. E. (2018). Beyond the "30 million word gap": Children's conversational exposure is associated with language-related brain function. *Psychological Science, 29*(5), 700–710.

Romeo, R. R., Segaran, J., Leonard, J. A., Robinson, S. T., West, M. R., Mackey, A. P., . . . Gabrieli, J. (2018). Language exposure relates to structural neural connectivity in childhood. *Journal of Neuroscience, 38*(36), 7870–7877.

Roseberry, S., Hirsh-Pasek, K., & Golinkoff, R. M. (2014). Skype me!: Socially contingent interactions help toddlers learn language. *Child Development, 85*(3), 956–970.

Rowe, M. L. (2008). Child-directed speech: Relation to socioeconomic status, knowledge of child development and child vocabulary skill. *Journal of Child Language, 35*(1), 185–205.

Rowe, M. L. (2012). A longitudinal investigation of the role of quantity and quality of child-directed speech in vocabulary development. *Child Development, 83*(5), 1762–1774.

Rowe, M. L. (2018). Understanding socioeconomic differences in parents' speech to children. *Child Development Perspectives, 12,* 122–127.

Rowe, M. L., Coker, D., & Pan, B. A. (2004). A comparison of fathers' and mothers' talk to toddlers in low-income families. *Social Development, 13*(2), 278–291.

Rowe, M. L., & Leech, K. A. (2019). A parent intervention with a growth mindset approach improves children's early gesture and vocabulary development. *Developmental Science, 22*(4), 1–10.

Rowe, M. L., Leech, K. A., & Cabrera, N. (2017). Going beyond input quantity: Wh-questions matter for toddlers' language and cognitive development. *Cognitive Science, 41,* 162–179.

Rowe, M. L., Pan, B. A., & Ayoub, C. (2005). Predictors of variation in maternal talk to children: A longitudinal study of low-income families. *Parenting: Science and Practice, 5*(3), 259–283.

Rowe, M. L., & Snow, C. E. (2020). Analyzing input quality along three dimensions: Interactive, linguistic, and conceptual. *Journal of Child Language, 47*(1), 5–21.

Rowe, M. L., & Weisleder, A. (2020). Language development in context. *Annual Review of Developmental Psychology, 2,* 201–223.

Snow, C. E. (1991). The theoretical basis for relationships between language and literacy in development. *Journal of Research in Childhood Education, 6*(1), 5–10.

Snow, C. E., & Uccelli, P. (2009). The challenge of academic language. In D. R. Olson & N. Torrance (Eds.), *The Cambridge handbook of literacy* (pp. 112–133). Cambridge University Press.

Stephens, G., & Matthews, D. (2014). The communicative infant from 0–18 months: The social-cognitive foundations of pragmatic development. In D. Matthews (Ed.), *Pragmatic development in first language acquisition* (pp. 13–35). John Benjamins.

Surrain, S. (2021). "Spanish at home, English at school": How perceptions of bilingualism shape family language policies among Spanish-speaking parents of preschoolers. *International Journal of Bilingual Education and Bilingualism, 24*(8), 1163–1177.

Tomasello, M. (1988). The role of joint attentional processes in early language development. *Language Sciences, 10*(1), 69–88.

Tomasello, M., & Farrar, M. J. (1986). Joint attention and early language. *Child Development, 57,* 1454–1463.

Tomasello, M., & Todd, J. (1983). Joint attention and lexical acquisition style. *First Language, 4*(12), 197–211.

Tremblay, P., & Dick, A. S. (2016). Broca and Wernicke are dead, or moving past the classic model of language neurobiology. *Brain and Language, 162,* 60–71.

Uccelli, P., Ece Demir-Lira, Rowe, M. L., Levine, S. C., & Goldin-Meadow, S. (2019). Children's early decontextualized talk predicts academic language proficiency in midadolescence. *Child Development, 90,* 1650–1663.

Vasilyeva, M., Huttenlocher, J., & Waterfall, H. (2006). Effects of language intervention on syntactic skill levels in preschoolers. *Developmental Psychology, 42*(1), 164–174.

Vygotsky, L. S. (1978). *Mind in society: The development of higher psychological processes.* Harvard University Press.

Westby, C. E. (1991). Learning to talk-talking to learn: Oral-literate language differences. In C. Simon (Ed.), *Communication skills and classroom success: Therapy methodologies for language learning disabled students* (pp. 181–218). College-Hill Press.

Yu, C., & Smith, L. B. (2012). Embodied attention and word learning by toddlers. *Cognition, 125*(2), 244–262.

CHAPTER 3

Prioritizing Dual Language Learners' Language Comprehension Development to Support Later Reading Achievement

Jeannette Mancilla-Martinez

Dual Language Learners in the United States: Diversity Disguised

U.S. children from homes in which a language other than—or in addition to—English is used are referred to by many terms, but one feature remains at the forefront: English proficiency. For example, *non-English language background* is the school-designated term for school-age children (K–12) from linguistically diverse homes, independent of the student's own language proficiency. The gross dichotomization of students' home language environment as English-monolingual or not English-monolingual is just the tip of the iceberg that serves to disguise immense diversity in this population of learners. The bottom line is that language proficiency, across the home language and English, varies widely and is not an all-or-none phenomenon. A more asset-based term that acknowledges the duality (or multiplicity) of language learning and does not privilege English has gained traction in the United States over the years: *dual language learners* (DLLs). This term is most often used in reference to children from birth to age 8 who are learning more than one language and it specifically recognizes that children within the birth to age 8 developmental span are effectively developing their language skills, in one or more languages. I use the

term DLL throughout in reference to all children who are not from monolingual English-speaking homes, but I note whether findings are specific to DLL subgroups (e.g., English learners). The bulk of findings focus on DLLs from Spanish-speaking homes given the volume of research findings based on this population of DLLs, and the developmental scope spans research from the toddlerhood to the early elementary years (second to third grade) given this handbook's early childhood focus.

Diversity within the DLL Population

The sociodemographic characteristics of DLLs in the United States are immensely varied, and the "superdiversity" within members of this population has significant implications for effectively serving their strengths and needs (Park, Zong, & Batalova, 2018). For instance, hundreds of languages are spoken in the homes of DLLs, family country of origin spans the globe, family nativity varies widely, and family socioeconomic status encompasses all possible ranges, yet a common and misguided narrative is that being a DLL is synonymous with being a foreign-born, recent immigrant to the United States. While family nativity indeed varies widely and some DLLs and/or their families are foreign-born and/or recent immigrants, the vast majority of DLLs, especially DLLs in the birth to age 8 range, are U.S.-born, U.S. citizens. In fact, less than 5% of DLLs are foreign-born (Park et al., 2018). Thus, most DLLs have been instructed in U.S. classrooms since formal school entry. Furthermore, the instructional language in U.S. classrooms for all students is almost exclusively English (Bialik, Scheller, & Walker, 2018).

Somewhat less frequently discussed is the changed demographic landscape in U.S. schools across all regions of the nation. Historically, DLLs and their families have resided in "traditional destination states" (e.g., California, Texas, Illinois). But DLLs and their families reside in all 50 states and so-called "new destination states" in the American South (e.g., Alabama, Kentucky, Tennessee) have experienced unprecedented growth of DLL populations over the past decade (Romo, Thomas, & García, 2018).Diversity in the American South has traditionally centered on racial, not on linguistic and/or cultural, differences. This is a central point to understand—and one to which we will return—as the noted demographic shifts experienced by "new destination states" may have outpaced the development of school infrastructure to accommodate linguistic and cultural differences, in turn potentially limiting educational equity for the rapidly growing population of DLLs in these regions of the country (Krogstad, 2020).

DLLs from Spanish-Speaking Homes

Recognition and appreciation for the vast diversity within the DLL population in the United States does not contradict the fact that DLLs from Spanish-speaking homes continue to be the largest segment of the DLL population (Migration Policy Institute, 2020). Of the roughly 11 million DLLs in the United States (32% of the nation's age 0–8 population), the great majority speak Spanish as their native language (Migration Policy Institute, 2020). Furthermore, families from Spanish-speaking homes originate from multiple countries, but Mexico is the country of origin for most DLLs (Romo et al., 2018). Given their expansive representation across the nation and the comparatively scant research base on DLLs from other language backgrounds, the primary focus of this chapter is on DLLs from Spanish-speaking homes. But before moving forward, it is necessary to explicitly address the often used "at-risk" label in reference to U.S. DLLs.

DLLs and the "At-Risk" Label

The "at-risk" label, broadly referring to students considered to have a higher likelihood for compromised academic outcomes, is ubiquitous in the field of education (Zimmerman, Rodriguez, Rewey, & Heidemann, 2008). For DLLs, the duality of their language skills and their accompanying language status in schools (e.g., non-English language background) have been characterized as de facto "risk" factors for compromised educational outcomes (e.g., low reading comprehension, school dropout). The at-risk label is cause for concern, as multilingualism is not a risk factor for any negative life outcome. Yet the at-risk label for DLLs promotes and perpetuates deficit orientations by focusing on what students lack (i.e., an English-only language background; for a related discussion, see Patton Terry, Bingham, Berryman, Clay, & Caton, Chapter 33, this volume). Low reading comprehension (RC) among DLLs is often positioned as stemming directly from their language status. In this line of reasoning, English monolingual students would encounter few, if any, academic struggles simply because they are English monolingual. However, English monolinguals encounter significant reading challenges, and this has been the case for decades; on average, one in three students in fourth grade can read at or above the *proficient* level (Hussar et al., 2020). But national trends by student groups are more alarming: One in four Black and Latino students, fewer than one in four students eligible for the National School Lunch Program, and fewer than one in nine English learner students read at or above the *proficient* level. This sampling of sobering statistics underscores that race/ethnicity, income, and English proficiency, to name just a few factors, individually influence children's opportunities to learn in general and likelihood of RC success specifically. What might we expect the reading achievement to be for Latino students from low-income, Spanish-speaking homes who are not yet proficient in English? Their intersecting identities represent multiplicative risk factors for compromised RC. But poverty—not language—is at the crux of the matter. Not only do DLLs from Spanish-speaking homes disproportionally live in or near poverty, but they also generally attend underresourced segregated schools that are taught by underprepared teachers with lower rates of certification, fewer years of teaching experience, and limited experience working with DLLs (Samson & Lesaux, 2015). Poverty has been an established risk factor for a wide array of negative life outcomes for decades (Duncan & Hoynes, 2021), and it is beyond the scope of this chapter to address the complex relationship between poverty and race/ethnicity. But we must recognize that language status represents a complex factor that is confounded with poverty and race/ethnicity in the United States.

A silver lining lies in the role of schools in supporting children's RC. At the risk of oversimplifying the complex role of schooling as it relates to equality, there are two key arguments: (1) Schools can help reduce inequalities, and (2) schools can further exacerbate inequalities. Ultimately, for schools to effectively support *all* students, instructional efforts must be aligned with what we know to be the most effective approaches. When it comes to the science of early reading, there is a wealth of accumulated and growing research to help guide efforts to ensure that all students are positioned as capable learners that are expected to thrive. But this is not sufficient. There must be an understanding of the scientific process of early reading development, which is more similar than different for monolingual learners and DLLs.

The Science of Early Reading: The Centrality of Language

Language development is a remarkably dynamic developmental feat. Children typically learn to talk if provided with interactive opportunities to hear and engage with language. Furthermore, the types of opportunities to engage with language and the types of interactions children have with language are not structured in a didactic, formal way. In sharp contrast to language development, there is significant and ongoing debate concerning reading development. If read to, will children naturally learn to read? No. Formal and explicit reading instruction is usually necessary. But how much and which types of formal and explicit reading instruction are necessary are questions that hinge on multiple factors, especially on language, the foundation for reading.

The well-known simple view of reading (SVR) model (Gough & Tunmer, 1986) posits that language comprehension and word reading are necessary for successful RC. The *goal* of reading at every point in development is comprehension and knowledge development is severely limited if stu-

dents struggle to comprehend the text they are expected to read (Smith, Snow, Serry, & Hammond, 2021). By placing the goal of reading at the forefront, we may more readily recognize that there are more similarities than what appear to be irreconcilable differences in what we know about reading and its development. Yet reference to the "science of reading" (SOR) tends to be contentious, as it is often conceptualized as a sterile, recipe-like, skill-and-drill, and phonics-only approach to teaching reading. It is not. The SOR refers to research-informed insight into how children learn to read, stemming from empirical evidence and, in turn, into best practices for supporting reading development. Given that the goal of reading is always comprehension and that this does not change depending on children's developmental stage, *knowledge development* should underpin all reading instructional efforts: All students should receive sustained language comprehension support throughout the duration of their schooling (Justice & Jiang, Chapter 11, this volume). However, the instructional emphasis placed on word reading should typically not be sustained throughout the duration of schooling. Rather, word-reading instruction should be tailored to students' skills level, typically—though not exclusively—during the early elementary grades.

Still, the sterile-like conceptualization of the SOR has led some researchers to advocate for more contextualized instructional approaches. This may sound reasonable, even laudable, but there is limited guidance on what such an approach tangibly looks like instructionally. It is essential to have a tangible reading instructional plan, especially for DLLs whose educational needs have historically been underserved. Non-negotiable tangibles include language comprehension and word reading. However, a major challenge is that reading programs have focused heavily on phonics-centered instructional approaches and, in turn, phonics-centered assessments, while reading programs that intentionally and explicitly support students' language comprehension development in the service of requisite knowledge development for RC remain scarce; there is a dearth of language comprehension assessments. This is a long-standing but serious problem, as assessment results should guide instructional efforts. The preponderance of phonics-centered assessments results in an uneven emphasis on phonics-centered instruction, even though we know that language comprehension is pivotal for RC. Penetrating language comprehension has proven much more elusive, even though intentional and explicit attention to supporting language comprehension is necessary for knowledge development. Below, I synthesize key findings from my research, with language comprehension as the unifying thread.

Prioritizing DLLs' Language Comprehension Development

Traditional Language Comprehension Operationalization and Assessment

Language comprehension is a developmental process that requires the orchestration of multiple language components, including the ability to automatically associate meaning to speech sounds. As a broad construct, language comprehension measurement is distinctly complex, especially for DLLs who negotiate more than one language. Challenges in identifying and supporting DLLs who go on to struggle with RC are at least partly rooted in the assessments used for identifying reading difficulties, as schools typically rely on measures of word reading (Mancilla-Martinez & Lesaux, 2017; Spencer & Wagner, 2017). This is not surprising, as assessing language comprehension is generally more difficult than assessing word reading. The need to account for more than one language among DLLs introduces unique complexities in assessing language comprehension, and specific guidance on how to attend to native language proficiency for identification purposes is generally lacking and without empirical validation (Francis et al., 2019). Results from a meta-analysis reveal that nearly all studies rely on English-only measures to identify RC difficulties among DLLs, different types of language comprehension measures differentially predict RC difficulties, and most studies are cross-sectional (Spencer & Wagner, 2017). Findings from the few longitudinal studies to date suggest that it may be possible to identify DLLs who later struggle with RC based on a skills profile in which low language comprehension skills—most commonly proxied by vocabulary measures—are evident *during* the primary grades despite age-appropriate word reading skills (Mancilla-Martinez & Lesaux, 2011, 2017); that is, it may be unnecessary to wait until RC can be assessed after the primary grade years. This means we must *assess* DLLs' language comprehension. Yet, language assessments in schools are almost exclusively used as screeners to identify students who may have limited English proficiency (i.e., to identify English learners). This is troubling, as students whose parents report that they speak a language other than English at home are *assumed* to have inadequate English language skills. In contrast to the intent of the provision of English learner services, DLLs who receive English learner services often face a cycle of watered-down instruction (Murphy & Torff, 2019). Without a concerted effort to ensure that language comprehension is prioritized and becomes a standard component of school-based assessment for all students, our knowledge base on how best to support students' language comprehension development for successful RC will remain sorely limited. Yet we know that early language comprehension skills predict later RC outcomes.

Early Language Skills Predict Later RC Outcomes

The contributions of word reading and language comprehension are expected to change over the course of development: Word reading tends to exert a stronger influence on RC during the early elementary grade years, when students are developing age-appropriate word-reading skills, and language comprehension tends to take over as the stronger predictor after the early elementary grade years, when students have typically developed age-appropriate word-reading skills (e.g., Scarborough, 1998). For DLLs from Spanish-speaking homes, however, the influence of language comprehension on RC emerges much later, at the outset of high school entry (Mancilla-Martinez & Lesaux, 2017); that is, the developmental shift to reliance on language comprehension skills once word reading is automatized does not typically occur for struggling DLLs from Spanish-speaking homes at the late-elementary level (Mancilla-Martinez & Lesaux, 2010). These findings highlight the unique process of skills development among DLLs from Spanish-speaking homes. While DLLs from Spanish-speaking homes tend to develop word-reading skills on par with national norms, their language comprehension skills remain well below the national average (Mancilla-Martinez & Lesaux, 2011). Again, these findings suggest it may be possible to identify DLLs who may later struggle with RC based on this skills profile during the primary grade years (i.e., age-appropriate word reading and low language comprehension) rather than *wait* until RC can be assessed.

Because RC hinges on language ability, targeting language comprehension, and its assessment, is crucial to equitably support DLLs' RC.

Challenging Traditional Language Comprehension Conceptualization and Assessment

Several factors complicate our understanding of DLLs' language comprehension development and achievement that limit best supporting their RC. One factor is that English-only language skills are typically assessed, although DLLs' linguistic resources are not English-only. Another factor is that when DLLs' language skills are assessed in both Spanish and English, the measures used are generally designed for monolinguals, whether Spanish monolinguals or, more commonly, English monolinguals. A third factor centers on the predominantly English-based instructional context in the United States that necessarily limits DLLs' Spanish language and literacy development. Taken together, it is unsurprising that findings reveal a persistent pattern of low Spanish-only and low English-only language skills among DLLs, prior to formal school entry and during the formal school-age years (e.g., Gross, Buac, & Kaushanskaya, 2014; Mancilla-Martinez & Lesaux, 2011, 2017; Mancilla-Martinez & Vagh, 2013). The "at-risk" depiction plagues DLLs early on despite their predominantly English-only instructional context, and this pattern ensues during the formal school years. DLLs continue to evidence depressed oral language skills relative to national monolingual norms in Spanish and in English from ages 4.5 to 11 (Mancilla-Martinez & Lesaux, 2017). Given that DLLs' language skills, in Spanish and in English, appear to need further development to reach monolingual expectations, questions emerge about the potential need for specialized support services, such as special education (SPED). The multitude of factors that lead to the typical characterization of DLLs as somehow deficient in their language skills and in RC resist simple solutions, but a basic starting point is to consider the language development instructional supports and opportunities afforded to DLLs.

DLLs' School-Based Language-Learning Opportunities

Instructional use of Spanish and English does not impede DLLs' English language development and can in fact support English language and reading development (e.g., National Academies of Sciences, Engineering, and Medicine, 2017; Ortiz & Fránquiz, 2019). Yet classroom use of Spanish remains limited (Franco et al., 2019; Jacoby & Lesaux, 2017; McClain, Mancilla-Martinez, Flores, & Buckley, 2021). One line of research I have focused on examines DLLs' preschool language environments (McClain et al., 2021). We examined teachers' quantifiable speech patterns and offered qualitative contextualization and interpretation of those speech patterns. Our results showed that Spanish was rarely used in classrooms, though there was variability, and questions were also rarely posed, limiting DLLs' access to linguistically responsive supports. These results are concerning, because use of Spanish in the classroom is a foundational feature for high-quality language environments for DLLs (Mancilla-Martinez & Jacoby, 2018; Ortiz & Fránquiz, 2019). Indeed, teachers' use of Spanish and use of translanguaging strategies positively related to use of questions, in particular open-ended questions. This speech pattern offered unique affordances for enhancing DLLs' participation in instructional interactions to facilitate extended discourse with and among students. Like all students, DLLs are capable learners, and it is our responsibility to provide a strengths-based approach to their education, including the provision of rigorous and sophisticated language-learning experiences. To avoid deficit framings, educators' beliefs about and expectations for DLLs' dual language development and learning must be research-grounded.

Beliefs about DLLs' Language Development and Learning

It would be a mistake to assume that parents who share a similar cultural, linguistic, and economic background—in this case, Latino, Spanish-speaking parents from low-income homes—share similar beliefs about children's learning and language development and similar home language use practices (Hwang, Mancilla-Martinez, Flores, & McClain, 2022; Mancilla-Martinez & Lesaux, 2014). Not only is there heterogeneity in parental beliefs, but parents' beliefs relate to home language use practices and to their children's vocabulary achievement (Hwang et al., 2022). It is thus essential to provide parents with accurate, research-based information on dual language development. It would also be a mistake to expect that all educators have research-based knowledge on DLLs' language development (Oh & Mancilla-Martinez, 2021). Yet teacher beliefs are significant predictors of DLLs' English RC. The importance of professional development and training opportunities to cultivate research-informed teacher beliefs about DLLs' language development and learning seems clear and urgent to equitably support DLLs' reading achievement and development. But this is not an easy task and requires that educators commit to understanding the *scientific* process of language development among DLLs.

Scientific Understanding of DLLs' Language Development: Targeting Conceptual Knowledge

My research draws on tenets of the shared (distributed) asymmetrical model proposed by Dong and colleagues (2005), a model that incorporates features of the most prominent models of the bilingual mental lexicon (e.g., the distributed model, the revised hierarchical model, and the conceptual mediation model). The shared (distributed) asymmetrical model serves as a useful framework for understanding and supporting DLLs' language comprehension acquisition and development. According to the shared (distributed) asymmetrical model, there is (1) shared storage for conceptual representations of the bilingual's two vocabularies and (2) asymmetrical (i.e., distributed or separate) links between concepts and lexical names in the two languages. The shared (distributed) asymmetrical model also suggests that proficiency in one language supports proficiency in another language, in line with previous work (e.g., Bilson, Yoshida, Tran, Woods, & Hills, 2015). Furthermore, not only are semantic representations postulated to be shared across languages, but context also plays a central role, with bilinguals selectively activating either the first (e.g., Spanish) or the second (e.g., English) language. Similarly, the knowledge hypothesis (Anderson & Freebody, 1981) holds that students who have amassed a large vocabulary store have also likely amassed a large store of conceptual knowledge, and vocabulary is an integral part of general conceptual knowledge. Contrasting earlier, monolingual (or fractional) views of bilingualism (see Grosjean, 1989), the shared (distributed) asymmetrical model and the knowledge hypothesis suggest that DLLs' knowledge of *concepts* likely represent a more

scientifically based reflection of their overall language knowledge. Thus, reliance on traditional measures designed to elicit a match between language-specific lexical labels to concepts separately in DLLs' two languages is not aligned with what we know about bilingual language acquisition and development. Accordingly, language comprehension assessments that apply conceptual scoring may represent a more equitable approach for assessing and supporting DLLs' language comprehension.

Language comprehension entails much more than vocabulary, but vocabulary can serve as a proxy for language comprehension. By tapping DLLs' knowledge of concepts independent of the lexical label (e.g., Spanish or English) assigned to the concepts, we may obtain a better proxy of their overall language-independent vocabulary knowledge. In fact, though lexical development can differ, conceptual development is similar among monolinguals and bilinguals, and encounters with concepts rather than with lexical labels contribute more to early vocabulary development (Jardak & Byers-Heinlein, 2019). Additionally, children growing up speaking two or more languages reach language acquisition milestones at different developmental stages relative to their monolingual age-matched peers (for a review, see Kovács, 2015). Due to this developmental timing difference, comparing DLLs against age-based standardized language measures only in only one language may exaggerate discrepancies in performance.

Conceptually scored assessments reflect vocabulary knowledge in terms of known concepts, as students can respond in *either* language and credit is given for labeling the concept, whether the label is produced in Spanish (*semilla*) or in English (seed). Thus, the language in which the label for the concept is known is not the focal target. Use of conceptually scored vocabulary measures is not new, but previous research in this area, including my earlier work, has largely utilized *adapted* measures rather than measures designed for and normed on Spanish–English bilinguals (e.g., Mancilla-Martinez, Pan, & Vagh, 2011; Pearson, Fernández, & Oller, 1995). Newer research in this area helps fill this assessment gap by utilizing *standardized* vocabulary measures with both preschool (Mancilla-Martinez, Greenfader, & Ochoa, 2018a, 2018b) and school-age DLLs (e.g., Hwang, Mancilla-Martinez, McClain, Oh, & Flores, 2020; Mancilla-Martinez, Hwang, Oh, & Pokowitz, 2020).

Results underscore the utility of these measures, and it is also the case that conceptually scored measures predict English RC among elementary-age DLLs from Spanish-speaking homes, over and above the effects of English academic language (Hwang et al., 2020). These results suggest schools can capitalize on the conceptual knowledge DLLs bring to support their RC. These findings offer insight into cultivating more asset-based views of DLLs' knowledge and capabilities as learners.

Moving Forward

Building on current findings, several lines of research could benefit from further study, including language comprehension assessments, language and reading development support for the educator workforce, classroom language-learning opportunities for DLLs, and early identification of DLLs with or at-risk for language and reading disabilities.

Language Comprehension Assessments

Even when assessments are available in DLLs' home language, it is challenging to have personnel with the language proficiency and experience necessary to assess students. These challenges have not received adequate attention in research despite the fact that assessment selection matters for equitable instruction (Mancilla-Martinez, Hwang, & Oh, 2021). Language comprehension assessments for use with DLLs should allow DLLs to use their full linguistic knowledge when responding (e.g., Mancilla-Martinez, Hwang, Oh, & McClain, 2020; Oh & Mancilla-Martinez, 2021). However, there is a need for investigations of the utility and validity of such measures beyond Spanish. Furthermore, there is a need for the development of language comprehension measures designed for and normed on DLLs that tap a wider range of skills (e.g., oral narrative ability). The development and study of psychometrically validated language comprehension measures for DLLs will require strong multidisciplinary collaborations. There is much that can be learned about the affordances of methodologies that challenge traditional conceptualizations of language comprehension and allow for scientifically based, rigorous evaluations of DLLs' language comprehension acquisition and development for successful RC.

Language and Reading Development Support for the Educator Workforce

Our approach to understanding and supporting DLLs' reading development and achievement cannot be abstract, ambiguous, or arbitrary. No matter how asset-based and equity-minded educators' intentions might be, the approach must be scientifically grounded, systematic, and sustained or the very inequities we aim to eliminate may inadvertently be perpetuated. As developmental processes, the benefits of a strong language foundation on later RC may not become evident until the upper elementary grades and beyond. But this should not deter efforts to ensure that language comprehension support is provided early on and is sustained throughout the school years. Though the need to better support DLLs' language comprehension skills is non-negotiable, recent findings from new immigrant contexts raise new questions that warrant further investigation. For example, DLLs' word reading skills may need further support during the primary grade years (Mancilla-Martinez, Hwang, Oh, & McClain, 2020). Despite ensuing debates over the SOR, what does seem clear is that if we are to mitigate later reading and overall academic difficulties, we must be resolute about supporting DLLs' language comprehension and word reading development early on, and sustaining that support.

To this end, U.S. educators, not just a specialized subset of educators, must be provided with the necessary training and ongoing professional development to understand the scientific process of language and reading development among DLLs. National reports also reveal a persistent shortage of a qualified workforce to work with DLLs in the United States (National Academies of Sciences, Engineering, and Medicine, 2017), and preliminary evidence shows that some educators hold deficit-oriented beliefs, with those beliefs negatively related to DLLs' RC (Oh & Mancilla-Martinez, 2021). This raises equity concerns. Because reading is language-based and there is a need to better support DLLs' language comprehension skills, it is prudent to ensure that educators develop expertise in (dual) language development to equitably support DLLs' reading development and achievement. Thus, studies that investigate the effects of ongoing professional development opportunities anchored in the scientific process of (second) language and literacy acquisition and linguistically and culturally responsive language and reading assessments have strong potential to inform research-grounded educator beliefs and practices that promote equitable instruction for DLLs.

Classroom Language Learning Opportunities for DLLs

There is little question that classroom-based language-learning opportunities can be further strengthened across our nation's classrooms, especially for DLLs (Phillips Galloway & Lesaux, Chapter 24, this volume). Indeed, DLLs are typically afforded limited opportunities to engage in classroom talk (McClain et al., 2021). Research on how teachers can be supported to provide sophisticated language-learning opportunities to help build DLLs' conceptual understanding in the service of RC is necessary. DLLs have experienced opportunities and learning gaps pre-pandemic and the recent COVID-19 pandemic has disproportionally affected DLLs (Sugarman & Lazarín, 2020; U.S. Department of Education, 2021). During COVID-19, DLLs were less engaged in online learning, educators reported feeling underprepared to meet DLLs' needs, and DLLs' chronic absenteeism rate more than tripled (Patrick, Woods, Bala, & Santelli, 2021). DLLs' learning trajectories can be expected to be set back ("slide") or remain stagnant ("slow down"), referred to as the "COVID slide" or "COVID slowdown," respectively (Kuhfeld & Tarasawa, 2020). A complex task prepandemic, remote learning due to the pandemic has further compromised the quantity and quality of language supports afforded to DLLs that influence their RC outcomes, requiring scientifically grounded, data-driven guidance for accelerating their learning post-pandemic.

DLLs with or at Risk for Disabilities

SPED placement decisions are an issue of educational equity for all students, and more research examining the complex intersection of language status and potential learning disabilities (LD) is needed, including the referral and identification process for DLLs within the response-to-intervention (RTI) framework. RTI is designed to be an equitable approach for identifying LD (Fuchs & Fuchs, 2007), but linguistic and cultural differences must be considered (Klingner & Edwards, 2011). Of concern, DLLs' representation in SPED remains highly contentious (e.g., Artiles, Rueda, Salazar, & Higareda, 2005;

Morgan et al., 2015). If DLLs are not provided with appropriate language support services, we can expect that their RC will be compromised, significantly impacting knowledge acquisition. This is a cycle that can endure. Some researchers have pointed to educators' limited training and expertise in this area as contributing to DLLs' disproportionality in SPED (e.g., Artiles, 2015), and a recent study reveals that exclusionary factors, such as English proficiency, are potentially associated with rates of SPED identification (Mancilla-Martinez, Oh, Luk, & Rollins, 2022). There is a pressing need to invest in personnel with the language proficiency and experience necessary to assess students in their native language, and to provide them with ongoing professional development support.

Conclusion

Reading is a language-based, complex, developmental process. Precisely due to its parsimonious nature, the SVR (Gough & Tunmer, 1986) represents a highly useful model of reading by highlighting the non-negotiable roles of language comprehension and word reading for English monolinguals and DLLs. Despite this knowledge base, the reading instruction support afforded to DLLs is not always research-grounded. DLLs in the United States, in general, tend to struggle with reading to a greater degree than their English monolingual peers throughout the formal school-age years. There are numerous factors that contribute to this generally low reading achievement profile, some of which have been discussed in this chapter, but we cannot underestimate the importance of ensuring that the approach to reading instruction is not arbitrary, however well intentioned. Reading instruction for DLLs must attend, at minimum, to building well-developed word-reading skills and to providing sustained language comprehension support, as the goal is always comprehension. If we deny DLLs the opportunity to develop strong word reading and language comprehension skills, it seems inevitable that further inequities will persist.

References

Anderson, R. C., & Freebody, P. (1981). Vocabulary knowledge. In J. Guthrie (Ed.), *Comprehension and teaching: Research reviews* (pp. 77–117). International Reading Association.

Artiles, A. J. (2015). Beyond responsiveness to identity badges: Future research on culture in disability and implications for response to intervention. *Educational Review, 67,* 1–22.

Artiles, A. J., Rueda, R., Salazar, J., & Higareda, I. (2005). Within-group diversity in minority disproportionate representation: English language learners in urban school districts. *Exceptional Children, 71,* 283–300.

Bialik, K., Scheller, A., & Walker, K. (2018, October 25). *6 facts about English language learners in U.S. public schools.* Pew Research Center. Retrieved from *www.pewresearch.org/fact-tank/2018/10/25/6-facts-about-english-language-learners-in-u-s-public-schools.*

Bilson, S., Yoshida, H., Tran, C. D., Woods, E. A., & Hills, T. T. (2015). Semantic facilitation in bilingual first language acquisition. *Cognition, 140,* 122–134.

Dong, Y., Gui, S., & MacWhinney, B. (2005). Shared and separate meanings in the bilingual mental lexicon. *Bilingualism: Language and Cognition, 8,* 221–238.

Duncan, G. J., & Hoynes, H. (2021). Reducing child poverty can promote children's development and productivity in adulthood (Child Evidence Brief No. 11). *Society for Research in Child Development.*

Francis, D. J., Rojas, R., Gusewski, S., Santi, K. L., Khalaf, S., Hiebert, L., & Bunta, F. (2019). Speaking and reading in two languages: On the identification of reading and language disabilities in Spanish-speaking English learners. In D. J. Francis (Ed.), *Identification, classification, and treatment of reading and language disabilities in Spanish-speaking EL students* (pp. 15–42). Jossey-Bass.

Franco, X., Bryant, D. M., Gillanders, C., Castro, D. C., Zepeda, M., & Willoughby, M. T. (2019). Examining linguistic interactions of dual language learners using the Language Interaction Snapshot (LISn). *Early Childhood Research Quarterly, 48,* 50–61.

Fuchs, L. S., & Fuchs, D. (2007). Model for implementing responsiveness to intervention. *Teaching Exceptional Children, 39,* 14–20.

Gough, P. B., & Tunmer, W. E. (1986). Decoding, reading, and reading disability. *Remedial and Special Education, 7,* 6–10.

Grosjean, F. (1989). Neurolinguists, beware: The bilingual is not two monolinguals in one person. *Brain and Language, 36,* 3–15.

Gross, M., Buac, M., & Kaushanskaya, M. (2014). Conceptual scoring of receptive and expressive vocabulary measures in simultaneous and sequential bilingual children. *American Journal of Speech-Language Pathology, 23,* 574–586.

Hussar, B., Zhang, J., Hein, S., Wang, K., Roberts, A., Cui, J., . . . Dilig, R. (2020). The condition of education 2020 (NCES 2020-144). Retrieved from *https://nces.ed.gov/pubsearch/pubsinfo.asp?pubid=2020144.*

Hwang, J. K., Mancilla-Martinez, J., Flores, I., & McClain, J. B. (2022). The relationship among home language use, parental beliefs, and Spanish-speaking children's vocabulary. *International Journal of Bilingual Education and Bilingualism, 25,* 1175–1193.

Hwang, J. K., Mancilla-Martinez, J., McClain, J., Oh, M., & Flores, I. (2020). Spanish-speaking English learners' English language and literacy skills: The predictive role of conceptually scored vocabulary. *Applied Psycholinguistics, 41,* 1–24.

Jacoby, J. W., & Lesaux, N. K. (2017). Language and literacy instruction in preschool classes that serve Latino dual language learners. *Early Childhood Research Quarterly, 40,* 77–86.

Jardak, A., & Byers-Heinlein, K. (2019). Labels or concepts?: The development of semantic networks in bilingual two-year-olds. *Child Development, 90,* 212–229.

Klingner, J. K., & Edwards, P. A. (2011). Cultural considerations with response to intervention models. *Reading Research Quarterly, 41,* 108–117.

Kovács, Á. M. (2015). Cognitive adaptations induced by a multi-language input in early development. *Current Opinion in Neurobiology, 35,* 80–86.

Krogstad, J. M. (2020). Hispanics have accounted for more than half of total U.S. population growth since 2010. Retrieved from *www.pewresearch.org/fact-tank/2020/07/10/hispanics-have-accounted-for-more-than-half-of-total-u-s-population-growth-since-2010.*

Kuhfeld, M., & Tarasawa, B. (2020). The COVID-19 slide: What summer learning loss can tell us about the potential impact of school closures on student academic achievement. Retrieved from *www.nwea.org/content/uploads/2020/05/collaborative-brief_covid19-slide-apr20.pdf.*

Mancilla-Martinez, J., Greenfader, C. M., & Ochoa, W. (2018a). Spanish-speaking preschoolers' conceptual vocabulary knowledge: Towards more comprehensive assessment. *NHSA Dialog: A Research-to-Practice Journal for the Early Childhood Field, 21.*

Mancilla-Martinez, J., Greenfader, C. M., & Ochoa, W. (2018b). Assessing preschoolers' conceptual vocabulary. *Head Start Dialog: Research-to-Practice Journal for the Early Childhood Field, 21.*

Mancilla-Martinez, J., Hwang, J. K., & Oh, M. H. (2021). Assessment Selection Matters for Understanding and Supporting Multilingual Learners' Reading Comprehension. *Reading Teacher, 75,* 351–362.

Mancilla-Martinez, J., Hwang, J. K., Oh, M. H., & McClain, J. B. (2020). Early elementary grade dual language learners from Spanish-speaking homes struggling with English reading comprehension: The dormant role of language skills. *Journal of Educational Psychology, 112,* 880–894.

Mancilla-Martinez, J., Hwang, J. K., Oh, M. H., & Pokowitz, E. L. (2020). Patterns of development in Spanish–English conceptually-scored vocabulary among elementary-age dual language learners. *Journal of Speech, Language, and Hearing Research, 63,* 3084–3099.

Mancilla-Martinez, J., & Jacoby, J. W. (2018). The influence of risk factors on preschoolers' Spanish vocabulary development in the context of Spanish instruction. *Early Education and Development, 29,* 563–580.

Mancilla-Martinez, J., & Lesaux, N. K. (2010). Predictors of reading comprehension for struggling readers: The case of Spanish-speaking language minority learners. *Journal of Educational Psychology, 102,* 701–711.

Mancilla-Martinez, J., & Lesaux, N. K. (2011). The gap between Spanish-speakers' word reading and word knowledge: A longitudinal study. *Child Development, 82,* 1544–1560.

Mancilla-Martinez, J., & Lesaux, N. K. (2014). Spanish-speaking parents' beliefs about their young children's learning and language development. *NHSA Dialog, 17.*

Mancilla-Martinez, J., & Lesaux, N. K. (2017). Early indicators of later reading comprehension outcomes among Spanish-speaking language minority learners. *Scientific Studies of Reading, 5,* 428–448.

Mancilla-Martinez, J., Oh, M., Luk, G., & Rollins, A. (2022). Language and special education status: 2009–2019 Tennessee trends. *Educational Researcher.*

Mancilla-Martinez, J., Pan, B., & Vagh, S. B. (2011). Assessing the productive vocabulary of Spanish–English bilingual toddlers from low-income families. *Applied Psycholinguistics, 32,* 333–357.

Mancilla-Martinez, J., & Vagh, S. B. (2013). Growth in toddlers' Spanish, English, and conceptual vocabulary knowledge. *Early Childhood Research Quarterly, 28,* 555–567.

McClain, J., Mancilla-Martinez, J., Flores, I., & Buckley, L. (2021). Translanguaging to support emergent bilingual students in English dominant preschools: An explanatory sequential mixed-method study. *Bilingual Research Journal, 44,* 158–173.

Migration Policy Institute. (2020). The patchy landscape of state English learner policies under ESSA. Retrieved from *www.migrationpolicy. org/research/state-english-learner-policies-essa.*

Morgan, P. L., Farkas, G., Hillemeier, M. M., Mattison, R., Maczuga, S., & Li, H. (2015). Minori-ties are disproportionately underrepresented in special education: Longitudinal evidence across five disability conditions. *Educational Researcher, 5,* 278–292.

Murphy, A. F., & Torff, B. (2019). Teachers' beliefs about rigor of curriculum for English language learners. *The Educational Forum, 83,* 90–101.

National Academies of Sciences, Engineering, and Medicine. (2017). *Promoting the educational success of children and youth learning English: Promising futures.* National Academies Press.

Oh, M. H., & Mancilla-Martinez, J. (2021). Elementary school teachers' bilingual development beliefs and English learners' English reading comprehension achievement. *Elementary School Journal, 122,* 165–190.

Ortiz, A. A., & Fránquiz, M. E. (2019). Co-editors' introduction: Challenges to the success of English learners in the context of language instruction educational programs. *Bilingual Research Journal, 42,* 1–5.

Park, M., Zong, J., & Batalova, J. (2018). Growing superdiversity among young U.S. dual language learners and its implications. Retrieved from *www.migrationpolicy.org/sites/default/files/ publications/superdiversityamongdlls_final.pdf.*

Patrick, S. K., Woods, S. C., Bala, N., & Santelli, F. A. (2021). Schooling during COVID-19: Fall semester trends from six Tennessee districts. Retrieved from *https://peabody.vanderbilt.edu/ tera/files/covid19_fall_semester_trends_final. pdf.*

Pearson, B. Z., Fernández, S. C., & Oller, D. K. (1995). Cross-language synonyms in the lexicons of bilingual infants: One language or two? *Journal of Child Language, 22,* 345–368.

Romo, H. D., Thomas, K. J. A., & García, E. E. (2018). Changing demographics of dual language learners and English learners: Implications for school success. *Social Policy Report, 31*(2), 1–35.

Samson, J. F., & Lesaux, N. K. (2015). Disadvantaged language minority students and their teachers: A national picture. *Teachers College Record, 117,* 1–26.

Scarborough, H. S. (1998). Predicting future achievement of second graders with reading disabilities: Contributions of phonemic awareness, verbal memory, rapid naming and IQ. *Annals of Dyslexia, 48,* 115–136.

Smith, R., Snow, P., Serry, T., & Hammond, L. (2021). The role of background knowledge in reading comprehension: A critical review. *Reading Psychology, 42,* 214–240.

Spencer, M., & Wagner, R. K. (2017). The comprehension problems for second-language learners with poor reading comprehension despite adequate decoding: A meta-analysis. *Journal of Research in Reading, 40,* 199–217.

Sugarman, J., & Lazarín, M. (2020). Educating

English learners during the COVID-19 pandemic. Retrieved from *www.migrationpolicy.org/sites/default/files/publications/mpi-english-learners-covid-19-final.pdf.*

U.S. Department of Education. (2021). ED COVID-19 handbook: Roadmap to reopening safely and meeting all students' needs. Retrieved from *www2.ed.gov/documents/coronavirus/reopening-2.pdf.*

Zimmerman, S. S., Rodriguez, M. C., Rewey, K. L., & Heidemann, S. L. (2008). The impact of an early literacy initiative on the long-term academic success of diverse students. *Journal of Education for Students Placed at Risk, 13,* 452–481.

CHAPTER 4

Early Literacy, Response to Intervention, and Multi-Tiered Systems of Support

Dayna Russell Freudenthal, Mai W. Zaru, and Stephanie Al Otaiba

The Individuals with Disabilities Education Improvement Act of 2004 allowed local education agencies to use response-to-intervention (RTI) approaches for early identification and remediation of reading difficulties to reduce the numbers of students who need ongoing intensive intervention. RTI was intended to replace traditional approaches that utilized IQ–achievement discrepancy for identification, which were criticized for essentially requiring students to fall far enough behind their peers to qualify for supports, as a "wait to fail" approach (e.g., Fletcher, Coulter, Reschly, & Vaughn, 2004; Vellutino, Scanlon, Small, & Fanuele, 2006). The principal components of RTI are evidence-based core reading instruction, universal screening, tiered interventions, and formative progress monitoring (cf. Gersten et al., 2009). These components have been embodied in broader multi-tiered systems of support (MTSS), defined in the Every Student Succeeds Act (2015) as a "continuum of evidence-based, systemic practices to support a rapid response to students' needs, with regular observation to facilitate data-based instructional decision making" (Title IX, Sec. 8002[33]). MTSS are intended to provide a broad array of instruction and interventions beyond academic skills, and many chapters in this handbook focus on a wide range of supports, including language development (Phillips, Chapter 12, this volume,

and Zucker, Yeomans-Maldonado, Surrain, & Landry, Chapter 22, this volume).

Our purpose in this chapter is to describe promising early literacy interventions that can be used within RTI and MTSS approaches for kindergarten through third grade (for a review on preschool MTSS approaches, see Carta & Greenwood, Chapter 28, this volume). First, we describe our theoretical and empirical framework. Next, we describe the effects of recent studies (2017–2020) of early literacy interventions ranging from standardized to more data-guided instruction provided by researchers or teachers (see Table 4.1). Then we summarize major implications, describe limitations, and discuss directions for research. We provide resources in Table 4.2 for ongoing and updated information about MTSS resources.

Theoretical and Empirical Framework

In writing this chapter, we drew on the simple view of reading (SVR; Gough & Tunmer, 1986) as a theoretical framework to contextualize the foundational, code-focused instructional elements (phonemic awareness, grapheme–phoneme correspondence, phonics, word recognition, and fluency) and the meaning-focused instructional elements (vocabulary, oral language, listening

TABLE 4.1. Study Characteristics

Tier	Study	GL	Participants	Intervention	Measures	Findings
			Standard (*n* = 6)			
			Researcher-implemented (*n* = 5)			
1	Maki et al. (2021) (RCT)	3	T: (*n* = 21 scored below AIMSweb benchmark); BAU (*n* = 24).	Classwide intervention (10 sessions and three to 10 partner readings) and Reading Mastery offered to BAU.	ORF	Effect for T was higher than BAU (η^2 = 0.11) on ORF.
2	Al Otaiba et al. (2018) (RCT)	K–2	Scored <100 on standardized reading comp measure: T_1 (*n* = 56), T_2 (*n* = 55), T_3 (*n* = 61).	TEXTs (T_1: sequence, T_2: compare and contrast, T_3: cause and effect) 16-session small-group intervention.	[RM] ETSS: Expository Text Structure Screener	Effects on trained text structures on ETSS for T_1, T_2, and T_3, *d* = 1.9, 1.5, 1.8.
2	Vadasy & Sanders (2020) (RCT)	K–1	Study 1: K (*n* = 34) fewer than three letter names/sounds, grade 1 (*n* = 31) < 50th percentile on K spring literacy assessment. Study 2: K (*n* = 61) < 11 letter sounds [winter].	Intervention was 1:1, 5 weeks, 4 sessions/ week. Study 1: fast or slow rate of single- and two-letter GPC introduction. Study 2: single or mixed GPC introduction at fast rate.	[RM] measures of letter sounds, letter-sound writing, word reading	Study 1 effects of fast rate on letter sounds, letter-sound writing, word reading (*d* = 0.84, 0.59, 0.30). Study 2: no main effects.
2	Steacy et al. (2020) (QED)	1	Teacher-identified at-risk; composite score on measures of letter naming, decoding, and word recognition (*n* = 93).	Decoding and fluency in MTSS study; 1:1 tutoring (63 sessions) followed by 1–3 minutes of sight word challenge.	TOWRE	Students required on average 5.65 exposures for mastery word length.
2–3	Bouton et al. (2018) (QED)	1	Students with low responsiveness to Tier 1 (*n* = 24).	Students received Tier 3 (*n* = 24) or traditional RTI (*n* = 24): Direct to Tier 3 from Tier 1; 42 sessions on word-level reading.	TOWRE[f]	Large effects favoring direct to Tier 3 on sight word efficiency and word ID (*d* = 0.87, 0.74).
			Teacher-implemented (*n* = 1)			
2	Fogarty et al. (2020) (RCT)	3	Students at/below 41st percentile on GMRT-4 subtest (MacGinitie, MacGinitie, Maria, & Dreyer, 2010) and at least 25 wcpm (*n* = 200).	Students received T (*n* = 100): Web-based vocabulary intervention, or BAU (*n* = 100).	[RM] proximal measure of vocabulary, reading comprehension	Moderate to large effects on measure of vocabulary (*g* = 0.52–0.78), near measures of comprehension (*g* = 0.28–0.65).
			Hybrid (*n* = 9)			
			Researcher-implemented (*n* = 6)			
2	Foorman et al. (2018) (RCT)	K–2	Students below 30th percentile on vocabulary and reading skills (T_1: *n* = 1,653, T_2: *n* = 1,764).	Students received T_1: stand-alone (81 sessions) in small groups, or T_2: foundational instruction aligned with the core reading program.	FRA (Foorman et al., 2015)	T_1 and T_2 started below 10th and improved to 20th percentile; K students experienced the largest growth.

TABLE 4.1. *(continued)*

Tier	Study	GL	Participants	Intervention	Measures	Findings
2	Coyne, Oldham, et al. (2018) (QED; RDD)	1–3	Tier 2 (T: n = 318) 1 below grade on NWF, 2 and 3 below ORF benchmark. Tier 1 (BAU: n = 360).	Students in T received: supplemental for 4 days/week, November–June, or BAU.	ORF; WRMT-R[l]	Effects favored T on phonemic awareness and decoding (ES = 0.39, 0.36).
2	Burns et al. (2018) (QED, no control)	2–3	ELLs (n = 201) scored below on the ORF benchmark.	Students received targeted interventions (fluency or phonics) in small groups; all students received vocabulary.	ORF	Effects favored students with the lowest ELP (η^2 = 0.05).
2	Burns et al. (2020) (QED)	2–3	Students below 10th percentile on ORF, not SpEd (T: n = 92). SpEd (n = 22). Tier 1: (BAU: n = 385).	Students received T: small-group intervention in phonics or fluency; SpEd: school-delivered services; BAU (Reading Mastery).	PRESS decoding (Path to Reading Excellence in School Sites Research Group, 2014); ORF	Effects favored T over SpEd, and BAU over SpEd on reading growth (g = 0.74, 0.68).
2	Lovett et al. (2017) (QED)	1–3	Scored at/below 85 on reading measure (T: n = 172, BAU: n = 47)	Students received T: small-group 100–125 sessions of PHAST + RAVE-O; or BAU (typical instruction).	[RM], PIAT-R (Lazarus, 1990); SRI-2[e]; WRMT,[k] TOWRE, GORT-4[c]	Effects favored T on [RM] measures (d = 1.44–1.82), and code-focused (d = 0.57–1.39) and meaning-focused norm-referenced (d = 0.63–0.90).
2	Christodoulou et al. (2017) (RCT)	1–3	Students (n = 47) T: n = 23, waiting list: n = 24); below 25th percentile on 2+ subtests of WRMT,[l] TOWRE.[g]	Intensive small-group intervention, 6-week summer program, 4 hours/day; waiting-list control.	ORF; Symbol Imagery Test (Bell, 2010)	Effects favored T on ORF and Symbol Imagery (d = 0.76, 1.32).

Teacher-implemented (n = 3)

Tier	Study	GL	Participants	Intervention	Measures	Findings
1–2	Coyne, McCoach, et al. (2018) (RCT)	K	At-risk (T: n = 825, BAU: n = 781) scored < 30th percentile PPVT-4. R: not at risk (n = 741).	Students received T: small-group (88 sessions) vocabulary intervention + whole-class instruction. BAU: Tier 1; R: reference [Tier 1].	[RM] Expressive target word, Listening comp; PPVT-4[d]	Effects favored T on [RM] measure for target words and listening comp. (g = 1.07, 0.41).
1–2	Solari et al. (2018) (RCT)	1	At-risk ($T_1 + T_2$: n = 61) < 4 wrc and at-risk on listening comprehension (Texas Primary Reading Inventory); BAU (n = 37).	Supplemental Reading Rules [RR] (68 sessions) Tier 1 whole-class, Tier 2 small-group word study, comprehension, and fluency: T_1 = coached teachers, T_2 = uncoached, BAU = typical.	Phoneme Segmentation (Yopp, 1995); WJ-III[h]	Moderate effects favoring RR conditions on word reading, fluency, and comprehension (g = 0.41–0.72)

(continued)

TABLE 4.1. (continued)

Tier	Study	GL	Participants	Intervention	Measures	Findings
2	Fien et al. (2021) (RCT)	1	At-risk (10th–30th percentile) on SAT-10 (Harcourt Educational Measurement, 2002): (n = 757).	Students received T (n = 406): Tier 2 Enhanced Core Reading Instruction [ECRI] aligned with Tier 1 or BAU (n = 406).	DIBELS NWF,[b] ORF, WRMT[i]	Effects favored T on NWF and word attack (g = 0.31, 0.48).

Individualized (n = 7)

Researcher-implemented (n = 2)

Tier	Study	GL	Participants	Intervention	Measures	Findings
2	Savage et al. (2018) (QED)	1	Students (T: n = 119; CBP: n = 82) < 30th percentile on WRAT-4.	Small groups received (22–24 sessions) T: Direct Mapping and Set Variability of phonics, or CBP: current best practices.	WRAT-4,[j] WJ-III,[b] ORF, PPVT-4[d]	Effects favored T on word reading, vocab, spelling, sight word, ORF (d = 0.08–0.41); delayed posttest (d = 0.18–0.30).
2–3	Didion et al. (2020) (SCD)	3	Students below 25th percentile on TOWRE-2 and receive Tier 2 and Tier 3 supports (n = 12).	Data Mountain program (pilot: 21 sessions, 15 for replication): oral reading fluency, self-monitoring, and motivation training.	ORF	Between-case effects on ORF for pilot (ES = 0.54, 0.17), and replication (ES = 0.63).

Teacher-implemented (n = 5)

Tier	Study	GL	Participants	Intervention	Measures	Findings
2	Vernon-Feagans et al. (2018) (RCT)	K–1	Students < 35th percentile 1 or more WJ-III-DRB[i]; T (n = 305), BAU (n = 251).	Students received T: TRI (17 sessions) 1:1 (rereading fluency, word work, guided oral reading, and pocket phrases), or BAU.	WJ-III-DRB[i]	Effects favored T on letter-word, word attack, spelling, and comp (g = 0.26, 0.28, 0.26, 0.16).
2	Bratsch-Hines et al. (2020) (RCT)	K–1	Students < 35th percentile on 1 or more WJ-III-DRB[i]: T (n = 298); BAU (n = 247) dichotomized for low/high PA and vocab.	Students received T: 1:1 TRI (17 sessions) rereading fluency, word work, guided oral reading, and pocket phrases; or BAU.	WJ-III-DRB[i]	Outcomes favored T on all measures, lower initial PA negatively related to decoding, spelling, and comp.
2	Sutter et al. (2019) (QED)	3	Scored < 20th percentile (n = 5,042), or above (n = 17,920) on ISIP-ER.	Students received ISIP-ER [Istation Indicators of Progress-Early Reading], a computer-adaptive reading program (CARP).	ISIP-ER (Mathes et al., 2011)	Effects favored students < 20th percentile (d = 1.4); increased 18 points on reading on average.
3	Weiser et al. (2019) (QED)	K–8	Students (n = 452) with reading disabilities in SpEd or resource rooms.	Teachers (n = 44) were randomized in one of three coaching groups (face-to-face, on demand, and technology based).	CTOPP;[a] TOWRE-2,[g] ORF, TWS-5 (Larsen et al., 2013), WJ-III[b]	Effects favored students with teachers in tech-coaching on their phonemic awareness, decoding, fluency, writing, spelling (d = 0.22–1.01). (continued)

TABLE 4.1. *(continued)*

Tier	Study	GL	Participants	Intervention	Measures	Findings
3	Partanen et al. (2019) (QED)	3	Students < 25th percentile on KTEA-II; T_1: intensive ($n = 40$), T_2: small-group ($n = 42$), R: good readers ($n = 76$).	T_1: 3-month intervention with 1:1 and small-group, 3.75 hours/day; T_2: small-group, three times/week ; R: district, evidenced-based core reading.	KTEA-II (Kaufman, 2004)	Interaction effects favored the T_1 intensive group on word reading and decoding fluency.

Note. GL, grade level; ES, effect size; small, medium, and large effects: η^2 (0.01, 0.06, 0.14, respectively); Cohen's d or Hedges's (0.2, 0.5, 0.8, respectively); ORF, oral reading fluency; RCT, randomized controlled trial; QED, quasi-experimental design; RDD, regression discontinuity design; T, treatment; R, reference; BAU, business as usual; NR, not reported. ELP, English language proficiency; SpEd, special education; NWF, nonsense word fluency; PA, phonological awareness; vocab, vocabulary; GPC, grapheme–phoneme correspondence; wrc, words read correctly; [RM], researcher-made; TRI, targeted reading intervention; GMRT-4, Gates–MacGinitie Reading Test; FRA, Florida Center for Reading Research Reading Assessment (Foorman et al., 2015); PHAST, Phonological and Strategy Training; PIAT-R, Peabody Individual Achievement Test—Revised; SAT-10, Stanford Achievement Test, 10th edition; KTEA-II, Kaufman Test of Education Achievement.

[a]Comprehensive Test of Phonological Processing (CTOPP; Wagner et al., 1999); [b]Dynamic Indocators of Basic Early Literacy Skills Nonsense Word Fluency (DIBELS NWF; Kaminski & Good, 1996); [c]Gray Oral Reading Tests (GORT 4; Wiederholt & Bryant, 2001); [d] Peabody Picture Vocabulary Test (PPVT-4; Dunn & Dunn, 2007); [e]Standardized Reading Inventory (SRI-2; Newcomer, 1999); [f]Test of Word Reading Efficiency (TOWRE; Torgesen et al., 1999); [g]Test of Word Reading Efficiency, Second Edition (TOWRE-2; Torgesen et al., 2012); [h]Woodcock–Johnson III Tests of Achievement (WJ-III; Woodcock et al., 2001); [i]Woodcock–Johnson III Diagnostic Reading Battery (WJ-III DRB; Woodcock et al., 2004); [j] Wide Range Achievement Test (WRAT-4; Wilkinson & Robertson, 2006); [k]Woodcock Reading Mastery Tests (WRMT; Woodcock, 1987); [l]Woodcock Reading Mastery Tests—Revised (WRMT-R; Woodcock, 1998).

and reading comprehension) and the measures used in the studies reviewed. Other chapters in this book include more complex frameworks that incorporate executive function or aspects of linguistics and comprehension. Another aspect of our framework is data-based decision making to inform RTI (Fuchs, Fuchs, & Malone, 2018) given that schools need reliable and valid data to identify students who are below grade-level benchmarks and plan interventions. The foundation for successful RTI is implementing an evidence-based Tier 1 core reading program consistent with the science of reading (e.g., Foorman et al., 2016; National Reading Panel, 2000). If the core is not explicit and systematic, or if it excludes key instructional elements, too many students will need intensive interventions. Ideally, at most schools, Tier 1 should help roughly 80% of students read at grade level (Gersten et al., 2009); those who are below grade level or who demonstrate slow growth should receive intensive interventions (Tier 2) delivered more frequently, in smaller groups, explicitly targeting specific skills or multiple reading components. Providing interventions that increase in intensity is another essential RTI/MTSS component, as is frequent progress monitoring, so that if Tier 2 does not accelerate students' growth, these data can be used formatively to determine

who needs even more intensive intervention (Tier 3) (Fuchs et al., 2018). Tier 3 may include a standardized intervention program, or it may be individualized based on student needs, which is referred to as *data-based individualization.* There is preliminary evidence that students might benefit from receiving Tier 3 immediately if their needs are very intensive. Al Otaiba et al. (2014) found that when students in grade 1 received Tier 2 or 3 immediately, rather than following a typical Tier 1–2–3 progression, their reading outcomes were significantly improved (effect size = 0.31). This study used progress monitoring data to determine whether students needed to remain in a tier, progress to a more intensive tier, or were easily remediated and no longer needed intervention. Data from delayed follow-up testing at the end of third grade revealed that students who were easy to remediate had similar reading skills as peers in Tier 1, who never needed intervention. By contrast, some students who had required sustained interventions had standard scores below 90 on word identification, oral reading fluency, and comprehension (7.9, 39.4, and 24.5%, respectively), suggesting they needed ongoing interventions.

There is also a policy element to our framework, because student response data may be used, with diagnostic data, to inform referral

TABLE 4.2. Additional Resources

Resource	Author/funding	Key features	Website
Colorín Colorado	WETA Public Broadcasting	Provides bilingual, research-based information and activities for teachers and families of English learners.	*colorincolorado.org*
Division for Learning Disabilities (DLD)	DLD, Council for Exceptional Children	Provides information and resources for implementing evidence-based intervention with students with learning disabilities.	*www.teachingld.org*
Florida Center for Reading Research	Florida State University	Conducts research and disseminates information and resources to support evidence-based practices.	*fcrr.org*
International Dyslexia Association	International Dyslexia Association	Provides information for families and teachers of students with dyslexia and knowledge and practice standards for teachers of reading.	*http://dyslexiaida.org/ knowledge-and-practice*
International Literacy Association	International Literacy Association	Connects research and practice for the purpose of improving the quality of literacy instruction worldwide.	*www.literacyworldwide. org*
IRIS Center	IRIS, Peabody College Vanderbilt University	Online resources for evidenced-based practices, assessment, differentiated instruction, and MTSS/RTI.	*iris.peabody.vanderbilt. edu/resources/iris-resource-locato*
National Center for Improving Literacy	U.S. Department of Education	Provides access to evidence-based approaches to screen, identify, and teach students with literacy-related disabilities.	*improvingliteracy.org*
National Center on Intensive Intervention	U.S. Department of Education Office of Special Education	Supports stakeholders to implement intensive intervention for students with severe and persistent academic and behavior needs through data-based individualization.	*intensiveintervention.org*
Reading Rockets	U.S. Department of Education	Provides resources about reading for parents and teachers along with topical research briefs and reports.	*readingrockets.org*
Regional Educational Laboratories	Institute of Education Sciences	Works in partnership with educators and policymakers to develop and use research to improve outcomes for students.	*ies.ed.gov/ncee/edlabs ies.ed.gov/ncee/edlabs/ regions/southeast/plc.asp*
The Reading League	The Reading League	Promotes the advancement of literacy education and reading instruction rooted in science with researchers and educators.	*thereadingleague.org*
UFLI Virtual Teaching Resource Hub	University of Florida Literacy Institute	Provides teachers with tools and resources to explore new ways to teach foundational reading skills using technology.	*education.ufl.edu/ufli/ virtual-teaching/main*
What Works Clearinghouse: Intervention Reports and Practice Guides	Institute of Education Sciences through U.S. Department of Education	Provides reviews of effectiveness of programs and guides for implementing evidence-based instruction across K–12 including students with disabilities and English learners.	*ies.ed.gov/ncee/wwc* Practice Guides: *ies. ed.gov/ncee/wwc/ practiceguides*

and identification processes for dyslexia services and special education. Increasingly, over the past decade, changes in state-level dyslexia legislation require early screening for risk and providing students with targeted intensive interventions (cf. Stevens et al., 2021). However, there has been variability in guidance and policy; some legislation specified the use of particular screeners, other legislation specified that interventions must be multisensory approaches, and still others required that teachers be trained to provide reading instruction based on the science of reading. All 50 states support RTI or MTSS approaches as part of the referral and identification process for special education; however, researchers have noted wide variability across and within states regarding the screening methods for eligibility and the focus and intensity of tiered interventions (e.g., Berkeley, Scanlon, Bailey, Sutton, & Sacco, 2020). Researchers have also cautioned that school-implemented RTI approaches may not be effective if they do not adhere to evidence-based practices (e.g., Balu et al., 2015). The Office of Special Education Programs warned that RTI should not delay referrals for special education. These admonitions are important because data indicate that only about one-third of all fourth graders achieve proficient reading levels (U.S. Department of Education, National Center for Education Statistics [NCES], 2019) and among students identified as having a specific learning disability (SLD), only 33% perform at even a basic level (NCES, 2019).

A recent review of reviews provides an empirical framework for understanding effective interventions (Al Otaiba, McMaster, Wanzek, & Zaru, 2022). This review synthesized meta-analyses and systematic reviews conducted over the past decade that described the effects of reading interventions for students with or at-risk for reading difficulties in grades K–3. The effects of these interventions were generally positive, with moderate effect sizes ranging from 0.41 to 0.62 on standardized measures of foundational code-based reading skills, and with relatively smaller effect sizes ranging from 0.32 to 0.36 on standardized measures of reading comprehension skills. While an effect of 0.32 is small, researchers generally consider that an effect larger than 0.22 may be practically important and educationally meaningful (What Works Clearinghouse [WWC], 2020). In general, interventions were delivered in small groups or one-

to-one instructional settings; the intervention focus included explicit and systematic instruction targeting multiple foundational skills, and a majority of studies were conducted in the early grades (kindergarten and first grade), with fewer in grades 2–3. Al Otaiba et al. (2022) reported that when meta-analyses had enough studies to conduct moderation analyses, the effectiveness of interventions did not statistically differ based on the size of the small group, who implemented interventions, or the intervention dosage. Interestingly, in light of a trend of increased state-level legislation that requires or recommends multisensory interventions for students with dyslexia, one of the meta-analyses reviewed (Stevens et al., 2021) found no statistically significant differences in reading outcomes favoring multisensory approaches and noted a need for future and more robust studies.

Despite the large corpus of research synthesized in their review of reviews, Al Otaiba et al. (2022) reported several limitations of the existing empirical base on reading interventions for struggling readers. First, few studies provided information about the Tier 1 core instruction students received in addition to their intervention. Second, limited research compared the effects of standardized interventions to data-guided individualized interventions; relatedly, there were few studies of Tier 3 interventions. Third, there was considerable variation in screening tools and the criteria (below a percentile or below a benchmark) used to establish pretreatment risk levels, and there was variation in how adequate response was defined. Prior research has noted that pretreatment characteristics have been related to student response (e.g., Al Otaiba & Fuchs, 2002; Lam & McMaster; 2014), and that "responsiveness" may vary depending on the specific reading construct being assessed and the developmental stage for that construct (i.e., a greater proportion of students might be responders if the criterion was word reading rather than comprehension). Fourth, there was less research conducted in grades 2–3, by which time students might have experienced "failure," and samples might be expected to include more students who had not benefited from preventive interventions and students who have been identified with dyslexia or SLDs. Finally, few studies in the corpus included ongoing progress monitoring for growth, movement among tiers, or evidence of longer-term intervention effects through follow-up data.

Effects of More Recent Studies of Early Literacy Interventions

In this next section, we describe recent research examining the effects of early literacy interventions in grades K–3 that could be implemented within an RTI or MTSS framework. We conducted an electronic search of databases to locate peer-reviewed intervention studies published between 2018 and 2021. The search yielded 361 peer-reviewed articles after duplicates were removed. We excluded a few studies that focused only on predicting student response, did not include a control group, or did not adequately explain the counterfactual or business-as-usual (BAU) conditions. We included 22 studies, which we categorized as providing standardized interventions, hybrid interventions (combining a standardization intervention with some individualization), or data-guided individualized interventions (see Table 4.1). We further categorized these studies as researcher-implemented or school- and teacher-implemented, then ordered them by intervention tier and grade level within grades K–3.

Effects of Standardized, Researcher-Implemented Interventions

Five studies evaluated the effects of researcher-implemented standardized interventions on reading outcomes (one study examined the effects of a Tier 1-only intervention, three provided Tier 2-only, and one examined Tiers 2–3.) Maki et al.'s (2021) study illustrated the positive effect of a brief, supplemental, classwide Tier 1 partner reading intervention within an MTSS model. This small-scale study involved two third-grade classrooms in one urban school in which a majority of students' median oral reading fluency (ORF) scores were about 10 points below benchmark. For 2 weeks, students participated in a 20-minute daily partner reading with paragraph shrinking adapted from the Peer-Assisted Learning Strategy (PALS; Fuchs, Fuchs, Mathes, & Simmons, 1997). Students in the control classroom continued their core instruction (Reading Mastery; SRA/McGraw Hill, 2008). Although students in both classrooms increased their ORF scores, a significant moderate effect ($[\varepsilon\tau\alpha]^2 = 0.11$) favored the treatment students.

Another brief study examined the effects of meaning-focused interventions; Al Otaiba, Connor, and Crowe (2018) provided a small-group expository text structure intervention to students in grades K–2 with low-average vocabulary and comprehension skills. In this randomized controlled trial (RCT), students were assigned to three text structure treatment conditions (sequencing, cause–effect, or compare–contrast). Interventionists explicitly taught signal words specific to each text structure, read-aloud or supported repeated reading, and modeled the use of text structure graphic organizers. Researchers developed a proximal text structures test. Students scored highest on items within their targeted text structure, with large effects (ranging from 1.49 to 1.9). In the cause–effect and compare–contrast conditions, students demonstrated significant gains on standardized vocabulary and listening and reading comprehension measures. Findings from this study extend prior research on the positive effect of text structure interventions with older students and suggest their promise and feasibility for early RTI.

The next two standardized studies involved code-focused interventions. Their findings provide guidance for optimizing the rate of grapheme–phoneme instruction and inform practice exposures required to master sight words. Vadasy and Sanders (2020) examined the effect of grapheme–phoneme training that varied by rate (slow vs. fast) and unit size (*single* letter-only vs. *mixed* two letters). Findings favored the faster rate of introduction on letter-sound ($d = 0.84$), letter-sound writing ($d = 0.59$), and word reading ($d = 0.30$). Kindergartners in the mixed condition made greater gains across measures (median $d = 0.86$). Steacy et al. (2020) provided sight word training within a larger MTSS study in grade 1. Students read high-frequency sight words for 1 minute (presented in order from most to least frequent); tutors provided corrective feedback. On average, students needed approximately 5.65 exposures to master these sight words, and poor readers tended to rely more on semantic properties.

The last study in this section was conducted by Bouton, McConnell, Barquero, Gilbert, and Compton (2018), who used propensity score matching to identify pairs of students who had participated in two different RTI approaches. In the direct approach, students who demonstrated inadequate response (to 6 weeks of Tier 1) were immediately provided intensive intervention; they realized significantly greater growth than students in the traditional RTI approach on standardized measures of sight word efficiency and word identification (d = 0.87, d = 0.74, respectively) but had similar gains on decoding. The effectiveness of immediately providing the most intensive intervention converges with prior research (Al Otaiba et al., 2014).

Effects of Standardized, School- and Teacher-Implemented Intervention

We found only one study that included a standardized intervention implemented by teachers, and this involved a technology-based vocabulary intervention (Fogarty et al., 2020). The Vocabulators program delivered explicit training and practice for vocabulary related to literal and inferential comprehension. Lessons included frequent opportunities to respond, obtain corrective feedback (via videos from a "coach"), and receive motivation supports (e.g., goal setting, earning badges). Grade 3 teachers received brief professional development (PD) and weekly support. Eligible students were randomly assigned within classrooms to treatment or a typical instruction condition. Treatment students demonstrated significantly greater growth on several measures of taught vocabulary (effect sizes ranged from g = 0.51 to 0.78) and on near transfer measures of comprehension (effect sizes ranged from g = 0.28 to 0.65), but not on standardized measures of vocabulary or comprehension. On average, students completed only about half of the 57 intended lessons (range 7–57), suggesting that technology-mediated interventions may show promise for struggling readers but teachers may need more guidance to ensure adequate dosage.

Effects of Hybrid, Researcher-Implemented Interventions

We examined six researcher-implemented studies that included Tier 2 hybrid interventions incorporating standardized and individualized elements (i.e., using screening data to select programs and mastery or progress monitoring data to adjust pacing or grouping). Several studies were implemented as part of large-scale school-improvement MTSS initiatives with researchers collaborating to support low-performing schools. The first study of this type was an RCT conducted by Foorman, Herrera, and Dombek (2018) in 55 schools that compared the effects of two Tier 2 treatments: a supplemental intervention using materials provided by the Tier 1 core curriculum publishers vs. a combination

of three stand-alone interventions. Researchers hired and trained interventionists and provided ongoing coaching to support fidelity. Students in grades K–2 received identical Tier 1 interventions in addition to interventions daily across the year; both conditions yielded similar growth in reading and language-related outcomes. On average, students began the year below the 10th percentile on foundational reading and improved to the 20th percentile. Kindergarten students demonstrated the largest gains in word reading and sentence reading, supporting the importance of early intervention. Researchers concluded that the Tier 2 intervention that accompanied the Tier 1 core instruction may be more feasible and cost-effective.

The next study, conducted by Coyne, Oldham, et al. (2018), was part of a statewide initiative that provided additional training, resources, and infrastructure to support MTSS. Using a regression discontinuity design (RDD), they evaluated the effects of a supplemental research-validated Tier 2 explicit reading intervention provided to struggling readers in grades 1–3. Researchers hired interventionists and provided PD and ongoing coaching to ensure fidelity of implementation. Results revealed a significant impact on phonemic awareness (effect size = 0.39) and decoding outcomes (effect size = 0.36) but not on fluency or comprehension. The authors noted differences between their positive findings and the null or negative effects in the Balu et al. (2015) RDD study of MTSS that took place under less supported, real-world conditions.

The following two studies by Burns and his team (Burns et al., 2018; Burns, Maki, Brann, McComas, & Helman, 2020) examined the effects of Tier 2 interventions in six urban, low-performing schools in partnership with a research team and a statewide service organization that provided the interventionists. First, Burns et al. (2018) focused on three project schools with relatively high proportions of English language learners (ELLs). They provided students in grades 2 and 3 one of six decoding interventions and one of two fluency interventions enhanced with a vocabulary component. Students with the lowest English proficiency experienced the greatest increase in reading, with significant and moderate effects ($[\eta]^2$ = 0.05). Next, Burns et al. (2020) included all six schools and provided intervention to students with severe reading difficulties who were not receiving special education. They compared these students' growth to students in special education and in Tier 1-only. Students received one of six decoding interventions or one of two fluency interventions for up to 18 weeks; they demonstrated significantly greater reading growth on ORF ($g = 0.74$) than students in special education (SPED). Students in Tier 1 also demonstrated significantly stronger growth than students in SPED ($g = 0.68$). None of the students with severe reading difficulties caught up to their Tier 1 peers, evidencing the need for sustained intensive intervention.

Lovett et al.'s (2017) large project included students in grades 1–2 who scored below a standardized reading score of 85 and spoke English as their primary language. Trained research staff members provided small-group (1:4) intervention (ranging from 100 to 125 hours) in a multicomponent program that integrated decoding and comprehension strategies of the Phonological and Strategy Training (PHAST) Reading Program (Lovett, Lacerenza, & Borden, 2000) with the fluency, orthography, vocabulary, syntax, and morphology activities of Retrieval, Automaticity, Vocabulary, Engagement–Orthography (RAVE-O; Wolf et al., 2009). Groups that mastered lessons progressed more quickly through the program. Treatment students had significantly stronger reading performance, with larger effects on researcher-made measures ($d = 1.44$ to $d = 1.82$) than for norm-referenced reading measures ($d = 0.57$ to $d = 1.39$). The effects were higher for code-focused measures ($d = 0.57$ to $d = 1.39$) relative to meaning-focused measures ($d = 0.63$ to $d = 0.90$). These effects were some of the largest seen in any of the studies reviewed, and significantly more treatment students achieved normalized standardized scores (SS; > 90 SS in word identification, word attack, and passage comprehension). Follow-up testing (only for the treatment students, until grade 4) revealed superior growth for students who had received intervention in grade 1 rather than in grade 2, underscoring the need for early intensive intervention.

The Christodoulou et al. (2017) study evaluated the effects of an intensive summer intervention (provided 4 hours daily for 6 weeks) for students with or at risk for reading disabilities. Participants were 6- to 9-year-olds identified through local school and community outreach. Most (26/43) students had a language-based learning disability. Interventionists provided intensive small-group instruction focused on visual and phonological processing via explicit instruction, including letters, syllables, words, and connected text. Instruction was monitored and modified as needed by staff. Significant differences favored the intervention group over the waiting-list controls, but most differences were due to the declining scores of the control students, indicating the need for robust interventions to counteract summer recidivism.

Effects of Hybrid School- and Teacher-Implemented Interventions

In three studies, researchers collaborated with teachers and school personnel to guide their Tier 1 and Tier 2 implementation using mastery or progress monitoring data to adjust pacing or grouping. Coyne, McCoach, et al. (2018) conducted a large-scale study in 48 elementary schools that examined the effects of Tier 1 and Tier 2 vocabulary instruction within an MTSS framework. Participants included six to eight kindergarten students per classroom with below-average vocabulary, who were divided into two small groups assigned to Tier 2 or Tier 1-only conditions. Researchers trained classroom teachers to provide all students with an evidence-based classwide Tier 1 vocabulary instructional program and trained school-based interventionists to provide supplemental small-group Tier 2 vocabulary intervention for 88 sessions (4 days per week over 22 weeks). Both Tier 1 and Tier 2 were implemented with fidelity. Students in the Tier 2 condition outperformed controls ($g = 1.07$) and caught up to their not-at-risk peers on the researcher-made tests of targeted words. There was also a main effect ($g = 0.41$) favoring treatment students on a researcher-made listening comprehension measure, but not on standardized vocabulary measures. Students with relatively higher initial vocabulary knowledge showed stronger responses on researcher-made measures. The researchers noted that students with lower overall language abilities may need even more intensive, Tier 3 interventions to accelerate language development.

In the next study, Solari, Denton, Petscher, and Haring (2018) examined the feasibility of grade 1 classroom teachers implementing classwide Tier 1 and small group Tier 2 focused on decoding and listening comprehension. Teachers nominated struggling readers, and researchers confirmed the students had poor decoding performance (reading four or fewer words on a word reading screener) and impaired listening comprehension. Four to five students per classroom qualified. Teachers were randomly assigned to condition (Reading Rules [RR] plus coaching, RR without coaching, or BAU [typical school reading instruction and intervention]). RR teachers received 4 days of PD about RTI, intervention implementation, small-group instruction, and modification of instruction guided by mastery data. RR teachers provided Tier 1 comprehension strategy instruction during a brief (15-minute) whole-class read-aloud and supplemental Tier 2 small-group lessons (phonemic awareness, phonics, fluent text reading, and comprehension). Students in both RR treatment conditions performed similarly, and they outperformed students in the BAU classrooms, with moderate effects on word reading, fluency, and passage comprehension (ranging from $g = 0.41$ to $g = 0.72$). A quantile regression revealed students in the lowest quantile experienced the strongest impacts related to word reading and decoding but remained very low-performing; the authors suggested that they may have needed more intensive intervention. Teachers implemented instruction with acceptable fidelity but did not provide the full dosage (66% of lessons) and may have benefited from support to implement data-based modifications to adjust grouping and pacing.

Fien et al. (2021) also examined the effects of supporting teachers to implement Tier 1 and Tier 2 in grade 1. Schools were recruited that were already conducting MTSS and were willing to use a comprehensive core reading program (Tier 1 for 90 minutes daily), conduct universal screening, and provide Tier 2 small-group intervention for struggling students (scoring between the 10th and the 30th percentile on a standardized reading achievement test. Schools were assigned to the BAU MTSS or to enhanced core reading instruction (ECRI) MTSS condition. In ECRI schools, researchers provided specialized PD and ongoing coaching, along with materials to support explicit teaching routines aligned across Tiers 1 and 2, with Tier 2 preteaching key content emphasizing foundational reading skills. They also trained teachers to follow data-based decision-making protocols. Significant differences from fall to spring favored struggling readers in the ECRI schools on phonemic decoding, ORF, word identification, and word attack, with effect sizes ranging from small to moderate ($g = 0.25$ to $g = 0.48$). Response was related to initial skills; students with relatively higher fall reading scores demonstrated greater decoding and reading fluency gains. Fien and colleagues noted that

when schools have evidence that Tiers 1 and 2 are effective for most, inadequate response could more reliably inform eligibility for special education or dyslexia services.

Effects of Data-Guided and Individualized, Researcher-Implemented Interventions

We reviewed two studies that described the effects of researcher-implemented interventions; these were the relatively most data-guided and individualized interventions. Savage, Georgiou, Parrila, and Maiorino (2018) contrasted the effects of two reading interventions on reading outcomes of first grade students identified as being at risk. Researchers developed both interventions, which were administered in small-group format but differed in focus for teaching phonics. The direct mapping and set-for-variability (DMSfV) intervention incorporated instruction in (1) direct mapping of grapheme–phoneme correspondence, including multiple vowel pronunciations, (2) teaching strategies for being flexible (and self-correcting erroneous pronunciations) while decoding vowels with variable digraph pronunciations (e.g., mouth vs. shoulder), (3) shared reading of text with these patterns, and (4) individualization of practice to ensure mastery. The second intervention was designed as a best practice approach, including explicit and systematic small-group literacy instruction (grapheme–phoneme, word reading, and text reading, but without DMSfV aspects). While students made gains in both treatments conditions, results indicated an advantage for students in the treatment DMSfV condition on standardized reading measures (word reading, vocabulary, spelling, sight word reading, and ORF), with small to moderate effect size at the immediate posttest ($d = 0.08-0.41$) and again at a delayed posttest ($d = 0.18-0.30$). Most effects decreased slightly at the delayed posttest, except word attack, which grew from 0.08 to 0.18.

Didion, Toste, and Benz (2020) conducted the only single-case design study we reviewed, using a multiple baseline design to track ORF growth during two experimental phases of Data Mountain training: (1) self-monitoring and goal setting, then (2) motivation training. During the pilot study, the between-case standardized mean difference indicated a moderate effect on ORF of 0.54 in Phase 1 and a smaller effect of 0.17 in Phase 2. The average growth of 31 words correct per minute (wcpm) across 6 weeks was higher than projected (i.e., national norms suggest 1.5 words per week as an acceptable rate of improvement). Across the replication study, when self-monitoring, goal-setting, and motivation training were combined, the effect of Data Mountain on ORF was 0.63 (growth of 18 wcpm across 3 weeks). Didion et al. reported a high level of fidelity of implementation (99%) and established the social validity of the intervention, with all participants reporting they "always" liked using Data Mountain.

Effects of Data-Guided and Individualized, Teacher-Implemented Interventions

We reviewed five teacher-implemented individualized intervention studies. The first two tested the effects of an evidence-based virtual/webcam professional development program designed for use in rural schools, the *targeted reading intervention* (TRI; Vernon-Feagans et al., 2012). TRI coaches trained classroom teachers to provide targeted, 1:1 diagnostic reading intervention to struggling readers in grades K–1, including phonological awareness, decoding, fluency, oral language, and comprehension activities. In their 2018 study, Vernon-Feagans, Bratsch-Hines, Varghese, Cutrer, and Garwood asked teachers to implement TRI daily, but teachers provided a lower dosage (twice weekly). Despite this limitation, and even if teachers were participating in their first or second year of TRI, students made significantly greater gains than controls on letter-word identification ($g = 0.26$), word attack ($g = 0.28$), spelling of sounds ($g = 0.26$), and passage comprehension ($g = 0.16$). In their next study, the TRI researchers examined the program's efficacy for students with lower initial skills (bottom quartile on phonological awareness or vocabulary) compared with students in the top three quartiles (Bratsch-Hines, Vernon-Feagans, Pedonti, & Varghese, 2020). The researchers noted that students with lower initial vocabulary scores demonstrated stronger treatment effects for decoding and suggested this pattern was related to TRI's emphasis on teaching word meanings during decoding. However, students with low initial phonological awareness scores demonstrated weaker outcomes.

The next study is unusual within the overall corpus of our chapter: It had the largest sample size ($n = 22,962$), it was intended for students at all reading levels, and it was the only study to implement a computer-adaptive reading program (CARP) used in school and at home (Sutter, Campbell, & Lambie, 2019). The study compared the reading achievement growth of third-grade students who scored below the 20th percentile to those who scored above this cut-point on the Istation's Indicators of Progress, Early Reading (ISIP-ER; Mathes, Torgesen, & Herron, 2011). The CARP addressed students' individual needs in component areas of phonemic awareness, alphabetic knowledge, vocabulary, comprehension, and fluency. The program informed teachers about individualized instructional planning based on student progress monitoring data. The effect of CARP was similar regardless of initial skills levels; therefore, the overall gap in reading performance did not close. The recommended CARP dosage for students with scores under the 20th percentile was 90 minutes per week at school and at home, and stronger gains were associated with completing the at-home recommended component.

Weiser, Buss, Sheils, Gallegos, and Murray (2019) compared the effects of three teacher coaching conditions on student reading outcomes: (1) technology-based coaching, (2) in-person coaching, or (3) on-demand in-person coaching. Researchers trained special education teachers to individualize reading instruction guided by ongoing progress monitoring data (ORF and Istation ISIP data). Students in all three conditions experienced gains, but students whose teachers were in the technology training condition demonstrated significantly greater reading growth, with effects ranging from $d = 0.22$ to $d = 1.01$ on several standard measures (i.e., phonemic awareness, decoding, fluency, writing, and spelling). Teachers in this condition also showed greater gains on a test of the science of reading ($d = 0.93$) than peers.

The final study was a program evaluation conducted by Partanen, Siegel, and Giaschi (2019), who examined reading growth for two types of poor readers. The most impaired readers, who scored at least one standard deviation below age-based standard scores, were invited to participate in a 3-month-long, intensive Tier 3 intervention at another campus. They received 3.75 hours per day of individual and a very small-group literacy intervention incorporating a variety of evidence-based instructional programs tailored to their needs. The other group of poor readers continued in small-group interventions in their schools three times per week (40-minute sessions). Partanen and colleagues confirmed that at pretest, students in the intensive program performed worse than peers who remained in school-delivered intervention, but at posttest, both groups performed similarly on word recognition and decoding fluency. They also conducted a follow-up test a year later, when the intensive Tier 3 students were only receiving the school-delivered intervention, and found that these students' reading performance had declined from their posttest performance (although they did not regress to pretreatment levels of performance).

Discussion

Our purpose in this chapter has been to describe effective and promising early literacy interventions for use within RTI and MTSS approaches in grades K–3. We used the SVR to frame our thinking about whether interventions had primarily a code focus on foundational skills such as phonemic awareness, phonics, word recognition, and ORF, or meaning-focused skills such as vocabulary, linguistic comprehension, and reading comprehension, or a multicomponent focus. Findings from a recent large review of existing meta-analysis and syntheses of experimental and quasi-experimental studies spanning into upper elementary school (Al Otaiba et al., 2022) served as an empirical framework. That review indicated positive effects of literacy interventions that were larger for foundational skills (effect sizes ranging from 0.41 to 0.62 on standardized measures) than for reading comprehension (effect sizes = 0.32 to 0.36). Within that review, a few meta-analyses had enough studies to test moderation, but effects were generally not different based on group size, who delivered the intervention, or even the intervention dosage. Some limitations of the research made it challenging to contextualize findings for MTSS or RTI, because few studies described information about Tier 1 core reading instruction students received during or before intervention; most studies were preventive rather than remedial (conducted in grades K–1), and there was limited research that included Tier 3.

Therefore, we synthesized findings from 22 more recent studies published between 2017 and 2020. Most studies were conducted as Tier 2 interventions (the sole supplemental Tier 1 intervention was conducted by Maki et al., 2021). We found that research regarding Tier 3 remains fairly limited; only four research teams described their interventions as Tier 3 or a mix of Tiers 2

and 3 (Bouton et al., 2018; Didion et al., 2020; Partanen et al., 2019; Weiser et al., 2019). Given concerns in the field that RTI not become another "wait to fail" approach and some evidence indicating students with the lowest initial skills in vocabulary or word reading showed the weakest response to intervention, it was notable that only Bouton et al. (2018) tested the efficacy of providing immediate Tier 3 intensive interventions. We did not find any studies that both trained teachers to implement data-based individualization and provided school systems support for ongoing data-based decision making to inform Tier 3 or referrals for special education. Although Fien et al. (2021) mentioned training teachers to use data, they did not report how data were used. Their study also did not analyze students' reading growth in Tier 3 (those who began the study at or below the 10th percentile). Future research should examine how best to utilize technology to monitor the screening data and progress monitoring data that link to the interventions students receive (cf. Fuchs, Fuchs, Hamlett, & Stecker, 2021).

As mentioned previously, Table 4.1 shows how we categorized all interventions as standardized, hybrid (that began with a standardized program but provided some individualization elements such as selecting among programs to meet a students' needs, changing grouping, or altering pacing within small groups), or individualized (content for each child was based on data about their instructional needs in a very small-group one-to-one setting). Researchers implemented a majority (five of six) of the standardized and hybrid (six of nine) interventions, but only two of the seven individualized interventions. Similar to studies in Al Otaiba et al.'s review of reviews (2022), most of these studies were preventive, with six studies in grades K or K–2, five studies in grade 1, five studies spanned grades 1–3 or 2–3, and five studies in grade 3 only. In terms of the SVR, only four studies focused primarily on meaning-focused interventions (Al Otaiba, Connor, & Crowe, 2018; Coyne, Oldham, et al., 2018; Coyne, McCoach, et al., 2018; Maki et al., 2021). These studies demonstrated moderate to large effects on various researcher-made measures of text-structure knowledge or vocabulary, or ORF, indicating students learned the target vocabulary or skills, which is encouraging given that research has shown these skills predict reading comprehension (e.g., Nagy & Wagner, 2007); but there were generally no significant differences on norm-referenced measures. Most interventions were code-focused or offered multiple components, and similar to Al Otaiba et al.'s review (2021), we found stronger effects on norm-referenced measures for code-focused skills of phonemic awareness, word reading, and ORF (effect sizes ranging from 0.19 to 1.31) than for meaning-focused skills of vocabulary, listening, or reading comprehension (0.16 to 0.90).

There was a trend for effects to be higher within the hybrid interventions, with the largest consistent effects reported in the researcher-implemented study by Lovett et al. (2017). Notably, Lovett et al. also found that a larger proportion of treatment students demonstrated normalized reading than did controls, with stronger growth trajectories for students who received intervention during grade 1 rather than grade 2. Their longitudinal findings were encouraging and contrasted diminishing effects over summer for controls (Christodoulou et al., 2017), declining trends in reading after students completed an intensive intervention and returned to typical school supports (Partanen et al., 2019), and diminishing effects at follow-up (Savage et al., 2018).

Among the other hybrid intervention studies, several were conducted in the context of large initiatives to shore up the foundation of RTI by focusing on Tiers 1 and 2; some were implemented by researcher-hired staff and some by trained teachers and school staff. A couple of studies utilized technology to provide web-based student instruction, and others used technology to coach teachers to individualize instruction. We noted a trend that teachers with less support struggled to provide the entire intended dosage of intervention. Nevertheless, it was encouraging that the alignment of content and routines could make Tiers 1 and 2 more feasible for teachers. Often, Tier 2 interventions pretaught key skills in small-group settings, with more explicit and targeted practice. Whether researcher- or teacher-implemented, studies shared two common elements: Students were screened for risk, and research staff or school teachers (or aides) received training for the Tier 1 and 2 programs for MTSS and about data-based individualization. Some studies also provided ongoing coaching. Across these studies, the pattern of positive effects contrasts with the Balu et al.'s (2015) RTI evaluation, which found null or negative effects for Tier 2 interventions. Perhaps this is because their evaluation examined school-implemented

RTI, and schools did not use consistent benchmarks for universal screeners, select evidence-based interventions, or train/coach personnel to implement with fidelity for the intended dosage.

This newer corpus of studies provides directions for future RTI research about individualizing early interventions. For example, findings from the Vadasy and Sanders study (2020) suggest a fast rate of presentation for grapheme–phoneme correspondence was effective. Findings from Steacy et al. (2020) suggest it may take about six practice cycles for struggling first graders to read sight words automatically. Findings from Savage et al. (2018) and Lovett et al. (2017) indicate that it is fruitful to teach students strategies for thinking flexibly about decoding words with complex vowel patterns and providing practice reading words in decodable texts. In these two studies, there was an element of motivation or attribution training to help students apply strategies and recognize when the strategies worked; these motivational elements were also intervention components in studies by Didion et al. (2020) and Fogarty et al. (2020).

Conclusion

Effective RTI/MTSS implementation requires an efficient and organized school system for data-based decision making, with teachers who have the knowledge and skill to implement instruction and intensive interventions. We hope our chapter supports researchers, leaders, and teachers in working collaboratively to collect, analyze, and interpret data to guide instructional decision making and problem solving at a schoolwide level.

References

An asterisk (*) indicates this study was in the corpus reviewed for this chapter.

*Al Otaiba, S., Connor, C. M., & Crowe, E. (2018). Promise and feasibility of teaching expository text structure: A primary grade pilot study. *Reading and Writing, 31*(9), 1997–2015.

Al Otaiba, S., Connor, C. M., Folsom, J. S., Wanzek, J., Greulich, L., Schatschneider, C., & Wagner, R. K. (2014). To wait in Tier 1 or intervene immediately: A randomized experiment examining first-grade response to intervention in reading. *Exceptional Children, 81*(1), 11–27.

Al Otaiba, S., & Fuchs, D. (2002). Characteristics of children who are unresponsive to early literacy intervention: A review of the literature. *Remedial and Special Education, 23*(5), 300–316.

Al Otaiba, S., McMaster, K., Wanzek, K., & Zaru, M. (2022). What we know and need to know about literacy interventions for elementary students with reading difficulties and disabilities, including dyslexia. *Reading Research Quarterly.*

Balu, R., Zhu, P., Doolittle, F., Schiller, E., Jenkins, J., & Gersten, R. (2015). *Evaluation of response to intervention practices for elementary school reading (NCEE 2016–4000).* National Center for Education Evaluation and Regional Assistance.

Bell, N. (2010). *Symbol Imagery Test.* Gander Educational Publishing.

Berkeley, S., Scanlon, D., Bailey, T. R., Sutton, J. C., & Sacco, D. M. (2020). A snapshot of RTI implementation a decade later: New picture, same story. *Journal of Learning Disabilities, 53*(5), 332–342.

*Bouton, B., McConnell, J. R., Barquero, L. A., Gilbert, J. K., & Compton, D. L. (2018). Upside-down response to intervention: A quasi-experimental study. *Learning Disabilities Research and Practice, 33*(4), 229–236.

*Bratsch-Hines, M., Vernon-Feagans, L., Pedonti, S., & Varghese, C. (2020). Differential effects of the targeted reading intervention for students with low phonological awareness and/or vocabulary. *Learning Disability Quarterly, 43*(4), 214–226.

*Burns, M. K., Frederick, A., Helman, L., Pulles, S. M., McComas, J. J., & Aguilar, L. (2018). Relationship between language proficiency and growth during reading interventions. *Journal of Educational Research, 110*(6), 581–588.

*Burns, M. K., Maki, K. E., Brann, K. L., McComas, J. J., & Helman, L. A. (2020). Comparison of reading growth among students with severe reading deficits who received intervention to typically achieving students and students receiving special education. *Journal of Learning Disabilities, 53*(6), 444–453.

*Christodoulou, J. A., Cyr, A., Murtagh, J., Chang, P., Lin, J., Guarino, A. J., . . . Gabrieli, J. D. (2017). Impact of intensive summer reading intervention for children with reading disabilities and difficulties in early elementary school. *Journal of Learning Disabilities, 50*(2), 115–127.

*Coyne, M. D., McCoach, D. B., Ware, S., Austin, C. R., Loftus-Rattan, S. M., & Baker, D. L. (2018). Racing against the vocabulary gap: Matthew effects in early vocabulary instruction and intervention. *Exceptional Children, 85*(2), 163–179.

*Coyne, M. D., Oldham, A., Dougherty, S. M., Leonard, K., Koriakin, T., Gage, N. A., . . . Gillis, M. (2018). Evaluating the effects of supplemental reading intervention within an MTSS or RTI reading reform initiative using a regression discontinuity design. *Exceptional Children, 84*(4), 350–367.

*Didion, L., Toste, J. R., & Benz, S. A. (2020). Self-determination to increase oral reading fluency performance: Pilot and replication single-case design studies. *Learning Disabilities Research and Practice, 35*(4), 218–231.

Dunn, L. M., & Dunn, D. M. (2007). *PPVT-4: Peabody Picture Vocabulary Test.* Pearson Assessments.

Every Student Succeeds Act of 2015, 20 U.S.C. § 7801 (2015).

*Fien, H., Nelson, N. J., Smolkowski, K., Kosty, D., Pilger, M., Baker, S. K., & Smith, J. L. M. (2021). A conceptual replication study of the Enhanced Core Reading Instruction MTSS-reading model. *Exceptional Children, 87*(3), 265–288.

Fletcher, J. M., Coulter, W. A., Reschly, D. J., & Vaughn, S. (2004). Alternative approaches to the definition and identification of learning disabilities: Some questions and answers. *Annals of Dyslexia, 54*(2), 304–331.

*Fogarty, M., Coyne, M. D., Simmons, L. E., Simmons, D. C., Henri, M., Kwok, O. M., . . . Wang, H. (2020). Effects of technology-mediated vocabulary intervention for third-grade students with reading difficulties. *Journal of Research on Educational Effectiveness, 13*(2), 271–297.

Foorman, B., Beyler, N., Borradaile, K., Coyne, M., Denton, C. A., Dimino, J., . . . Wissel, S. (2016). *Foundational skills to support reading for understanding in kindergarten through 3rd grade* (Educator's Practice Guide, NCEE 2016–4008). What Works Clearinghouse.

*Foorman, B. R., Herrera, S., & Dombek, J. (2018). The relative impact of aligning Tier 2 intervention materials with classroom core reading materials in grades K–2. *Elementary School Journal, 118*(3), 477–504.

Foorman, B., Petscher, Y., & Schatschneider, C. (2015). *Florida Center for Reading Research (FCRR) Reading Assessment: Technical manuals.* Florida Center for Reading Research. Retrieved from *www.fcrr.org/for-researchers/fra.aspx.*

Fuchs, D., Fuchs, L. S., Mathes, P. G., & Simmons, D. C. (1997). Peer-assisted learning strategies: Making classrooms more responsive to diversity. *American Educational Research Journal, 34*(1), 174–206.

Fuchs, L. S., Fuchs, D., Hamlett, C. L., & Stecker, P. M. (2021). Bringing data-based individualization to scale: A call for the next-generation technology of teacher support. *Journal of Learning Disabilities, 54,* 319–333.

Fuchs, L. S., Fuchs, D., & Malone, A. S. (2018).

The taxonomy of intervention intensity. *Teaching Exceptional Children, 50*(4), 194–202.

Gersten, R., Compton, D., Connor, C. M., Dimino, J., Santoro, L., Linan-Thompson, S., & Tilly, W. D. (2009). *Assisting students struggling with reading: Response to intervention (RtI) and multi-tier intervention in the primary grades (NCEE 2009–4045).* National Center for Education Evaluation and Regional Assistance, Institute of Education Sciences, U.S. Department of Education.

Gough, P. B., & Tunmer, W. (1986). Decoding, reading, and reading disability. *Remedial and Special Education, 7,* 6–10.

Harcourt Educational Measurement. (2002). *Stanford Achievement Test (SAT-10).* Harcourt Brace & Company.

Individuals with Disabilities Education Improvement Act, H.R. 1350, 108th Cong. (2004).

Kaminski, R. A., & Good, R. H. (1996). Toward a technology for assessing basic early literacy skills. *School Psychology Review, 25,* 215–227.

Kaufman, A. S. (2004). *Kaufman Test of Educational Achievement (KTEA-II).* American Guidance Service.

Lam, E. A., & McMaster, K. L. (2014). Predictors of responsiveness to early literacy intervention: A 10-year update. *Learning Disability Quarterly, 37*(3), 134–147.

Larsen, S. C., Hammill, D. D., & Moats, L. (2013). *Test of Written Spelling, 5th Edition* (TWS-5). PRO-ED.

Lazarus, B. D. (1990). Peabody Individual Achievement Test—Revised (PIAT-R). *Diagnostique, 15,* 135–148.

*Lovett, M. W., Frijters, J. C., Wolf, M., Steinbach, K. A., Sevcik, R. A., & Morris, R. D. (2017). Early intervention for children at risk for reading disabilities: The impact of grade at intervention and individual differences on intervention outcomes. *Journal of Educational Psychology, 109*(7), 889–914.

Lovett, M. W., Lacerenza, L., & Borden, S. L. (2000). Putting struggling readers on the PHAST track: A program to integrate phonological and strategy-based remedial reading instruction and maximize outcomes. *Journal of Learning Disabilities, 33,* 458–476.

MacGinitie, W. H., MacGinitie, R. K., Maria, K., & Dreyer, L. G. (2010). *Gates-MacGinitie reading tests* (4th ed.). Itasca, IL: Riverside Publishing.

*Maki, K. E., Ittner, A., Pulles, S. M., Burns, M. K., Helman, L., & McComas, J. J. (2021, January). *Effects of an abbreviated class-wide reading intervention for students in third grade.* Contemporary School Psychology.

Mathes, P., Torgesen, J., & Herron, J. (2011). *Istation's Indicators of Progress, Early Reading: Computer adaptive testing system for continuous progress monitoring of reading growth for students pre-K to grade 3 (Technical manual).* Istation.

Nagy, W., & Wagner, R. K. (2007). Metalinguistic awareness and the vocabulary–comprehension connection. In R. K. Wagner, A. E. Muse, & K. R. Tannenbaum (Eds.), *Vocabulary acquisition: Implications for reading comprehension* (pp. 52–77). Guilford Press.

National Reading Panel (U.S.), National Institute of Child Health, & Human Development (U.S.). (2000). *Teaching children to read: An evidence-based assessment of the scientific research literature on reading and its implications for reading instruction: Reports of the subgroups.* National Institute of Child Health and Human Development, National Institutes of Health.

Newcomer, P. L. (1999). *SRI-2 examiner's manual.* Pro-Ed.

*Partanen, M., Siegel, L. S., & Giaschi, D. E. (2019). Longitudinal outcomes of an individualized and intensive reading intervention for third grade students. *Dyslexia, 25*(3), 227–245.

Path to Reading Excellence in School Sites Research Group. (2014). *PRESS intervention manual.* Minnesota Center for Reading Research.

*Savage, R., Georgiou, G., Parrila, R., & Maiorino, K. (2018). Preventative reading interventions teaching direct mapping of graphemes in texts and set-for-variability aid at-risk learners. *Scientific Studies of Reading, 22*(3), 225–247.

*Solari, E. J., Denton, C. A., Petscher, Y., & Haring, C. (2018). Examining the effects and feasibility of a teacher-implemented Tier 1 and Tier 2 intervention in word reading, fluency, and comprehension. *Journal of Research on Educational Effectiveness, 11*(2), 163–191.

SRA/McGraw-Hill. (2008). *Reading mastery 1.* McGraw-Hill Education.

*Steacy, L. M., Fuchs, D., Gilbert, J. K., Kearns, D. M., Elleman, A. M., & Edwards, A. A. (2020). Sight word acquisition in first grade students at risk for reading disabilities: An item-level exploration of the number of exposures required for mastery. *Annals of Dyslexia, 70*(2), 259–274.

Stevens, E. A., Austin, C., Moore, C., Scammacca, N., Boucher, A. N., & Vaughn, S. (2021). Current state of the evidence: Examining the effects of Orton–Gillingham reading interventions for students with or at risk for word-level reading disabilities. *Exceptional Children, 87*(4), 397–417.

*Sutter, C. C., Campbell, L. O., & Lambie, G. W. (2019). Computer-adaptive reading to improve reading achievement among third-grade students at risk for reading failure. *Journal of At-Risk Issues, 22*(2), 31–38.

Texas Education Agency and the University of

Texas System. (2004–2006). *Texas Primary Reading Inventory*. Texas Reading Instruments.

Torgesen, J., Wagner, R., & Rashotte, C. (1999). *Test of Word Reading Efficiency*. American Guidance Service.

Torgesen, J. K., Wagner, R. K., & Rashotte, C. A. (2012). *Test of Word Reading Efficiency, Second Edition (TOWRE-2)*. PRO-ED.

U.S. Department of Education, Institute of Education Sciences, National Center for Education Statistics (2019). *Explore results for the 2019 NAEP reading assessment*. National Center for Education Statistics, Institute for Education Sciences, U.S. Department of Education. Retrieved from *www.nationsreportcard.gov/reading/?grade=4*.

*Vadasy, P. F., & Sanders, E. A. (2020). Introducing grapheme–phoneme correspondences (GPCs): Exploring rate and complexity in phonics instruction for kindergarteners with limited literacy skills. *Reading and Writing, 34*(1), 109–138.

Vellutino, F. R., Scanlon, D. M., Small, S., & Fanuele, D. P. (2006). Response to intervention as a vehicle for distinguishing between children with and without reading disabilities: Evidence for the role of kindergarten and first-grade interventions. *Journal of Learning Disabilities, 39*(2), 157–169.

*Vernon-Feagans, L., Bratsch-Hines, M., Varghese, C., Cutrer, E. A., & Garwood, J. D. (2018). Improving struggling readers' early literacy skills through a Tier 2 professional development program for rural classroom teachers: The targeted reading intervention. *Elementary School Journal, 118*(4), 525–548.

Vernon-Feagans, L., Kainz, K., Amendum, S., Ginsberg, M., Wood, T., & Bock, A. (2012). Targeted reading intervention: A coaching model to help classroom teachers with struggling readers. *Learning Disability Quarterly, 35*(2), 102–114.

Wagner, R. K., Torgesen, J. K., & Rashotte, C. A. (1999). *Comprehensive Test of Phonological Processing*. PRO-ED.

*Weiser, B., Buss, C., Sheils, A. P., Gallegos, E., & Murray, L. R. (2019). Expert reading coaching via technology: Investigating the reading, writing, and spelling outcomes of students in grades K–8 experiencing significant reading learning disabilities. *Annals of Dyslexia, 69*(1), 54–79.

What Works Clearinghouse. (2020). *What Works Clearinghouse procedures handbook*. Retrieved from *https://ies.ed.gov/ncee/wwc/handbooks*.

Wiederholt, J. L., & Bryant, B. R. (2001). GORT 4: *Gray Oral Reading Tests examiner's manual*. PRO-ED.

Wilkinson, G. S., & Robertson, G. J. (2006). *WRAT 4: Wide Range Achievement Test*. Psychological Assessment Resources.

Wolf, M., Barzillai, M., Gottwald, S., Miller, L., Spencer, K., Norton, E., . . . Morris, R. (2009). The RAVE-O intervention: Connecting neuroscience to the classroom. *Mind, Brain and Education, 3*, 84–93.

Woodcock, R. W. (1987). *Woodcock Reading Mastery Tests—Revised (WRMT-R)*. American Guidance Service.

Woodcock, R. W. (1998). *Woodcock Reading Mastery Tests—Revised, examiner's manual*. American Guidance Service.

Woodcock, R. W., Mather, N., & Schrank, F. A. (2004). *Woodcock–Johnson III Diagnostic Reading Battery*. Riverside.

Woodcock, R. W., McGrew, K. S., & Mather, N. (2001). *Woodcock–Johnson III Tests of Achievement*. Riverside.

Yopp, H. K. (1995). A test for assessing phonemic awareness in young children. *Reading Teacher, 49*(1), 20–29.

CHAPTER 5

The Neuroscience
of Early Literacy Development

Rachel R. Romeo

Over recent decades, advances in neuroimaging techniques have allowed researchers a window into the human brain *in vivo*. This has yielded numerous discoveries about how adult readers seamlessly translate printed text into words and concepts, and how children learn these skills. Although this process takes less than a second in a skilled reader, it is no small feat. In the time line of human evolution, reading and writing are relatively recent cultural inventions, having begun only in the last 5,000 years (Seidenberg, 2017). This required the brain to transform parts of visual cortex to specialize in text processing, and to reinforce connections with evolutionarily older language processing regions (Dehaene & Cohen, 2007). The recency of this phenomenon is why children must be explicitly taught how to read rather than picking it up by mere exposure (as with language acquisition), and presumably, it is also why many children struggle to learn to read (Dehaene, 2009). Cognitive neuroscience has helped to illuminate these processes, and continuing discoveries are poised to support the optimization of literacy acquisition and instruction.

In this chapter, I first review the neuroanatomy of the reading brain as revealed by neuroscience studies, followed by how the brain develops as literacy is acquired. I then discuss both the causes and consequences of subtle individual differences in the neural architecture that supports reading,

with a particular focus on socioeconomic differences. Ultimately, I conclude that better understanding the heterogeneity of early neurodevelopment has the propensity to reduce disparities in literacy development.

The Neurobiology of Reading

Reading is a complex, multifaceted process that requires the integration and coordination of multiple brain regions specialized for linguistic and visual processing. The three core regions involved include the left inferior frontal gyrus, the left temporoparietal cortex, and the left occipitotemporal cortex (Figure 5.1). These regions, connected by dorsal and ventral white-matter tracks, make up the brain's reading network. In skilled readers, the reading network is largely lateralized to the left hemisphere (Martin, Schurz, Kronbichler, & Richlan, 2015). Although regions in the right hemisphere are also involved in reading—especially in beginning and struggling readers (Chyl, Fraga-González, Brem, & Jednoróg, 2021)—right-hemisphere contributions to typical reading are less well understood. The follow section briefly reviews the contribution of each of these regions to the reading process, focusing both on structural properties (i.e., physical shape, size, and integrity) and functional significance (i.e., the behavioral skills supported).

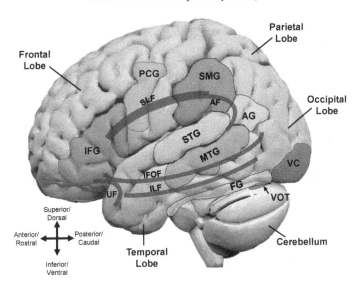

FIGURE 5.1. The neural reading network. Cortical regions comprising the canonical reading network are outlined on a lateral view of the left hemisphere. Thick lines represent interhemispheric white-matter tracts with the greatest contributions to the reading; these are located deep to the cortex but are overlaid in their approximate location for visualization. Additional neural regions (not shown) contribute reading in indirect ways. Exact locations of all regions vary slightly from person to person. Cortical regions: AG, angular gyrus; FG, fusiform gyrus; IFG, inferior frontal gyrus; MTG, middle temporal gyrus; PCG, precentral gyrus; SMG, supramarginal gyrus; STG, superior temporal gyrus; VC, visual vortex; VOT, ventral occipitotemporal cortex. White-matter tracts: AF, arcuate fasciculus; ILF, inferior longitudinal fasciculus; IFOF, inferior fronto-occipital fasciculus; UF, uncinate fasciculus; SLF, superior longitudinal fasciculus.

Inferior Frontal Cortex

The inferior frontal gyrus (IFG), located in the lateral ventral portion of the frontal lobe, is best known for playing a critical role in a variety of language functions. Often referred to as "Broca's area," the IFG is classically responsible for storing and sequencing the articulatory representations of words and planning the motoric aspects of speech (Burns & Fahy, 2010), a necessary precursor to speech production, which is executed by the parts of the precentral gyrus (the motor strip) dedicated to the articulators. However, brain imaging research has revealed a broader involvement of the IFG in several language-relevant processes (for review, see Friederici, 2011), including both semantic and syntactic processing (Rodd, Vitello, Woollams, & Adank, 2015). Other work suggests that Broca's area may function as a convergence or integration zone, in which small elements of language (e.g., sounds, words) are unified into a coherent representa-

tion (Hagoort, 2005). For the purposes of reading, all these functions may come into play—the IFG appears to be involved in the sequencing of sounds in words, especially before reading aloud, as well as the semantic comprehension of what is read (Coltheart, Rastle, Perry, Langdon, & Ziegler, 2001; Dehaene, 2009).

Temporoparietal Cortex

The temporoparietal region of the brain lies at the junction of the posterior temporal lobe and the and inferior parietal lobe. The posterior portion of the superior temporal gyrus (STG) contains a region known as "Wernicke's area," regarded as the brain's primary speech processing region. Being adjacent to the auditory cortex, Wernicke's area is involved in extracting phonemes (speech sounds) from speech (Hickok, 2009); however, it is similarly active in sign language processing, suggesting a broader role of the STG in linguistic processing beyond auditory speech (MacSweeney, Capek, Campbell, & Woll, 2008). Just anterior to the STG in the inferior parietal lobe, the supramarginal gyrus (SMG) is highly involved in phonological processing, and especially the process of sound–symbol mapping, in which graphemes (i.e., letters) are linked to corresponding phonemes (Oberhuber et al., 2016; Sliwinska, Khadilkar, Campbell-Ratcliffe, Quevenco, & Devlin, 2012). For this reason, the temporoparietal region is considered the decoding hub of the reading network and is critically involved in learning to read.

Two other structures in the temporoparietal region contribute to the comprehension aspect of language and reading. The middle temporal gyrus (MTG), located just posterior to the STG, is critically involved in semantic processing, or the mapping of language to the underlying meaning and concepts (Binder, Desai, Graves, & Conant, 2009). The angular gyrus (AG) lies posterior to both the STG and MTG and also plays a role in semantic processing, as well as the integration of linguistic information (Seghier, 2013). Although these are two of the core regions involved in language comprehension, semantic processing is a highly distributed process that involves a number of brain regions, including the IFG and the anterior temporal lobe (Binder et al., 2009).

Occipitotemporal Cortex

While the inferior frontal and temporoparietal regions contribute to language processing, no matter whether the information is spoken or written, the occipitotemporal cortex is uniquely involved in processing *written* language. This region bridges the visual cortex in the occipital lobe (which receives input from the eyes) with the rest of the temporal lobe. The fusiform gyrus (FG) lies on the ventral (underside) of the inferior temporal lobe and is involved in higher-level processing of visual information. Specific subregions of the FG are dedicated to the recognition of faces, body parts, shapes, and other objects and features important to human functioning. A posterior region of the FG near the occipital lobe, known as the ventral occipital temporal (VOT) region, is specialized for processing prelexical representations of letter and word patterns within text (McCandliss, Cohen, & Dehaene, 2003). For this reason, the VOT is often called the "visual word form area" (Cohen et al., 2000). Because reading is a relatively modern cultural invention that is not shared by all humans, this region is presumed to be a general object recognition region that is "recycled" during reading acquisition to specialize in text processing (Dehaene & Cohen, 2007, 2011).

White-Matter Tracts

The inferior frontal, temporoparietal, and occipitotemporal cortices are integrated into a reading network by white-matter pathways. The "dorsal route" comprises the arcuate fasciculus (AF) and the superior longitudinal fasciculus (SLF), which connect the IFG and posterior STG through the temporoparietal cortex (Catani, Jones, & ffytche, 2005). As the primary pathway connecting Broca's and Wernicke's areas, the AF/SLF joins receptive and expressive language processing hubs, and tract integrity is strongly associated with both language and reading proficiency (Friederici, 2009). Additionally, the "ventral route" contains several fiber pathways connecting language and reading regions through the inferior portion of the brain (Hickok & Poeppel, 2007). The uncinate fasciculus (UF) is a short U-shaped pathway that connects the IFG to the anterior temporal lobe (Von Der Heide, Skipper, Klobusicky, & Olson, 2013), while the inferior longitudinal fasciculus (ILF) extends throughout the temporal lobe connecting anterior and posterior regions, and a portion of the ILF connects to the VOT (Yeatman, Rauschecker, & Wandell, 2013). The inferior fronto-occipital fasciculus (IFOF) connects the IFG directly to the occipitotemporal cortex, though there is disagreement on whether this is truly a separable tract (Schmahmann & Pandya, 2007). Together, the dorsal and ventral routes link language networks and visual networks into a reading network.

Dual Routes for Reading

When the brain encounters a word, retinotopic cortices in the occipital lobe send the visual input to the VOT, at which point it may take either the ventral or dorsal route. These two pathways are described by the dual-route cascaded model (Coltheart et al., 2001). Because the dorsal route traverses sound processing regions, it is often referred to as the *phonological route*. Readers use this route when they encounter unfamiliar words that they must decode (i.e., map the letters to their sounds) before linking the sound pattern with the word's meaning (Jobard, Crivello, & Tzourio-Mazoyer, 2003). Because this route is relatively slow and systematic, it is also called the *indirect route*. Alternatively, if readers are very familiar with the encountered word, they may activate the ventral route—also known as the *lexical route*—to bypass phonological regions and match the printed word directly with its meaning (Taylor, Rastle, & Davis, 2013). Because this route is relatively faster, it is often called the *direct route*. Skilled readers utilize both routes depending on the familiarity and regularity (i.e., how well it conforms to phoneme–grapheme correspondence rules) of the words they encounter.

Development of the Reading Brain

Neuroimaging studies with children of various ages have provided invaluable insight into how the brain learns to read. Before children can make sense of written words, they must first have a language system on which to map it. Even before birth, fetuses can process basic acoustic properties of speech (Partanen et al., 2013) using left-lateralized language networks (Dehaene-Lambertz, Dehaene, & Hertz-Pannier, 2002) Maturation of the left superior temporal regions in the first year of life allows infants to segment phonological word forms and map them to semantic concepts, and maturation of inferior frontal regions throughout childhood allow for greater top-down processing of language (for review, see Skeide & Friederici, 2016).

Also during the first years of life, regions of the FG become increasingly specialized for visual objects that are important to humans (Deen et al., 2017). Before children (or preliterate adults) learn to read, the brain treats letters as arbitrary visuospatial symbols, processed primarily by right-lateralized fusiform regions (Dehaene et al., 2010; Dehaene-Lambertz, Monzalvo, & Dehaene, 2018). But very quickly as literacy instruction begins, letters become meaningful visual categories representing speech sounds, and they are increasingly processed by the left VOT (Brem et al., 2010; Dehaene-Lambertz et al., 2018). This general principle of right-to-left lateralization is seen across the reading network as children become increasingly skilled readers, suggesting a specialization process that promotes efficiency between left-hemisphere pathways for both language and reading (Chyl et al., 2021).

In addition to leftward lateralization, as children become more skilled readers, they exhibit a shift in reliance on left anterior regions to a greater engagement of left posterior brain regions (Booth et al., 2004; Turkeltaub, Gareau, Flowers, Zeffiro, & Eden, 2003). In addition to language functions, the inferior frontal cortex also supports executive processes such as focused attention and working memory. When children first begin to read, it requires intentional effort, but as reading becomes more automatic, children rely less on effortful prefrontal systems (Martin et al., 2015). Similarly, as children begin to recognize words more fluently, without the need for phonemic decoding, there is also a shift from reliance on temporoparietal regions to greater activation of the VOT (Church, Coalson, Lugar, Petersen, & Schlaggar, 2008).

As children learn to read, they also exhibit structural brain changes, especially in white-matter pathways. Both the AF and the ILF exhibit microstructural changes indicative of stronger frontotemporal directionality (Thiebaut de Schotten, Cohen, Amemiya, Braga, & Dehaene, 2012; Yeatman, Dougherty, Ben-Shachar, & Wandell, 2012), indicating greater connectivity between anterior and posterior language and reading regions. These changes occur very rapidly, within weeks of reading instruction (Huber, Donnelly, Rokem, & Yeatman, 2018), and appear to be strongly related to children's phonological skills (Saygin et al., 2013; Vandermosten, Boets, Wouters, & Ghesquiere, 2012; Yeatman et al., 2011). Furthermore, structural properties of these tracts predict children's later reading skills (Gullick & Booth, 2015; Hoeft et al., 2011; Ozernov-Palchik et al., 2019), highlighting the importance of these pathways in the development of the reading network.

Together, the functional and structural neuroimaging findings indicate that learning to read builds on a foundation of existing language and visual processing networks. With reading instruction, these circuits experience significant experience-dependent tuning—including greater reliance on left posterior regions and stronger frontotemporal connections—that allow children to develop skilled and fluent reading.

Individual Differences in the Development of the Reading Brain

Although the basic architecture of the reading network is the same across individuals, individual differences in both brain structure and function do exist. Often, these differences are meaningful and are related to variation in concurrent reading skill and proficiency or predict later reading development. At the extreme, sometimes these differences may be related to reading disorders with lifelong effects. Other times, there is no clear relation between neural heterogeneity and reading outcomes—in these scenarios, it is unclear whether this is simply natural variation, or if neuroscience has simply not yet revealed the meaning behind these differences.

Our research group is interested in both the *causes* and *consequences* of individual differences in the developing brain's reading and language networks. Potential causes include both *endogenous* influences, which are inherent to the individual, such as a genetic predisposition for a reading disorder, and *exogenous* influences, which are external to the individual, such as variation in early language and literacy experiences and instruction (Rowe, Romeo, & Leech, Chapter 2, this volume). In terms of the consequences—or outcomes—of neural heterogeneity, I provide evidence that cognitive neuroscience can predict trajectories of reading development, and I suggest that the field may soon be able to harness neural patterns to make instructional recommendations.

Sources of Heterogeneity in the Reading Network

the most studied individual differences in the reading brain are those associated with developmental dyslexia, which is a persistent reading difficulty that cannot be explained by another disability or insufficient instruction (American Psychiatric Association, 2022 and which affects approximately 5–17% of school-age children (Lyon, Shaywitz, & Shaywitz, 2003). Although the precise cause(s) of dyslexia are unknown, it is highly heritable (40–60%), and several candidate genes have been identified (Fisher & DeFries, 2002; Raskind, Peter, Richards, Eckert, & Berninger, 2013). A thorough review of the neural basis of dyslexia is outside the scope of this chapter (see D'Mello & Gabrieli, 2018, for a recent review). In brief, individuals with dyslexia tend to exhibit reduced activation in temporoparietal and occipitotemporal regions during reading and phonological tasks consistent with reduced phonological awareness and decoding skills, and increased frontal activation, possibly indicating greater effort during these tasks (Martin et al., 2015; Richlan, Kronbichler, & Wimmer, 2011). Even after successful remediation, children with

previous reading disorders often exhibit a greater reliance on the right hemisphere, suggesting compensatory strategies (Hoeft et al., 2011; Waldie, Haigh, Badzakova-Trajkov, Buckley, & Kirk, 2013). Structurally, children with dyslexia also exhibit reduced gray matter in temporoparietal and occipitotemporal regions (Richlan, Kronbichler, & Wimmer, 2013), as well as reduced integrity of the AF, SLF, and ILF (Vandermosten et al., 2012), suggesting inefficient connections. Importantly, many of these brain differences are apparent before children learn to read (Raschle, Chang, & Gaab, 2011; Raschle, Zuk, & Gaab, 2012), suggesting that they may be endogenous sources of reading difficulties rather than the result of altered reading experiences.

There is also a growing literature demonstrating that the brain's reading network is sensitive to environmental experiences, which has critical implications because experiences are modifiable (Romeo, Imhof, Bhatia, & Christodoulou, 2020). Socioeconomic status (SES)—an index of an individual's educational, financial, and social resources—is one of the strongest predictors of a child's reading development (Bradley & Corwyn, 2002). SES is associated with the structure and function of brain regions associated with a number of cognitive domains (for review, see Farah, 2017), including multiple parts of the reading network. Children from higher SES backgrounds exhibit greater left IFG lateralization during phonological processing (Raizada, Richards, Meltzoff, & Kuhl, 2008), and among children with reading disorders, SES more strongly predicts the thickness of left IFG gray matter than clinically relevant reading scores (Romeo, Christodoulou, et al., 2018). Higher SES is also associated with greater structural and functional connectivity of left-hemisphere reading regions (Ozernov-Palchik et al., 2019; Su, Li, Zhou, & Shu, 2021). Interestingly, SES also *moderates* relationships between reading skills and measures of brain structure and function, such that children from higher and lower SES backgrounds exhibit different neural patterns associated with the same reading proficiency (Gullick, Demir-Lira, & Booth, 2016; Noble, Wolmetz, Ochs, Farah, & McCandliss, 2006; Romeo, Perrachione, et al., 2022; Younger, Lee, Demir-Lira, & Booth, 2019). This suggests that there may be no universal brain pattern indicative of successful reading development, and perhaps that different individuals may rely on slight variations in cognitive skills to acquire literacy.

Why is SES related to the reading network? According to the bioecological model of development (Bronfenbrenner & Ceci, 1994), SES is a distal factor that influences neurocognitive development through children's proximal, day-to-day experiences. One such experience is children's early home literacy environment, or their exposure to literacy-related resources, interactions, and attitudes (Sénéchal & LeFevre, 2002). Independent of SES, young children who experience greater exposure to reading at home exhibit greater activation in temporoparietal regions during passive language processing (Hutton et al., 2015) and in both inferior frontal and occipitotemporal regions during phonological processing (Powers, Wang, Beach, Sideris, & Gaab, 2016). Home literacy is also associated with higher microstructural integrity of left frontotemporal white-matter pathways (Hutton, Dudley, Horowitz-Kraus, DeWitt, & Holland, 2020). In addition to literacy exposure, children's experience with oral language is also associated with brain networks for reading and language, including IFG activation during language processing (Romeo, Leonard, et al., 2018), thickness of superior temporal regions (Merz, Maskus, Melvin, He, & Noble, 2020), neural oscillations indicative of brain maturity (Brito et al., 2020; Pierce, Reilly, & Nelson, 2021; Romeo, Choi, et al., 2022), structural and functional frontotemporal connectivity (King, Camacho, Montez, Humphreys, & Gotlib, 2021; Romeo, Segaran, et al., 2018), and frontotemporal plasticity (Romeo, Leonard, et al., 2021). These studies highlight everyday experiences in children's lives that may contribute to heterogeneity in the neurodevelopment of the reading network, as well as malleable targets that may reduce disparities language and literacy outcomes.

Implications of Heterogeneity in the Reading Network

What are the effects of individual differences in the brain's reading network? As mentioned earlier, some variation may not have observable consequences on cognitive skills or developmental trajectories, at least as they are currently measured. However, some neural differences do have meaningful sequelae. At the extreme, children with lesions to parts of the reading network may experience anything from complete loss of reading, writing, and language abilities (alexia, agraphia, and aphasia, respectively) to minimal or nonexistent impairment, depending on when in development the lesion was acquired—the earlier, the better prognosis for plasticity. However, more subtle differences, known as "biomarkers," may also predict reading outcomes. Several studies have indicated that reduced integrity of the left AF and SLF predict poorer reading outcomes and even later diagnoses of dyslexia (Borchers et al., 2019; Gullick & Booth, 2015; Myers et al., 2014; Vanderauwera, Wouters, Vandermosten, & Ghesquière, 2017); however, in children with dyslexia or those at familial risk of developing it, increased integrity of right-hemisphere frontotemporal tracts predict more positive reading outcomes (Hoeft et al., 2011; Zuk et al., 2021). Similarly, reduced left-hemispheric activation during phonological and reading tasks predicts worse reading outcomes (Centanni et al., 2019; Chyl et al., 2018; Preston et al., 2015; Yu et al., 2018), while in children with reading disorders, greater right-hemispheric activation predicts relatively better outcomes (Hoeft et al., 2011; Yu et al., 2020). Together, these studies suggest that disruptions to the canonical left-lateralized reading network often forecast future reading struggle, but compensatory development in the right hemisphere may be protective against the worst outcomes.

In addition to reading outcomes, individual differences in brain development may also be able to predict which instructional or intervention strategies are optimal for each learner. It is important to note that there is much evidence and agreement for certain literacy instructional practices, such as a core foundation in phonics (Foorman, Chapter 6, this volume). However, individual differences in the reading network, whether a result of endogenous or exogenous influences, may predispose some students to learn better from subtle educational modifications. In one study, we found that struggling readers from lower-SES backgrounds (as compared to a higher-SES group) exhibited greater reading gains and associated temporoparietal cortical plasticity following an intensive summer intervention combining phonological strategies with visual word form memory exercises (Romeo, Christodoulou, et al., 2018). While there are myriad possible explanations, including intervention timing, intensity, or content, further investigations suggest that beginning readers from lower-SES backgrounds may rely more on visual word form imagery to successfully acquire literacy than their peers from more advantaged backgrounds (Romeo, Perrachione, et al., 2022). Perhaps then, this intervention strategy leveraged a relative skill born out of varying early experiences. If so, then reading instruction may be moving away from an outdated "one size fits all" approach toward something more akin to precision medicine (Gabrieli, Ghosh, & Whitfield-Gabrieli, 2015). Although it is still too soon to use neuroimaging to select individualized instruction, this remains a promising avenue to reduce disparities and support optimal literacy development across different learners.

Future Directions

This is an exciting time in the field of developmental cognitive neuroscience. We are able to image the brain at work with remarkable spatial and temporal precision, and track dynamic neural changes across the entire developmental trajectory from fetus to adulthood. Based on the advances summarized earlier, I suggest that the greatest strides will be made by embracing heterogeneity for what it can teach us about how reading develops—both universally, and individually—and how we can leverage this knowledge to optimize literacy instruction.

First, we must investigate a greater variety of early experiences and how these influence the development of the reading network. Human neuroscience, and especially developmental science, is plagued by a literature focused on an astonishingly small slice of the human experience—typically individuals from wealthy, educated, and Western societies (Nielsen, Haun, Kartner, & Legare, 2017). There is increasing evidence that our understanding of even basic neurodevelopmental trajectories may be distorted by representation bias in the groups examined (e.g., LeWinn, Sheridan, Keyes, Hamilton, & McLaughlin, 2017). This is especially important for a field such as reading development, which is undoubtedly influenced by variations in the properties of the language and orthography being acquired, and as demonstrated earlier, also by societal, educational, and familial differences. Only by investigating a broader variety of early experiences across cultures can we begin to understand what gives rise to the measurable neural heterogeneity.

Second, we must further investigate brain measures that pose translational value to education and intervention. By providing a "look under the hood," neuroscience is well poised to provide insight into the *mechanisms* of reading development. For example, two struggling readers may perform very similarly on behavioral reading assessments but struggle for very different reasons. Neuroimaging can help reveal how children process phonology, orthography, and semantics, and where in the reading network a breakdown arises. Similarly, there has been a recent surge in investigations of biomarkers to predict which children will exhibit reading difficulties. I suggest that similar approaches be applied to investigate biomarkers of treatment response, or whether a student will exhibit improvement in response to a specific intervention. Of particular interest are *dynamic* biomarkers that indicate how the brain has changed in response to a perturbation and may predict further outcomes. Such measures may help in the evaluation of adaptive interventions that aim to maximize intervention efficiency during times of heightened neural plasticity.

In conclusion, cognitive neuroscience has provided invaluable insight into how the brain learns to read, including both overarching developmental mechanisms and subtle individual differences. By embracing this heterogeneity and investigating both its causes and consequences, neuroscience is well poised to make further great advances in support of the successful reading development of all children.

References

American Psychiatric Association. (2022). *Diagnostic and statistical manual of mental disorders* (5th ed., text rev.). Author.

Binder, J. R., Desai, R. H., Graves, W. W., & Conant, L. L. (2009). Where is the semantic system?: A critical review and meta-analysis of 120 functional neuroimaging studies. *Cerebral Cortex, 19*(12), 2767–2796.

Booth, J. R., Burman, D. D., Meyer, J. R., Gitelman, D. R., Parrish, T. B., & Mesulam, M. M. (2004). Development of brain mechanisms for processing orthographic and phonologic representations. *Journal of Cognitive Neuroscience, 16*(7), 1234–1249.

Borchers, L. R., Bruckert, L., Dodson, C. K., Travis, K. E., Marchman, V. A., Ben-Shachar, M., & Feldman, H. M. (2019). Microstructural properties of white matter pathways in relation to subsequent reading abilities in children: A longitudinal analysis. *Brain Structure and Function, 224*(2), 891–905.

Bradley, R. H., & Corwyn, R. F. (2002). Socio-economic status and child development. *Annual Reviews in Psychology, 53,* 371–399.

Brem, S., Bach, S., Kucian, K., Kujala, J. V., Guttorm, T. K., Martin, E., . . . Richardson, U. (2010). Brain sensitivity to print emerges when children learn letter–speech sound correspondences. *Proceedings of the National Academy of Sciences USA, 107*(17), 7939–7944.

Brito, N. H., Troller-Renfree, S. V., Leon-Santos, A., Isler, J. R., Fifer, W. P., & Noble, K. G. (2020). Associations among the home language environment and neural activity during infancy. *Developmental Cognitive Neuroscience, 43,* Article 100780.

Bronfenbrenner, U., & Ceci, S. J. (1994). Nature-nuture reconceptualized in developmental perspective: A bioecological model. *Psychological Review, 101*(4), 568–586.

Burns, M. S., & Fahy, J. (2010). Broca's area: Rethinking classical concepts from a neuroscience perspective. *Topics in Stroke Rehabilitation, 17*(6), 401–410.

Catani, M., Jones, D. K., & ffytche, D. H. (2005). Perisylvian language networks of the human brain. *Annals of Neurology, 57*(1), 8–16.

Centanni, T. M., Norton, E. S., Ozernov-Palchik, O., Park, A., Beach, S. D., Halverson, K., . . . Gabrieli, J. D. E. (2019). Disrupted left fusiform response to print in beginning kindergartners is associated with subsequent reading. *NeuroImage: Clinical, 22,* Article 101715.

Church, J. A., Coalson, R. S., Lugar, H. M., Petersen, S. E., & Schlaggar, B. L. (2008). A developmental fMRI study of reading and repetition reveals changes in phonological and visual mechanisms over age. *Cerebral Cortex, 18*(9), 2054–2065.

Chyl, K., Fraga-González, G., Brem, S., & Jednoróg, K. (2021). Brain dynamics of (a)typical reading development—a review of longitudinal studies. *NPJ Science of Learning, 6*(1), Article 4.

Chyl, K., Kossowski, B., Dębska, A., Łuniewska, M., Banaszkiewicz, A., Żelechowska, A., . . . Jednoróg, K. (2018). Prereader to beginning reader: Changes induced by reading acquisition in print and speech brain networks. *Journal of Child Psychology and Psychiatry, 59*(1), 76–87.

Cohen, L., Dehaene, S., Naccache, L., Lehéricy, S., Dehaene-Lambertz, G., Hénaff, M.-A., & Michel, F. (2000). The visual word form area: Spatial and temporal characterization of an initial stage of reading in normal subjects and posterior split-brain patients. *Brain, 123*(2), 291–307.

Coltheart, M., Rastle, K., Perry, C., Langdon, R., & Ziegler, J. (2001). DRC: A dual route cascaded model of visual word recognition and reading aloud. *Psychological Review, 108*(1), 204–256.

Deen, B., Richardson, H., Dilks, D. D., Takahashi, A., Keil, B., Wald, L. L., . . . Saxe, R. (2017). Organization of high-level visual cortex in human infants. *Nature Communications, 8*(1), Article 13995.

Dehaene, S. (2009). *Reading in the brain: The new science of how we read.* Penguin.

Dehaene, S., & Cohen, L. (2007). Cultural recycling of cortical maps. *Neuron, 56*(2), 384–398.

Dehaene, S., & Cohen, L. (2011). The unique role of the visual word form area in reading. *Trends in Cognitive Sciences, 15*(6), 254–262.

Dehaene, S., Pegado, F., Braga, L. W., Ventura, P., Nunes Filho, G., Jobert, A., . . . Cohen, L. (2010). How learning to read changes the cortical networks for vision and language. *Science, 330*(6009), 1359–1364.

Dehaene-Lambertz, G., Dehaene, S., & Hertz-Pannier, L. (2002). Functional neuroimaging of speech perception in infants. *Science, 298*(5600), 2013–2015.

Dehaene-Lambertz, G., Monzalvo, K., & Dehaene, S. (2018). The emergence of the visual word form: Longitudinal evolution of category-specific ventral visual areas during reading acquisition. *PLoS Biology, 16*(3), Article e2004103.

D'Mello, A. M., & Gabrieli, J. D. E. (2018). Cognitive neuroscience of dyslexia. *Language, Speech, and Hearing Services in Schools, 49*(4), 798–809.

Farah, M. J. (2017). The neuroscience of socioeconomic status: Correlates, causes, and consequences. *Neuron, 96*(1), 56–71.

Fisher, S. E., & DeFries, J. C. (2002). Developmental dyslexia: Genetic dissection of a complex cognitive trait. *Nature Reviews Neuroscience, 3*(10), 767–780.

Friederici, A. D. (2009). Pathways to language: Fiber tracts in the human brain. *Trends in Cognitive Sciences, 13*(4), 175–181.

Friederici, A. D. (2011). The brain basis of language processing: From structure to function. *Physiological Reviews, 91*(4), 1357–1392.

Gabrieli, J. D. E., Ghosh, S. S., & Whitfield-Gabrieli, S. (2015). Prediction as a humanitarian and pragmatic contribution from human cognitive neuroscience. *Neuron, 85*(1), 11–26.

Gullick, M. M., & Booth, J. R. (2015). The direct segment of the arcuate fasciculus is predictive of longitudinal reading change. *Developmental Cognitive Neuroscience, 13,* 68–74.

Gullick, M. M., Demir-Lira, Ö. E., & Booth, J. R. (2016). Reading skill–fractional anisotropy relationships in visuospatial tracts diverge depending on socioeconomic status. *Developmental Science, 19*(4), 673–685.

Hagoort, P. (2005). On Broca, brain, and binding: A new framework. *Trends in Cognitive Sciences, 9*(9), 416–423.

Hickok, G. (2009). The functional neuroanatomy

of language. *Physics of Life Reviews, 6*(3), 121–143.

Hickok, G., & Poeppel, D. (2007). The cortical organization of speech processing. *Nature Reviews Neuroscience, 8*(5), 393–402.

Hoeft, F., McCandliss, B. D., Black, J. M., Gantman, A., Zakerani, N., Hulme, C., . . . Gabrieli, J. D. (2011). Neural systems predicting long-term outcome in dyslexia. *Proceedings of the National Academy of Sciences USA, 108*(1), 361–366.

Huber, E., Donnelly, P. M., Rokem, A., & Yeatman, J. D. (2018). Rapid and widespread white matter plasticity during an intensive reading intervention. *Nature Commununications, 9*(1), Article 2260.

Hutton, J. S., Dudley, J., Horowitz-Kraus, T., DeWitt, T., & Holland, S. K. (2020). Associations between home literacy environment, brain white matter integrity and cognitive abilities in preschool-age children. *Acta Paediatrica, 109*(7), 1376–1386.

Hutton, J. S., Horowitz-Kraus, T., Mendelsohn, A. L., DeWitt, T., Holland, S. K., & C-MIND Authorship Consortium. (2015). Home reading environment and brain activation in preschool children listening to stories. *Pediatrics, 136*(3), 466–478.

Jobard, G., Crivello, F., & Tzourio-Mazoyer, N. (2003). Evaluation of the dual route theory of reading: A metanalysis of 35 neuroimaging studies. *NeuroImage, 20*(2), 693–712.

King, L. S., Camacho, M. C., Montez, D. F., Humphreys, K. L., & Gotlib, I. H. (2021). Naturalistic language input is associated with resting-state functional connectivity in infancy. *Journal of Neuroscience, 41*(3), 424–434.

LeWinn, K. Z., Sheridan, M. A., Keyes, K. M., Hamilton, A., & McLaughlin, K. A. (2017). Sample composition alters associations between age and brain structure. *Nature Communications, 8*(1), Article 874.

Lyon, G. R., Shaywitz, S. E., & Shaywitz, B. A. (2003). A definition of dyslexia. *Annals of Dyslexia, 53*(1), 1–14.

MacSweeney, M., Capek, C. M., Campbell, R., & Woll, B. (2008). The signing brain: The neurobiology of sign language. *Trends in Cognitive Sciences, 12*(11), 432–440.

Martin, A., Schurz, M., Kronbichler, M., & Richlan, F. (2015). Reading in the brain of children and adults: A meta-analysis of 40 functional magnetic resonance imaging studies. *Human Brain Mapping, 36*(5), 1963–1981.

McCandliss, B. D., Cohen, L., & Dehaene, S. (2003). The visual word form area: Expertise for reading in the fusiform gyrus. *Trends in Cognitive Sciences, 7*(7), 293–299.

Merz, E. C., Maskus, E. A., Melvin, S. A., He, X., & Noble, K. G. (2020). Socioeconomic disparities in language input are associated with children's language-related brain structure and reading skills. *Child Development, 91*(3), 846–860.

Myers, C. A., Vandermosten, M., Farris, E. A., Hancock, R., Gimenez, P., Black, J. M., . . . Hoeft, F. (2014). White matter morphometric changes uniquely predict children's reading acquisition. *Psychological Science, 25*(10), 1870–1883.

Nielsen, M., Haun, D., Kartner, J., & Legare, C. H. (2017). The persistent sampling bias in developmental psychology: A call to action. *Journal of Experimental Child Psychology, 162*, 31–38.

Noble, K. G., Wolmetz, M. E., Ochs, L. G., Farah, M. J., & McCandliss, B. D. (2006). Brain–behavior relationships in reading acquisition are modulated by socioeconomic factors. *Developmental Science, 9*(6), 642–654.

Oberhuber, M., Hope, T. M. H., Seghier, M. L., Parker Jones, O., Prejawa, S., Green, D. W., & Price, C. J. (2016). Four functionally distinct regions in the left supramarginal gyrus support word processing. *Cerebral Cortex, 26*(11), 4212–4226.

Ozernov-Palchik, O., Norton, E. S., Wang, Y., Beach, S. D., Zuk, J., Wolf, M., . . . Gaab, N. (2019). The relationship between socioeconomic status and white matter microstructure in pre-reading children: A longitudinal investigation. *Human Brain Mapping, 40*(3), 741–754.

Partanen, E., Kujala, T., Näätänen, R., Liitola, A., Sambeth, A., & Huotilainen, M. (2013). Learning-induced neural plasticity of speech processing before birth. *Proceedings of the National Academy of Sciences USA, 110*(37), 15145–15150.

Pierce, L. J., Reilly, E., & Nelson, C. A. (2021). Associations between maternal stress, early language behaviors, and infant electroencephalography during the first year of life. *Journal of Child Language, 48*(4), 737–764.

Powers, S., Wang, Y., Beach, S., Sideris, G, & Gaab, N. (2016). Examining the relationship between home literacy environment and neural correlates of phonological processing in beginning readers with and without a familial risk for dyslexia: An fMRI study. *Annals of Dyslexia, 66*, 337–360.

Preston, J. L., Molfese, P. J., Frost, S. J., Mencl, W. E., Fulbright, R. K., Hoeft, F., . . . Pugh, K. R. (2015). Print–speech convergence predicts future reading outcomes in early readers. *Psychological Science, 27*(1), 75–84.

Raizada, R. D., Richards, T. L., Meltzoff, A., & Kuhl, P. K. (2008). Socioeconomic status predicts hemispheric specialisation of the left inferior frontal gyrus in young children. *NeuroImage, 40*(3), 1392–1401.

Raschle, N. M., Chang, M., & Gaab, N. (2011). Structural brain alterations associated with dyslexia predate reading onset. *NeuroImage, 57*(3), 742–749.

Raschle, N. M., Zuk, J., & Gaab, N. (2012). Functional characteristics of developmental dyslexia in left-hemispheric posterior brain regions predate reading onset. *Proceedings of the National Academy of Sciences USA, 109*(6), 2156–2161.

Raskind, W., Peter, B., Richards, T., Eckert, M., & Berninger, V. (2013). The genetics of reading disabilities: From phenotypes to candidate genes. *Frontiers in Psychology, 3*, Article 601.

Richlan, F., Kronbichler, M., & Wimmer, H. (2011). Meta-analyzing brain dysfunctions in dyslexic children and adults. *NeuroImage, 56*(3), 1735–1742.

Richlan, F., Kronbichler, M., & Wimmer, H. (2013). Structural abnormalities in the dyslexic brain: A meta-analysis of voxel-based morphometry studies. *Human Brain Mapping, 34*(11), 3055–3065.

Rodd, J. M., Vitello, S., Woollams, A. M., & Adank, P. (2015). Localising semantic and syntactic processing in spoken and written language comprehension: An activation likelihood estimation meta-analysis. *Brain and Language, 141*, 89–102.

Romeo, R. R., Choi, B., Gabard-Durnam, L. J., Wilkinson, C. L., Levin, A. R., Rowe, M. L., . . . Nelson, C. A., III. (2022). Parental language input predicts neuroscillatory patterns associated with language development in toddlers at risk of Autism. *Journal of Autism and Developmental Disorders, 52*, 2717–2731.

Romeo, R. R., Christodoulou, J. A., Halverson, K. K., Murtagh, J., Cyr, A. B., Schimmel, C., . . . Gabrieli, J. D. E. (2018). Socioeconomic status and reading disability: Neuroanatomy and plasticity in response to intervention. *Cerebral Cortex, 28*(7), 2297–2312.

Romeo, R. R., Imhof, A. M., Bhatia, P., & Christodoulou, J. A. (2020). Relationships between socioeconomic status and reading development: Cognitive outcomes and neural mechanisms. In C. Stevens, E. Pakulak, M. Soledad Segretin, & S. J. Lipina (Eds.), *Neuroscientific Perspectives on Poverty* (pp. 153–182). Ettore Majorana Foundation for Scientific Culture.

Romeo, R. R., Leonard, J. A., Grotzinger, H. M., Robinson, S. T., Takada, M. E., Mackey, A. P., . . . Gabrieli, J. D. E. (2021). Neuroplasticity associated with changes in conversational turn-taking following a family-based intervention. *Developmental Cognitive Neuroscience, 49*, Article 100967.

Romeo, R. R., Leonard, J. A., Robinson, S. T., West, M. R., Mackey, A. P., Rowe, M. L., & Gabrieli, J. D. E. (2018). Beyond the "30 million word gap": Children's conversational exposure is associated with language-related brain function. *Psychological Science, 29*(5), 700–710.

Romeo, R. R., Perrachionne, T. K., Olson, H. A.,

Halverson, K. K., Gabrieli, J. D. E., & Christodoulou, J. A. (2022). Socioeconomic dissociations in the neural and cognitive bases of reading disorders. *Developmental Cognitive Neuroscience, 58*, 101175.

Romeo, R. R., Segaran, J., Leonard, J. A., Robinson, S. T., West, M. R., Mackey, A. P., . . . Gabrieli, J. D. E. (2018). Language exposure relates to structural neural connectivity in childhood. *Journal of Neuroscience, 38*(36), 7870–7877.

Saygin, Z. M., Norton, E. S., Osher, D. E., Beach, S. D., Cyr, A. B., Ozernov-Palchik, O., . . . Gabrieli, J. D. E. (2013). Tracking the roots of reading ability: White matter volume and integrity correlate with phonological awareness in prereading and early-reading kindergarten children. *Journal of Neuroscience, 33*(33), 13251–13258.

Schmahmann, J. D., & Pandya, D. N. (2007). The complex history of the fronto-occipital fasciculus. *Journal of the History of Neurosciences, 16*(4), 362–377.

Seghier, M. L. (2013). The angular gyrus: Multiple functions and multiple subdivisions. *Neuroscientist, 19*(1), 43–61.

Seidenberg, M. S. (2017). *Language at the speed of sight: How we read, why so many can't, and what can be done about it.* Basic Books.

Sénéchal, M., & LeFevre, J. (2002). Parental involvement in the development of children's reading skill: A five-year longitudinal study. *Child Development, 73*(2), 445–460.

Skeide, M. A., & Friederici, A. D. (2016). The ontogeny of the cortical language network. *Nature Reviews Neuroscience, 17*(5), 323–332.

Sliwinska, M. W., Khadilkar, M., Campbell-Ratcliffe, J., Quevenco, F., & Devlin, J. (2012). Early and sustained supramarginal gyrus contributions to phonological processing. *Frontiers in Psychology, 3*, Article 161.

Su, M., Li, P., Zhou, W., & Shu, H. (2021). Effects of socioeconomic status in predicting reading outcomes for children: The mediation of spoken language network. *Brain and Cognition, 147*, Article 105655.

Taylor, J. S., Rastle, K., & Davis, M. H. (2013). Can cognitive models explain brain activation during word and pseudoword reading?: A meta-analysis of 36 neuroimaging studies. *Psychological Bulletin, 139*(4), 766–791.

Thiebaut de Schotten, M., Cohen, L., Amemiya, E., Braga, L. W., & Dehaene, S. (2012). Learning to read improves the structure of the arcuate fasciculus. *Cerebral Cortex, 24*(4), 989–995.

Turkeltaub, P. E., Gareau, L., Flowers, D. L., Zeffiro, T. A., & Eden, G. F. (2003). Development of neural mechanisms for reading. *Nature Neuroscience, 6*(6), 767–773.

Vanderauwera, J., Wouters, J., Vandermosten, M., & Ghesquière, P. (2017). Early dynamics of white matter deficits in children developing dyslexia. *Developmental Cognitive Neuroscience, 27*, 69–77.

Vandermosten, M., Boets, B., Wouters, J., & Ghesquiere, P. (2012). A qualitative and quantitative review of diffusion tensor imaging studies in reading and dyslexia. *Neuroscience and Biobehavioral Reviews, 36*(6), 1532–1552.

Von Der Heide, R. J., Skipper, L. M., Klobusicky, E., & Olson, I. R. (2013). Dissecting the uncinate fasciculus: Disorders, controversies and hypothesis. *Brain, 136*(6), 1692–1707.

Waldie, K. E., Haigh, C. E., Badzakova-Trajkov, G., Buckley, J., & Kirk, I. J. (2013). Reading the wrong way with the right hemisphere. *Brain Sciences, 3*(3), 1060–1075.

Yeatman, J. D., Dougherty, R. F., Ben-Shachar, M., & Wandell, B. A. (2012). Development of white matter and reading skills. *Proceedings of the National Academy of Sciences USA, 109*(44), E3045–E3053.

Yeatman, J. D., Dougherty, R. F., Rykhlevskaia, E., Sherbondy, A. J., Deutsch, G. K., Wandell, B. A., & Ben-Shachar, M. (2011). Anatomical properties of the arcuate fasciculus predict phonological and reading skills in children. *Journal of Cognitive Neuroscience, 23*(11), 3304–3317.

Yeatman, J. D., Rauschecker, A. M., & Wandell, B. A. (2013). Anatomy of the visual word form area: adjacent cortical circuits and long-range white matter connections. *Brain and Language, 125*(2), 146–155.

Younger, J. W., Lee, K. W., Demir-Lira, O. E., & Booth, J. R. (2019). Brain lateralization of phonological awareness varies by maternal education. *Developmental Science, 22*(6), Article e12807.

Yu, X., Raney, T., Perdue, M. V., Zuk, J., Ozernov-Palchik, O., Becker, B. L. C., . . . Gaab, N. (2018). Emergence of the neural network underlying phonological processing from the prereading to the emergent reading stage: A longitudinal study. *Human Brain Mapping, 39*(5), 2047–2063.

Yu, X., Zuk, J., Perdue, M. V., Ozernov-Palchik, O., Raney, T., Beach, S. D., . . . Gaab, N. (2020). Putative protective neural mechanisms in prereaders with a family history of dyslexia who subsequently develop typical reading skills. *Human Brain Mapping, 41*(10), 2827–2845.

Zuk, J., Dunstan, J., Norton, E., Yu, X., Ozernov-Palchik, O., Wang, Y., . . . Gaab, N. (2021). Multifactorial pathways facilitate resilience among kindergarteners at risk for dyslexia: A longitudinal behavioral and neuroimaging study. *Developmental Science, 24*(1), Article e12983.

PART II

DEVELOPMENT AND INSTRUCTION OF CODE-RELATED LITERACY SKILLS

CHAPTER 6

Learning the Code

Barbara R. Foorman

This chapter is about how English-speaking children learn to encode and decode their written language, that is, their alphabetic orthography. With the learning loss and growing achievement gap during the COVID-19 pandemic, this topic is highly significant in spite of decades of research and consensus reports documenting the compelling evidence for explicit and systematic teaching of the alphabetic code. First, characteristics of the English alphabetic orthography are described. Second, how children learn to identify and recognize words is explained. Third, two cognitive theories of reading are presented. Fourth, evidence-based instructional practices are discussed, as well as challenges to their implementation. Along the way, common misconceptions about learning the alphabetic code, such as the utility of the three-cueing systems, are pointed out.

Characteristics of the English Alphabetic Orthography

The English alphabetic orthography consists of 26 letters, called *graphemes,* and approximately 41–44 phonemes. The number of phonemes varies due to regional dialect. For example, in the Southern part of the United States the *oi* diphthong in *oil* is often pronounced as a single phoneme rather than two, so that the word sounds like *all.* The way that orthographic units (graphemes) map onto spoken units (phonemes) is called the *alphabetic principle.*

The Alphabetic Principle

A child faces several challenges in grasping the alphabetic principle. First, phonemes are psychological abstractions. As Liberman, Shankweiler, and Liberman (1989) point out, spectrographic analysis reveals the word *bag* to be one burst of sound rather than three separate phonemes. The way a child discovers the three separate phonemes is by contrasting /bag/ with other spoken words that differ in initial, medial, and final phonemes. For example, /bag/ differs from /sag/ in the initial phoneme; /bag/ differs from /bat/ in the final phoneme; and /bag/ differs from /big/ in the medial phoneme. By segmenting and blending phonemes in words, the child develops *phonemic awareness* and can learn to manipulate phonemes in speech and play rhyming, alliteration, and Pig Latin games.

A second challenge to grasping the alphabetic principle is learning the inconsistent mappings between phonology and orthography. In consistent or shallow orthographies, such as Finnish, Italian, Spanish, German, and Greek, grapheme–phoneme mappings are readily accessible and efficient, and word reading accuracy is near ceiling by the middle of first grade (Seymour,

Aro, & Erskine, 2003). However, English is an opaque, or deep, orthography that has inconsistent mappings. Ziegler, Stone, and Jacobs (1997) found that 69.3% of monosyllabic English words are consistent in grapheme-to-phoneme mappings and 30.7% of the phoneme-to-grapheme mappings are consistent. In spite of the depth of English orthography, researchers estimate that approximately 80% of English monosyllabic words can be pronounced using a relatively small set of phonics rules relating phonology and spelling (Coltheart, Rastle, Perry, Langdon, & Ziegler, 2001) and only about 4% are truly irregular, such as *aisle* and *yacht*, and must be memorized (Hanna, Hanna, Hodges, & Rudorf, 1966).

A third challenge to learning the alphabetic principle is that although orthography encodes phonology, encounters with print require engagement of the visual system as input to the phonological system (Dehaene, 2010). Therefore, the visual distinctiveness of the orthographic units (i.e., graphemes) must be learned. For example, the fact that a 180-degree rotation of the letter *d* yields a different grapheme (i.e., *b*), which can then yield yet another grapheme (i.e., *p*) when rotated 180 degrees in a different direction—all with their own associated phoneme—is something that must be learned. Learning the distinctive features occurs through the visual–motor practice of encoding (i.e., writing) each grapheme, then contrasting similar graphemes so that decoding the letter–sounds becomes efficient (Seidenberg, 2017). Thus, mastering the alphabetic principle entails learning both the visual distinctiveness of letters (i.e., orthography) and the mappings of orthography to sound (i.e., phonology). It is not surprising, therefore, that the multimodal challenge of handwriting fluency has large effects on written composition in both first and fourth grades (e.g., Wagner et al., 2011).

Phonological-Orthographic Mappings

The alphabetic principle is a key intellectual insight that graphemes relate intentionally and conventionally to sound segments in speech (i.e., phonemes). This insight is just the beginning of a gradual learning process in which the child computes the mappings while encoding and decoding graphemes, aided by phonemic awareness, concepts of print, and feedback from a literate person such as a family member, caregiver, or teacher (Foorman, 1994; Share, 1995). This

process of learning the statistical structures of orthography and phonology and the mappings between them is aided by explicit instruction in grapheme–phoneme connections (Seidenberg, 2017), which includes practicing the connections across all positions within words (Beck & Beck, 2013). Phonics instruction is discussed in later sections, but first the knowledge to be learned about these phonological–orthographic structures is presented.

There are three key points to understanding how the child computes phonological–orthographic mappings in English. First, the English alphabetic code is more accurately described as an alphabetic cipher for speech (Gough, Juel, & Griffith, 1992) because a cipher is based on systematic algorithms for arranging letters, whereas a code substitutes arbitrary symbols for components of a message and requires a codebook to decode. These algorithms underlie the probabilities of certain letters co-occurring and having particular pronunciations. With multiple exposures to the sound–spelling patterns in English, the child computes the frequency of phonological–orthographic structures that occur in words at various "grain sizes"—whole word, onset–rime, and phoneme (Ziegler & Goswami, 2005). Within a syllable, the *onset* refers to the initial phoneme such as /s/ in *seam* or phonemes in *steam* (/s/ /t/) or *stream* (/s/ /t/ /r/), and the *rime* (*-eam*) refers to the medial vowel and remaining consonants. Orthographic rimes facilitate prediction of the pronunciation of vowel teams. For example, the child learns that the rime *-eat* in the highly frequent word *great* has a different pronunciation than in the more regular pattern in *meat, seat,* and *heat.* By computing the frequency with which these orthographic neighbors occur, the child can derive probable pronunciations for units larger than grapheme-to-phoneme. Thus, instead of decoding *struck* as five separate phonemes, it can be chunked into *str-uck.* Similarly, *invisible* can be chunked into *in-vis-ible.* The child also computes legal statistical patterns such as double letters occurring at the end of words, as in *mitt* and *floss,* but not at the beginning of words (except for names such as *llama* or *Llewellyn*).

Second, English orthography is more accurately described as morphophonemic because both sound and meaning are represented (Chomsky & Halle, 1968). Meaning is preserved with or without a change in spelling or in pronunciation. In *kindness,* the suffix *-ness* is added to the base morpheme, *kind,* without a spelling change. In *vineyard* or *signal,* morphemes are combined with a phonological change in the morphemes *vine* and *sign.* In the word *theoretical,* there is a shift in both spelling and phonology as the base morpheme *theory* is changed into an adjective by a spelling change (*y* to *i*) and the addition of the suffixes *-ic* and *-al* (Carlisle & Stone, 2005).

Third, English orthography can be described in historical terms by its etymology, that is, by the language of origin—Anglo-Saxon, Latin, and Greek. Words of Anglo-Saxon origin tend to be the most common and frequent words in English (numbers, work-related words, body parts, animals) and function words (*a, the, you, would, to*). They comprise the list of the 100 most used words in English and often consist of single syllables. The consonant and vowel sound–symbol correspondences of English mostly stem from Anglo-Saxon. In contrast, the influence of Latin and Greek is most apparent in morphology—prefixes, suffixes, roots, and plurals. The influence of Greek is also apparent in words that combine scientific morphemes (*astro* + *logy*; *thermos* + meter) and in phonology—the *ph* for /f/ in *phone*; the *y* in *gym*, the /k/ pronunciation of *ch* in *chrome* (Moats, 2021).

In summary, English orthography is a deep morphophonemic cipher whose phonological-orthographic structure can be computed through statistical learning aided by phonemic awareness and feedback from a literate adult (Compton et al., Chapter 25, and Kemp & Treiman, Chapter 9, this volume). Challenges children have in learning the linguistic knowledge sources that underlie this structure are illustrated by the spelling errors noted in Table 6.1.

As shown in Table 6.1, omission of the *r* when writing *hurt* reflects lack of awareness of this phoneme. Hence, phonics instruction includes explicit instruction on the "*r*-controlled vowels" of *ir* (*bird*), *er* (*her*), *ur* (*hurt*), *ar* (*park*), and *or* (*for*). Alphabetic knowledge is relevant to correct representation of the *tch* in *patch*, the *wr* in *wrapper*, and the *c* spelling for the /k/ in *cosmology*. Morphological knowledge is relevant to preservation of the base morpheme (*heal*) in *health* and to the Latin and Greek roots and affixes in *attention, cosmology,* and *mnemonic*. Because of the prevalence of Greek and Latin roots and affixes in multisyllabic English words, English language arts standards in the United States typically mandate their teaching in third through eighth grades.

Finally, the errors in Table 6.1 in words reflecting spelling conventions remind us of why spelling needs to be taught in elementary school (Foorman, Breier, & Fletcher, 2003). Remember that phoneme-to-grapheme mappings in monosyllabic English words are only 30.7% consistent (Ziegler et al., 1997). Consider the many spelling patterns for "long *e*" (*me, heed, meat, grief, these, key*), "long *a*" (*main, brave, clay, eight, great, they, vein*), "long *i*" (*dime, by, die, light, stifle, guy, heist*), or "long *o*" (*home, coat, go, toe, glow, fold, open, though*). Consider also that *could, cook,* and *put* all have the same vowel sound and that *boo, stew, cube, blue, fruit,* and *judo* all have the same vowel sounds. In addition to spelling variants for vowel teams, there

TABLE 6.1. Linguistic Knowledge Sources Relevant to Reading and Spelling English Words

Word	Error	Knowledge source
hurt	hut	phonemic awareness
patch	pach	alphabetic
writer	ridr	alphabetic; morphological
health	helth	morphological
guess	gues	spelling convention (consonant doubling at end of word)
beginning	begining	spelling convention (consonant doubling when adding *-ing*)
tried	tryed	spelling convention (change *y* to *i* when adding *-ing*)
give	giveing	spelling convention (drop final *-e* when adding *-ing*)
attention	atenshun	morphological (Latin root, prefix, and suffix)
cosmology	kosmology	alphabetic; morphology (Greek root and suffix)
mnemonic	nemonik	morphology (Greek root and suffix)

are irregular spellings of highly frequent words (*of, is, you, said, was*) to be learned. Moreover, there are spelling conventions regarding inflectional endings to be taught. Consonants are doubled when inflectional endings are added to single-syllable words ending in a consonant—*beginning, stopped, runner.* When adding *-ed, y* is changed to *i* (*tried, cried*). When adding *-ing*, final *-e* is dropped (*giving, breathing*). Other conventions to be taught are contractions (*don't, we've, wouldn't*), plurals (*cats* vs. *dishes*), and possessives (*mine, yours, day's work, children's books, chickens' eggs*). Finally, in addition to teaching the meaning of words with Latin and Greek roots and affixes, the spelling shifts that occur with the addition of affixes also need to be taught.

Learning to Identify and Recognize Words

The complexity of English orthography just described makes it clear that children learn to read by being taught, unlike how children acquire language, which develops naturally among members of a speech community before formal schooling. Children cannot memorize the approximately 300,000 words in a dictionary. However, memorizing the 220 highly frequent words on the Dolch List (Dolch, 1953) is a manageable task when the words are sprinkled throughout primary-grade reading instruction.

Given that English is a quasi-regular orthography with approximately 80% consistent grapheme-to-phoneme correspondences (Coltheart et al., 2001), children can learn the alphabetic principle by learning to decode and encode through phonics instruction. Children can be taught variant correspondences (inconsistent vowel teams, *r*-controlled vowels, diphthongs), with attention to onsets and rimes, final *-e*, silent letters, spelling rules, and morphological elements. Instruction on highly reliable syllable patterns such as "open" syllables in which the first vowel has a "short" sound as in *insect* makes sense, but not on unreliable patterns such as closed syllables in which the first vowel has a "long" sound, such as in *moment* (Kearns, 2020).

A central goal for children learning to identify and recognize words is to bind words' spellings to their pronunciations and their meanings in memory through a process called *orthographic mapping*, so that words can be recognized automatically by sight (Ehri, 2020). Ehri's expla-

nation of sight-word reading as orthographic mapping corrects practitioners' notions of sight words as highly frequent words to be memorized and the three-cueing system's advice that meaning be given equal weight to the graphophonic and syntactic cues in reading words. Conceptually, the three-cueing system stems from Goodman's (1976) notion of reading as a psycholinguistic guessing game whereby readers focus on graphic cues and search memory for related syntactic, semantic, and phonological cues in order to ascertain meaning. The three-cueing system became popularized as an instructional approach in the 1990s (e.g., Routman, 1994) and is still widely used despite lack of evidence of effectiveness. As Ehri (2020) points out, context helps confirm meaning rather than guess meaning. In summary, context cannot replace a primary emphasis on learning the alphabetic code if children are to become independent readers (e.g., Duke, 2020; Landi, Perfetti, Bolger, Dunlap, & Foorman, 2005; Scanlon & Anderson, 2020).

Cognitive Theories of Learning to Read

Rapid recognition of words is fundamental to cognitive theories of reading. Here, two enduring theories are highlighted: the simple view of reading (Gough & Tunmer, 1986) and Perfetti's reading systems framework (Perfetti & Helder, 2022).

The Simple View of Reading

The simple view of reading posits that reading comprehension is a product of decoding and linguistic comprehension. Both decoding and linguistic comprehension are necessary components; neither is sufficient alone (Rayner, Foorman, Perfetti, Pesetsky, & Seidenberg, 2001). Over time, associations between decoding and reading comprehension will decrease, whereas associations between linguistic comprehension and reading comprehension will increase (Hoover & Gough, 1990). A recent meta-analysis found that studies based on the simple view of reading had an average explained variance in reading comprehension of 60% (Quinn & Wagner, 2018).

Support for the increasing role played by linguistic comprehension in the simple view of reading has also been found in latent variable modeling studies (Foorman, Petscher, & Herrera, 2018; Foorman, Wu, Quinn, & Petscher,

2020; Lonigan, Burgess, & Schatschneider, 2018). Foorman, Petscher, et al. (2018) found in their cross-sectional study in grades 1–10 that the unique contribution of decoding to reading comprehension decreased from 14% in grade 1 to 1% in grades 6–10, whereas the unique contribution of linguistic comprehension to reading comprehension increased from 8% in grade 1 to 58% in grade 6 and 66% in grade 10. Throughout the grades, there was a large percentage of common variance between the decoding and linguistic comprehension factors, ranging from 46% in grade 1, to 40% in grade 6, to 32% in grade 10 (see Figure 2 in Bailey, Duncan, Cunha, Foorman, & Yeager, 2020).

In summary, the simple view of reading is an enduring heuristic but requires elaboration to account for the large amount of overlapping variance between decoding and linguistic comprehension in predicting reading comprehension in grades 1–10. This large overlap also suggests that reading instruction needs to integrate language and decoding skills if children are to understand what they read.

Perfetti and Helder's Reading Systems Framework

Perfetti and Helder's (2022) reading systems framework is useful in its depiction of the linguistic and orthographic knowledge required for reading comprehension. There are three knowledge systems in their framework: orthographic knowledge (mapping to language); linguistic knowledge (phonology, syntax, and morphology); and general knowledge (including text structure). The processes of reading are word identification, meaning and form identification, sentence parsing, inferencing, and comprehension monitoring. These processes use the knowledge sources in both constrained ways (e.g., word identification uses linguistic and orthographic knowledge but not general knowledge) and interactive ways (e.g., inferences are drawn from meaning extracted from sentences and from general knowledge). These processes take place within a cognitive architecture with limited attentional and memory capacity. A key focus of the framework is the lexicon—the mental store of words a reader has. The lexicon is a central connection point between the word identification system and the comprehension system. Thus, the quality of a reader's orthographic and phonological representation of a word in the lexicon ensures that words are identified accurately

and efficiently, with the correct meaning and grammatical function in sentences. This way, words move from a functional to an autonomous lexicon, and the process of decoding, encoding, and understanding words become efficient (Perfetti, 2007).

In summary, there is compelling evidence on how children learn to read in English. Mastering the alphabetic system is a necessary but not sufficient condition for reading comprehension. Proficiency in linguistic comprehension, adequate cognitive skill, and deep background knowledge are essential if children are to understand what they read (Castles, Rastle, & Nation, 2018; Petscher et al., 2020). Moreover, if children are to become readers, they must have the opportunity to read (National Research Council, 1998) and be motivated to engage in reading (e.g., Guthrie et al., 2007). An obvious question is whether this compelling evidence is apparent in evidence-based instructional strategies and programs for teaching children to read.

Evidence-Based Practices for Teaching the Alphabetic Code and Implementation Challenges

Consensus documents (National Institute of Child Health and Human Development [NICHD] 2000; National Research Council, 1998; RAND Reading Study Group, 2002) and recent systematic reviews of the evidence base (Foorman et al., 2016; Gersten et al., 2020; Wanzek et al., 2016) support the use of explicit, systematic phonics in a variety of curricula. The meta-analysis on phonics conducted as part of the NICHD (2000) National Reading Panel report compared phonics programs with programs without phonics and found an effect size of 0.41 favoring phonics programs (Ehri, Nunes, Stahl, & Willows, 2001; see Foorman & Connor, 2011, for response to criticism). Ehri et al. (2001) did not find a significant difference between programs that taught grapheme–phoneme correspondences (synthetic phonics) or onset–rimes (analytic phonics, embedded phonics, or word families). Mathes et al. (2005) also did not find a difference between synthetic phonics and analytic phonics in a grade 1 intervention study. Similarly, Foorman and colleagues did not find differences in an experimental grade 1 intervention study (Haskell, Foorman, & Swank, 1992) or in a quasi-experimental field study in eight schools and 66 classrooms in grades 1 and 2 (n = 285; Foorman, Francis, Fletcher, Schatschneider, & Mehta, 1998). The design of the field study contrasted a commercial synthetic phonics program, an embedded phonics approach, a research-based whole-language approach, and the district's usual whole-language approach. Children receiving synthetic phonics improved in word reading at a significantly faster rate and had significantly higher word recognition skills than those receiving the whole-language approaches (and comprehension outcomes paralleled these findings but were less robust). Initial levels of phonemic awareness both predicted and moderated these effects. The lack of differences between synthetic and analytic phonics is not surprising given the importance of teaching grapheme–phoneme correspondences as part of the alphabetic cipher and the importance of teaching onset–rimes to anchor inconsistent vowel teams to their orthographic neighbors.

Elements Critical to Effective Phonics Programs

The What Works Clearinghouse (WWC) practice guide *Foundational Skills to Support Reading for Understanding in Kindergarten through 3rd Grade* provides four recommendations for teaching reading in the primary grades (Foorman et al., 2016). This practice guide is based on more than 4,500 citations from 2000 through 2014 that yielded 235 eligible studies to review using WWC's group design standards. From this subset, 56 studies met WWC's rigorous standards. The panel of experts for this practice guide made the following recommendations based on the evidence from these well-designed studies:

1. Teach students academic language skills, including the use of inferential and narrative language, and vocabulary knowledge.
2. Develop awareness of the segments of sounds in speech and how they link to letters.
3. Teach students to decode words, analyze word parts, and write and recognize words.
4. Ensure that each student reads connected text every day to support reading accuracy, fluency, and comprehension.

Many practitioners believe that they are following these recommendations by teaching vocabulary, phonemic awareness, incidental phonics, and guided reading of text. However, in these so-called "balanced" literacy approaches that emphasize meaningful context, curricula are often improvised with text leveled by word frequency, word count, and picture cues rather than being *explicit* and *systematic* with text designed to practice the sound–spelling patterns taught. The word *explicit* means that teaching of sound–spelling correspondences is direct rather than indirect or incidental, as in the three-cueing system. Incidental teaching often results in children using a strategy of pronouncing the first letter and then guessing at the word based on context (Rayner et al., 2001). The word *systematic* suggests a carefully designed scope and sequence of phonic elements with plenty of opportunity to practice each sound–spelling pattern in word lists and in connected text, and selection of words based on their oral and printed frequency. Hiebert (2007) argues that to create fluent readers a word-zone fluency curriculum needs to be developed that controls words for printed word frequency and orthographic and morphological structure. She suggests that the rise in dysfluent readers is due to the loss of control on the sublexical features in text for beginning readers that began in the mid-1980s as texts were leveled by the number and frequency of words and the presence of pictures.

The Need for Core Reading Programs Based on Theories of Learning

As useful as a core reading program is when compared to practitioners' improvised balanced literacy approach, not all core reading programs are designed with attention to how children learn. Foorman and colleagues examined the design of six grade 1 core reading programs published between 1995 and 2000 (Foorman, Francis, Davidson, Harm, & Griffin, 2004): Harcourt, Houghton Mifflin, Open Court (1995, 2000 editions), Success for All, and Reading Mastery. They created a relational database of the words in the student anthologies and calculated the printed and oral frequency, length, grammatical complexity, number of unique and total words, and repetition of words. They also created a phonics look-up table to check whether a word was holistically taught, decodable now, decodable later, or never decodable when it was first and last encountered in the student anthology. Reading Mastery stood out as having the most repetitions of a word—a median of five times, which mirrors Reitsma's (1983) study of the number of times a beginning reader needs to be exposed to a word before automatic recognition occurs. Additionally, Reading Mastery had the highest relative frequency and smallest corpus of unique words (i.e., 370), least printed and oral vocabulary demands, least grammatically complex sentences, and highest decodability (69.46% at first presentation and 69.73% at last presentation). Thus, a program such as Reading Mastery may be appropriate for remedial reading if users do not mind that text does not appear until Lesson 91.

Harcourt and Houghton Mifflin had relatively large numbers of total words (59,347 and 21,410, respectively) and numbers of unique words (2,843 and 2,696, respectively). These two programs also had the lowest percentages of words that were decodable now (25.78 and 15.97%, respectively), improving at last presentation to 35.57 and 29.02%, respectively. In these two programs, over half of the unique words were never decodable at first or last presentation. An example of the incoherent phonics approach in Houghton Mifflin was that variant pronunciations for *oo* (*too* vs. *look*), variant spelling patterns for the vowel phoneme in *too* (*clue*, *chew*, *soup*), variant pronunciations for *ou* (*soup*, *house*), and "long o" for *ow* (*throw*) were all presented within the same lesson. In contrast, in the two editions of Open Court, decodability indices were relatively strong at first presentation (48.76 and 56.75%, respectively) and increased to 64.67 and 70.52% at last presentation, respectively. Words with variant sound–spelling patterns were first presented separately and then contrasted. Establishing such a set for diversity is sound pedagogical practice (Gibson & Levin, 1976). In addition, a blending strategy was taught to minimize mispronunciations and maximize access to meaning (e.g., /c/, /ca/, /cat/ rather than /c/ /a/ /t/). Moreover, vocabulary and grammatical demands of Open Court text increased gradually across the year. Thus, these editions of Open Court appeared to have lexical and text features based on learning theory (Rayner et al., 2001): Students had the opportunity to practice and contrast the sound–spelling patterns taught and were given a blending strategy to aid in accessing meaning, and vocabulary and grammatical complexity in passages gradually increased across the year. Because of these advantageous features of Open Court, Foorman and colleagues (2006) controlled for curriculum in their analysis of how instructional practice interacted with initial reading ability in grades 1 and 2 in predicting reading and spelling outcomes.

In summary, the Foorman et al. (2004) analysis of the variability in decodability, vocabulary, and grammatical complexity of core reading programs considered for state adoption over 20 years ago is valuable for several reasons. First, no such comprehensive investigation has been conducted since. Second, all of these programs are still in use. Houghton Mifflin and Harcourt merged in 2007, and the subsequent core reading program, HMH *Journeys*, continues to exhibit some of the lack of coherence and consistency seen in the previous editions (Foorman, Herrera, & Dombek, 2018; Foorman, Herrera, et al., 2020). Third, curriculum matters to literacy outcomes.

Implementation Challenges

Well-designed reading curricula are necessary but not sufficient for teaching children to become successful readers. Knowledgeable teachers need to implement well-designed curricula in an effective manner. As described earlier, Foorman et al. (2006) found that teaching quality affected first and second graders' reading and spelling outcomes through interactions of effectiveness ratings and time allocation with students' initial reading ability. Teaching quality can be improved through program-specific professional development and coaching (e.g., Folsom, Smith, Burk, & Oakley, 2017). Teachers often need support in how to assess children's learning so that their instruction is differentiated through flexible small groups, meaningful center-based activities, peer-assisted learning, and appropriate independent work (e.g., Connor, Morrison, Fishman, Schatschneider, & Underwood, 2007). Literacy coaches can create professional learning communities to keep teachers abreast of evidence-based practices (see Foorman, Smith, & Lee, 2020, for links to literacy resources). Literacy coaches can also assist in establishing multitiered systems of support in the school, so that students not responding to classroom instruction (i.e., Tier 1) receive appropriate interventions in Tiers 2 and/or 3. Literacy coaches need school leaders to commit to K–3 reading as a school's top priority and to engage them in the creation of a schoolwide reading improvement plan. Ideally, such plans and support for their implementation should exist at the district and even state level, and preservice teacher preparation programs should be integrated into these plans as well (Foorman, 2020; St. Martin, Vaughn, Troia, Fien, & Coyne, 2020).

During the COVID-19 pandemic, the need for district and school literacy plans to include options for remote and safe in-person learning became apparent. Unfortunately, the evidence base for distance-learning reading programs is weak for primary grade students (e.g., Sahni et al., 2021). Moreover, social distancing, desk shields, and mask wearing in school means that teachers cannot easily hear students read aloud in order to correct their reading errors, and that students cannot see teachers' mouths as an aid to word pronunciation—both critical strategies to teaching beginning reading. Thus, it falls to parents and caregivers to provide this feedback as their children read at home.

Conclusion

Children naturally acquire language in order to communicate with other members of their speech community. Supported by literate adults, children develop linguistic comprehension, concepts of print, phonemic awareness, and gradually learn to compute the statistical structures that underlie their alphabetic cipher and morphophonemic orthography. Systematic reviews and meta-analyses provide strong support for explicit, systematic phonics instruction in well-designed curricula implemented through ongoing professional development in multi-tiered systems of support. The value of systematic phonics instruction is to improve decoding skill, which indirectly improves comprehension by making decoding more accurate and, eventually, more efficient. These indirect effects allow students to advance only so far in understanding complex text. Building students' proficiency in language and their knowledge of the world are important to the broader goal of improving reading comprehension.

References

Bailey, D., Duncan, G., Cunha, F., Foorman, B., & Yeager, D. (2020). Persistence and fade-out of educational-intervention effects. *Psychological Science in the Public Interest, 21*(2), 55–97.

Beck, I., & Beck, M. (2013). *Making sense of phonics* (2nd ed.). Guilford Press.

Carlisle, J. F., & Stone, C. A. (2005). Exploring the role of morphemes in word reading. *Reading Research Quarterly, 40*, 428–449.

Castles, A., Rastle, K., & Nation, K. (2018). Ending the reading wars: Reading acquisition from novice to expert. *Psychological Science in the Public Interest, 19*(1), 5–51.

Chomsky, N., & Halle, M. (1968). *The sound patterns of English*. Harper & Row.

Coltheart, M., Rastle, K., Perry, C., Langdon, R., & Ziegler, J. (2001). DRC: A dual route cascaded model of visual word recognition and reading aloud. *Psychological Review, 108*, 204–256.

Connor, C. M., Morrison, F. J., Fishman, B. J., Schatschneider, C., & Underwood, P. (2007). THE EARLY YEARS: Algorithm-guided individualized reading instruction. *Science, 315*(5811), 464–465.

Dehaene, S. (2010). *Reading in the brain: The new science of how we read*. Penguin.

Dolch, E. (1953). *The Dolch basic sight word list*. Garrard.

Duke, N. (2020). When young readers get stuck. *Educational Leadership, 78*(3), 26–33.

Ehri, L. C. (2020). The science of learning to read words: A case for systematic phonics instruction. *Reading Research Quarterly, 55*(Suppl. 1), S45–S60.

Ehri, L. C., Nunes, S., Stahl, S., & Willows, D. (2001). Systematic phonics instruction helps students learn to read: Evidence from the National Reading Panel's meta-analysis. *Review of Educational Research, 71*, 393–447.

Folsom, J., Smith, K., Burk, K, & Oakley, N. (2017). Educator outcomes associated with implementation of Mississippi's K–3 early literacy professional development initiative (REL 2017–270). Retrieved February 10, 2022, from *https://ies.ed.gov/ncee/edlabs/regions/southeast/pdf/REL_2017270.pdf*.

Foorman, B. (1994). The relevance of a connectionist model of reading for "The Great Debate." *Educational Psychology Review, 6*, 25–47.

Foorman, B. (2020). State policy levers for improving literacy. Retrieved February 10, 2022, from *https://compcenternetwork.org/sites/default/files/archive/statepolicyleversforimprovingliteracy.pdf*.

Foorman, B., Beyler, N., Borradaile, K., Coyne, M., Denton, C., Dimino, J., . . . Wissel, S. (2016). *Foundational skills to support reading for understanding in kindergarten through 3rd grade* (NCEE 2016–4008). Retrieved February 10, 2022, from *https://ies.ed.gov/ncee/wwc/docs/practiceguide/wwc_foundationalreading_070516.pdf*.

Foorman, B., Herrera, S., & Dombek, J. (2018). The relative impact of aligning Tier 2 intervention materials to classroom core reading materials in grades K–2. *Elementary School Journal, 118*(3), 477–504.

Foorman, B., Herrera, S., Dombek, J., Wood, C., Gaughn, L., & Doughtery-Underwood, L.

(2020). The impact of word knowledge instruction on literacy outcomes in grade 5 (REL 2020–083). Retrieved February 10, 2022, from *https://ies.ed.gov/ncee/edlabs/regions/southeast/pdf/REL_2021083.pdf*.

Foorman, B., Petscher, Y., & Herrera, S. (2018). Unique and common effects of decoding and language factors in predicting reading comprehension in grades 1–10. *Learning and Individual Differences, 63,* 12–23.

Foorman, B., Smith, K., & Lee, L. (2020). Implementing evidence-based literacy practices in K–3 classrooms. *Education and Treatment of Children, 43,* 49–55.

Foorman, B., Wu, Y-C., Quinn, J., & Petscher, Y. (2020). How do latent decoding and language predict latent reading comprehension: Across two years in grades 5, 7, and 9? *Reading and Writing, 33,* 2281–2309.

Foorman, B. R., Breier, J. I., & Fletcher, J. M. (2003). Interventions aimed at improving reading success: An evidence-based approach. *Developmental Neuropsychology, 24*(2 & 3), 613–639.

Foorman, B. R., & Connor, C. (2011). Primary reading. In M. Kamil, P. D. Pearson, & E. Moje (Eds.), *Handbook on reading research* (Vol. IV, pp. 136–156). Taylor & Francis.

Foorman, B. R., Francis, D. J., Davidson, K., Harm, M., & Griffin, J. (2004). Variability in text features in six grade 1 basal reading programs. *Scientific Studies in Reading, 8*(2), 167–197.

Foorman, B. R., Francis, D. J., Fletcher, J. M., Schatschneider, C., & Mehta, P. (1998). The role of instruction in learning to read: Preventing reading failure in at risk children. *Journal of Educational Psychology, 90,* 37–55.

Foorman, B. R., Schatschneider, C., Eakin, M. N., Fletcher, J. M., Moats, L. C., & Francis, D. J. (2006). The impact of instructional practices in grades 1 and 2 on reading and spelling achievement in high poverty schools. *Contemporary Educational Psychology, 31,* 1–29.

Gersten, R., Haymond, K., Newman-Gonchar, R., Dimino, J., & Jayanthi, M. (2020). Meta-analysis of the impact of reading interventions for students in the primary grades. *Journal of Research on Educational Effectiveness, 13*(4), 401–427.

Gibson, E., & Levin, H. (1976). *The psychology of reading* (3rd ed). MIT Press.

Goodman, K. (1976). Reading: A psycholinguistic guessing game. In H. Singer & R. Ruddell (Eds.), *Theoretical models and processes of reading* (2nd ed., pp. 497–508). International Reading Association.

Gough, P., Juel, C., & Griffith, P. (1992). Reading, spelling, and the orthographic cipher. In P. Gough, L. Ehri, & R. Treiman (Eds.), *Reading acquisition* (pp. 35–48). Erlbaum.

Gough, P., & Tunmer, W. (1986). Decoding, reading, and reading disability. *Remedial and special Education, 7,* 6–10.

Guthrie, J., Hoa, A. L., Wigfield, A., Tonks, S., Humenick, N., & Littles, E. (2007). Reading motivation and reading comprehension growth in the later elementary years. *Contemporary Educational Psychology, 32*(3), 282–313.

Hanna, P., Hanna, J., Hodges, R., & Rudorf, E., Jr. (1966). Phoneme–grapheme correspondences as cues to spelling improvement (USDOE Publication No. 32008). Retrieved February 10, 2022, from *https://files.eric.ed.gov/fulltext/ed128835.pdf*.

Haskell, D. W., Foorman, B. R., & Swank, P. R. (1992). Effects of three orthographic/phonological units on first grade reading. *Remedial and Special Education, 13,* 40–49.

Hiebert, E. H. (2007). The fluency curriculum and text elements that support it. In P. Schwanenflugel & M. Kuhn (Eds.), *Fluency instruction for shared reading: Two whole class approaches* (pp. 36–54). Guilford Press.

Hoover, W., & Gough, P. (1990). The simple view of reading. *Reading and Writing, 2,* 127–160.

Kearns, D. (2020). Does English have useful syllable division patterns? *Reading Research Quarterly, 55*(Suppl. 1), S145–S160.

Landi, N., Perfetti, C., Bolger, D., Dunlap, S., & Foorman, B. (2005). The role of discourse context in developing word form representation: A paradoxical relation between reading and learning. *Journal of Experimental Child Psychology, 94,* 114–133.

Liberman, I., Shankweiler, D., & Liberman, A. (1989). The alphabetic principle and learning to read. In D. Shankweiler & I. Liberman (Eds.), *Phonology and reading disability: Solving the reading puzzle (International Academy for Research in Learning Disabilities Monograph Series, 6,* 1–33). University of Michigan Press.

Lonigan, C., Burgess, S., & Schatschneider, C. (2018). Examining the simple view of reading with elementary school children: Still simple after all these years. *Remedial and Special Education, 39*(5), 260–273.

Mathes, P. G., Denton, C. A., Fletcher, J. M., Anthony, J. L., Francis, D. J., & Schatschneider, C. (2005). The effects of theoretically different instruction and student characteristics on the skills of struggling readers. *Reading Research Quarterly, 40*(2), 148–182.

Moats, L. (2021). *Speech to print* (3rd ed.). Brookes.

National Institute of Child Health and Human Development. (2000). *National Reading Panel–Teaching children to read: Reports of the subgroups* (NIH Pub. No. 00–4754). U.S. Department of Health and Human Services.

National Research Council. (1998). *Preventing reading difficulties in young children* (C. E.

Snow, M. S. Burns, & P. Griffin, Eds.). National Academy Press.

Perfetti, C. (2007). Reading ability: Lexical quality to comprehension. *Scientific Studies of Reading, 11*(4), 357–383.

Perfetti, C., & Helder, A. (2022). Progress in reading science: Word identification, comprehension, and universal perspectives. In M. Snowling, C. Hulme, & K. Nation (Eds.), *The science of reading: A handbook* (2nd ed., pp. 5–35). Wiley-Blackwell.

Petscher, Y., Cabell, S., Catts, H., Compton, Foorman, B., Hart, S., . . . Wagner, R. (2020). How the science of reading informs 21st-century education. *Reading Research Quarterly, 55*(1), S267–S282.

Quinn, J. M., & Wagner, R. K. (2018). Using meta-analytic structural equation modeling to study developmental change in relations between language and literacy. *Child Development, 89*(6), 1956–1969.

RAND Reading Study Group. (2002). *Reading for understanding.* RAND.

Rayner, K., Foorman, B. R., Perfetti, C. A., Pesetsky, D., & Seidenberg, M. S. (2001). How psychological science informs the teaching of reading. *Psychological Science in the Public Interest, 2*(2), 31–74.

Reitsma, P. (1983). Printed word learning in beginning readers. *Journal of Experimental Child Psychology, 36*, 321–339.

Routman, R. (1994). *Invitations: Changing as teachers and learners, K–12.* Heinemann.

Sahni, S., Polanin, J., Zhang, Q., Michaelson, L., Caverly, S., Polese, M., & Yang, J. (2021). *A What Works Clearinghouse rapid evidence review of distance learning programs* (WWC 2021–005). U.S. Department of Education, Institute of Education Sciences, National Center for Education Evaluation and Regional Assistance, What Works Clearinghouse. Retrieved February 10, 2022, from *https://ies.ed.gov/ncee/wwc/ Docs/ReferenceResources/Distance_Learning_ RER_508c.pdf*

Scanlon, D., & Anderson, K. (2020). Using context as an assist in word solving: The contributions of 25 years of research on the interactive strategies approach. *Reading Research Quarterly, 55*(Suppl. 1), S19–S34.

Seidenberg, M. (2017). *Language at the speed of sight.* Basic Books.

Seymour, P. H. K., Aro, M., & Erskine, J. M. (2003). Foundation literacy acquisition in European orthographies. *British Journal of Psychology, 94*, 143–174.

Share, D. (1995). Phonological recoding and self teaching: Sine qua non of reading acquisition. *Cognition, 55*, 151–218.

St. Martin, K., Vaughn, S., Troia, G., Fien, H., & Coyne, M. (2020). *Intensifying literacy instruction: Essential practices.* MIMTSS Technical Assistance Center, Michigan Department of Education. Retrieved February 10, 2022, from *https://intensiveintervention.org/resource/ intensifying-literacy-instruction-essential-practices*

Wagner, R., Puranik, C., Foorman, B., Foster, E., Wilson, L. G., Tschinkel, E., & Kantor, P. T. (2011). Modeling the development of written language. *Reading and Writing, 24*, 203–220.

Wanzek, J., Vaughn, S., Scammacca, N., Gatlin, B., Walker, M., & Capin, P. (2016). Meta-analyses of the effects of Tier 2 type reading interventions in grades K–3. *Educational Psychology Review, 28*(3), 551–576.

Ziegler, J., & Goswami, U. (2005). Reading acquisition, developmental dyslexia, and skilled reading across languages: A psycholinguistic grain size theory. *Psychological Bulletin, 131*(1), 3–29.

Ziegler, J., Stone, G., & Jacobs, A. (1997). What is the pronunciation for *-ough* and the spelling for /u/?: A database for computing feedforward and feedback consistence in English. *Behavior Research Methods, Instruments, & Computers, 29*(4), 600–618.

CHAPTER 7

The Science of Early Alphabet Instruction

What We Do and Do Not Know

Shayne B. Piasta

In alphabetic orthographies such as English, one of the first tasks for beginning readers and writers is cracking the alphabetic code. For very young children, this includes recognizing that printed words comprise letters, and these letters correspond to the sounds (phonemes) heard when the word is read aloud. Understanding this concept—the alphabetic principle—comprises the basis for decoding and spelling (Ehri, 2015; Foorman, Chapter 6, this volume) and is grounded in children's early alphabet knowledge (Byrne & Fielding-Barnsley, 1989).

Alphabet knowledge consists of children's understanding of letter forms, names, and associated sounds. Young children's alphabet knowledge is an important predictor of later reading and spelling skills (Georgiou, Torppa, Manolitsis, Lyytinen, & Parrila, 2012; National Early Literacy Panel [NELP]; 2008) and, conversely, also an indicator of future reading difficulties (Piasta, Petscher, & Justice, 2012; Torppa, Poikkeus, Laakso, Eklund, & Lyytinen, 2006). Given the theoretical and empirical ties between early alphabet knowledge and later literacy, expectations for letter name and sound learning are included in state and national guidelines pertaining to preschool and kindergarten. Head Start, for instance, sets benchmarks of knowing 18 uppercase and 15 lowercase letter names (Administration for Children and Families, 2015; see also Piasta et al., 2012), and the Common Core

State Standards recommend knowing the names of all uppercase and lowercase letters as well as all basic letter–sound correspondences by the end of kindergarten (National Governors Association Center for Best Practices & Council of Chief State School Officers, 2010). This emphasis on supporting young children's alphabet knowledge aligns with emerging evidence that children's trajectories of early alphabet learning, not just mastering letter names and sounds by first grade, may be important for literacy success (Piasta, Logan, Farley, Strang, & Justice, 2021; Torppa et al., 2006).

How can children's alphabet learning be supported? For some children, alphabet knowledge may be acquired in incidental ways as they sing their "ABCs," play with magnetic letters and other materials, learn to write their names, and engage in other activities at home and school (McGee & Richgels, 1989). For example, shared reading can promote children's alphabet knowledge (Mol, Bus, & de Jong, 2009), particularly when the adult engages in what is called *print referencing*—pointing to, talking about, and otherwise calling attention to the letters in the printed text (Justice & Ezell, 2002). Such adult mediation has been noted as a critical factor in children's alphabet learning (Justice & Ezell, 2002; Levin & Aram, 2012). The extent to which adults engage in these types of practices to support children's alphabet learning, however, varies (Bindman,

Skibbe, Hindman, Aram, & Morrison, 2014; Treiman et al., 2015). Moreover, adults do not equally attend to letter names and sounds during their interactions with children, with adults in the United States tending to focus on letter names (Ellefson, Treiman, & Kessler, 2009; Gerde, Skibbe, Goetsch, & Douglas, 2019). Thus, intentionally and effectively supporting children's learning through early alphabet instruction is also important. Yet many widely used curricula do not have evidence of promoting children's alphabet knowledge (Preschool Curriculum Evaluation Research Consortium, 2008).

Until recently, research to identify effective practices for supporting children's alphabet learning was relatively limited. The National Early Literacy Panel (2008) found a positive effect of code-focused instruction, in general, on alphabet knowledge outcomes but was able to draw few conclusions regarding the effects of alphabet instruction specifically, due to the limited availability of relevant studies. A subsequent meta-analysis found only 10 studies focused on alphabet instruction, yielding modest effect sizes, and also provided few insights to practices or components that improve alphabet learning (Piasta & Wagner, 2010a). Fortunately, as reviewed below, researchers have increasingly attended to this issue and extended what we know about the science of alphabet instruction.

The Science of Early Alphabet Instruction

Supporting children's alphabet learning requires consideration of *what* to teach and *how* to teach those concepts. Below, I review what we know about alphabet instruction with respect to both of these aspects. I primarily focus on the science of alphabet instruction as it applies to teaching the English alphabet to children in U.S. classrooms; however, I include studies of other alphabetic languages when these provide additional insights. I mainly consider experimental and other causally interpretable studies of alphabet instruction. I include some noncausal research that has implications for what and how we teach about the alphabet but note that we do not (yet) know whether these suggested instructional practices are effective. In describing what we do and do not know about the science of alphabet instruction, I summarize the state of this field and identify limitations, unanswered questions, and future directions.

Teaching Names versus Sounds

Children are generally expected to be able to associate letter forms with both English letter names (e.g., the letter *B*) and corresponding sounds (e.g., /b/). In the United States, children tend to acquire letter-name knowledge ahead of letter-sound knowledge (Ellefson et al., 2009). Yet, arguably, being able to associate letters with sounds is the key element that affords decoding and spelling in alphabetic languages (Hulme, Bowyer-Crane, Carroll, Duff, & Snowling, 2012). This gives rise to questions concerning the sequencing and content of alphabet instruction with respect to teaching letter names and sounds.

Roberts, Vadasy, and Sanders (2019) tested three versions of alphabet instruction and found an advantage of teaching letter sounds before names on U.S. preschoolers' letter-sound learning for the version that emphasized paired-associate learning (i.e., explicitly teaching children by showing them a letter while saying the name and sound). There were no differences for letter-sound learning in the other versions (in which paired-associate learning was combined with articulatory or orthographic learning), and no differences for letter-name learning in any version. Results were the same for English monolingual children and dual language learners. In a prior study, Levin, Shatil-Carmon, and Asif-Rave (2006) found no overall differences in Israeli children's learning of Hebrew letter names or sounds based on whether they were taught names or sounds first.

Two additional studies have tested the effects of teaching letter names and sounds together or separately. Piasta, Purpura, and Wagner (2010) found an advantage of combined letter name and sound instruction on U.S. preschoolers' alphabet learning, compared to instruction on letter sounds only. Roberts, Vadasy, and Sanders (2018) found that combined letter-name and -sound instruction, as well as instruction in letter names only, increased U.S. preschoolers' letter-name learning relative to instruction in letter sounds only. Instruction in letter sounds, whether alone or combined with letter-name instruction, promoted letter-sound learning. These findings held regardless of dual language learner status. In both studies, letter-sound instruction was no more effective for letter-sound learning than jointly teaching names and sounds together, and only combined letter-name and -sound instruction was more effective than typical instruction.

In part, these studies suggest that children learn what they are taught—names, sounds, or both. Yet they also suggest that teaching letter names and sounds together may be desirable, particularly if the goal involves learning both names and sounds. This also aligns with evidence suggesting that children may use their knowledge of letter names, together with their phonological awareness skills, to derive the associated letter sound for those letters whose names include cues to those sounds (e.g., /b/ in *B*; /k/ in *K*; Cardoso-Martins, Mesquita, & Ehri, 2011; Piasta & Wagner, 2010b).

Teaching Uppercase versus Lowercase

Preschool and kindergarten children in the United States are generally more knowledgeable about uppercase than lowercase letters (Anthony, Chen, Williams, Cen, & Erazo, 2021; Treiman & Kessler, 2004). Correlational research indicates that children are more likely to know the name of a lowercase letter when they are already familiar with the uppercase form, particularly when letters are visually similar (e.g., *Pp, Ss;* Huang & Invernizzi, 2014; Pence Turnbull, Bowles, Skibbe, Justice, & Wiggins, 2010; Treiman & Kessler, 2004). This suggests that children use their uppercase letter knowledge to learn lowercase letters. An instructional implication may be that uppercase letters should be taught first, or that uppercase and lowercase letters should be taught simultaneously. Although both practices are commonly reported by early childhood teachers (Gerde et al., 2019), this premise has yet to be tested.

Other Instructional Sequencing Issues

In general, there is little causal evidence to inform decisions regarding the specific sequence in which letters are taught. Jones, Clark, and Reutzel (2013) propose six different teaching sequences based on (1) letters that appear in children's names, (2) alphabetic order, (3) whether letter names include sound cues, (4) consonant sound acquisition order, (5) letter frequency, and (6) visual similarity. Each of these is based on descriptive and correlational research identifying patterns as to which letters children are more or less likely to know. For example, children tend to be most familiar with the letters in their first names (Huang, Tortorelli, & Invernizzi, 2014; Piasta, Phillips, Williams, Bowles, & Anthony,

2016; Treiman & Kessler, 2004), leading to recommendations to focus on these letters when beginning alphabet instruction. Similarly, children are more likely to know letters earlier in the alphabetic sequence (e.g., *A, B, C* vs. *X, Y, Z;* Huang et al., 2014; Phillips, Piasta, Anthony, Lonigan, & Francis, 2012) and, as noted earlier, those letters whose names include cues to their sounds (Piasta & Wagner, 2010b; Treiman, Tincoff, Rodriguez, Mouzaki, & Francis, 1998). Children also are more likely to know consonant letters whose sounds are acquired earlier in development (Justice, Pence, Bowles, & Wiggins, 2006). These findings lead to suggestions to teach in alphabetic order or otherwise start with letters that may be more familiar to children and thus easier to learn. Alternatively, based on evidence that children are less likely to know letters that do not appear frequently in printed text (e.g., *Q, Y;* Huang et al., 2014; Kim, Petscher, Treiman, & Kelcey, 2021), Jones et al. (2013) also suggest starting with these less frequent and perhaps more challenging letters. The relative effectiveness of these various instructional sequences, however, has not been tested.

Jones et al.'s (2013) final sequence considers the extent to which letters have similar versus distinctive shapes. Children may be less familiar with letters that are visually (e.g., *E* and *F, b* and *d*)—or phonologically (e.g., *M* and *N*, /ě/ and /ĭ/)—similar to other letters (Carnine, 1976; Huang & Invernizzi, 2014; Treiman & Kessler, 2003; Treiman, Kessler, & Pollo, 2006). Some researchers have tested the effects of teaching visually or phonologically similar letters together, to facilitate comparison, or separately, to avoid confusion. For example, Carnine (1976) found that U.S. first graders were more likely to produce the correct sounds for *E* and *I* when these letters were not taught within the same session than when taught together, and found a similar advantage for separating the introduction of these letters for preschool children. Carnine (1980) found that U.S. preschoolers learned to match letters more quickly when introduced alongside non-visually similar letters and then in the context of visually similar letters, as compared to first introducing alongside visually similar letters. In these studies, separating instruction for potentially confusable letters appeared most beneficial. An important caveat, however, is that these studies relied on paradigms (rote training, trials-to-criterion) that do not necessarily reflect the alphabet instructional practices or learning outcomes typical of early childhood classrooms. Altogether, current research does not identify any optimal teaching sequence but does suggest possible benefits of introducing potentially confusing letters separately.

Instructional Pacing

Traditional approaches to early alphabet instruction have often taken the form of "letter-of-the-week" (Gerde et al., 2019; Neuman, 2006). Yet, as Jones and colleagues (Jones & Reutzel, 2012; Jones et al., 2013) argue, principles of learning imply that increasing opportunities for exposure, repetition, and distributed practice should enhance alphabet learning. This suggests that introducing letters at a quicker pace may be advantageous. In an initial study, Jones and Reutzel (2012) found that U.S. kindergartners taught one new letter per day through brief, explicit alphabet lessons, followed by cycles of review, were more likely to meet end-of-year letter-name fluency benchmarks compared to those who experienced traditional letter-of-the-week instruction. Although these results must be interpreted cautiously given methodological limitations, two more recent studies also suggest benefits of quicker pacing. Vadasy and Sanders (2021) found that U.S. kindergarteners and first graders demonstrated greater letter-sound learning when letters and digraphs were introduced at a faster rate (two to four per week) as compared to a slower rate (one to three per week). Similarly, in a correlational study of Norwegian 6-year-olds, Sunde, Furnes, and Lundetræ (2020) showed an association between a faster pace of letter introduction and children's subsequent lowercase letter-sound knowledge, word reading, and spelling.

Evidence also supports distributed practice as important for letter-sound learning. Kryznowski and Carnine (1980) found that U.S. first graders were more likely to produce the correct sounds for E and I when these letters were taught in a "spaced" format (i.e., interspersed with teaching sounds for other letters). Volpe, Burns, DuBois, and Zaslofsky (2011) showed positive effects of incremental rehearsal, which applies similar principles, on letter-sound knowledge and fluency.

Explicit Teaching

Explicit teaching, in which the instructor shows the letter form and provides the corresponding name and/or sound, is featured in many alphabet instruction studies. Most of these studies show an advantage for children's alphabet learning relative to comparison conditions, in which alphabet learning opportunities may also be explicit or may be more incidental (Piasta, Park, Fitzgerald, & Libnoch, 2022; Piasta et al., 2010; Roberts et al., 2018). Explicit teaching may be especially important for alphabet learning due to its alignment with *paired-associate learning*. Paired-associate learning is a cognitive process in which visual symbols (e.g., letters) are attached to verbal labels (e.g., names and sounds) through repeated pairings of this information (i.e., opportunities to see a letter while hearing/saying its name and sound; for example, showing a child the printed letter B and saying, "This is the letter B. It represents the /b/ sound"). This process is critical for alphabet learning, as demonstrated by Roberts et al. (2019). In this study, U.S. preschoolers who were monolingual English speakers demonstrated greater alphabet learning when they experienced instruction that emphasized paired-associate learning as compared to instruction that included additional articulatory (e.g., teaching children to attend to mouth shapes while saying sounds) or orthographic (e.g., letter writing) activities. Paired-associate learning also appeared beneficial for children who were dual language learners, as they were more likely to learn letters taught using paired-associate learning (alone or in combination with articulatory or orthographic activities) than untaught letters; the additional articulatory or orthographic activities also might have been helpful for these children given that there were no statistically significant differences among these three instructional conditions. Notably, counter to notions of explicit teaching as rote drill and memorization, the instruction provided in Roberts et al. and other studies consisted of quick-paced, engaging alphabet activities that children found fun and engaging (Piasta, Logan, et al., 2022; Roberts et al., 2018; Roberts, Vadasy, & Sanders, 2020), with little evidence that such instruction was negatively associated with motivation (Roberts & Sadler, 2019).

Teaching in Context

A common instructional recommendation is to teach letters in meaningful contexts, such as during shared book reading or by linking them to children's own names. As noted, children can gain alphabet knowledge through adult-mediated shared storybook reading (Justice & Ezell, 2002; Mol et al., 2009; cf. NELP, 2008). Additional work has considered learning from alphabet books in particular, with somewhat inconclusive results. Greenewald and Kulig (1995) found that U.S. kindergartners who experienced shared alphabet book reading learned more letter names than those who experienced shared storybook reading, whereas Willoughby, Evans, and Nowak (2015) found no differences when comparing the alphabet learning of preschool-age Canadian children who experienced traditional alphabet books, alphabet eBooks, or storybook reading. Both-de Vries and Bus (2014) found that alphabet books improved Dutch kindergartners' letter learning compared to typical classroom activities. They also found some evidence that illustrations using anthropomorphic figures to represent letter sounds (e.g., *bear* for *B, cat* for *C*) may distract children and lead to less alphabet learning than illustrations of objects (e.g., *box* for *B, coat* for *C*), which might partially explain contradictory results across studies.

Roberts et al. (2020) directly tested whether U.S. preschoolers' letter-name and -sound learning differed when taught in context versus not in context. Children who experienced lessons in which letters were presented in context (as part of children's names, at the beginning of familiar words, or within a storybook) learned fewer letter sounds and were less successful in identifying initial sounds in words than those who experienced lessons in which letters were presented in isolation. There were no differences on letter naming or letter fluency, and results were the same for children who were monolingual English-speaking and dual language learners. Ratings of children's engagement during lessons indicated that engagement was higher when letters were presented in isolation. These findings suggest that children do not necessarily benefit from teaching letters in context, nor does teaching letters without context undermine children's participation or interest in alphabet instruction. A related, but unanswered, question is whether opportunities to apply acquired alphabet knowledge to authentic reading and writing activities facilitates continued alphabet learning in any way (see Savage, Georgiou, Parrila, & Maiorino, 2018).

Teaching through Writing

Writing is another meaningful context that has been investigated as it may support alphabet

learning. Hall, Toland, Grisham-Brown, & Graham (2014) found that interactive writing lessons improved U.S. preschoolers' letter name, but not sound, knowledge relative to typical instruction. In initial studies of peer-assisted writing strategies, Puranik, Patchan, Lemons, and Al Otaiba (2017) and Puranik, Petscher, Otaiba, and Lemons (2018) found preliminary evidence that this approach may facilitate U.S. kindergarteners' letter writing and letter naming fluency, although effects appeared conditional on school-level literacy achievement. Piasta, Logan, et al. (2022) found positive effects on U.S. preschoolers' letter-name learning, letter-sound learning, and letter writing in a pilot study of alphabet lessons that taught all of these components. These studies suggest that children can learn about the alphabet within the context of writing. As all studies included attention to letter names and sounds in addition to writing, however, they do not address whether writing activities specifically promote alphabet learning. Roberts et al. (2019) tested this by comparing alphabet instruction that emphasized only paired-associate learning to that which also included letter-writing activities. The paired-associate learning (only) instruction resulted in better letter-name and -sound learning for U.S. preschoolers who were monolingual English speakers. There was no difference between conditions for dual language learners, nor was there a difference in letter writing between the conditions. These results suggest that explicit attention to letter names and sounds, rather than writing specifically, may be the mechanism for learning names and sounds. As this work is replicated, it will be important to disentangle effects on letter writing, which is a key learning goal for young children (Cabell, Tortorelli, & Gerde, 2013; Gerde et al., 2019), as it is currently unclear whether both instructional approaches were equally effective or ineffective in promoting this outcome.

Teaching Articulatory Awareness

Roberts et al. (2019) also studied articulatory awareness as a component of alphabet instruction. Letter sounds are characterized by how each is produced, which includes mouth position and movement, airflow, and voicing (i.e., whether the vocal cords vibrate). Increasing awareness of how sounds are produced may help children differentiate and remember sounds, and instruction that draws children's attention to articulatory features may benefit children's phonological awareness, reading, and spelling (Boyer & Ehri, 2011; Torgesen et al., 1999). Roberts et al. (2019), however, did not find an advantage for alphabet instruction that included explicit attention to mouth position and movement (i.e., having children watch the instructor's mouth or using mirrors to watch their own mouths). U.S. preschoolers who were monolingual English speakers exhibited better letter-name and -sound learning when they experienced instruction that emphasized paired-associate learning (only) compared to instruction the combined paired-associate learning with articulation instruction. There were no significant differences between the two conditions for preschoolers who were dual language learners.

Multisensory Teaching

Writing and articulatory awareness instruction are often components of multisensory instruction more generally. Multisensory instruction provides opportunities for children to use multiple sensory modalities during learning. With respect to alphabet instruction, which typically attends to visual (i.e., seeing printed letters) and auditory modalities (i.e., hearing letter names and sounds) by default, multisensory instruction often adds kinesthetic and/or tactile learning opportunities (e.g., tracing or writing, use of letter manipulatives and gross motor movements, attending to articulatory gestures). Evidence concerning multisensory alphabet instruction is currently limited, with rather mixed findings. Bara, Gentaz, and Colé (2007) found that French kindergartners had better letter recognition when physical exploration of foam letters was added to alphabet instruction, but a prior study had not shown this advantage (Bara, Gentaz, Colé, & Sprenger-Charolles, 2004). Labat, Escalle, Baldy, and Magnan (2014) found that adding physical exploration of letters and letter tracing to alphabet instruction did not yield any advantage for French kindergartners' letter-sound learning, although the letter tracing may have facilitated letter writing (despite other studies not showing benefits of tracing; Beech, Pedley, & Barlow, 1994; Kratochwill, Severson, & Demuth, 1978). McMahon, Rose, and Parks (2003) reported improved alphabet learning for children who used body movements to represent letter shapes, and DiLorenzo, Rody, Bucholz, and Brady (2011) claimed benefits of an over-all multisensory alphabet instruction program; both studies, however, are less than conclusive given methodological limitations. As noted earlier, Roberts et al. (2019) did not find benefits of adding articulatory awareness or letter-writing components to alphabet instruction, and a study by Schlesinger and Gray (2017), albeit with second graders and letter-like symbols, also found no clear advantage of multisensory over non-multisensory instruction. Thus, despite theoretical rationales as to how multisensory instruction may promote alphabet learning (see Labat et al., 2014; Schlesinger & Gray, 2017), more research in this area is needed.

Embedded Mnemonics

Evidence supports embedded mnemonics as an effective strategy for teaching letter sounds. Embedded mnemonics integrate the letter shape into familiar objects, actions, and/or characters that also reflect the letter sound (e.g., a snake drawn in the shape of an *S* that hisses /s/); note that such embedded mnemonics are different than the anthropomorphic figures representing letter sounds (e.g., *bear* for *B*) used in some alphabet books and found to be distracting to children in the Both-de Vries and Bus (2014) study. Ehri, Deffner, and Wilce (1984) found that U.S. kindergartners exhibited greater letter-sound learning when taught letters using pictures integrating the letter shape and sound than when taught (1) using pictures of the same objects that did not incorporate the letter shape or (2) without using pictures. First graders also showed a similar benefit on letter-sound learning, plus an advantage of embedded mnemonics on letter writing. In a subsequent study, Shmidman and Ehri (2010) replicated these findings with English-speaking preschoolers who were taught Hebrew letters. Roberts and Sadler (2019) expanded this work by studying alphabet instruction that included not only embedded mnemonics in which the letter shape was integrated into a drawing of a character that also represented the sound (e.g., dippy duck) but also narrative stories about these characters that provided additional exposures to the sound. Preschoolers who experienced this instruction learned more letter sounds and were better able to identify the initial sounds in words as compared to those who experienced instruction that did not feature embedded mnemonics or stories but provided the same exposure to the letters and sounds.

Notably, alphabet instruction commonly features mnemonics that are not embedded (e.g., a snake to represent *S* and /s/ but not shaped like an *S*; jumping for *J*). Ehri et al.'s (1984) findings suggested that nonembedded picture mnemonics were no more effective than not using pictures. Marsh and Desberg (1978) found that U.S. kindergartners were better able to recall letter sounds during instruction that provided pictures to represent letter sounds than when no pictures were provided. However, this benefit was no longer apparent when the letters were presented in isolation (i.e., without the accompanying pictures). They had similar findings when using action mnemonics rather than picture mnemonics. Hetzroni and Shavit (2002), in contrast, found benefits of nonembedded picture mnemonics for Israeli children learning Hebrew letters, although they studied older children (ages 10–15 years) with intellectual disabilities. In most of this work, children's learning and retention was tested over a very brief period of time (e.g., one "training trial" per letter and all letters taught within a week). As research in this area continues, attention to action mnemonics and more ecologically valid instructional practices is warranted.

Alphabet and Phonological Awareness Instruction

Correlational studies suggest that alphabetic knowledge and phonological awareness are reciprocally related (Caravolas, Hulme, & Snowling, 2001; Lerner & Lonigan, 2016), and combining alphabet and phonological awareness instruction may be advantageous for phonemic awareness and reading outcomes (Bus & van IJzendoorn, 1999; cf. NELP, 2008). Is such combined instruction also effective for alphabet learning? Meta-analyses have shown significant effects of combined instruction on alphabet knowledge but, due to the limited studies available, could not conclude whether this was more effective than alphabet instruction alone (NELP, 2008; Piasta & Wagner, 2010a). A few primary studies have directly tested this. Schneider, Roth, and Ennemoser (2000) found no differences in alphabet learning between German kindergarteners who experienced letter-sound instruction alone versus letter-sound plus phonological awareness instruction. Likewise, Lonigan et al. (2013) did not find any advantage of combined alphabet and phonological awareness instruction versus alphabet instruction on U.S. preschoolers' alphabet learning (with all instruction also

featuring dialogic reading). Castles, Coltheart, Wilson, Valpied, and Wedgwood (2009) examined whether providing phonemic awareness instruction, versus alternative instruction, prior to letter-sound instruction affected Australian preschoolers' letter-sound learning. They found no benefits on a letter-sound production task but small benefits on a letter-sound recognition task (cf. Cardoso-Martins et al., 2011). Taken together, this literature does not provide strong evidence that teaching phonological awareness ahead of or combined with alphabet instruction benefits alphabet learning. Yet results also do not suggest that providing phonological awareness instruction hinders alphabet learning. This is important because, in reality, it may not be possible to completely separate alphabet and phonological awareness instruction, as strategies for teaching letter sounds often involve asking children to identify these sounds at the beginning of words and similar activities.

Technology

Emerging evidence suggests that young children can learn about the alphabet through technology, particularly when such technology incorporates design features known to enhance engagement and learning. For example, Schmitt, Hurwitz, Sheridan Duel, and Nichols Linebarger (2018) found that U.S. preschoolers and kindergartners who played literacy games on an educational website had improved alphabet outcomes relative to those who played nonliteracy games. Similarly, Neumann (2018) found that Australian preschoolers taught about the alphabet using iPad apps improved their letter-name and -sound knowledge, but not letter writing abilities, relative to those who did not use the apps, and Elimelech and Aram (2020) found an advantage in alphabet learning, including on a task assessing letter writing/emergent writing, for Israeli preschoolers who played a digital computer game in which they selected letters that mapped to sounds and spelled words. These studies, however, do not address the relative effectiveness of teaching the alphabet via technology versus more typical instruction. In contrast, D'Agostino, Rodgers, Harmey, and Brownfield (2016) tested the effects of using an iPad app in lieu of magnetic letters for the alphabet-focused portion of Reading Recovery lessons. U.S. first graders who used the app made greater gains in letter-naming fluency, letter identification, and using letters to represent sounds in words as compared to those taught using magnetic letters. These results suggest possible affordances of using technology for alphabet instruction, although this deserves further attention including the role of adult mediation.

Differentiation

Although not yet realized, a promising application of technology could be its use to differentiate alphabet instruction. *Differentiation* refers to modifying instructional content, process, and/or products to respond to differing learning needs (Tomlinson, 2014). Differentiation is especially relevant to alphabet instruction given substantial individual differences in young children's alphabet knowledge, such that some children may have mastered letters that others are still learning (Piasta, 2014; Piasta, Logan, et al., 2022). Moreover, descriptive work suggests that letters vary in their difficulty (Phillips et al., 2012; Piasta, Phillips, Williams, Bowles, & Anthony, 2016), due to differences in visual and phonological similarity, inclusion of sound cues in letter names, and other factors referenced earlier in this chapter. This implies that certain letters may be easier or more challenging to learn and that instruction should be adjusted accordingly. A recent meta-analysis showed positive effects of differentiated literacy instruction generally (Puzio, Colby, & Algeo-Nichols, 2020), but research specific to alphabet instruction is limited. Piasta, Park, et al. (2022) provide proof-of-concept for differentiating the content of alphabet instruction (i.e., which letters are taught), finding positive impacts of alphabet lessons designed for this purpose on letters individually selected for children based on an initial alphabet screening. This work also empirically tested the instructional implications surrounding letter difficulty. Piasta, Park, et al. found that letter difficulty affected children's letter-name, but not letter-sound, learning. More difficult letters (e.g., *Q, U*) may require greater instructional intensity than less difficult letters (e.g., *O, B*), requiring differention of instructional processes. An important next step is to directly test whether such differentiated instruction is more or less effective than nondifferentiated approaches, such as letter-of-the-week.

Conclusion

In summary, practices such as combining letter-name and -sound instruction, including explicit instruction and embedded mnemonics, and utilizing quicker pacing seem promising as ways to promote early alphabet learning, whereas available evidence does not necessarily support multisensory techniques, teaching within context, or combined alphabet and phonological awareness instruction as improving alphabet outcomes. Knowing what practices do and do not facilitate young children's alphabet learning—the science of early alphabet instruction—is critical for ensuring that alphabet instruction is not only effective but also efficient. Parents and teachers are supporting children's learning across many aspects of language and literacy, as well as across multiple other domains. Spending a disproportionate amount of time on alphabet instruction limits other learning opportunities (Neuman, 2006; Snow & Matthews, 2016) and, as indicated, not all children—or letters—may require the same instruction (Piasta, 2014). The emerging evidence reviewed in this chapter suggests that letter-of-the-week approaches may not be efficient, although more research is needed to determine effectiveness relative to other approaches. Differentiated alphabet instruction, in particular, is a notable area for future research, including how this might be afforded through use of technology.

Understanding what we do not (yet) know from the science of early alphabet instruction is also important. Despite suggestions concerning teaching uppercase and lowercase letters and sequences for alphabet instruction based on descriptive and correlational data, such instructional implications have yet to be tested. There are also many other unanswered questions. These include those related to best supporting letter writing and effects of nonembedded mnemonics, as well as other questions not addressed in the literature to date. Many of these questions, including addressing mixed evidence concerning multisensory instruction, require careful attention to counterfactual conditions and to the applicability to classroom settings. Much of the current research also needs to be replicated, particularly with more linguistically, ethnically, and socially diverse samples. Nevertheless, the small but growing science of early alphabet instruction yields important insights that can support young children's acquisition of alphabet knowledge as a critical foundation for continued literacy success.

References

Administration for Children and Families, & U.S. Department of Health and Human Services. (2015). *Head Start early learning outcomes framework: Ages birth to five.* Author.

Anthony, J. L., Chen, Y.-J. I., Williams, J. M., Cen, W., & Erazo, N. A. (2021). U.S. children's understanding of the English alphabet: Its acquisition, conceptualization, and measurement. *Journal of Educational Psychology, 113*(6), 1073–1087.

Bara, F., Gentaz, E., & Colé, P. (2007). Haptics in learning to read with children from low socioeconomic status families. *British Journal of Developmental Psychology, 25*(4), 643–663.

Bara, F., Gentaz, E., Colé, P., & Sprenger-Charolles, L. (2004). The visuo-haptic and haptic exploration of letters increases the kindergarten-children's understanding of the alphabetic principle. *Cognitive Development, 19*(3), 433–449.

Beech, J. R., Pedley, H., & Barlow, R. (1994). Training letter-to-sound connections: The efficacy of tracing. *Current Psychology, 13*(2), 153–164.

Bindman, S. W., Skibbe, L. E., Hindman, A. H., Aram, D., & Morrison, F. J. (2014). Parental writing support and preschoolers' early literacy, language, and fine motor skills. *Early Childhood Research Quarterly, 29*(4), 614–624.

Both-de Vries, A. C., & Bus, A. G. (2014). Visual processing of pictures and letters in alphabet books and the implications for letter learning. *Contemporary Educational Psychology, 39*(2), 156–163.

Boyer, N., & Ehri, L. C. (2011). Contribution of phonemic segmentation instruction with letters and articulation pictures to word reading and spelling in beginners. *Scientific Studies of Reading, 15*(5), 440–470.

Bus, A. G., & van IJzendoorn, M. H. (1999). Phonological awareness and early reading: A meta-analysis of experimental training studies. *Journal of Educational Psychology, 91*(3), 403–414.

Byrne, B., & Fielding-Barnsley, R. (1989). Phonemic awareness and letter knowledge in the child's acquisition of the alphabetic principle. *Journal of Educational Psychology, 81*(3), 313–321.

Cabell, S. Q., Tortorelli, L. S., & Gerde, H. K. (2013). How do I write . . . ? Scaffolding preschoolers' early writing skills. *Reading Teacher, 66*(8), 650–659.

Caravolas, M., Hulme, C., & Snowling, M. J. (2001). The foundations of spelling ability: Evidence from a 3-year longitudinal study. *Journal of Memory and Language, 45*(4), 751–774.

Cardoso-Martins, C., Mesquita, T. C. L., & Ehri, L. (2011). Letter names and phonological awareness help children to learn letter–sound relations. *Journal of Experimental Child Psychology, 109*(1), 25–38.

Carnine, D. W. (1976). Similar sound separation and cumulative introduction in learning letter–sound correspondences. *Journal of Educational Research, 69*(10), 368–372.

Carnine, D. W. (1980). Two letter discrimination sequences: High-confusion-alternatives first versus low-confusion-alternatives first. *Journal of Reading Behavior, 12*(1), 41–47.

Castles, A., Coltheart, M., Wilson, K., Valpied, J., & Wedgwood, J. (2009). The genesis of reading ability: What helps children learn letter–sound correspondences? *Journal of Experimental Child Psychology, 104*(1), 68–88.

D'Agostino, J. V., Rodgers, E., Harmey, S., & Brownfield, K. (2016). Introducing an iPad app into literacy instruction for struggling readers: Teacher perceptions and student outcomes. *Journal of Early Childhood Literacy, 16*(4), 522–548.

DiLorenzo, K. E., Rody, C. A., Bucholz, J. L., & Brady, M. P. (2011). Teaching letter–sound connections with picture mnemonics: "Itchy's alphabet" and early decoding. *Preventing School Failure, 55*(1), 28–34.

Ehri, L. C. (2015). How children learn to read words. In A. Pollatsek & R. Treiman (Eds.), *The Oxford handbook of reading* (pp. 293–310). Oxford University Press.

Ehri, L. C., Deffner, N. D., & Wilce, L. S. (1984). Pictorial mnemonics for phonics. *Journal of Educational Psychology, 76*(5), 880–893.

Elimelech, A., & Aram, D. (2020). Using a digital spelling game for promoting alphabetic knowledge of preschoolers: The contribution of auditory and visual supports. *Reading Research Quarterly, 55*(2), 235–250.

Ellefson, M., Treiman, R., & Kessler, B. (2009). Learning to label letters by sounds or names: A comparison of England and the United States. *Journal of Experimental Child Psychology, 102*, 323–341.

Georgiou, G. K., Torppa, M., Manolitsis, G., Lyytinen, H., & Parrila, R. (2012). Longitudinal predictors of reading and spelling across languages varying in orthographic consistency. *Reading and Writing, 25*(2), 321–346.

Gerde, H. K., Skibbe, L. E., Goetsch, M., & Douglas, S. N. (2019). Head Start teachers' beliefs and reported practices for letter knowledge. *NSHA Dialog, 22*(2), 1–21.

Greenewald, M. J., & Kulig, R. (1995). Effects of repeated reading of alphabet books on kindergarteners' letter recognition. *Yearbook of the National Reading Conference, 44*, 231–235.

Hall, A. H., Toland, M. D., Grisham-Brown, J., & Graham, S. (2014). Exploring interactive writing as an effective practice for increasing Head Start students' alphabet knowledge skills. *Early Childhood Education Journal, 42*(6), 423–430.

Hetzroni, O. E., & Shavit, P. (2002). Comparison of two instructional strategies for acquiring form and sound of Hebrew letters by students with mild mental retardation. *Education and Training in Mental Retardation and Developmental Disabilities, 37*(3), 273–282.

Huang, F. L., & Invernizzi, M. A. (2014). Factors associated with lowercase alphabet naming in kindergarteners. *Applied Psycholinguistics, 35*(6), 943–968.

Huang, F. L., Tortorelli, L. S., & Invernizzi, M. A. (2014). An investigation of factors associated with letter-sound knowledge at kindergarten entry. *Early Childhood Research Quarterly, 29*(2), 182–192.

Hulme, C., Bowyer-Crane, C., Carroll, J. M., Duff, F. J., & Snowling, M. J. (2012). The causal role of phoneme awareness and letter-sound knowledge in learning to read: Combining intervention studies with mediation analyses. *Psychological Science, 23*(6), 572–577.

Jones, C. D., Clark, S., & Reutzel, D. R. (2013). Enhancing alphabet knowledge instruction: Research implications and practical strategies for early childhood educators. *Early Childhood Education Journal, 41*(2), 81–89.

Jones, C. D., & Reutzel, D. R. (2012). Enhanced alphabet knowledge instruction: Exploring a change of frequency, focus, and distributed cycles of review. *Reading Psychology, 33*(5), 448–464.

Justice, L. M., & Ezell, H. K. (2002). Use of storybook reading to increase print awareness in at-risk children. *American Journal of Speech–Language Pathology, 11*(1), 17–29.

Justice, L. M., Pence, K., Bowles, R. B., & Wiggins, A. (2006). An investigation of four hypotheses concerning the order by which 4-year-old children learn the alphabet letters. *Early Childhood Research Quarterly, 21*(3), 374–389.

Kim, Y.-S. G., Petscher, Y., Treiman, R., & Kelcey, B. (2021). Letter features as predictors of letter-name acquisition in four languages with three scripts. *Scientific Studies of Reading, 25*, 453–469.

Kratochwill, T. R., Severson, R. A., & Demuth, D. M. (1978). Children's learning as a function of variation in stimulus characteristics and motor involvement. *Contemporary Educational Psychology, 3*(2), 144–153.

Kryznowski, J., & Carnine, D. (1980). The effects of massed versus spaced formats in teaching sound–symbol correspondences to young children. *Journal of Reading Behavior, 12*(3), 225–229.

Labat, H., Ecalle, J., Baldy, R., & Magnan, A. (2014). How can low-skilled 5-year-old children benefit from multisensory training on the acquisition of the alphabetic principle? *Learning and Individual Differences, 29*, 106–113.

Lerner, M. D., & Lonigan, C. J. (2016). Bidirectional relations between phonological awareness and letter knowledge in preschool revisited: A growth curve analysis of the relation between two code-related skills. *Journal of Experimental Child Psychology, 144*, 166–183.

Levin, I., & Aram, D. (2012). Mother–child joint writing and storybook reading and their effects on kindergartners' literacy: An intervention study. *Reading and Writing, 25*(1), 217–249.

Levin, I., Shatil-Carmon, S., & Asif-Rave, O. (2006). Learning of letter names and sounds and their contribution to word recognition. *Journal of Experimental Child Psychology, 93*(2), 139–165.

Lonigan, C. J., Purpura, D. J., Wilson, S. B., Walker, P. M., & Clancy-Menchetti, J. (2013). Evaluating the components of an emergent literacy intervention for preschool children at risk for reading difficulties. *Journal of Experimental Child Psychology, 114*(1), 111–130.

Marsh, G., & Desberg, P. (1978). Mnemonics for phonics. *Contemporary Educational Psychology, 3*(1), 57–61.

McGee, L. M., & Richgels, D. J. (1989). "K is Kristen's": Learning the alphabet from a child's perspective. *Reading Teacher, 43*(3), 216–225.

McMahon, S. D., Rose, D. S., & Parks, M. (2003). Basic reading through dance program: The impact on first-grade students' basic reading skills. *Evaluation Review, 27*(1), 104–125.

Mol, S. E., Bus, A. G., & de Jong, M. T. (2009). Interactive book reading in early education: A tool to stimulate print knowledge as well as oral language. *Review of Educational Research, 79*, 979–1007.

National Early Literacy Panel. (2008). *Developing early literacy.* National Institute for Literacy.

National Governors Association Center for Best Practices & Council of Chief State School Officers. (2010). *Common core state standards for English language arts and literacy in history/social studies, science, and technical subjects.* Authors.

Neuman, S. B. (2006). N is for nonsensical. *Educational Leadership, 64*(2), 28–31.

Neumann, M. M. (2018). Using tablets and apps to enhance emergent literacy skills in young children. *Early Childhood Research Quarterly, 42*, 239–246.

Pence Turnbull, K. L., Bowles, R. P., Skibbe, L. E., Justice, L. M., & Wiggins, A. K. (2010). Theoretical explanations for preschoolers' lowercase alphabet knowledge. *Journal of Speech, Language, and Hearing Research, 53*(6), 1757–1768.

Phillips, B. M., Piasta, S. B., Anthony, J. L., Lonigan, C. J., & Francis, D. J. (2012). IRTs of the ABCs: Children's letter name acquisition. *Journal of School Psychology, 50*(4), 461–481.

Piasta, S. B. (2014). Moving to assessment-guided differentiated instruction to support young children's alphabet knowledge. *Reading Teacher, 68*(3), 202–211.

Piasta, S. B., Logan, J. A. R., Farley, K. S., Strang, T. M., & Justice, L. M. (2022). Profiles and predictors of children's growth in alphabet knowledge. *Journal of Education for Students Placed at Risk, 27*, 1–26.

Piasta, S. B., Park, S., Fitzgerald, L. R., & Libnoch,

H. A. (2022). Young children's alphabet learning as a function of instruction and letter difficulty. *Learning and Individual Differences, 93,* Article 102113.

Piasta, S. B., Petscher, Y., & Justice, L. M. (2012). How many letters should preschoolers in public programs know? The diagnostic efficiency of various preschool letter-naming benchmarks for predicting first-grade literacy achievement. *Journal of Educational Psychology, 104*(4), 945–958.

Piasta, S. B., Phillips, B. M., Williams, J. M., Bowles, R. P., & Anthony, J. L. (2016). Measuring young children's alphabet knowledge: Development and validation of brief letter-sound knowledge assessments. *Elementary School Journal, 116*(4), 523–548.

Piasta, S. B., Purpura, D. J., & Wagner, R. K. (2010). Fostering alphabet knowledge development: A comparison of two instructional approaches. *Reading & Writing, 23,* 607–626.

Piasta, S. B., & Wagner, R. K. (2010a). Developing emergent literacy skills: A meta-analysis of alphabet learning and instruction. *Reading Research Quarterly, 45*(1), 8–38.

Piasta, S. B., & Wagner, R. K. (2010b). Learning letter names and sounds: Effects of instruction, letter type, and phonological processing skill. *Journal of Experimental Child Psychology, 105,* 324–344.

Preschool Curriculum Evaluation Research Consortium. (2008). *Effects of preschool curriculum programs on school readiness: Report from the Preschool Curriculum Evaluation Research initiative.* Institute of Education Sciences.

Puranik, C. S., Patchan, M. M., Lemons, C. J., & Al Otaiba, S. (2017). Using peer assisted strategies to teach early writing: Results of a pilot study to examine feasibility and promise. *Reading and Writing, 30*(1), 25–50.

Puranik, C. S., Petscher, Y., Otaiba, S. A., & Lemons, C. J. (2018). Improving kindergarten students' writing outcomes using peer-assisted strategies. *Elementary School Journal, 118*(4), 680–710.

Puzio, K., Colby, G. T., & Algeo-Nichols, D. (2020). Differentiated literacy instruction: Boondoggle or best practice? *Review of Educational Research, 90*(4), 459–498.

Roberts, T. A., & Sadler, C. D. (2019). Letter sound characters and imaginary narratives: Can they enhance motivation and letter sound learning? *Early Childhood Research Quarterly, 46,* 97–111.

Roberts, T. A., Vadasy, P. F., & Sanders, E. A. (2018). Preschoolers' alphabet learning: Letter name and sound instruction, cognitive processes, and English proficiency. *Early Childhood Research Quarterly, 44,* 257–274.

Roberts, T. A., Vadasy, P. F., & Sanders, E. A.

(2019). Preschoolers' alphabet learning: Cognitive, teaching sequence, and English proficiency influences. *Reading Research Quarterly, 54*(3), 413–437.

Roberts, T. A., Vadasy, P. F., & Sanders, E. A. (2020). Preschool instruction in letter names and sounds: Does contextualized or decontextualized instruction matter? *Reading Research Quarterly, 55*(4), 573–600.

Savage, R., Georgiou, G., Parrila, R., & Maiorino, K. (2018). Preventative reading interventions teaching direct mapping of graphemes in texts and set-for-variability aid at-risk learners. *Scientific Studies of Reading, 22*(3), 225–247.

Schlesinger, N. W., & Gray, S. (2017). The impact of multisensory instruction on learning letter names and sounds, word reading, and spelling. *Annals of Dyslexia, 67*(3), 219–258.

Schmitt, K. L., Hurwitz, L. B., Sheridan Duel, L., & Nichols Linebarger, D. L. (2018). Learning through play: The impact of web-based games on early literacy development. *Computers in Human Behavior, 81,* 378–389.

Schneider, W., Roth, E., & Ennemoser, M. (2000). Training phonological skills and letter knowledge in children at risk for dyslexia: A comparison of three kindergarten intervention programs. *Journal of Educational Psychology, 92*(2), 284–295.

Shmidman, A., & Ehri, L. (2010). Embedded picture mnemonics to learn letters. *Scientific Studies of Reading, 14*(2), 159–182.

Snow, C. E., & Matthews, T. J. (2016). Reading and language in the early grades. *The Future of Children, 26*(2), 57–74.

Sunde, K., Furnes, B., & Lundetræ, K. (2020). Does introducing the letters faster boost the development of children's letter knowledge, word reading and spelling in the first year of school? *Scientific Studies of Reading, 24*(2), 141–158.

Tomlinson, C. A. (2014). *The differentiated classroom: Responding to the needs of all learners* (2nd ed.). Association for Supervision and Curriculum Development.

Torgesen, J. K., Wagner, R. K., Rashotte, C. A., Rose, E., Lindamood, P., Conway, T., & Garvan, C. (1999). Preventing reading failure in young children with phonological processing disabilities: Group and individual responses to instruction. *Journal of Educational Psychology, 91*(4), 579–593.

Torppa, M., Poikkeus, A.-M., Laakso, M.-L., Eklund, K., & Lyytinen, H. (2006). Predicting delayed letter knowledge development and its relation to grade 1 reading achievement among children with and without familial risk for dyslexia. *Developmental Psychology, 42*(6), 1128–1142.

Treiman, R., & Kessler, B. (2003). The role of letter names in the acquisition of literacy. In H. W.

Reese & R. Kail (Eds.), *Advances in child development and behavior* (Vol. 31, pp. 105–135). Academic Press.

Treiman, R., & Kessler, B. (2004). The case of case: Children's knowledge and use of upper and lowercase letters. *Applied Psycholinguistics, 25*(3), 413–428.

Treiman, R., Kessler, B., & Pollo, T. C. (2006). Learning about the letter name subset of the vocabulary: Evidence from U.S. and Brazilian preschoolers. *Applied Psycholinguistics, 27*(2), 211–227.

Treiman, R., Schmidt, J., Decker, K., Robins, S., Levine, S. C., & Demir, Ö. E. (2015). Parents' talk about letters with their young children. *Child Development, 86*(5), 1406–1418.

Treiman, R., Tincoff, R., Rodriguez, K., Mouzaki, A., & Francis, D. J. (1998). The foundations of literacy: Learning the sounds of letters. *Child Development, 69*(6), 1524–1540.

Vadasy, P. F., & Sanders, E. A. (2021). Introducing grapheme–phoneme correspondences (GPCs): Exploring rate and complexity in phonics instruction for kindergarteners with limited literacy skills. *Reading and Writing, 34*(1), 109–138.

Volpe, R. J., Burns, M. K., DuBois, M., & Zaslofsky, A. F. (2011). Computer-assisted tutoring: Teaching letter sounds to kindergarten students using incremental rehearsal. *Psychology in the Schools, 48*(4), 332–342.

Willoughby, D., Evans, M. A., & Nowak, S. (2015). Do ABC ebooks boost engagement and learning in preschoolers?: An experimental study comparing ebooks with paper ABC and storybook controls. *Computers and Education, 82,* 107–117.

CHAPTER 8

Invented Spelling

An Integrative Review of Descriptive, Correlational, and Causal Evidence

Monique Sénéchal, Gene Ouellette, and H. N. Lam Nguyen

It is now well documented that individual differences in literacy skills present early and remain relatively stable over time. In an effort to better understand contributing factors to these differences, researchers have focused on both internal processes and environmental influences on development, including the home environment and early school experiences. Home and school literacy experiences vary in terms of formality and their focus on print (e.g., Sénéchal & LeFevre, 2014), and also with respect to the role of the child, ranging from passive observational learning to more highly active participation (e.g., Hamilton, Hayiou-Thomas, Hulme, & Snowling, 2016). In this chapter, the focus is on invented spelling, which by nature, is an active, child-generated, exploration of print (see also Kemp & Treiman, Chapter 9, this volume).

Young children often attempt to represent words in print prior to receiving formal literacy instruction (Read, 1971). Such attempts are not always conventional in how they capture the phonology of words and change over time as a child progresses on the journey of acquiring literacy skills. Therefore, these invented spellings offer insights into children's early and changing understanding of the relation between spoken and written language. A review of those insights is presented in this chapter, organized as a function of the strength of the evidence.

A scientific approach to the study of early literacy typically involves three incremental steps. Applied to the study of invented spelling, the first step consists of thorough descriptions of children's attempts at spelling. These descriptions yield information about commonalities and differences in the complexity of children's early spellings and how these spellings change across development. The second step builds on descriptive studies to assess, via correlational studies, the associations among invented spelling, other important early literacy skills, as well as reading and accurate spelling. Third, intervention research is necessary to provide the strongest evidence that invented spelling can play a causal role in the acquisition of more advanced literacy skills. In this chapter, research findings for each of these steps are reviewed.

Descriptive Evidence

Read (1971, 1975) argued that the increasing sophistication of invented spellings reflects children's developing knowledge of how sounds within spoken words are represented in print (see also Chomsky, 1971; Clay, 1972; Ferreiro & Teberosky, 1982). This can be seen in the developmental progression of early spelling in relation to phonology, which begins with initial nonalphabetic markings, followed by printing letters randomly, to a gradual representation of the phonology of words in print (Gentry, 1982; Gentry & Gillet, 1993; Henderson, 1981; Treiman, 1993). A typical progression would be as follows: Children's early attempts to capture words in print consist of the initial sounds of words (e.g., spelling *pretty* with *P*), followed by the addition of final consonant sounds (e.g., PT), then the marking of medial vowel sounds (e.g., PIT or PET). Interestingly, children can make use of both letter names and letter sounds in attempts to capture words in print. For instance, in the example just presented, the second syllable in *pretty* can be captured with the letter name for *T* alone. Alternatively, children who might know the sound of the letter *T* might mark the final syllable as TE. Marking the consonant blend tends to appear later as in PRET or PRIT, with fewer children representing the blend without the main vowel (PRT). Whether invented spelling naturally leads to conventional spelling is a matter of debate, as will be discussed subsequently.

Of special importance is the fact that spelling phonologically does not require prior knowledge of how to read (Ehri & Wilce, 1987; Ouellette & Sénéchal, 2008a). As such, invented spelling begins prior to children receiving formal literacy instructions (Read, 1971) and, more specifically, before they become practiced readers (Gentry & Gillet, 1993); therefore, it is a very early aspect of literacy acquisition, and one that offers a window into development.

The qualitative description of children's invented spellings provided the basis for researchers to develop quantitative measures that are sensitive to the developmental progressions observed. Such measures are necessary to examine the relations between children's invented spelling sophistication and other literacy skills. There are at least three types of scoring rubric. For instance, Mann, Tobin, and Wilson (1987) scored spelling attempts on a 4-point scale that closely resembled the progression described earlier, because it awarded 1 point for the initial phoneme; 2 points for including the initial and final phonemes; 3 points for capturing the phonetic structure of the word, albeit in an unconventional manner; and 4 points for the conventionally correct spelling (for a similar rubric, see Morris & Perney, 1984). A second example is from Tangel and Blachman (1992, 1995), who developed a 6-point scale to capture the number of phonemes represented, with 1 point representing a salient phoneme and 6 points the correct spelling (e.g., Ouellette & Sénéchal, 2008a, 2008b). A third example is that of Kessler's (2009) computerized program that scores each letter sequentially as a function of how far it is from the conventional spelling (e.g., Treiman et al., 2019). With these types of rubrics, researchers could examine the associations between invented spelling sophistication and other early literacy skills.

Before reviewing the correlational literature, however, it is necessary to comment on one common aspect of the scoring rubrics. In each rubric, the highest invented spelling score corresponds to the accurate spelling. Although it can be assumed that young children can, through exploration, spell words accurately when their phonology-to-orthography mappings are entirely consistent (e.g., *bat*), exploration alone might not be sufficient to spell words that include inconsistent orthographic patterns (e.g., including the silent *a* in *boat*). Justly, the inclusion of accurate spelling when measuring invented spelling has been criticized because it may confound research conclusions; that is, it is not possible to ascertain whether it is the early unconventional phonological spelling or the more advanced conventional spelling that is the behavior responsible for any relation with other variables. Should accurate spellings be rarely observed, however, then their inclusion might not affect the patterns of obtained findings. Indeed, there is some evidence that correct spellings are relatively rare in kindergarten. For instance, Morris and Perney (1984) found that correct spellings represented only 9% of the 1,350 spellings produced by the 75 participating children in September of grade 1. Sénéchal and LeFevre (2014) also found that correct spellings were rare: Children spelled accurately 1.2 and 3.0% of the 1,329 and 1,121 words spelled in kindergarten and the beginning of grade 1, respectively. Despite the apparent rarity of correct spellings, we have noted in the remainder of the chapter whether the measurement of invented spelling included accurate spelling, and, whenever possible, it is also noted whether the findings were replicated when accurate spellings were removed from the invented spelling analysis.

Correlational Evidence

Examining the relations between invented spelling and its building blocks, or the component skills, is necessary to construct accurate models of how it develops, as well as how early individual differences in literacy skills arise (Ouellette & Sénéchal, 2008a). In order for children to capture the sounds of words in print, they must possess some level of phoneme awareness and alphabet knowledge. Phoneme awareness is required for children to be able to segment the sounds within a word to be spelled, be it at the level of syllables, onsets and rimes, or phonemes. Moreover, knowledge of letter shapes, names, and/or sounds is necessary to represent these sounds in print. To some extent, children's invented spelling should be a reflection of their developing phoneme awareness and alphabet knowledge. Consequently, there should be differences in children's invented spellings as a function of their ability to segment words at different levels (e.g., syllabic vs. phonemic levels), as well as between children who only know letter names compared to those who also have letter-sound knowledge. Invented spelling is more than the sum of its components, however. Invented spelling provides practice at deciding which letters best capture the sounds that a child detected in a word. It can be viewed as a problem-solving task that consists of mapping the sounds in a word to known letters. As such, invented spelling provides insight and practice in the alphabetic principle. It follows that invented spelling is a more advanced skill than are its building blocks (Ouellette & Sénéchal, 2017). This section describes two meta-analyses conducted to synthesize the cumulative correlational evidence. This is followed by a more detailed description of three longitudinal studies that examined the contribution of invented spelling to reading and spelling.

If the assumption is that practice with the alphabetic principle afforded by invented spelling can lead to accurate orthographic representations for consistent parts of words, then it follows that invented spelling should also be related to accurate spelling; that is, while the accuracy of invented spellings is constrained by whether words or parts of words are consistent in their sound-to-letter mapping, invented spelling may still play a facilitative role in spelling acquisition. Consistent with other theories of early literacy acquisition (Ehri, 2005; Perfetti & Hart, 2002; Share, 1995), complete and accurate orthographic representations require sufficient accurate reading experience, which provides repeated exposure to accurate spellings. Evidence for this is reviewed in the last section of this chapter.

Researchers have been particularly interested in studying the impact of invented spelling on literacy acquisition (e.g., Caravolas, Hulme, & Snowling, 2001; Ehri, 1989, 2005; Ehri & Wilce, 1987; Richgels, 1995). As described, invented spelling creates opportunities for children to explore sound–letter mappings, thus providing practice with and eventual understanding of the alphabetic principle. It follows that invented spelling should facilitate learning to read and spell once in grade school. This hypothesis was examined here by conducting meta-analyses of the longitudinal research that included measures of invented spelling in kindergarten or the beginning of grade 1, and measured reading and/or spelling at a later point in time. To be included in the analyses, studies needed to meet the following criteria: (1) measure *invented spelling,* defined as plausible but unconventional spellings; (2) measure word reading and/or conventional spelling at a later point in time (e.g., end of grade 1); (3) have a sample of 50 children or more to yield reliable correlation coefficients; and (4) be published in English or French. In cases where both concurrent and longitudinal correlation coefficients were reported, only the longitudinal coefficients were included in the meta-analysis. Finally, in cases where reading or spelling was assessed with two or more tests, the averaged correlation coefficient with invented spelling was included in the meta analysis. The studies, their sample sizes, measures, and correlation coeffi cients are reported in Table 8.1.

The first meta-analysis assessed whether invented spelling would be longitudinally related to children's reading once they were in grade school. The analysis, including eight studies, yielded a significant heterogeneity index indicating that the variability across studies was greater than chance ($Q = 48.64$, $p < .001$). As can be seen in Table 8.1, the coefficient for Shatil, Share, and Levin (2000) was small compared to those for the remaining studies. As suggested by Cooper, Hedges, and Valentine (2009), the analysis was repeated without this study. Removing this study resulted in a heterogeneity index that was not statistically significant ($Q = 12.69$, $p > .08$). This latter analysis with seven studies, representing 1,579 children, showed that invented spelling was longitudinally and significantly linked to eventual reading skills. The estimated correlation was .60 ($p < .001$, 95% confidence interval = 0.54–0.66), and its magnitude suggests a strong association between invented spelling and later reading.

TABLE 8.1. Correlations among Invented Spelling Measured at Time 1 and Reading and Accurate Spelling at the End of Grades 1 and/or 2

Study	Pub Year	G1 Read	G1 AS	G2 Read	G2 AS	N	IS measure includes AS	Lang	Country
Caravolas et al.	2001	0.73	0.75	0.60	0.47	148	Yes	E	UK
Charbel et al.	2021	0.58		0.57	0.41	93	No	E	Canada
Mann	1993	0.68				78	Yes	E	USA
McBride-Chang	1998			0.66	0.50	93	Yes	E	USA
Morris & Perney	1984	0.68				75	Yes	E	USA
Ouellette & Sénéchal	2017	0.48	0.46			171	Yes[a]	E	Canada
Sénéchal	2012	0.51	0.54			97	No	E	Canada
Shatil et al.	2000	0.30	0.41			278	Yes	H	Israel
Treiman et al.	2019	0.61		0.53		970	Yes	E	USA

Note. Lang, language; E, English; H, Hebrew; Grades: G, grade; Measures: IS, invented spelling; R, reading; AS, accurate spelling.

[a]Accurate spelling was excluded in supplemental analyses.

The second meta-analysis assessed whether invented spelling would be longitudinally related to children's accurate spelling once they were in grade school. The analysis, including six studies, revealed that the coefficients across studies were relatively homogeneous as revealed by a nonstatistically significant heterogeneity index ($Q = 7.0$, $p = .22$). This analysis with six studies, representing 882 children, showed that invented spelling was longitudinally and positively linked to eventual spelling skills (estimated correlation = .48, $p < .001$, 95% confidence interval = 0.40–0.56). This small body of research is consistent with the hypothesis that invented spelling is moderately to strongly linked to eventual reading and spelling.

These correlational meta-analyses, based on longitudinal data, are in accord with the view that invented spelling facilitates the acquisition of reading and spelling. Yet they do not demonstrate whether these positive effects are entirely due to invented spelling as opposed to well-known predictors. Reviewed next are three longitudinal studies in which more stringent analyses were conducted to document the unique role of invented spelling in learning to read and spell. The key hypothesis tested is that invented spelling builds on phoneme awareness and alphabet knowledge; therefore, invented spelling should mediate the relations between these building blocks and the advanced literacy skills that are reading and conventional spelling.

Ouellette and Sénéchal (2017) examined whether children's invented spelling in kindergarten predicted reading and conventional spelling in grade 1, over and above phonological awareness and alphabet knowledge. In the study, 171 children were tested on phonological awareness, alphabet knowledge, invented spelling, and word reading in early kindergarten, as well as on reading (a composite of word reading and decoding) and conventional spelling halfway through grade 1. Path models predicting grade 1 reading and spelling were then built and tested. In these models, phoneme awareness and alphabet knowledge were directly linked to invented spelling and early word reading, which in turn were linked to grade 1 reading and spelling. The results for grade 1 reading were consistent with the model with one exception: Alphabet knowledge was linked to invented spelling, but not directly to early reading (rather indirectly through invented spelling). Regarding spelling, both alphabet knowledge and phoneme awareness were significantly linked to invented spelling, and invented spelling linked to conventional spelling. Notably, excluding accurate spellings from the analysis did not change the pattern of results. Taken together, these findings are consistent with the correlational meta-analyses in showing that invented spelling seems to play a facilitative role in the acquisition of more advanced literacy skills, which appears to be beyond that explained by other well-known predictors.

Sénéchal (2017) also tested the facilitative role of invented spelling in another longitudinal study in which 107 children participated at the beginning of kindergarten and at the beginning and end of grade 1. Children's alphabet knowledge, phoneme awareness, invented spelling, and early reading were assessed in kindergarten and the beginning of grade 1, whereas a standardized test of word reading and decoding was administered at the end of grade 1. Noteworthy, in this study accurate spellings were excluded from the analysis. Moreover, the invented spelling measure at the beginning of grade 1 was corrected as follows: Invented spelling was the total score on four words (*boat*, *chain*, *people*, and *rough*) that children never spelled correctly, and correct spelling was the sum of the correct spellings for the remaining six words that were spelled accurately by one or more children (*angry*, *bed*, *color*, *fish*, *name*, and *lady*). Thus, the same task yielded invented spelling scores that were independent from the accurate spelling scores.

The first hypothesis tested was that invented spelling mediates the relations among alphabet knowledge, phoneme awareness, and later reading. Sénéchal (2017) found partial support for this prediction: Kindergarten invented spelling provided full mediation between phoneme awareness and reading at the beginning of grade 1, but partial mediation between alphabet knowledge and reading. These longitudinal findings are important, because word reading measured at the beginning of grade 1 cannot be solely attributed to formal instruction. As for reading at the end of grade 1, unique predictors were beginning of grade 1 invented spelling and early reading. Although beginning of grade 1 conventional spelling was strongly correlated with the end of grade 1 reading ($r = .514$), it was not a unique predictor in this stringent regression analysis. This latter finding is important, because it clarifies the distinctive role of invented spelling as opposed to early conventional spelling.

A third longitudinal study by Charbel, Sénéchal, Ouellette, and LeFevre (2021) added more evidence to the hierarchical embeddedness of early skills to more advanced literacy skills. It also confirmed the facilitative role of invented spelling to reading. Ninety-three English-speaking children, who were nonreaders in kindergarten, were followed from the beginning of kindergarten until the end of grade 2. Alphabet knowledge, phoneme awareness, invented spelling (i.e., nonconventional phonological spellings

only), and reading were assessed in kindergarten; invented spelling and reading were assessed at the beginning of grade 1; reading was measured at the end of grades 1 and 2, and spelling at the end of grade 2. Receptive vocabulary measured thrice was used as a control measure in all analyses. There are four key findings to note. First, kindergarten alphabet knowledge and phoneme awareness predicted growth in invented spelling at the beginning of grade 1. Second, invented spelling mediated the relation between alphabet knowledge, phoneme awareness, and reading growth from the beginning to the end of grade 1. Third, invented spelling also predicted reading growth from the end of grade 1 to grade 2. And fourth, the positive association between invented spelling in grade 1 and accurate spelling in grade 2 was mediated by children's grade 1 reading abilities. As expected, children's early accurate spelling was rare, and it was not a unique predictor of advanced skills. The findings support the notion that invented spelling facilitates the growth of reading skills, which are then required for developing accurate spelling.

In summary, the longitudinal correlational evidence reviewed in the meta-analyses and in more stringent studies is in accord with the view that children's early spelling attempts provide insight into the alphabetic principle, which, in time, facilitates reading and spelling acquisition. Moreover, the results of the Charbel et al. (2021) study show that reading skills are necessary for the development of conventional spelling, presumably via opportunities for orthographic learning to establish accurate lexical representations, as discussed in subsequent sections of this chapter.

A Note on Printing Skills

Invented spelling is most often assessed in research by asking children to write words that are dictated to them (e.g., Milburn et al., 2017; Ouellette & Sénéchal, 2008a, 2008b; Uhry, 1999). However, whether early printing skills impact children's spelling outcomes has yet to be explored in invented spelling research. Previous research indicates that early writing skills, including name writing and letter writing, have been linked to children's spelling ability to some extent (Kim, Al Otaiba, Puranik, Folsom, & Gruelich, 2014; Lonigan, Schatschneider, & Westberg, 2008; Puranik, Lonigan, & Kim, 2011). Notably, research suggests that children's experience with writing may play a role in their performance on different spelling tasks. Puranik and Apel (2010) found that children's spelling performance differed significantly between a letter tile task, an oral task, and a written task, but only for children who were less proficient at writing. Once children reached a certain threshold in their writing ability (i.e., being able to write at least 19 letters, or a majority, of the alphabet), such an effect was no longer found; instead, they performed equally well across the three tasks. Further exploration of an age effect revealed that differences in performance between spelling tasks were found in 3- and 4-year-olds but not 5-year-olds. That younger children performed best on the letter tile task, followed by the oral task, then the written task suggests that motor demands may be a constraining factor in children's spelling performance for these age groups. However, for older children, the lack of differences in performance between spelling tasks indicates that early writing skills are a reflection of not merely children's motor skills but also their letter knowledge. Given that invented spelling research is often conducted between preschool and early elementary school years, more consideration of different spelling tasks for different age groups may paint a more complete picture of children's invented spelling development.

Causal-Based Evidence: A Meta-Analysis of Intervention Research

In educational science, the strongest evidence that a variable plays a causal role in subsequent learning comes from intervention research. In this section, meta-analytic techniques used to combine findings from intervention studies assessed whether invented spelling plays a causal role in children's literacy acquisition. The design of intervention studies is strongest when one group of children receives training in invented spelling and a control group of children participates in an alternative activity, preferably one that is purported to also influence the dependent variable. Good designs are ones that control for possible social-desirability effects by having the control group participate in an alternative activity not related to the dependent variable, for example, a drawing activity. Finally, the weakest design is one in which members of a control group remains in their regular classroom. Although the intention was to consider the quality of research

designs in the body of research included in the meta-analysis, the number of studies that met criteria was too small to do so statistically.

An extensive review of the published literature was conducted to find intervention studies that focused on invented spelling or phonetic spelling, and for which the dependent measure was reading and/or spelling. To be included in the meta-analysis, the intervention studies needed to include these five minimal criteria: (1) have a control group; (2) use a pretest–posttest research design; (3) have a minimum of 10 children per condition; (4) provide the necessary data to allow the computation of effect sizes; (5) be published in English or French.

The search of the literature yielded 15 studies that met the five criteria. Three of these studies included four experimental conditions for which two could be considered invented spelling interventions. Given this, the two invented spelling conditions were randomly paired with the two remaining conditions. This procedure added three more studies, bringing the total to 18. Notably, some studies included three conditions, in which case the alternative condition judged to provide the strongest control was selected. Following the earlier description of study design strength, the selected control condition would be the one in which children received phoneme awareness training as opposed to one in which children remained in their kindergarten classrooms. In cases in which the two alternative treatments were equivalent, one was randomly selected. The next step was to calculate the effect sizes using Hedges's g, a standardized difference score between the intervention and control groups that is adjusted for sample size. The effect sizes for each study are presented in Table 8.2, as a function of outcome variables, namely, children's invented spelling, reading, and conventional spelling.

The first meta-analysis verified whether invented spelling interventions actually worked; that is, did they improve children's invented spelling? The initial analysis, which included 14 studies, yielded a significant heterogeneity index, indicating that the variability across studies was greater than chance ($Q = 120.58$, $p < .001$). As can be seen in Table 8.2, the effect sizes of Alves Martins, Salvador, Albuquerque, and Silva (2016) and Ehri and Wilce (1987) were large as compared to those of the remaining studies. Following Cooper et al. (2009), the analysis was repeated without these two studies.

Table 8.2. Effect Sizes for Invented Spelling, Reading, and/or Spelling for the Meta-Analysis

Study	Pub Year	Effect Size			Interv Group Feedback	Control Group	Instructor	N	Lang
		Inv spell	Read	Spell					
Alves Martins et al.	2013			2.79	Proxi	Draw	2	108	P
Alves Martins et al.	2016	2.56			Proxi	K act	2	160	P
Clark	1988		0.40	0.61	Proxi	T spell	1	100	E
Hofslundsengen et al.	2016		0.36	0.65	Proxi	None	1	105	N
Ehri & Wilce [a]	1987	3.15	0.37		Proxi+1	ABCs	2	20	E
Levin & Aram 1	2013	0.36			Conv+1	T spell	2	98	H
Levin & Aram 2	2013	0.11			Spell P	None	2	99	H
Møller et al. [a]	2022		0.72	0.68	Ph Spell	ABCs	1	34	D
Morin & M.-G.	2007			0.37	Proxi	None	1	90	F
O'Connor & Jenkins	1995	0.96			Proxi	PA	3	10	E
Ouellette & Sénéchal	2008b	0.59	0.57		Proxi	PA	3	46	E
Ouellette et al.	2013	0.21	0.65		Proxi	PA	1	40	E
Pulido & Morin 1	2018		0.58	0.59	Proxi	T spell	1	60	F
Pulido & Morin 2	2018		0.09	0.22	Proxi+1	None	1	69	E
Rieben et al. 1	2005	0.06	0.24	0.16	None	C spell	1	73	F
Rieben et al. 2	2005	0.36	0.57	0.34	Conv	Draw	1	74	F
Santoro et al.	2006	0.86	1.02		Conv+2	Read	2	76	E
Sénéchal et al.	2012	0.38	0.40		Proxi	PA	1	37	E

Note. All children were in kindergarten except those in Clark (1988), who were in grade 1. The effect sizes are adjusted based on the sample size. inv, invented; Instr, Instructor; 1, teacher or trained research assistant; 2, researcher; 3, researcher and teacher; Pub, publication; Interv feed, intevention feedback; Proxi, invented spelling with proximal instructions; Proxi+1, invented spelling with proximal instructions and conventional spelling; Conv, conventional spelling; Conv+1, conventional spelling, sound by sound; Spell P, spelling practice no feedback; Ph Spell, phonetic spelling; Conv+2, conventional spelling with reading instruction; ABCs, letter-sound production; K act, kindergarten activities; T spell, traditional spelling; PA, phonological awareness training. Lang, Language; P, Portuguese; E, English; N, Norwegian; H, Hebrew; D, Danish.
[a] All children received phonics training.

Doing so confirmed that these two studies were outliers, because their removal resulted in a heterogeneity index that was no longer statistically significant (12 studies: $Q = 11.09$, $p = .44$). This latter analysis, representing 867 children, showed that training did improve children's invented spelling, and that the statistically significant effect size (ES) was moderately large (ES = 0.39, $SE = 0.07$, $p < .01$, 95% confidence interval = 0.24–0.54). In the context of educational studies, an effect size of 0.39 is equivalent to a gain of 15 percentiles for children receiving the invented spelling intervention, when all participating children are assumed to be at the 50th percentile at pretest.

The second meta-analysis evaluated whether invented spelling interventions facilitated children's word reading. In these studies, all children received word-reading training at the end of the intervention. The hypothesis is that learning to read words would be easier for children in the invented spelling condition as compared to the control children. Once combined, the 12 studies ($N = 724$ children) showed that invented spelling training facilitated learning to read words as compared to the control condition, and the variability across studies was not greater than expected by chance (heterogeneity index $Q = 6.41$, $p = .84$). This statistically significant effect was moderately large at .43 ($p < .01$, 95% confidence interval = 0.30–0.56), and is equivalent to a gain of 17 percentiles for the children receiving the invented spelling intervention when all participating children are assumed to be at the 50th percentile at pretest.

The third and final analysis assessed whether invented spelling interventions facilitated children's word-spelling accuracy. Combining the seven studies that measured accurate spelling revealed that the studies were heterogeneous, with the effect sizes of Alves Martins et al. (2016) being extreme when compared to the remaining studies ($Q = 67.98$, $p < .01$). Removing this study from the sample confirmed that it was an outlier, because the heterogeneity index was no longer statistically significant ($Q = 4.77$, $p = .44$). Representing 337 children, this analysis showed that invented spelling training did improve children's conventional spelling, and that the statistically significant effect was moderately large (ES = 0.48, $SE = .11$, $p < .01$, 95% confidence interval = 0.20–0.75). An effect size of 0.48 is equivalent to a gain of 18 percentiles for the children receiving the invented spelling intervention, with the assumption that all children in the study were at the 50th percentile at pretest.

In summary, this body of intervention studies provides the strongest evidence that young children's exploration of the alphabetic code through early spelling attempts can have a facilitative effect on literacy acquisition. It allows children to actively integrate their budding alphabetic knowledge with their awareness of the phonology of spoken language. These intervention studies suggest that children's explorations of the written script, accompanied by helpful mediation, can be encouraged in kindergarten. Given that a single study has been conducted with students in grade 1 (Clark, 1988), an explicit recommendation for that grade is more guarded at present.

Closing Comments on Invented Spelling and Accurate Orthographic Representations

The invented spellings that children produce may coincide with the conventional spelling of words when there are consistent sound-to-letter mappings. For example, French-speaking kindergartners could spell the French word *ami* (/ami/; friend) accurately, because each phoneme consistently maps onto the corresponding letter name (Morin, 2007). In fact, studies by Ehri and Wilce (1987) as well as Møller, Mortensen, and Elbro (2022) showed that kindergartners could spell phonetically when the English or Danish orthography was modified to be consistent. However, children should find it difficult to produce accurate spellings for words or parts of words that include sound-to-letter inconsistencies (Caravolas, Kessler, Hulme, & Snowling, 2005). This

would certainly be the case in languages such as English, French, or Danish, which have inconsistent orthographies. One worry, therefore, is that invented spelling might have a pervasive negative impact on accurate spelling and reading. However, both correlational and training studies reviewed earlier have shown this not to be the case; invented spelling has been confirmed to facilitate, not hinder, subsequent spelling and reading. Furthermore, Charbel et al. (2021) showed that reading skills were needed to develop more accurate spelling skills, and relatedly, Ouellette and Sénéchal (2017) argued that the development of complete and accurate orthographic representations, as needed for accurate spelling and reading, requires reading skills. Further support for this view comes from learning studies demonstrating that children acquire word-specific orthographic representations as they encounter words in print during reading.

Indeed, there is now considerable research supporting the contention that orthographic representations are acquired via reading exposure. In their work with students in elementary school, Conrad and colleagues (Conrad, Harris, & Williams, 2013; Conrad & Deacon, 2016) reported that reading accuracy and efficiency predicted gains in lexical orthographic knowledge, independent of phonological awareness. Other studies have examined the role of reading in building orthographic representations directly, by teaching students new (often non-) words in a repeated reading paradigm and then assessing visual recognition, reading, and spelling of the newly taught items. Such studies have shown robust orthographic learning to come from reading in grades 1 and beyond (e.g., Cunningham, 2006; Share, 1999), consistent with much developmental and cognitive theory describing word-reading acquisition (Ehri, 2005; Perfetti, 2007; Share, 2004).

Further research into just how reading allows orthographic learning to proceed has highlighted the interplay between written and oral language when it comes to building orthographic representations. Ouellette (2010) had students in grade 2 and grade 4 (Ouellette & Fraser, 2009) repeatedly read novel (non-) words, some of which were accompanied by additional semantic information (in the form of a definition and picture). Both cohorts showed robust orthographic learning from reading, with more detailed representations stored when words were supported by semantics, and the most pronounced boost observed in the younger readers. These findings suggest that reading practice brings about the building of orthographic representations by binding together phonology (pronunciation) and orthography (spelling) while being supported by oral language vocabulary knowledge.

Orthographic learning is also impacted by external factors during reading. Martin-Chang, Ouellette, and Bond (2017) directly examined such factors in a training study in which they manipulated whether words were encountered in context or as isolated words, and whether the children received feedback during their reading. This was accomplished in a carefully designed, fully counterbalanced, within-participant study with students in grade 2. Reading in context boosted reading accuracy initially, and the external support garnered from feedback resulted in heightened reading accuracy throughout training, as well as on a delayed posttest 1 week later. When students were tested on their spelling of the exposed words, a different picture emerged: The highest spelling scores were observed when children had practiced reading words in isolation versus in context. In summary, providing feedback and/or context helps children read words accurately, which in turn seems to create initial orthographic representations, but these may not be fully specified as to allow for accurate spelling. However, reading words in isolation seems to produce orthographic representations that are higher in quality and therefore better able to support precise spelling. These findings reflect how orthographic representations are built incrementally and can vary in detail and accuracy. Initially stored representations gleaned from reading may not all be complete—some may be "good enough" to support reading but not spelling (Martin-Chang et al., 2017). Continued opportunities for encountering these words in print, via word reading and other literacy activities, would support further refinement of stored representations.

Together with the earlier reviewed studies on invented spelling, these results all speak to the developmental sequence and coordination of reading and spelling acquisition, along with the building of orthographic representations. In young children, invented spelling has facilitative effects on early spelling and reading. The emergence of reading ability then allows for the learning of orthographic representations, which may be refined in terms of accuracy over time through continued exposure to the printed word.

It is interesting to note that once this sequence is established, spelling then affords an additional, powerful means of acquiring and refining representations. In an initial teaching study, Conrad (2008) had students in grade 2 practice reading or spelling words, then posttested learning in both domains. While both types of practice led to gains in reading, only the children who practiced spelling were equally able to read and spell the words; the students who practiced only reading showed more variable performance with spelling. These results suggest that more accurate orthographic representations may be gleaned from spelling practice, relative to repeated reading alone. Ouellette (2010) further tested this possibility by incorporating a repeated spelling practice condition directly into an orthographic learning paradigm and reported that students in grade 2 showed superior orthographic learning from spelling practice relative to repeated reading. These findings have recently been replicated (Conrad, Kennedy, Saoud, Scallion, & Hanusiak, 2019) and found in languages other than English as well (e.g., see Shahar-Yames & Share, 2008). Studies with skilled, adolescent, and adult readers have also shown that training in spelling can result in more accurate orthographic representations and faster word reading as a result, on a word-specific basis (Ouellette, Martin-Chang, & Rossi, 2017; Rossi, Martin-Chang, & Ouellette, 2019).

Conclusion

Invented spelling has been described as a highly analytical, child-directed, literacy activity that integrates phonological and orthographic processes (Ouellette & Sénéchal, 2017), and repeated spelling practice with children once they begin to read provides a similar experience. Spelling affords the opportunity for a student to focus on word structure, evoking metalinguistic processing of expected and unanticipated spelling–pronunciation links. In this respect, it is not entirely surprising that spelling instruction has been found to benefit reading outcomes across the school grades (see meta-analysis by Graham & Santangelo, 2014) and can be used as an effective means of teaching reading (see Gentry & Ouellette, 2019). In the early years, invented spelling can be viewed as an important and unique literacy experience, one that is amendable to inclusion across home and school environments.

Acknowledgments

The research conducted by Sénéchal and/or Ouellette was funded by the Social Sciences and Humanities Research Council of Canada.

References

Alves Martins, M., Albuquerque, A., Salvador, L., & Silva, C. (2013). The impact of invented spelling on early spelling and reading. *Journal of Writing Research, 5*(2), 215–237.

Alves Martins, M., Salvador, L., Albuquerque, A., & Silva, C. (2016). Invented spelling activities in small groups and early spelling and reading. *Educational Psychology, 36*(4), 738–752.

Caravolas, M., Hulme, C., & Snowling, M. J. (2001). The foundations of spelling ability: Evidence from a 3-year longitudinal study. *Journal of Memory and Language, 45*(4), 751–774.

Caravolas, M., Kessler, B., Hulme, C., & Snowling, M. (2005). Effects of orthographic consistency, frequency, and letter knowledge on children's vowel spelling development. *Journal of Experimental Child Psychology, 92*(4), 307–321.

Charbel, R., Sénéchal, M., Ouellette, G., & LeFevre, J.-A. (2021). *Testing a nested skills model of literacy from kindergarten to grade 2.* Poster presentation at the 28th Annual Meeting of the Society for the Scientific Study of Reading, Irvine, CA.

Chomsky, C. (1971). Write first, read later. *Childhood Education, 47,* 296–300.

Clark, L. K. (1988). Invented versus traditional spelling in first graders' writings: Effects on learning to spell and read. *Research in the Teaching of English, 22*(3), 281–309.

Clay, M. M. (1972). *Reading: The patterning of complex behaviour.* Heinemann Educational Books.

Conrad, N. J. (2008). From reading to spelling and spelling to reading: Transfer goes both ways. *Journal of Educational Psychology, 100*(4), 869–878.

Conrad, N. J., & Deacon, S. H. (2016). Children's orthographic knowledge and their word reading skill: Testing bidirectional relations. *Scientific Studies of Reading, 20*(4), 339–347.

Conrad, N. J., Harris, N., & Williams, J. (2013). Individual differences in children's literacy development: The contribution of orthographic knowledge. *Reading and Writing, 26*(8), 1223–1239.

Conrad, N. J., Kennedy, K., Saoud, W., Scallion, L., & Hanusiak, L. (2019). Establishing word representations through reading and spelling: Comparing degree of orthographic learning. *Journal of Research in Reading, 42*(1), 162–177.

Cooper, H., Hedges, L. V., & Valentine, J. C. (Eds.). (2009). *The handbook of research synthesis and meta-analysis* (2nd ed.). Russell Sage Foundation.

Cunningham, A. E. (2006). Accounting for children's orthographic learning while reading text: Do children self-teach? *Journal of Experimental Child Psychology, 95*(1), 56–77.

Ehri, L. C. (1989). The development of spelling knowledge and its role in reading acquisition and reading disability. *Journal of Learning Disabilities, 22*(6), 356–365.

Ehri, L. C. (2005). Learning to read words: Theory, findings, and issues. *Scientific Studies of Reading, 9*(2), 167–188.

Ehri, L. C., & Wilce, L. S. (1987). Does learning to spell help beginners learn to read words? *Reading Research Quarterly, 22*(1), 47–65.

Ferreiro, E., & Teberosky, A. (1982). *Literacy before schooling.* Heinemann Educational Books.

Gentry, J. R. (1982). An analysis of developmental spelling in "GNYS AT WRK." *Reading Teacher, 36*(2), 192–200.

Gentry, J. R., & Gillet, J. W. (1993). *Teaching kids to spell.* Heinemann Educational Books.

Gentry, J. R., & Ouellette, G. P. (2019). *Brain words: How the science of reading informs teaching.* Stenhouse.

Graham, S., & Santangelo, T. (2014). Does spelling instruction make students better spellers, readers, and writers?: A meta-analytic review. *Reading and Writing, 27*(9), 1703–1743.

Hamilton, L. G., Hayiou-Thomas, M. E., Hulme, C., & Snowling, M. J. (2016). The home literacy environment as a predictor of the early literacy development of children at family-risk of dyslexia. *Scientific Studies of Reading, 20*(5), 401–419.

Henderson, E. H. (1981). *Learning to read and spell: The child's knowledge of words.* Northern Illinois University Press.

Hofslundsengen, H., Hagtvet, B. E., & Gustafsson, J.-E. (2016). Immediate and delayed effects of invented writing intervention in preschool. *Reading and Writing, 29*(7), 1473–1495.

Kessler, B. (2009). Ponto [Computer software]. Retrieved from *http://spell.psychology.wustl.edu/ponto.*

Kim, Y.-S., Al Otaiba, S., Puranik, C., Folsom, J. S., & Gruelich, L. (2014). The contributions of vocabulary and letter writing automaticity to word reading and spelling for kindergartners. *Reading and Writing, 27*(2), 237–253.

Levin, I., & Aram, D. (2013). Promoting early literacy via practicing invented spelling: A comparison of different mediation routines. *Reading Research Quarterly, 48*(3), 221–236.

Lonigan, C. J., Schatschneider, C., & Westberg, L. (2008). Identification of children's skills and abilities linked to later outcomes in reading, writing, and spelling. In *Developing early literacy: Report of the National Early Literacy Panel* (pp. 55–106). National Institute for Literacy.

Mann, V. A., Tobin, P., & Wilson, R. (1987). Measuring phonological awareness through the invented spellings of kindergarten children. *Merrill–Palmer Quarterly, 33*(3), 365–391.

Mann, V. A. (1993). Phoneme awareness and future reading ability. *Journal of Learning Disabilities, 26*(4), 259–269.

Martin-Chang, S., Ouellette, G., & Bond, L. (2017). Differential effects of context and feedback on orthographic learning: How good is good enough? *Scientific Studies of Reading, 21*(1), 17–30.

McBride-Chang, C. (1998). The development of invented spelling. *Early Education and Development, 9*(2), 147–160.

Milburn, T. F., Hipfner-Boucher, K., Weitzman, E., Greenberg, J., Pelletier, J., & Girolametto, L. (2017). Cognitive, linguistic and print-related predictors of preschool children's word spelling and name writing. *Journal of Early Childhood Literacy, 17*(1), 111–136.

Møller, H. L., Mortensen, J. O., & Elbro, C. (2022). Effects of integrated spelling in phonics instruction for at-risk children in kindergarten. *Reading and Writing Quarterly, 38*, 67–82.

Morin, M.-F. (2007). Linguistic factors and invented spelling in children: The case of French beginners in Canada. *L1-Educational Studies in Language and Literature, 7*(3), 173–189.

Morin, M.-F., & Montésinos-Gelet, I. (2007). Effet d'un programme d'orthographes approchées en maternelle sur les performances ultérieures en lecture et en écriture d'élèves à risque. *Revue des sciences de l'éducation, 33*(3), 663–683.

Morris, D., & Perney, J. (1984). Developmental spelling as a predictor of first-grade reading achievement. *Elementary School Journal, 84*(4), 440–457.

O'Connor, R. E., & Jenkins, J. R. (1995). Improving the generalization of sound/symbol knowledge: Teaching spelling to kindergarten children with disabilities. *Journal of Special Education, 29*(3), 255–275.

Ouellette, G. (2010). Orthographic learning in learning to spell: The roles of semantics and type of practice. *Journal of Experimental Child Psychology, 107*(1), 50–58.

Ouellette, G., & Fraser, J. R. (2009). What exactly is a yait anyway: The role of semantics in orthographic learning. *Journal of Experimental Child Psychology, 104*(2), 239–251.

Ouellette, G., Martin-Chang, S., & Rossi, M. (2017). Learning from our mistakes: Improvements in spelling lead to gains in reading speed. *Scientific Studies of Reading, 21*(4), 350–357.

Ouellette, G., & Sénéchal, M. (2008a). A window into early literacy: Exploring the cognitive and linguistic underpinnings of invented spelling. *Scientific Studies of Reading, 12*(2), 195–219.

Ouellette, G., & Sénéchal, M. (2008b). Pathways to literacy: A study of invented spelling and its role in learning to read. *Child Development, 79*(4), 899–913.

Ouellette, G., & Sénéchal, M. (2017). Invented spelling in kindergarten as a predictor of reading and spelling in grade 1: A new pathway to literacy, or just the same road, less known? *Developmental Psychology, 53*(1), 77–88.

Ouellette, G., Sénéchal, M., & Haley, A. (2013). Guiding children's invented spellings: A gateway into literacy learning. *Journal of Experimental Education, 81*(2), 261–279.

Perfetti, C. A. (2007). Reading ability: Lexical quality to comprehension. *Scientific Studies of Reading, 11*(4), 357–383.

Perfetti, C. A., & Hart, L. (2002). The lexical quality hypothesis. In L. Verhoeven, C. Elbro, & P. Reitsma (Eds.), *Precursors of functional literacy* (pp. 189–213). John Benjamins.

Pulido, L., & Morin, M.-F. (2018). Invented spelling: What is the best way to improve literacy skills in kindergarten? *Educational Psychology, 38*(8), 980–996.

Puranik, C., & Apel, K. (2010). Effect of assessment task and letter writing ability on preschool children's spelling performance. *Assessment for Effective Intervention, 36*(1), 46–56.

Puranik, C. S., Lonigan, C. J., & Kim, Y.-S. (2011). Contributions of emergent literacy skills to name writing, letter writing, and spelling in preschool children. *Early Childhood Research Quarterly, 26*(4), 465–474.

Read, C. (1971). Pre-school children's knowledge of English phonology. *Harvard Educational Review, 41*(1), 1–34.

Read, C. (1975). *Children's categorization of speech sounds in English*. National Council of Teachers of English.

Richgels, D. J. (1995). Invented spelling ability and printed word learning in kindergarten. *Reading Research Quarterly, 30*(1), 96–109.

Rieben, L., Ntamakiliro, L., Gonthier, B., & Fayol, M. (2005). Effects of various early writing practices on reading and spelling. *Scientific Studies of Reading, 9*(2), 145–166.

Rossi, M., Martin-Chang, S., & Ouellette, G. (2019). Exploring the space between good and poor spelling: Orthographic quality and reading speed. *Scientific Studies of Reading, 23*(2), 192–201.

Santoro, L. E., Coyne, M. D., & Simmons, D. C. (2006). The reading–spelling connection: Developing and evaluating a beginning spelling intervention for children at risk of reading disability. *Learning Disabilities Research and Practice, 21*(2), 122–133.

Sénéchal, M. (2017). Testing a nested skills model of the relations among invented spelling, accurate spelling, and word reading, from kindergarten to grade 1. *Early Child Development and Care, 187*(3–4), 358–370.

Sénéchal, M., & LeFevre, J. (2014). Continuity and change in the home literacy environment as predictors of growth in vocabulary and reading. *Child Development, 85*, 1535–1551.

Sénéchal, M., Ouellette, G., Pagan, S., & Lever, R. (2012). The role of invented spelling on learning to read in low-phoneme awareness kindergartners: A randomized-control-trial study. *Reading and Writing, 25*(4), 917–934.

Shahar-Yames, D., & Share, D.L. (2008). Spelling as a self-teaching mechanism in orthographic learning. *Journal of Research in Reading, 31*(1), 22–39.

Share, D. L. (1995). Phonological decoding and self-teaching: Sine qua non of reading acquisition. *Cognition, 55*(2), 151–218.

Share, D. L. (1999). Phonological recoding and orthographic learning: A direct test of the self-teaching hypothesis. *Journal of Experimental Child Psychology, 72*(2), 95–129.

Share, D. L. (2004). Orthographic learning at a glance: On the time course and developmental onset of self-teaching. *Journal of Experimental Child Psychology, 87*(4), 267–298.

Shatil, E., Share, D. L., & Levin, I. (2000). On the contribution of kindergarten writing to grade 1 literacy: A longitudinal study in Hebrew. *Applied Psycholinguistics, 21*(1), 1–21.

Tangel, D. M., & Blachman, B. A. (1992). Effect of phoneme awareness instruction on kindergarten children's invented spelling. *Journal of Literacy Research, 24*(2), 233–261.

Tangel, D. M., & Blachman, B. A. (1995). Effect of phoneme awareness instruction on the invented spelling of first-grade children: A one-year follow-up. *Journal of Literacy Research, 27*(2), 153–185.

Treiman, R. (1993). *Beginning to spell*. Oxford University Press.

Treiman, R., Hulslander, J., Olson, R. K., Willcutt., E. G., Byrne, B., & Kessler, B. (2019). The unique role of early spelling in the prediction of later literacy performance. *Scientific Studies of Reading, 23*(5), 437–444.

Uhry, J. K. (1999). Invented spelling in kindergarten: The relationship with finger-point reading. *Reading and Writing, 11*(5), 441–464.

CHAPTER 9

Early Spelling Development

Influences, Theory, and Educational Implications

Nenagh Kemp and Rebecca Treiman

Play qeschns. Go otside and play hidenseck. Rede. Hav ise creem. Travl rod the weld.

These suggestions were added, in a scrawling hand, to the to-do list I had left on my desk during the writing of this chapter. The culprit was my (NK) 5-year-old daughter, who is learning how to turn spoken language into written symbols that others can (sometimes) decipher for meaning. The task of learning to read has received a century of research interest, but only in more recent decades has as much attention been turned to the task of learning to write, and particularly, to spell.

Background

Spelling is an important part of writing and requires the integration of a number of skills. Across the world, the most common spelling system is the alphabet, in which each sound, or phoneme, is written with a letter or letter combination. Some children must instead learn writing systems that represent consonants but omit vowels (e.g., Arabic) or that show the vowels as part of their consonants (e.g., the Devanagari script used for Hindi). Many children are taught the logographic system of Chinese, in which each character contains a unit of meaning (and usually sound), and some must master a syllabary

(e.g., Japanese katakana), in which each character signifies one syllable. In this chapter we focus on alphabetic systems, particularly English.

Children learning an alphabet must come to understand that written language is represented by a set of conventional symbols, arranged in a particular direction, denoting the sounds of their language in the appropriate order. Some alphabetic orthographies have simple correspondences between sounds and letters. In both Italian and Finnish, for example, the vowel sound /i/ is almost always spelled *i*, as in *minuti* (Italian) or *minuutti* (Finnish), the word for *minute/s*. Such regularity means that learners of these systems can progress relatively quickly in learning to spell. Other alphabets, such as English and French, have more complex sound–letter relationships. In English, /i/ can be spelled in several ways, as in *meet*, *meat*, and *mete*; in French it may appear as in *midi* (*midday*) or *stylo* (*pen*). The choice among alternative spellings of a sound can be influenced by multiple factors, including the sound's position in a word, the letters and sounds around it, and whether it signals a grammatical feature such as a plural.

Because of the multiple influences on some spelling systems, including English, it can take years for children to learn to spell conventionally. However, children from all linguistic backgrounds begin to learn about some of aspects of their writing system even before they start formal literacy instruction. This chapter reviews children's early years of spelling development and describes theories about the process, educational implications, and directions for future research.

Children's Spelling Development: What the Research Tells Us

Marks and Scribbles

If given the opportunity, children make marks and scribbles on a surface as early as 1 or 2 years of age (Trivette, Hamby, Dunst, & Gorman, 2013). Most people would probably agree that although toddlers might attempt to draw, they do not yet attempt to write. However, young children seem to show some differentiation of drawing and writing at an early age. For example, Levin and Bus (2003) asked Dutch and Israeli children, ages 2½ to 4½, to draw pictures of things such as birds and mothers, and to write the corresponding words. Dutch and Israeli mothers performed above the level expected by random guessing at classifying these outputs as drawing (for both groups) or writing (for the Israeli group) for the 4-year-olds, although not for the younger children. The main distinction between the two types of outputs was that writing was more likely to contain small units, arranged in a line. Treiman and Yin (2011) saw distinctions in even younger children's productions when they asked 2- to 6-year-old Chinese children to draw and write several items. Chinese adults could classify these attempts as drawing versus writing at a level above that expected by chance, even for the 2- and 3-year-olds. Examination of the children's productions revealed that their drawings were larger, denser, more curved, and more often colored-in than their writing.

Text is laid out on the page in different ways in different writing systems, and young children begin to learn about their culture's convention. Treiman, Cohen, Mulqueeny, Kessler, and Schechtman (2007) found that U.S. 3- to 5-year-old nonreaders judged their own names to be written appropriately more often when they were presented in a horizontal arrangement than in other, non-English arrangements (vertically, diagonally, or randomly). To find out whether children would generalize this knowledge beyond their own names to text in general, Treiman, Mulqueeny, and Kessler (2015) presented nonreading U.S. 3- to 5-year-olds with pairs of letter strings with different arrangements and asked them which item of each pair looked more like a word. Children showed a tendency to choose horizontal print that, although not perfect, was significantly above chance.

Other studies suggest that children use this understanding of the visual appearance of writing in their own output. Brenneman, Massey, Machado, and Gelman (1996) reported that about 70% of a group of U.S. children approaching 5 years of age wrote letters horizontally, rising to 96% in a group of children approaching 6 years. Children's productions also show an increasing knowledge about the direction in which writing should go. At 3 years, children tend to produce marks that are scattered on the page, but this improves by age 4, and by age 5 years the majority of children write in the correct direction for their language, whether it is left to right (e.g., French; Gombert & Fayol, 1992), or right to left (Hebrew; Tolchinsky-Landsmann & Levin, 1985).

Adults in countries such as the United States and Australia often teach young children about the symbols of their writing system ("A is for *ant*"; "Your name begins with A, Anna!"), but they do not usually teach nonreaders about the general visual characteristics, layout, and direction of writing. How have even 3-year-olds internalized some of this knowledge? The most plausible suggestion is that children use *statistical learning*: the implicit ability to learn how often things in the environment occur, singly or together. Statistical learning occurs across the lifespan, and across domains of learning (for a review, see Bogaerts, Frost, & Christiansen, 2020). It probably helps explain infants' rapid acquisition of spoken language, as babies are adept at learning which novel spoken syllables are likely to occur together in a stream of nonsense syllables (Saffran, Aslin, & Newport, 1996). Similarly, from the books, signs, and other environmental print they see, children tacitly learn about the appearance of their language's symbols and their arrangement and direction on the page. Thus, statistical learning can help to explain how children learn about many of the characteristics of written language's visual *outer form*.

Prephonological Writing

Knowledge of the *inner function* of writing, its ability to represent language, takes some time to acquire (Zhang, Yin, & Treiman, 2017). Children who are *prephonological* writers produce at least some of the symbols of their (alphabetic) language but do not yet consistently use the appropriate symbols for the intended sounds. Prephonological spelling can lead to the production of apparently random spellings for words, such as MDR for "birthday cake." However, a growing knowledge of the outer form of writing is also evident in children's use of common letter sequences and their tendency to use varied letters within and between words. Each language has certain orders and sequences of letters that are common and others that are less common or nonexistent. Ganopole (1987) found that even 3-year-olds are sensitive to a range of such *graphotactic* patterns: They identified letter strings as "something for reading" when they were longer than a single letter, when they did not simply repeat a letter (e.g., "hhhh") or a *digram* (a two-letter sequence, e.g., "ebebe"), and when they were not interrupted by geometric shapes (e.g., "fΘt"). However, with only three stimuli per pattern in that study, it is hard to be sure how much of the children's performance was due to chance.

More systematic research has confirmed that despite its apparently random nature, prephonological spelling reflects some of the most common graphotactic patterns of a language. Writing systems differ in their typical word length and frequencies of different letter patterns, and these differences are apparent even in children's early attempts at writing. When Pollo, Kessler, and Treiman (2009) examined the productions of U.S. and Brazilian prephonological spellers about 4½ years old, they found that the Brazilian children tended to use more vowel letters and more consonant–vowel digrams than U.S. children. These differences reflect the features of written Portuguese and English. Furthermore, both U.S. and Brazilian children produced the more common letters of their writing system more often than the less common letters, and both tended to avoid double letters, which are less common than nondouble letters in both writing systems. Since it is unlikely that adults had pointed out these features to the children, it is suggested that the children had picked them up via statistical learning.

Additional evidence of early graphotactic knowledge and the role of statistical learning comes from Treiman, Kessler, Boland, Clocksin, and Chen (2018), who collated the outputs of one hundred seventy-nine 3- to 5-year-old prephonological spellers. The authors compared the younger and older children in their sample, on the assumption that older prephonological spellers, who have had more exposure to written language than younger children, have had more opportunity to learn graphotactic patterns. This assumption was borne out in the results. Compared to the younger group, the older group produced writing whose features better reflected the distributions of written English in terms of word length and common and uncommon digrams.

If children are sensitive to the patterns of letters they see in written language, we might expect the letter sequences that they see most often to be most influential. One letter sequence that occurs frequently in children's experience is the written alphabet in sequential order. Pollo et al. (2009) found that U.S. and Brazilian prephonological spellers produced digrams in which the letters were in alphabetical order (e.g., "ab," "bc") more often than would be expected by chance. This result suggests that children were picking up this order from the environment. Other sequences of letters that children see often are their own names. Adults often draw attention to a child's name and to other words beginning with the first letter of that name ("Look, Dad and Dana both start with D!") (Treiman et al., 2015). The first letter of children's names appears particularly often in their early writing, but children use the other letters from their names as well. For example, several studies show that name letters make up nearly half of the letters in prephonological spellers' productions (e.g., Both-de Vries & Bus, 2008; Kessler, Pollo, Treiman, & Cardoso-Martins, 2013). Taken together, the results described here show that children learn a remarkable amount about the outer form of writing before beginning to learn about the inner form, or how to use writing to represent the language.

Phonological Writing

An important step in learning to spell in an alphabetic writing system is learning to segment a word into sounds (e.g., *dig* as /d/ /ɪ/ /g/), and to represent each sound with a letter or letter group ("d-i-g"). This task may seem trivial to skilled spellers, but it takes time and effort for many children to achieve (Sénéchal, Ouellette, & Nguyen, Chapter 8, this volume). Children may start off writing only the first one or two sounds of a word. For example, they might write *Mummy* as "M." The first letter of a child's own name is often the first to be used be used correctly for its sound (Zhang & Treiman, 2020), while other letters continue to be used in unconventional ways. Thus, a girl called Rosie might write *run* as "RTO." Giving children practice in writing their names might strengthen their understanding of the links between letters and their sounds and help them to start writing words on the basis of their sounds (Both-de Vries & Bus, 2008).

Another prompt for phonological spelling can come from children's knowledge of letters' names, which in the United States and some other countries are often learned at an early age. Children may benefit from their knowledge that, for example, "P" is called /pi/ to write "p" in *peach*. Indeed, U.S. preschoolers were shown to use more phonologically appropriate letters to spell words that began with a letter name, such as *peach*, than words that did not, such as *patch* (Treiman & Wolter, 2020). Researchers have also reported letter-name spelling in children learning to write in Brazilian Portuguese (Pollo et al., 2005) and Hebrew (Levin, Patel, Margalit, & Barad, 2002).

Even while children's phonological spelling improves, errors of various types remain. Early spellings sometimes include *intrusions* of letters that do not belong, such as the second letter in "MRAP" for *map*. Intrusive letters are likely to be those with which children are most familiar, such as letters that occur frequently in the print environment and letters from their own name (Treiman, Kessler, & Bourassa, 2001). Children may also *omit* some letters, even when most of the word is represented. For example, they often fail to include a vowel letter when spelling a *syllabic consonant* (a consonant that forms a syllable on its own), as in "travl" for *travel* in our chapter-opening example. Other omissions arise when children produce just one consonant of a cluster (Bruck & Treiman, 1990), writing "scarf and boots," for example, as "saf and boos." Omissions of nasal sounds such as /m/ and /n/ in final consonant clusters (e.g., "roud" for *round*) may reflect children's perception of nasalization as a characteristic of the vowel rather than a separate segment (Treiman, 1993).

Substitutions are another frequent type of error in phonological spelling. Some substitutions represent an accurate perception of the word's sounds, one that is not reflected in the conventional spelling. For example, "chrumpet" for *trumpet* reflects the fact that the first sound of word-initial "tr" is pronounced very much like /tʃ/, which is often conventionally spelled "ch" (Treiman, 1993). Other substitutions reflect a child's dialect. When Kemp (2009) asked children to spell words whose vowel pronunciations differed by dialect, she found that British and Australian children of 6–8 years showed mirror-image error patterns. For words that they pronounced with a final /ɪ/, such as *rabbit* and *rocket*, British children were more likely to write "rabbit" but "rockit." Australian children, who pronounce these words with a final /ə/, were more likely to write "rocket" but "rabbet." There are many other cases in which there are several conventional ways to represent a sound and the child chooses the wrong one. This can result in outputs such as "ise creem" and "froot." Adults may find it useful to consider, and where relevant to praise, the phonological accuracy of children's early spelling attempts before pointing out the conventionally correct version.

Graphotactic Patterns

At the same time as they are learning how to represent the sounds of their language in writing, children are continuing to accumulate knowledge of graphotactic patterns. Some such patterns are specifically taught at school, but others are not. In English, as in other alphabetic languages, there are conventions about which letters may double and where. Treiman (1993) noted that in their classroom writing, U.S. first graders used frequently doubled consonants such as "bb" more often than illegal ones such as "hh," and largely avoided doubling consonants in word-initial position, in line with English spelling conventions. Following up on these findings, Cassar and Treiman (1997) asked U.S. children to choose which of two nonwords looked more like a word. Kindergartners performed above chance in terms of doublet position, choosing a nonword with a doublet at the end (e.g., "foll") more often than one with a doublet at the beginning (e.g., "ffol"). First graders also performed above chance in terms of doublet identity, choosing a nonword with a legal doublet (e.g., "teff") over an illegal one (e.g., "tehh").

Children's early spelling productions reflect their growing sensitivity to more complex graphotactic patterns as well. The spelling of some vowels is *conditioned*, or partially determined, by the adjacent consonant letters. For instance, at the start of a word, /k/ is usually written with "c" when it precedes "e" or "i" (as in *keg* and *kid*), but as "c" before other vowel letters (as in *cap, cop,* and *cup*). Hayes, Treiman, and Kessler (2006) reported that, even in grade 2, children's spelling of the initial consonants of nonwords such as /kɪmp/ ("cimp"/"kimp") and /kʌmp/ ("cump"/"kump") showed evidence of context conditioning in that children were more likely to use "k" for the former than for the latter.

Graphotactic patterns apply not only to the letters used to represent language but also to how those letters are shown on the page. As well as spatial layout, children need to learn about conventions such as capitalization, spacing, and punctuation. Treiman and Kessler (2004) reported that U.S. children tended to use capital letters in their early spellings, but wrote most letters in lowercase by grade 2. In a study of children in grades 3 to 4, Kemp and Evans (2017) found that children incorrectly omitted 66% of capital letters and incorrectly capitalized 22% of words that did not require them. Punctuation marks also represent a challenge to young writers. Beginning writers do not often use them (Hall, 1999) and, when they do, may do so unconventionally (Cordeiro, 1988). Apostrophes present particular difficulty, with children of 8–10 years using them correctly only half the time (Bryant, Nunes, & Bindman, 2000; Kemp & Evans, 2017). There is the limited research on nonletter-based graphotactic knowledge such as capitals and apostrophes, but it seems that knowledge about these matters develops slowly and incompletely across the school years.

Morphology: Word Structure and Meaning

The spelling of a great many English words is partially determined by their *morphology*: their structure, form, and meaning. A *base* or root word such as *sign* can be extended with an *inflectional* morpheme, which adds a grammatical property to a word, such as tense or number. Examples of inflected words include *signing, signs,* and *signed*. A base word can also undergo a more fundamental *derivational* change, which can change the word's grammatical category and/or its meaning. For example, *undersigned* is a word derived from *sign*. The spelling of a base word often remains the same across word forms, despite changes in pronunciation.

Researchers have shown that children appear to represent some aspects of morphology even in their early spelling. Children's tendency to maintain the spelling of base words across derived forms is one potential indicator of this ability. In U.S. English, "t" and "d" in the middle of many two-syllable words such as *pretty* and *giddy* are pronounced with a *tap*, in which the tongue quickly flaps against the back of the teeth. Treiman, Cassar, and Zukowski (1994) showed that U.S. children in grades 1–4 used the correct letter ("t" or "d") more often to spell taps in two-morpheme words, such as *cuter* or *louder,* than in otherwise similar one-morpheme words, such as *quarter* and *ladder*. Similar findings come from U.K. children spelling the middle /z/ sound more accurately in two-morpheme words such as *frozen* than one-morpheme words such as *dozen* (Kemp, 2006). These studies suggest that children use their knowledge of the base form (e.g., the "t" of *cute* in *cuter,* or the "z" of *froze* in *frozen*) to choose the correct spelling in two-morpheme words. One-morpheme words (e.g., *quarter* or *dozen*) have no base form from which to derive this extra information, which can explain children's greater difficulty in deciding which letter is needed.

Other evidence for children's use of morphology comes from examining their spelling of consonant clusters. As noted earlier, children often fail to represent both consonants in a cluster. However, children even as young as 5 or 6 years of age tend to omit consonants less often from two-morpheme words (e.g., *tuned*) than from one-morpheme words (e.g., *band*) (e.g., Bourassa, Treiman, & Kessler, 2006; although this was not replicated by Larkin & Snowling, 2008). These findings have been interpreted to suggest that children consider the final letter of a base form (e.g., *tune*) when spelling its past-tense form (*tuned*), which is not possible for a one-morpheme word such as *band*.

Cases in which pronunciation changes from base to derived forms seem particularly challenging for children. For example, Carlisle (1988) showed that by grade 4, children generally maintained the spelling of base forms when they had obvious derived forms, as in *warm* and *warmth*. However, when the relations between the base word and the derived words were less obvious because of a change in base word pronunciation (e.g., *equal, equality*), even children in grades 6 and 8 did not consistently retain the base spellings.

The shared meaning of a base word across its derivations is often fairly accessible even to young children, especially if pronunciation does not change. However, the shared meaning of *bound morphemes* (units of meaning that cannot exist on their own, such as "un-" and "-ed") seems harder for young children to notice. The varying pronunciations of some bound morphemes add to the challenge. For example, the plural ending is consistently written "s," whether pronounced /z/ as in *signs*, /s/ as in *sights*, or /əz/ as in *sizes*, and the regular past-tense ending is always "ed," whether pronounced /d/ as in *signed*, /t/ as in *sliced*, or /əd/ as in *sighted*. Children seem to start off spelling the regular past-tense verb ending "ed" as it sounds: They might write "smild" for *smiled* but "laft" for *laughed* (e.g., Beers & Beers, 1992; Larkin & Snowing, 2008). According to one study (Nunes, Bryant, & Bindman, 1997), it takes at least 2 years for children to learn to use "ed" for past-tense verbs and not for similar-sounding nonverbs (e.g., "sofed" for *soft*), and another year or so more to confine "ed" to past-tense verbs that are regular (e.g., *laughed* but not "lefed" for *left*).

Multiple cues may contribute to a child's spelling of a particular unit. For example, even young writers tend to spell the regular plural "s" ending correctly, despite the three possible pronunciations listed above (/z/, /s/, /əz/) (Beers & Beers, 1992; Leong, 2009). It seems straightforward to conclude that children understand that plurals are spelled with "s." However, more systematic testing highlights the greater influence of graphotactic than morphological knowledge. Kemp and Bryant (2003) showed, for example, that children get plurals right more often when their final letters create common sequences rather than illegal ones. Specifically, when a nonword presented as a singular noun ends in a consonant (e.g., /vɪl/, which could be written "vill"), children are likely to correctly write its plural with "s" (e.g., "vills"). However, when a singular nonword ends in a vowel (e.g., /blaɪ/, which could be written "bly"), children are less likely to use "s" for the plural form, instead using a variety of endings (e.g., "blise" and "blize" as well as "blies"). For a word ending in /lz/ (as in /vɪlz/), the only graphotactically acceptable way to spell the /z/ sound is "s," as in the spelling "vills." Word-final "ls" is appropriate; "lz" is not. For a word ending in a vowel plus /z/ (as in /blaɪz/), several letter combinations are graphotactically acceptable, and so this item could be written "blies," "blize," or "blise." The findings of Kemp and Bryant sug-

gest that graphotactic cues trump morphological cues in at least some situations.

Models of Spelling Development

Theorists have devised several different approaches to explain the process of spelling development. One is the constructivist theory pioneered by Ferreiro and Teberosky (1982), which is grounded in Piaget's view of cognitive development. In this view, children take an active role in predicting and testing abstract ideas about how reading and writing work. Even before they start writing phonologically, children are seen to hold assumptions such as that the letters in a word must be different from each other and that different words should be spelled differently. As we mentioned earlier, there is some evidence for these assumptions (e.g., Ganopole, 1987). There is also some support (e.g., Zhang & Treiman, 2015) for Ferreiro and Teberosky's (1982) suggestion that children think that larger objects should have larger or longer written representations than smaller objects. However, there is little experimental evidence for the constructivist idea that children go through a stage of thinking that each letter of a word represents a syllable (Cardoso-Martins, Corrêa, Lemos, & Napoleão, 2006; Treiman, Pollo, Cardoso-Martins, & Kessler, 2013).

A better-known set of models of spelling development are stage and phase theories. These models vary in the number of stages or phases and the exact characteristics of each, but they share a view of a linear progress through spelling strategies of increasing sophistication. Frith's (1985) model begins with a *logographic* stage, in which children build up their knowledge of rote-learned whole words (e.g., the "STOP" on a stop sign). As this memorized set of words expands, children notice the individual letters and sounds, which leads them into the *alphabetic* stage. As young writers master sound-based spelling, they can enter the *orthographic* stage, in which they begin to incorporate graphotactic patterns and morphological conventions. Ehri's model (e.g., 2000, 2020) begins with a *prealphabetic* phase, in which children use random letters (and other symbols). In the *partial alphabetic* phase, children represent some but not all sounds in words using the conventional name and sound values of letters. The *full alphabetic* phase heralds the consistent, linear representation of the sounds of a word with plausible letters, which may result in correct or incorrect spellings (e.g., "reed" for *read*). In the final, *consolidated alphabetic* phase, children begin integrating graphotactic and morphological patterns in their spelling.

There is no disputing the heavy reliance on phonology in children's early spelling, and children's knowledge of graphotactics and morphology does increase as they progress through school. However, characterizing spelling development in a stage- or phase-like way overlooks some important aspects of development. As we have seen, there is robust evidence for early knowledge of writing's outer form. Children also incorporate some graphotactic and morphological cues into even their early spellings. Stage or phase models of spelling development necessarily lump together a range of spelling attempts: For example, attempts at spelling *question* ranging from "k" to "ksn" to "qeschn" would all be allocated to Ehri's partial alphabetic phase, despite their differences in sophistication. Finally, stage and phase models cannot explain why some sounds are more likely to be omitted or misspelled than others.

A contrasting approach to the descriptive nature of stage and phase models is to consider how the spelling of individual words occurs. Dual-route models attempt to explain this process (e.g., Barry, 1994; Houghton & Zorzi, 2003). The first of the two routes is a lexical route, which is used when a writer spells a familiar word on the basis of the orthographic form that they have stored in their mental lexicon. The nonlexical route is used when an unfamiliar word is encountered. The writer has no stored form to consult, and must instead break down the word into its sounds and link those sounds to appropriate letters. These two routes work in parallel. For so-called *regular* words such as *left* (whose sounds are written with their most common letters), both the lexical and nonlexical routes lead to the same spelling outcome. For *irregular* words such as *laughed* (not all of whose sounds are written with their most common letters), the nonlexical route cannot generate the conventional spelling, and so only the lexical route will be successful. Learners of writing systems such as English and French are seen to rely first on the nonlexical route (e.g., Sprenger-Charolles, Siegel, & Bonnet, 1998). As they learn more words, children use the lexical route more heavily. For languages with simpler letter–sound relationships, such as Italian, the non-lexical

route is seen as more important from the beginning.

Although dual-route models have advanced our knowledge of reading and writing, the division of words into regular and irregular categories is overly simple. Some of the sounds in irregular words are spelled with their most common spelling (e.g., the /l/ in *laughed*) and the spellings of some so-called "irregular" words can be explained on the basis of graphotactic and other considerations (e.g., the final "e" of *have* prevents the word from ending with "v," which does not normally appear at the ends of English words). It seems unlikely that irregular words must be represented only as whole forms or that simple letter–sound correspondences are the only patterns that spellers can use. Also, the contributions of graphotactics and morphology are not easily accounted for in current dual-route views of spelling.

An alternative to these views of spelling is the integration of multiple patterns framework (IMP; Treiman & Kessler, 2014). IMP takes into account children's knowledge of both the visual appearance of written words (the outer form) and of how letters/symbols relate to linguistic units (the inner form). A major aspect of understanding the inner form is learning about how the sounds of language are represented in writing, but IMP also includes the important role of graphotactics and morphology. The theory also points to the role of statistical learning, in addition to that of direct instruction, in the acquisition of spelling. One important idea is that children will find learning easier when multiple spelling cues converge, and more difficult when cues conflict. As discussed earlier, for example, U.S. children tend to use the correct letter ("t" or "d") to spell taps in the middle of words which have a base form to refer to (e.g., *dirt* in *dirty*) than when they do not. This result is interpreted to show the influence of morphology on early spelling. However, phonology seems to play a role as well: because the tap is voiced, it sounds more like "d," and so children are more likely to use "d" than "t" overall. Evidence from several languages (Dutch: de Bree, van der Ven, & van der Maas, 2017; French: Pacton, Fayol, & Perruchet, 2005; English: Kemp & Bryant, 2003) supports the idea that children learn spellings more easily with converging than conflicting cues. IMP is a relatively new framework for accounting for spelling and its development, and there is scope for further testing and refining of its tenets in future work.

Implications for the Teaching of Spelling

The models of spelling development we have just discussed lead to different implications for the best ways to teach spelling in schools. For example, as Deacon and Bryant (2006) pointed out, a stage- or phase-model approach might encourage teachers to avoid introducing graphotactic or morphological patterns until children have been writing for several years and become more skilled at phonology-based writing. In contrast, a view aligned with IMP (Treiman & Kessler, 2014) would support the decision to teach patterns that go beyond phonology from the beginning of spelling instruction.

Typically developing children with opportunities for print exposure are good but not perfect at picking up statistical patterns without instruction (Hayes et al., 2006). Teachers can accelerate students' learning by explicitly pointing out a range of common patterns, rather than waiting for children to build up this knowledge implicitly. For example, a teacher could ask students to compare the spelling of words whose sound /ɑ/ (often written "o") is preceded by /w/ (e.g., *what, wand*) to those whose /ɑ/ is preceded by a different sound (e.g., *hot, pond*). If children are encouraged to notice that /ɑ/ is often spelled "a" rather than the usual "o" after /w/, this could help them achieve the correct spellings of words such as *wad* and *quarrel*. It could also encourage them to notice how the spellings of other sounds are influenced by the surrounding context. Explicit instruction has been shown to improve children's spelling of numerous patterns, from the graphic features of written language (Reutzel, Oda, & Moore, 1989) to the use of derivational relations (Nunes, Bryant, & Olsson, 2003) and apostrophes (Kemp & Evans, 2017).

Literate adults, teachers included, can be so familiar with words' conventional spellings that they fail to appreciate the phonological accuracy of children's spelling attempts. For example, a teacher who knows the spelling of *rich* and *itch* might feel that these words' different final spellings mean that they are pronounced differently. If a child makes the phonologically plausible spelling attempt "ritch" or "ich," the teacher might tell a child to listen carefully to the sounds in the word to get the right spelling, when in fact the child has represented the sounds perfectly well, but needs instruction on the alternative ways of spelling word-final /tʃ/. If teachers are given training on these nonintuitive skills, their ability to understand and teach this knowledge to children can improve (McCutchen et al., 2002; Spear-Swerling & Brucker, 2004).

One important finding for the teaching of spelling is that children with *dyslexia* (specific difficulties in reading and spelling; Compton et al., Chapter 25, this volume) make spelling errors that are very similar to those made by typically developing, but younger, children (e.g., Bernstein, 2009; Protopapas, Fakou, Drakopoulou, Skaloumbakas, & Mouzaki, 2013). For example, children with dyslexia, like other children, find it difficult to discern and represent all the consonants of consonant clusters. However, children with dyslexia need to put in more time and effort than typically developing children to succeed in spelling these clusters. A systematic review and meta-analysis found that children with dyslexia gained the most benefit from small-group and individual interventions, and from programs that incorporated phonics, graphotactics, and morphological conventions (Galuschka et al., 2020). Findings such as these are important for improving support for children with specific spelling difficulty.

More broadly, it is important to bear in mind that many of the conclusions from the studies discussed in this chapter, as in most research, are based on group averages. Individual children will progress in their spelling development at different rates and pick up some patterns and conventions more easily than others. As far as possible in the busy classroom environment, teaching should be adjusted for each child's level of knowledge and ability. It is also important to bear in mind that, although spelling is an important skill, it is by no means the only aspect of good writing (Gerde & Bingham, Chapter 20, and McMaster, Birinci, Shanahan, & Lembke, Chapter 10, this volume). Teachers should aim for their students to develop the ability to write fluently, persuasively, logically, and engagingly. This goal is more easily achieved if the writer can spell most words automatically, without having to stop to think, consult a dictionary, or choose another, easier word to use instead.

Future Directions

Most of the research on spelling, as well as on reading, has been conducted on English. Much of the rest has focused on European alphabetical systems such as French and Finnish. Today there is growing interest in studying spelling development in alphabets beyond the European context and in nonalphabetic systems. Understanding the acquisition and use of a wider range of systems will help us to identify the universal aspects of learning to write, as well as those more specific to individual scripts and languages. This is an important area for future research. Different writing systems have different conventions for spacing, punctuation, and (if they distinguish case), the use of lowercase and uppercase letters. The learning of these conventions also needs further study.

Young children have traditionally been exposed only to the conventional writing style encountered in children's books and at school. With the rise of digital communication in the last few decades, other forms of writing have become more common. At younger and younger ages, children see casual exchanges that lack many of the traditions of grammar, punctuation and spelling and that may include visual expressions of emotion. For example, children may see their mothers type, "hi sarah hope ur still on for fri :-)" and must reconcile the conventions of this message with those they have seen in books and at school. Exposure to this digital writing style has not been shown to damage conventional writing skill, and may even help to improve it (see Wood, Kemp, & Plester, 2014, for a review). However, the children of today, and of the future, are certain to see such ways of writing at earlier ages than in the past. The relationship between children's spelling and their exposure to different styles of writing is another important topic for future research.

References

Barry, C. (1994). Spelling routes (or roots or rutes). In G. D. A. Brown & N. C. Ellis (Eds.), *Handbook of spelling: Theory, process and intervention* (pp. 27–49). Wiley.

Beers, C. S., & Beers, J. W. (1992). Children's spelling of English inflectional morphology. In S. Templeton & D. R. Bear (Eds.), *Development of orthographic knowledge and the foundations of literacy: A memorial Festschrift for Edmund H. Henderson* (pp. 231–251). Erlbaum.

Bernstein, S. E. (2009). Phonology, decoding, and lexical compensation in vowel spelling errors made by children with dyslexia. *Reading and Writing, 22*(3), 307–331.

Bogaerts, L., Frost, R., & Christiansen, M. H. (2020). Integrating statistical learning into cog-

nitive science. *Journal of Memory and Language, 115,* Article 104167.

Both-de Vries, A. C., & Bus, A. G. (2008). Name writing: A first step to phonetic writing? Does the name have a special role in understanding the symbolic function of writing? *Literacy Teaching and Learning, 12*(2), 37–55.

Bourassa, D., Treiman, R., & Kessler, B. (2006). Use of morphology in spelling by children with dyslexia and typically developing children. *Memory & Cognition, 34,* 703–714.

Brenneman, K., Massey, C., Machado, S. F., & Gelman, R. (1996). Young children's plans differ for writing and drawing. *Cognitive Development, 11*(3), 397–419.

Bruck, M., & Treiman, R. (1990). Phonological awareness and spelling in normal children and dyslexics: The case of initial consonant clusters. *Journal of Experimental Child Psychology, 50*(1), 156–178.

Bryant, P., Nunes, T., & Bindman, M. (2000). The relations between children's linguistic awareness and spelling: The case of the apostrophe. *Reading and Writing, 12,* 253–276.

Cardoso-Martins, C., Corrêa, M. F., Lemos, L. S., & Napoleão, R. F. (2006). Is there a syllabic stage in spelling development?: Evidence from Portuguese-speaking children. *Journal of Educational Psychology, 98*(3), 628–641.

Carlisle, J. F. (1988). Knowledge of derivational morphology and spelling ability in fourth, sixth, and eighth graders. *Applied Psycholinguistics, 9*(3), 247–266.

Cassar, M., & Treiman, R. (1997). The beginnings of orthographic knowledge: Children's knowledge of double letters in words. *Journal of Educational Psychology, 89,* 631–644.

Cordeiro, P. (1988). Children's punctuation: An analysis of errors in period placement. *Research in the Teaching of English, 22,* 62–74.

Deacon, S. H., & Bryant, B. (2006). Getting to the root: Young writers' sensitivity to the role of root morphemes in the spelling of inflected and derived words. *Journal of Child Language, 33,* 401–417.

de Bree, E., van der Ven, S., & van der Maas, H. (2017). The voice of Holland: Allograph production in written Dutch past tense inflection. *Language Learning and Development, 13*(3), 215–240.

Ehri, L. C. (2000). Learning to read and learning to spell: Two sides of a coin. *Topics in Language Disorders, 20,* 19–36.

Ehri, L. C. (2020). The science of learning to read words: A case for systematic phonics instruction. *Reading Research Quarterly, 55,* S45–S60.

Ferreiro, E., & Teberosky, A. (1982). *Literacy before schooling.* Heinemann.

Frith, U. (1985). Beneath the surface of developmental dyslexia. In K. Patterson, J. Marshall, & M. Coltheart (Eds.), *Surface dyslexia: Neuropsychological and cognitive studies of phonological reading* (pp. 301–330). Erlbaum.

Galuschka, K., Görgen, R., Kalmar, J., Haberstroh, S., Schmalz, X., & Schulte-Körne, G. (2020). Effectiveness of spelling interventions for learners with dyslexia: A meta-analysis and systematic review. *Educational Psychologist, 55*(1), 1–20.

Ganopole, S. J. (1987). The development of word consciousness prior to first grade. *Journal of Reading Behavior, 19*(4), 415–436.

Gombert, J. E., & Fayol, M. (1992). Writing in preliterate children. *Learning and Instruction, 2*(1), 23–41.

Hall, N. (1999). Young children's use of graphic punctuation. *Language and Education, 13*(3), 178–193.

Hayes, H., Treiman, R., & Kessler, B. (2006). Children use vowels to help them spell consonants. *Journal of Experimental Child Psychology, 94*(1), 27–42.

Houghton, G., & Zorzi, M. (2003). Normal and impaired spelling in a connectionist dual-route architecture. *Cognitive Neuropsychology, 20*(2), 115–162.

Kemp, N. (2006). Children's spelling of base, inflected, and derived words: Links with morphological awareness. *Reading and Writing, 19*(7), 737–765.

Kemp, N. (2009). The spelling of vowels is influenced by Australian and British English dialect differences. *Scientific Studies of Reading, 13*(1), 53–72.

Kemp, N., & Bryant, P. (2003). Do beez buzz? Rule-based and frequency-based knowledge in learning to spell plural -*s*. *Child Development, 74*(1), 63–74.

Kemp, N., & Evans, J. (2017). *Mark's marks: An intervention study on children's use of apostrophes and capital letters.* Paper presented April, 2017, at Language, Literacy and Learning Conference, Perth, Australia.

Kessler, B., Pollo, T. C., Treiman, B., & Cardoso-Martins, C. (2013). Frequency analyses of prephonological spellings as predictors of success in conventional spelling. *Journal of Learning Disabilities, 46*, 252–259.

Larkin, R. F., & Snowling, M. J. (2008). Morphological spelling development. *Reading and Writing Quarterly, 24*(4), 363–376.

Leong, C. K. (2009). The role of inflectional morphology in Canadian children's word reading and spelling. *Elementary School Journal, 109*(4), 343–358.

Levin, I., & Bus, A. G. (2003). How is emergent writing based on drawing?: Analyses of children's products and their sorting by children

and mothers. *Developmental Psychology, 39*(5), 891–904.

Levin, I., Patel, S., Margalit, T., & Barad, N. (2002). Letter names: Effect on letter saying, spelling, and word recognition in Hebrew. *Applied Psycholinguistics, 23*, 269–300.

McCutchen, D., Abbott, R. D., Green, L. B., Beretvas, S. N., Cox, S., Potter, N. S., . . . Gray, A. L. (2002). Beginning literacy: Links among teacher knowledge, teacher practice, and student learning. *Journal of Learning Disabilities, 35*(1), 69–86.

Nunes, T., Bryant, P., & Bindman, M. (1997). Morphological spelling strategies: Developmental stages and processes. *Developmental Psychology, 33*, 637–649.

Nunes, T., Bryant, P., & Olsson, J. (2003). Learning morphological and phonological spelling rules: An intervention study. *Scientific Studies of Reading, 7*(3), 289–307.

Pacton, S., Fayol, M., & Perruchet, P. (2005). Children's implicit learning of graphotactic and morphological regularities. *Child Development, 76*(2), 324–339.

Pollo, T. C., Kessler, B., & Treiman, R. (2005). Vowels, syllables, and letter names: Differences between young children's spelling in English and Portuguese. *Journal of Experimental Child Psychology, 92*, 161–181.

Pollo, T. C., Kessler, B., & Treiman, R. (2009). Statistical patterns in children's early writing. *Journal of Experimental Child Psychology, 104*(4), 410–426.

Protopapas, A., Fakou, A., Drakopoulou, S., Skaloumbakas, C., & Mouzaki, A. (2013). What do spelling errors tell us? Classification and analysis of errors made by Greek schoolchildren with and without dyslexia. *Reading and Writing, 26*(5), 615–646.

Reutzel, D. R., Oda, L. K., & Moore, B. H. (1989). Developing print awareness: The effect of three instructional approaches on kindergarteners' print awareness, reading readiness, and word reading. *Journal of Reading Behavior, 21*, 197–217.

Saffran, J. R., Aslin, R. N., & Newport, E. L. (1996). Statistical learning by 8-month-old infants. *Science, 274*(6640), 1926–1928.

Spear-Swerling, L., & Brucker, P. O. (2004). Preparing novice teachers to develop basic reading and spelling skills in children. *Annals of Dyslexia, 54*(2), 332–364.

Sprenger-Charolles, L., Siegel, L. S., & Bonnet, P. (1998). Reading and spelling acquisition in French: The role of phonological mediation and orthographic factors. *Journal of Experimental Child Psychology, 68*(2), 134–165.

Tolchinsky-Landsmann, L., & Levin, I. (1985).

Writing in preschoolers: An age-related analysis. *Applied Psycholinguistics, 6*(3), 319–339.

Treiman, R. (1993). *Beginning to spell: A study of first-grade children*. Oxford University Press.

Treiman, R., Cassar, M., & Zukowski, A. (1994). What types of linguistic information do children use in spelling? The case of flaps. *Child Development, 65*(5), 1318–1337.

Treiman, R., Cohen, J., Mulqueeny, K., Kessler, B., & Schechtman, S. (2007). Young children's knowledge about printed names. *Child Development, 78*(5), 1458–1471.

Treiman, R., & Kessler, B. (2004). The case of case: Children's use and knowledge of upper and lowercase letters. *Applied Psycholinguistics, 25,* 413–428.

Treiman, R., & Kessler, B. (2014). *How children learn to write words*. Oxford University Press.

Treiman, R., Kessler, B., Boland, K., Clocksin, H., & Chen, Z. (2018). Statistical learning and spelling: Older prephonological spellers produce more wordlike spellings than younger prephonological spellers. *Child Development, 89*(4), e431–e443.

Treiman, R., Kessler, B., & Bourassa, D. (2001). Children's own names influence their spelling. *Applied Psycholinguistics, 22,* 555–570.

Treiman, R., Mulqueeny, K., & Kessler, B. (2015). Young children's knowledge about the spatial layout of writing. *Writing Systems Research, 7*(2), 235–244.

Treiman, R., Pollo, T. C., Cardoso-Martins, C., & Kessler, B. (2013). Do young children spell words syllabically? Evidence from learners of Brazilian Portuguese. *Journal of Experimental Child Psychology, 116*(4), 873–890.

Treiman, R., & Wolter, S. (2020). Use of letter names benefits young children's spelling. *Psychological Science, 31*(1), 43–50.

Treiman, R., & Yin, L. (2011). Early differentiation between drawing and writing in Chinese children. *Journal of Experimental Child Psychology, 108*(4), 786–801.

Trivette, C. M., Hamby, D. W., Dunst, C. J., & Gorman, E. (2013). Emergent writing among young children from twelve to sixty months of age. *CELL Reviews, 6*(2), 1–18.

Wood, C., Kemp, N., & Plester, B. (2014). *Text messaging and literacy: The evidence*. Routledge.

Zhang, L., & Treiman, R. (2015). Writing dinosaur large and mosquito small: Prephonological spellers' use of semantic information. *Scientific Studies of Reading, 19*(6), 434–445.

Zhang, L., & Treiman, R. (2020). Learning to spell phonologically: Influences of children's own names. *Scientific Studies of Reading, 24*(3), 229–240.

Zhang, L., Yin, L., & Treiman, R. (2017). Chinese children's early knowledge about writing. *British Journal of Developmental Psychology, 35*(3), 349–358.

CHAPTER 10

Supporting Students' Early Writing Development through Data-Based Instruction

Kristen L. McMaster, Seyma Birinci, Emma Shanahan, and Erica Lembke

Writing is not an easy task, even for the most accomplished authors. It might seem simple enough: All you need is an idea for a story or a topic in mind, and then you start writing! Of course, writing is much more complex than that. To be successful, one must set a purpose for the text to be written, consider the audience that will read it, draw on background knowledge or experiences, select the right words to express thoughts and ideas, transcribe those words and string them into grammatically correct sentences and coherent paragraphs, evaluate the text for style and clarity, and so on. This process is typically iterative, recursive, and requires persistence.

For students who experience significant difficulty with this multidimensional process, the impact of their struggles can be significant and lifelong. Learning to write is critical for literacy development (Biancarosa & Snow, 2004), for integrating and communicating learned content (Shanahan, 2004), and for overall success in school, as well as postsecondary education and employment (Graham & Perin, 2007). To ensure that students at risk for difficulties with writing have opportunities for success, early identification, intervention, and ongoing assessment are paramount (Berninger, Nielsen, Abbott, Wijsman, & Raskind, 2008).

In this chapter, we describe early (grades 1–3) writing assessment and intervention research using a data-based instruction (DBI) approach. We draw on scientific evidence regarding components of early writing development, validated instructional approaches that align with those components, and how teachers can use these approaches within a data-based decision-making framework to improve young students' writing outcomes. First, we outline a "simple view" of early writing, followed by an overview of DBI. Then, we describe a program of research in which we have applied these early writing and DBI frameworks to support teachers' individualization of instruction. We end by highlighting implications and future directions for this work.

The Simple View of Writing

The "simple view of writing" (Berninger & Amtmann, 2003) provides a framework for understanding young children's writing development. In this view, children develop three sets of component skills needed to produce written text: *text generation*, in which writers generate and translate ideas into language representations in their working memory (Berninger et al., 1992); *transcription*, which enables writers to translate their language representations into orthographic symbols (Berninger, Fuller, & Whitaker, 1996) through handwriting or typing, spelling, and mechanics; and *self-regulation*, in which students use strategies to set goals (what they will write), make plans to reach their goals (how they will write), and monitor their progress (Harris

& Graham, 1992; Zimmerman & Reisenberg, 1997). These components are constrained by cognitive resources: If lower-level skills are not automatic, fewer cognitive resources are available for higher-level writing processes such as composition (McCutchen, 2006).

The simple view of writing helps clarify the dimensions of early writing that teachers should assess and target during instruction to support students' overall writing development. For instance, focusing on handwriting and spelling skills early on could help students build the automaticity needed to transcribe text effortlessly. Then, they can devote more cognitive resources to idea generation and other process-oriented skills involved in written composition. Indeed, empirical evidence has indicated that when children receive explicit transcription instruction, the quality and quantity of their written composition improves (see McMaster, Kunkel, Shin, Jung, & Lembke, 2018, for a review). Thus, this framework informs the types of "data" and "instruction" that teachers might use in a DBI framework to support students who struggle with early writing.

Data-Based Instruction

DBI is a framework in which teachers systematically monitor students' academic progress, analyze students' responsiveness to instruction, and individualize instruction when progress is insufficient (Deno & Mirkin, 1977; Fuchs, McMaster, Fuchs, & Al Otaiba, 2013; Freudenthal, Zaru, & Al Otaiba, Chapter 4, this volume). DBI consists of multiple steps: (1) Establish a student's present level of performance; (2) set a long-term goal for the student to achieve by the end of an instructional period; (3) implement high-quality, evidence-based instruction aligned with the student's needs with high fidelity; (4) monitor student progress toward the goal on a regular basis using validated assessments; (5) use decision rules to evaluate instructional effectiveness; (6) generate hypotheses about student needs to make instructional changes as needed; (7) implement the changes and continuing monitoring progress; (8) repeat the process for as long as necessary, until the student reaches the long-term goal. Evidence indicates that when teachers use this process with fidelity, they make high-quality instructional changes and students' outcomes improve (Jung, McMaster, Kunkel, Shin, & Stecker, 2018; Stecker, Fuchs, & Fuchs, 2005).

Unfortunately, DBI is not implemented extensively in practice (Fuchs et al., 2013; Lemons, Al Otaiba, Conway, & Mellado De La Cruz, 2016)—which at least in part is likely due to teachers' lack of preparation to tailor instruction based on individual student needs (e.g., Roehrig, Duggar, Moats, Glover, & Mincey, 2008; Stecker et al., 2005), particularly in the area of writing (Helfrich & Clark, 2016). In fact, national surveys indicate that teachers do not feel prepared to teach writing in general (Brenner & McQuirk, 2019; Troia & Graham, 2016; for related discussion on preschool teachers, see Gerde & Bingham, Chapter 20, this volume). Perhaps as a result, teachers do not spend as much time teaching writing as other academic areas (Brindle, Graham, Harris, & Hebert, 2016) and report using evidence-based writing practices infrequently (Gilbert & Graham, 2010). Teachers' limited implementation of writing instruction—let alone individualization for children who experience writing difficulties—can lead to negative long-term consequences for many students. This problem motivated our ongoing program of research that became the Early Writing Project.

Evolution of the Early Writing Project

The Early Writing Project is a comprehensive professional development (PD) system that provides teachers with tools, learning opportunities, and ongoing collaborative supports needed to implement DBI to improve early writing outcomes of students with intensive needs (i.e., students in grades 1–3 identified as needing individualized support in writing to succeed within the general education curriculum—typically students receiving special education with specific individualized education plans that include writing goals). Below, we describe the evolution of the Early Writing Project, starting with our initial search for progress monitoring tools for beginning writers, which led to development of a PD system to support teachers' use of these tools, followed by tests of the system's efficacy and exploration of factors that contribute to student outcomes and teachers' successful and sustained use of DBI.

In Search of the "Data" for DBI: Curriculum-Based Measurement in Writing

Our initial interest in early writing was driven by the need for assessment tools that teachers could use to monitor young children's performance and progress in writing to provide effective intervention for those students with intensive needs. One approach to assessment, curriculum-based measurement (CBM; Deno, 1985), is well suited for progress monitoring, and substantial research supports its use in a DBI framework (Stecker et al., 2005). Deno (1985) specified four criteria for CBM tasks to be used for data-based decision making: They must (1) produce *reliable and valid* data; (2) be *simple and efficient,* so that teachers can use them on a frequent basis; (3) *produce easily understandable data* that can be communicated to teachers, students, and parents; and (4) be *inexpensive* given that multiple forms are needed to monitor progress over time. Researchers who conducted initial research on CBM in writing identified several writing tasks and scoring metrics with evidence of reliability and validity for children in grades 3 to 6, but technical adequacy evidence was relatively weak for children in the primary grades (McMaster & Espin, 2007). Thus, we (among other researchers; see McMaster, Ritchey, & Lembke, 2011) set out to identify measures that are appropriate for beginning writers.

Within a DBI framework, it was critical to identify *general outcome indicators* of overall early writing proficiency, such that teachers could monitor progress toward important writing goals over time. The simple view of writing (Berninger & Amtmann, 2003) helped guide identification of potential tasks for this purpose. For young writers, *transcription* was important to consider, as early writers must develop fluent handwriting and spelling skills (Ritchey et al., 2016) to have cognitive capacity to engage in higher-order processes involved in text generation and self-regulation. *Text generation* also seemed important to capture, as young writers move from producing text at the word level to the sentence and passage levels (Whitaker, Berninger, Johnston, & Swanson, 1994). We considered *self-regulation* in the context of supports to promote writing in short periods of time, such as writing prompts and think time to promote planning.

This work started out as somewhat independent lines of research focusing on young writers. First, Lembke, Deno, and Hall (2003) identified word and sentence dictation tasks scored using quantitative indices as promising indicators of second-graders' overall writing performance. Later, McMaster, Du, and Pétursdóttir (2009) developed and compared additional tasks and various quantitative scoring metrics to determine which approaches showed the strongest technical adequacy for first graders. Both sets of researchers also examined the capacity of the various measures to monitor progress, by determining which measures were sensitive to growth over relatively short time periods (Hampton & Lembke, 2016; McMaster et al., 2011).

From this work, a set of three types of CBM tasks emerged that had evidence of reliability, validity, and sensitivity to growth, and that aligned with the components of the simple view of writing (see Ritchey et al., 2016): word dictation, picture–word, and story prompts. *Word dictation* is designed to capture transcription skills at the word level, and is appropriate for students just beginning to write words. Word dictation is individually administered for 3 minutes. The examiner dictates words (using spelling patterns identified in core standards) with one repeat, and students write each word. Scores include words written (WW), words spelled correctly (WSC), correct letter sequences (CLS; any two adjacent letters that are correctly placed according to the correct spelling of the word), and correct minus incorrect letter sequences (CILS). *Picture–word prompts* are designed to capture transcription and text generation at the sentence level, and are appropriate for students learning to connect words into sentences. Each group-administered prompt consists of words with a picture above. After providing students with practice, the examiner instructs them to write sentences using the prompts. After 3 minutes, the examiner instructs students to stop, and scores the writing sample for WW, WSC, and correct word sequences (CWS; two adjacent words spelled correctly that were used correctly in the context of the sentence). *Story prompts* capture transcription and text generation at the discourse level. Story prompts are designed to reflect experiences that students attending U.S. schools will be able to relate to, and to have simple vocabulary and sentence structure. Each prompt is printed at the top of a page, followed by lines to write on. The examiner provides 30 seconds for students to think about what they will write, then 3 minutes to respond to the prompt. Students' samples are scored for WW, WSC, and CWS.

All of these tasks have multiple forms designed to be of equivalent difficulty, such that progress can be monitored over time. For students with intensive early writing needs, teachers are encouraged to select the task that best matches the students' targeted level of writing (at the word, sentence, or discourse level), and administer and score the task weekly, graphing the data on a regular basis to determine whether students are on track to meet their goals.

Supporting Teachers' Use of CBM Writing Data to Individualize Instruction

As we developed and refined CBM tasks for early writing, teachers expressed a great deal of enthusiasm for the measures. However, many teachers shared that they were unsure of what to do when student data indicated a need for more intensive instruction. In fact, some teachers cited their administration of the CBM tasks as their *only* writing instruction, which was not its intended use. We realized that teachers needed a more comprehensive set of tools, including instructional tools and a framework for using data to inform instruction, to realize the potential impact of CBM. They would also likely require ongoing support to be able to use the tools with fidelity. Thus, we sought funding from the Institute of Education Sciences (IES), U.S. Department of Education, to develop such a comprehensive system. We called this system "DBI-TLC," designed to provide Tools, Learning opportunities, and Collaborative supports to promote teachers' successful implementation of an integrated DBI approach in early writing.

Our development of DBI-TLC was guided by a theory of change (Lembke et al., 2018; McMaster et al., 2020), which posits that effective "TLC" to support teachers' use of DBI should lead to increased teacher knowledge, skill, and self-efficacy; which should lead to teachers' implementation of all DBI components with fidelity; which in turn should result in improved student outcomes. This theory of change is supported by evidence that teachers who use CBM in a DBI framework are more likely to act on data, change their instructional practices, and improve student outcomes when they receive support (e.g., from a peer or coach, or via technology; see Gesel, LeJeune, Chow, Sinclair, & Lemons, 2020; Jung et al., 2018; Stecker et al., 2005, for reviews). Below, we describe each of the DBI-TLC components, with supporting evidence from research.

DBI Tools

DBI tools included all the necessary materials needed for implementing DBI in early writing with fidelity, including progress monitoring tools, intervention tools, and decision-making tools to guide teachers to examine individual student data and make timely and appropriate instructional decisions based on that data.

PROGRESS MONITORING TOOLS

We selected CBM tasks and metrics that emerged from earlier research as having sufficient evidence of reliability, validity, and sensitivity to growth in short time periods at the word (word dictation), sentence (picture–word) and passage (story prompt) levels. We established normative information (expected performance levels and rates of growth for students in grades 1–3; e.g., Allen et al., 2020) to provide guidance for goal setting. We also refined administration and scoring instructions for teachers to make them as clear and replicable as possible, based on feedback from teachers and researchers. In addition, we designed a graphing tool in which teachers could easily enter student data to produce graphs automatically, with goals and trend lines to aid decision making.

INSTRUCTIONAL TOOLS

To identify research-based early writing instruction that targets the components of the simple view of writing, we conducted a best-evidence synthesis (McMaster et al., 2018). This review identified several transcription (handwriting and spelling) interventions with evidence of positive effects on students' written composition—specifically, that explicit systematic instruction in handwriting and spelling can improve the quantity and quality of students' written composition. In addition, interventions that combined text generation and self-regulation strategies, such as self-regulated strategy development (SRSD; Harris & Graham, 1992), indicated improved students' composition quantity and quality.

Based on these findings, we developed a set of transcription and text-generation mini-lessons that teachers could mix and match to create comprehensive, tailored writing intervention plans to meet individual student needs. Transcription mini-lessons include activities that support accurate and automatic letter formation, building words using onsets and rimes, and spelling words, with durations ranging from 5 to 20 minutes. Text generation mini-lessons include activities to support constructing and combining sentences and to improve writing fluency, with durations ranging from 10 to

20 minutes. All mini-lessons incorporate explicit instructional design, including segmenting complex skills, modeling, systematic fading of support, opportunities to respond and receive feedback, and purposeful guided and independent practice (Hughes, Morris, Therrien, & Benson, 2017).

In addition to mini-lessons, we created other tools to help teachers identify their students' current level of writing and to match the mini-lessons with these needs. A diagnostic tool helps teachers to identify their students' needs and strengths, and helps to identify a set of appropriate mini-lessons for the targeted needs. A basic writing instruction plan (WIP) provides a template for teachers to create weekly plans that incorporate the selected mini-lessons for their students. An "instructional alignment tool" helps teachers ensure that their WIPs are aligned to student needs, the simple view of writing, and relevant state English Language Arts standards.

DECISION-MAKING TOOLS

To assist teachers in using early writing data to individualize instruction, we provide a guide that walks teachers through a series of decision rules and questions to help them determine *when* to make instructional changes and *what* instructional changes to make. The guide prompts teachers to inspect individual student graphs when they have six to eight data points and to evaluate whether student progress is sufficient to meet the long-term goal (based on level, trend, and variability of the data in relation to the goal line). Teachers are guided to increase the goal if progress is steeper than the goal line, change instruction if it is flatter, or keep instruction as is if progress is in line with the goal line. If the decision is to change instruction, teachers are prompted to determine whether they need to (1) adjust fidelity, (2) change the content or focus, or (3) intensify instruction, depending on their hypotheses about the source of students' difficulties. Further guidance is provided depending on the teachers' decisions, including ways to intensify instruction using Fuchs, Fuchs, and Malone's (2017) taxonomy of intervention intensity (e.g., increasing dosage, alignment, attention to transfer, explicitness of instruction, or behavioral supports).

Learning

Teachers learn about the DBI process and how to use the assessment and instructional tools

through a series of learning modules, delivered via in-person, daylong workshops offered "just in time" for when teachers are ready to use the content in their own practice. The modules are offered in the following sequence: (1) *DBI Overview and Introduction to CBM for Beginning Writers*, in which teachers learn to administer, score, and graph CBM; (2) *Implementing High Quality Writing Intervention, Part 1*, in which teachers learn to implement high quality, research-based instruction; (3) *Implementing High Quality Writing Intervention, Part 2*, in which teachers learn to design instructional plans based on students' strengths and needs; and (4) *Data-Based Decision Making*, in which teachers learn to use student data to make instructional decisions.

COLLABORATIVE SUPPORT

Collaborative support occurs in the form of coaching (thus far provided by members of our research team) and includes opportunities for teachers to review DBI procedures and ask questions, share data, be observed implementing DBI with students, receive feedback, problem solve, and identify interventions in collaboration with their coach and with peers. We included key PD elements identified by Desimone (2009), including (1) *focus on content*, by emphasizing knowledge and skills needed to implement each DBI step; (2) *active learning opportunities over an extended duration*, by providing multiple chances to view models, practice, and apply content with feedback during Learning Modules and in the classroom; (3) *coherence,* by ensuring that DBI components align with theory and core standards and are integrated into existing instructional routines; and (4) *collective participation*, by ensuring that teachers have frequent opportunities to collaborate with coaches and peers.

Examining the Efficacy of DBI-TLC

We developed DBI-TLC over 3 years using an iterative process of development and field trials with classroom teachers who provided feedback about how to ensure that all elements are usable and feasible in real-world contexts, and revision and refinement of all components (see Lembke et al., 2018 for details). We then conducted a small, randomized controlled trial (RCT; see McMaster et al., 2020), in which special education teachers from 19 classrooms in two Midwestern states were assigned randomly to treatment (received all components of DBI-TLC) or to a business-as-usual control group (received PD at the end of the study). All teachers completed pre- and posttests of DBI knowledge, skills, and self-efficacy, and we assessed treatment teachers' fidelity of DBI implementation. Students (most of whom were receiving special education services) in grades 1–3 ($N = 57$) were identified by their teachers as having significant early writing needs. For each teacher, we selected the two or three lowest performing students based on word dictation and picture–word scores. They completed pre- and posttests of early writing CBM tasks and a standardized writing measure. Treatment teachers outperformed controls at posttest on DBI knowledge and skills (Hedges's $g = 2.88$). Their fidelity of implementation was, on average, 84% for CBM administration, 79% for writing instruction, and 52% for decision making. Treatment students showed stronger (but statistically nonsignificant) writing performance compared to controls on CBM, with effect sizes of 0.23 to 0.40, but not on the standardized measure (effect size = 0.02–0.13). We are now conducting a fully powered multisite, multiyear efficacy trial to replicate these promising findings.

Exploring Factors Related to Student Outcomes

In addition to examining the overall efficacy of DBI-TLC, we are exploring various factors related to student outcomes and teachers' implementation of DBI. For instance, Bresina and McMaster (2020) used data from the RCT described earlier to identify predictors of student growth in early writing (as measured by weekly CBM progress). Teachers' DBI knowledge and skills at posttest related strongly to student growth, as did the number of weeks of writing intervention that students received. The relation between fidelity of writing instruction and student growth, while significant, was weaker. These results suggest that writing instruction fidelity may be relatively less important to student progress in writing intervention, or that more time is needed for teachers' improved knowledge and skills to affect their fidelity (which in turn might have an even greater impact on student outcomes). Alternatively, our fidelity tool may not have been sensitive enough to capture fidelity of intensive writing instruction. More research is needed to understand contributions of teacher-level factors related to student writing outcomes.

Exploring Factors That Influence Teachers' Implementation and Sustainment of DBI

We have also explored teachers' perceptions of facilitators and barriers to DBI implementation and sustainability over time. In a mixed-methods study using data gathered during the initial RCT (Poch, McMaster, & Lembke, 2020), we found that a majority of teachers reported coaching as a facilitator, specifically, the accountability and implementation support that coaches provided. Teachers also generally appreciated that the structure of DBI aligned well with their existing instructional programming, their students' needs, and their priorities related to DBI. The most commonly identified barrier was the accessibility of DBI tools, specifically finding the materials in the online database. Teachers also reported external barriers, such as testing and student absences. Despite these challenges, teachers implemented DBI components with fidelity and reported that the amount of time they spent on DBI activities decreased each week. These findings suggest that the supports made available to teachers allowed DBI to be a usable and feasible practice for teachers. Teachers' feedback about project-related challenges informed further revisions to the DBI-TLC package (e.g., a more accessible website with all the materials).

In recent work, we have also begun developing an initial understanding of what it takes to sustain DBI in early writing (Shanahan & Birinci, 2021). Thus far, we have found that teachers tend to continue using only certain components of DBI following a year of participation in the current ongoing efficacy trial of the Early Writing Project. Teachers sustained each component (CBM, writing instruction, and decision making) to different extents and for different reasons.

In a survey of their sustained use, 75% of our first cohort of treatment teachers who responded ($N = 20$) reported that they continued using CBM in writing beyond their study year. Observations revealed that they continued administering CBM with high fidelity (on average, 99.3%). In interviews, teachers reported that they appreciated that CBM data helped them in the individualized education plan (IEP) process as a means of goal setting, progress monitoring, and communicating with stakeholders. Progress monitoring likely was sustained at high levels, because it already exists in special education teachers' repertoires in other subjects such as reading.

Writing instruction was also sustained (75%

of teachers reporting, observations indicating an average of 79.3% fidelity). Teachers cited the primary reason for sustaining writing instruction was that the mini-lessons aligned with their existing instructional practices. Specifically, they often integrated the writing lessons into their typical reading instruction. For example, one teacher used a letter-writing mini-lesson to reinforce students' acquisition of letter names and sounds. Other teachers highlighted the need to integrate reading and writing instruction due to limited instructional time; they were able to continue using the writing lessons that also targeted reading goals. Overall, teachers identified that a pathway to ensure their students received intensive support in both literacy domains was to merge their instruction. Thus, the answer of what it takes to sustain writing instruction may lie at least in part in teachers' capacity to integrate reading and writing practice.

In contrast to their strong sustained use of the CBM and instruction components of DBI, few teachers (20%) reported sustaining the decision-making component. This lack of sustainment is concerning given that making consistent, systematic decisions related to instruction is core to the individualization process (D. Fuchs & Fuchs, 2015). However, teachers did not report lack of interest or skill to make instructional decisions as the reason for not sustaining the decision-making component. Rather, teachers preferred to make decisions based on their informal evaluation of student progress. In interviews, teachers often explained their decision-making process as going with their "gut" or just "looking at the data." One teacher explained, "I still feel like I'm doing it, just maybe not in as concise and organized a manner."

Teachers' reasons for preferring to "eyeball" decisions are likely multifaceted. Teachers reported that they were not always able to collect the data needed to make timely decisions due to external factors such as snow days and student absences. Without this step in the process, teachers may have felt that they needed to deviate from the decision-making protocol. Additionally, teachers may require additional support to understand, practice, and internalize steps of the decision-making process. Teachers may lack the skills needed to interpret CBM progress data in order to make appropriate decisions (Espin, Wayman, Deno, McMaster, & de Rooij, 2017). However, we suspect that even with appropriate data and knowledge of how to interpret

graphs, other barriers to sustaining a systematic decision-making process exist. CBM graphs are not the only source of data that teachers access. In working directly with students, they are also collecting informal observational data that can influence and inform, whether positively or negatively, their decisions. Teachers may also not be convinced that a systematic approach to decision making, as opposed to a more creative or informal approach, will result in better student outcomes. To understand what it will take to sustain decision making, we must first understand whether and how these hypothesized factors influence teachers' choice or inability to sustain.

Implications

Among a number of implications of this work, we believe two are central to both the strengths of the Early Writing Project and opportunities for improvement: (1) the importance of PD and coaching supports, and (2) the need to strengthen the decision-making component.

Importance of PD and Coaching

As we discussed in the introduction, PD plays a key role in increasing teachers' knowledge and self-efficacy toward implementing new practices or teaching in general. McMaster et al. (2020) demonstrated that DBI-TLC for early writing resulted in an increase in teachers' knowledge and skills results. In addition, Bresina and McMaster (2020) found that students whose teachers had higher knowledge and skills were more likely to make greater weekly CBM growth—partially supporting our theory of change.

These positive outcomes likely can be attributed to the formal workshops provided, but perhaps more so to the ongoing coaching that teachers received. These findings are consistent with previous literature that has emphasized the importance of coaching to improve teachers' implementation of evidence-based practices in general (e.g., Kretlow & Bartholomew, 2010) as well as DBI, more specifically. For example, a meta-analysis of the effects of DBI for students with intensive learning needs (Jung et al., 2018) indicated that the effects of DBI varied depending on the type and frequency of support provided for teachers, with the largest effects in support that incorporated collaborative problem solving ($g = 0.86$; Jung, McMaster, & delMas,

2017). Teachers themselves have attributed their success with DBI at least in part to coaching (Poch et al., 2020). As one teacher said, "Having someone to help you assess the problems and determine the direction to take the students was so valuable." While more research is needed to identify the specific components of coaching that can facilitate improved DBI implementation, we believe these results indicate the value in providing ongoing support.

A Need to Strengthen Teachers' Decision Making

Some of our less positive findings include the low fidelity of teachers' decision making, along with evidence that teachers are sustaining the decision-making component of DBI much less than the CBM and instruction components. These results are consistent with previous researchers' findings that teachers do not always use the data they collect to respond to student progress (Stecker et al., 2005).

Researchers have observed that teachers have difficulty understanding graphs, interpreting data, and linking the data to instruction (Espin et al., 2017; van den Bosch, Espin, Chung, & Saab, 2017; Wagner, Hammerschmidt-Snidarich, Espin, Seifert, & McMaster, 2017). Even though CBM graphs are designed to be simple and easy to interpret (Deno, 1985), understanding and interpreting graphs in general is a complex process (Shah & Hoeffner, 2002). Interpreting CBM graphs includes understanding x and y axes and relationships between data points, student's current level of performance and long-term goal, and levels of performance and progress in each intervention phase. Researchers have demonstrated that when PD targets these dimensions, teachers' understanding and interpretation of CBM graphs can be improved (van den Bosch, Espin, Pat-El, & Saab, 2019). Decision making is the last component that we introduce in the Early Writing Project (about 2 months into implementation), and teachers have two or three opportunities at most to make decisions with their own students' data. Likely, teachers need practice in this skill beyond what we have provided thus far.

Future Directions

Much work is needed to continue to learn how best to support teachers in their individualization of early writing instruction to improve out-comes for students with intensive needs. Below, we describe three areas that we believe warrant particular attention.

A Focus on Teacher Preparation

Much of our focus thus far has been on inservice PD and support to improve teachers' individualization of early writing intervention. We believe, however, that we must not overlook preservice teacher preparation programs given their important role in preparing future teachers to use and adapt evidence-based practices in their teaching. A well-designed teacher preparation program should build teachers' knowledge in writing to learn about evidence-based writing approaches and have opportunities to practice them. Gaining the necessary knowledge and skills should in turn increase preservice teachers' self-efficacy toward teaching writing (Graham, Harris, MacArthur, & Fink, 2002). In addition to knowing how to teach writing, teachers also need to feel ready to tailor the instruction based on students' responses. Surveys that focused on preservice teachers' perceptions suggest that preservice teachers do not have high self-efficacy when it comes to tailoring writing instruction according to students' specific needs (Helfrich & Clark, 2016). Future work should focus on improving teacher preparation programs such that future teachers are familiar with current evidence-based practices and have sufficient practice to implement them.

A Focus on Technology

As the field of education evolves, the mechanisms to implement DBI in early writing (as well as other areas) will need to evolve with it. The COVID-19 pandemic has underscored the need for increased technology integration for teachers to implement the DBI process in flexible ways. In a survey of teachers' sustained use of DBI during the 2020–2021 school year, 80.6% of teachers reported implementing its components less frequently than the previous year due to COVID-19. Among teachers who were implementing instruction remotely, most found the Early Writing Project materials incompatible, or only partially compatible, with their instruction. These teachers also reported making more adaptations to the materials than teachers who were instructing in hybrid or in-person modes. Even as K–12 education returns primarily to in-person instruction, technology integration into the DBI process could allow for a more efficient and user-friendly implementation experience.

One area in which technology could be integrated into DBI is in the decision-making process—an area already highlighted as a particular challenge for teachers. An interactive, computer-based system could allow teachers to synthesize multiple relevant sources of data, along with CBM data, to more easily arrive at instructional decisions. This concept of automated decision making was explored by Lynn and Douglas Fuchs and colleagues decades ago (e.g., L. S. Fuchs, Fuchs, & Hamlett, 1989; L. S. Fuchs, Fuchs, Hamlett, & Ferguson, 1992). They found that computerized "diagnostic feedback" or "expert system consultation" led teachers to make more individualized instructional programs for students, and led to improved student outcomes. These efforts to create a computerized decision-making system were not continued, and technology has evolved considerably since this time, so additional work is needed to reenvision such a system—particularly for writing.

A Focus on the Reading-Writing Connection

Despite the well-established connection between reading and writing development for struggling readers and writers (e.g., Graham et al., 2020), more research is needed to understand how to connect skills in both domains as part of intensive instruction. As noted in our work, external pressures often prevent teachers from implementing writing instruction. Reading is generally more valued than writing (Fitzgerald & Shanahan, 2000), and with limited instructional time available to teachers, they often must deprioritize writing. This state of affairs is deeply concerning given that writing instruction can increase reading outcomes for struggling early readers and writers (Graham & Hebert, 2011). Graham (2020) called on researchers to integrate the sciences of reading and writing in several ways, including the investigation of how teachers bring reading and writing together in the classroom. Future work in this area is needed to understand reading and writing as a collaborative act.

Conclusion

Scientific evidence from early writing research provides a framework of early writing development (the simple view of writing; Berninger &

Amtmann, 2003) that can inform theoretically sound approaches to assessment and instruction. In our work, we have used this framework to apply a DBI approach to early writing—by creating CBM tools that teachers can use to monitor students' early writing progress and instructional tools based on the best evidence from research regarding effective interventions to promote early writing growth. Furthermore, we have demonstrated that a comprehensive PD package with tools, learning opportunities, and collaborative supports can improve teacher knowledge and skills, and shows promise for students' improved early writing outcomes. More research could shed further light on how to support pre- and inservice teachers' early writing practices, particularly their data-based decision making. We believe that a focus on both preservice preparation and inservice PD and supports is critical, and that advances in technology and in connecting reading and writing hold great promise to improve outcomes for students with the most intensive early writing needs.

Acknowledgments

Coauthors Seyma Birinci and Emma Shanahan contributed equally to this chapter and are listed in random order. The research reported here was supported in part by the Institute of Education Sciences, U.S. Department of Education, through Grant Nos. R324A130144 and R324A170101 to the University of Minnesota. The opinions expressed are those of the authors and do not represent views of the Institute or the U.S. Department of Education.

References

Allen, A. A., Jung, P.-G., Poch, A. L., Brandes, D., Shin, J., Lembke, E. S., & McMaster, K. L. (2020). Technical adequacy of curriculum-based measures in writing in grades 1–3. *Reading and Writing Quarterly, 36,* 563–587.

Berninger, V., & Amtmann, D. (2003). Preventing written expression disabilities through early and continuing assessment and intervention for handwriting and/or spelling problems: Research into practice. In H. L. Swanson, K. Harris, & S. Graham (Eds.), *Handbook of research on learning disabilities* (pp. 345–363). Guilford Press.

Berninger, V., Yates, C., Cartwright, A., Rutberg, J., Remy, E., & Abbott, R. (1992). Lower-level developmental skills in beginning writing. *Reading and Writing, 4,* 257–280.

Berninger, V. W., Fuller, F., & Whitaker, D. (1996). A process model of writing development across the life span. *Educational Psychology Review, 8,* 193–218.

Berninger, V. W., Nielsen, K. H., Abbott, R. D., Wijsman, E., & Raskind, W. (2008). Writing problems in developmental dyslexia: Under-recognized and under-treated. *Journal of School Psychology, 46,* 1–21.

Biancarosa, G., & Snow, C. (2004). *Reading next: A vision for action and research in middle and high school literacy: A report to Carnegie Corporation of New York.* Alliance for Excellence in Education.

Brenner, D., & McQuirk, A. (2019). A snapshot of writing in elementary teacher preparation programs. *The New Educator, 15,* 18–29.

Bresina, B. C., & McMaster, K. L. (2020). Exploring the relation between teachers' factors and student growth in early writing. *Journal of Learning Disabilities, 53,* 311–324.

Brindle, M., Graham, S., Harris, K. R., & Hebert, M. (2016). Third and fourth grade teacher's classroom practices in writing: A national survey. *Reading and Writing, 29,* 929–954.

Deno, S. L. (1985). Curriculum-based measurement: The emerging alternative. *Exceptional Children, 52,* 219–232.

Deno, S. L., & Mirkin, P. K. (1977). *Data-based program modification: A manual.* Council for Exceptional Children.

Desimone, L. M. (2009). Improving impact studies of teachers' professional development: Toward better conceptualizations and measures. *Educational Researcher, 38,* 181–199.

Espin, C. A., Wayman, M. M., Deno, S. L., McMaster, K. L., & de Rooij, M. (2017). Data-based decision-making: Developing a method for capturing teachers' understanding of CBM graphs. *Learning Disabilities Research and Practice, 32,* 8–21.

Fitzgerald, J., & Shanahan, T. (2000). Reading and writing relations and their development. *Educational Psychologist, 35,* 39–50.

Fuchs, D., & Fuchs, L. S. (2015). Rethinking service delivery for students with significant learning problems: Developing and implementing intensive instruction. *Remedial and Special Education, 36,* 105–111.

Fuchs, L. S., Fuchs, D., & Hamlett, C. L. (1989). Monitoring reading growth using student recalls: Effects of two teacher feedback systems. *Journal of Educational Research, 83,* 103–110.

Fuchs, L. S., Fuchs, D., Hamlett, C. L., & Ferguson, C. (1992). Effects of expert system consultation within curriculum-based measurement, using a reading maze task. *Exceptional Children, 58,* 436–450.

Fuchs, L. S., Fuchs, D., & Malone, A. S. (2017). The taxonomy of intervention intensity. *Teaching Exceptional Children, 50,* 194–202.

Fuchs, D., McMaster, K. L., Fuchs, L. S., & Al Otaiba, S. (2013). Data-based individualization as a means of providing intensive instruction to students with serious learning disorders. In L. Swanson, K. R. Harris, & S. Graham (Eds.), *Handbook of learning disabilities* (2nd ed., pp. 526–544). Guilford Press.

Gesel, S. A., LeJeune, L. M., Chow, J. C., Sinclair, A. C., & Lemons, C. J. (2021). A meta-analysis of the impact of professional development on teachers' knowledge, skill, and self-efficacy in data-based decision-making. *Journal of Learning Disabilities, 54,* 269–283.

Gilbert, J., & Graham, S. (2010). Teaching writing to elementary students in grades 4–6: A national survey. *Elementary School Journal, 110,* 494–518.

Graham, S. (2020). The sciences of reading and writing must become more fully integrated. *Reading Research Quarterly, 55,* S35–S44.

Graham, S., Aitken, A. A., Hebert, M., Camping, A., Santangelo, T., Harris, K. R., . . . Ng, C. (2020). Do children with reading difficulties experience writing difficulties?: A meta-analysis. *Journal of Educational Psychology, 113,* 1–26.

Graham, S., Harris, K. R., MacArthur, C., & Fink, B. (2002). Primary grade teachers' theoretical orientations concerning writing instruction: Construct validation and a nationwide survey. *Contemporary Educational Psychology, 27,* 147–166.

Graham, S., & Hebert, M. (2011). Writing to read: A meta-analysis of the impact of writing and writing instruction on reading. *Harvard Educational Review, 81,* 710–744.

Graham, S., & Perin, D. (2007). A meta-analysis of writing instruction for adolescent students. *Journal of Educational Psychology, 99,* 445–476.

Hampton, D. D., & Lembke, E. S. (2016). Examining the technical adequacy of progress monitoring using early writing curriculum-based measures. *Reading & Writing Quarterly, 32,* 336–352.

Harris, K. R., & Graham, S. (1992). *Self-regulated strategy development: A part of the writing process.* In M. Pressley, K. R. Harris, & J. T. Guthrie (Eds.), *Promoting academic competence and literacy in school* (pp. 277–309). Academic Press.

Helfrich, S. R., & Clark, S. K. (2016). A comparative examination of pre-service instruction. *Reading Psychology, 37,* 943–961.

Hughes, C. A., Morris, J. R., Therrien, W. J., & Benson, S. K. (2017). Explicit instruction: Historical and contemporary contexts. *Learning Disabilities Research and Practice, 32,* 140–148.

Jung, P. G., McMaster, K. L., & delMas, R. C. (2017). Effects of early writing intervention delivered within a data-based instruction framework. *Exceptional Children, 83,* 281–297.

Jung, P. G., McMaster, K. L., Kunkel, A. K., Shin, J., & Stecker, P. M. (2018). Effects of data-based individualization for students with intensive learning needs: A meta-analysis. *Learning Disabilities Research and Practice, 33*, 144–155.

Kretlow, A. G., & Bartholomew, C. C. (2010). Using coaching to improve the fidelity of evidence-based practices: A review of studies. *Teacher Education and Special Education, 33*(4), 279–299.

Lembke, E., Deno, S. L., & Hall, K. (2003). Identifying an indicator of growth in early writing proficiency for elementary school students. *Assessment for Effective Intervention, 28*, 23–35.

Lembke, E. S., McMaster, K. L., Smith, R. A., Allen, A., Brandes, D., & Wagner, K. (2018). Professional development for data-based instruction in early writing: Tools, learning, and collaborative support. *Teacher Education and Special Education, 41*, 106–120.

Lemons, C. J., Al Otaiba, S., Conway, S. J., & Mellado De La Cruz, V. (2016). Improving professional development to enhance reading outcomes for students in special education. *New Directions for Child and Adolescent Development, 154*, 87–104.

McCutchen, D. (2006). Cognitive factors in the development of children's writing. In C. A. MacArthur, S. Graham, & J. Fitzgerald (Eds.), *Handbook of writing research* (pp. 115–130). Guilford Press.

McMaster, K., & Espin, C. (2007). Technical features of curriculum-based measurement in writing: A literature review. *Journal of Special Education, 41*, 68–84.

McMaster, K. L., Du, X., & Pétursdóttir, A. L. (2009). Technical features of curriculum-based measures for beginning writers. *Journal of Learning Disabilities, 42*, 41–60.

McMaster, K. L., Du, X., Yeo, S., Deno, S. L., Parker, D., & Ellis, T. (2011). Curriculum-based measures of beginning writing: Technical features of the slope. *Exceptional Children, 77*, 185–206.

McMaster, K. L., Kunkel, A., Shin, J., Jung, P. G., & Lembke, E. (2018). Early writing intervention: A best evidence synthesis. *Journal of Learning Disabilities, 51*, 363–380.

McMaster, K. L., Lembke, E. S., Shin, J., Poch, A. L., Smith, R. A., Jung, P.-G., . . . Wagner, K. (2020). Supporting teachers' use of data-based instruction to improve students' early writing skills. *Journal of Educational Psychology, 112*, 1–21.

McMaster, K. L., Ritchey, K. D., & Lembke, E. (2011). Curriculum-based measurement for beginning writers: Recent developments and future directions. In T. E. Scruggs & M. A. Mastropieri (Eds.), *Assessment and intervention: Advances in learning and behavioral disabilities* (Vol. 24, pp. 111–148). Emerald.

Poch, A. L., McMaster, K. L., & Lembke, E. S. (2020). Usability and feasibility of data-based instruction for students with intensive writing

needs. *Elementary School Journal, 121*, 197–223.

Ritchey, K. D., McMaster, K. L., Al Otaiba, S., Puranik, C. S., Kim, Y., Parker, D. C., & Ortiz, M. (2016). Indicators of fluent writing in beginning writers. In K. Cummings & Y. Petcher (Eds.), *The fluency construct* (pp. 21–66). Springer.

Roehrig, A. D., Duggar, S. W., Moats, L., Glover, M., & Mincey, B. (2008). When teachers work to use progress monitoring data to inform literacy instruction: Identifying potential supports and challenges. *Remedial and Special Education, 29*, 364–382.

Shah, P., & Hoeffner, J. (2002). Review of graph comprehension research: Implications for instruction. *Educational Psychology Review, 14*, 47–69.

Shanahan, T. (2004). Overcoming the dominance of communication. In T. L. Jetton & J. A. Dole (Eds.), *Adolescent literacy research and practice* (pp. 59–64). Guilford Press.

Shanahan, E., & Birinci, S. (2021, March 8). *Going the distance: Teachers sustain data-based instruction beyond their participation in research.* Conference presentation at the Council for Exceptional Children L.I.V.E. 2021, Virtual.

Stecker, P. M., Fuchs, L.S., & Fuchs, D. (2005). Using curriculum-based measurement to improve student achievement: Review of research. *Psychology in the Schools, 42*, 795–819.

Troia, G. A., & Graham, S. (2016). Common core writing and language standards and aligned state assessments: A national survey of teacher beliefs and attitudes. *Reading and Writing, 29*, 1719–1743.

van den Bosch, R. M., Espin, C. A., Chung, S., & Saab, N. (2017). Data-based decision-making: Teachers' comprehension of curriculum-based measurement progress-monitoring graphs. *Learning Disabilities Research & Practice, 32*, 46–60.

van den Bosch, R. M., Espin, C. A., Pat-El, R., & Saab, N. (2019). Improving teachers' comprehension of curriculum-based measurement progress-monitoring graphs. *Journal of Learning Disabilities, 52*, 413–427.

Wagner, D. L., Hammerschmidt-Snidarich, S., Espin, C. A., Seifert, K., & McMaster, K. L. (2017). Pre-service teachers' interpretation of CBM progress monitoring data. *Learning Disabilities Research & Practice, 32*, 22–31.

Whitaker, D., Berninger, V., Johnston, J., & Swanson, L. (1994). Intraindividual differences in level of language in intermediate grade writers: Implications for the translating process. *Learning and Individual Differences, 6*, 107–130.

Zimmerman, B., & Reisenberg, R. (1997). Becoming a self-regulated writer: A social cognitive perspective. *Contemporary Educational Psychology, 22*, 73–101.

PART III

DEVELOPMENT AND INSTRUCTION OF MEANING-RELATED LITERACY SKILLS

CHAPTER 11

Language Is the Basis
of Skilled Reading Comprehension

Laura M. Justice and Hui Jiang

Any caregiver of young children will likely agree that children's explosive growth in language skills is one of the most impressive feats of early childhood. From about 1 year of age to the fifth birthday, when many children are on the cusp of entering kindergarten and their first foray into formal schooling, children's language skills grow at an astonishing pace: Whereas at the first birthday the child is saying a few recognizable words (Mommy, Daddy, up, bye-bye), by age 5 the child is likely producing complex utterances and commentaries on any number of matters. For instance, a 4-year-old girl scanning the pages of a storybook in which the protagonist loses his teddy bear in a forest might note, "He looking. He looking in there to find his lost teddy. Oh, he's so sad. Poor, poor Buddy." In so doing, the child displays such sophisticated skill with language that she is able to *pronominalize* (using the pronoun *he* to refer to Buddy), produce infinitive verb forms (*to find*) and adverbial phrases (*in there*), and to contract copular verb forms (*he's so sad*). These refined language skills not only allow the child to clearly convey her ideas to others as a principal tool of human communication, but these also serve as the basis for learning across the curriculum as she enters into, and progresses through, formal schooling in the years to come. In this chapter, we discuss the role of language as the basis for skilled reading in the later primary grades.

For some time, experts have emphasized the importance of language skill to children's reading comprehension based on longitudinal research studies. For instance, Storch and Whitehurst (2002) reported results of a longitudinal study involving 626 4-year-olds followed through fourth grade. Annual assessments evaluated children's language skills (e.g., vocabulary), literacy skills (e.g., alphabet knowledge), and, at later grades, their reading skills in both decoding and reading comprehension. Study findings showed a strong positive progression of language skills measured in the first 4 years of schooling (preschool through second grade) and reading comprehension measured in third and fourth grade, indicating consistent positive interrelations between children's language skills and reading comprehension. Nonetheless, the details of this study also suggested that children's decoding skills at second grade were slightly more influential to third- and fourth-grade reading comprehension than children's earlier language skills, a finding reported in other salient studies of the same epoch (Lonigan & Shanahan, 2009).

Findings such as this indicate that reading comprehension in the later primary grades is influenced by both early language and decoding skills, a phenomenon set forth by the "simple view of reading," which proposes that reading comprehension is—simply—the product of both decoding and linguistic comprehension (i.e., language skills; Gough & Tunmer, 1986). Recent work by the Language and Reading Research Consortium (LARRC; 2015a) revealed that the contribution of language skills to reading comprehension relative to decoding increases substantially over the first years of primary school (grades 1 to 3 in the United States). Specifically, by about 10 years of age, children's language skills contribute more strongly to their reading ability than their decoding skills. Thus, among fluent readers, one might argue that language *is* the basis for skilled reading comprehension, a premise that was foundational to the work of the LARRC, a consortium of reading investigators that sought to explore the role of language skill in reading comprehension.

The LARRC was established in 2010 via funding provided by the Institute of Education Sciences via the Reading for Understanding Initiative (see also Phillips, Chapter 12, this volume). It was a consortium of 14 investigators across five universities who sought to understand the specific dimensions of language skills that may be more or less influential to skilled reading. In addition, the LARRC was interested in exploring the *malleability* of language skills through refinements to classroom instruction and determining whether improvements in language skills could lead to improvements in reading comprehension via mediating processes. The inaugural consortium investigators are listed in the Acknowledgments at the end of this chapter. In the remainder of this chapter we highlight key findings from the LARRC's research activities.

Findings from the LARRC

The LARRC investigators conducted a set of studies over a 5-year period that focused on understanding the role of language skills in reading comprehension, with a particular interest in the role of lower- and higher-level language skills as potentially discrete dimensions of language ability. Scientifically, LARRC investigators sought to assess a variety of hypotheses regarding the linguistic basis of reading comprehension using a variety of research methodologies. As discussed in Farquharson, Murphy, and LARRC (2016), LARRC investigators conducted a core set of studies involving a 5-year longitudinal study and a 2-year experimental study that, collectively, involved thousands of PreK to third-grade children across multiple states. By combining correlational research with experimental methods, the LARRC was able to examine the relations between language skill and reading comprehension in complementary ways.

The longitudinal study of PreK to third-grade children was launched in 2010 and featured a cohort design: In the first year, 915 children across these five grades were enrolled, then followed until third grade, thus yielding both cross-sectional data and longitudinal data. The children completed an assessment battery annually of more than 50 measures designed to comprehensively measure an array of language, reading, and ancillary skills, such as attention and memory. Given the study design, concurrent and predictive relations between constituent language skills such as vocabulary, grammar, and morphology, and children's reading comprehension could be assessed. The experimental study featured a two-cohort randomized controlled trial (RCT) conducted in 2014 and 2015, in which children across these same grades were assigned to receive one of two variations of a language-focused curriculum relative to a control curricula. The language-focused curriculum was designed explicitly to teach a broad set of constituent language skills, and the study methods permitted causal evaluation of the effects of this curriculum on children's language and reading skills. Results from this set of studies allow several key claims to be made concerning the language bases of reading comprehension.

Lower- and Higher-Level Language Skills Are Distinct Dimensions of Language Ability

Theoretically, language skills are often differentiated into those that are lower-level and those that are higher-level within the context of reading comprehension. Lower-level skills are automatically derived and highly efficient processes that readers use to construct the literal meaning of a text, referred to by some as the *textbase* (Kintsch & Kintsch, 2005). These skills are necessary but not sufficient for engaging in reading for understanding, which requires *higher-level language skills,* which serve to create a mental model of the text that integrates the text with one's prior knowledge and organizes its multiple propositions into an integrated whole (Kintsch & Kintsch, 2005). Also referred to as *higher-level comprehension processes* and *higher-level meaning construction skills,* these language skills enable readers to combine word meanings to construct a coherent mental model of the text.

Higher-level language skills proposed as particularly influential to skilled comprehension include inferencing, comprehension monitoring, and use of text structure knowledge (Cain & Oakhill, 1999; Cain, Oakhill, & Bryant, 2004; Perfetti, 2007). *Inferencing* within the context of reading for meaning involves the reader filling in gaps within the literal presentation of text; for instance, presented text noting that "Tommy bundled up his coat and headed outside," the reader is likely to infer that the weather is cold, even though this is not explicitly stated. Readers also may find themselves predicting future events in a text, which also involves inferencing. Experts suggest that inferencing is a critical higher-level process involved with constructing meaning from text, and that inferencing skill differentiates good and poor readers with respect to comprehension (Cain & Oakhill, 1999; Cain, Oakhill, Barnes, & Bryant, 2001). *Comprehension monitoring* involves ongoing self-assessment of one's own comprehension of a text, as well as application of corrective strategies when comprehension is suffering. For instance, for a reader who arrives at an unknown word in a text, as with *spoliation* in "Jorge alerted the court to possible spoliation," the act of comprehension monitoring would signal the degradation of meaning given the unknown word, signaling to the reader to apply some sort of repair strategy, such as looking up the word in an online dictionary (Cain et al., 2001). Finally, *text-structure knowledge* concerns readers' understanding of the organizational nature of written texts, such as the way in which cause-and-effect and problem-solution texts are commonly organized and how key words (e.g., first, then) are used for textual organization. Text-structure knowledge is positively associated with reading comprehension (Cain et al., 2001).

The cross-sectional research conducted by the LARRC allowed for rigorous empirical evaluation of the extent to which lower- and higher-level language skills represent distinct dimensions of language skill; that is, although experts often referenced lower- and higher-level language skill as discrete dimensions, this had yet to be scientifically validated. Using data from 14 different measures of language skill administered to children in PreK through third grade, LARRC investigators found that by second and third grade, higher-level language skill (which they referred to as "discourse") is indeed a skill that is distinct skill from lower-level skills such as grammar and vocabulary (LARRC, 2015b). This work indicates that language skill in the early primary grades is multidimensional, comprising both lower- and higher-level skills.

LARRC investigators also explored the contribution of these distinct dimensions of language skills to reading comprehension among third graders (Logan & LARRC, 2017). Across the continuum of reading comprehension ability, lower-level language skills comprising vocabulary and grammar were uniquely influential to reading comprehension, as was higher-level language skills based on measures of inferencing, comprehension monitoring, and text-structure knowledge. For the average reader, in terms of comprehension ability, lower- and higher-level language skills accounted for more variance in comprehension skills than decoding and memory skills. Such findings are important for demonstrating that language skills are a critical basis for reading comprehension by third grade, and also that both lower- and higher-level language skills play key roles in reading for understanding.

Explicit Teaching of Lower- and Higher-Level Language Skills

Given the positive predictive relations between lower- and higher-level language skills and reading comprehension in the primary grades (Logan & LARRC, 2017), it is important to identify strategies for improving the teaching of these skills in PreK to third grade. Furthermore, it is likewise necessary to determine whether teaching lower- and higher-level language skills serves to improve reading comprehension given the predictive relations between these sets of skills. LARRC sought to address both of these limitations in the extant literature at the time.

First, the LARRC investigators developed and tested curricular supplements (essentially, "add-ons" to the language arts curriculum in place) that supported teachers' explicit instruction in lower- and higher-level language skills. Prior to the LARRC studies, the available evidence on explicit teaching of language skills in PreK through third-grade classrooms suggested that teachers would benefit from curricular tools that would improve their explicit teaching of language skills. For instance, an assessment of the quality of language instruction in PreK settings showed that the average teacher used very few strategies that accelerated young children's language learning, such as modeling advanced vocabulary words (Justice, Mashburn, Hamre, & Pianta, 2008). Likewise, an in-depth examination of third-grade language arts instruction by Connor, Morrison, and Slominski (2006) suggested that teachers' provision of explicit higher-order comprehension instruction, which would likely include teaching of lower- and higher-level language skills, occurred at very low rates of less than 10 minutes per day. Although there have been thoughtful demonstrations in the scientific literature of approaches to support teachers' explicit teaching of higher-level language skills, in particular Williams, Hall, and Lauer (2004) and Williams et al. (2005), it is not clear whether these approaches can be readily adopted in everyday language arts instruction.

To facilitate teaching of lower- and higher-level language skills in PreK through third-grade classrooms, LARRC investigators developed a thematically based curricular supplement Let's Know!, which was designed to teach academic vocabulary, inferencing, comprehension monitoring, and text-structure knowledge, among other language skills. Developed using formative design research activities over a 3-year period, Let's Know! featured a structured sequence of lessons organized into four units, three of which were to last about 7 weeks and the final to last about 4 weeks (25 weeks total). Each of the four units comprised a series of sequential lessons designed to explicitly teach targeted language skills. The three primary lesson types were Words to Know, which targeted academic vocabulary; Integration, which targeted inferencing and comprehension monitoring; and Text Mapping, which targeted text-structure knowledge. Lessons were also included that provided students with opportunities to read texts and to complete progress monitoring tasks. Each lesson was designed to follow a structured gradual release of responsibility model, in which teachers first present the goals of the lesson and models of targeted skills, followed by student practice with the teacher and then independently.

In a pilot study involving 60 PreK through third-grade teachers, the teachers implemented Let's Know! lessons across the academic year, and periodic observations were conducted to examine the extent to which teachers explicitly taught the targeted language skills (LARRC, Pratt, & Logan, 2014). The observations focused specifically on explicit teaching of targeted language skills during language arts instruction, including the higher-level language skills of inferencing, comprehension monitoring, and text-structure knowledge. In total, 18 discrete teaching targets were coded, representing a range of language skills and teaching foci (e.g., cause and effect, compare and contrast). Table 11.1 provides a comparison of the frequency with which teachers implementing Let's Know! were observed teaching three targeted higher-level language skills compared to control teachers, namely, inferencing, comprehension monitoring, and text-structure knowledge—the three higher-level language skills explicitly targeted in Let's Know!. The values represent the number of 30-second intervals (out of 12) in which teachers were observed teaching each of the targeted skills. As indicated in the data in Table 11.1, Let's Know! teachers were observed teaching each of these three higher-level skills more frequently than those in control classrooms during observed language arts lessons, although overall the frequency of teaching these skills was quite low. We did not test for significant differences for these three skills specifically, although visual inspection of the data (see Table 11.1) suggest that Let's Know! teachers explicitly taught comprehension monitoring and text-structure knowledge more frequently than did control teachers.

The Mediating Role of Language Skills for Improved Reading Comprehension

Given the contribution of language skills to the development of reading comprehension, researchers have proposed that instruction directly targeting language skills can potentially result in improved reading comprehension (Bowyer-Crane et al., 2008). An early test of this theory was a seminal study by Beck, Perfetti, and McKeown (1982) that involved explicit, systematic teaching of academic vocabulary words to fourth-grade students. Findings showed that explicit vocabulary instruction had a positive, significant effect on not only vocabulary skills but also students' reading comprehension. This study, along with others (Cirino, Pollard-Durodola, Foorman, Carlson, & Francis, 2007; Zipke, Ehri, & Cairns, 2009) provide preliminary, but compelling, evidence that instruction explicitly targeting language skills can positively impact children's reading comprehension.

TABLE 11.1. Teaching of Three Higher-Level Language Skills

Higher-level language skill	Let's Know! teachers' mean (standard deviation)	Control teachers' mean (standard deviation)
Inferencing	0.37 (1.00)	0.33 (0.13)
Comprehension monitoring	0.27 (0.98)	0.00 (0.57)
Text-structure knowledge	1.17 (2.57)	0.39 (0.52)

Whereas efforts to impact reading comprehension via language instruction typically focus on one specific language skill, such as vocabulary or inference making, extant research indicates that reading comprehension is associated with a variety of language skills, including vocabulary, grammar abilities, inferencing skills, text-structure knowledge, and comprehension monitoring (Cain & Oakhill, 1999, 2014; Cain et al., 2004). Relatively few multicomponent language interventions have been examined for effects on reading comprehension. One exception is the work by Williams, Stafford, Lauer, Hall, and Pollini (2009), who developed a supplemental classroom intervention for second-grade students that targeted a variety of language skills, including vocabulary, grammar, and text-structure knowledge. Compared to children in control conditions, children who received language-focused instruction showed not only improved vocabulary skills but also better reading comprehension on distal (transfer) tasks. Another RCT conducted by Clarke, Snowling, Truelove, and Hulme (2010) also demonstrated promising results of language-focused instruction with 8- to 9-year-old students. Students who received instruction that targeted vocabulary, narrative ability, and listening comprehension outperformed those in a control condition on a standardized measure of reading comprehension, and the gains were maintained at an 11-month follow-up. This study lends convincing evidence to the causal role of language skills in reading comprehension. However, with the intervention delivered by trained research staff on an individual basis, it was unclear whether such work could generalize to the classroom setting, and whether language-focused intervention can be delivered by teachers.

Similar to the intervention tested by Clarke and colleagues (2010), LARRC used an RCT design to examine the effects of Let's Know! on the language skills and reading comprehension of first- to third-grade students (LARRC, Jiang, & Logan, 2019). This study also involved PreK and kindergarten students, for which impacts were examined separately due to use of different measures. An important aspect of the LARRC RCT is that Let's Know! was implemented by classroom teachers and delivered to the entire classroom. Using a sample of 938 first- through third-grade students from 160 classrooms, LARRC investigators first examined the direct impacts of Let's Know! on students' language skills over an academic year, specifically, academic vocabulary, comprehension monitoring, and text comprehension (narrative and exposition). Measurement of these curriculum-aligned outcomes relied on LARRC-developed tools given that there were few validated tools available addressing these constructs. Measures of inferencing were also collected but not analyzed due to measurement concerns. Results indicated that students who received Let's Know! instruction significantly outperformed those assigned to the control condition in curriculum-aligned measures of academic vocabulary and comprehension monitoring across all three grades. Third graders in the Let's Know! condition also scored significantly higher in the narrative text comprehension tasks compared to those in the control group.

The theory of change inherent to the design of Let's Know! contends that intervention targeting children's language skills would transfer to effects on reading comprehension skills, which is another major hypothesis tested in the present study. To test this hypothesis, the LARRC administered three distal measures of reading comprehension, represented as a latent construct, and used multilevel structural equation modeling to examine the effects of Let's Know! on the curriculum-aligned measures and, in turn, their influence on reading comprehension. Modeling was conducted for each of the three grades separately, and results indicated a positive mediated effect whereby Let's Know! significantly improved children's reading comprehension via its effect on the curriculum-aligned measures, most prominently via academic vocabulary. Therefore, these results converge with a small but growing line of research showing that explicit instruction focusing on lower- and/or higher-language skills can contribute to reading comprehension as well (e.g., Clarke et al., 2010; Williams et al., 2004, 2009). Importantly, the LARRC RCT was the first to examine the impact of language-focused instruction on students' reading comprehension with instruction delivered by teachers within the context of whole-class instruction. Furthermore, this work highlighted the strong mediating role of vocabulary skills in transferring the effects of language-focused instruction to reading comprehension. The promising results provide an impetus for ongoing investments into leveraging students' language skills as a vehicle to improving reading comprehension.

Important Implications

Given evidence suggesting that language skills are the basis of skilled reading comprehension, consistent with the simple view of reading, reading instruction in the early primary grades should include explicit teaching of lower- and higher-level language skills. The Let's Know! curricular supplement, which targets a range of language skills to include, for instance, academic vocabulary and comprehension monitoring, is one freely available educational resource that can be used by teachers to ensure systematic coverage of language skills as part of the foundational reading curriculum (it is available at *https://larrc.ehe. osu.edu/curriculum*). Although Let's Know! can be used in PreK and kindergarten classrooms, evaluation of impacts at these grades has not yet been completed.

An important implication of this work, as well as other studies of the importance of language-focused instruction, is the need to ensure that educators have sufficient expertise in language development and instruction to effectively use such resources. If we view teaching language as an essential aspect of reading instruction, then language itself becomes the subject matter. Some experts have argued that many educators have only limited subject matter expertise with respect to language (e.g., Washburn, Joshi, & Binks-Cantrell, 2011), and empirical research has shown that college students majoring in education have more limited knowledge of language structures than their peers in linguistics and speech–hearing sciences (Justice & Ezell, 1999). Given that courses on language acquisition are routinely available on college campuses in disciplines such as psychology and communication science and disorders, requiring these within teacher credentialing programs could be readily explored.

Future Directions

There are considerable research opportunities that can build upon the work of the LARRC. First, the effectiveness of Let's Know! can continue to be evaluated to determine the extent to which it positively affects language and reading outcomes for students in a variety of settings and of various backgrounds. Researchers can determine whether its effects are generalizable, thus determining the extent to which the curriculum can be potentially scaled for broader use. Second, tools for evaluating students' lower- and higher-level language skills, particularly those that can be readily used by educators, need to be developed and evaluated for psychometric qualities. To effectively teach language as a subject matter, teachers need tools that allow them to formatively assess students' skills development. Third, there is a need to understand teachers' knowledge about language as a subject matter and to determine if improving knowledge about language enhances language-focused instruction. Presumably, teachers with heightened knowledge about language will be able to deliver language-focused instruction more effectively than those whose knowledge is limited, although this premise requires careful evaluation. Ensuring that teachers have sufficient knowledge about language to promote students' reading comprehension should be a fundamental goal of teaching credentialing programs worldwide.

Acknowledgments

The inaugural investigators of LARRC are as follows: the *Ohio State University (lead)*—Laura Justice (Principal Investigator), Richard Lomax, Ann O'Connell, Stephen Petrill, and Shayne Piasta; *Arizona State University*—Shelley Gray (Site Principal Investigator) and Maria Adelaida Restrepo; *Lancaster University, United Kingdom*—Kate Cain (Site Principal Investigator); *University of Kansas*—Hugh Catts (Site Principal Investigator), Mindy Bridges, and Diane Nielson; *University of*

Nebraska–Lincoln—Tiffany Hogan (Site Principal Investgator), Jim Bovaird, and Ron Nelson.

References

Beck, I., Perfetti, C. A., & McKeown, M. (1982). Effects of long-term vocabulary instruction on lexical access and reading comprehension. *Journal of Educational Psychology, 74*(4), 506–521.

Bowyer-Crane, C., Snowling, M. J., Duff, F. J., Fieldsend, E., Carroll, J. M., Miles, J., . . . Hulme, C. (2008). Improving early language and literacy skills: Differential effects of an oral language versus a phonology with reading intervention. *Journal of Child Psychology and Psychiatry, 49*(4), 422–432.

Cain, K., & Oakhill, J. (1999). Inference making ability and its relation to comprehension failure in young children. *Reading and Writing, 11*(5–6), 489–503.

Cain, K., & Oakhill, J. (2014). Reading comprehension and vocabulary: Is vocabulary more important for some aspects of comprehension? *L'Année Psychologique, 114,* 647–662.

Cain, K., Oakhill, J., Barnes, M. A., & Bryant, P. E. (2001). Comprehension skill, inference-making ability, and their relation to knowledge. *Memory & Cognition, 29*(6), 850–859.

Cain, K., Oakhill, J., & Bryant, P. (2004). Children's reading comprehension ability: Concurrent prediction by working memory, verbal ability, and component skills. *Journal of Educational Psychology, 96*(1), 31–42.

Cirino, P. T., Pollard-Durodola, S. D., Foorman, B. R., Carlson, C. D., & Francis, D. J. (2007). Teacher characteristics, classroom instruction, and student literacy and language outcomes in bilingual kindergartners. *Elementary School Journal, 107*(4), 341–364.

Clarke, P. J., Snowling, M. J., Truelove, E., & Hulme, C. (2010). Ameliorating children's reading-comprehension difficulties: A randomized controlled trial. *Psychological Science, 21*(8), 1106–1116.

Connor, C. M., Morrison, F. J., & Slominski, L. (2006). Preschool instruction and children's emergent literacy growth. *Journal of Educational Psychology, 98*(4), 665–689.

Farquharson, K., Murphy, K. A., & Language and Reading Research Consortium. (2016). Ten steps to conducting a large, multi-site, longitudinal investigation of language and reading in young children. *Frontiers in Psychology, 7,* Article 419.

Gough, P. B., & Tunmer, W. E. (1986). Decoding, reading, and reading disability. *Remedial and Special Education, 7*(1), 6–10.

Justice, L., & Ezell, H. (1999). Knowledge of syntactic structures: A comparison of speech–language pathology graduate students to those in related disciplines. *Contemporary Issues in Communication Science and Disorders, 26,* 119–127.

Justice, L. M., Mashburn, A. J., Hamre, B., & Pianta, R. C. (2008). Quality of language and literacy instruction in preschool classrooms serving at-risk pupils. *Early Childhood Research Quarterly, 23*(1), 51–68.

Kintsch, W., & Kintsch, E. (2005). *Comprehension:* Routledge.

Language and Reading Research Consortium. (2015a). Learning to read: Should we keep things simple? *Reading Research Quarterly, 50,* 151–169.

Language and Reading Research Consortium. (2015b). The dimensionality of language skills in young children. *Child Development, 86,* 1948–1965.

Language and Reading Research Consortium, Pratt, A., & Logan, J. (2014). Improving language-focused comprehension instruction in primary-grade classrooms: Impacts of the let's know! experimental curriculum. *Educational Psychology Review, 26,* 357–377.

Language and Reading Research Consortium, Jiang, H., & Logan, J. (2019). Improving reading comprehension in the primary grades: Mediated effects of a language-focused classroom intervention. *Journal of Speech, Language, and Hearing Research, 62*(8), 2812–2828.

Logan, J., & Language and Reading Research Consortium. (2017). Pressure points in reading comprehension: A quantile multiple regression analysis. *Journal of Educational Psychology, 109,* 451–464.

Lonigan, C., & Shanahan, T. (2009). *Developing early literacy: Report of the National Early Literacy Panel. Executive Summary. A scientific synthesis of early literacy development and implications for intervention.* National Institute for Literacy.

Perfetti, C. (2007). Reading ability: Lexical quality to comprehension. *Scientific Studies of Reading, 11*(4), 357–383.

Storch, S. A., & Whitehurst, G. J. (2002). Oral language and code-related precursors to reading: Evidence from a longitudinal structural model. *Developmental Psychology, 38*(6), 934–947.

Washburn, E. K., Joshi, R. M., & Binks-Cantrell, E. S. (2011). Teacher knowledge of basic language concepts and dyslexia. *Dyslexia, 17*(2), 165–183.

Williams, J. P., Hall, K. M., & Lauer, K. D. (2004). Teaching expository text structure to young at-risk learners: Building the basics of comprehension instruction. *Exceptionality, 12*(3), 129–144.

Williams, J. P., Hall, K. M., Lauer, K. D., Stafford,

K. B., DeSisto, L. A., & deCani, J. S. (2005). Expository text comprehension in the primary grade classroom. *Journal of Educational Psychology, 97*(4), 538–550.

Williams, J. P., Stafford, K. B., Lauer, K. D., Hall, K. M., & Pollini, S. (2009). Embedding reading comprehension training in content-area instruc-

tion. *Journal of Educational Psychology, 101*(1), 1–20.

Zipke, M., Ehri, L. C., & Cairns, H. S. (2009). Using semantic ambiguity instruction to improve third graders' metalinguistic awareness and reading comprehension: An experimental study. *Reading Research Quarterly, 44*(3), 300–321.

CHAPTER 12

Language Interventions in Early Childhood

Summary and Implications from a Multistudy Program of Research

Beth M. Phillips

Few developmental accomplishments may have more significance for children's ultimate academic and interpersonal outcomes than the achievement of robust receptive and expressive oral language skills (Hulme, Snowling, West, Lervåg, & Melby-Lervåg, 2020). Such competencies, representing highly interrelated components, relate to content (i.e., semantics), form (i.e., syntax, morphology, phonology) and use (i.e., pragmatics). Whereas some aspects of language (e.g., certain elements of grammar) can approximate adult-like forms by school entry, other aspects continue developing well after. Unfortunately, many children face challenges in acquiring language skills on typical time lines. Because of the interconnectedness among component skills, many children have weaknesses across areas, although some present with more heterogeneous profiles. Although for some children, early language delays are transient, for too many others early weaknesses foreshadow longstanding difficulties that can spread across academic and other domains.

In relation to reading, core language skills lay the foundation for more applied linguistic capabilities such as inferencing and comprehension monitoring that, collectively with the foundational components, facilitate understanding of speech, text read aloud to children, and, once decoding skills are in place, text children read themselves. Although many children read-

ily achieve language milestones and have little difficulty eventually using these abilities for successful reading comprehension, many other children struggle early to master multiple elements of language, then struggle again later to derive meaning from what they decode. Numerous longitudinal studies draw direct links between early language skills and later reading comprehension (e.g., Lonigan, Schatschneider, & Westberg, 2008). The challenges faced by children with gaps in their language competencies likely grow as the diversity of vocabulary increases and texts include more decontextualized styles of sentence structure and discourse.

Given the need for schools to support all children's development, a growing number of researchers working in early childhood education (ECE) have identified the critical need to support language skills among young children who by their preschool years are demonstrating substantial gaps relative to peers (e.g., Hulme, Snowling, West, Lervåg, & Melby-Lervåg, 2020). Many have called for improvements in Tier 1 ECE settings through professional development and enhanced curricula, noting the need for more intentional language instruction in classrooms (e.g., Dobinson & Dockrell, 2021; Phillips, Zhao, & Weekley, 2018). In addition, many, including our team at the Florida Center for Reading Research (FCRR), have worked to develop supplemental instructional content designed to both remediate and accelerate children's language beyond what may be possible in the general educational context alone (Law et al., 2017; Rogde, Hagen, Melby-Lervåg, & Lervåg, 2019).

A Language Intervention Program of Research

This chapter summarizes approximately 15 years of an ongoing program of research supported by funding from the Institute of Education Sciences (IES) and the National Institute of Child Health and Human Development (NICHD) on small-group, supplemental language-focused interventions for children in preschool and kindergarten (e.g., Lonigan, Purpura, Wilson, Walker, & Clancy-Menchetti, 2013; Lonigan & Phillips, 2016; Phillips et al., 2021; Phillips, Lonigan, Kim, Clancy, & Connor, 2022). Related work is ongoing in new projects. A large team of investigators, developers, project coordinators, and many others have contributed to this work over time; thus, the sole authorship of this chapter belies the extensive collaboration underpinning all projects discussed. This work has also been informed by lessons learned over an even longer period of time developing and evaluating several Tier 1 preschool comprehensive curricula (e.g., Lonigan, Farver, Phillips, & Clancy-Menchetti, 2011; Lonigan et al., 2015). The majority of the work discussed centers around multiple Tier 2 language interventions developed within the context of the Reading for Understanding (RFU) project awarded to a large group of investigators at Florida State University by IES (see also Justice & Jiang, Chapter 11, this volume). Among the many diverse interventions this team developed (e.g., Connor et al., 2014, 2018; Phillips et al., 2021), those most relevant for this chapter include three modular interventions targeting semantics, syntax, narrative text structure, and listening comprehension: Dialogic Reading—Extended (DR-E), Language in Motion (LIM), and Comprehension Monitoring and Providing Awareness of Story Structure (COMPASS); their development was spearheaded by Lonigan and Clancy, Phillips, and Kim, respectively (Kim & Phillips, 2016; Phillips et al., 2021). In the sections below, I first describe the population of children targeted by the series of projects and highlight key instructional design features of these interventions, before summarizing broad findings and key implications and discussing future directions.

Broadening the Reach of Language Interventions

The preschool and kindergarten period represents a primary, and critical, opportunity to identify and provide robust support to the many children who arrive in these classrooms with substantial needs related to their language skills, both within oral interactions and in the application of language skills to the reading process. To enhance equity and opportunity from the very beginning of formal schooling experiences, we have centered much of our work on early intervention, with the primary goal of preventing the development or exacerbation of language delays and disorders, and the negative consequences that can accrue for children whose language abilities are mismatched with increasing academic expectations.

A relatively small percentage of students, those for whom a language impairment has been diagnosed or is strongly suspected, receive supportive language therapies during school hours to help remediate their delayed development. This population is certainly in significant need of, and can benefit from, intensive and sustained language support (Bishop, Snowling, Thompson, Greenhalgh, & Catalise Consortium, 2016; Curran & Hogan, Chapter 26, this volume). However, especially if one conceptualizes instructional supports as being on a continuum of intensity, this group of children represents only a portion of those who might benefit from language and vocabulary instruction of greater intentionality, explicitness, and frequency given that children with language skills above a clinical threshold at one time point sometimes subsequently fall behind and can still face substantial concurrent and later challenges (Law et al., 2017). When we initiated this program of research, these "bubble" children were rarely among those receiving special attention in ECE, including in research projects, whose inclusion criteria have often mirrored those of schools and clinicians (although see some comparability in the program of intervention work being pursued by Melby-Lervåg and colleagues [e.g., Hagen, Melby-Lervåg, & Lervåg, 2017; Melby-Lervåg, Hagen, & Lervåg, 2020]). Therefore, across numerous projects, we have intentionally included *children with a wide range of language abilities,* defined as those with scores in both low-average and below-average ranges on standardized language instruments, as eligible participants in supplemental intervention projects. Whereas intervention with nearly (or in many of our studies, over) 50% of children is not likely feasible if provided only by specialists, as elaborated below, it is feasible when designed for implementation by a broader set of educators.

Our intention in having inclusive eligibility criteria is because we envision a dual purpose for these interventions. The first purpose is to "shore up" recently acquired language skills at a moment when they are particularly important (i.e., at the outset of formal schooling) to enhance children's likelihood of taking full advantage of the learning opportunities provided in the Tier 1 context and minimize the potential for losing ground relative to peers. The second purpose is to remediate language skills for children who are already moderately to substantially below average. We do not see these goals as being mutually exclusive; thus, across multiple studies, selected inclusion criteria (and instructional design elements) allowed pursuit of both aims simultaneously. Our intentional inclusion of children with a wide range of initial language scores also has facilitated evaluation of whether and how these baseline abilities moderate their response, and whether the interventions are an appropriate fit to children across the range; such analyses have been highlighted in recent publications (e.g., Phillips et al., 2021).

Theoretical and Instructional Design Underpinnings of Our Language Interventions

The theoretical framework for all of our interventions derives from a conceptualization of the young child as an *active* language learner, whose skill development can be supported or partially impeded by the environmental contexts to which she or he is exposed (e.g., Harris, Golinkoff, & Hirsh-Pasek, 2011). Children with comparatively weaker language skills by age 4 or 5 include those with intrinsic language learning difficulties and those whose capacity for language acquisition is intact but has been suppressed by limited language learning opportunities (Rogde et al., 2019). Some children represent both of these subgroups (Bishop et al., 2016). While acknowledging that the most impaired children will likely need alternative, or at least additional types of support, we have conceptualized these language interventions as appropriate for children who arrive at preschool or kinder-

garten with poor language skills via either of these routes. What all such children need, we have theorized, is both an *acceleration* of their language growth trajectory to try to close some or all of the gap with peers, and, perhaps more importantly, a *repairing* of their capacity to fully benefit from the incidental and implicit opportunities for typical language growth in their naturalistic home and classroom environments. Explicit, systematic intervention during the preschool and kindergarten periods that leads to substantive increases in language skills may help children break out of the developmental inertia of their early language growth, increasing their further growth capacity.

To accomplish such lofty goals, the core features of all our language interventions have included highly interactive structured lessons in which the primary goal is to elicit increasingly complex language from the children in ways they find fun and attention grabbing. Although more structured than guided play, our lessons meet the design recommendations of Hirsh-Pasek et al. (2015) of incorporating active, engaged, meaningful, and social features. Along a continuum of play, we would characterize these lessons as both game-based and playful instruction (Zosh et al., 2018). For example, across different interventions, design features that stimulate active engagement include board games, puppets, and manipulation of two- and three-dimensional props. All interventions have been exclusively situated in small groups, as we deemed this the optimal context for scaffolded support, sufficient participation turns, and the possibility of benefiting from peer models.

The design priority we set for ourselves was to develop highly scaffolded instruction on challenging concepts that could be provided with consistency across many small groups and simultaneously demonstrate responsiveness to individual children within those groups. As an example, within LIM, all multiday lessons follow a systematic progression that involves first modeling, then requesting receptive responses (e.g., prop manipulation), and ultimately expressive responses related to each new linguistic feature being taught. Surrounding this core structure, however, are repeated opportunities, signaled in the written lessons, for interventionists to provide simplification or increased challenge to individual children. Similar differentiation features are embedded in the design architecture of both DR-E and COMPASS, with, for example, the individualized expansions and prompts provided.

Another core element of our interventions, particularly those developed within RFU, has been the mandate that children would, along with the language targets, be able to learn about the world from participating in our small groups. All interventions, regardless of whether the linguistic focus is on vocabulary, syntax, or narrative, are built around topic areas that give the groups something meaningful and useful to read and talk about (Cabell & Hwang, Chapter 15, this volume). By infusing all lessons with that unit's content focus we aimed to (1) build topical background knowledge (and thus future inferential competencies) related to highly accessible schemas such as food preparation and playground activities, along with slightly less routine topics such as community helpers, geography and science concepts; (2) support breadth and depth of lexical knowledge within the semantic networks underpinning the content; and (3) support children in developing the habit of active, purposeful listening to learn new information.

Many interventions targeting language skills are designed by and for implementation by individuals with professional training in speech and language development, or at least by certified teachers (e.g., Brinchman, Hjetland, & Lyster, 2016). In contrast, we have deliberately developed and evaluated our small-group interventions with implementation by researcher-supervised interventionists who were preferred, but not required, to have a postsecondary degree and were therefore most comparable to paraprofessionals and teaching assistants who are commonly hired directly by schools. The intention has been to maximize the feasibility of ultimately scaling these interventions for delivery by school personnel and to be mindful of the wide range of teacher education levels in diverse preschool contexts. For comparable reasons, all interventions have been scripted, although to degrees varying from suggested wording to more structured, standardized phrasing of instructional language, depending on the lesson's linguistic targets. Certainly, it seems likely (e.g., Kim et al., 2017) that many classroom teachers and intervention providers, once they develop expertise in and experience with the content, may be successful at individualizing intervention pacing, delivery, and even content. Yet the experience of deploying hundreds of interventionist teachers indicates that they generally welcome and rely on the structured lesson plans as their own scaffold. The standardization also has ensured that all participating children are comparably exposed to the carefully crafted, child-friendly definitions, explanations and examples of syntactic features, and other instructional design elements that the design teams have developed. All interventionists also have been amply guided by initial and ongoing professional development support to maximize fidelity of implementation and, critically, to provide the educative opportunities for these personnel to build their pedagogical understanding of why and how the intervention content is being delivered. Alongside all lessons, the professional development components have been repeatedly implemented and refined in anticipation of future uptake by school personnel.

Process and Findings from a Systematic Program of Research

Early work on dialogic reading as a modular intervention and as woven into a comprehensive Tier 1 preschool curriculum (e.g., Lonigan et al., 2011, 2013) provided the conceptual, and, in some cases, instructional design foundation for the development of our small-group interventions. We initiated the series of studies explicitly targeting children with low- to below-average language skills through an NICHD-funded project. This first project was conceptualized as response to intervention (RTI) in PreK, in that all children eligible for inclusion represented classrooms with an evidence-based Tier 1 curriculum but were still deemed insufficiently responsive to this intervention by midyear (see also Carta & Greenwood, Chapter 28, this volume). Across two consecutive school years we developed and tested two versions of small-group language interventions that primarily addressed vocabulary but also included some attention to syntax (e.g., prepositional phrases, elaborating noun phrases with adjectives, use of comparing words) using randomized trials. In the first year, we organized the intervention around storybooks and embedded an abbreviated version of the repeated reading and questioning process of dialogic reading. Results were underwhelming, and we concluded that, in fact, given our multiple language targets, the book-reading aspect used up valuable time and limited children's opportunities to respond. Thus, in the second year, we moved away from books and designed the intervention around hands-on interaction with props (e.g., moving bears in, out, behind, and between cups to learn prepositional phrases) that afforded substantially more opportunities for children to practice expressive responses to prompts of increasing challenge. This activity-based framework soon after became the model for the development of LIM. The second year generated more promising impacts on both proximal (i.e., curriculum-linked) and standardized measures, although results for vocabulary skills were stronger than for expressive or receptive language (Lonigan & Phillips, 2016). Specifically, we obtained significant impacts on both a proximal and a distal standardized measure of vocabulary, but on only the proximal and not the distal measures of language.

Shortly after completing this series of studies, a group of researchers at FCRR were funded through the RFU initiative to develop and evaluate a set of supplemental interventions with the common aim of ultimately improving, or staving off, difficulties with reading comprehension. These interventions were designed to work within, but do not require formal use of, a multi-tiered system of supports. Within a larger scope of work, in a series of systematically sequenced studies, the early childhood versions of DR-E, LIM, and COMPASS were evaluated separately, and in combination, for preschool and kindergarten participants. The initial steps were to conceptualize and design both LIM and COMPASS, complete small-scale pre–post design trials of each instructional unit, and conduct small, randomized trials of both new interventions separately (e.g., Phillips, 2014; Phillips, Tabulda, Burris, Sedgwick, & Chen, 2016). These years of incremental work afforded opportunities not only to revise the content and materials, but also, equally as critical, to explore written and in-person training support necessary to ensure high-quality implementation that brought to life the vision of the design teams. Ultimately, refined versions of both new interventions demonstrated promise on proximal and near-transfer measures (e.g., novel listening comprehension passages with embedded syntax and vocabulary targets) with both preschool and kindergarten children. During this time period, we also refined existing dialogic reading practices into the enhanced (with additional picture cards and small-group games complementing the interactive reading) version we call DR-E, and readied a version for preschool.

Following these smaller studies, we initiated simultaneous larger randomized trials for

DR-E, LIM, and COMPASS in preschool, kindergarten, or both grades (and others; Connor et al., 2018). In samples of over 300 and 800 children in preschool and kindergarten, respectively, we evaluated the impact of these interventions on standardized measures of vocabulary, syntax, and listening comprehension and on a researcher-developed measure of comprehension monitoring, in the form of inconsistency detection (Phillips et al., 2021). Given the focus on impacts we believed educators would see as more relevant (but cf. Clemens & Fuchs, 2022) we did not include proximal (i.e., targeted vocabulary or syntax) measures in this trial. Our primary questions were whether each intervention would impact construct-matched outcome measures (i.e., a standardized syntax measure for LIM given its targeting of syntax) and whether any of these interventions would show generalized impacts on outcomes less directly matched to instructional targets (e.g., for LIM, standardized vocabulary assessments). Overall, results indicated that 12-week versions of DR-E and LIM, and a 10-week version of COMPASS had significant impacts on matching measures, but that there were no generalized impacts in kindergarten and only generalized impacts in preschool within the context of multiple significant moderation findings. For example, LIM had a significant positive impact on a standardized measure of vocabulary, but only for children who were above the mean child age at screening.

Given the limited generalized impacts, our subsequent study in these two grades explored the possibility that combining two of these three interventions, in all possible pairings, and extending the overall intervention duration to 18 weeks, would generate broader impacts relative to business as usual. To accomplish this aim, we developed an adapted version of DR-E for kindergarten with somewhat more advanced texts and target vocabulary. Unlike in the prior study, we now evaluated impacts on both proximal and standardized measures. Findings from samples of over 700 qualified (i.e., screened-in based on low to low-average listening comprehension) and randomized participants in each grade indicated significant, and in some cases, large, impacts from all paired component interventions on both proximal and standardized measures matched to the targeted language elements (Phillips et al., 2022), with some evidence of moderation based on component sequencing that, in some cases, indicated recency effects.

Whereas significant and educationally meaningful results for this longer intervention with the paired component interventions were more extensive than in the previous study in which each component intervention was evaluated separately, we remained somewhat dissatisfied by the extent to which impacts generalized and by the number of children who still demonstrated language weaknesses at posttest. As a result, we conceptualized a more logistically ambitious trial to evaluate the benefits of receiving paired intervention components (DR-E and LIM) in preschool only, kindergarten only, or both. There are compelling arguments to be made for the double duration, as well as for why timing might be optimized in each grade (e.g., to potentiate later implicit learning by intervening in preschool or, in contrast, to better synchronize with reading instruction by intervening in kindergarten). Our design explores all of these contrastive possibilities. Once completed, results will inform the future steps in this program of research and strengthen understanding of mechanisms by which language instruction may be optimized.

Key Implications

Promise of Impacts on Standardized Language Outcomes

Across multiple design, small-scale, and large-scale intervention trials, the language-focused interventions described here have consistently yielded impacts on proximal measures of targeted skills and on near-transfer measures (e.g., Kim & Phillips, 2016; Phillips, Tabulda, et al., 2016). Furthermore, the set of interventions described here have yielded, in multiple studies, significant impacts on distal measures (Phillips et al., 2021, 2022). Most notably, these effects have been identified on broad vocabulary, narrative comprehension, and syntax measures that have minimal overlap with the interventions' linguistic targets.

Although we are not able to fully deconstruct our interventions to identify the specific mechanisms by which they have led to significant impacts, there are some very plausible candidates. First, the small-group, highly structured, and relatively explicit design of these interventions likely supports children's grasp of what they are intended to learn and therefore guides their attention and efforts to these targets. Consistent with this premise, two recent systematic

reviews indicate greater impact on language outcomes when instruction is at least partially delivered in small-group or individual settings (Herrera, Phillips, Newton, Dombek, & Hernandez, 2021; Rogde et al., 2019). The small-group context facilitates time on task and may better permit the teacher to ascertain each child's understanding and provide differentiated support and feedback.

This context also likely relates to the second plausible mechanism, which is the high frequency of opportunities to respond by each child during the intervention sessions. The earlier RTI project and the three component interventions within RFU studies were designed to facilitate highly active linguistic engagement during every lesson, including multiple opportunities for children to participate chorally and individually (Connor et al., 2014; Phillips et al., 2021). Numerous intervention studies and reviews emphasize the value of opportunities to respond for children's acquisition of specific linguistic and other academic targets (attentional engagement) and reduction in disruptive behaviors (e.g., MacSuga-Gage & Simonsen, 2015). The focus on expressive language, and how children are asked to respond may be of critical importance (Dobinson & Dockrell, 2021). Within each of these interventions, there is a clear focus on eliciting, and providing scaffolded feedback to, multiword utterances from children as they are asked to retell, explain, and describe text and live behaviors (e.g., prop manipulation modeled by interventionists or enacted by children themselves).

The third plausible design feature that may be facilitating impacts on distal language measures is the exposure of children within each intervention session to the sophisticated vocabulary and sentence structures of the carefully selected trade books and researcher-composed texts within each intervention. Large-, and especially small-group shared reading in Tier 1 preschool and kindergarten classrooms are neither as ubiquitous nor necessarily as attentionally engaging as some might assume (Dynia & Justice, 2015; Phillips et al., 2018). Thus, highly interactive, and purpose-driven engagement in listening to and discussing texts during intervention lessons may support language acquisition not only through explicit vocabulary instruction but also via the more systematic exposure to novel vocabulary (Montag, Johnes, & Smith, 2015). Relatedly, all described interventions include redundant focus on the targeted semantic, syntactic, and narrative features. Planned repetitions, cumulative review activities, and explicitly described connections between new and prior targets may help consolidate learning.

Modularity of Impacts

Although it has yielded consistent, meaningful impacts on measures aligned with instruction (both proximal and distal), this program of research demonstrates that in 30 hours or less of intervention, impacts do not as readily generalize to other, even highly related language skills (Phillips et al., 2021, 2022). The results reveal a paradox in light of our and others' parallel work on the structure of language (e.g., LARRC, 2015; Lonigan & Milburn, 2017); that is, whereas the numerous investigations consistently highlight the interconnected nature of early language skills, revealed in factor-analytic models as one or two highly correlated latent variables, our intervention results indicate relatively modular impacts where children grow relative to children in comparison groups on the targeted language elements but do not consistently show generalized improvements in nontargeted language elements. A comparable paradox has been revealed in similar intervention work by others in which, despite being indistinguishable in multiple structural models (e.g., Lonigan & Milburn, 2017), some find stronger effects or effects more generalized on receptive than expressive measures or the opposite (Gonzalez et al., 2010; Melby-Lervåg et al., 2020). We continue to explore, through ongoing longitudinal and intervention studies, what might lead to such a contrast in developmental versus instructional findings, including whether the high interconnectedness of the underlying language construct is, ironically, working against broader impacts from instruction. Analogizing language skills to muscles throughout the human body, exercising and strengthening one's biceps will not automatically translate into muscle mass gains elsewhere in the body. This may be because powerful personal and/or environmental influences that led to the entire body being weak in the first place are still in effect. We continue to investigate whether certain individual differences within children and certain design characteristics within instruction might offset the stability of language skills. Some of our moderation findings suggest greater generalization in subgroups of children (e.g., those relatively older for their grade level), but the patterns are uneven and require new, carefully designed experiments to build on identified trends.

Likely Need for Sustained Support

Despite the clear promise of explicit, intensive language interventions to improve young children's skills in this area (Hulme et al., 2020), it is undeniable that even the most effective interventions are not closing the gaps for all children. One tentative conclusion is that sustained and broad impacts on distal language skills require greater longevity of support than many shorter-term, single-year interventions may include, although see Rogde et al. (2019) for meta-analytic findings that may contradict this conclusion. Our recent multiyear intervention trial will be illuminating regarding the possibility that extended duration across two distinct school years is more beneficial, although we did not include a contrast controlling for the total dosage in two different delivery periods (i.e., all possible weeks of intervention in a single school year). It may be that the myriad influences on early language skills, and the relative stability of such skills, preclude a goal of full remediation via early intervention. Rather, similar to the analogy of reading interventions as "insulin" or "inoculation" presented by multiple authors (e.g., Coyne, Kame'enui, Simmons, & Harn, 2004), and mindful of evidence for the fade out of many interventions (e.g., Bailey, Duncan, Cunha, Foorman, & Yeager, 2020), it may be more appropriate to consider supplemental early language lessons as just the first, yet critical, installment of supports necessary to sustain impacts of intervention, and bolster and advance skills as the linguistic challenges increase across years of schooling. Whereas Coyne et al. (2004) in fact reported findings consistent with an at least short-term inoculation effect, they also highlighted the many individual differences that influence how firmly the early intervention benefits take hold.

Given the increasing stability of language skills, an intervention that alters a child's trajectory of growth in language skills enough to preclude his or her need for future supports may require initiation with even younger children. Perhaps newly acquired language is at its most malleable; however, the highly diverse early language trajectories of children before age 3 may increase the challenge of identifying those in need of extra attention (Law et al., 2017). Much more research is needed on the timing, duration, focus, and content of language interventions to identify those components and design features most likely to achieve inoculative impacts.

Future Research Directions

Intervention Content

One central question the field continues to grapple with centers on whether there is a particular set of vocabulary words or syntactical or morphological components that is most likely to be directly generative of further linguistic progress (Coyne et al., 2019; Melby-Lervåg et al., 2020). That is, might certain content or forms, once mastered, generate autonomous acquisition of additional words and structures, promoting a version of self-teaching? Ideally, researchers will ultimately determine specific root morphological and syntactic structures (e.g., high-frequency affixes, particular syntactic sentence frames) that once acquired are generative of competence with newly encountered texts, including those taught structures *and* other semantic and grammatic elements (Brinchmann et al., 2016).

Seminal work by Biemiller (e.g., 2005) suggested a focus on teaching particular root words in a deliberate sequence to help optimize vocabulary growth rates. In results potentially consistent with this premise, Melby-Lervåg et al. (2020) reported that effects on distal oral language measures were mediated by acquisition of taught vocabulary. Their study also indicated that it was specifically expressive mastery of targeted words, selected to be age-appropriate and to fit the concept of a "Tier Two word" (e.g., Beck, McKeown, & Kucan, 2002) that seemed to facilitate better performance on distal measures. However, in a study with somewhat older dual language learners, even long-term sustained impact on a set of carefully chosen root words was not sufficient to transfer to generalized vocabulary growth (Vadasy, Sanders, & Nelson, 2015). Mixed findings such as these indicate that more longitudinal work is needed to identify what exactly is, and can be, generalized from instruction, and whether teaching specific content and forms at particular moments in time can maximize impacts on vocabulary breadth and depth and on broader linguistic competencies. Realistically, it is also plausible that there are no especially generative instructional targets, and that answers lie instead in improving children's uptake and the instructional contexts surrounding the intervention experiences that may promote or impede maintenance of progress.

An alternative but not mutually exclusive goal may be to focus more on how much progress children make during intervention windows. Perhaps what is most needed is to accelerate the rate of growth beyond some velocity threshold, such that a new, permanently faster growth trajectory takes hold and can sustain even without further specialized support. Evidence at least generally consistent with this idea is reported by Vadasy et al. (2013) in their longer-term follow-up of a vocabulary intervention for dual language learners in kindergarten, where immediate gains predicted long-term status. One aspect of this approach may be to increase the immediate instructional intensity of interventions rather than (or in addition to) their duration to better serve as a true "disruption" of preceding growth patterns. Typically, early childhood language interventions to date have provided 20- to 45-minute lessons 3–5 days per week (Foorman, Herrera, & Dombek, 2018; Phillips et al., 2021; Rogde et al., 2019). Substantially longer instructional periods may be needed to counteract the much larger amount of daily time children are experiencing less dense and supportive language input. Relatedly, closer linkages in the sequencing and content of Tier 1 and Tier 2 instruction may facilitate the desired intensity and sustaining environment (Coyne et al., 2019; Foorman et al., 2018). More investigation is needed to identify follow-on experiences that maximize the longevity of intervention impacts.

Beyond enhancing foundational language skills, and akin to ongoing inquiries focused on reading comprehension (e.g., Elleman & Compton, 2017), there remains a key question of whether comprehension of text read aloud is best supported by direct instruction of "listening comprehension strategies" such as how to draw causal inferences, shoring up of the foundational skills underpinning this application of oral language skills (e.g., Kim, 2016), or both. For example, more research is needed to examine the benefits from being explicitly taught, and given repeated guided practice, on how to apply foundational language skills to the task of comprehending when listening to connected texts or to oral narratives. A 2017 meta-analysis by Pesco and Gagné (2017) supports the benefit of explicit instruction on narrative production and narrative comprehension but leaves open questions of whether impacts are sustained, and whether they ultimately transfer to reading comprehension. Within our own research, the component intervention targeting comprehension monitoring and narrative text structure shows promise in supporting listening comprehension, especially when delivered in combination with components targeting vocabulary or syntax (Kim & Phillips, 2016; Phillips et al., 2021, 2022). However, we do not yet have clear evidence of transfer of gains to reading comprehension once children are older and reading independently.

Intervention Participants

As described earlier, the language-focused interventions we have developed across time have been, cumulatively, evaluated with thousands of children, in samples representing numerous aspects of diversity. These characteristics have included a range of home socioeconomic backgrounds, rural and urban school contexts, and, to some extent, racial diversity with substantial proportions of African American participants across studies. Our samples also have included many children already with, or highly likely to subsequently have been given, a language delay classification (e.g., children with multiple standardized language scores at or below the 10th percentile) and children with self-regulatory weaknesses. Work is underway exploring specific impacts for this latter group of children (e.g., Lonigan et al., 2022). Yet, especially given the increasing diversity of the U.S. population, it is imperative that we and others continue to expand the scope of participant groups and to more deeply explore how factors such as dual language status, dialect use, developmental language disorder, and comorbid behavioral disorders affect the uptake and sustained benefits of small-group language interventions.

To this end, we have initiated multiple investigations of diverse participant groups within the large archive generated by these studies. For example, promising secondary analyses of preschool children in our trial of paired interventions indicated comparable, if not greater, impacts among the proportion of the sample with the lowest baseline language scores (Phillips, Lonigan, & Kim, 2016). However, all children in our series of studies have had sufficient expressive language skills to be able to provide valid responses to assessment measures and to participate with at least single-word responses in the interventions. It is an open question whether

our interventions would benefit children with greater language impairments or the social interaction challenges often seen among those with autism spectrum disorder (ASD). Single subject adaptations of dialogic reading to children with ASD have yielded promising findings (e.g., Fleury & Schwartz, 2017), but larger trials and more varied intervention structures targeting this population are clearly needed (Whalon & Fleury, Chapter 27, this volume).

Beyond these efforts, much remains to be learned about how to ensure that language-focused interventions are genuinely inclusive, appropriately adaptive, and, ultimately, accessible in all school contexts. For example, although many prior study participants have been African American, we have not yet conducted careful assessment and analyses of the ways that children's varying degrees of African American English dialect use, and children's concurrent or increasing facility with Mainstream American English dialect, might influence children's response to intervention (Patton Terry, Gatlin, & Johnson, 2018). Similarly, we recently initiated a project evaluating the combined LIM and DR-E interventions with children who are Spanish-speaking dual language learners. As prior studies have included too few dual language learners in any one grade, only in this newest project will we be able to comprehensively assess how initial levels of Spanish and English language skills moderate uptake of our language interventions.

Conclusion

The program of intervention development and evaluation summarized here has spanned over a decade and many individual studies, and has included thousands of participating children and a large team of contributors. Our efforts have yielded not only success but also a clear understanding of the substantial challenges posed when attempting to remediate and accelerate early language development. Evidence suggests the importance of highly interactive lessons with many opportunities for children to practice new words and language forms in a context with ample individualized scaffolding. Evidence also suggests the need to ensure that the lessons and associated professional development support implementers' understanding of the what, why, and how of the instructional content to maximize impact. Ongoing studies continue to expand the reach of our interventions and further the goal of making evidence-based small-group lessons accessible across the landscape of early childhood education.

Acknowledgments

Research summarized in this chapter was funded by the Reading for Understanding Network Grant No. R305F100027 from the U.S. Department of Education, Institute of Education Sciences, and by Learning Disabilities Research Center Grant No. HD052120 from the Eunice Kennedy Shriver National Institute of Child Health and Human Development. The opinions expressed are the author's and do not represent the views of the funding agencies.

References

Bailey, D. H., Duncan, G. J., Cunha, F., Foorman, B. R., & Yeager, D. S. (2020). Persistence and fade-out of educational-intervention effects: Mechanisms and potential solutions. *Psychological Science in the Public Interest, 21*(2), 55–97.

Beck, I. L., McKeown, M. G., & Kucan, L. (2002). *Bringing words to life: Robust vocabulary instruction* (1st ed.). Guilford Press.

Biemiller, A. (2005). Size and sequence in vocabulary development: Implications for choosing words for primary grade vocabulary instruction. In E. F. Hiebert & M. L. Kamil (Eds.), *Teaching and learning vocabulary: Bringing research to practice* (pp. 223–242). Erlbaum.

Bishop, D. V., Snowling, M. J., Thompson, P. A., Greenhalgh, T., & Catalise Consortium. (2016). CATALISE: A multinational and multidisciplinary Delphi consensus study: Identifying language impairments in children. *PLOS ONE, 11*(7), Article e0158753.

Brinchmann, E. I., Hjetland, H. N., & Lyster, S. A. H. (2016). Lexical quality matters: Effects of word knowledge instruction on the language and literacy skills of third-and fourth-grade poor readers. *Reading Research Quarterly, 51*(2), 165–180.

Clemens, N. H., & Fuchs, D. (2022). Commercially developed tests of reading comprehension: Gold standard or fool's gold? *Reading Research Quarterly, 57*, 385–397.

Connor, C. M., Phillips, B. M., Kaschak, M., Apel, K., Kim, Y-S., Al Otaiba, S., . . . Lonigan, C. J. (2014). Comprehension tools for teachers: Reading for understanding from pre-kindergarten through fourth grade. *Educational Psychology Review, 26*, 379–401.

Connor, C. M., Phillips, B. M., Kim, Y.-S. G.,

Lonigan, C. J., Kaschak, M. P., Crowe, E., . . . Al Otaiba, S. (2018). Examining the efficacy of targeted component interventions on language and literacy for third and fourth graders who are at risk of comprehension difficulties. *Scientific Studies of Reading, 22*(6), 462–484.

Coyne, M. D., Kame'enui, E. J., Simmons, D. C., & Harn, B. A. (2004). Beginning reading intervention as inoculation or insulin: First-grade reading performance of strong responders to kindergarten intervention. *Journal of Learning Disabilities, 37*(2), 90–104.

Coyne, M. D., McCoach, D. B., Ware, S., Austin, C. R., Loftus-Rattan, S. M., & Baker, D. L. (2019). Racing against the vocabulary gap: Matthew effects in early vocabulary instruction and intervention. *Exceptional Children, 85*(2), 163–179.

Dobinson, K. L., & Dockrell, J. E. (2021). Universal strategies for the improvement of expressive language skills in the primary classroom: A systematic review. *First Language, 41*(5), 527–554.

Dynia, J. M., & Justice, L. M. (2015). Shared-reading volume in early childhood special education classrooms, *Reading Psychology, 36*(3), 232–269.

Elleman, A. M., & Compton, D. L. (2017). Beyond comprehension strategy instruction: What's next? *Language, Speech, and Hearing Services in Schools, 48*(2), 84–91.

Fleury, V. P., & Schwartz, I. S. (2017). A modified dialogic reading intervention for preschool children with autism spectrum disorder. *Topics in Early Childhood Special Education, 37*(1), 16–28.

Foorman, B. R., Herrera, S., & Dombek, J. (2018). The relative impact of aligning Tier 2 intervention materials with classroom core reading materials in grades K–2. *Elementary School Journal, 118*(3), 477–504.

Gonzalez, J. E., Pollard-Durodola, S., Simmons, D. C., Taylor, A. B., Davis, M. J., Kim, M., & Simmons, L. (2010). Developing low-income preschoolers' social studies and science vocabulary knowledge through content-focused shared book reading. *Journal of Research on Educational Effectiveness, 4*(1), 25–52.

Hagen, Å. M., Melby-Lervåg, M., & Lervåg, A. (2017). Improving language comprehension in preschool children with language difficulties: A cluster randomized trial. *Journal of Child Psychology and Psychiatry, 58*, 1132–1140.

Harris, J., Golinkoff, R. M., & Hirsh-Pasek, K. (2011). Lessons from the crib for the classroom: How children really learn vocabulary. In S. B. Neuman & D. K. Dickinson (Eds.), *Handbook of early literacy research* (Vol. 3, pp. 49–65). Guilford Press.

Herrera, S., Phillips, B. M., Newton, Y., Dombek, J. L., & Hernandez, J. A. (2021). *Effectiveness of early literacy instruction: Summary of 20 years of research* (REL 2021–084). U.S. Department of Education, Institute of Education Sciences, National Center for Education Evaluation and Regional Assistance, Regional Educational Laboratory Southeast.

Hirsh-Pasek, K., Zosh, J. M., Golinkoff, R. M., Gray, J. H., Robb, M. B., & Kaufman, J. (2015). Putting education in "educational" apps: Lessons from the science of learning. *Psychological Science in the Public Interest, 16*(1), 3–34.

Hulme, C., Snowling, M. J., West, G., Lervåg, A., & Melby-Lervåg, M. (2020). Children's language skills can be improved: Lessons from psychological science for educational policy. *Current Directions in Psychological Science, 29*(4), 372–377.

Kim, J. S., Burkhauser, M. A., Quinn, D. M., Guryan, J., Kingston, H. C., & Aleman, K. (2017). Effectiveness of structured teacher adaptations to an evidence-based summer literacy program. *Reading Research Quarterly, 52*(4), 443–467.

Kim, Y.-S. (2016). Direct and mediated effects of language and cognitive skills on comprehension or oral narrative texts (listening comprehension) for children. *Journal of Experimental Child Psychology, 141,* 101–120.

Kim, Y.-S., & Phillips, B. M. (2016). 5 minutes a day to improve comprehension monitoring in oral language contexts: An exploratory intervention study with prekindergartners from low income families. *Topics in Language Disorders, 36,* 356–367.

Language and Reading Research Consortium. (2015). The dimensionality of language ability in young children. *Child Development, 86,* 1948–1965.

Law, J. Charlton, J., Dockrell, J., Gascoigne, M., McKean, C., & Theakston, A. (2017). *Early language development: Needs, provision, and intervention for preschool children from socioeconomically disadvantaged backgrounds.* A report for the Education Endowment Foundation.

Lonigan, C. J., Farver, J. M., Phillips, B. M., & Clancy-Menchetti, J. (2011). Promoting the development of preschool children's emergent literacy skills: A randomized evaluation of a literacy-focused curriculum and two professional development models. *Reading and Writing, 24*(3), 305–337.

Lonigan, C. J., Hand, E. D., Spiegel, J. A., Morris, B. M., Jungersen, C. M., Alfonso, S. V., & Phillips, B. M. (2022). Does preschool children's self-regulation moderate the impacts of instructional activities?: Evidence from a randomized intervention study. *Journal of Experimental Child Psychology, 216,* Article 105321.

Lonigan, C. J., & Milburn, T. F. (2017). Identifying the dimensionality of oral language skills of children with typical development in preschool through fifth grade. *Journal of Speech, Language, and Hearing Research, 60*(8), 2185–2198.

Lonigan, C. J., & Phillips, B. M. (2016). Response to instruction in preschool: Results of two randomized studies with children at risk of reading disabilities. *Journal of Educational Psychology, 108*(1), 114–129.

Lonigan, C. J., Phillips, B. M., Clancy, J. L., Landry, S. H., Swank, P. R., Assel, M., . . . School Readiness Consortium. (2015). Impacts of a comprehensive school readiness curriculum for preschool children at risk for educational difficulties. *Child Development, 86*(6), 1773–1793.

Lonigan, C. J., Purpura, D. J., Wilson, S. B., Walker, P. M., & Clancy-Menchetti, J. (2013). Evaluating the components of an emergent literacy intervention for preschool children at risk for reading difficulties. *Journal of Experimental Child Psychology, 114*(1), 111–130.

Lonigan, C. J., Schatschneider, C., & Westberg, L. (2008). Identification of children's skills and abilities linked to later outcomes in reading, writing, and spelling. In *Developing early literacy: Report of the National Early Literacy Panel* (pp. 55–106). National Institute for Literacy.

MacSuga-Gage, A. S., & Simonsen, B. (2015). Examining the effects of teacher-directed opportunities to respond on student outcomes: A systematic review of the literature. *Education and Treatment of Children, 38,* 211–239.

Melby-Lervåg, M., Hagen, Å. M., & Lervåg, A. (2020). Disentangling the far transfer of language comprehension gains using latent mediation models. *Developmental Science, 23*(4), Article e12929.

Montag, J. L., Jones, M. N., & Smith, L. B. (2015). The words children hear: Picture books and the statistics for language learning. *Psychological Science, 26*(9), 1489–1496.

Patton Terry, N. P., Gatlin, B., & Johnson, L. (2018). Same or different: How bilingual readers can help us understand bidialectal readers. *Topics in Language Disorders, 38*(1), 50–65.

Pesco, D., & Gagné, A. (2017). Scaffolding narrative skills: A meta-analysis of instruction in early childhood settings. *Early Education and Development, 28*(7), 773–793.

Phillips, B. M. (2014). Promotion of syntactical development and oral comprehension: Development and initial evaluation of a small-group intervention. *Child Language Teaching and Therapy, 30,* 63–77.

Phillips, B. M., Kim, Y.-S. G., Lonigan, C. J., & Connor, C. M., Clancy, J., & Al Otaiba, S. (2021). Supporting language and literacy development with intensive small-group interventions: An early childhood efficacy study. *Early Childhood Research Quarterly, 57,* 75–88.

Phillips, B. M., Lonigan, C. J., & Kim, Y. S. (2016, February). *Young children with low language skills: Can Tier 2 language interventions help?* Presentation at Annual Meeting of the Pacific Coast Research Conference, Pacific Coast Research Conference, Coronado, CA.

Phillips, B. M., Lonigan, C. J., Kim, Y.-S. G., Clancy, J., & Connor, C. M. (2022). *Impact of multi-component early childhood language interventions.* Manuscript under review.

Phillips, B. M., Tabulda, G., Burris, P. W., Sedgwick, T. K., & Chen, S. (2016). Literate language intervention with high-need prekindergarten children: A randomized trial. *Journal of Speech Language and Hearing Research, 59,* 1409–1420.

Phillips, B. M., Zhao, Y., & Weekley, M. J. (2018). Teacher language in the preschool classroom: Initial validation of a classroom environment observation tool. *Early Education and Development, 29,* 379–397.

Rogde, K., Hagen, Å. M., Melby-Lervåg, M., & Lervåg, A. (2019). The effect of language comprehension training on standardized tests: A systematic review. *Campbell Systematic Reviews, 15*(4), Article e1059.

Vadasy, P. F., Nelson, J. R., & Sanders, E. A., (2013). Longer term effects of a Tier 2 kindergarten vocabulary intervention for English learners. *Remedial and Special Education, 34*(2) 91–101.

Vadasy, P. F., Sanders, E. A., & Nelson, J. R. (2015). Effectiveness of supplemental kindergarten vocabulary instruction for English learners: A randomized study of immediate and longer-term effects of two approaches. *Journal of Research on Educational Effectiveness, 8*(4), 490–529.

Zosh, J. M., Hirsh-Pasek, K., Hopkins, E. J., Jensen, H., Liu, C., Neale, D., . . . Whitebread, D. (2018). Accessing the inaccessible: Redefining play as a spectrum. *Frontiers in Psychology, 9,* Article 1124.

CHAPTER 13

Content Literacy

Integrating Social Studies and Language

Sharolyn D. Pollard-Durodola and Jorge E. Gonzalez

The social studies curriculum has evolved to represent a broad interdisciplinary corpus of knowledge (e.g., geography, economics, civics, peace education) (Mangram & Watson, 2011; Yarrow, 2008), with integrated topics from the humanities (e.g., philosophy) and the social sciences (e.g., psychology) to ensure a more nuanced understanding of the external and internal influences that shape how children exist in relationship with others in society (National Council for the Social Studies [NCSS], 2019). The specific curricular objectives, rooted in the human experience (Mindes, 2005; Saxe, 2004), build knowledge that can equip students to make well-informed decisions as problem-solvers while developing a deep understanding of their unique relationship with the earth (environment), other people, and institutions in society (NCSS, 1994) while fostering intellectual abilities and dispositions that are necessary for citizenship and civic competence (NCSS, 1994, 2010). As such, the social studies discipline has been conceptualized as a "curricula anchor" (Mindes & Newman, 2021, p. 1) for all students with the instructional aims of the early years (e.g., PreK to third grade), providing a foundation for more expansive knowledge-building in the later grades.

In this vein, NCSS recommends that a daily period of time, similar to the time allotment for other subject areas, be dedicated to elementary school social studies instruction (NCSS, 2017).

Tyner and Kabourek (2020), however, followed more than 18,000 kindergarten students through fifth grade and found that grade 1–5 students spend an average of 28 minutes daily in social studies instruction, documenting the limited school time devoted to social studies that has been previously reported (Fitchett, Heafner, & Lambert, 2014; Heafner & Fitchett, 2012; Saxe, 2004), even in early childhood settings (e.g., less than 90 minutes a week) (Burstein, Hutton, & Curtis, 2006). A recurring theme, therefore, in the social studies literature is the persistent marginalization of the social studies discipline during the elementary school years due in part to the passing of regulatory legislation (e.g., No Child Left Behind, Race to the Top, Every Student Succeeds Act) that has contributed to the reprioritization of English language arts (ELA) and mathematics, subject areas that are now afforded additional instructional time because they are associated with mandatory assessments and increased teacher accountability (Au, 2013; Burstein et al., 2006; D'Souza & Kullberg, 2018; Huck, 2019; Strachan, 2015).

Tyner and Kabourek (2020), however, also found that students from lower socioeconomic status (SES) communities, in addition to those who spoke a non-English language at home—students who often have limited access to quality instruction (Camburn & Han, 2011; Fitchett, 2010)—benefited the most from an additional

30 minutes of daily social studies teaching. Specifically, the students who engaged in an additional brief allotment of daily social studies instruction outperformed those with less social studies time by 15% of a standard deviation on a fifth-grade reading assessment, underscoring the critical connection between content knowledge (social studies) and reading comprehension (Cabell & Hwang, 2020; Cervetti & Hiebert, 2018; Cervetti & Wright, 2020; Verhoeven & Perfetti, 2011). This connection, however, is dismally reflected in the current downward trends in social studies knowledge (e.g., U.S. history, geography) and parallel fourth- and eighth-grade reading scores (Hussar et al., 2020; National Assessment of Educational Progress [NAEP], 2018). As such, students may require early robust opportunities to participate in well-structured social studies instruction that systematically builds domain knowledge through networks of schemas that can be used to expand their background knowledge (e.g., prior life experiences, previous knowledge). This makes comprehension more achievable, because content knowledge unlocks the meaning of new vocabulary and concepts present in academic discussions and materials (August & Shanahan, 2006; Kim, Relyea, Burkhauser, & Scherer, 2021; Nagy & Townsend, 2012; O'Reilly, Wang, & Sabatini, 2019) by helping students understand the context of reading (Tyner & Kabourek, 2020)—a skill utilized by literate adults (Hirsch, 2006).

Much attention has been directed, therefore, to how to improve early social studies instruction. This includes the evolution of elementary social studies teaching from a traditional stand-alone curricular subject organized by thematic units and lessons to content that is most often integrated during ELA (Burstein et al., 2006; Huck, 2019; Kim et al., 2021; Strachan, 2015; Wright & Neuman, 2014). This content integration approach, initially popularized in the 1930s (Knudsen, 1937), has been the focus of ongoing debates about its potential benefits (Brophy, Alleman, & Knighton, 2009; Fitchett et al., 2014). More recently, one meta-analysis (Hwang, Cabell, & Joyner, 2022) reported positive K–5 outcomes (vocabulary, content, comprehension) for students who participated in an integrated literacy and content approach in comparison to students who received literacy and content instruction separately, demonstrating a potential benefit for content integration (Cabell & Hwang, Chapter 15, this volume).

Referred to as a *content literacy practice* or *disciplinary literacy*, this integrative approach is "rooted in making connections" (e.g., across concepts, vocabulary, big ideas) (Huck, 2019, p. 6) and may complement the interdisciplinary aims of the Common Core State Standards (CCSS), which purposely combine ELA and literacy in history/social studies (National Governors Association Center for Best Practices & Council of Chief State School Officers, 2010), and the *Social Studies for the Next Generation: Purposes, Practices, and Implications for College, Career, and Civic Life Framework for Social Studies State Standards* (NCSS, 2013). The supporting framework for early grade implementation of these standards is veritably language-based with discipline-specific discourse opportunities (e.g., asking, explaining, arguing) (Wright & Domke, 2019; Wright & Gotwals, Chapter 14, this volume), rigorous and deeper vocabulary-learning expectations (e.g., using new words acquired from being read to and through conversations, analyzing words) (Baker et al., 2015), and analytical thinking/talking priorities to prepare K–12 students for the future language and literacy demands of college and life (Mindes, 2015).

Accelerating topic-driven social studies knowledge through more language-based pedagogies, however, may especially benefit preschool and kindergarten children who may not yet be able to read but who are able to listen to and interact in rich adult–child and peer discussions (e.g., asking questions, sharing ideas, using discipline specific vocabulary) when social studies-related books are read to them (Gonzalez et al., 2014; Peck & Herriot, 2015; Pinkham, 2012; Strachan, 2015; Strachan & Block, 2020; Tyner & Kabourek, 2020; Wright & Domke, 2019).

For this reason, preschool and kindergarten content literacy practices continue to be the focus of research to determine more effective ways to integrate social studies learning during ELA with critical thinking opportunities in which interactive shared book reading is the conduit for early learning (Gonzalez et al., 2011, 2014; Pollard-Durodola, Gonzalez, Simmons, & Simmons, 2015; Pollard-Durodola et al., 2016, 2018; Strachan, 2015; Kim et al., 2021). *Content-enriched shared book reading* discussions, for example, can undergird the early development of "information capital" (Neuman & Celano, 2012, p. 105), a rich knowledge base that supports social studies aims (e.g., critical thinking, problem solving), while expanding young children's vocabulary knowledge and their ability to discuss new concepts (Kim et al., 2021; Neuman & Kaefer, 2018; Silverman & Hines, 2009; Spycher, 2009; Strachan, 2015). Oral vocabulary as a critical component of oral language development plays an important role in children's ability to acquire domain knowledge (e.g., social studies) (Hirsch, 2006). In this vein, reading and discussing conceptually related books across several days in a topic immersion approach may provide the multiple explicit exposures to content-related vocabulary that can maximize limited social studies time—even in preschool.

This chapter examines content literacy practices that have been utilized in a preschool social studies intervention implemented first in general education classrooms with children who were native English speakers (Gonzalez et al., 2011, 2014) and later in dual language bilingual education settings where Spanish-speaking emergent bilinguals, in the initial stages of English proficiency, acquired social studies knowledge in English as a second language (Pollard-Durodola et al., 2016, 2018). Interactive shared book reading served as the early learning platform with the underpinning belief that world knowledge (e.g., social studies) could be accelerated by focusing students' attention on domain-specific vocabulary found within conceptually related texts—especially informational books that can broaden children's initial background knowledge (Duke, Pearson, Strachan, & Billman, 2011)—to build extensive knowledge networks important for comprehension (listening, reading) (Neuman, 2006). Although content-enriched literacy practices have the potential to accelerate social studies knowledge when educators struggle to include all content in the instructional day, evidence suggests that typical practices may be casually constructed (Strachan, 2015), and that guidance for more structured frameworks that can accelerate broad knowledge connections are warranted (Huck, 2019).

Content-Enriched Shared Book Reading: Social Studies and Vocabulary Development

Project Words of Oral Reading and Language Development (WORLD) aimed to equalize opportunities for young children, primarily from lower-SES communities and households in which a non-English language was spoken, by

building high-priority social studies knowledge through a carefully sequenced 18-week interactive shared book-reading intervention with daily 20-minute small-group topic-immersion discussions around the broad social studies theme *People, Places, and the Environment*. As a language-based pedagogy, *interactive shared book reading* reinforced social studies learning during the back-and-forth adult–child interactions and dialogues that occurred while reading and discussing books—a prominent feature of interactive shared book reading approaches (What Works Clearinghouse [WWC], 2015), while reinforcing young children's oral language development with explicit attention on a small group of semantically related content vocabulary to simultaneously support language and conceptual knowledge growth. There is evidence that emergent bilinguals especially benefit from intensive attention on a small set of academic vocabulary over several days using varied strategies (e.g., listening, speaking) to reinforce content learning (Baker et al., 2014).

The key to the WORLD content literacy approach was how instruction was organized. Vygotsky (1978) emphasizes that *organized learning* stimulates cognitive development in ways that may not be possible when instructional planning does not intentionally integrate opportunities for adult guidance and feedback. As such, researchers investigated the most effective way to organize and structure interactive shared book reading vocabulary tasks and the supporting materials though a 3-year design experiment (Bradley & Reinking, 2012) in collaboration with preschool teachers in general and bilingual education classrooms, so that the culminating approach and materials would have ecological value for content learning in the field (see Gonzalez et al., 2011; Pollard-Durodola, Gonzalez, & Simmons, 2014; Pollard-Durodola et al., 2015).

The Building Blocks for Maximizing Social Studies Learning via Responsive Language Practices

Building knowledge occurs while building language (vocabulary) because "knowledge is intimately related to language" (Cabell & Hwang, 2020; p. 101). Students who understand the words *meadow* and *valley* are likely to understand that the earth is made of diverse landforms that support life in varied ways. Emergent bilinguals who learn content vocabulary in English are likely to make connections to these words when learning the same concept in Spanish: "I have observed that the students use the vocabulary they learned in daily conversations or in other subjects when that topic comes up. . . . Even when we are learning a particular subject in Spanish, they will recognize the words or pictures and discuss that particular word we were learning [in English WORLD]" (Bilingual Teacher 13 in Pollard-Durodola et al., 2021, p. 15). Below we summarize how daily content-literacy lessons can be organized through broad knowledge connections facilitated by high levels of student engagement, adult–child and peer interactions, and multiple occasions for analytical thinking.

Instructional Design Principles

The WORLD intervention integrated validated interactive, shared book-reading practices with a six-principle instructional design framework built around critical features of effective instruction that have been used in varied academic contexts with diverse learners (Coyne, Kame'enui, & Carnine, 2011; Simmons, Pollard-Durodola, Gonzalez, Davis, & Simmons, 2008): (1) big ideas (the essential knowledge to be taught: social studies concepts and vocabulary, oral language standards); (2) conspicuous strategies (the explicit routine and strategies for teaching new concepts and vocabulary); (3) mediated scaffolding (intentional adult guidance and material scaffolds: text visuals that depict content word meanings); (4) strategic integration (the thoughtful planning or sequence for connecting new information with what the student already knows); (5) judicious review (a cumulative approach that ensures generalizable applications of new knowledge); and (6) primed background knowledge (assistance that enables the learner to draw on previous life experiences and knowledge to reinforce learning new information).

We extended the original six principles to include a seventh principle, intentional opportunities for language interaction (Simmons et al., 2008). This principle prioritized purposeful opportunities for generating and sustaining focused talk around high-priority social studies content within a small group of six students with planned distributed discussion tasks (e.g., before, during, after book reading) for the whole group in addition to individual turns with feedback. The smaller group discussions afforded greater

intensity, especially for emergent bilinguals who required frequent structured listening and speaking interactions with an English proficient adult who could provide feedback while discussing social studies concepts (Bedore, Peña, Griffin, & Hixon, 2016; Hur, Snyder, & Reichow, 2020; Larson et al., 2020; Pollard-Durodola et al., 2021). Sheer exposure (e.g., only listening) to a second language during content instruction is not sufficient to develop the advanced language (e.g., sentence structure, language functions, correct use of content-related terms) that is required for academic learning (Salinas, Rodriguez, & Blevins, 2017).

All children benefited from the systematic use of evidence-based language interaction opportunities (e.g., language extensions, open-ended questions) with high-demand talk (e.g., making inferences) supported by scaffolds (e.g., thematic visuals representing content vocabulary) and life applications that can make "challenging concepts more concrete and meaningful" (Strachan, 2015, p. 209). These interactions were distributed across the week in a 5-day routine and across the daily 20-minute thematically organized lessons, with talking points occurring before, during, and after reading the text.

Thematically Organized Shared Book-Reading Structure and Routine

The intervention structure provided a platform for adult–child and peer partner discussions around conceptually related text sets that comprised a storybook paired with an informational text and organized around two broad social studies themes, *Places Where We Live and Go* and *The Earth,* with smaller anchoring topics (e.g., The Earth topics: land, water) that were used to organize one instructional unit or week of instruction and guided the selection of commercially available children's books that met the following criteria: (1) They could be read and discussed in 20-minute sessions, (2) they included a sufficient number of vocabulary (approximately three words per text) associated with the social studies themes and smaller topics, (3) target vocabulary words were depicted in the text illustrations/visuals, and (4) the text structure exposed children to academic terms (e.g., characters, main idea) associated with storybooks and informational text features (e.g., life cycles, clearly constructed figures) to clarify abstract concepts.

Furthermore, a range of lower and higher cognitive tasks and open-ended question types (literal, inferential) were carefully sequenced to provide multiple analytical thinking opportunities that generated discussions around word associations (e.g., Challenge Questions: "Could you swim across an *ocean*? Why or why not?") that may indicate how well young children can deeply process new concepts (Beck, McKeown, & Kucan, 2013). Overall, thematic organization of daily shared book-reading lessons can provide an intellectual structure that more easily generates deep networks of knowledge that expand and deepen content and vocabulary learning (Kim et al., 2021).

The thematic sequence was rooted in a 5-day routine that integrated the following validated shared book-reading practices, allowing multiple opportunities for children to ask questions, use new social studies vocabulary, and engage in analytical thinking with knowledge extensions: repeated text readings (Spychner, 2009), brief in-context definitions (Justice, Meier, & Walpole, 2005), distributed interactions (e.g., before, during, or after reading the book) (Wasik, Bond, & Hindman, 2006), open-ended questions (Sénéchal, 1997), higher cognitive strategies (e.g., comparing, explaining, associating) (Dickinson & Smith, 1994), and directing children's attention to key features depicted in visuals (e.g., illustrations, visual representations of words) (Kaefer, 2018).

The following instructional episode exemplifies the daily distributed routine: Before reading the storybook *No Jumping on the Bed* (Arnold, 1996), in the *Places Where we Live and Go* theme, the *Homes* unit was introduced with a thematic poster to prime children's background knowledge (e.g., "We've been learning about places where we live and go. Today we will learn about homes") before previewing new words (*ceiling, apartment*) by using a naturalistic visual card for each word as a discussion prompt. Children listened to and repeated the words and asked questions. The storybook was introduced while pointing to text illustrations to help children make a prediction in a brief partner discussion (e.g., "Tell your friend about what you will learn about the ceiling on this page"). While reading the book, the teacher stopped on specific pages to engage children briefly in a discussion about the depicted target words (e.g., "A *ceiling* is the part of the room that is on top. Why is Walter falling through the *ceiling*?"). After reading

the storybook, there were activities to talk about the character, the main thing that happened, and to make life connections ("What do you think would happen if someone fell through the *ceiling* at home?").

On Day 2, the book was reread, with opportunities to apply new knowledge and words in discourse games with individual turns to talk (Magic Mirror: "Luis, look into the mirror and tell us about the *ceiling* that you see! What do you see on the *ceiling*?") and analytical discussions to deeply process new concepts (e.g., Challenge Questions: "Why do we have *apartments* in *cities*? Would you have a neighbor if you lived in an *apartment*? Why or why not?") with two different visual cards as scaffolds. The routine was repeated on Days 3 and 4, expanding and deepening knowledge about places to live within a community with the complementary information text *House* (Schaefer, 2003), two new words (*roof, basement*), and additional discourse and analytical life applications through rich expansive associative talk with adult scaffolding (e.g., Challenge Questions: "Would a *basement* have a lot of sunlight? Why or why not? What is the difference between a *roof* and a *ceiling*?"). Day 5 included rich cumulative review opportunities to integrate social studies knowledge and vocabulary learned across texts, the week, and previous lessons. Furthermore, new information was connected to previously taught ideas (e.g., concepts, vocabulary) across the 18 weeks.

Knowledge Networks

Although words may represent labels for specific concepts or ideas, the concepts represent deeper networks of knowledge (Anderson & Freebody, 1981; Neuman, 2006) that bolster schema development and the transfer of children's learning (Fitzgerald, Elmore, Relyea, & Stenner, 2020). Thematically organizing the shared book-reading content (e.g., broad themes, weekly topics) and materials (visuals that depict vocabulary) allowed teachers to focus children's attention on the interconnected knowledge across conceptually related text sets and genres (storybooks, information texts) in which semantically organized words (e.g., *ceiling, roof, basement*) were selected to build and extend new knowledge (e.g., buildings in the community have useful structures) in the small-group discussion. Clustering vocabulary semantically taps into word connections that represent how young children naturally acquire conceptually related words (Hadley & Mendez, 2021; Neuman & Dwyer, 2011) while facilitating word retrieval (Neuman & Kaefer, 2018). Building knowledge networks provides explicit attention to the connections between taught words (Mancilla-Martinez & McClain, 2020) which are links to topic-driven concepts (Stahl & Nagy, 2006). The *knowledge hypothesis* (Stahl & Nagy, 2006) provided a theoretical framework for how to build networks of knowledge during the thematic shared book-reading approach. This theory posits that new words can be accrued when children are immersed (e.g., over several days) in learning about a new topic in which the broader concepts that are associated with the word are the focus of attention (Nagy, 2007). In this manner, vocabulary knowledge becomes a "proxy" (Mancilla-Martinez & McClain, 2020, p. 217) for the development of domain knowledge, because students construct deeper understandings of the associated concepts as they map new information on their initial understandings.

Associative Talk and Analytical Thinking

The positive impact on language learning conferred by shared book reading is largely dependent on the intentionality and quality of the shared reading by adult readers (Sembiante, Dynia, Kaderavek, & Justice, 2018). The level of cognitive challenge that engages children in inferential thinking exposes them to varying levels of abstraction through contextualized and decontextualized opportunities to interact with vocabulary, thus deepening the processing of words (Gonzalez et al., 2014). High-demand questions (e.g., Earth theme, Land topic: "What happens to a *riverbank* when we have a lot of rain?") that require children to associate text elements with prior knowledge that goes beyond the book reading is especially beneficial to deeper processing of words (Lenhart, Suggate, Lenhad, & Vaahtoranta, 2020). Inferencing, for example, a key, higher-order questioning strategy, actively requires children to make associations between words, concepts, and ideas both in and beyond the book, and is important to reading comprehension (Sembiante et al., 2018). Indeed, Gonzalez et al. (2014) found that not only question type but also placement and duration of talk mattered for young children's vocabulary growth.

Specifically, the extended teacher talk about vocabulary (e.g., "What is the difference between a tree *trunk* and *twigs*? Would a tree trunk be found underground? Why or why not?") that occurred after reading the book was positively associated with children's end-of-year expressive vocabulary growth, while the *duration* of teachers' associative vocabulary talk was positively related to children's receptive language outcomes. Perhaps the extratextual talk after reading the book permitted children the additional time for the challenging demand of comprehending, connecting, analyzing, and discussing the association between new vocabulary and concepts taught. It is also possible that the extratextual discussions, primarily occurring after the second reading of the text, when most of the inferential talk occurred, functioned as a cue to instantiate mental representations or *schemas* constructed by the preschoolers, thus retrieving existing lexical networks for deeper active analysis of new words (Gonzalez et al., 2014). Last, the cumulative nature of the WORLD curriculum ensured multiple listening and speaking episodes and exposures to associative talk in which teachers could be responsive to the nuances of children's receptive and expressive linguistic abilities. Linguistic responsivity is essential in the language (native language, English as a second language) learning process (Lucas & Villegas, 2011).

Future Considerations

The WORLD studies demonstrated that scaffolding children's textual and extratextual conversations around challenging associative talk provides numerous opportunities for teachers to leverage book discussions as a linchpin in children's deeper learning of words across a wide spectrum of learning abilities (Sembiante et al., 2018). Developing teachers' abilities to adjust the challenge level of associate talk to accommodate varying language abilities would greatly assist teachers to modulate discussions by using both literal- and inferential-level questions and thereby address the needs of a wide array of children. Relatedly, varying the type, demand level, and placement of questions (e.g., after reading the book) alone may not be sufficient to produce language effects. As noted by Lenhart and colleagues (2020), it may be necessary to support teachers to augment open-ended questions with rich and meaningful discussions supported with immediate feedback, language modeling, and, where appropriate, elaborations.

Furthermore, although the structured shared book-reading lesson routines ensured consistency in teaching the critical social studies content with embedded small-group language interactions, preschool teachers' ability to respond to the nuances of children's performance may have required more customized support, with adequate dedicated time to internalize some of the intensive approaches (Gusky & Yoon, 2009), especially when engaging emergent bilinguals in social studies learning in English as a second language (e.g., beginning-of-year analytical discussions). Findings from *Promoting the Educational Success of Children and Youth Learning English: Promising Futures* (National Academies of Sciences, Engineering, and Medicine [NASEM], 2017) confirm that previous interventions that cultivated English language use during content instruction included important professional development components such as customized coaching to simultaneously support content learning and oral language development (e.g., Spycher, 2009).

Conclusion

Educators must plan with the "end in mind" (McTighe & Wiggins, 1998, p. 7) in not only the judicious sequencing of integrated instruction during the early years but also in maintaining a "long-range viewpoint" (Huck, 2019, p. 6) of the desired learning outcome: Students will acquire knowledge in school that will be of future benefit in their own life and prepare them to address the perplexing concerns characteristic of a modern society. The current and long-standing sociodynamics, rooted in U.S. history (Wilkerson, 2020), warns that our children require a more substantive knowledge base in which the central social studies' aim is not diluted: Cultivate civic competence in youth to make critical decisions aligned with democratic values, with a respect for diversity and inclusivity. As such, we cannot turn a blind eye to the social justice concerns of the present era and the "failed citizenship" (Banks, 2017) discourses that continue to ignore the paradoxes that exist in U.S. society (Subedi, 2019; Iruka et al., Chapter 29, this volume). Overall, teachers have a unique role in sculpting the "nature of knowledge" (Subedi, 2008, p. 417) that all children, especially those from marginalized ethnic groups, are exposed to, creating opportunities for critical dialogues (conversing across differences) that may circumvent racist microaggressions and "linguistic bullying" (Subedi, 2008, p. 431), episodes that silence students of color, and that young children recognize and participate in (e.g., "Go back to your country") during social studies instruction. In this specific scenario, a teacher of Indian immigrant ancestry utilized a content-literacy approach, integrating book reading and reflective writing responses to provide opportunities for perspective taking for children to understand concepts of prejudice and bias experienced by a Japanese American character (historical fiction). As exemplified in this lesson, social studies teaching cannot be detached from broader societal values and concerns, because educational institutions serve as a microcosm of the existing societal structures, history, and tensions (Pittman, 2010). A lingering question, therefore, is what happens in a society when social studies is no longer a valued curricular anchor during the early years? Perhaps, we are witnessing the outcome.

References

Anderson, R. C., & Freebody, P. (1981). Vocabulary knowledge. In J. Guthrie (Ed.), *Comprehension and teaching: Research reviews* (pp. 77–117). International Reading Association.

Arnold, T. (1996). *No jumping on the bed.* Penguin Books.

Au, W. (2013). Coring social studies within corporate education reform: The Common Core State Standards, social justice, and the politics of knowledge in U.S. schools. *Critical Education, 4*(5), 1–16.

August, D., & Shanahan, T. (2006). *Developing literacy in second-language learners: A report on the National Literacy Panel on language minority children and youth.* Erlbaum.

Baker, D. L., Santoro L., Ware, S., Cuéllar, D., Oldham, A., Cuticelli, M., Coyne, M., . . . McCoach, B. (2015). Understanding and implementing the Common Core vocabulary standards in kindergarten. *Council for Exceptional Children, 47*(5), 264–271.

Baker, S., Lesaux, N., Jayanthi, M., Dimino, J., Proctor, C. P., Morris, J., & Newman-Gonchar, R. (2014). Teaching academic content and literacy to English learners in elementary and middle school (NCEE 2014–4012). Retrieved April 18, 2021 from *https://files.eric.ed.gov/fulltext/ED544783.pdf.*

Banks, J. A. (2017). Failed citizenship and transformative civic education. *Educational Researcher, 46*(7), 366–377.

Beck, I. L., McKeown, M. G., & Kucan, L. (2013). *Bringing words to life: Robust vocabulary instruction* (2nd ed.). Guilford Press.

Bedore, L. M., Peña, E. D., Griffin, Z. M., & Hixon, J. G. (2016). Effects of age of English exposure, current input/output, and grade on bilingual language performance. *Journal of Child Language, 43*(3), 687–706.

Bradley, B. A., & Reinking, D. (2012). Enhancing research and practice in early childhood through formative and design experiments. *Early Child Development and Care, 181*, 305–319.

Brophy, J., Alleman, J., & Knighton, B. (2009). *Inside the social studies classroom*. Routledge.

Burstein, J. H., Hutton, I. A., & Curtis, R. (2006). The state of elementary social studies teaching in one urban district. *Journal of Social Studies Research, 30*(1), 15–21.

Cabell, S. Q., & Hwang, H. (2020). Building content knowledge to boost comprehension in the primary grades. *Reading Research Quarterly, 55*(Suppl. 1), S99–S107.

Camburn, E. M., & Han, S. W. (2011). Two decades of generalizable evidence on U.S. instruction from national surveys. *Teachers College Record, 113*(3), 561–610.

Cervetti, G. N., & Hiebert, E. H. (2018). Knowledge at the center of English language arts instruction. *Reading Teacher, 72*, 499–507.

Cervetti, G. N., & Wright, T. S. (2020). The role of knowledge in understanding and learning from text. In E. B. Moje, P. Afflerbach, P. Encisco, & N. K. Lesaux (Eds.), *Handbook of reading research* (Vol. 5, pp. 237–260). Routledge.

Coyne, M. D., Kame'enui, E. J., & Carnine, D. W. (2011). *Effective teaching strategies that accommodate diverse learners*. Pearson.

Dickinson, D. K., & Smith, M. W. (1994). Long-term effects of preschool teachers' book readings on low-income children's vocabulary and story comprehension. *Reading Research Quarterly, 29*, 104–122.

D'Souza, L., & Kullberg, M. (2018). Developing future citizens of America: Repositioning social studies education in an era of accountability. *Social Studies Education Review, 7*(2), 1–14.

Duke, N. K., Pearson, P. D., Strachan, S. L., & Billman, A. K. (2011). Essential elements of fostering and teaching reading comprehension. In S. J. Samuels & A. E. Farstrup (Eds.), *What research has to say about reading instruction* (4th ed., pp. 51–93). International Reading Association.

Fitchett, P. G. (2010). A profile of twenty-first century social studies teachers. *Journal of Social Studies Research, 34*, 229–265.

Fitchett, P. G., Heafner, T. I., & Lambert, R. G. (2014). Examining elementary social studies marginalization: A multilevel model. *Education Policy, 28*(1), 40–68.

Fitzgerald, J., Elmore, J., Relyea, J. E., & Stenner, A. J. (2020). Domain-specific academic vocabulary network development in elementary grades core disciplinary textbooks. *Journal of Educational Psychology, 112*(5), 855–879.

Gonzalez, J. E., Pollard-Durodola, S., Simmons, D. C., Taylor, A. B., Davis, M. J., Fogarty, M., & Simmons, L. (2014). Enhancing preschool children's vocabulary: Effects of teacher talk before, during and after shared reading. *Early Childhood Research Quarterly, 29*(2), 214–226.

Gonzalez, J. E., Pollard-Durodola, S. D., Taylor, A., Simmons, D. C., Davis, M., & Simmons, L. (2011). Developing low-income preschooler's social studies and science vocabulary through content-focused shared book reading. *Journal of Research on Educational Effectiveness, 4*, 25–52.

Gusky, T. R., & Yoon, K. S. (2009). What works in professional development? *Phi Delta Kappan, 90*(7), 495–500.

Hadley, H. B., & Mendez, K. Z. (2021). A systematic review of word selection in early childhood vocabulary instruction. *Early Childhood Research Quarterly, 54*, 44–59.

Heafner, T. L., & Fitchett, P. G. (2012). Tipping the scales: National trends of declining social studies instructional time in elementary schools. *Journal of Social Studies Research, 36*(2), 190–215.

Hirsch, E. D. (2006). Building knowledge: The case for bringing content into the language arts block and for knowledge-rich curriculum core for all children. *American Educator, 30*(1), 8–18.

Huck, A. (2019). Elementary social studies content integration in CCLS: An analysis of content integration. *The Social Studies, 110*(1), 1–16.

Hur, J. H., Snyder, P., Reichow, B. (2020). Systematic review of English early literacy interventions for children who are dual language learners. *Topics in Early Childhood Special Education, 40*(1), 6–23.

Hussar, B., Zhang, J., Hein, S., Wang, K., Roberts, A., Cui, J., . . . Dilig, R. (2020). The Condition of Education 2020 (NCES 2020-144). Retrieved April 14, 2021, from *https://nces.ed.gov/pubsearch/pubsinfo. asp?pubid=2020144.*

Hwang, H., Cabell, S. Q., & Joyner, R. E. (2022). Effects of integrated literacy and content-area instruction on vocabulary and comprehension in the elementary years: A meta-analysis. *Scientific Studies of Reading, 26*, 223–249.

Justice, L. M., Meier, J., & Walpole, S. (2005). Learning new words from storybooks: An efficacy study with at-risk kindergarteners. *Language, Speech, and Hearing Services in Schools, 36*, 17–32.

Kaefer, T. (2018). The role of topic-related background knowledge in visual attention to illustration and children's word learning during shared book reading. *Journal of Research in Reading, 41*(3), 582–596.

Kim, J. S., Relyea, J. E., Burkhauser, M. A., & Scherer, E. (2021). Improving elementary grade students' science and social studies vocabulary knowledge depth, reading comprehension, and argumentative writing: A conceptual replication. *Educational Psychology Review, 33*, 1935–1964.

Knudsen, C. W. (1937). What do educators mean by integration? *Harvard Educational Review, 7*, 15–26.

Larson, A. L., Cyeyk, L. M., Carta, J. J., Hammer, C. S., Baralkt, M. Uchikoshi, Y., . . . Wood, C. (2020). A systematic review of language-focused interventions for young children from culturally and linguistically diverse backgrounds. *Early Childhood Research Quarterly, 50*(1), 157–178.

Lenhart, J., Suggate, S., Lenhard, W., & Vaahtoranta, E. (2020). Shared-reading in small groups: Examining the effects of question demand level and placement. *Cognitive Development, 55*, 2–17.

Lucas, T., & Villegas, A. M. (2011). A framework for preparing linguistically responsive teachers. In T. Lucas (Ed.), *Teacher preparation for linguistically diverse classrooms: A resource for teacher educators* (pp. 55–72). New York: Routledge.

Mancilla-Martinez, J., & McClain, J. B. (2020). What do we know today about the complexity of vocabulary gaps and what do we not know? In E. B. Moje, P. Afflerbach, P. Enciso, & N. K. Lesaux (Eds.), *Handbook of reading research* (5th ed., pp. 216–230). Routledge.

Mangram, J. A., & Watson, A. (2011). Us and them: Social studies teachers' talk about global education. *Journal of Social Studies Research, 35*(1), 95–116.

McTighe, J., & Wiggins, G. (1998). *Understanding by design*. Association for Supervision and Curriculum Development.

Mindes, G. (2005). Social studies in today's early childhood curricula. *Young Children, 60*(5), Article 12.

Mindes, G. (2015). Preschool through grade 3: Pushing up the social studies from early childhood education to the world. *Young Child, 70*(3), 10–15.

Mindes, G., & Newman, M. (2021). *Social studies for young children: Preschool and primary curriculum anchor*. Rowman & Littlefield.

Nagy, W. (2007). Metalinguistic awareness and the vocabulary–comprehension connection. In R. K. Wagner, A. E. Muse, & K. R. Tannenbaum (Eds.), *Vocabulary acquisition: Implications for reading comprehension* (pp. 52–77). Guilford Press.

Nagy, W., & Townsend, D. (2012). Words as tools: Learning academic vocabulary as language acquisition. *Reading Research Quarterly, 47*(1), 91–108.

National Academies of Sciences, Engineering, and Medicine. (2017). *Promoting the Educational success of children and youth learning English: Promising futures*. National Academies Press.

National Assessment of Educational Progress. (2018). Civics, geography, and U.S. history assessments. Retrieved April 14, 2021, from *www.nationsreportcard.gov/highlights/civics/2018*.

National Council for the Social Studies. (1994). *Expectations of excellence: Curriculum standards for social studies*. Author.

National Council for the Social Studies. (2010). *National curriculum standards for social studies: A framework for teaching, learning, and assessment*. Author.

National Council for the Social Studies. (2013). *Social studies for the next generation: Purposes, practices, and implications of the college, career, and civic life (C3): Framework for social studies state standards*. Author.

National Council for the Social Studies. (2017). Powerful, purposeful pedagogy in elementary school social studies: A position statement of the National Council for the Social Studies. *Social Education, 81*(3), 186–189.

National Council for the Social Studies. (2019). Early childhood in the social studies context: A position statement of the National Council for the Social Studies. *Social Education, 83*(3), 167–170.

National Governors Association Center for Best Practices & Council of Chief State School Officers. (2010). *Common Core State Standards for English language arts and literacy in history/social studies, science, and technical subjects*. Authors.

Neuman, S. B. (2006). How we neglect knowledge—and why. *American Educator, 30*(1), 24–27.

Neuman, S. B., & Celano, D. C. (2012). *Giving our children a fighting chance: Poverty, literacy, and the development of information capital*. Teachers College Press.

Neuman, S. B., & Dwyer, J. (2011). Developing vocabulary and conceptual knowledge for low-income preschoolers: A design experiment. *Journal of Literacy Research, 43*(2), 103–129.

Neuman, S. B., & Kaefer, T. (2018). Developing low-income children's vocabulary and content knowledge through a shared book reading program. *Contemporary Educational Psychology, 52*, 15–24.

O'Reilly, T., Wang, Z., & Sabatini, J. (2019). How much knowledge is too little?: When a lack of knowledge becomes a barrier to comprehension. *Psychological Science, 30*(9), 1344–1351.

Peck, C. L., & Herriot, L. (2015). Teachers' beliefs about social studies. In H. Fives & M. G. Gill (Eds.), *International handbook of research on teachers' beliefs* (pp. 387–402). Routledge.

Pinkham, A. M. (2012). Learning by the book—the importance of picture books for children's knowledge acquisition. In A. M. Pinkham, T. Kaefer, & S. B. Neuman (Eds.), *Knowledge development in early childhood* (pp. 90–108). Guilford Press.

Pittman, C. T. (2010). Race and gender oppression in the classroom: The experiences of women faculty of color with white male students. *Teaching Sociology, 38*(3), 183–196.

Pollard-Durodola, S. D., Gonzalez, J. E., Saenz, L., Resendez, N., Kwok, O., Zhu, L., & Davis, H. (2018). The effects of content enriched shared book reading vs. vocabulary-only discussions on the vocabulary outcomes of preschool dual language learners. *Early Education and Development, 29*(2), 245–265.

Pollard-Durodola, S. D., Gonzalez, J. E., Saenz, L., Soares, D., Resendez, N., Kwok, O., . . . Zhu, L. (2016). The effects of content-related shared book reading on the language development of preschool dual-language learners. *Early Childhood Research Quarterly, 36*, 106–121.

Pollard-Durodola, S. D., Gonzalez, J. E., Saenz, L., Soares, D., Resendez, N., & Zhu, L. (2021, July 5). The social validity of content enriched shared book reading vocabulary instruction and preschool DLLs' language outcomes. *Early Education and Development*. [Epub ahead of print] doi:10.1080/10409289.2021.1946761

Pollard-Durodola, S. D., Gonzalez, J. E., & Simmons, D. (2014). Accelerating preschoolers' content vocabulary: Designing a shared book intervention in collaboration with teachers. *NHSA Dialog, 17*(3), 49–75.

Pollard-Durodola, S. D., Gonzalez, J. E., & Simmons, D. C., & Simmons, L. (2015). *Accelerating language skills and content knowledge via shared book reading*. Brookes.

Salinas, C. S., Rodriguez, N. N., & Blevins, B. (2017). Emergent bilinguals in the social studies. In M. M. Manfra & C. M. Bolick (Eds.), *Handbook of social studies research* (pp. 440–460). Wiley.

Saxe, D. W. (2004). On the alleged demise of social studies: The eclectic curriculum in times of standardization—A historical sketch. *International Journal of Social Education, 18*(2), 93–102.

Schaefer, L. M. (2003). *House*. Heinemann.

Sembiante, S. F., Dynia, J. M., Kaderavek, J. N., & Justice, L. M. (2018). Teachers' literal and Inferential1 talk in early childhood and special education classrooms. *Early Education and Development, 29*(1), 14–30.

Sénéchal, M. (1997). The differential effect of storybook reading on preschoolers' acquisition of expressive and receptive vocabulary. *Journal of Child Language, 24*, 123–138.

Silverman, R., & Hines, S. (2009). The effects of multimedia-enhanced instruction on the vocabulary of English-language learners and non-English-language learners in pre-kindergarten through second grade. *Journal of Educational Psychology, 101*(2), 305–314.

Simmons, D. C., Pollard-Durodola, S. D., Gonzalez, J. E., Davis, M., & Simmons, L. (2008). Shared book reading interventions. In S. B. Neuman (Ed.), *Educating the other America* (pp. 187–212). Brookes.

Spycher, P. (2009). Learning academic language through science in two linguistically diverse kindergarten classes. *Elementary School Journal, 109*(4), 359–379.

Stahl, S. A., & Nagy, W. E. (2006). *Teaching word meanings*. Erlbaum.

Strachan, S. L. (2015). Kindergarten students' social studies and content literacy learning from interactive read-alouds. *Journal of Social Studies Research, 39*, 207–223.

Strachan, S. L., & Block, M. K. (2020). Approaching interdisciplinary teaching: Using informational texts during social studies. *Young Children, 75*(4), 38–44.

Subedi, B. (2008). Fostering critical dialogue across cultural differences: A study of immigrant teachers' interventions in diverse schools. *Theory and Research in Social Education, 36*(4), 413–440.

Subedi, B. (2019). Narrating loss, anxiety, and hope: Immigrant youth's narratives of belonging and citizenship. *Journal of Social Studies Research, 43*, 109–121.

Tyner, T., & Kabourek, S. (2020). *Social Studies instruction and reading comprehension: Evidence from the Early Childhood Longitudinal Study*. Thomas B. Fordham Institute.

Verhoeven, L., & Perfetti, C. A. (2011). Second language reading acquisition. Introduction to this special issue: Vocabulary growth and reading skill. *Society for the Scientific Study of Reading, 15*(1), 1–7.

Vygotsky, L. S. (1978). *Mind in society: The development of higher psychological processes*. Harvard University Press.

Wasik, B. A., Bond, M. A., & Hindman, A. (2006). The effects of language and literacy intervention on Head Start children and teachers. *Journal of Educational Psychology, 98*, 63–74.

What Works Clearinghouse. (2015). Intervention report: Shared book reading. Retrieved from *https://ies.ed.gov/ncee/wwc/evidencesnapshot/458*.

Wilkerson, I. (2020). *Caste: The origins of our discontents*. Random House.

Wright, T. S., & Domke, L.M. (2019). The role of language and literacy in K–5 science and social studies standards. *Journal of Literacy Research, 51*(1), 5–29.

Wright, T. S., & Neuman, (2014). Paucity and disparity in kindergarten oral vocabulary instruction. *Journal of Literacy Research, 46,* 330–357.

Yarrow, A. L. (2008). Beyond civics and the 3 R's: Teaching economics in the schools. *History of Education Quarterly, 48*(3), 397–431.

CHAPTER 14

Supporting Integrated Instruction in Science and Literacy in K–2 Classrooms

Tanya S. Wright and Amelia Wenk Gotwals

There is growing agreement about the importance of integrating science and literacy (i.e., oral and written language practices) learning in the elementary grades (e.g., Cervetti, 2021). This focus on integrated science and literacy development aligns with theories of text comprehension (e.g., Kintsch's [1998] construction–integration model), which state that knowledge (e.g., science knowledge) is critical for text comprehension; that is, even if children can decode words, if they have limited knowledge and vocabulary related to the topic of a text, they are likely to have difficulty comprehending the text (e.g., for reviews see Wright & Cervetti, 2017; Cervetti & Wright, 2020). This suggests that if we want children to comprehend texts about science, we should promote integration of science and literacy from the start of elementary school while children are learning to read independently. Our work has focused on this integration in early elementary grades as a way to promote both literacy goals and learning goals that science educators have for young children (e.g., Wright & Gotwals, 2017a; Gotwals, Wright, Domke, & Anderson, 2022).

In this chapter, we begin by situating our work in the broader research on science and literacy integration and explain why we have taken a disciplinary literacy perspective in our work. We then highlight our research and consider challenges and opportunities for future research in this area.

Ways to Integrate Science and Literacy

Many schools maintain a siloed view of elementary learning, in which more time on English language arts (ELA) means less attention to other subjects, typically pushing out science from the enacted curriculum (Blank, 2013; Plumley, 2019). In response, scholars have focused on integrating science and literacy learning in order to support learning goals for both subjects, while reducing the competition for time in the elementary school day (Cervetti, 2021). There are two primary ways that researchers have thought about the integration of science with literacy. One of these has been to focus on building science knowledge and vocabulary as part of or to supplement the ELA curriculum, sometimes referred to as "content-rich" or "knowledge-building" ELA approaches (e.g., see Cabell & Hwang, 2020, for a review; Cabell & Hwang, Chapter 15, this volume). For young children, educators have worked to supplement the ELA curriculum with reading opportunities that build knowledge and vocabulary in a content area. Studies with young children that have focused specifically on building children's science vocabulary through shared book reading revealed that young children learned a substantial number of sophisticated science words that were taught (e.g., Neuman, Newman, & Dwyer, 2011) and that knowledge of these words can support children in expressing understanding of science concepts (Spycher, 2009).

For example, Spycher (2009) compared the effectiveness of explicit and implicit approaches to science vocabulary instruction for kindergartners during read-alouds. Spycher found that kindergarteners who participated in the explicit intervention (including child-friendly definitions, examples, generating sentences with words, answering questions) had higher scores on vocabulary measures and were better able to articulate science concepts than peers who listened solely to science read-alouds. While there is evidence that these content-rich ELA approaches support literacy goals by building knowledge and vocabulary for reading science texts, these programs do not attend to the full range of learning goals for children's science learning.

Children's Science Learning

The Framework for K–12 Science Education (National Research Council [NRC], 2012), which informed the Next Generation Science Standards (NGSS; Next Generation Science Standards Lead States, 2013), summarized research that suggests that students learn science best when they are engaged in the practices of science rather than learning about science content separately from the "doing of" science. In order to support this shift in instruction, the Framework outlines three dimensions of science that were interwoven to create the standards: (1) science and engineering practices (SEPs); (2) disciplinary core ideas

(DCIs); and (3) crosscutting concepts (CCCs). The SEPs represent the multiple ways of knowing and doing that scientists and engineers use to study the natural and designed world. The DCIs include rich concepts that have broad importance within the discipline and provide a key for understanding and investigating complex ideas and solving problems. The CCCs are concepts that can provide an organizational framework to connect the disciplines to support a coherent view of the world. See Table 14.1 for details on each dimension.

The goal of NGSS is to promote "three-dimensional" instruction such that all dimensions are woven together to support rich opportunities for making sense of phenomena (i.e., events that occur in the universe that can be explained or predicted using science knowledge; NRC, 2012). For example, in one of our curricular units, students begin by looking at pictures of plants growing in unusual places (e.g., cracks in a sidewalk, out of buildings) and work to make sense of how this could happen. This focus on scientific sensemaking (Schwarz, Braaten, Haverly, & de los Santos, 2021), and engaging in the practices of scientists and engineers, opens up opportunities for young children to be introduced to disciplinary literacy practices that support both science and literacy learning (Wright & Domke, 2019). For example, as students attempt to figure out how plants grow in unusual places, they need to ask questions, design and carry out investigations, analyze data, and obtain information from texts. Therefore, reading about science (i.e., obtaining

TABLE 14.1. Three Dimensions of the Next Generation Science Standards

Science and engineering practices	Disciplinary core ideas	Crosscutting concepts
1. Asking questions (for science) and defining problems (for engineering)	1. Physical sciences	1. Patterns
2. Developing and using models	2. Life sciences	2. Cause and effect: mechanism and explanation
3. Planning and carrying out investigations	3. Earth and space sciences	3. Scale, proportion, and quantity
4. Analyzing and interpreting data	4. Engineering, technology, and application of science	4. Systems and system models
5. Using mathematical and computational thinking		5. Energy and matter: flows, cycles, and conservation
6. Constructing explanations (for science) and designing solutions (for engineering)		6. Structure and function
7. Engaging in argument from evidence		7. Stability and change
8. Obtaining, evaluating, and communicating information		

information from texts) reflects only a small part of science learning for young children, and integrating readings on science topics into ELA could never replace opportunities for children to engage in three-dimensional science learning.

These understandings led us to our focus on integrating opportunities for supporting oral and written language practices into science. Our work on the SOLID Start project (Science, Oral Language, and Literacy Development from the Start of Elementary School; *solidstart.msu.edu*)[1] uses a disciplinary literacy framework to consider the ways that science instruction might enhance opportunities for literacy learning in the elementary grades, with a particular focus on developing these learning opportunities from kindergarten through second grade children.

Why Disciplinary Literacy for Young Children?

Scholars who focus on disciplinary literacy conceptualize the use of written texts and oral language practices as ways of communicating within a discipline (e.g., Fang, 2012; Fang & Schleppegrell, 2010; Lemke, 1990; Schleppegrell, 2001; C. Shanahan, Shanahan, & Misischia, 2011). Disciplinary literacies are considered cultural practices of the discipline (e.g., Engle & Conant, 2002; Moje, 2007). Fang (2012) defined *disciplinary literacy* as "the ability to engage in social, semiotic, and cognitive practices consistent with those of content experts" (p. 19) and that it is "grounded in the beliefs that reading and writing are integral to disciplinary practices and that disciplines differ not only in content but also in the ways this content is produced, communicated, and critiqued" (pp. 19–20). Therefore, as part of participating in disciplinary learning, students need to learn about the literacies of that discipline. ELA instruction may not support students in learning these discipline-specific oral and written language practices (e.g., T. Shanahan & Shanahan, 2008).

Our work builds on theoretical frameworks that view disciplinary literacies as cultural practices, but we focus specifically on understanding the ways that young children can begin to engage in the practices of the science community as novices. Although much of the literature on disciplinary literacy has focused on adolescent learners (e.g., Fang & Schleppegrell, 2010; Moje, 2015; T. Shanahan & Shanahan, 2008), recently scholars have argued that young children should be apprenticed into disciplinary

literacy practices from an early age in a developmentally appropriate manner (C. Shanahan & Shanahan, 2014; Wright & Gotwals, 2017a, 2017b). We argue that early elementary teachers *can* and *should* support children's participation in disciplinary literacy practices as children engage in science learning and that a focus on *sense-making* allows for this integration of science and disciplinary literacy practices, because it involves using ideas, language, evidence, and experiences to figure out how and why the world works (Gotwals et al., 2022; Schwarz et al., 2021; Wright & Gotwals, 2017a). This type of sense-making involves engaging in oral and written language practices of the discipline (e.g., Lee, 2019; Wright & Domke, 2019). For example, beginning in kindergarten, the NGSS expects children to be able to "share observations" and "construct an argument supported by evidence."

However, without teacher support, children are unlikely to adopt general or more specific epistemic norms of science discourse (NRC, 2007, 2012). Therefore, elementary teachers need to provide opportunities for children to construct science knowledge by engaging in science practices (e.g., investigating science phenomena) and also to make explicit the disciplinary literacy practices of the science community. For example, Danish and Saleh (2015) studied a class of first- and second-grade students as they learned to critique and discuss their peers' scientific representations in terms of how well they conveyed scientific information. The teacher asked what the creators were aiming to communicate before the class critiqued and discussed their work, and teachers supported students to co-construct a list of criteria for what constitutes a good science representation before students discussed which of two drawings was the better scientific drawing and why. Children voted on which drawing best met the criteria. Over time, children moved from voting for drawings based on personal preference toward using scientific criteria for useful and meaningful representations. Thus, students were not just asked to engage in literacy practices (e.g., make a representation that conveys meaning), but they also discuss what makes this practice discipline-specific (i.e., What type of representation works for science?).

Our SOLID Start Approach

While these theories support our understanding of the learning we would like to see for young children, supporting this type of integrated science and literacy instruction is difficult, especially for early elementary teachers, many of whom do not have strong backgrounds in science or access to curricular resources (Davis, Petish, & Smithey, 2006). Therefore, in our work, we have explored what it looks like for young children to participate in the disciplinary literacy practices of science while they are still learning to read and write independently, and how to support teachers in creating these opportunities for young children.

Just as "content-rich" programs that integrate science content into ELA cannot replace opportunities for science learning, our work cannot replace opportunities for intensive focus on foundational literacy skills and on reading and writing literature that are crucial for literacy development in the early grades and that we would expect to be addressed during ELA times. In our work, we do not focus on teaching children to decode texts, nor do we work with fictional texts during science learning (i.e., because if we take a disciplinary literacy perspective, it would be atypical for scientists to use fiction as part of science practices). We address standards for speaking, listening, language, and informational text reading and writing as these align with science learning.

Our Research

A critical first step in our work has been trying to learn more about the opportunities for literacy development that also support science learning for young children (Wright & Domke, 2019). As we worked to gain this understanding, we engaged in a content analysis of the *Framework for K–12 Science Education* (NRC, 2012), which provides the theoretical basis for the NGSS, as well as of performance expectations for children in the elementary grades (NGSS Lead States, 2013). The goal of this work was to understand messages about the role of literacy in science learning. Our findings showed a substantial emphasis on supporting literacy for science learning. For example, in the *Framework*, we found and analyzed 723 sentences that addressed literacy out of 4,137 sentences, or approximately 17% of this text that serves as guidance for science education. We found a heavy emphasis on terms that align with literacy practices, such as *model/representation, explain/design solutions,*

argue, ask questions/define problems, communicate, discuss, text, describe, all of which indicate a clear need for oral and written language practices. The authors of this consensus document clearly state:

> Any education in science and engineering needs to develop students' ability to read and produce domain-specific text. As such, every science or engineering lesson is in part a language lesson, particularly reading and producing the genres of texts that are intrinsic to science and engineering. (NRC, 2012, p. 76)

The *Framework* documents also emphasize the importance of apprenticing young children into discipline-specific practices through discussion, beginning in the elementary grades, for example, that "students need to understand how to participate in scientific discussions, how to adopt a critical stance while respecting the contributions of others, and how to ask questions and revise their own opinions" (NRC, 2012, p. 252). When we analyzed performance expectations for elementary students in NGSS, we found that these reflected the emphasis of the framework. Table 14.2 shows typical expectations for K–2 students, and phrases are highlighted to emphasize the need for science-specific oral and written language to accomplish these learning goals. Overall, it is clear from these analyses that meeting science standards will require new and challenging oral and written language practices for young children, and instruction for young children will need to address disciplinary literacy beginning in kindergarten. Yet elementary teachers may not have the supports that they need (e.g., curriculum materials, professional learning opportunities) to enact this type of ambitious instruction in K-2 classrooms.

Development of the SOLID Start Curriculum

In response to the lack of integrated and standards-aligned science and disciplinary literacy curriculum materials for K–2, we have developed open-access curricular units that engage young children in scientific sense-making and disciplinary literacy (*solidstart.msu.edu*; Wright & Gotwals, 2017a, 2017b). Our units are structured around intriguing and accessible anchoring phenomena and unit-driving questions that can be answered using data from explorations and informational texts (i.e., including digital media).

TABLE 14.2. Sample Performance Expectations from NGSS That Emphasize Disciplinary Literacy Practices

K-ESS2-2. *Construct an argument* supported by evidence for how plants and animals (including humans) can change the environment to meet their needs.

K-ESS3-3. *Communicate solutions* that will reduce the impact of humans on the land, water, air, and/or other living things in the local environment.

1-LS1-2. *Read texts and use media* to determine patterns in behavior of parents and offspring that help offspring survive.

1-ESS1-1. Use observations of the sun, moon, and stars to *describe patterns* that can be predicted.
1-PS4-2. Make observations *to construct an evidence-based account* that objects can be seen only when illuminated.

2-ESS2-2. *Develop a model to represent* the shapes and kinds of land and bodies of water in an area.

K-2-ETS1-1. *Ask questions*, make observations, and *gather information* about a situation people want to change to define a simple problem that can be solved through the development of a new or improved object or tool.

Note. Standards that start with K are for kindergarten, those starting with 1 are for first grade, and those starting with 2 are for second grade. Engineering standards are for K–2.

For example, a first-grade unit, entitled Reading Under Cover, begins with a driving question of "How can I read under the covers when it's dark?" Over the course of the unit, children engage in science and disciplinary literacy practices to figure out that one needs a light source to read under the covers at night. In addition, children also investigate how opaque objects can create shadows and how some reflective objects can act as mirrors. Each lesson within the unit is guided by a set of five instructional strategies (Wright & Gotwals, 2017a, 2017b): *Ask, Explore, Read, Write,* and *Synthesize.* We describe each of these instructional strategies and use examples from the Reading Under Cover unit to illustrate what this looks like in the SOLID Start curriculum.

Ask

As noted earlier, the units are centered on anchoring phenomena and driving questions that are related to real-world problems, and direct children to ask questions about and build explanations of phenomena. In addition, each lesson begins with a smaller-grain-size driving question, which focuses children on the piece of the phenomenon they will work to make sense of in that lesson. For example, lesson-level driving questions for the Reading Under Cover unit include "What happens when we try to read in bed under covers?"; "What happens when we shine light on different objects?"; "What happens when our bodies block light?"; and "What materials create the best shadows?" The last lesson-driving question of the unit, "How can we communicate what we have figured out about

reading under the covers to next year's class?" focuses on the science practice of "communicating information" while also providing the children with an audience for whom to explain their new understandings.

Explore

In each lesson, children actively participate in the science practices (NRC, 2012) to explore phenomena and use oral and written language to make sense of the explorations and their connection to the anchoring phenomenon (Bismack, West, Wright, & Gotwals, 2020; West, Wright, Gotwals, 2020; Wright, Haverly, West, & Gotwals, 2019). Exploration of phenomena is critical, because it facilitates young children's science learning, while increasing their interest in science. For example, in the first lesson of the Reading Under Cover unit, children build forts with a range of materials (e.g., a heavy blanket, a sheet, a clear shower curtain) and share their initial ideas about why it is easier to read under some materials compared to others. Over the course of the unit, children shine flashlights on different materials and keep track of what happens. All of the explorations allow children to work toward an answer to the unit-level driving question.

Read

The ability to read and comprehend science text is critical for engaging in science (Cervetti, Pearson, Bravo, & Barber, 2006; Krajcik & Southerland, 2010; NRC, 2012). While many K–2 children can read some informational texts independently, the texts that we select for SOLID Start focus on ideas that are intended to enhance children's sense-making about phenomena; therefore, we select texts that are more appropriate as read-alouds for this age group. We use texts to support exploration of concepts that children may not be able to directly observe or manipulate and to introduce new vocabulary that helps children to talk about what they have discovered in their explorations (Edwards, Gotwals, & Wright, 2020; Gotwals & Wright, 2017; Wright, 2019, 2020). For example, in the first lesson of the Reading Under Cover unit, the teacher reads aloud a few pages of the book *What Are Shadows and Reflections?* (Johnson, 2014). The teacher stops at certain points during the read-aloud to support students' understanding of vocabulary such as *light source,* and to encourage discussion that makes connections between the text and the exploration for the day (e.g., by saying, "The author talks about many different light sources. What was the light source in our exploration today? If we could change our light source, would it change our observations? How?").

Write

Young children can engage in writing and drawing to support science practices (e.g., keep track of evidence, develop models; Schwartz et al., 2009). Children's written work can provide a meaningful context for teachers to support children's sense-making and press them for evidence-based explanations. Therefore, in SOLID Start curriculum units, young children have opportunities to write as part of engagement in science practices. This includes opportunities for children to draw and write, as well as to engage in shared writing opportunities (i.e., the teacher models science writing or scribes children's ideas). For example, in the first lesson of the Reading Under Cover unit, children draw and label models. Children learn that scientists use models to "show how something looks or how it works to help them make sense of their observations." Figure 14.1 provides an example of Eleanor's model of her findings from the first exploration in the *Reading Under Cover* unit. During the exploration, she tried reading a book under forts made of different materials—a thick blanket, a thin blanket, a sheet, and a clear shower curtain—and has used the model in Figure 14.1 to show which materials work best for reading. While she labels most materials in her representation with "I can read," she writes, "I cant read" for the "thik blanket." Over the course of the unit, students revisit their initial models and revise them based on new information from explorations and readings. For example, they consider what happens when shining a flashlight through each material and label the materials with new vocabulary words such as *opaque* or *transparent.*

Synthesize

Finally, the curriculum materials support teachers in leading discussions at the end of each lesson aimed at helping children make connections within the lesson and across a unit (West, Wright, & Gotwals, 2021; Wright et al., 2019). Discussion about specific investigations, read-alouds, and writing happen as children are engaged in these activities; however, there are also opportunities at the end of each lesson for teachers to support children in synthesizing their ideas by engaging in the disciplinary literacy practices of explanation and argumentation (Duschl & Osborne, 2002; Kim & Hand, 2015; Windschitl, Thompson, Braaten, & Stroupe, 2012). As a way of supporting this type of sense-making, teachers and children make class "summary tables" where they keep track of what they have figured out in each lesson (e.g., using a combination of writing, photographs, and drawing) and refer back to these charts over the course of the unit. For example, in each lesson in the Reading Under Cover unit, the teacher may return to the unit-level driving question and ask children, "What did we figure out today?" And as children suggest answers, the teacher may prompt them with questions such as "How did we figure that out?" or "What is your evidence?"

Curriculum Research Findings

We conducted a study that compared students in seven kindergarten classrooms who used these materials with six business-as-usual (BAU) control classrooms in a community with a high percentage of students growing up in poverty. After a 4-week unit, children in SOLID Start classrooms were significantly more likely to engage in science discourse, make claims and provide evidence-based support for their claims, and apply new science vocabulary in the context of answering questions compared to their BAU peers (Wright & Gotwals, 2017a, 2017b). Holding

FIGURE 14.1. Child's written model from the Reading Undercover Unit.

constant both prior science knowledge (as measured by the SOLID Start preinterview) and oral language ability (as measured by the Peabody Picture Vocabulary Test), children who participated in the SOLID Start curriculum scored, on average, almost 1.6 standard deviations higher on the posttest than students in the comparison group for one unit and 1.2 standard deviations higher for a second SOLID Start unit. While students' prior knowledge in science and their oral language abilities were significant predictors of posttest scores in both models, the effect sizes were minimal to small compared to the effects of the intervention. These findings align with those of other researchers who have engaged children in science learning with integrated literacy opportunities (e.g., Samarapungavan, Patrick, & Mantzicopoulos, 2011).

Development of SOLID Start PD

While we documented significant student learning when teachers used SOLID Start curriculum materials, like others (e.g., Arias, Davis, Marino, Kademian, & Palinscar, 2016), we found that even with these materials, K–2 teachers were not comfortable engaging children in sense-making talk and struggled to support conversations that probed or synthesized children's ideas (Wright & Gotwals, 2017a). Thus, the next step in our project was to design online professional development (PD), which included virtual instructional coaching to support K–2 teachers in integrating science talk into their classroom instruction.

Supporting Talk during Elementary Science

A central component of this initial work was to build a shared vision for high-quality science talk that could be translated into a formative observational tool (i.e., the SOLID Start Tool) for use in PD and instructional coaching. To do this, we engaged in a systematic literature review of 48 studies to understand the characteristics of high-quality science talk in elementary classrooms and research-based instructional strategies for promoting this type of science talk (Gotwals et al., 2022). We used the findings from this literature review to build the SOLID Start Tool (Gotwals & Wright, 2021). Our analysis revealed three major themes about key domains of science talk with instructional strategies to support these themes:

- *Theme 1: Talk that supports equitable student participation and engagement in science.*

The instructional strategies associated with this theme tended to be "domain-general" in the sense that the strategies could be useful across disciplines. For example, instructional strategies included having explicit routines to support student participation in science talk (e.g., Monteira & Jiménez-Aleixandre, 2016), promoting discussion of ideas between teacher and student, as well as between students (e.g., Chen, Hand, & Norton-Meier, 2017), and encouraging students to share their ideas, including their home and community experiences, during science talk (e.g., Pappas, Varelas, Barry, & Rife, 2003). We found that almost all of the studies in our literature review included Theme 1 in the description of high-quality talk, indicating the importance of providing *all* students with rich opportunities to engage in science and disciplinary literacy practices.

- *Theme 2: Talk that supports deepening of science understanding within and across activities.* Instructional strategies associated with this theme included scaffolding talk that supports students in figuring out science phenomena and engineering design problems, supporting the purposeful engagement in science and engineering practices through talk by encouraging students to discuss *why* they are doing certain activities in particular ways, and promoting unit and lesson-level coherence by supporting talk that makes connections between activities within a lesson and/or from lesson to lesson within a unit. For example, Monteira and Jiménez-Aleixandre (2016) studied a kindergarten classroom's 5-month investigation of snails. Their findings emphasized the importance of the teacher's scaffolding of *purposeful observation,* which they defined as, "prolonged systematic observation that has a clear focus, is guided by the teacher, recorded, explicitly discussed, and used to test claims and revise initial models" (p. 1253). During instruction, the teacher led discussions that allowed students to make sense of their observations and experiences in light of their questions. In addition, they found that the teacher explicitly supported discussion of evidence, hypotheses, claims, and testing, and emphasized the need for evidence when making a claim. With this explicit support, children were better able to use evidence in support of their claims about the structures and behaviors of snails during discussions. In addition, Monteira and Jiménez-Aleixandre discussed the importance of *recurrence,* or addressing select questions and topics multiple times in order to allow students to integrate evidence from their experiments, informational texts, and purposeful observation. This continual revisiting of central topics allowed students to better integrate their ideas and revise their understandings during science talk.

- *Theme 3: Talk that develops disciplinary literacy for science.* The instructional strategies in this theme included having contextualized and child-friendly supports for introducing science oral language and vocabulary, scaffolding students' use of science language and vocabulary when engaging in science learning, and providing explicit supports for disciplinary literacy practices. For example, in one study, the authors described how students and teachers discussed multiple meanings of the word *matter* (Pappas et al., 2003) and in another study, teachers supported children in deepening their understanding of what is meant in science by the term *claim,* and what counts as *evidence* as children engaged in oral argumentation (Chen et al., 2017). All studies focused on the contextualized nature of learning science terminology, teaching, and deepening understanding of word meanings, as they were important for students' learning and engagement in science practices. Kerwalla, Petrou, and Scanlon (2013) found that providing sentence stems supported students in planning investigations (e.g., "We will change . . . "; "We will measure . . . "). Studies also supported student attempts at science-specific ways of creating and using text or representations to obtain, evaluate, and communicate information, including discussion of why and how text and representations support science practices (e.g., Danish & Selah, 2015; described earlier).

Tool Development and Initial Findings

We focused on the development of the SOLID Start Tool because research suggests that observational tools like this can effectively provide feedback to support teacher learning, guide viewing of high-quality exemplars of new practices, provide shared criteria to support individualized feedback and instructional coaching, and guide opportunities to engage with other teachers enacting the same new practices through PD communities (Fishman, Marx, Best, & Tal, 2003; Hill, Lynch, Gonzalez, & Pollard, 2020). A main activity in the SOLID Start PD is that teachers work with a coach and within a professional learning community (PLC) to plan for teaching a science lesson; teachers then teach and video-record the science lesson, and then teachers and coaches meet one-on-one and use the SOLID Start Tool to reflect on their lesson. The SOLID Start Tool has been piloted for 2 years with cohorts involved in the SOLID Start PD. Pilot studies indicate that teachers and coaches were able to use the Tool to guide online discussions about instruction in PLC groups and one-on-one coaching sessions. Teachers and coaches used the SOLID Start Tool both to reflect on the lessons that they had taught and to plan for future instruction. The Tool helped to focus these conversations around important characteristics of high-quality science talk and consider instructional strategies that the teachers could try to improve the science talk in their classrooms.

While the first two cohorts of PD provided initial evidence that work with the Tool could support improvements in classroom talk, this work also pointed to key challenges. The biggest challenge was that teachers' ability to enact their learning about science talk was related to the curriculum materials they were using. For this pilot PD work, teachers could work on science talk using the existing science curriculum in their classroom; however, curriculum materials differ substantially in their alignment with NGSS, including whether children are provided with opportunities to engage in both science and disciplinary literacy practices. In a case study of one participating teacher in our PD (Anderson, 2020), the teacher used different curriculum materials across videotaped lessons. In the first lesson, she used materials from Teachers Pay Teachers; in the second lesson, material from a commonly used science curriculum, and her third lesson was downloaded from the SOLID Start website. The curriculum materials in use enhanced or constrained opportunities for facilitating the types of science talk that were learned in the SOLID Start PD, suggesting that PD and coaching alone may not support enactment of science or disciplinary literacy practices if this work is not combined with the use of high-quality curriculum materials.

Future Directions

There is substantial evidence that both science and disciplinary literacy are neglected in the early years of schooling, particularly in schools serving a high percentage of children growing up in poverty (Blank, 2013; Plumley, 2019; Wright & Neuman, 2014). However, our research (Wright & Gotwals, 2017a) and that of others (e.g., Monteira & Jiménez-Aleixandre, 2016) demonstrate learning gains for young children in science and literacy when they engage in rich science learning experiences that include opportunities to engage in disciplinary literacy practices. Our SOLID Start work has shown that young children in kindergarten through second grade can and should be engaged in learning that integrates disciplinary literacy into science at the start of elementary schools, and that we can provide this instruction in ways that are developmentally appropriate. We do not have to wait for children to be able to read and write independently to begin this work. Young children can participate in the practices of the science community as novices, including being introduced to science and disciplinary literacy practices right from the start of school (National Academies of Sciences, Engineering, and Medicine [NASEM], 2021). This work can be done in ways that support both science and literacy learning standards for young children. In contrast to the belief that time on science limits literacy learning opportunities for young children, our work demonstrates that time on science provides and enhances opportunities for supporting oral and written language goals.

Still, there are numerous challenges to the ambitious vision for science and literacy learning described in this chapter. First among these is the persistent belief that time spent on science limits opportunities for supporting early literacy goals. In fact, science is rarely taught in elementary schools (Blank, 2013), and when elementary students are taught science, it often involves disconnected hands-on activities (Plumley, 2019). There is much work to do to convince educators that, in fact, time on science opens opportunities for children's literacy learning, including opportunities to use and practice skills they learn during ELA, as well as opportunities to learn new ways of using literacy that are particularly important to the ways that scientists communicate. In our project, we typically have to work hard to convince educators to try our curriculum materials (even though these materials can be downloaded for free), because of the prevailing view that time spent on science will limit opportunities for children's literacy development. For example, time spent on science may stand in contrast to third-grade reading policies that reflect more limited views of the science of reading and promote the idea that the best way to support children's success is to spend large blocks of time on isolated components of reading (Cummings, 2021). Instead, we argue that an integrated approach enables children to receive additional instruction in many literacy standards when they have opportunities to learn and practice these *both* during ELA and during science instruction.

There continue to be few studies on ways to integrate science and literacy for diverse communities of children from birth through age 8. Our work has focused on schools with a high percentage of children growing up in poverty because of repeated evidence of inequitable instructional opportunities in these schools. Other research teams have found that meaningful experiences with science that emphasize the use of oral and written language for sense-making are particularly supportive for multilingual learners (Lee, 2019) and Indigenous learners (e.g., Bang, Brown, Calabrese-Barton, Rosebery, & Warren, 2017). Also, while there has been some work in this area for young children before elementary school (e.g., French, 2004), future research should continue to explore ways that integrated and interdisciplinary learning can be supportive for preschool children's science and early literacy learning (Clements & Wright, 2022). Therefore, a critical goal for future research is to build on the funds of knowledge that children bring to school as we provide opportunities for engaging young children of diverse cultural and linguistic backgrounds in the work and discourse of science (Bang et al., 2017; Buxton & Lee, 2014; Moll, Amanti, Neff, & Gonzalez, 2006).

Another challenge is that supporting this type of integrated science and literacy instruction is difficult, especially for early elementary teachers, many of whom do not have strong backgrounds in science or access to curricular resources (Davis et al., 2006). Researchers have found mixed results in how curriculum materials and PD have separately led to changes in teachers' instruction (e.g., Arias et al., 2016). We found that teachers engaged young children in more science discourse when provided with SOLID Start curriculum materials. However, the teachers also expressed discomfort with, and often skipped parts of lessons that focused specifically on explanation and argumentation (Wright & Gotwals, 2017a). Curriculum materials alone were not enough to support these practices. Similarly, PD alone has had mixed results on improving teachers' instruction but it can be supportive if situated in teachers' own instructional needs and related to the curriculum they intend to teach (e.g., Anderson, 2020; Hill et al., 2020). Therefore, elementary teachers need coherent systems of support in order to enact the ambitious view of science and disciplinary literacy instruction that we have argued for in this chapter.

Despite some understanding of how to support this teacher learning, results suggest that reforms often fall short of providing meaningful PD that promotes change (e.g., Darling-Hammond, Wei, Andree, Richardson, & Orphanos, 2009; Cunningham, Firestone, & Zegers, Chapter 18, this volume). One reason for these inconsistent findings may be that teacher learning opportunities have relied on individual tools (e.g., curricula or observational protocols or coaching) rather than on coherent systems of support. For example, a recent meta-analysis emphasizes the importance of combining curriculum resources with PD and coaching to support teachers' science, technology engineering, and mathematics (STEM) instruction (Hill et al., 2020). Yet few studies have examined how coherent systems of PD can improve integrated science and disciplinary literacy instruction in grades K–2. Thus, future research must focus on investigating how to best combine curriculum and PD opportunities to support early elementary teachers' instruction over time as they engage children in science and disciplinary literacy practices.

Acknowledgments

The material of SOLID Start project is based on work supported by the National Science Foundation under Grant No. DRL-1620580. Any opinions, findings, and conclusions or recommendations expressed in this material are those of the author(s) and do not necessarily reflect the views of the National Science Foundation. Our SOLID Start research has also been funded by the Spencer Foundation, and the CREATE for STEM Institute at MSU.

Note

1. This material is based on work supported by the National Science Foundation under Grant No. DRL-1620580. Any opinions, findings, and conclusions or recommendations expressed in this

material are those of the author(s) and do not necessarily reflect the views of the National Science Foundation. Our SOLID Start research has also been funded by the Spencer Foundation, and the CREATE for STEM Institute at MSU.

References

Anderson, B. E. (2020). *Investigating the nature of teachers' vocabulary and science talk during science instruction in early-elementary classrooms* (Publication No. 28025870). Doctoral dissertation, Michigan State University. ProQuest Dissertations Publishing.

Arias, A. M., Davis, E. A., Marino, J.-C., Kademian, S. M., & Palincsar, A. S. (2016). Teachers' use of educative curriculum materials to engage students in science practices. *International Journal of Science Education, 38*(9), 1504–1526.

Bang, M., Brown, B. A., Calabrese-Barton, A., Rosebery, A. S., & Warren, B. (2017). Toward more equitable learning in science: Expanding relationships among students, teachers, and science practices. In C. V. Schwarz, C. Passmore, & B. J. Reiser (Eds.), *Helping students make sense of the world using next generation science and engineering practices* (pp. 33–58). NSTA Press.

Bismack, A., West, J. M., Wright, T. S., & Gotwals, A. G. (2020). Science and literacy team-up to support young children: SOLID Start science curriculum materials. *Michigan Science Teachers Association Journal, 65*(2), 33–42.

Blank, R. K. (2013). Science instructional time is declining in elementary schools: What are the implications for student achievement and closing the gap? *Science Education, 97*, 830–847.

Buxton, C. A., & Lee, O. (2014). English learners in science education. In N. G. Lederman & S. K. Abell (Eds.), *Handbook of research on science education* (Vol. II, pp. 204–222). Routledge, Taylor & Francis.

Cabell, S. Q., & Hwang, H. (2020). Building content knowledge to boost comprehension in the primary grades. *Reading Research Quarterly, 55*, S99–S107.

Cervetti, G. N. (2021). Science–literacy integration: Content-area literacy or disciplinary literacy? *Language Arts, 98*(6), 340–351.

Cervetti, G. N., Pearson, P. D., Bravo, M. A., & Barber, J. (2006). Reading and writing in the service of inquiry-based science. In R. Douglas, M. Klentschy, & K. Worth (Eds.), *Linking science and literacy in the K–8 classroom* (pp. 221–244). NSTA Press.

Cervetti, G. N., & Wright, T. S. (2020). The role of knowledge in understanding and learning from text. *Handbook of Reading Research, 5*, 237–260.

Chen, Y. C., Hand, B., & Norton-Meier, L. (2017). Teacher roles of questioning in early elementary science classrooms: A framework promoting student cognitive complexities in argumentation. *Research in Science Education, 47*(2), 373–405.

Clements, D. H., & Wright, T. S. (2022). Teaching content in early childhood. In *Developmentally appropriate practice in early childhood programs: Serving children from birth to age 8* (4th ed., pp. 63–72). National Association for the Education of Young Children.

Cummings, A. (2021). Making early literacy policy work in Kentucky: Three considerations for policymakers on the "Read to Succeed" Act. Retrieved from *http://nepc.colorado.edu/publication/literacy*.

Danish, J. A., & Saleh, A. (2015). The impact of classroom context upon 1st and 2nd grade students' critical criteria for science representations. *Instructional Science, 43*(6), 665–682.

Darling-Hammond, L., Wei, R. C., Andree, A., Richardson, N., & Orphanos, S. (2009). Professional learning in the learning profession: A status report on teacher development in the United States and abroad. Retrieved from *www.learningforward.org/docs/pdf/nsdcstudy2009.pdf*.

Davis, E. A., Petish, D., & Smithey, J. (2006). Challenges new science teachers face. *Review of Educational Research, 76*(4), 607–651.

Duschl, R. A., & Osborne, J. (2002). Supporting and promoting argumentation discourse in science education. *Studies in Science Education, 38*, 39–72.

Edwards, K., Gotwals, A. W., Wright, T. S. (2020). The Boxcar Challenge unit: Integrating engineering design, science, and literacy for kindergarten. *Science and Children, 57*(5), 47–53.

Engle, R. A., & Conant, F. R. (2002). Guiding principles for fostering productive disciplinary engagement: Explaining an emergent argument in a community of learners classroom. *Cognition and Instruction, 20*, 399–483.

Fang, Z. (2012). Language correlates of disciplinary literacy. *Topics in Language Disorders, 32*(1), 19–34.

Fang, Z., & Schleppegrell, M. J. (2010). Disciplinary literacies across content areas: Supporting secondary reading through functional language analysis. *Journal of Adolescent and Adult Literacy, 53*, 587–597.

Fishman, B. J., Marx, R. W., Best, S., & Tal, R. T. (2003). Linking teacher and student learning to improve professional development in systemic reform. *Teaching and Teacher Education, 19*, 643–658.

French, L. (2004). Science as the center of a coherent, integrated early childhood curriculum. *Early Childhood Research Quarterly, 19*(1), 138–149.

Gotwals, A. W., & Wright, T. S. (2017). From "Plants don't eat" to "Plants are producers": The role of vocabulary in scientific sense-making. *Science and Children, 55*(3), 44–50.

Gotwals, A. W., Wright, T. S., Domke, L., & Anderson, B. (2022). Science talk in elementary classrooms: A synthesis of the literature. *Elementary School Journal, 122*, 642–673.

Gotwals, A. W., & Wright, T. S. (2021, April). *The Development of the SOLID Start Formative Observation Tool: Promoting Science, Oral Language and Literacy in K–2*. Presented at the National Association of Research in Science Teaching Conference.

Hill, H. C., Lynch, K., Gonzalez, K. E., & Pollard, C. (2020). Professional development that improves STEM outcomes. *Phi Delta Kappan, 101*(5), 50–56.

Johnson, R. (2014). *What are shadows and reflections?* Crabtree.

Kerawalla, L., Petrou, M., & Scanlon, E. (2013). Talk Factory: Supporting "exploratory talk" around an interactive whiteboard in primary school science plenaries, *Technology, Pedagogy and Education, 22*(1), 89–102.

Kim, S., & Hand, B. (2015). An analysis of argumentation discourse patterns in elementary teachers' science classroom discussions. *Journal of Science Teacher Education, 26*, 221–236.

Kintsh, W. (1998). *Comprehension: A paradigm for cognition*. Cambridge University Press.

Krajcik, J. S., & Sutherland, L. M. (2010). Supporting students in developing literacy in science, *Science, 328*(5977), 456–459.

Lee, O. (2019). Aligning English language proficiency standards with content standards: Shared opportunity and responsibility across English learner education and content areas. *Educational Researcher, 48*(8), 534–542.

Lemke, J. L. (1990). *Talking science: Language, learning, and values*. Ablex.

Moll, L., Amanti, C., Neff, D., & Gonzalez, N. (2006). Funds of knowledge for teaching: Using a qualitative approach to connect homes and classrooms. In N. Gonzalez, L. Moll, & C. Amanti (Eds.), *Funds of knowledge* (pp. 83–100). Routledge.

Monteira, S. F., & Jiménez-Aleixandre, M. P. (2016). The practice of using evidence in kindergarten: The role of purposeful observation. *Journal of Research in Science Teaching, 53*(8), 1232–1258.

Moje, E. B. (2007). Developing socially just subject-matter instruction: A review of the literature on disciplinary literacy teaching. *Review of Research in Education, 31*(1), 1–44.

Moje, E. B. (2015). Doing and teaching disciplinary literacy with adolescent learners: A social and cultural enterprise. *Harvard Educational Review, 85*, 254–278.

National Academies of Sciences, Engineering, and Medicine. (2021) *Science and engineering in preschool through elementary grades: The brilliance of children and the strengths of educators*. National Academies Press.

National Research Council. (2007). *Taking science to school: Learning and teaching science in grades K–8*. National Academies Press.

National Research Council. (Ed.). (2012). *A framework for K–12 science education: Practices, crosscutting concepts, and core ideas*. National Academies Press.

Neuman, S. B., Newman, E. H., & Dwyer, J. (2011). Educational effects of a vocabulary intervention on preschoolers' word knowledge and conceptual development: A cluster-randomized trial. *Reading Research Quarterly, 46*, 249–272.

Next Generation Science Standards (NGSS) Lead States. (2013). Next Generation Science Standards: For states, by states. Retrieved from *www.nextgenscience.org/search-standards-dci*.

Pappas, C. C., Varelas, M., Barry, A., & Rife, A. (2003). Dialogic inquiry around information texts: The role of intertextuality in constructing scientific understandings in urban primary classrooms. *Linguistics and Education, 13*(4), 435–482.

Plumley, C. L. (2019). *2018 NSSME+: Status of elementary school science*. Horizon Research.

Samarapungavan, A., Patrick, H., & Mantzicopoulos, P. (2011). What kindergarten students learn in inquiry-based science classrooms. *Cognition and Instruction, 29*(4), 416–470.

Schleppegrell, M. J. (2001) Linguistic features of the language of schooling. *Linguistics and Education, 12*, 431–459.

Schwarz, C., Reiser, B, Davis, B., Kenyon, L, Acher, A., Fortus, D., . . . Krajcik, J. (2009). Developing a learning progression for scientific modeling: Making scientific modeling accessible and meaningful for learners. *Journal for Research in Science Teaching, 6*, 632–654.

Schwarz, C. V., Braaten, M., Haverly, C., & de los Santos, E. X. (2021). Using sense-making moments to understand how elementary teachers' interactions expand, maintain, or shut down sense-making in science. *Cognition and Instruction, 39*, 113–148.

Shanahan, C., & Shanahan, T. (2014). Does disciplinary literacy have a place in elementary school? *Reading Teacher, 67*, 636–639.

Shanahan, C., Shanahan, T., & Misischia, C. (2011). Analysis of expert readers in three disciplines history, mathematics, and chemistry. *Journal of Literacy Research, 43*, 393–429.

Shanahan, T., & Shanahan, C. (2008). Teaching disciplinary literacy to adolescents: Rethinking content-area literacy. *Harvard Educational Review, 78*, 40–59.

Spycher, P. (2009). Learning academic language through science in two linguistically diverse kindergarten classes. *Elementary School Journal, 109*(4), 359–379.

West, J. M., Wright, T. S., & Gotwals, A. W. (2021). Supporting discussions: Moving kindergarteners' conversations forward. *Reading Teacher, 74*(6) 703–712.

Windschitl, M., Thompson, J., Braaten, M., & Stroupe, D. (2012). Proposing a core set of instructional practices and tools for teachers of science. *Science Education, 96*, 878–903.

Wright, T. S. (2019). Reading to learn from the start: The power of interactive read-alouds. *American Educator, 42*, 4–8.

Wright, T. S. (2020). *A teacher's guide to vocabulary development across the day (K–3): The Classroom Essentials Series*. Heinemann.

Wright, T. S., & Cervetti, G. N. (2017). A systematic review of the research on vocabulary instruction that impacts text comprehension. *Reading Research Quarterly, 52*(2), 203–226.

Wright, T. S., & Domke, L. M. (2019). The role of language and literacy in K–5 science and social studies standards. *Journal of Literacy Research, 51*(1), 5–29.

Wright, T. S., Haverly, C., West, J., & Gotwals, A. W. (2019). Discussion supports sense-making within and across lessons: Promoting coherent learning about weather forecasting in kindergarten. *Science and Children, 57*, 50–56.

Wright, T. S., & Gotwals, A. W. (2017a). Supporting kindergartners' science talk in the context of an integrated science and disciplinary literacy curriculum. *Elementary School Journal, 117*, 513–537.

Wright, T. S., & Gotwals, A. W. (2017b). Supporting disciplinary talk from the start of school: Teaching children to think and talk like scientists. *Reading Teacher, 71*, 189–197.

Wright, T. S., & Neuman, S. B. (2014). Paucity and disparity in kindergarten oral vocabulary instruction. *Journal of Literacy Research, 46*, 330–357.

CHAPTER 15

Leveraging Content-Rich English Language Arts Instruction in the Early Grades to Improve Children's Language Comprehension

Sonia Q. Cabell and HyeJin Hwang

Customarily six to eight ushers create the arch. The ushers may be commissioned officers from different branches of service and, thus, in different uniforms. If that many ushers are not needed, other military guests may be asked in advance to assist the ushers in performing the service. (Crossley & Keller, 1996, p. 258)

Do you understand this passage? You might understand all the words in the passage, but do you really know what it is trying to communicate? When presenting this passage to educators during professional development workshops, many have thought that it describes a funeral. However, it actually describes the Arch of Sabers ceremony at the end of a military wedding. To comprehend this passage, we need to not only understand the language used in the passage (e.g., vocabulary, syntax), but also need to have and use relevant background knowledge about the topic to make inferences (e.g., what service is being described) and learn from the text (e.g., a military wedding ceremony; Kintsch, 1998). When we don't have the background knowledge for a given text, it becomes difficult to understand it, or learn from it.

Oral language skills underlie our ability to comprehend text we read or that is read aloud to us (e.g., Language and Reading Research Consortium [LARRC], Jiang, & Logan, 2019; Jus-tice & Jiang, Chapter 11, this volume). Also, the knowledge that we bring to a text is the key determinant in how much we understand that text (Anderson & Pearson, 1984). For young children in the early grades, the integration of oral language and content knowledge instruction may be a more powerful approach to improving language comprehension than traditional instruction, which siloes instruction within subjects (i.e., language and literacy teaching in the English language arts [ELA] subject and content knowledge teaching within science and social studies; Hwang, Cabell, & Joyner, 2022a). We consider *content-rich ELA instruction* as instruction that integrates both literacy and science and/or social studies within the ELA instructional setting. ELA is simultaneously leveraged for building content knowledge (i.e., knowledge of the social and natural world) and literacy learning. For the purposes of this chapter, we define *literacy* to broadly encompass both oral language skills and code-related skills. However, it is important to note that the integration that takes place in content-rich ELA instruction in the early grades primarily involves oral language skills; therefore, we focus attention on efforts to improve language comprehension (and not decoding) per the simple view of reading (Gough & Tunmer, 1986).

We begin by describing efforts to improve children's oral language skills in school-based settings, with a particular emphasis on the utility of teacher–child conversations. We then discuss how content-rich ELA instruction can potentially improve teacher–child conversations in ways that can promote oral language development, particularly in the interactive read-aloud context. Next, we provide evidence regarding the effects of integrated approaches more generally, and content-rich ELA approaches more specifically, in elementary school settings, describing common instructional features of content-rich ELA approaches among studies. Finally, we highlight preliminary findings from two recent randomized controlled trials conducted by our research team of a widely used content-rich ELA curriculum in kindergarten classrooms, and we recommend future research directions.

Efforts to Improve Oral Language Skills

Language comprehension is an essential aspect of reading ability that enables an individual to read for understanding (Gough & Tunmer, 1986; Petscher et al., 2020), with the ultimate purpose of reading being to simultaneously extract and construct meaning from text (RAND Reading Study Group, 2002). *Language comprehension* is often characterized by the oral language skills that comprise it, both lower-level or foundational skills (e.g., vocabulary, syntactical knowledge) and higher-level language skills (e.g., inferencing, comprehension monitoring; Justice & Cabell, 2022). When considering their relation to literacy, lower- and higher-level oral language skills allow children to both understand and use the formal language that is commonly privileged in school environments and in texts (sometimes referred to as *academic language;* Foorman et al., 2016). Evidence indicates that strong oral language skills in the early years support language comprehension, which in turn supports reading comprehension (Kendeou, van den Broek, White, & Lynch, 2009; LARRC, 2015; LARRC, Jiang, & Logan, 2019; Scarborough, 2001; Storch &

Whitehurst, 2002; Vellutino, Tunmer, Jaccard, & Chen, 2007).

The Importance of Conversations

The development of oral language begins at birth, as children engage in daily interactions with caregivers around them. They incrementally learn language as a result of a multitude of conversations, with understandings of concepts deepening over time with multiple experiences with words and ideas (Rowe, Romeo, & Leech, Chapter 2, this volume). Thus, the early childhood period is an essential time for improving children's oral language skills in ways that promote later success in literacy. Preschool and kindergarten teachers' complexity of language use in the classroom is well correlated with growth in children's vocabulary and syntax (Farrow, Wasik, & Hindman, 2020; Huttenlocher, Vasilyeva, Cymerman, & Levine, 2002). One reason for this may be that children are likely to mirror the complexity of teachers' utterances and vice versa (Justice, McGinty, Zucker, Cabell, & Piasta, 2013). Consequently, much research has sought to improve the quality of teacher–child conversations (e.g., Cabell et al., 2011; Zucker et al., 2019).

Both theory and research indicate that adult–child conversational interactions are central to language learning (Rowe & Snow, 2020), playing a more salient role in classroom language environments than the volume of words children hear (Duncan et al., 2020). Indeed, most programs that seek to improve young children's oral language skills involve teacher–child conversations, at least to some degree. Through both informal and structured conversations, children can learn and use novel words (Christ, Wang, & Chiu, 2011) and connect them to other semantically related words (Neuman & Kaefer, 2018). Target vocabulary words can be explicitly taught and discussed with children as part of instructional routines (Beck & McKeown, 2001). Teachers can also use responsive strategies to promote children's active participation in conversations and provide exposure to advanced language models (Dickinson & Porche, 2011; Girolametto, Weitzman, & Greenberg, 2003; Piasta et al., 2012; Wasik & Iannone-Campbell, 2012). In particular, strategies to elicit and extend talk promote back-and-forth responsive conversations. One way to *elicit* children's talk is to ask open-ended questions, which typically cannot be answered adequately by a single-word response (Justice, Weber, Ezell, & Bakeman, 2002). Teachers can follow a child's contribution to a conversation by using an *extension* that continues the child's conversational topic and provide more information and explanation. The use of elicitations and extensions not only maintains conversational turns between speakers but can also promote vocabulary learning (Cabell, Justice, McGinty, DeCoster, & Forston, 2015; McCathren, Yoder, & Warren, 1995). In addition to the frequency of strategy use being related to general vocabulary learning in PreK children (Cabell et al., 2011), Cabell and colleagues (2015) further demonstrated that when elicitations and extensions are concentrated within conversations (i.e., back-and-forth turns that remained on a single topic), this topic-focused use is uniquely related to general vocabulary development.

Interactive read-alouds can serve as an instructional context for conversations that are topic-focused. Extratextual conversations (i.e., talk that goes beyond the text) that takes place before, during, and after reading aloud to children relates to children's vocabulary development not only in PreK but also through the end of kindergarten (Cabell et al., 2019; Gonzalez et al., 2014; Zucker, Cabell, Justice, Pentimonti, & Kaderavek, 2013). One reason for this relation may be that the read-aloud context affords teachers the opportunity for concentrated episodes of conversation around particular topics that expose children to academic vocabulary and help to build semantic networks of related words and ideas. Teachers can leverage texts to explicitly teach vocabulary words, involving children in discussion about the meanings of words (e.g., Zucker et al., 2019). Beyond vocabulary learning, texts read aloud to children often feature more complex syntax than texts students are reading on their own. Further, informational texts, which provide information about the social or natural world (Duke, Caughlan, Juzwik, & Martin, 2012), appear to influence teacher-child conversations by promoting the use of inferential language for both teachers and children (Price, Bradley, & Smith, 2012; Zucker, Justice, Piasta, & Kaderavek, 2010).

Yet research on improving children's oral language skills in school-based settings has demonstrated an uneven landscape (Dickinson, Freiberg, & Barnes, 2011). There are indeed positive effects of oral language instruction on young children's learning (Silverman, Johnson, Keane, & Khanna, 2020). However, findings have consistently demonstrated that although proximal skills are improved, it is difficult to for learning to transfer to more distal standardized measures of oral language (Cabell et al., 2011; Marulis & Neuman, 2010; Piasta et al., 2012). For example, a common research finding in PreK and kindergarten settings is that students learn the words that are taught when teachers explicitly teach target vocabulary words, but this doesn't often transfer to more generalized vocabulary learning (e.g., Coyne et al., 2022; Marulis & Neuman, 2010; with a few notable exceptions, including Gonzalez et al., 2011; Lonigan, Farver, Phillips, & Clancy-Menchetti, 2011; Neuman & Kaefer, 2018; Wasik & Hindman, 2020). In addition to vocabulary outcomes, Piasta et al. (2012) demonstrated that a conversational responsivity intervention improved the complexity of PreK children's language (i.e., syntax) within conversations but not more generally on distal, standardized language outcomes (Cabell et al., 2011). These findings are in keeping with meta-analytic findings for a wider grade band (K–5) showing that language comprehension interventions do not demonstrate impact on standardized measures of vocabulary and listening comprehension (Silverman et al., 2020). In short, efforts to improve the component oral language skills contributing to young children's language comprehension could be considerably strengthened.

Building Content Knowledge to Boost Language Comprehension

We posit that one way to boost language comprehension outcomes is to integrate oral language and content knowledge instruction. Despite theoretical and empirical evidence that building content knowledge is important for language comprehension (Cabell & Hwang, 2020), the majority of efforts to improve young children's oral language skills do not place an emphasis on simultaneously building oral language skills and content knowledge. For example, when content words (i.e., words related to science and social studies topics) are taught, they are often introduced to students apart from content knowledge with which the words are associated. Despite growing recognition of the importance of teaching vocabulary, few vocabulary programs have deeply leveraged the connection between vocabulary and content knowledge (Neuman & Kaefer, 2018; Neuman, Samudra, & Danielson, 2021; Williams, Stafford, Lauer, Hall, & Pollini, 2009).

Content-area instruction appears to offer a facilitative context for children to build language skills through meaningful back-and-forth, teacher–child conversations about specific topics (Cabell, DeCoster, LoCasale-Crouch, Hamre, & Pianta, 2013; Kook & Greenfield, 2021). Cabell and colleagues (2013) compared teacher–child interactions across different contexts (i.e., read-aloud, literacy, math, science, social studies, aesthetics) within 314 PreK classrooms. Findings demonstrated that PreK teachers' language modeling was most robust during science instruction (followed by the read-aloud context), suggesting that the science context may lend itself to conversations that feature academic language use by teachers and children, including discussion of vocabulary and ideas that are interrelated. Indeed, Wright and Gotwals (2017) demonstrated that a curriculum that integrates science and literacy improves kindergarten students' science talk (e.g., making claims, using science vocabulary; Wright & Gotwals, Chapter 14, this volume).

It is unclear whether social studies affords a similar benefit as the science context, but it is important to note that in the Cabell et al. (2013) study, the coding of the social studies context was broad and encompassed any time that teachers and children were talking about the social world around them. Other work has demonstrated an impact on children's vocabulary learning using focused social studies curricula (e.g., Gonzalez et al., 2011; Pollard-Durodola & Gonzalez, Chapter 13, this volume). The idea of content-area instruction as potentially facilitative of quality conversational interactions is an important one, as research has demonstrated that teachers have difficulty in improving conversational quality with children without structured support such as a curriculum (Cabell et al., 2011, 2015). In short, quality conversational interactions that promote language learning can more readily take place within integrated literacy and content-area approaches, such as during content-rich ELA instruction.

The Impact of Content-Rich ELA Approaches in Elementary School Settings

Effects of Integrated Literacy and Content-Area Instruction

Before narrowing our focus to the extant research on content-rich ELA instruction in the early grades, we first provide a broader view of integrated approaches. We define *integrated literacy and content-area instruction* as "instruction in which literacy activities (reading and/or writing) serve as a tool to cultivate content knowledge (science and/or social studies) while, at the same time, content teaching serves as a lever to facilitate literacy skills (vocabulary and/or comprehension)" (Hwang, Cabell, & Joyner, 2022a, p. 224). Our definition of integrated instruction is broader than, but inclusive of, content-rich ELA instruction in that both are based on the promise of building content knowledge in supporting language comprehension, deriving from theories and research indicating the facilitative role of content knowledge in comprehension (Hwang, 2019, 2020; Hwang & Duke, 2020; Kendeou, Butterfuss, Kim, & Van Boekel, 2019; Kintsch, 1998).

A meta-analysis by Hwang et al. (2022a) synthesized the effects of integrated literacy and content-area instruction on comprehension (listening and reading) and vocabulary in the elementary years (K–5). The overall effects for comprehension and vocabulary obtained from 35 experimental or quasi-experimental research studies were significant (effect size [ES] = 0.40 for comprehension and ES = 0.91 for vocabulary). Importantly, integrated literacy and content-area instruction was observed to improve students' comprehension in general (ES = 0.25; measured with standardized comprehension measures), in addition to comprehension about a topic students learned during the integrated-approach intervention (ES = 0.54; measured with proximal, researcher-developed comprehension measures). Both effect sizes for comprehension outcomes were large based on Kraft's (2020) benchmark of interpreting effect sizes in the field of education research and are considered to be of policy interest (Hedges & Hedberg, 2007).

For vocabulary outcomes, the effect size was significant for vocabulary knowledge of words taught during the intervention (ES = 0.81) but not for vocabulary in general (i.e., standardized measures). The nonsignificant effect size for general vocabulary knowledge might be partially due to the fact that there were only a few studies that included standardized outcome measures. In addition, a supplementary analysis indicated that integrated literacy and content-area instruction can enhance students' knowledge of content taught in the intervention, which might indicate the potential of integrated approaches in enhancing not only vocabulary and comprehension but also content knowledge.

Effects of Content-Rich ELA Instruction

While *integrated approaches* comprehensively refer to instruction that integrates support for literacy and support for content areas, regardless of the instructional context in which integrated approaches take place (e.g., ELA time, science time, or both ELA and science time), content-rich ELA instruction can be characterized as instruction that centers around building students' content-knowledge *during ELA*. A systematic review was conducted to investigate the effects of content-rich ELA instruction in K–5 settings on comprehension (listening and reading) and vocabulary (Hwang, Cabell, & Joyner, 2022b). The review quantified the overall effects by examining content-rich ELA interventions that exclusively focused on building content knowledge (rather than ELA interventions that also emphasized other components such as motivation) and those that met the quality standards for (quasi-)experimental research design, as delineated by the What Works Clearinghouse (Institute of Education Science [IES], 2017). The results of the meta-analysis of five content-rich ELA interventions were similar to those from the meta-analysis of integrated literacy and content-area instruction. The content-rich ELA interventions were observed to improve comprehension when standardized and proximal measures were considered together (ES = 0.24) and vocabulary being taught during the intervention (ES = 0.29). Moreover, a supplementary analysis showed that content-rich ELA interventions can support content knowledge taught during the intervention (ES = 1.23) and in general (ES = 0.91).

Features of Content-Rich ELA Instruction

The systematic review also analyzed the common characteristics of content-rich ELA approaches and found instructional characteristics that distinguish content-rich ELA instruction from traditional ELA instruction (see also Hwang, Lupo, Cabell, & Wang, 2021). Content-rich ELA instruction is centered on building content knowledge (Cervetti & Hiebert, 2019) by organizing instructional sessions and texts to reflect connections among different pieces of information around content being taught. For example, when content-rich ELA instruction aims to teach content related to economics, such as *exchanges*, instruction sessions would focus on different aspects of exchanges such as *needs and wants* and *products and services*, and students

would interact with conceptually coherent texts about the different aspects of exchanges across instructional sessions. Also, explicit vocabulary instruction is a common feature that teaches words related to content and the relationships among words around the content. This way, instruction can provide multiple opportunities for students to leverage what they know to comprehend new, but related, texts and to learn vocabulary related to one another around content. In addition to engaging students in discussions about content-related texts (often through interactive read-alouds in the primary grades), some interventions involved students in writing about content they learned (e.g., Connor et al., 2017) and engaged in hands-on activities related to content being taught (e.g., Vitale & Romance, 2011, 2012). For example, instruction engaged students in examining different liquids such as water and oil (hands-on activity) when the content goal was to develop knowledge about differences between liquid and solid; then instruction involved students in writing about what they observed during the hands-on activity in their science journals.

In summary, integrated approaches more broadly and content-rich ELA instruction specifically have promise to provide a boost to comprehension outcomes, when compared with traditional instruction. The potential of these approaches has been leveraged to support literacy and content knowledge in mid- or upper-elementary students more than students in K–2, even though the extent which these approaches can support comprehension, vocabulary, and content knowledge appears to be similar across the grades in the elementary years (e.g., Hwang et al., 2022a). Though interventions vary, there are common features of instruction across content-rich ELA approaches that include organization of instruction around science and social studies topics; use of conceptually coherent text sets for interactive read-alouds (particularly in the early grades); explicit vocabulary teaching that includes instruction on the relationships among words; discussion and writing that support knowledge building; and use of hands-on activities.

Evaluating Widely Used Content-Rich ELA Programs

In the past decade, there has been a proliferation of content-rich ELA programs in elementary school settings, and significant public attention has been given to building content knowledge to improve literacy outcomes (Wexler, 2019). Yet, to date, there are only a handful of (quasi-) experimental studies that have examined content-rich ELA instruction in the primary grades (Connor et al., 2017; Duke, Halvorsen, Strachan, Kim, & Konstantopoulos, 2021; Gray, Sirinides, Fink, & Bowden, 2022; Kim, Burkhauser, et al., 2021; Kim, Relyea, Burkhauser, Scherer, & Rich, 2021; Neuman & Kaefer, 2018; Neuman et al., 2021; Vitale & Romance, 2012). Moreover, of the widely used commercially available core ELA programs in the United States, only *ARC Core Kindergarten* (formerly *Zoology One: Kindergarten Research Labs*; American Reading Company) has been rigorously evaluated (Gray et al., 2022). Although results from the Gray et al. study indicated a positive and significant impact on a standardized measure of reading comprehension, it is difficult to parse effects of decoding instruction from language comprehension instruction on that measure for kindergarten children, particularly since the program includes instruction in both code-related and oral language skills. In addition, the study didn't measure effects on components of language comprehension (e.g., vocabulary, listening comprehension). This is an area of great importance to the field of education, as content-rich ELA curricula are being widely used across the nation.

Core Knowledge Language Arts Efficacy Trials

Core Knowledge Language Arts: Knowledge Strand (CKLA: Knowledge; Core Knowledge Foundation & Amplify Education, Inc., 2017) is a widely used ELA program that includes most of the common features distinguishing content-rich ELA instruction from typical literacy instruction in the early grades. The program is designed to build content knowledge and oral language skills within ELA instruction through the vehicle of teacher–child conversations before, during, and after interactive read-alouds of coherent text sets, ordered to sequentially build knowledge across science and social studies topics. In primary grade classrooms (K–2), CKLA: Knowledge is decouplable from the complementary CKLA: Skills Strand, which focuses on decoding instruction. Our team evaluated the CKLA: Knowledge Strand only, and treatment schools were asked to maintain their existing phonics program but replace language comprehension instruction with CKLA: Knowledge. We briefly describe the preliminary results of two randomized controlled trials (RCTs) of CKLA: Knowledge in kindergarten classrooms (Cabell & Hwang, 2020).

The trials took place in two large urban districts in the United States during the 2017–2018 and 2018–2019 school years. In both studies, school-level random assignment resulted in about half of schools assigned to the treatment condition ($n = 11$, $n = 12$) or business-as-usual control condition ($n = 12$, $n = 12$). Kindergarten teachers in treatment schools implemented CKLA: Knowledge for approximately one semester, with science and social studies topics including The Five Senses, Plants, Farms, Native Americans, Seasons and Weather, and Colonial Towns and Townspeople. When combining data across studies to increase statistical power to detect effects, findings indicated that the content-rich ELA curriculum delivered by classroom teachers significantly impacted vocabulary and content knowledge on proximal, researcher-created measures (ES = 0.26–0.93). Notably, a significant effect of the intervention was found on a distal, standardized measure of expressive vocabulary (ES = 0.09) that indexes generalized learning. Significant effects were not found on standardized measures of receptive vocabulary, listening comprehension, and content knowledge. This work not only makes a notable scientific contribution to the scant extant literature based on this topic in kindergarten settings, but it may also have policy and practice implications as one of the first projects to examine the effects of a widely used, content-rich ELA curriculum on children's language comprehension.

Future Directions

The evidence suggests that integrated literacy and content-area instruction offer more of a literacy benefit than traditional siloed instruction (Hwang et al., 2022a). Yet more work is needed to evaluate commercially available, content-rich ELA curricula that are currently in wide use in the United States in the early grades. To our knowledge, there have only been two experimental efforts (Cabell & Hwang, 2020; Gray et al., 2022), and both were in kindergarten only. Multiyear trials of widely used content-rich ELA curricula are needed to examine the impact of building oral language and content knowledge on the components of language comprehension, and eventual reading comprehension. Multiyear trials in the area of language comprehension are rare, with Silverman et al.'s (2020) meta-analysis reporting only one in their corpus of studies (Tong, Irby, Lara-Alecio, Yoon, & Mathes, 2010).

In our review of the extant literature of content-rich ELA instruction, as in other research (Marulis & Neuman, 2010), there remains an limited impact on standardized measures of language. But as Elleman, Lindo, Morphy, and Compton (2009) note, distal measures shouldn't be considered the sole benchmark for determining the utility of an intervention; the value of proximal measures should not be dismissed. And although Silverman et al. (2020) found no effects on standardized measures, "custom measures" of listening comprehension did not reflect what was directly taught and were therefore distal to some degree. Thus, careful attention to the selection of language measures is indispensable.

Much of our interest in this topic has been about whether content-rich ELA instructions "work" to improve language comprehension. Indeed, there is growing evidence to affirmatively answer this question. In addition to intervention research, we need to better understand *why* integrated approaches might work, exploring the mechanisms underlying the relation between an integrated approach and an increase in outcomes in the early primary grades. Prior research in PreK settings provides clues to one potential mechanism—that the content-area context may better facilitate high-quality language interactions (including vocabulary) among teachers and children (Cabell et al., 2013). This finding is important, because if science instruction is indeed a naturally facilitative context for quality language interactions, it could inform the focus of professional development efforts to improve the notoriously hard-to-shift classroom language environment in ways that would accelerate language learning for children and lead to subsequent comprehension improvement. Gray et al. (2022) and Kim, Burkhauser, et al. (2021) highlight student motivation as another potential mechanism (Guthrie et al., 2004, 2009), as content-area learning can be a natural motivator for increased participation in discussions and activities that build knowledge and language.

If the field can better understand the benefit of integrated approaches, these insights could usher in a profound shift in how elementary school programming is considered. In the current U.S. public school system, as early as kindergarten, teachers use distinct curriculum materials for each subject, whose content does not often connect across a given day. Although content-rich ELA curricula in wide use today seek to integrate content and literacy, they are not necessarily designed to replace science and social studies curricula. There may be other ways to consider integration and cohesion across subject areas (Duke, Lindsey, & Wise, Chapter 16, this volume). Rather than having separate ELA, science, and social studies curricula, innovative comprehensive curricula (used beyond the ELA instructional block) could be embraced that provide children with a coherent learning experience across disciplines that also boosts their language and literacy skills. These curricula, and associated professional development, could support teachers in improving the quality of literacy instruction for all children.

Acknowledgments

Portions of this work were funded by the Institute of Education Sciences (IES), U.S. Department of Education (Grant No. R305A170635; Principal Investigator: Sonia Cabell). The opinions expressed are those of the authors and do not represent views of the IES or the U.S. Department of Education. We offer special thanks to James Kim and Thomas White, who served as co-Investigators, and Charles Gale, who assisted in analyses. We also thank Rhonda Raines, who provided insightful feedback on drafts of this chapter.

References

Anderson, R. C., & Pearson, P. D. (1984). A schema-theoretic view of basic processes in reading comprehension. In P. D. Pearson, R. Barr, M. L. Kamil, & P. Mosenthal (Eds.), *Handbook of reading research* (pp. 255–291). Longman.

Beck, I. L., & McKeown, M. G. (2001). Text talk: Capturing the benefits of read-aloud experiences for young children. *Reading Teacher, 55*(1), 10–20.

Cabell, S. Q., DeCoster, J., LoCasale-Crouch, J., Hamre, B. K., & Pianta, R. C. (2013). Variation in the effectiveness of instructional interactions across preschool classroom settings and learning activities. *Early Childhood Research Quarterly, 28*(4), 820–830.

Cabell, S. Q., & Hwang, H. (2020). Building content knowledge to boost comprehension in the primary grades. *Reading Research Quarterly, 55*(1), S99–S107.

Cabell, S. Q., Justice, L. M., McGinty, A. S., DeCoster, J., & Forston, L. D. (2015). Teacher–child conversations in preschool classrooms: Contributions to children's vocabulary development. *Early Childhood Research Quarterly, 30,* 80–92.

Cabell, S. Q., Justice, L. M., Piasta, S. B., Curenton, S. M., Wiggins, A., Turnbull, K. P., & Petscher, Y. (2011). The impact of teacher responsivity education on preschoolers' language and literacy skills. *American Journal of Speech–Language Pathology, 20*(4), 315–330.

Cabell, S. Q., Zucker, T. A., DeCoster, J., Melo, C., Forston, L., & Hamre, B. (2019). Prekindergarten interactive book reading quality and children's language and literacy development: Classroom organization as a moderator. *Early Education and Development, 30*(1), 1–18.

Cervetti, G. N., & Hiebert, E. H. (2019). Knowledge at the center of English language arts instruction. *Reading Teacher, 72*(4), 499–507.

Christ, T., Wang, X. C., & Chiu, M. M. (2011). Using story dictation to support young children's vocabulary development: Outcomes and process. *Early Childhood Research Quarterly, 26*(1), 30–41.

Connor, C. M. D., Dombek, J., Crowe, E. C., Spencer, M., Tighe, E. L., Coffinger, S., . . . Petscher, Y. (2017). Acquiring science and social studies knowledge in kindergarten through fourth grade: Conceptualization, design, implementation, and efficacy testing of content-area literacy instruction (CALI). *Journal of Educational Psychology, 109*(3), 301–320.

Core Knowledge Foundation and Amplify Education, Inc. (2017). *Core Knowledge Language Arts: Knowledge Strand.* Author.

Coyne, M. D., McCoach, D. B., Ware, S. M., Loftus-Rattan, S. M., Baker, D. L., Santoro, L. E., & Oldham, A. C. (2022). Supporting vocabulary development within a multitiered system of support: Evaluating the efficacy of supplementary kindergarten vocabulary intervention. *Journal of Educational Psychology, 114,* 1225–1241.

Crossley, A., & Keller, C. A. (1996). *The Army wife handbook: A complete social guide.* ABI Press.

Dickinson, D. K., Freiberg, J. B., & Barnes, E. M. (2011). Why are so few interventions really effective?: A call for fine-grained research methodology. In S. B. Neuman & D. K. Dickinson (Eds.), *Handbook of early literacy research* (Vol. 3, pp. 337–357). Guilford Press.

Dickinson, D. K., & Porche, M. V. (2011). Relation between language experiences in preschool classrooms and children's kindergarten and fourth-grade language and reading abilities. *Child Development, 82*(3), 870–886.

Duke, N. K., Caughlan, S., Juzwik, M. M., & Martin, N. M. (2012). *Reading and writing genre with purpose in K–8 classrooms.* Heinemann.

Duke, N. K., Halvorsen, A. L., Strachan, S. L., Kim, J., & Konstantopoulos, S. (2021). Putting PjBL to the test: The impact of project-based learning on second graders' social studies and literacy learning and motivation in low-SES school settings. *American Educational Research Journal, 58*(1), 160–200.

Duncan, R. J., King, Y. A., Finders, J. K., Elicker, J., Schmitt, S. A., & Purpura, D. J. (2020). Prekindergarten classroom language environments and children's vocabulary skills. *Journal of Experimental Child Psychology, 194,* Article 104829.

Elleman, A. M., Lindo, E. J., Morphy, P., & Compton, D. L. (2009). The impact of vocabulary instruction on passage-level comprehension of school-age children: A meta-analysis. *Journal of Research on Educational Effectiveness, 2*(1), 1–44.

Farrow, J., Wasik, B. A., & Hindman, A. H. (2020). Exploring the unique contributions of teachers' syntax to preschoolers' and kindergarteners' vocabulary learning. *Early Childhood Research Quarterly, 51,* 178–190.

Foorman, B., Beyler, N., Borradaile, K., Coyne, M., Denton, C.A., Dimino, J., . . . Wissel, S. (2016). *Foundational skills to support reading for understanding in kindergarten through 3rd grade* (NCEE 2016–4008). National Center for Education Evaluation and Regional Assistance, Institute of Education Sciences, U.S. Department of Education.

Girolametto, L., Weitzman, E., & Greenberg, J. (2003). Training day care staff to facilitate children's language. *American Journal of Speech–Language Pathology, 12*(3), 299–311.

Gonzalez, J. E., Pollard-Durodola, S., Simmons, D. C., Taylor, A. B., Davis, M. J., Fogarty, M., & Simmons, L. (2014). Enhancing preschool children's vocabulary: Effects of teacher talk before, during and after shared reading. *Early Childhood Research Quarterly, 29*(2), 214–226.

Gonzalez, J. E., Pollard-Durodola, S., Simmons, D. C., Taylor, A. B., Davis, M. J., Kim, M., & Simmons, L. (2011). Developing low-income preschoolers' social studies and science vocabulary knowledge through content-focused shared book reading. *Journal of Research on Educational Effectiveness, 4*(1), 25–52.

Gough, P. B., & Tunmer, W. E. (1986). Decoding, reading, and reading disability. *Remedial and Special Education, 7*(1), 6–10.

Gray, A. M., Sirinides, P. M., Fink, R. E., & Bowden, A. B. (2022). Integrating literacy and science instruction in kindergarten: Results from the efficacy study of *Zoology One. Journal of*

Research on Educational Effectiveness, 15(1), 1–27.

Guthrie, J. T., McRae, A., Coddington, C. S., Lutz Klauda, S., Wigfield, A., & Barbosa, P. (2009). Impacts of comprehensive reading instruction on diverse outcomes of low- and high-achieving readers. *Journal of Learning Disabilities, 42*(3), 195–214.

Guthrie, J. T., Wigfield, A., Barbosa, P., Perencevich, K. C., Taboada, A., Davis, M. H., . . . Tonks, S. (2004). Increasing reading comprehension and engagement through concept-oriented reading instruction. *Journal of Educational Psychology, 96*(3), 403–423.

Hedges, L. V., & Hedberg, E. C. (2007). Intraclass correlation values for planning group-randomized trials in education. *Educational Evaluation and Policy Analysis, 29*(1), 60–87.

Huttenlocher, J., Vasilyeva, M., Cymerman, E., & Levine, S. (2002). Language input and child syntax. *Cognitive Psychology, 45*(3), 337–374.

Hwang, H. (2019). The role of science domain knowledge and reading motivation in predicting informational and narrative reading comprehension in L1 and L2: An international study. *Learning and Individual Differences, 76*, Article 101782.

Hwang, H. (2020). Early general knowledge predicts English reading growth in bilingual and monolingual students throughout the elementary years. *Elementary School Journal, 121*(1), 154–178.

Hwang, H., Cabell, S. Q., & Joyner, R. E. (2022a). Effects of integrated literacy and content-area instruction on vocabulary and comprehension in the elementary years: A meta-analysis. *Scientific Studies of Reading, 26*, 223–249.

Hwang, H., Cabell, S. Q., & Joyner, R. E. (2022b). Does cultivating content knowledge during literacy instruction support vocabulary and comprehension in the elementary school years? A systematic review. *Reading Psychology.*

Hwang, H., & Duke, N. K. (2020). Content counts and motivation matters: Reading comprehension in third-grade students who are English learners. *AERA Open, 6*(1), 1–17.

Hwang, H., Lupo, S. M., Cabell, S. Q., & Wang, S. (2021). What research says about leveraging the literacy block for learning. *Reading in Virginia, XLII* (2020–2021), 35–48.

Institute of Education Sciences. (2017). *What Works Clearinghouse standards handbook* (Version 4.0). Retrieved from *https://ies.ed.gov/ncee/wwc/docs/referenceresources/wwc_standards_handbook_v4.pdf.*

Justice, L. M., & Cabell, S. Q. (2022). Educational interventions targeting language development. In J. Law, S. Reilly, & C. McKean (Eds.), *Language development: Individual differences in a social context* (pp. 519–538). Cambridge University Press.

Justice, L. M., McGinty, A. S., Zucker, T., Cabell, S. Q., & Piasta, S. B. (2013). Bi-directional dynamics underlie the complexity of talk in teacher–child play-based conversations in classrooms serving at-risk pupils. *Early Childhood Research Quarterly, 28*(3), 496–508.

Justice, L. M., Weber, S. E., Ezell, H. K., & Bakeman, R. (2002). A sequential analysis of children's responsiveness to parental print references during shared book-reading interactions. *American Journal of Speech–Language Pathology, 11*, 30–40.

Kendeou, P., Butterfuss, R., Kim, J., & Van Boekel, M. (2019). Knowledge revision through the lenses of the three-pronged approach. *Memory & Cognition, 47*(1), 33–46.

Kendeou, P., van den Broek, P., White, M. J., & Lynch, J. S. (2009). Predicting reading comprehension in early elementary school: The independent contributions of oral language and decoding skills. *Journal of Educational Psychology, 101*, 765–778.

Kim, J. S., Burkhauser, M. A., Mesite, L. M., Asher, C. A., Relyea, J. E., Fitzgerald, J., & Elmore, J. (2021). Improving reading comprehension, science domain knowledge, and reading engagement through a first-grade content literacy intervention. *Journal of Educational Psychology, 113*(1), Article 3.

Kim, J. S., Relyea, J. E., Burkhauser, M. A., Scherer, E., & Rich, P. (2021). Improving elementary grade students' science and social studies vocabulary knowledge depth, reading comprehension, and argumentative writing: A conceptual replication. *Educational Psychology Review, 33*(4), 1935–1964.

Kintsch, W. (1998). *Comprehension: A paradigm for cognition.* Cambridge University Press.

Kook, J. F., & Greenfield, D. B. (2021). Examining variation in the quality of instructional interaction across teacher-directed activities in head start classrooms. *Journal of Early Childhood Research, 19*(2), 128–144.

Kraft, M. A. (2020). Interpreting effect sizes of education interventions. *Educational Researcher, 49*(4), 241–253.

Language and Reading Research Consortium. (2015). Learning to read: Should we keep things simple? *Reading Research Quarterly, 50*(2), 151–169.

Language and Reading Research Consortium, Jiang, H., & Logan, J. (2019). Improving reading comprehension in the primary grades: Mediated effects of a language-focused classroom intervention. *Journal of Speech, Language, and Hearing Research, 62*, 2812–2828.

Lonigan, C. J., Farver, J. M., Phillips, B. M., &

Clancy-Menchetti, J. (2011). Promoting the development of preschool children's emergent literacy skills: A randomized evaluation of a literacy-focused curriculum and two professional development models. *Reading and Writing, 24*(3), 305–337.

Marulis, L. M., & Neuman, S. B. (2010). The effects of vocabulary intervention on young children's word learning: A meta-analysis. *Review of Educational Research, 80*(3), 300–335.

McCathren, R. B., Yoder, P. J., & Warren, S. F. (1995). The role of directives in early language intervention. *Journal of Early Intervention, 19*(2), 91–101.

Neuman, S. B., & Kaefer, T. (2018). Developing low-income children's vocabulary and content knowledge through a shared book reading program. *Contemporary Educational Psychology, 52*, 15–24.

Neuman, S. B., Samudra, P., & Danielson, K. (2021). Effectiveness of scaling up a vocabulary intervention for low-income children, pre-K through first grade. *Elementary School Journal, 121*(3), 385–409.

Petscher, Y., Cabell, S. Q., Catts, H. W., Compton, D. L., Foorman, B. R., Hart, S. A., . . . Wagner, R. K. (2020). How the science of reading informs 21st-century education. *Reading Research Quarterly, 55*, S267–S282.

Piasta, S. B., Justice, L. M., Cabell, S. Q., Wiggins, A. K., Turnbull, K. P., & Curenton, S. M. (2012). Impact of professional development on preschool teachers' conversational responsivity and children's linguistic productivity and complexity. *Early Childhood Research Quarterly, 27*(3), 387–400.

Price, L. H., Bradley, B. A., & Smith, J. M. (2012). A comparison of preschool teachers' talk during storybook and information book read-alouds. *Early Childhood Research Quarterly, 27*(3), 426–440.

RAND Reading Study Group. (2002). *Reading for understanding: Toward an R&D program in reading comprehension.* RAND.

Rowe, M. L., & Snow, C. E. (2020). Analyzing input quality along three dimensions: Interactive, linguistic, and conceptual. *Journal of Child Language, 47*(1), 5–21.

Scarborough, H. S. (2001). Connecting early language and literacy to later reading (dis)abilities: Evidence, theory, and practice. In S. B. Neuman & D. K. Dickinson (Eds.), *Handbook for research in early literacy* (pp. 97–110). Guilford Press.

Silverman, R. D., Johnson, E., Keane, K., & Khanna, S. (2020). Beyond decoding: A meta-analysis of the effects of language comprehension interventions on K–5 students' language and literacy outcomes. *Reading Research Quarterly, 55*(Suppl. 1), S207–S233.

Storch, S. A., & Whitehurst, G. J. (2002). Oral language and code-related precursors to reading: Evidence from a longitudinal structural model. *Developmental Psychology, 38*, 934–947.

Tong, F., Irby, B. J., Lara-Alecio, R., Yoon, M., & Mathes, P. G. (2010). Hispanic English learners' responses to longitudinal English instructional intervention and the effect of gender: A multilevel analysis. *Elementary School Journal, 110*(4), 542–566.

Vellutino, F. R., Tunmer, W. E., Jaccard, J. J., & Chen, R. (2007). Components of reading ability: Multivariate evidence for a convergent skills model of reading development. *Scientific Studies of Reading, 11*(1), 3–32.

Vitale, M. R., & Romance, N. R. (2011). Adaptation of a knowledge-based instructional intervention to accelerate student learning in science and early literacy in grades 1 and 2. *Journal of Curriculum and Instruction, 5*(2), 79–93.

Vitale, M. R., & Romance, N. R. (2012). Using in-depth science instruction to accelerate student achievement in science and reading comprehension in grades 1–2. *International Journal of Science and Mathematics Education, 10*(2), 457–472.

Wasik, B. A., & Hindman, A. H. (2020). Increasing preschoolers' vocabulary development through a streamlined teacher professional development intervention. *Early Childhood Research Quarterly, 50*, 101–113.

Wasik, B. A., & Iannone-Campbell, C. (2012). Developing vocabulary through purposeful, strategic conversations. *Reading Teacher, 66*(4), 3321–3332.

Wexler, N. (2019). *The knowledge gap: The hidden cause of America's broken education system—and how to fix it.* Avery.

Williams, J., Stafford, K. B., Lauer, K., Hall, K., & Pollini, S. (2009). Embedding reading comprehension training in content-area instruction. *Journal of Educational Psychology, 101*(1), 1–20.

Wright, T. S., & Gotwals, A. W. (2017). Supporting kindergartners' science talk in the context of an integrated science and disciplinary literacy curriculum. *Elementary School Journal, 117*(3), 513–537.

Zucker, T. A., Cabell, S. Q., Justice, L. M., Pentimonti, J. M., & Kaderavek, J. N. (2013). The role of frequent, interactive prekindergarten shared reading in the longitudinal development of language and literacy skills. *Developmental Psychology, 49*(8), 1425–1439.

Zucker, T. A., Carlo, M. S., Landry, S. H., Masood-Saleem, S. S., Williams, J. M., & Bhavsar, V.

(2019). Iterative design and pilot testing of the Developing Talkers tiered academic language curriculum for pre-kindergarten and kindergarten. *Journal of Research on Educational Effectiveness, 12*(2), 274–306.

Zucker, T. A., Justice, L. M., Piasta, S. B., & Kaderavek, J. N. (2010). Preschool teachers' literal and inferential questions and children's responses during whole-class shared reading. *Early Childhood Research Quarterly, 25*(1), 65–83.

CHAPTER 16

Feeding Two Birds with One Hand

Instructional Simultaneity in Early Literacy Education

Nell K. Duke, Julia B. Lindsey, and Crystal N. Wise

As evidenced throughout this volume, a great deal is known about specific foci of instruction, instructional strategies, interventions, and programs that foster early literacy development. In fact, to practitioners, it can feel that too much is known. As a thought experiment, consider a first-grade teacher working to build a research-aligned school day. Imagine that he or she has access to research-tested programs and practices as follows: 10 minutes per day for phonemic awareness instruction; 20 minutes for whole-class phonics instruction; various interventions and approaches to small-group reading instruction at 15 minutes per group times four groups per day; 20 minutes for a whole-class interactive read-aloud and discussion of a literary text; 20 minutes for whole-class reading and discussion of an informational text; 20 minutes for a vocabulary intervention; 15 minutes for a research-tested spelling intervention; 10 minutes for handwriting instruction and practice; and 35 additional minutes of writing instruction and experience in order to meet, along with the handwriting and spelling instruction, the expectation of 1 hour per day of writing instruction from the What Works Clearinghouse Practice Guide on developing effective elementary writers (Graham et al., 2012). Next, consider allocating 60 minutes for mathematics instruction, the recommended 45 minutes for social studies (Council of Chief State School Officers, 2018), and 45 minutes for science and engineering (for which there is not a consensus time allocation but which should be taught "comprehensively, frequently, and consistently taught in all preschool through elementary settings"; National Academies of Sciences, Engineering, and Medicine, 2021). Many scholars recommend that a portion of the day be devoted to an evidence-based social and emotional learning program, in addition to the infusion of work on social and emotional learning throughout the day (e.g., Center for Advancing Social and Emotional Learning, n.d.). For that purpose, we estimate 20 minutes per day. Recommendations for daily recess time vary substantially, from 20 to 60 minutes (Council on School Health, 2013). For the sake of this thought experiment, we set aside 40 minutes. For lunch, the Centers for Disease Control and Prevention (2019) recommends 30 minutes. There is no consensus on the range, amount of time, or weekly number of "specials" (e.g., art, library, music, physical education). We estimate just one special per day at 45 minutes, acknowledging that in some schools there are more (e.g., physical education meets three times per week). At this point, we are up to 8 hours and 15 minutes, nearly 25% more time than the average length of a school day in the United States (6 hours and 40 minutes; National Center for Education Statistics, 2007–2008). Furthermore, we have not necessarily addressed all important instructional targets (e.g., presentation skills, digital literacy) nor have we accounted for transition times between these many parts of the day, transitions to other parts of the school building (e.g., for lunch and specials), time for children to get settled in the morning and to pack up at the end of the day, time for school public address announcements, time for bathroom breaks if those are done as a whole group, and so on. Even with a very efficient approach to these various transitions, the teacher is likely to be at least 2.5 hours a day short. There are quite literally not enough hours in the day.

Perhaps the most obvious solution for inadequate time in the school day is to lengthen the day. However, quite a lot of lengthening would be required—even the states with the longest average school day do not have a day that is nearly long enough for the scenario presented in the previous paragraph (National Center for Education Statistics, 2007–2008). Furthermore, a day that is that long may not be developmentally appropriate for young children. An alternative solution is to cut some portions of the day entirely. In fact, research suggests that this is the de facto response in many places, for example, with social studies receiving less and less attention in early education (e.g., Fitchett & Heafner, 2010). However, for any portion of the day to be cut, there are scholars and advocates who argue that that the loss is unacceptable. For example, there is strong a bipartisan support for instruction in social studies beginning in early education (e.g., Winthrop, 2020). It seems that there are no simple solutions to the problem of inadequate time in the school day.

All domains—academic, social, emotional, and health—should be concerned about how to address the time problem. However, we posit that the field of literacy education has a particular role to play in this dilemma, because it has generated such a large number of research-tested programs, practices, and instructional foci, and because it is often the domain that consumes the largest portion of the school day. Indeed, P. David Pearson has referred to literacy as a "curricular bully" in U.S. classrooms (Cervetti, Pearson, Bravo, & Barber, 2006).

Fortunately, literacy can serve as a leader in tackling the problem of inadequate time in the school day. Literacy has a long history of research documenting the value of addressing more than one instructional target at once, combining instructional targets and practices such that a single portion of the day is achieving multiple instructional goals at once—a phenomenon we are calling *instructional simultaneity*. In this chapter, we discuss research on four forms of instructional simultaneity: (1) addressing multiple reading foundational skills simultaneously, (2) developing literacy bridging processes, (3) addressing multiple language arts processes simultaneously, and (4) providing literacy and content-area instruction simultaneously. We document that each of these forms of instructional simultaneity can indeed achieve the goal of impacting achievement in multiple areas concurrently, thus lightening at least some of the pressure on time in the school day. We conclude with directions for research and practice.

Addressing Multiple Reading Foundational Skills Simultaneously

One area in which benefits of instructional simultaneity are evident is reading foundational skills—concepts of print, phonemic awareness, phonics and word recognition, and fluency (National Governors Association Center for Best Practices & Council of Chief State School Officers, 2010). Most reading foundational skills can be understood as skills that, when used in concert, lead to accurate word recognition. Consider the act of reading a page of an unknown text designed for kindergarten readers, shown in Figure 16.1. To read the two sentences on that page, a reader must understand how to navigate written text embedded in a speech bubble, understand the direction in which we read (left to right in English), identify how words are separated one from the other in print, and understand how punctuation operates (i.e., command of many print concepts). Thus, although print awareness or concepts of print are sometimes viewed as part of language comprehension (Scarborough, 2001), they are essential to word recognition. Other reading foundational skills are also needed in order to read the page in Figure 16.1. To read an unknown single-syllable word, such as *tag,* a reader needs to identify letter forms and their corresponding sounds (phonics or orthographic knowledge) and how to blend those sounds, or phonemes, to pronounce the word (phonemic awareness). To learn to read an irregularly spelled word on the page, such as *you,* efficiently, the child needs to have had previous experience segmenting the word (phonemic awareness) and associating the segmented sounds with the letters that spell them (/y/ spelled *y,* /oo/

spelled *ou*; phonics or orthographic knowledge). Then the child needs to apply the resulting orthographic mapping in order to recognize the word when reading.

We could look at this example as evidence that word reading simply involves adding component skills together, and you could draw the conclusion that teaching each component in isolation will lead to proficiency. However, this does not fit with research findings regarding the development of reading foundational skills. Research suggests that reading foundational skills are reciprocally related (e.g., Clayton, West, Sears, Hulme, & Lervåg, 2020). Rather than adding together completely separate skills, reading foundational skills function in harmony with one another as readers simultaneously apply information about print, phonemic awareness, phonics, and word recognition.

Instructional simultaneity in reading foundational skills already exists in multiple research-based and -tested instructional routines such as high-quality shared reading (e.g., Wesseling, Christmann, & Lachmann, 2017; Zucker, Cabell, Justice, Pentimonti, & Kaderavek, 2013) and interactive writing (e.g., Roth & Guinee, 2011). For example, in interactive writing, the teacher leads the writing of a text, with children contributing to parts of the writing. Interactive writing provides a context in which the teacher

can provide explicit instruction and modeling of print concepts (e.g., where to start writing), phonemic awareness (e.g., segmenting a word to spell it), phonics/spelling, and other aspects of literacy development (e.g., building knowledge of the genre of the text). Well-designed instruction using shared reading and interactive writing techniques can support children's development in a range of reading foundational skills, including phonological awareness, spelling, sound–spelling knowledge, and print concepts. Furthermore, these activities, with the right texts and instructional purposes, can also contribute to children's language and knowledge development.

Many reading researchers have emphasized the critical role of phonemic awareness in learning to read and the importance of including explicit phonemic awareness instruction in early reading acquisition (e.g., Ehri et al., 2001). Phonemic awareness is believed to facilitate children's ability to connect letters and spellings to sounds in order to decode and encode words. Despite decades of research suggesting that children who know some letters are best served by practicing phonemic awareness with letters (National Early Literacy Panel [NELP], 2008; National Reading Panel [NRP], 2000), in practice, many educators and programs continue to separate these skills, with large-swaths of instructional time devoted to oral-only phonemic awareness practice. In fact, in a

FIGURE 16.1. Excerpt from *Tag at the Park* by Julia Lindsey, Illustrated by Diana Galicia Heredia, published in the Great First Eight Curriculum. Copyright © 2022 Regents of the University of Michigan. Reprinted by permission.

recent commentary entitled *They Say You Can Do Phonemic Awareness Instruction "in the Dark," but Should You?: A Critical Evaluation of the Trend Toward Advanced Phonemic Awareness Training,* Clemens and colleagues (2021) express concern about the amount of phonemic awareness instruction occurring independent of letters.

Instructional simultaneity with phonemic awareness and phonics is likely most impactful when phonemic awareness and phonics instruction are well aligned (NRP, 2000). In one lesson, for example, children learning to read regular consonant–vowel–consonant words might review the short sound of the letter *a* while looking at the letter *a*, orally blend segmented sounds into consonant–vowel–consonant words with a medial short *a,* spell and read such words, then read a decodable text with a high proportion of consonant–vowel–consonant words. This type of lesson is not new and should not be seen as controversial: Many research studies focused on foundational reading include protocols like this one (e.g., Denton et al., 2013; Fien et al., 2015). Instructional simultaneity in reading foundational skills is not just a way to save instructional time, it is likely to be far more impactful than isolated activities aiming to target just one of these skills at a time.

Developing Bridging Processes

The simple view of reading, and many variations thereof, depict reading as a product of word recognition and language comprehension (e.g., Gough & Tunmer, 1986; Hoover & Tunmer, 2020). Duke and Cartwright (2021) contend

that reading is better depicted as involving not only word recognition and language comprehension but also a set of bridging processes that are related to both constructs (Orcutt, Johnson, & Kendeou, Chapter 17, this volume). Addressing bridging processes can be seen as another form of instructional simultaneity, as it can foster development of both word recognition and language comprehension in the same instructional activity.

The archetypal bridging process is graphophonological semantic cognitive flexibility. This construct entails the ability to concurrently attend to and actively switch between the letter(s)–sound (graphophonological) relationships and meaning (semantics) of words. For example, a common task to measure and develop graphophonological semantic cognitive flexibility involves sorting words into a two-by-two matrix in which words are related by meaning horizontally and by initial grapheme and phoneme vertically (or vice versa) (see Figure 16.2). Research reveals that this skill is related to reading comprehension, and that interventions to improve it lead to improvements in reading comprehension (e.g., Cartwright, Hodgekiss, & Isaac, 2008; Cartwright et al., 2020).

Although not always recognized as such, vocabulary knowledge also acts as a bridging process. Vocabulary knowledge is certainly implicated in language comprehension, but studies suggest it is also implicated in word recognition (e.g., Ouellette, 2006; Ricketts, Natlon, & Bishop, 2007). Even children who have been identified as having dyslexia, a difficulty primarily associated with difficulties in the word recognition side of the simple view of reading (e.g., Catts, Kamhi, & Adlof, 2012), benefit from instruction

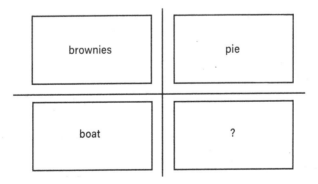

FIGURE 16.2. A sample matrix for measuring and developing graphophonological semantic cognitive flexibility. From Duke, Ward, and Pearson (2021). Copyright © 2021 John Wiley & Sons, Inc. Reprinted by permission.

that attends to semantic as well as graphophonological features of words. For example, in a study of fourth- and fifth-grade students with dyslexia, researchers found that word-meaning instruction along with word-reading instruction significantly improved the students' accurate and fluent word reading in comparison to word reading instruction alone (Austin, Vaughn, Clemens, Pustejovsky, & Boucher, 2022). This study, although outside the age-range focus of this volume, does suggest the benefits of simultaneously attending to meaning as well as word recognition in early reading development.

Simultaneously attending to vocabulary knowledge development and word-reading development may be particularly important for developing efficiency in reading orthographically irregular words. In a study conducted with fourth graders, Ouellette (2006) found that higher-level vocabulary knowledge (specifically, expressive knowledge rather than only receptive knowledge) is predictive of reading words that do not follow general orthographic rules (e.g., *yacht*). Similarly, Ricketts et al. (2007) found that with 8- to 10-year-olds, vocabulary knowledge was related to reading words that presented exceptions to general orthographic rules. In a study with children in first grade that investigated the relationships among oral vocabulary, decoding, irregular word recognition, and other language skills, researchers also found that vocabulary knowledge predicted irregular word recognition (Ouellette & Beers, 2010). This finding led the researchers to theorize that rich semantic knowledge is supportive of irregular word reading.

As expected, interventions that teach children to draw on both graphophonological and semantic knowledge when reading can be beneficial to children's word reading abilities, specifically of irregular words (e.g., Dyson, Best, Solity, & Hulme, 2017). In Colenbrander, Wang, Arrow, and Castle's (2020) review of research on teaching irregular words, the authors note that existing research does not provide clear answers regarding how to teach irregular word reading given the limited number of studies in this area. However, based on research that has been done, they suggest teaching irregular word recognition by providing instruction that builds grapheme–phoneme knowledge and knowledge of the words' spellings, while also focusing children's attention on their existing vocabulary knowledge and the sentence context. In a study with children ages 5–7, Dyson et al. (2017) taught children to

read irregular words by correctly pronouncing mispronounced words, learning the meaning of mispronounced words, matching the irregular word to a picture, thinking of words that rhyme with the irregular word, and writing the first letter of the irregular word. Children who participated in this 4-week intervention improved in their ability to correct mispronunciations and to read and explain the meanings of the words taught. The intervention also had positive effects on children's general ability to explain word meanings of untaught words. In accordance with this study's findings, teachers may find it helpful to use the steps below to support developing readers' flexibility and independence in reading irregular words. These steps build on the five-step process suggested in Dyson et al.'s study:

1. Have the child pronounce the word based on the letters he or she sees.
2. Ask, "Is it a word you've heard before?"
3. Ask, "Does the word make sense in the sentence?"
4. If pronounced correctly, move to step 6.
5. If mispronounced, provide the correct pronunciation of the irregular word. Have the child repeat the pronunciation.
6. Provide an explanation of the word and image that represents the word's meaning.
7. Point out any letters that may map onto the sounds of the word.
8. Spell the word with the child.
9. Have the child write the word (may differentiate to writing the first letter of the word, if appropriate).
10. Read the sentence again with the correctly pronounced word.

Notice that this procedure addresses both word recognition and vocabulary development. Although this practice alone cannot constitute the entirety of daily reading foundational skills and vocabulary instruction, it does offer one opportunity to address multiple instructional foci simultaneously.

Addressing Multiple Language Arts Processes Simultaneously

Reciprocity is not limited to foundational skills and bridging processes. Entire language arts processes—reading, writing, speaking, listening, viewing, and visually representing (e.g., National

Governors Association Center for Best Practices & Council of Chief State School Officers, 2010)—are also reciprocally related and can be taught concurrently. For example, consider a series of lessons in which children practice delivering effective presentations (speaking) while learning to comprehend and critique their classmates' presentations (listening). If children's presentations include posters or slides, then reading (for the audience) and writing (for the presenter) are also involved. If presentations incorporate visual elements, such as diagrams and graphs, as informational texts often do (Guo, Wright, & McTigue, 2018; Roberts et al., 2013), then viewing and visually representing are also entailed. In other words, one series of lessons within the classroom could address six language arts processes.

The combination of two language arts processes—reading and writing—has been the subject of the most research. Researchers have concluded that reading and writing "draw on common sources of knowledge and cognitive processes, involve meaning making, and can be used conjointly to accomplish important learning goals" (Graham et al., 2018, p. 279). For example, reading mentor texts is widely recommended for improving writing (Laminak, 2017), although this practice is surprisingly underresearched, particularly in reference to young writers. Writing has been found in many studies to improve reading (e.g., Hebert, Simpson, & Graham, 2013).

Despite their reciprocity, in our experience, reading and writing are often taught in different parts of the day in the primary grades and sometimes in preschool as well. Furthermore, it is not uncommon for reading and writing to be separated not only temporally—typically with reading in the morning, writing in the afternoon—but also conceptually. For example, reading instruction might be focused on reading fictional narrative text, while writing that same day might be focused on writing a completely different genre. Or reading instruction might focus on the strategy of chunking words to read them, but writing instruction might miss the opportunity to teach or remind children of the value of chunking words to spell them. Aside from not taking advantage of possible synergies in instruction across reading and writing, entirely separating reading and writing contributes to the central problem presented in this chapter: inadequate time in the school day for all that needs to occur.

Fortunately, as in other areas we have discussed, research suggests that reading and writing can be fruitfully taught simultaneously. In an innovative meta-analysis, Graham and colleagues (2018) examined 47 studies in which students were taught reading and writing in an integrated fashion (what the authors referred to as a "balanced" fashion, not to be confused with common use of the term *balanced literacy*). They included studies in preschool through secondary school in which no more than 60% of instructional time was spent on either reading or writing and excluded studies in which reading and writing were taught sequentially or focused on just one aspect of reading and writing. The meta-analysis documented statistically significant effects when reading measures were averaged (weighted effect size [ES] = 0.39) and when writing measures were averaged (ES = 0.37). Measures of more specific constructs also showed effects: on decoding (ES = 0.53), reading comprehension (ES = 0.39), reading vocabulary (ES = 0.35), writing quality (ES = 0.47), writing mechanics (ES = 0.18), and writing output (ES = 0.69).

Seventeen of the studies included in the meta-analysis involved entirely or primarily children in preschool through grade 1. Of those, seven studies tested the impact of integrated reading and writing instruction on total reading performance, with 83% of them having a positive effect size. Six of the studies tested the impact on total writing performance of young children, with 100% of them having a positive effect size. The researchers described reading/writing approaches they categorized as "early literacy" as follows:

> Reading and writing instruction focuses on fostering emerging literacy skills of preschool through grade 1 students. Interactive reading and writing involving the teacher and students is emphasized, with movement toward more student independence with each of these processes. Instruction to foster basic literacy skills, such as phonological awareness and word-reading skills, is provided. (Graham et al., 2018, p. 286)

That said, it is important to note that not all studies examined in the meta-analysis investigated the impacts of a program on both reading and writing, and not all programs studied were found to be effective. For these reasons, it is important for practitioners to examine any given program in relation to practices that have been shown to be effective in research. Furthermore, the researchers point out that just because integrated reading and writing is generally effective does not mean that they should always be taught together. There may be a place for separate reading and writing instruction. Still, integrated reading and writing instruction offers one strategy we can use to address the time challenge posed at the outset of this chapter.

Providing Literacy and Content-Area Instruction Simultaneously

The forms of instructional simultaneity that we have addressed up to this point in the chapter have all been within literacy; in this section, we turn to instructional simultaneity between literacy and another domain. In particular, we discuss research in which instruction in literacy and science or social studies are integrated. For example, Halvorsen, Duke, Strachan, and Johnson (2018) describe a project-based unit situated in the social studies discipline of history, in which children learn about schooling and transportation in the past and the present, conduct research about the history of their local community, and develop postcards about the history of their local community to sell, give to community members, or display in the community (e.g., at a local historical museum). This project involves building historical content knowledge and research skills (e.g., drawing inferences from primary source material). It also involves reading a variety of informational texts and learning about specific genres (biographies, postcards), text features (indexes, captions), and comprehension strategies (e.g., identifying the author's purpose, using context clues to ascertain the meaning of unfamiliar words from context). The project also involves developing writing skills as children work to write postcard captions with an introduction, facts and definitions about the topic, and a conclusion. In a cluster randomized controlled trial, Duke, Halvorsen, Strachan, Kim, and Konstantpoulos (2021) examined the impact of this and three similar, project-based units as compared to business-as-usual social studies and literacy instruction, finding statistically significant impacts on both literacy and social studies.

Findings from the Duke, Halvorsen, et al. (2021) study mirror those of a meta-analysis of studies of integrated literacy and content area

instruction. Hwang, Cabell, and Joyner (2022) identified 35 studies in kindergarten through fifth grade in which integrated instruction was compared to instruction in which literacy and a content area were taught separately. Studies found statistically significant impacts on both literacy (Hedges's g for comprehension = 0.40) and content knowledge (ES = 0.89). Thirteen of the studies focused on kindergarten to grade 2; results of those studies were not different from those of the larger group (Cabell & Hwang, Chapter 15, this volume).

Regarding preschool-age children, to our knowledge, research has not compared integrated to separated instruction. However, research does suggest the potential for simultaneously fostering development in literacy and another domain in the preschool years. For example, Sarama, Lange, Clements, and Wolfe (2012) found that a mathematics intervention designed to incorporate intentional use of language fostered not only mathematics development but also development of oral language on several measures. Gonzalez et al. (2010) used shared reading, which has a long record of fostering literacy development, to develop knowledge of specific science and social studies concepts/vocabulary words (e.g., *water, liquid, frozen*), finding positive effects on both receptive and expressive vocabulary knowledge (Pollard-Durodola & Gonzalez, Chapter 13, this volume). There is good reason to believe that instructional simultaneity across literacy and content areas can be efficacious throughout the early childhood years.

Future Directions

In this chapter, we have outlined a significant problem of practice in early literacy education: inadequate time in the day for all of the instructional targets, programs, and practices that research suggests merit inclusion. We have proposed that one way to address this problem is to engage in four forms of instructional simultaneity: (1) addressing multiple reading foundational skills simultaneously, (2) developing literacy bridging processes, (3) addressing multiple language arts processes simultaneously, and (4) providing literacy and content-area instruction simultaneously. We have documented that each of these forms of instructional simultaneity can indeed achieve the goal of impacting achievement in multiple areas concurrently. That said, it is important to note that the research is far from indicating that we should *always* engage in instructional simultaneity. Sometimes, a singular instructional focus may be most suited to children's needs.

In simultaneously addressing multiple instructional foci, we must maintain the integrity of each target. For example, efforts to integrate literacy into content-area instruction should not be allowed to wash out important characteristics of effective content-area instruction, and content-rich English language arts instruction should be designed only in partnership with experts in the content areas (Wright & Gotwals, Chapter 14, this volume). We must not lose sight of what we know about effective instruction when combining multiple instructional targets. For example, historically and culturally responsive pedagogical practices (e.g., Muhammad, 2020) remain crucial whether addressing one or multiple instructional targets. Similarly, explicit, systematic instructional practices should continue to be a mainstay of literacy instruction (e.g., Foorman et al., 2016; Shanahan et al., 2010).

Researchers should turn a great deal more attention to the problem of inadequate time in the school day. It is tempting to design interventions for our particular research focus—vocabulary, for example, or informational text—with little concern for whether there is realistically enough time to include them in the school day in the long term. But doing so places the burden on teachers to decide what to include and what to let go. It is also tempting to think that if something is good for children, then more of it is better for children, but much like vitamins, there can be too much of a good thing. Any allocation of instructional time for one focus comes at the cost of less instructional time for something else. As a field, we need to take a "Name that Tune" approach to the development of programs and practices—working to achieve instructional goals in the least possible amount of time.

Research is also needed on how to allocate time across an entire school day. The three of us are involved in a project to develop a full-day birth-to-age-8 curriculum called *The Great First Eight Curriculum*. In designing the school day for this curriculum, there was remarkably little research on which to draw. We were certainly aware of the need to avoid practices and transitions that waste time (Brinkerhoff & Roehrig, 2014), but left unanswered were many questions about how much time to devote to each instructional focus and practice over the course of the day. Like the teacher in the thought experiment presented at the outset of this chapter, we found ourselves struggling to fit in all that we had hoped. We were grateful for practices, such as integrated content-area and literacy instruction, that address multiple instructional foci simultaneously, feeding multiple birds with one hand. Still, we look forward to more research in the years to come that can inform the complex process of building a school day. For us, among the most pressing questions in literacy research is not how to teach, but how to teach it all.

References

Austin, C. R., Vaughn, S., Clemens, N. H., Pustejovsky, J. E., & Boucher, A. N. (2022). The relative effects of instruction linking word reading and word meaning compared to word reading instruction alone on the accuracy, fluency, and word meaning knowledge of 4th–5th grade students with dyslexia. *Scientific Studies of Reading, 26*, 204–222.

Brinkerhoff, E. H., & Roehrig, A. D. (2014). *No more sharpening pencils during work time and other time wasters*. Heinemann.

Cartwright, K., Hodgekiss, M. D., & Isaac, M. C. (2008). Graphophonological–semantic flexibility: Contributions to skilled reading across the lifespan. In K. B. Cartwright (Ed.), *Literacy processes: Cognitive flexibility in learning and teaching*. Guilford Press.

Cartwright, K. B., Bock, A. M., Clause, J. H., Coppage August, E. A., Saunders, H. G., & Schmidt, K. J. (2020). Near- and far-transfer effects of an executive function intervention for 2nd to 5th grade struggling readers. *Cognitive Development, 56*, Article 100932.

Catts, H. W., Kamhi, A. G., & Adlof, S. M. (2012). Defining and classifying reading disabilities. In A. G. Kamhi & H. G. Catts (Eds.), *Language and reading disabilities* (3rd ed.). Pearson.

Center for Advancing Social and Emotional Learning. (n.d.). Adopt an evidence-based program for SEL. Retrieved from *https://schoolguide.casel.org/focus-area-3/school/adopt-an-evidence-based-program-for-sel*.

Centers for Disease Control and Prevention. (2019). Making time for school lunch. Retrieved from *www.cdc.gov/healthyschools/nutrition/school_lunch.htm*.

Cervetti, G., Pearson, P. D., Bravo, M. A., & Barber, J. (2006). Reading and writing in the service of inquiry-based science. In R. Douglas, M. P. Klentschy, & K. Worth (Eds.), *Linking science and literacy in the K–8 classroom* (pp. 221–244). National Science Teachers Association.

Clayton, F. J., West, G., Sears, C., Hulme, C., & Lervåg, A. (2020). A longitudinal study of early reading development: Letter–sound knowledge, phoneme awareness and RAN, but not letter-sound integration, predict variations in reading development. *Scientific Studies of Reading, 24*(2), 91–107.

Clemens, N., Solari, E., Kearns, D. M., Fien, H., Nelson, N. J., Stelega, M., . . . Hoeft, F. (2021). They say you can do phonemic awareness instruction "in the dark," but should you?: A critical evaluation of the trend toward advanced phonemic awareness training. Retrieved from *https://doi.org/10.31234/osf.io/ajxbv.*

Colenbrander, D., Wang, H., Arrow, T., & Castles, A. (2020). Teaching irregular words: What we know, what we don't know, and where we can go from here. *Educational and Developmental Psychologist, 37*(2), 97–104.

Council of Chief State School Officers. (2018). The marginalization of social studies. Retrieved from *https://ccsso.org/sites/default/files/2018-11/elementary%20ss%20brief%2045%20minute%20version_0.pdf.*

Council on School Health: Murray, R., Ramstetter, C., Devore, C., Allison, M., Ancona, R., . . . Young, T. (2013). The crucial role of recess in school. *Pediatrics, 131*(1), 183–188.

Denton, C. A., Tolar, T. D., Fletcher, J. M., Barth, A. E., Vaughn, S., & Francis, D. J. (2013). Effects of Tier 3 intervention for students with persistent reading difficulties and characteristics of inadequate responders. *Journal of Educational Psychology, 105*(3), 633–648.

Duke, N. K., & Cartwright, K. B. (2021). The science of reading progresses: Communicating advances beyond the simple view of reading. *Reading Research Quarterly, 56*(Suppl. 1), S25–S44.

Duke, N. K., Halvorsen, A-L., Strachan, S. L., Kim, J., & Konstantopoulos, S. (2021). Putting PjBL to the test: The impact of project-based learning on second-graders' social studies and literacy learning and motivation in low-SES school settings. *American Educational Research Journal, 58*(1), 160–200.

Duke, N. K., Ward, A. E., & Pearson, P. D. (2021). The science of reading comprehension instruction. *Reading Teacher, 74*(6), 663–672.

Dyson, D., Best, W., Solity, J., & Hulme, C. (2017). Training mispronunciation correction and word meanings improves children's ability to read words. *Scientific Studies of Reading, 21*(5), 392–407.

Ehri, L. C., Nunes, S. R., Willows, D. M., Schuster, B. V., Yaghoub-Zadeh, Z., & Shanahan, T. (2001). Phonemic awareness instruction helps children learn to read: Evidence from the National Reading Panel's meta-analysis. *Reading research quarterly, 36*(3), 250–287.

Fien, H., Smith, J. L., Smolkowski, K., Baker, S. K., Nelson, N. J., & Chaparro, E. (2015). An examination of the efficacy of a multitiered intervention on early reading outcomes for first grade students at risk for reading difficulties. *Journal of Learning Disabilities, 48*(6), 602–621.

Fitchett, P. G., & Heafner, T. L. (2010). A national perspective on the effects of high-stakes testing and standardization on elementary social studies marginalization. *Theory and Research in Social Education, 38*(1), 114–130.

Foorman, B., Beyler, N., Borradaile, K., Coyne, M., Denton, C. A., Dimino, J., et al. (2016). *Foundational skills to support reading for understanding in kindergarten through 3rd grade* (NCEE 2016-4008). National Center for Education Evaluation and Regional Assistance, Institute of Education Sciences, U.S. Department of Education.

Gonzalez, J. E., Pollard-Durodola, S., Simmons, D. C., Taylor, A. B., Davis, M. J., Kim, M., & Simmons, L. (2010). Developing low-income preschoolers' social studies and science vocabulary knowledge through content-focused shared book reading. *Journal of Research on Educational Effectiveness, 4*(1), 25–52.

Gough, P. B., & Tunmer, W. E. (1986). Decoding, reading, and reading disability. *Remedial and Special Education, 7*(1), 6–10.

Graham, S., Bollinger, A., Booth Olson, C., D'Aoust, C., MacArthur, C., McCutchen, D., & Olinghouse, N. (2012). *Teaching elementary school students to be effective writers: A practice guide* (NCEE 2012-4058). National Center for Education Evaluation and Regional Assistance, Institute of Education Sciences, U.S. Department of Education.

Graham, S., Liu, X., Aitken, A., Ng, C., Bartlett, B., Harris, K.R., & Holzapfel, J. (2018). Effectiveness of literacy programs balancing reading and writing instruction: A meta-analysis. *Reading Research Quarterly, 53*(3), 279–304.

Guo, D., Wright, K. L., & McTigue, E. M. (2018). A content analysis of visuals in elementary school textbooks. *Elementary School Journal, 119*(2), 244–269.

Halvorsen, A.-L., Duke, N. K., Strachan, S. L., & Johnson, C. M. (2018). Engaging the community with a project-based approach. *Social Education, 82*(1), 24–29.

Hebert, M., Simpson, A., & Graham, S. (2013). Comparing effects of different writing activities on reading comprehension: A meta-analysis. *Reading and Writing, 26,* 111–138.

Hoover, W. A., & Tunmer, W. E. (2020). *The cognitive foundations of reading and its acquisition.* Springer.

Hwang, H., Cabell, S. Q., & Joyner, R. E. (2022). Effects of integrated literacy and content-area instruction on comprehension and vocabulary in the elementary years: A meta-analysis. *Scientific Studies of Reading, 26,* 223–249.

Laminack, L. (2017). Mentors and mentor texts: What, why, and how? *Reading Teacher, 70*(6), 753–755.

Muhammad, G. (2020). *Cultivating genius: An equity framework for culturally and historically responsive literacy.* Scholastic.

National Academies of Sciences, Engineering, and Medicine. (2021). *Science and engineering in preschool through elementary grades: The brilliance of children and the strengths of educators.* National Academies Press.

National Center for Education Statistics. (2007–2008). *Schools and staffing survey.* Author.

National Early Literacy Panel. (2008). *Developing early literacy: Report of the National Early Literacy Panel.* National Institute for Literacy.

National Governors Association Center for Best Practices & Council of Chief State School Officers. (2010). *Common Core State Standards for English language arts and literacy in history/social studies, science, and technical subjects.* Authors.

National Reading Panel. (2000). *Report of the National Reading Panel: Teaching children to read: An evidence-based assessment of the scientific research literature on reading and its implications for reading instruction: Reports of the subgroups.* NICHD Clearinghouse.

Ouellette, G. (2006). What's meaning got to do with it: The role of vocabulary in word reading and reading comprehension. *Journal of Educational Psychology, 98*(3), 554–566.

Ouellete, G., & Beers, A. (2010). A not-so-simple view of reading: How oral vocabulary and visual-word recognition complicate the story. *Reading and Writing, 23,* 189–208.

Ricketts, J., Nation, K., & Bishop, D. V. (2007). Vocabulary is important for some, but not all reading skills. *Scientific Studies of Reading, 11*(3), 235–257.

Roberts, K. L., Norman, R. R., Duke, N. K., Morsink, P., Martin, N. M., & Knight, J. A. (2013). Diagrams, timelines, & tables, oh my!: Concepts and comprehension of graphics. *Reading Teacher, 61,* 12–24.

Roth, K., & Guinee, K. (2011). Ten minutes a day: The impact of interactive writing instruction on first graders' independent writing. *Journal of Early Childhood Literacy, 11*(3), 331–361.

Sarama, J., Lange, A. A., Clements, D. H., Wolfe, C. B. (2012). The impacts of an early mathematics curriculum on oral language and literacy. *Early Childhood Research Quarterly, 27*(3), 489–502.

Scarborough, H. S. (2001). Connecting early language and literacy to later reading (dis)abilities: Evidence, theory, and practice. In S. B. Neuman & D. K. Dickinson (Eds.), *Handbook of early literacy research* (Vol. 1, pp. 97–110). Guilford Press.

Shanahan, T., Callison, K., Carriere, C., Duke, N. K., Pearson, P. D., Schatschneider, C., & Torgesen, J. (2010). *Improving reading comprehension in kindergarten through 3rd grade: A practice guide* (NCEE 2010–4038). National Center for Education Evaluation and Regional Assistance, Institute of Education Sciences, U.S. Department of Education.

Wesseling, P. B., Christmann, C. A., & Lachmann, T. (2017). Shared book reading promotes not only language development, but also grapheme awareness in German kindergarten children. *Frontiers in Psychology, 8,* 1–14.

Winthrop, R. (2020). The need for civic education in 21st-century schools. Retrieved from *www.brookings.edu/wp-content/uploads/2020/01/brookingspolicy2020_bigideas_winthrop_civiceducation.pdf.*

Zucker, T. A., Cabell, S. Q., Justice, L. M., Pentimonti, J. M., & Kaderavek, J. N. (2013). The role of frequent, interactive prekindergarten shared reading in the longitudinal development of language and literacy skills. *Developmental Psychology, 49*(8), 1425–1439.

CHAPTER 17

Comprehension

From Language to Reading

Ellen Orcutt, Victoria Johnson, and Panayiota Kendeou

The latest Nation's Report Card indicates that approximately one in three fourth graders reads below a basic proficiency level (National Assessment of Educational Progress, 2019); that is, they fail to make simple inferences and comprehend the overall meaning of texts. Despite the persistent efforts of researchers, policymakers, and educators to improve reading performance of all children in U.S. schools, this statistic has remained largely unchanged for several decades. Unfortunately, students who experience such reading difficulties are likely to struggle throughout their education and employment (Pearson et al., 2020; Snow, 2002).

In this chapter, we focus on *comprehension* as a generalized cognitive process and learning product. We situate comprehension in contemporary models of reading and language, and provide evidence for its generalizability. In this context, we also identify general and modality-specific processes. We argue that comprehension can be developed early on, across modalities, and can transfer from one modality to another via targeted instruction. We present a case model of how this theoretical approach to comprehension can translate into instructional design and conclude with future directions in this area of work.

Comprehension in Contemporary Reading Models

One of the most popular frameworks for understanding reading comprehension is Gough and Tunmer's (1986) Simple View of Reading (SVR), which posits that reading comprehension is the product of decoding and language comprehension, in which both skills are necessary and not alone sufficient for readers to understand what they read. The SVR has shaped how reading comprehension has been studied for decades (e.g., Byrne & Fielding-Barnsley, 1995; Garcia & Cain, 2014; Hogan, Adlof, & Alonzo, 2014; Kendeou, Savage, & van den Broek, 2009; Kendeou, van den Broek, White, & Lynch, 2009; Tilstra, McMaster, van den Broek, Kendeou, & Rapp, 2009). The need for explicit and systematic phonics instruction, which targets decoding skills, is often emphasized in early elementary grades. However, the emphasis on decoding-centric curricula does not negate the need for early comprehension instruction. In fact, language comprehension strategies can be taught even before children learn to read proficiently (Fricke, Bowyer-Crane, Haley, Hulme, & Snowling, 2013; Kendeou, Bohn-Gettler, White, & van den Broek, 2008; Kendeou et al., 2005; Lynch et al., 2008; van den Broek, Kendeou, Lousberg, & Visser, 2011). Given that reading comprehension is the product of decoding and language comprehension, if either skill is absent, reading comprehension suffers. Thus, it is critical that comprehension skills be taught in young children in conjunction with decoding-focused instruction.

It is important to note that various terms are often used in the literature to describe the comprehension component described in the SVR, including language comprehension, oral language, listening comprehension, and linguistic comprehension. We argue that although there are likely important differences in the ways researchers conceptualize comprehension, in the context of the SVR these terms have been perceived synonymous. Notably, Gough and Tunmer (1986) used "listening comprehension" and "linguistic comprehension" interchangeably in their seminal introduction of their framework. Moreover, the Language and Reading Research Consortium (LARRC; 2017) compared the constructs of "oral language comprehension" and "listening comprehension" in preschool through third-grade student populations and found evidence that supports treating them as the same construct. Therefore, we refer to this construct as "language comprehension" throughout this chapter.

Since the inception of the SVR, several other theoretical models have been proposed that expand and complicate the simple view (see Cervetti et al., 2020, for a review; Kim, Chapter 1, this volume). Duke and Cartwright (2021) have recently proposed the Active View of Reading, which expands on the SVR and incorporates contemporary empirical evidence on the development of reading comprehension. The model emphasizes the importance of decoding and language comprehension, but makes four important distinctions from the SVR. First, it allows for explanations of reading difficulties to extend beyond an inability to decode and/or comprehend, such as differences in cultural or vocabulary knowledge. Evidence suggests that differences in content knowledge can predict unique variance in reading ability above and beyond decoding and language comprehension (e.g., Cabell & Hwang, 2020; Hwang, 2020) and is separate from vocabulary knowledge (e.g., Ahmed et al., 2016). Second, the model recognizes that decoding and comprehension skills are not entirely separate constructs, and that their predictive variance of reading comprehension often overlaps (e.g., Lonigan, Burgess, & Schatschneider,

2018; Taboada Barber, Cartwright, Hancock, & Klauda, 2021). Third, the model includes other relevant contributors to reading comprehension, including executive function, motivation, engagement, and strategy use, as there is existing evidence that supports the unique contribution of each (Ahmed et al., 2016; Butterfuss & Kendeou, 2018; Cartwright et al., 2020; Cutting & Scarborough, 2012; Søndergaard Knudsen, Jensen de López, & Archibald, 2018). Finally, the model, which solely represents characteristics of the reader, also acknowledges the impact of the text, the task, and the sociocultural context in which the reading is taking place, thus staying close to the reading heuristic proposed by the Rand Study Research Group (Snow, 2002).

The Active View of Reading provides a more comprehensive and nuanced understanding of how reading comprehension develops. It reflects the complexity of reading comprehension and includes its multiple contributing factors. It is within this contemporary context that we situate our discussion of comprehension.

Comprehension as a Process and Product

One of the most influential early theoretical models of comprehension is the construction–integration model (Kintsch & van Dijk, 1978; Kintsch, 1991; van Dijk & Kintsch, 1983), providing a more detailed framework for understanding cognition behind comprehension (Butterfuss, Kim, & Kendeou, 2020; Kendeou & O'Brien, 2018; McNamara & Magliano, 2009). This model posits that comprehension involves two phases: construction and integration. *Construction* comprises the activation of information in a text along with the reader's background knowledge. Activated information can come from four different sources: current text input, the prior sentence, recently read text, and background knowledge. As information is activated, it is integrated into an interconnected network of nodes. *Integration* comprises the spreading of the activation within this network until activation settles. These processes occur iteratively while engaging with a text. These two phases result in the construction of a situation model, a mental representation of what the text is about in the reader's mind. Thus, this situation model is considered the final product of comprehension, while its construction involves the actual processes of comprehension.

The distinction between the processes and

products of comprehension is an important one (Kendeou & O'Brien, 2018; Kendeou, McMaster, & Christ, 2016; Kendeou, van den Broek, Helder, & Karlsson, 2014). The *products* of comprehension serve as indicators of what the reader understands and learns from the text at the completion of reading. The *processes* of comprehension are the cognitive processes readers use to arrive at those products that occur moment by moment as individuals read (McNamara & Kendeou, 2011; Rapp, van den Broek, McMaster, Kendeou, & Espin, 2007). This distinction is also important for both the development and instruction of comprehension. Developmentally, a focus solely on products limits our ability to identify underlying processes that can lead to changes in reading performance (Magliano, Millis, Ozuru, & McNamara, 2007). By considering both processes and products, researchers gain a deeper understanding of how to effectively facilitate comprehension. Instructionally, interventions are commonly driven by the belief that effective methods for helping readers should be designed so that they affect the processes that occur *during* reading.

However, interventions and assessments for comprehension are often grounded in measures that are product-based, focusing on recall or question tasks that are collected *after* reading (Kendeou et al., 2020). A focus on cognitive processes can be helpful in describing, explaining, and addressing the needs of struggling readers, as failures in particular processes can lead to comprehension difficulties and thus low performance on products of reading comprehension (McNamara & Kendeou, 2011). Research in the cognitive sciences can lead to a greater understanding of comprehension processes and the reasons these processes may fail under different contexts and for a variety of readers (Graesser, McNamara, & Louwerse, 2003). This work can then be informative in addressing the needs of struggling readers by knowing at which points and why the process fails, allowing for the design of appropriate interventions and learning materials (e.g., Gersten, Fuchs, Williams, & Baker, 2001; Graesser et al., 2003; Kendeou, van den Broek, White, & Lynch, 2007; Nesbit & Hadwin, 2006; Pressley, 2002; Pressley, Graham, & Harris, 2006).

Comprehension as General and Specific

While comprehension is most commonly studied in the context of reading in educational research,

it is an important cognitive outcome across many contexts and media formats. These formats can include plain text, static visuals (e.g., illustrated books, comics), dynamic visuals (e.g., videos), and multimodal representations (e.g., integrated text and video). We argue that comprehension can be conceptualized as a general skill that shares important common features across a variety of media formats. However, while comprehension across media is a generalized process that can be successfully leveraged in instruction, there are also media specific processes that must be considered.

Underlying the general comprehension processes is the ability to draw inferences and construct mental models (Kintsch & van Dijk, 1978). *Inference making* refers to the process of generating or retrieving information to "fill in" gaps (Kintsch, 1991; McNamara & Magliano, 2009). Assumed to be a two-stage process, the generation of an inference involves first the reactivation of previously acquired information. Then, the previously acquired information is integrated with the newly encoded information (Elbro & Buch-Iversen, 2013). These activation and integration processes of comprehension are parallel, asynchronous processes that are often viewed as continuous and overlapping (Kendeou, 2015).

The ability to draw inferences has been shown to be central to comprehension across the lifespan (e.g., Cain, Oakhill, Barnes, & Bryant, 2001; Lynch & van den Broek, 2007; Kendeou et al., 2007; Kendeou, van den Broek, et al., 2009; McNamara & Kendeou, 2011). In addition, inference making supports the construction of coherent mental models in both reading and non-reading contexts (e.g., Gernsbacher, 1990; Kendeou et al., 2008; Kendeou, van den Broek, et al., 2009). The generalizability of inference making does not mean that there are no processing differences across different media (these do exist; e.g., Magliano, Loschky, Clinton, & Larson, 2013); rather, what generalizes is the processes by which inferences are generated across different media, namely activation and integration (Kendeou, 2015). Due to this generalizability, inference making can be initially taught in non-reading contexts (e.g., illustrated books, audio books, videos) and then transferred to reading comprehension (Butterfuss, Kendeou, McMaster, Orcutt, & Bulut, 2022; Kendeou et al., 2016; McMaster et al., 2015).

Despite these shared processes, different media have different affordances that can also influence inference generation. According to Magliano et al. (2013), these differences center around units of meaning, multimodality, and demands on vocabulary and knowledge. For example, in text, the unit of meaning is letters and words, and without an ability to decode these words, comprehension of the text is virtually impossible (Gough & Tunmer, 1986). This is the fundamental argument behind the SVR and the primary rationale as to why phonics instruction is often prioritized in early elementary school. However, proficient ability to decode is not necessary for the comprehension of most age-appropriate dynamic narratives, such as videos, making decoding a *specific* cognitive process to reading comprehension (Lynch et al., 2008). Furthermore, in dynamic narratives, the integration of both visual and linguistic processing is necessary for comprehension (Magliano, Larson, Higgs, & Loschky, 2015). This visual processing, something that is not necessary for text-based reading, is another example of a specific comprehension process. Additionally, dynamic narratives can provide opportunities for generating inferences of higher complexity than plain texts, as they could involve either linguistic or visual information only, or the integration of linguistic and visual information.

We assert that the underlying generalized processes of comprehension, such as inference making, can be capitalized on to begin language comprehension instruction in early grade levels and across modalities, while taking into account the media-specific processes involved in each modality and placing particular emphasis on the transfer of the skills between media. The inferential language comprehension (iLC; Kendeou et al., 2019) framework serves as a theoretical guide for designing such curricula.

The iLC Framework: General Principles for Language Comprehension Instruction

The iLC framework (Kendeou et al., 2019) is used to personalize inference teaching for young students by leveraging the affordances of static and dynamic visual narratives. It is built on the idea that language comprehension development depends on a general inference skill that can transfer across contexts and media. The framework emphasizes that this instruction is optimized when it begins in early elementary grades, utilizes inferential questioning with scaffolding and feedback, includes vocabulary instruction, and is implemented across modalities with transfer as the ultimate goal.

The iLC framework provides a number of important considerations when designing language comprehension curricula. First and foremost is the necessity of language comprehension in young students. Educators need to include the systematic teaching of language comprehension skills in their classrooms as early as possible for students to build strong reading skills. However, students rarely are exposed to such instruction until later elementary grades, if at all (van Kleeck, 2003; Weiser & Mathes, 2011). The instruction need not be limited by a lack of early reading skill, as language-comprehension-specific instruction has been shown to improve literacy outcomes in elementary students (Silverman, Johnson, Keane, & Khanna, 2020). Evidence suggests that students can be taught comprehension skills, such as inference making, during their prereading years through the use of video and multimedia (Fricke et al., 2013; Kendeou et al., 2005, 2008; Lynch et al., 2008; van den Broek et al., 2011). Furthermore, language-focused instruction has been shown to improve reading comprehension outcomes (Connor et al., 2013, 2014; LARRC, Jiang, & Logan, 2019; LARRC, Pratt, & Logan, 2014; LARRC & Yeomans-Maldonado, 2017) and prevent long-term reading difficulties (National Early Literacy Panel, 2008; Silverman et al., 2020).

Multimodality, Gamification, and Technology

The iLC framework suggests that the gateway to language comprehension in the prereading years is through the use of static and dynamic visual narratives. Static narratives consist of picture books that can be used in read-aloud lessons. Dynamic narratives consist of videos that can be used in learning modules. Given the growing presence of technology in the classroom, video narratives are more accessible than ever. Additionally, there is overwhelming evidence that educational technology (e.g., games, interactive applications, intelligent tutoring systems) improves a variety of student-level outcomes such as motivation, engagement, and learning (e.g., Butler, Marsh, Slavinsky, & Baraniuk, 2014; D'Mello, 2013; Jackson & McNamara, 2013; VanLehn, 2011). As suggested in the Active View of Reading model (Duke & Cartwright, 2021), motivation and engagement are important determinants of overall reading comprehension. Gamifying comprehension instruction and matching students' interests are yet another benefit to utilizing technology in the classroom and individualizing instruction to best meet the needs of the student.

Inferences

At the heart of the iLC framework is inference making. Inferences are often considered the cornerstone of comprehension, as they support the reader's construction of coherent representations (Kintsch & van Dijk, 1978). Inference generation is a process that can be explicitly taught to young students (e.g., Fricke et al., 2013). Supporting the student's ability to make connections, both within and across the text and background knowledge, is at the heart of comprehension. Graesser and Franklin (1990) provided evidence that inference making can be prompted with questioning through their cognitive model of question answering, QUEST, which specifies the information sources and mechanisms that are at play when answering questions. Furthermore, there are numerous examples of questioning-based interventions that focus specifically on inference generation during reading in the primary grades (see McMaster & Espin, 2017, for a review). Questioning is a familiar practice to teachers, as it is often used during book-sharing interactions or "dialogic reading" to develop inferencing in preschoolers (van Kleeck, 2008; Zevenbergen & Whitehurst, 2003). Consistent with the conceptualization of inferences as the activation and integration of information, questions support inference generation because they help (re)activate relevant information, both inside and outside the text, and facilitate integration of that information in order to generate the inference.

Vocabulary Knowledge

An important component of comprehension instruction is the inclusion of vocabulary instruction (Duke & Cartwright, 2021; Silverman et al., 2020; Wright & Cervetti, 2017), as having a knowledge base of the words used in a text is foundational to understanding a text's meaning. Specifically, brief, direct instruction of words' meaning prior to engaging with a text has been shown to be an effective means of vocabulary instruction (Hawkins, Musti-Rao, Hale, McGuire, & Hailley, 2010). Furthermore,

the active processing of the vocabulary words, such as comparing words and relating words to various contexts, appears to be a more effective means of vocabulary instruction in comparison to a definition-only presentation (Wright & Cervetti, 2017). This is why the iLC includes explicit precursory vocabulary instruction and contextualizes each term to the content of the static or dynamic narrative.

Scaffolding and Feedback

Foundational to the iLC framework is the use of scaffolding and feedback, as demonstrated in Figure 17.1. Questions can prompt the activation of knowledge needed to generate an inference (knowledge that was acquired by watching the dynamic narrative or vocabulary knowledge instruction), but students can also benefit from appropriate scaffolding of the information to assist in their construction of inferences, and therefore, their overall mental representation and comprehension. Scaffolding typically incorporates cues, prompts, and corrective feedback (Golke, Dörfler, & Artelt, 2015). For example, scaffolded feedback can articulate whether a student was correct or incorrect in their inference attempt, and then elaborate upon what makes their attempt accurate or inaccurate, referencing explicit information from the narrative. Scaffolding has potential to support the generation of inferences because it re-activates the relevant information in a student's memory needed to make a connection and integrate that information to generate an inference. Furthermore, feedback on the accuracy of the inference made is an important component of scaffolded instruction (Hattie & Timperley, 2007; McMaster, Espin, & van den Broek, 2014). The delivery of feedback must be timely, as immediate feedback helps students to generate connections they missed, or update incorrect connections before they become entrenched in their mental representations and hinder further comprehension (Butler & Roediger, 2007; Roediger & Marsh, 2005).

Individualization

A final consideration in the iLC is the individualization or personalization of comprehension instruction. Individualization of instruction has a long history in education (Cronbach & Snow, 1977) and continues to be emphasized in today's literature (Pearson et al., 2020). Advances in

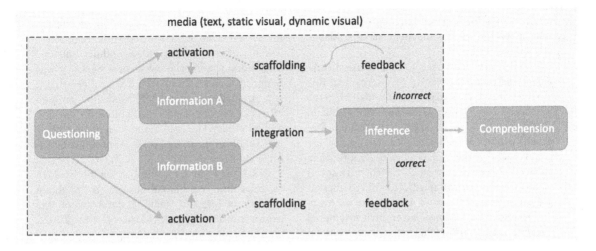

FIGURE 17.1. The inference process in the Inferential Language Comprehension (iLC) Framework. From Kendeou et al. (2019). Copyright © 2019 John Wiley & Sons, Inc. Reprinted by permission.

technology help improve the design and delivery of individualized instruction through the development of sophisticated algorithms (Connor et al., 2013) and intelligent tutoring systems (Graesser, Li, & Forsyth, 2014). Thus, individualized instruction through the means of technology in the context of comprehension instruction provides opportunities for self-paced, scaffolded development of core skills such as inference making, as well as opportunities for deliberate practice of those skills in various contexts (McNamara & Kendeou, 2022).

Transfer

Early comprehension instruction via multiple modalities is not complete until the issue of transfer is addressed. The ultimate goal of this instructional process is for students to transfer comprehension skills to different contexts. Given that comprehension is a general skill (Gernsbacher, 1990; Kendeou et al., 2019), the iLC emphasizes that comprehension instruction curricula address the transfer of this skill when interacting with different modes of information, ranging from literary texts, videos, and even daily social interactions. Evidence supports the transfer of these comprehension skills across media in both children and adults (Gernsbacher, 1990; Kendeou, 2015; Magliano et al., 2007, 2013). Specifically, there is evidence for the transfer of inference processes from a dynamic narrative context to a

static narrative context to a reading comprehension context (e.g., Kendeou et al., 2008). Thus, if students develop their inference-making in an oral language context (e.g., videos or read-aloud books), they may utilize this strategy in new contexts, such as reading.

The iLC Framework: Inference Galaxy as a Case Example

What Is Inference Galaxy?

Inference Galaxy is a suite of web-based instructional tools that were designed using the iLC framework. These tools serve to improve language and reading comprehension by focusing on inference making, a core language comprehension skill. Inference Galaxy is situated within the multi-tiered systems of support (MTSS) framework, in which both Tier 1 and Tier 2 instructions are provided based on students' needs, and an assessment tool is provided to inform placement. Inference Galaxy consists of three instructional programs: ELCII, a kindergarten Tier 1 instructional program; TeLCI, a first- and second-grade Tier 2 intervention program; and MIA, a K–2 assessment of inference-making skill. All tools are interactive and automated, capitalizing on the affordances of technology to easily individualize and adapt instruction and assessment to students' needs. Importantly, these tools pose no decoding demands to students, which allows for targeted language comprehension instruction that is independent of students' decoding ability.

ELCII (Early Language Comprehension Individual Instruction) consists of twenty learning modules in which students are guided through inferential video lessons with the assistance of an alien pedagogical agent. During the lessons, students learn academic vocabulary words that are key to ideas in the video, view age-appropriate videos that present content consistent with social studies and science standards, respond to inferential questions, and receive appropriate scaffolding and specific feedback after each attempted question. ELCII also includes twenty read-aloud lessons that take the form of a whole-class interactive book-reading and questioning activity led by a teacher. Read-aloud lessons are designed to reinforce inference-making skills learned during the learning video modules to promote transfer of inference generation skills to book contexts. Each week, for a total of 10 weeks, students complete two ELCII learning modules and participate in two read-aloud lessons. These core components reflect those outlined in the iLC framework and are displayed in Figure 17.2.

TeLCI (Technology-Based Early Language Comprehension Intervention) is designed similarly to ELCII, with the exception of consisting of 24 video modules and eight read-aloud lessons, paced at three video modules and one read-aloud lesson each week for 8 weeks. It was designed with a faster-paced dosage given that it is a targeted intervention for students identified at risk of comprehension difficulties in first and second grade. The read-aloud lessons take place in a small-group setting for a more direct learning experience with these students.

ELCII and TeLCI capitalize on both video modules and read-aloud lessons to facilitate transfer of inference making. Drawing on the extant transfer literature (Barnett & Ceci, 2002), the read-aloud lessons are designed so that they ensure transfer of the learned skill (i.e., inference making) across modalities (from video to listening comprehension), social context (from individual to whole-classroom interaction), and language complexity (from oral language to written language). Furthermore, a teacher read-aloud approach (as opposed to independent silent reading) ensures that ELCII will impose minimal decoding demands (Reed, Swanson, Petscher, & Vaughn, 2014), and thus free important cognitive resources for the students to focus on the targeted skill of inference making (Perfetti & Hart, 2002). Also, the use of open-ended ques-

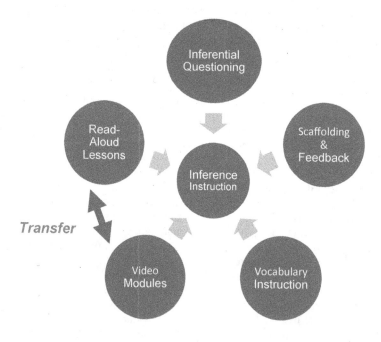

FIGURE 17.2. Core components of TELCI and ELCII.

tions ensures that students engage in language production through interaction with others for optimal learning to occur (Foorman et al., 2016; van Kleeck, 2008).

The Minnesota Inference Assessment (MIA) serves as a proximal pre- and posttest measure of inference making in the context of both ELCII and TeLCI. It comprises four video modules (two at pretest, two as posttest) that are constructed similarly to ELCII and TeLCI's modules. Each assessment module consists of a 5- to 6-minute video with eight inferential multiple-choice items presented throughout. Given that it is an assessment, no vocabulary instruction, scaffolding, or feedback is provided.

Evidence for Usability, Feasibility, and Promise of Inference Galaxy

Kendeou et al. (2019) articulated the iLC framework, which provides the theoretical rationale for the instructional design implemented in ELCII and TeLCI. McMaster et al. (2019) applied this framework to design-based research studies to develop and refine ELCII and TeLCI. In this phase, we collaborated with school partners (literacy specialists, teachers, and parents) and content experts to conceptualize, design, field-test, and refine these tools based on both observations of teachers and students during learning modules and read-alouds and explicit feedback from teachers on how to ensure its feasibility and usability in classroom contexts. We conducted a quasi-experimental study (Butterfuss et al., 2022) that compared the timing of questioning and identified that answering questions throughout the video as opposed to at its conclusion, is the optimal timing ($d = 0.12$). In this study, we also examined the extent to which ELCII and TeLCI had promise for improving inference ability from pre- to posttest on proximal ($d = 0.58$ for MIA) and distal measures ($d = 0.26$ for CELF-5 USP). We also analyzed the system log data of student responses to the inferential questions in the learning modules on a weekly basis to examine growth over time ($d = 0.80$) and as a function of the core components of scaffolding and feedback ($d = 1.25$), both demonstrating efficacy.

We also developed and validated the proximal measure, MIA (Kendeou et al., 2020). The results of the Rasch model indicated that a unidimensional vertical scale had a good fit to the data, also confirmed with a confirmatory factor analysis (comparative fit index = .90, Tucker–Lewis index = .90, root mean square error of approximation = .023), providing construct-validity evidence. MIA scores correlated with language and reading measures as expected (weak-to-moderate positive relations; Pearson et al., 2020), providing evidence for criterion-related validity. Currently, MIA has four parallel forms in the K–2 band, each with two videos, one fiction and one nonfiction, and a total of 16 questions. These forms have good internal consistency (all α's > .85).

Conclusion

In this chapter, we have emphasized the need for early language comprehension instruction to support later reading success, with a specific focus on inference generation. General language comprehension is a core component to reading comprehension and can be understood as both a generalized process and product. We identified the general and modality-specific comprehension processes that need to be accounted for when considering the transfer of skills across media. The iLC framework describes the necessary components needed to teach inference making, a foundational comprehension skill in young students, including questioning, vocabulary, scaffolding and feedback, and transfer of skills across modalities. The iLC framework informed the design of Tier 1 and Tier 2 instructional programs, in addition to an inference-making assessment for K–2. These tools are now fully integrated into the Inference Galaxy (*https://inferencegalaxy.com*), a digital system ready for large-scale implementation in K–2 settings. In future work, we need to understand better how transfer of inference skill across modalities and contexts can be accelerated in efforts to bridge persistent gaps and support all students' reading comprehension.

Acknowledgments

Writing of this chapter was funded in part by Grant Nos. R324A160064, R305A170242, and R305A220107 from the U.S. Department of Education to the University of Minnesota. The opinions are those of the authors and do not represent the policies of the U.S. Department of Education.

References

Ahmed, Y., Francis, D. J., York, M., Fletcher, J. M., Barnes, M., & Kulesz, P. (2016). Validation of the direct and inferential mediation (DIME) model of reading comprehension in grades 7 through 12. *Contemporary Educational Psychology, 44*(45), 68–82.

Barnett, S. M., & Ceci, S. J. (2002). When and where do we apply what we learn?: A taxonomy for far transfer. *Psychological Bulletin, 128*(4), 612–687.

Butler, A. C., Marsh, E. J., Slavinsky, J. P., & Baraniuk, R. G. (2014). Integrating cognitive science and technology improves learning in a STEM classroom. *Educational Psychology Review, 26*(2), 331–340.

Butler, A. C., & Roediger, H. L. (2007). Testing improves long-term retention in a simulated classroom setting. *European Journal of Cognitive Psychology, 19*(4–5), 514–527.

Buttersfuss, R., & Kendeou, P. (2018). The role of executive function in reading comprehension. *Educational Psychology Review, 30*, 801–826.

Butterfuss, R., Kendeou, P., McMaster, K. L., Orcutt, E., & Bulut, O. (2022). Question timing, language comprehension, and executive function in inferencing. *Scientific Studies of Reading, 26*, 61–78.

Butterfuss, R., Kim, J., & Kendeou, P. (2020). Reading comprehension [grantee submission]. In *Oxford Research Encyclopedia, Education.*

Byrne, B., & Fielding-Barnsley, R. (1995). Evaluation of a program to teach phonemic awareness to young children: A 2- and 3- year follow-up and a new preschool trial. *Journal of Educational Psychology, 87*, 488–503.

Cabell, S. Q., & Hwang, H. (2020). Building content knowledge to boost comprehension in the primary grades. *Reading Research Quarterly, 55*(Suppl. 1), S99–S107.

Cain, K., Oakhill, J. V., Barnes, M. A., & Bryant, P. E. (2001). Comprehension skill, inference-making ability, and their relation to knowledge. *Memory & Cognition, 29*(6), 850–859.

Cartwright, K. B., Lee, S. A., Taboada Barber, A., DeWyngaert, L. U., Lane, A. B., & Singleton, T. (2020). Contribution of executive function and intrinsic motivation to university students' reading comprehension. *Reading Research Quarterly, 55*(3), 345–369.

Cervetti, G., Pearson, P. D., Palincsar, A. S., Afflerbach, P., Kendeou,P., Biancarosa, G., . . . Berman, A. I. (2020). How reading for understanding research complicates the simple view of reading invoked in the science of reading. *Reading Research Quarterly, 55*(Suppl. 1), S161–S172.

Connor, C. M., Morrison, F. J., Fishman, B.,

Crowe, E. C., Al Otaiba, S., & Schatschneider, C. (2013). A longitudinal cluster-randomized controlled study on the accumulating effects of individualized literacy instruction on students' reading from first through third grade. *Psychological Science, 24*(8), 1408–1419.

Connor, C. M., Phillips, B. M., Kaschak, M., Apel, K., Kim, Y., Otaiba, S. A., . . . Lonigan, C. J. (2014). Comprehension tools for teachers: Reading for understanding from prekindergarten through fourth grade. *Educational Psychology Review, 26*(3), 379–401.

Cronbach, L. J., & Snow, R. E. (1977). *Aptitudes and instructional methods: A handbook for research on interactions.* Irvington.

Cutting, L. E., & Scarborough, H. S. (2012). Multiple bases for comprehension difficulties: The potential of cognitive and neurobiological profiling for validation of subtypes and development of assessments. In J. P. Sabatini, T. O'Reilly, & E. R. Albro (Eds.), *Reaching an understanding: Innovations in how we view reading assessment* (pp. 101–116). Rowman & Littlefield.

D'Mello, S. (2013). A selective meta-analysis on the relative incidence of discrete affective states during learning with technology. *Journal of Educational Psychology, 105*(4), 1082–1099.

Duke, N. K., & Cartwright, K. B. (2021). The science of reading progresses: Communicating advances beyond the simple view of reading. *Reading Research Quarterly, 56*(Suppl. 1), S25–S44.

Elbro, C., & Buch-Iversen, I. (2013). Activation of background knowledge for inference making: Effects on reading comprehension. *Scientific Studies of Reading, 17*(6), 435–452.

Foorman, B., Beyler, N., Borradaile, K., Coyne, M., Denton, C. A., Dimino, J., . . . Wissel, S. (2016). Foundational skills to support reading for understanding in kindergarten through 3rd grade. Retrieved from *https://ies.ed.gov/ncee/wwc/docs/practiceguide/wwc_foundational-reading_040717.pdf.*

Fricke, S., Bowyer-Crane, C., Haley, A. J., Hulme, C., & Snowling, M. J. (2013). Efficacy of language intervention in the early years. *Journal of Child Psychology and Psychiatry, 54*(3), 280–290.

Garcia, J. R., & Cain, K. (2014). Decoding and reading comprehension: A meta-analysis to identify which reader and assessment characteristics influence the strength of the relationship in English. *Review of Educational Research, 84*(1), 74–111.

Gernsbacher, M. A. (1990). *Language comprehension as structure building.* Erlbaum.

Gersten, R., Fuchs, L. S., Williams, J. P., & Baker, S. (2001). Teaching reading comprehension strategies to students with learning disabilities:

A review of research. *Review of Educational Research, 71*(2), 279–320.

Golke, S., Dörfler, T., & Artelt, C. (2015). The impact of elaborated feedback on text comprehension within a computer-based assessment. *Learning and Instruction, 39,* 123–136.

Gough, P., & Tunmer, W. (1986). Decoding, reading, and reading disability. *Remedial and Special Education, 7,* 6–10.

Graesser, A. C., & Franklin, S. P. (1990). QUEST: A cognitive model of question answering. *Discourse Processes, 13*(3), 279–303.

Graesser, A. C., Li, H., & Forsyth, C. (2014). Learning by communicating in natural language with conversational agents. *Current Directions in Psychological Science, 23*(5), 374–380.

Graesser, A. C., McNamara, D. S., & Louwerse, M. M. (2003). What do readers need to learn in order to process coherence relations in narrative and expository text. In A. P. Sweet & C. E. Snow (Eds.), *Rethinking reading comprehension* (pp. 82–98). Guilford Press.

Hattie, J., & Timperley, H. (2007). The power of feedback. *Review of Educational Research, 77*(1), 81–112.

Hawkins, R. O., Musti-Rao, S., Hale, A. D., McGuire, S., & Hailley, J. (2010). Examining listening previewing as a classwide strategy to promote reading comprehension and vocabulary. *Psychology in the Schools, 47*(9), 903–916.

Hogan, T. P., Adlof, S. M., & Alonzo, C. N. (2014). On the importance of listening comprehension. *International Journal of Speech–Language Pathology, 16,* 199–207.

Hwang, H. (2020). Early general knowledge predicts English reading growth in bilingual and monolingual students throughout elementary years. *Elementary School Journal, 121*(1), 154–178.

Jackson, G. T., & McNamara, D. S. (2013). Motivation and performance in a game-based intelligent tutoring system. *Journal of Educational Psychology, 105*(4), 1036–1049.

Kendeou, P. (2015). A general inference skill. In E. J. O'Brien, A. E. Cook, & R. F. Lorch (Eds.), *Inferences during reading* (pp. 160–181). Cambridge University Press.

Kendeou, P., Bohn-Gettler, C., White, M. J., & van den Broek, P. (2008). Children's inference generation across different media. *Journal of Research in Reading, 31,* 259–272.

Kendeou, P., Lynch, J. S., van den Broek, P., Espin, C. A., White, M. J., & Kremer, K. E. (2005). Developing successful readers: Building early comprehension skills through television viewing and listening. *Early Childhood Educational Journal, 33*(2), 91–98.

Kendeou, P., McMaster, K. L., Butterfuss, R., Kim, J., Bresina, B., & Wagner, K. (2019). The inferential language comprehension (iLC) framework:

Supporting Children's comprehension of visual narratives. *Topics in Cognitive Science, 12*(1), 256–273.

Kendeou, P., McMaster, K. L., Butterfuss, R., Kim, J., Slater, S., & Bulut, O. (2020). Development and validation of the Minnesota Inference Assessment. *Assessment for Effective Intervention, 47*(1), 47–52.

Kendeou, P., McMaster, K. L., & Christ, T. J. (2016). Reading comprehension: Core components and processes. *Policy Insights from the Behavioral and Brain Sciences, 3*(1), 62–69.

Kendeou, P., & O'Brien, E. J. (2018). Reading comprehension theories: A view from the top down. In M. F. Schober, D. N. Rapp, & M. A. Britt (Eds.), *The Routledge handbook of discourse processes* (pp. 7–21). Routledge/Taylor & Francis Group.

Kendeou, P., Savage, R., & van den Broek, P. (2009). Revisiting the simple view of reading. *British Journal of Educational Psychology, 79,* 353–370.

Kendeou, P., van den Broek, P., Helder, A., & Karlsson, J. (2014). A cognitive view of reading comprehension: Implications for reading difficulties. *Learning Disabilities Research and Practice, 29*(1), 10–16.

Kendeou, P., van den Broek, P., White, M. J., & Lynch, J. (2007). Comprehension in preschool and early elementary children: Skill development and strategy interventions. In D. S. McNamara (Ed.), *Reading comprehension strategies: Theories, interventions, and technologies* (pp. 27–45). Erlbaum.

Kendeou, P., van den Broek, P., White, M. J., & Lynch, J. S. (2009). Predicting reading comprehension in early elementary school: The independent contributions of decoding and oral language skills. *Journal of Educational Psychology, 101,* 765–778.

Kintsch, W. (1991). The role of knowledge in discourse comprehension: A construction–integration model. *Advances in Psychology, 79,* 107–153.

Kintsch, W., & van Dijk, T. A. (1978). Toward a model of text comprehension and production. *Psychological Review, 85*(5), 363–394.

Language and Reading Research Consortium. (2017). Oral language and listening comprehension: Same or different constructs? *Journal of Speech, Language, and Hearing Research, 60*(5), 1273–1284.

Language and Reading Research Consortium, Jiang, H., & Logan, J. (2019). Improving reading comprehension in the primary grades: Mediated effects of a language-focused classroom intervention. *Journal of Speech, Language, and Hearing Research, 62,* 2812–2828.

Language and Reading Research Consortium,

Pratt, A., & Logan, J. A. R. (2014). Improving language-focused comprehension instruction in primary-grade classrooms: Impacts of the Let's Know! experimental curriculum. *Educational Psychology Review, 26,* 357–377.

Language and Reading Research Consortium & Yeomans-Maldonado, G. (2017). Development of comprehension monitoring in beginner readers. *Reading and Writing, 30,* 2039–2067.

Lonigan, C. J., Burgess, S. R., & Schatschneider, C. (2018). Examining the simple view of reading with elementary school children: Still simple after all these years. *Remedial and Special Education, 39*(5), 260–273.

Lynch, J. S., & van den Broek, P. (2007). Understanding the glue of narrative structure: Children's on- and off-line inferences about characters' goals. *Cognitive Development, 22*(3), 323–340.

Lynch, J. S., van den Broek, P., Kremer, K., Kendeou, P., White, M. J., & Lorch, E. P. (2008). The development of narrative comprehension and its relation to other early reading skills. *Reading Psychology, 29*(4), 327–365.

Magliano, J. P., Larson, A. M., Higgs, K., & Loschky, L. C. (2015). The relative roles of visuospatial and linguistic working memory systems in generating inferences during visual narrative comprehension. *Memory & Cognition, 44*(2), 207–219.

Magliano, J. P., Loschky, L. C., Clinton, J. A., & Larson, A. M. (2013). Is reading the same as viewing?: An exploration of the similarities and differences between processing text- and visually based narratives. In B. Miller, L. Cutting, & P. McCardle (Eds.), *Unraveling the behavioral, neurobiological and genetic components of reading comprehension* (pp. 78–90). Brookes.

Magliano, J. P., Millis, K., Ozuru, Y., & McNamara, D. S. (2007). A multidimensional framework to evaluate reading assessment tools. In D. S. McNamara (Ed.), *Reading comprehension strategies: Theories, interventions, and technologies* (pp. 107–136). Erlbaum.

McMaster, K. L., & Espin, C. A. (2017). Reading comprehension instruction and intervention: Promoting inference making. In D. Compton, R. Partial, & K. Cain (Eds.). *Theories of reading development* (pp. 463–488). John Benjamins.

McMaster, K. L., Espin, C. A., & van den Broek, P. (2014). Making connections: Linking cognitive science and intervention research to improve comprehension of struggling readers. *Learning Disabilities Research and Practice, 29*(1), 17–24.

McMaster, K. L., Kendeou, P., Bresina, B., Slater, S., Wagner, K., White, M. J., . . . Umana, C. (2019). Developing an interactive software application to support young children's inference-making. *L1-Educational Studies in Languages and Literature, 19,* 1–30.

McMaster, K. L., van den Broek, P., Espin, C. A., Pinto, V., Janda, B., Lam, E., . . . van Boekel, M. (2015). Developing a reading comprehension intervention: Translating cognitive theory to educational practice. *Contemporary Educational Psychology, 40,* 28–40.

McNamara, D. S., & Kendeou, P. (2011). Translating advances in reading comprehension research to educational practice. *International Electronic Journal of Elementary Education, 4*(1), 33–46.

McNamara, D., & Kendeou, P. (2022). The early Automated Writing Evaluation (eAWE) Framework. *Assessment in Education: Principles, Policy and Practice, 29,* 150–182.

McNamara, D. S., & Magliano, J. (2009). Toward a comprehensive model of comprehension. In B. H. Ross (Eds.), *The psychology of learning and motivation* (pp. 297–384). Elsevier/Academic Press.

National Assessment of Educational Progress. (2019). The nation's report card. Retrieved from *www.nationsreportcard.gov/highlights/reading/2019.*

National Early Literacy Panel. (2008). Developing early literacy. Retrieved from *http://lincs.ed.gov/publications/pdf/nelpreport09.pdf.*

Nesbit, J. C., & Hadwin, A. F. (2006). Methodological issues in educational psychology. In P. A. Alexander & P. H. Winne (Eds.), *Handbook of educational psychology* (pp. 825–847). Erlbaum.

Pearson, P. D., Palincsar, A. S., Afflerbach, P., Cervetti, G. N., Kendeou, P., Biancarosa, G., . . . Berman, A. I. (2020). *Reaping the rewards for the reading for understanding initiative.* National Academy of Education.

Perfetti, C. A., & Hart, L. (2002). The lexical basis of comprehension skill. In D. S. Gorfein (Ed.), *On the consequences of meaning selection: Perspectives on resolving lexical ambiguity* (pp. 67–86). American Psychological Association.

Pressley, M. (2002). Metacognition and self-regulated comprehension. In A. E. Farstrup & S. J. Samuels (Eds.), *What research has to say about reading instruction* (3rd ed., pp. 291–309). International Reading Association.

Pressley, M., Graham, S., & Harris, K. (2006). The state of educational intervention research as viewed through the lens of literacy intervention. *British Journal of Educational Psychology, 76*(1), 1–19.

Rapp, D. N., van den Broek, P., McMaster, K. L., Kendeou, P., & Espin, C. A. (2007). Higher-order comprehension processes in struggling readers: A perspective for research and intervention. *Scientific Studies of Reading, 11*(4), 289–312.

Reed, D. K., Swanson, E., Petscher, Y., & Vaughn, S. (2014). The effects of teacher read-alouds and student silent reading on predominantly bilingual high school seniors' learning and retention of social studies content. *Reading and Writing, 27,* 1119–1140.

Roediger, H. L., & Marsh, E. J. (2005). The positive and negative consequences of multiple-choice testing. *Journal of Experimental Psychology: Learning, Memory, and Cognition, 31*(5), 1155–1159.

Silverman, R. D., Johnson, E., Keane, K., & Khanna, S. (2020). Beyond decoding: A meta-analysis of the effects of language comprehension interventions on K–5 students' language and literacy outcomes. *Reading Research Quarterly, 55*(Suppl. 1), S207–S233.

Snow, C. (2002). *Reading for understanding: Toward an R&D program in reading comprehension.* Rand Corporation.

Søndergaard Knudsen, H. B. S., Jensen de López, K., & Archibald, L. M. D. (2018). The contribution of cognitive flexibility to children's reading comprehension—the case for Danish. *Journal of Research in Reading, 41*(Suppl. 1), S130–S148.

Taboada Barber, A., Cartwright, K. B., Hancock, G. R., & Klauda, S. L. (2021). Beyond the simple view of reading: The role of executive functions in emergent bilinguals' and English monolinguals' reading comprehension. *Reading Research Quarterly, 56*(Suppl. 1), S45–S64.

Tilstra, J., McMaster, K., van den Broek, P., Kendeou, P., & Rapp, D. (2009). Simple but complex: Components of the simple view of reading across grade levels. *Journal of Research in Reading, 32,* 383–401.

van den Broek, P., Kendeou, P., Lousberg, S., & Visser, G. (2011). Preparing for reading comprehension: Fostering text comprehension skills in preschool and early elementary school children. *International Electronic Journal of Elementary Education, 4*(1), 259–268.

van Dijk, T. A., & Kintsch, W. (1983). *Strategies of discourse comprehension.* Academic Press.

van Kleeck, A. (2003). Research on book sharing: Another critical look. In A. van Kleeck, S. A. Stahl, & E. Bauer (Eds.) *On reading books to children: Parents and teachers* (pp. 271–320). Routledge.

van Kleeck, A. (2008). Providing preschool foundations for later reading comprehension: The importance of and ideas for targeting inferencing in storybook-sharing interventions. *Psychology in the Schools, 45*(7), 627–643.

VanLehn, K. (2011). The relative effectiveness of human tutoring, intelligent tutoring systems, and other tutoring systems. *Educational Psychologist, 46*(4), 197–221.

Weiser, B., & Mathes, P. (2011). Using encoding instruction to improve the reading and spelling performances of elementary students at risk for literacy difficulties: A best-evidence synthesis. *Review of Educational Research, 81*(2), 170–200.

Wright, T. S., & Cervetti, G. N. (2017). A systematic review of the research on vocabulary instruction that impacts text comprehension. *Reading Research Quarterly, 52*(2), 203–226.

Zevenbergen, A., & Whitehurst, G. (2003). Dialogic reading: A shared picture book reading intervention for preschoolers. In A. van Kleeck, S. A. Stahl, & E. Bauer (Eds.), *On reading to children: Parents and teachers* (pp. 177–200). Erlbaum.

PART IV

USING THE SCIENCE OF EARLY LITERACY IN PROFESSIONAL DEVELOPMENT AND FAMILY ENGAGEMENT

CHAPTER 18

Measuring and Improving Teachers' Knowledge in Early Literacy

Anne E. Cunningham, Allison R. Firestone, and Mónica Zegers

"I feel such a deeper sense of community and connection to what I'm learning in our small Teacher Study Groups," one member remarked to the group when comparing her experience to the district's large, workshop-style professional development, where she reported feeling lost and anonymous in a crowded setting. "Hmm, I wonder if that's how my children feel during circle time!?" her partner responded, highlighting the parallels in best practices in adult and child learning communities.
— Preschool teacher participants in Teacher Study Group program
(see Cunningham, Etter, Platas, Wheeler, & Campbell, 2015)

There are common features that support both children's learning in the classroom and teachers' learning in a professional development (PD) context. Just as children construct knowledge in a deep and meaningful way through thoughtfully designed learning experiences, teachers learn to implement high-quality classroom practices and meet students' needs when they engage in active learning experiences that simultaneously emphasize content and pedagogical content knowledge. Conducting PD in small groups over extended periods of time can meet teachers' individual needs and ensure their understanding of content, but developing deep networks of knowledge in teachers requires both well-designed professional learning opportunities and precise measures that can evaluate their effectiveness.

Why Should We Think about Teachers' Knowledge?

The field has been considering how best to support the development of deep networks of knowledge in teachers for some time. At the turn of the century, scholars began investigating teachers' knowledge as a potential lever for educational improvement. Although research had made significant progress in establishing what comprised effective reading instruction (see National Institute of Child Health and Human Development, 2000), many students—particularly those from marginalized groups (e.g., those with "atypical" learning needs, those who were not White, those who were learning English)—continued to struggle in becoming fluent, critical readers. In response to this disconnect between the existence of evidence-based literacy practices and teachers' ongoing struggle to support the reading development of all students, literacy scholars began to examine what Moats (1994) termed the *missing foundation in teacher education*: the requisite body of knowledge for teaching reading. It stood to reason that teachers who struggled to enact effective literacy instruction—particularly in as complex a task as reading, in as varied and dynamic a setting as a public school classroom—may lack a deep and flexible understanding of the subject. Thus, researchers investigated whether there was a body of knowledge that effective reading teachers drew on to implement evidence-based reading practices.

To ascertain whether an essential knowledge base for effective early literacy instruction existed, an initial wave of research built on Shulman's (1986, 1987) assertion that teachers need both subject-matter content (CK) and pedagogical content (PCK). *Subject-matter CK* refers to a teacher's understanding of a subject. Beyond memorized facts, CK is domain-specific expertise, akin to the deep agility within a subject accomplished through a college major. A teacher with deep CK in early literacy understands, for example, that spoken language comprises different-size units (e.g., phonemes) and how phonics connects to other foundational components in the reading acquisition trajectory. Early and recent research has established that effective literacy teachers possess a deep body of subject-specific CK that includes language knowledge (Phillips, Oliver, Tabulda, Wood, & Funari, 2020), linguistic knowledge (Fielding-Barnsley & Purdie, 2005; Wong Fillmore & Snow, 2018), phonological knowledge (McCutchen, Harry, et al., 2002), understanding of English orthography (Brady & Moats, 1997), understanding of phonics and decoding (Moats, 1994; Martinussen, Ferrari, Aitken, & Willows, 2015), and holistic knowledge of children's reading development (Cremin, Mottram, Bearne, & Goodwin, 2008; Wong Fillmore & Snow, 2018).

In this chapter, we define early literacy using Gough and Tunmer's (1986) widely accepted view that reading comprises two components: word recognition and language comprehension. This simple view of reading posits that strong reading comprehension cannot occur unless both decoding skills (i.e., word recognition) and language comprehension abilities are strong. Decoding includes the beginner's ability to convert letters to sounds to read a novel word and also the more mature reader's developed skill of instantly recognizing words (i.e., word recognition). This is not an easy task, however. The relational units of English orthography—the written symbols for sounds—are not simply single letters. English does not use a phonetic alphabet, wherein one letter represents a speech sound. It employs a *deep* alphabetic system that characterizes speech sounds and meaningful units in an often complex and varied manner.

As a result, beginning readers must acquire a conscious awareness of our sound system (i.e., phonology) to fluently anchor letters (i.e., graphemes) to sounds. Likewise, teachers must be conscious of these dimensions of oral language and their relation to English orthography to effectively teach this system to young children. Given the complexities of just this component of reading development, we focus exclusively in this chapter on the word recognition components related to early literacy instruction and teachers' associated knowledge.

As aforementioned, Shulman (1986, 1987) also articulated that effective teachers possess pedagogical content knowledge (PCK) given that "mere content knowledge is likely to be as useless pedagogically as content-free skill" (Shulman, 1986, p. 8). In addition to drawing on mutually exclusive bodies of knowledge on content and pedagogical practices, effective teachers leverage PCK—knowledge specifically associated with teaching a subject—that facilitates students' understanding of that subject area. Literacy research has since supported Shulman's argument (e.g., Griffith, Bauml, & Barksdale, 2015; Jordan, Bratsch-Hines, & Vernon-Feagans, 2018); it is with this subject-specific knowledge *for* teaching that teachers communicate their deep CK to students in a developmentally appropriate manner. For example, teachers who possesses PCK of linguistic structures communicate their CK to students through an accessible phonics lesson that provides instructive examples and nonexamples, precise feedback, and a nuanced analysis of student errors.

Given the criticality of both CK and PCK, our purpose in this chapter is to synthesize the extant research on teachers' knowledge in early literacy instruction (i.e., grades PreK–2), with an emphasis on the latest empirical work on the topic. We begin with a discussion of how research has expanded our understanding of why teachers' knowledge matters in early literacy instruction—and therefore why it is worth understanding—and we then synthesize recent findings regarding what today's teachers know. We also interrogate how teachers' knowledge has been measured across this body of work, with an emphasis on high-priority areas for future research and guidelines for evaluating the quality of existing measures. We conclude with a discussion of what the literature has indicated regarding effective practices for building teachers' knowledge.

Why Knowledge Matters

Knowledge Calibration

Knowledge calibration research has indicated that teachers' perceptions of their own knowledge are often inaccurate, overestimated, and thus insufficient proxies for actual knowledge—a fact that must be taken into account when planning coursework and PD. Knowledge calibration studies have long identified the disparate relationship between early literacy teachers' perceived and actual knowledge of children's literature, phonemic awareness, phonics, and overall reading-related CK (e.g., Cunningham, Perry, Stanovich, & Stanovich, 2004; Cunningham, Zibulsky, & Callahan, 2009). Echoing these findings more recently, both Stark, Snow, Eadie, and Goldfeld (2016) and Arrow, Braid, and Chapman (2019) found no relationship between teachers' self-rated and actual knowledge of early literacy concepts. Stark et al. (2016) found disparities among participants' requisite, perceived, and actual knowledge of basic linguistic constructs, and that no relationship existed between teachers' self-rated ability to teach phonemic awareness and phonics, and their demonstrated knowledge in those areas. Despite teachers rating their ability to teach early literacy skills as either moderate or very good, most displayed limited knowledge of these foundational components of early literacy.

Given these patterns, researchers (e.g., Cunningham et al., 2009; Cunningham & Ryan O'Donnell, 2015) have hypothesized that the discrepancy between actual and perceived knowledge may act as a barrier to professional learning. In fact, teachers' knowledge calibration does appear to impact the effectiveness of PD activities, suggesting that coherence with teachers' existing levels of knowledge must be taken into account when designing and implementing PD (see Firestone, Cruz, & Rodl, 2020), as well as the presence or lack of knowledge calibration. For example, Mathers (2021) assessed preschool teachers' pedagogical knowledge of oral language before and after participating in an intervention, and their findings demonstrated that the knowledge teachers possessed prior to the intervention explained the degree to which it impacted teachers' instruction.

Relatedly, Scarparolo and Hammond (2018) used preintervention assessment scores to tailor their PD to teachers' needs. The researchers shared teachers' scores with them prior to beginning the PD "to enable the teachers to accurately calibrate their current level of knowledge with their perceptions of what they knew and understood. This was done purposely to ensure that the participants would be more receptive to the information being presented" (p. 498). In doing so, the researchers drew teachers' attention to areas in which they demonstrated low to moderate knowledge. The authors posited that the significant improvements in teachers' knowledge and willingness to incorporate new practices into their instruction related to their being made aware of what they did not know prior to participation. This work suggests that accurately measuring and supporting calibration of teachers' knowledge is an important step in designing and implementing professional learning opportunities.

Teachers' Knowledge, Teachers' Practice, Student Outcomes: A Conceptual Framework

The relationship between teachers' knowledge, instruction, and student achievement is complex. Extant literature has suggested that teachers' knowledge impacts classroom instruction—and, conversely, that teachers' experiences during classroom instruction impact their knowledge—and that improved knowledge and practice enhance student outcomes (Desimone & Garet, 2015; Didion, Toste, & Filderman, 2020; Firestone et al., 2020; Piasta, Park, Farley, Justice, & O'Connell, 2020; Schachter, Spear, Piasta, Justice, & Logan, 2016; Shulman, 1987). We thus ground this discussion in a conceptual framework (see Figure 18.1) that acknowledges the dynamic way in which teachers' knowledge influences their practice and their students.

This framework rests on both seminal and contemporary reading research. For example, McCutchen, Abbott, et al. (2002) found a relationship between reading teachers' CK—of both literature and phonology—and instructional quality, and also between teachers' phonological knowledge and their students' reading achievement. Other findings have indicated the role of teachers' knowledge and practice in impacting students' reading development. McCutchen, Harry, et al.'s (2002) study on teachers' knowledge of early literacy found that when teachers became more knowledgeable about the roles of phonological and orthographic content in lit-

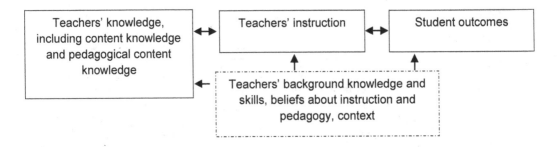

FIGURE 18.1. Relationship between teachers' knowledge, teachers' practice, and student outcomes. See Desimone (2009), Desimone and Garet (2015), and Firestone et al. (2020).

eracy instruction, they applied that knowledge to improve their classroom practice.

Recent research has both confirmed and provided a more nuanced picture of the role that teachers' knowledge plays in changing students' reading outcomes. For example, Cash, Cabell, Hamre, DeCoster, and Pianta (2015) examined prekindergarten teachers' beliefs and knowledge in relation to students' language and literacy development. Their analysis revealed that though teachers' beliefs did not predict skills development, teachers' knowledge of language positively predicted gains in children's expressive vocabulary skills. Additionally, they found that teachers' literacy knowledge predicted gains in children's print knowledge. Though this is not evidence of a linear, causal pathway from teachers' knowledge to student outcomes—given that some research has demonstrated changes in knowledge that have not been associated with changes in instruction or student outcomes (e.g., Gersten, Dimino, Jayanthi, Kim, & Santoro, 2010; Jayanthi et al., 2018; Neuman & Cunningham, 2009)—evidence exists in support of a dynamic interaction among teachers' knowledge, practice, and student learning.

What Do Teachers Know about Early Literacy?

In their foundational study, Moats and Foorman (2003) pinpointed common misconceptions in teachers' understanding of early literacy and indicated areas in which targeted learning was needed. Salient areas of misunderstanding included (1) the phoneme–grapheme relationship (e.g., identification of phonemes within words); (2) functional spelling units (e.g., digraphs, blends, and silent letter spellings);

(3) conventions of syllable deletion and syllable spelling; (4) linguistic components of sentences; (5) children's difficulties with phonological, orthographic, and syntactic learning; and (6) the relationships among components of early literacy instruction. In the two decades since publication of Moats and Foorman's study, research has shown that teachers' knowledge in oral language, phonological awareness, and phonics remains low (e.g., Schachter et al., 2016). However, research on new teachers entering the workforce (Clark, Helfrich, & Hatch, 2017; Tetley & Jones, 2014) and effective models of PD (e.g., Cunningham et al., 2015) hold promise for supporting knowledge acquisition in these critical areas.

Teachers' Knowledge of Early Literacy: The Building Blocks of Reading

First, early literacy teachers need deep knowledge of the structure of the English language given that language is foundational in learning to read and of particular importance in supporting emerging multilingual learners (e.g., Cunningham & Ryan O'Donnell, 2015; Foorman et al., 2016; Gough & Tunmer, 1986). In its broadest definition, *oral language* comprises phonology, grammar, morphology, vocabulary, discourse, and pragmatics. Certain components of oral language, such as phonology, morphology, and vocabulary, are directly linked to the code-related skills that help word reading develop and provide the foundation for development of the more advanced language skills needed for comprehension (Cain & Oakhill, 2007). Consequently, to support the development of oral language in young students and connect it to literacy, teachers must understand that spoken language comprises different-size units (e.g., phonemes) that may or may not correspond one-to-one with graphemes. Teachers must also understand that phonemes build morphemes, morphemes build words, words build phrases, and so on; in other words, they must possess knowledge of the building blocks of language. Yet oral language knowledge remains an area in which teachers need capacity building (Schachter et al., 2016).

Phonics and phonological awareness are additional areas of early literacy in which teachers need in-depth CK and PCK given that "the knowledge base for teaching speech to print relationships is hard to access and not gained simply through classroom experience or introspection" (Moats, 2009, p. 388). Both have been identified as high-need areas in terms of teachers' knowledge development (Carreker, Joshi, & Boulware-Gooden, 2010; Cheesman, McGuire, Shankweiler, & Coyne, 2009; Cunningham et al., 2004; Cunningham & Ryan O'Donnell, 2015; Cunningham & Zibulsky, 2009; Washburn, Joshi, & Binks-Cantrell, 2011a, 2011b). Knowledge of *phonological awareness*—the ability to perceive (e.g., hear) and manipulate (e.g., segment, blend) smaller units of sound (e.g., /c/ in *cat*) within words—is critical to ensure that all students establish decoding skills. This also includes a deep understanding of the alphabetic principle—in English, we have 26 letters (i.e., graphemes) that map onto 44 sounds (i.e., phonemes), and our written code is based on approximately 44 phonemes. These sounds can be represented in multiple ways (e.g., /f/ in *fan, cliff, phone, laugh*). The *method* of teaching the alphabetic principle to beginning readers is called *phonics* instruction. Accordingly, learning phonological awareness, the alphabetic principle, and all the associated phoneme–grapheme mappings, coupled with rapid automatic word recognition, is of particular importance in preventing early reading struggles (Foorman et al., 2016). Dispiritingly, research has suggested that teachers' knowledge remains low in these areas (e.g., Brady et al., 2009; Cohen, Mather, Schneider, & White, 2017; Cunningham et al., 2015; Puliatte & Ehri, 2018).

Preservice Teachers: Coursework and Exposure

Two additional studies, both focused on preservice teachers' knowledge, have suggested that the reading curricula to which teachers are exposed early on may influence their knowledge formation, and that preparatory coursework and practicum experiences play a role in building foundational CK and PCK. Tetley and Jones (2014) examined 224 preservice teachers' CK of language concepts and found that participants' scores on a knowledge survey were associated with exposure to particular curricula during classroom experiences. Those who had been exposed to Reading Recovery[1] had significantly lower phonological construct scores than those who had not, whereas those who had been exposed to a structured commercial phonics program demonstrated significantly higher phonological construct scores than those who had not. As the authors hypothesized, these findings suggest that experience with curriculum aligned with evidence-based recommendations for early literacy instruction (Foorman et al., 2016) supports understanding of phonological awareness and phonics. It is important to note, however, that research with practicing teachers has examined whether district curriculum predicts knowledge, and findings have indicated that the mere presence of a code-based program is not sufficient to build teachers' knowledge (Cohen et al., 2017). This work indicates that though required use of a curriculum is not a panacea, providing novice teachers with course-aligned, guided experiences with code-based curricula may support knowledge development.

Relatedly, Clark et al's (2017) study of preservice teachers underscored the influence of coursework on phonological awareness and phonics knowledge. Drawing participants from two different teacher preparation programs, they examined whether participants' knowledge varied based on required reading coursework (one program required five reading methods courses, whereas the other required just two). Despite the researchers' hypothesis to the contrary, participants from the two-course program scored significantly higher on a knowledge survey than those from the five-course program. These findings suggest that quality and depth of coursework rather than quantity mattered given the two-course program's tight focus on code-based instruction. This work suggests that preservice teachers' preparation—both in coursework and in practicum experiences—should be grounded in evidence-based phonological awareness and phonics instruction to prepare candidates with knowledge of these critical components in early reading and especially for word recognition processes (see also Jordan et al., 2018).

Knowledge for Teaching Struggling Readers

Finally, it is important to emphasize that teachers' CK and PCK support the enactment of high-quality learning experiences for *all* students across diversity spectra (e.g., cognitive, linguistic, racial/ethnic). In other words, supporting teachers' acquisition of research-based knowledge, as conceptualized in the previous sections, supports all learners by ensuring high-quality universal instruction and responsive intervention when needed (Gersten et al., 2008). Given that teachers' prior experience with code-based PD has been shown to predict their knowledge (e.g., Spear-Swerling & Cheesman, 2011), strengthening teachers' CK and PCK in oral language, phonological awareness, phonics, morphology, and orthography remains a powerful mechanism for improving outcomes among struggling readers. Furthermore, ensuring that teachers understand the value of a code-based approach to reading instruction enhances the likelihood that teachers will allocate instructional time accordingly (Cunningham et al., 2009; Spear-Swerling & Zibulsky, 2014), which is of particular importance for students who struggle to acquire early reading skills.

Measuring Teachers' Knowledge

Though research has enhanced our understanding of teachers' early literacy knowledge, there are measurement-precision issues within this body of work. Across studies, literacy-related constructs have not been clearly and consistently named, defined, and operationalized—a problem that Reutzel et al. (2011) highlighted a decade ago but remains unsolved. Inconsistencies in construct naming generate confusion: Is phonological awareness the same as phonological sensitivity? How about the alphabetic principle and phonics? For example, multiple articles have reported measuring "language constructs," but what comprises language constructs has varied. For Carlisle, Correnti, Phelps, and Zeng (2009), language constructs consisted of phonemic awareness, phonics, fluency, vocabulary, and reading comprehension, whereas for Binks-Cantrell, Joshi, and Washburn (2012) it encompassed phonological and phonemic awareness, phonics, and morphology. Similarly, reading comprehension as a construct has encompassed morphology, text analysis, and fluency (Carlisle, Kelcey, Rowan, & Phelps, 2011), though in other cases it has been defined as independent from fluency and phonics (Carlisle et al., 2009).

Another challenge related to measurement precision is the common practice of adapting existing measures for new studies and the often unaddressed requirement to establish evidence of reliability, validity, and fairness (American Educational Research Association [AERA], American Psychological Association, & National Council on Measurement in Education, 2014). *Validity* refers to the degree to which an instrument accurately measures what it purports to measure; *reliability* alludes to the consistency of scores across tasks, contexts, or raters; and *fairness* refers to actively reducing bias during each stage of test development. Though it is a common practice to adapt existing instruments to fit a study's purpose—for example, when assessing a new population in terms of sociocultural background, language, or expertise—it becomes problematic when evidence of validity and reliability for the adapted measure is not established. Researchers and administrators must keep these standards in mind when selecting, developing, adapting, and evaluating measures.

Use of Construct-Based Assessments

Construct-based assessments conceptualize learning as a progression along a dimension of interest (i.e., the construct), beginning by specifying a construct that describes a latent ability, such as learners' understanding of a concept or practice. This approach requires that a construct be clearly delineated, which results in a useful tool. Moreover, they use multiple items to assess the target construct. This, in turn, prevents construct underrepresentation, or "the extent to which a test fails to capture important aspects of the construct domain that the test is intended to measure" (AERA et al., 2014, p. 217), which can occur if a test attempts to measure a broad swath of knowledge with a small set of items. This does not mean that measures assessing multiple constructs should be avoided; rather, developers of such instruments must (1) clearly indicate the items assessing each construct, (2) establish that each dimension assessing a particular construct is valid and reliable, and (3) maintain awareness of within-item multidimensionality,[2] or that items may tap more than one construct (Wu, Adams, Wilson, & Haldane, 2007).

Early Literacy Measures Available by Construct

Our goal was to identify available measures that clearly delineated the constructs being assessed within the larger domain of teachers' knowledge of early literacy. We identified measures that met the following criteria: (1) used with English-speaking populations, (2) used with prekindergarten–2 preservice and practicing teachers, and (3) provided evidence of validity and reliability. These include the following criteria.

Phonological Awareness

Phonological awareness is the most assessed aspect of teachers' early literacy knowledge, which is unsurprising given the criticality of this skill in reading acquisition. Existing measures probe, for example, teachers' ability to define and indicate the importance of phonological awareness in reading development and the ability to identify, count, and delete phonemes. Among the measures identified, the Teacher's Knowledge and Perceptions of Knowledge (Binks-Cantrell et al., 2012) has good reliability ($\alpha = 0.90$) and provides a clear definition of phonological awareness. The Knowledge Test (McMahan, Oslund, & Odegard, 2019) has also shown high reliability in its two forms ($\alpha_{-A} = 0.86$ and $\alpha_{-B} = 0.87$), and it probes the common confusion between teachers' knowledge of phonemic awareness and higher-level phonological awareness activities. The Phonemic Awareness, Knowledge, and Skills test (Cheesman et al., 2009) has moderate to high reliability (Kuder–Richardson Formula 20 = 0.69; Spearman–Brown for longer version = 0.82) and includes items that assess knowledge, skills, and pedagogical expertise.

The Alphabetic Principle

As a foundational construct, most multidimensional measures include at least some items on phonetics and phonics. These constructs are usually assessed with items asking teachers to define phonemic awareness, indicate the importance of phonemic awareness for reading development, and apply knowledge in tasks such as counting phonemes and identifying phonemes in words spelled with complex graphemes. Five of the 28 measures that we identified also included items that assess teachers' perceived ability (Cunningham et al., 2004), and six also included PCK items (e.g., choosing which of three instructional activities focused on phonemic awareness). Overall, available multiconstruct measures have shown moderate to high reliability. Among the construct-based measures, the Phonics Knowledge Task (Cunningham et al., 2004) is based on a clear definition and operationalization of phonics (a method for teaching the alphabetic principle and grapheme–phoneme mappings) that distinguish between implicit and explicit knowledge. However, this measure should be used with caution, as only the implicit knowledge dimension has shown good reliability ($\alpha_{-} = 0.77$ vs. $\alpha_{-} = 0.40$).

Morphology

Morpheme knowledge has been assessed with surveys that ask for definitions and explanations, and require knowledge application, such as identifying and counting morphemes in written words. Apart from the Morpheme Counting Task (Spear-Swerling, Brucker, & Alfano, 2005), no measure has evaluated morpheme knowledge as an independent construct. Similarly, in PCK-specific assessments, morphology has been considered a dimension within comprehension (Carlisle et al., 2011; Phelps & Schilling, 2004) rather than an independent construct. Additional multi-item, construct-based measures are needed in this area.

Orthography and Spelling

Knowledge of orthography and rules of spelling is difficult to measure, as both encompass multiple dimensions of literacy knowledge. For example, spelling requires "knowledge of phonology, orthographic patterns, morphology, and the relationship between word form and word meaning" (Puliatte & Ehri, 2018, p. 246). Because spelling is a procedure, surveys and vignettes have assessed PCK by asking teachers to indicate best practices for teaching students to become proficient spellers (Carreker et al., 2010; Puliatte & Ehri, 2018). Occasionally, surveys have assessed teachers' CK on spelling rules, such as differentiating regularly spelled from irregularly spelled high-frequency words (Moats & Foorman, 2003; Puliatte & Ehri, 2018). Among existing measures, however, only two are clearly focused on evaluating spelling or orthographic knowledge: the Instructional Practices Questionnaire (IPQ; Puliatte & Ehri, 2018), which evaluates best practices to teach spelling, and the Spelling Instruction Assessment (SIA; Carreker et al., 2010), which evaluates proficiency in identifying students with spelling difficulties and best practices to ameliorate difficulties. However, the reliability of the SIA is moderate, and no reliability information was provided for the IPQ. Therefore, we recommend requesting reliability information and carefully reviewing these measures before using them.

Children's Literature

There are limited measures available to assess teachers' knowledge of children's literature, and the Title Recognition Test (TRT; Cunningham et al., 2004, 2009) was the only one identified with strong evidence of validity and reliability. The TRT asks teachers to identify known titles in a list of children's books that includes real titles and foils. Teachers with greater knowledge of children's literature score higher by identifying more actual titles of children's books and fewer foils. However, the TRT requires adaptation based on the population being assessed—in terms of the country of origin, language spoken, and grades taught—and existing versions must be periodically updated to include new books. Ideally, different versions of this measure will continue to emerge with sufficient evidence of validity and reliability (e.g., Kozak & Martin-Chang, 2019).

BOOK SHARING

Given that there are multiple ways to use a book, the limited number of measures we found have focused on different dimensions of a teacher's ability to share books as a learning tool. Piasta et al. (2010), for example, developed an observational rubric to assess teachers' print referencing (e.g., print meaning, print organization, attention to letters and words) during shared reading. Hsieh, Hemmeter, McCollum, and Ostrosky (2009) created an observational checklist to account for the strategies used during shared reading, and these were organized in three clusters: oral language (e.g., expanding children's information), alphabetic code (e.g., demonstrating and emphasizing characteristics of sounds and words), and print knowledge (e.g., pointing out print conventions). Additional research is needed to link these observational tools with teachers' literature CK.

Effective Practices for Building Teachers' Knowledge

Though there are open questions regarding measurement, it is clear that teachers are more likely to enact effective early literacy instruction when they possess deep, working knowledge of oral language, phonological awareness, and phonics. Therefore, there is continued demand for teacher preparation and PD that support construction of CK and PCK. Fortunately, researchers have examined a variety of models for doing so, including intensive PDs, instructional coaching, and growth-in-practice approaches.

Intensive PD and Coaching Models

We refer to *intensive PD* as that which is delivered by a researcher or PD professional within a constrained amount of time (e.g., a 1-day workshop). This is commonly considered the traditional model for professional learning, and it remains the prevalent form of PD in many districts (Tooley & White, 2018; Wei, Darling-Hammond, & Adamson, 2010). This model has been critiqued as a top-down, one-size-fits-all approach that treats teachers as passive recipients of knowledge (Lieberman & Miller, 2014; Little, 2003), and recent studies have addressed this by tailoring intensive PD to teachers' background knowledge and integrating more active learning experiences. For example, Scarparolo and Hammond's (2018) use of teachers' preassessment scores: "Teachers are at the core of the professional development, not an afterthought and this is reflected in the fact that the teachers' knowledge was sought prior to the professional development so that it could be tailored to their areas of need" (p. 494). In this way, the researchers individualized the PD, building on previous findings regarding knowledge calibration (e.g., Cunningham et al., 2009) and the impact of teachers' existing knowledge on intervention effectiveness (e.g., Brady et al., 2009).

Teachers participating in intensive PD that includes coaching have reported that coaches' demonstrations of teaching practices in their classrooms contributed to their growth. Coaching in combination with a knowledge-building PD has been shown to result in improvements in classroom practice (e.g., Ehri & Flugman, 2018; Goldfeld et al., 2020; Neuman & Cunningham, 2009), which suggests that classroom-based coaching can connect new knowledge to classroom practice—a finding that has relevance for teacher preparation (Hindman & Wasik, Chapter 19, this volume). Taken together with work that has indicated the positive impact of high-quality classroom experiences on novice teachers' knowledge (e.g., Tetley & Jones, 2014), those designing student teaching experiences may leverage the power of coaching in tandem with university coursework on early literacy. Given that most teacher preparation programs include funding and infrastructure for coaching—commonly in the form of university supervisors—there is an opportunity to connect the learning occurring in coursework to candidates' K–12 classroom experiences. University supervisors can demonstrate skills taught in coursework through instructional modeling in the classroom, which holds promise for building foundational knowledge of early literacy among preservice teachers.

Growth-in-Practice Models

Just as classroom learning is increasingly understood through the lens of teacher–child interactions, teachers' knowledge may also be conceptualized as constructed through relationship-based learning. Analyses have suggested that sustained, school-based models for learning—in which teachers actively connect new knowledge to their day to-day practice (Darling-Hammond, Wei, Andree, Richardson, & Orphanos, 2009, Kennedy, 2016)—may be more effective in improving knowledge and practice than intensive PDs. These approaches tend to frame teachers as agents actively constructing professional knowledge, best supported by learning to learn from their own practice (Darling-Hammond, Hyler, & Gardner, 2017; Lieberman & Miller, 2014). Common growth-in-practice models include professional learning communities (PLCs; e.g., Vescio, Ross, & Adams, 2008), Japanese lesson study (e.g., Doig & Groves, 2011), and teacher study groups (TSGs; e.g., Gersten et al., 2010). PLCs and lesson study groups tend to focus on a fluid array of member-selected topics, whereas TSGs focus on a single, preselected topic, such as emergent literacy (e.g., Cunningham et al., 2015). TSGs leverage expert input (e.g., a university faculty member or master teacher) to facilitate integration of new knowledge into teachers' collaborative discussions and application to practice. Many TSGs have focused on literacy, and this body of work has demonstrated a positive impact on teachers' knowledge. For example,

Cunningham et al. (2015) implemented a design experiment with three sequential, yearlong TSG cohorts. Participating teachers' CK and PCK were initially low, and both increased significantly after participating in the TSG. Larger, randomized TSGs have also demonstrated statistically significant, positive impacts on teachers' knowledge (Gersten et al., 2010; Jayanthi et al., 2018).

In terms of scaling this research to practice, the empirical work has suggested that particular components of TSGs may act as active ingredients that enhance teachers' knowledge in a way that improves their practice and, ultimately, student learning (Firestone et al., 2020). These components include (1) expert input, (2) a direct connection to teachers' daily practice, (3) the opportunity to learn through collaboration with colleagues, (4) coherence with existing knowledge and beliefs, and (5) sustained duration (e.g., over the course of an academic year). For example, teachers have specified that expert input—new content presented by a researcher or school-based facilitator—supported their acquisition and enactment of newly learned concepts (e.g., Hung & Yeh, 2013) and facilitated the emergence of a common knowledge base among colleagues (e.g., Englert & Tarrant, 1995). Though TSGs are a model primarily focused on teacher inquiry and collaboration, reserving a small portion of sessions for an expert to provide teachers with new content, answer questions, and provide contextually relevant examples appears to act as a scaffold that supports teachers in learning to identify and address problems of practice. Across studies, teachers have also described TSGs' connection to daily practice and the iterative experience of building knowledge through critical reflection as key in connecting new knowledge to sustained changes in their instruction. Finally, teachers have reported that ongoing collaboration with colleagues toward a shared goal, such as improving literacy instruction, is supportive in acquiring and enacting new knowledge.

From this work, we have begun to develop a more nuanced understanding of the components that underlie growth-in-practice models and facilitate their impact on teachers' knowledge. At the heart of this approach is that teaching is understood as dynamic and "unforgivingly complex," (Cochran-Smith et al., 2016, p. 71) and therefore requires ongoing collaboration and reflection.

Future Directions

In this chapter, we have summarized available research on teachers' knowledge of early literacy. We conclude that there are high-need areas for teachers' knowledge development, and that what we know about effective teacher learning can support knowledge acquisition in critical areas of early literacy. There is increasing evidence that relationship-based PD models enhance teachers' knowledge (e.g., Cunningham et al., 2015), and research with preservice teachers suggests that coaching in tandem with coursework on early literacy can positively impact novice teachers' knowledge (e.g., Tetley & Jones, 2014). Strengthening teachers' CK and PCK in early literacy is a powerful lever for improving outcomes for all learners, as it is a foundation for high-quality universal instruction.

However, there are issues that must be addressed in understanding, measuring, and building teachers' knowledge. We need to enhance precision in naming, defining, and operationalizing the constructs we measure, while also carefully designing—and choosing—measures with evidence of validity, reliability, and fairness. These efforts should focus on systematizing the information available on teachers' knowledge by methodically mapping how constructs are measured, how PD impacts teachers' knowledge, and how changes in knowledge correlate with children's literacy outcomes. Efforts in improving measurement should also develop measures for unexplored dimensions of teachers' knowledge, such as syntax and book use.

Teaching is a multifaceted intellectual endeavor requiring application of deep knowledge in contextualized decision making. As the field prioritizes inclusive models of instruction that support the engagement of all students in meaningful learning (Waitoller & King Thorius, 2016), ensuring that teachers have the foundational knowledge to do so remains of the utmost importance.

Notes

1. A reading intervention that emphasizes children's ability to use multiple cues (syntactic, semantic, visual, graphophonemic) to identify unfamiliar words and correct errors while reading connected text (Chapman & Tunmer, 2018; Clay, 1991).

2. Within-item multidimensionality may occur, for example, when evaluating knowledge of the alphabetic principle, which requires sensitivity to phonology. In this case, there is an overlap between these constructs.

References

American Educational Research Association, American Psychological Association, & National Council on Measurement in Education. (2014). *Standards for Educational and Psychological Testing*. American Educational Research Association.

Arrow, A. W., Braid, C., & Chapman, J. W. (2019). Explicit linguistic knowledge is necessary, but not sufficient, for the provision of explicit early literacy instruction. *Annals of Dyslexia, 69*(1), 99–113.

Binks-Cantrell, E., Joshi, R. M., & Washburn, E. K. (2012). Validation of an instrument for assessing teacher knowledge of basic language constructs of literacy. *Annals of Dyslexia, 62*(3), 153–171.

Brady, S., Gillis, M., Smith, T., Lavalette, M. Bronstein, L., Lowe, E., . . . Wilder, T. (2009). First grade teachers' knowledge of phonological awareness and code concepts: Examining gains from an intensive form of professional development and corresponding teacher attitudes. *Reading and Writing, 22*(4), 425–455.

Brady, S., & Moats, L. (1997). *Informed instruction for reading success: Foundations for teacher preparation* (Position Paper). International Dyslexia Association.

Cain, K., & Oakhill, J. (2007). Cognitive bases of children's language comprehension difficulties: Where do we go from here? In *Children's comprehension problems in oral and written language: A cognitive perspective* (pp. 283–295). Guilford Press.

Carlisle, J. F., Correnti, R., Phelps, G., & Zeng, J. (2009). Exploration of the contribution of teachers' knowledge about reading to their students' improvement in reading. *Reading and Writing, 22*(4), 457–486.

Carlisle, J. F., Kelcey, B., Rowan, B., & Phelps, G. (2011). Teachers' knowledge about early reading: Effects on students' gains in reading achievement. *Journal of Research on Educational Effectiveness, 4*(4), 289–321.

Carreker, S., Joshi, R. M., & Boulware-Gooden, R. (2010). Spelling-related teacher knowledge: The impact of professional development on identifying appropriate instructional activities. *Learning Disability Quarterly, 33*(3), 148–158.

Cash, A. H., Cabell, S. Q., Hamre, B. K., DeCoster, J., & Pianta, R. C. (2015). Relating prekindergarten teacher beliefs and knowledge to children's language and literacy development. *Teaching and Teacher Education, 48*, 97–105.

Chapman, J. W., & Tunmer, W. E. (2018). Reading Recovery's unrecovered learners: Characteristics and issues. *Review of Education, 7*(2), 237–265.

Cheesman, E., McGuire, J., Shankweiler, D., & Coyne, M. (2009). First-year teacher knowledge of phonemic awareness and its instruction. *Teacher Education and Special Education, 32*(3), 270–289.

Clark, S. K., Helfrich, S. R., & Hatch, L. (2017). Examining preservice teacher content and pedagogical content knowledge needed to teach reading in elementary school. *Journal of Research in Reading, 40*(3), 219–232.

Clay, M. (1991). Why is an inservice programme for Reading Recovery teachers necessary? *Reading Horizons: A Journal of Literacy and Language Arts, 31*(5), 355–372.

Cochran-Smith, M., Ell, F., Grudnoff, L., Haigh, M., Hill, M., & Ludlow, L. (2016). Initial teacher education: What does it take to put equity at the center? *Teaching and Teacher Education, 57*, 67–78.

Cohen, R. A., Mather, N., Schneider, D. A., & White, J. M. (2017). A comparison of schools: Teacher knowledge of explicit code-based reading instruction. *Reading and Writing, 30*(4), 653–690.

Cremin, T., Mottram, M., Bearne, E., & Goodwin, P. (2008). Exploring teachers' knowledge of children's literature. *Cambridge Journal of Education, 38*(4), 449–464.

Cunningham, A. E., Etter, K., Platas, L., Wheeler, S., & Campbell, K. (2015). Professional development in emergent literacy: A design experiment of teacher study groups. *Early Childhood Research Quarterly, 31*, 62–77.

Cunningham, A. E., Perry, K. E., Stanovich, K. E., & Stanovich, P. J. (2004). Disciplinary knowledge of K–3 teachers and their knowledge calibration in the domain of early literacy. *Annals of Dyslexia, 54*(1), 139–167.

Cunningham, A. E., & Ryan O'Donnell, C. (2015). Teacher knowledge in early literacy. In A. Pollatsek & R. Treiman (Eds.), *The Oxford handbook of reading* (pp. 447–462). Oxford University Press.

Cunningham, A. E., & Zibulsky, J. (2009). Introduction to the special issue about perspectives on teachers' disciplinary knowledge of reading processes, development, and pedagogy. *Special Issue on Teacher Knowledge: Reading and Writing: An Interdisciplinary Journal, 22*, 375–378.

Cunningham, A. E., Zibulsky, J., & Callahan, M. D. (2009). Starting small: Building preschool teacher knowledge that supports early literacy development. *Reading and Writing: An Interdisciplinary Journal, 22*(4), 487–510.

Darling-Hammond, L., Hyler, M. E., & Gardner, M. (2017). *Effective teacher professional development*. Learning Policy Institute.

Darling-Hammond, L., Wei, R. C., Andree, A., Richardson, N., & Orphanos, S. (2009). *Professional learning in the learning profession: A status report on teacher development in the United States and abroad*. School Redesign Network at Stanford University.

Desimone, L. M. (2009). Improving impact studies of teachers' professional development: Toward better conceptualizations and measures. *Educational Researcher, 38*(3), 181–199.

Desimone, L. M., & Garet, M. S. (2015). Best practices in teachers' professional development in the United States. *Psychology, Society, and Education, 7*(3), 252–263.

Didion, L., Toste, J. R., & Filderman, M. J. (2020). Teacher professional development and student reading achievement: A meta-analytic review of the effects. *Journal of Research on Educational Effectiveness, 13*(1), 29–66.

Doig, B., & Groves, S. (2011). Japanese lesson study: Teacher professional development through communities of inquiry. *Mathematics Teacher Education and Development, 13*(1), 77–93.

Ehri, L. C., & Flugman, B. (2018). Mentoring teachers in systematic phonics instruction: Effectiveness of an intensive year-long program for kindergarten through 3rd grade teachers and their students. *Reading and Writing, 31*(2), 425–456.

Englert, C. S., & Tarrant, K. L. (1995). Creating collaborative cultures for educational change. *Remedial and Special Education, 16*(6), 325–336.

Fielding-Barnsley, R., & Purdie, N. (2005). Teachers' attitude to and knowledge of metalinguistic in the process of learning to read. *Asia-Pacific Journal of Teacher Education, 33*(1), 65–76.

Firestone, A. R., Cruz, R. A., & Rodl, J. E. (2020). Teacher study groups: An integrative literature synthesis. *Review of Educational Research, 90*(5), 675–709.

Foorman, B., Beyler, N., Borradaile, K., Coyne, M., Denton, C. A., Dimino, J., . . . Wissel, S. (2016). *Foundational skills to support reading for understanding in kindergarten through 3rd grade: Educator's Practice Guide* (NCEE 2016–4008). What Works Clearinghouse.

Gersten, R., Compton, D., Connor, C. M., Dimino, J., Santoro, L., Linan-Thompson, S., & Tilly, W. D. (2008). *Assisting students struggling with reading: Response to Intervention and multi-tier intervention for reading in the primary grades. A practice guide* (NCEE 2009–4045). National Center for Education Evaluation and Regional Assistance, Institute of Education Sciences, U.S. Department of Education.

Gersten, R., Dimino, J., Jayanthi, M., Kim, J. S., & Santoro, L. E. (2010). Teacher study group:

Impact of the professional development model on reading instruction and student outcomes in first grade classrooms. *American Educational Research Journal, 47*(3), 694–739.

Goldfeld, S., Snow, P., Eadie, P., Munro, J., Gold, L., Orsini, F., . . . Shingles, B. (2020). Teacher knowledge of oral language and literacy constructs: Results of a randomized controlled trial evaluating the effectiveness of a professional learning intervention. *Scientific Studies of Reading, 25*(1), 1–30.

Gough, P. B., & Tunmer, W. E. (1986). Decoding, reading, and reading disability. *Remedial and Special Education, 7*(1), 6–10.

Griffith, R., Bauml, M., & Barksdale, B. (2015). In-the-moment teaching decisions in primary grade reading: The role of context and teacher knowledge. *Journal of Research in Childhood Education, 29*(4), 444–457.

Hsieh, W. Y., Hemmeter, M. L., McCollum, J. A., & Ostrosky, M. M. (2009). Using coaching to increase preschool teachers' use of emergent literacy teaching strategies. *Early Childhood Research Quarterly, 24*(3), 229–247.

Hung, H. T., & Yeh, H. C. (2013). Forming a change environment to encourage professional development through a teacher study group. *Teaching and Teacher Education, 36,* 153–165.

Jayanthi, M., Dimino, J., Gersten, R., Taylor, M. J., Haymond, K., Smolkowski, K., & Newman-Gonchar, R. (2018). The impact of teacher study groups in vocabulary on teaching practice, teacher knowledge, and student vocabulary knowledge: A large-scale replication study. *Journal of Research on Educational Effectiveness, 11*(1), 83–108.

Jordan, R. L. P., Bratsch-Hines, M., & Vernon-Feagans, L. (2018). Kindergarten and first grade teachers' content and pedagogical content knowledge of reading and associations with teacher characteristics at rural low-wealth schools. *Teaching and Teacher Education, 74,* 190–204.

Kennedy, M. M. (2016). How does professional development improve teaching? *Review of Educational Research, 86*(4), 945–980.

Kozak, S., & Martin-Chang, S. (2019). Preservice teacher knowledge, print exposure, and planning for instruction. *Reading Research Quarterly, 54*(3), 323–338.

Lieberman, A., & Miller, L. (2014). *Teachers in professional communities: Improving teaching and learning.* Teachers College Press.

Little, J. W. (2003). Inside teacher community: Representations of classroom practice. *Teachers College Record, 105,* 913–945.

Martinussen, R., Ferrari, J., Aitken, M., & Willows, D. (2015). Preservice teachers' knowledge of phonemic awareness: Relationship to perceived knowledge, self-efficacy beliefs, and expo-

sure to a multimedia-enhanced lecture. *Annals of Dyslexia, 65*(3), 142–158.

Mathers, S. J. (2021). Using video to assess preschool teachers' pedagogical knowledge: explicit and higher-order knowledge predicts quality. *Early Childhood Research Quarterly, 55,* 64–78.

McCutchen, D., Abbott, R. D., Green, L. B., Beretvas, N., Cox, S., Potter, N. S., . . . Gray, A. L. (2002). Beginning literacy: Links among teacher knowledge, teacher practice, and student learning. *Journal of Learning Disabilities, 35*(1), 69–86.

McCutchen, D., Harry, D., Cunningham, A. E., Cox, S., Sidman, S., & Covill, A. (2002). Content knowledge of teachers of beginning reading. *Annals of Dyslexia, 52*(1), 207–228.

McMahan, K. M., Oslund, E. L., & Odegard, T. N. (2019). Characterizing the knowledge of educators receiving training in systematic literacy instruction. *Annals of Dyslexia, 69*(1), 21–33.

Moats, L. C. (1994). The missing foundation in teacher education: Knowledge of the structure of spoken and written language. *Annals of Dyslexia, 44*(1), 81–102.

Moats, L. C. (2009). Knowledge foundations for teaching reading and spelling. *Reading and Writing, 22*(4), 379–399.

Moats, L. C., & Foorman, B. F. (2003). Measuring teachers' content knowledge of language and reading. *Annals of Dyslexia, 53*(1), 23–45.

National Institute of Child Health and Human Development. (2000). *Report of the National Reading Panel. Teaching Children to read: An evidence-based assessment of the scientific research literature on reading and its implications for reading instruction* (NIH Publication No. 00–479). U.S. Government Printing Office.

Neuman, S. B., & Cunningham, L. (2009). The impact of professional development and coaching on early language and literacy instructional practices. *American Educational Research Journal, 46*(2), 532–566.

Phelps, G., & Schilling, S. (2004). Developing measures of content knowledge for teaching reading. *Elementary School Journal, 105*(1), 31–48.

Phillips, B. M., Oliver, F., Tabulda, G., Wood, C., & Funari, C. (2020). Preschool teachers' language and vocabulary knowledge: Development and predictive associations for a new measure. *Dyslexia, 26*(2), 153–172.

Piasta, S. B., Dynia, J. M., Justice, L. M., Pentimonti, J. M., Kaderavek, J. N., & Schatschneider, C. (2010). Impact of professional development on preschool teachers' print references during shared read-alouds: A latent growth curve analysis. *Journal of Research on Educational Effectiveness, 3*(4), 343–380.

Piasta, S. B., Park, S., Farley, K. S., Justice, L. M., & O'Connell, A. A. (2020). Early childhood educators' knowledge about language and literacy: Associations with practice and children's learning. *Dyslexia, 26*(2), 137–152.

Puliatte, A., & Ehri, L. C. (2018). Do 2nd and 3rd grade teachers' linguistic knowledge and instructional practices predict spelling gains in weaker spellers? *Reading and Writing, 31*(2), 239–266.

Reutzel, D. R., Dole, J. A., Read, S., Fawson, P., Herman, K., Jones, C. D., . . . Fargo, J. (2011). Conceptually and methodologically vexing issues in teacher knowledge assessment. *Reading and Writing Quarterly, 27*(3), 183–211.

Scarparolo, G. E., & Hammond, L. S. (2018). The effect of a professional development model on early childhood educators' direct teaching of beginning reading. *Professional Development in Education, 44*(4), 492–506.

Schachter, R. E., Spear, C. F., Piasta, S. B., Justice, L. M., & Logan, J. A. (2016). Early childhood educators' knowledge, beliefs, education, experiences, and children's language- and literacy-learning opportunities: What is the connection? *Early Childhood Research Quarterly, 36*, 281–294.

Shulman, L. S. (1986). Those who understand: Knowledge growth in teaching. *Educational Researcher, 15*(2), 4–14.

Shulman, L. S. (1987). Knowledge and teaching: Foundations of the new reform. *Harvard Educational Review, 57*(1), 1–23.

Spear-Swerling, L., Brucker, P. O., & Alfano, M. P. (2005). Teachers' literacy-related knowledge and self-perceptions in relation to preparation and experience. *Annals of Dyslexia, 55*(2), 266–296.

Spear-Swerling, L., & Cheesman, E. (2011). Teachers' knowledge base for implementing response-to-intervention models in reading. *Reading and Writing, 25*(7), 1691–1723.

Spear-Swerling, L., & Zibulsky, J. (2014). Making time for literacy: Teacher knowledge and time allocation in instructional planning. *Reading and Writing, 27*(8), 1353–1378.

Stark, H. L., Snow, P. C., Eadie, P. A., & Goldfeld, S. R. (2016). Language and reading instruction in early years' classrooms: The knowledge and self-rated ability of Australian teachers. *Annals of Dyslexia, 66*(1), 28–54.

Tetley, D., & Jones, C. (2014). Preservice teachers' knowledge of language concepts: Relationships to field experiences. *Australian Journal of Learning Difficulties, 19*(1), 17–32.

Tooley, M., & White, T. (2018). *Rethinking relicensure: Promoting professional learning through teacher licensure renewal policies*. New America.

Vescio, V., Ross, D., & Adams, A. (2008). A review of research on the impact of professional learning communities on teaching practice and student learning. *Teaching and Teacher Education, 24*, 80–91.

Waitoller, F. R., & King Thorius, K. A. (2016). Cross-pollinating culturally sustaining pedagogy and universal design for learning: Toward an inclusive pedagogy that accounts for dis/ability. *Harvard Educational Review, 86*(3), 366–474.

Washburn, E. K., Joshi, R. M., & Binks-Cantrell, E. S. (2011a). Are preservice teachers prepared to teach struggling readers? *Annals of Dyslexia, 61*(1), 21–43.

Washburn, E. K., Joshi, R. M., & Binks-Cantrell, E. S. (2011b). Teacher knowledge of basic language concepts and dyslexia. *Dyslexia, 17*(2), 165–183.

Wei, R. C., Darling-Hammond, L., & Adamson, F. (2010). *Professional development in the United States: Trends and challenges* (Vol. 28). National Staff Development Council.

Wong Fillmore, L., & Snow, C. E. (2018). What teachers need to know about language. In C. T. Adger, C. E. Snow, & D. Christian (Eds.), *What teachers need to know about language* (2nd ed., pp. 8–51). Multilingual Matters.

Wu, M. L., Adams, R. J., Wilson, M. R., & Haldane, S. (2007). *ACER ConQuest 2.0: General item response modelling software* [Computer program manual]. Australian Council for Educational Research.

CHAPTER 19

Professional Development in Early Language and Literacy

Using Data to Balance Effectiveness and Efficiency

Annemarie H. Hindman and Barbara A. Wasik

Professional development (PD) is a linchpin in the successful translation of science of reading research into effective classroom instruction. Early oral language development is uniquely important for later reading success (Dickinson, Golinkoff, & Hirsh-Pasek, 2010), but classroom language environments, including those that emphasize vocabulary instruction, are often of modest quality (Deshmukh et al., 2019; Wright, 2012). To bolster early language development, our approach has been to provide teachers with PD that raises both their conceptual understanding and procedural knowledge regarding the use of research-based strategies in classrooms (e.g., Wasik & Hindman, 2020). Specifically, we help teachers refine their linguistic interactions with young children, with the goal of increasing children's language (especially vocabulary) and other early literacy outcomes.

We describe in this chapter, as background, research on the role(s) of language and vocabulary in learning to read. Next, we explore the limited language experiences in many early childhood classrooms and summarize current research on PD. We describe the multiple iterations of our PD model, refined over time and across varied contexts. Finally, we synthesize the

implications of our findings and highlight areas for future research.

A Framework for Early Literacy: Language as an Engine of Learning

The process of learning to read, for most children, is a long and complex interweaving of skill sets focused on both the code and meaning of print (Cain, Compton, & Parilla, 2017; Connor, 2016; Duke & Cartwright, 2021), most of which may begin to develop long before children start formal reading instruction (Anthony, Chen, Williams, Cen, & Erazo, 2021; Piasta, Logan, Farley, Strang, & Justice, 2022). Popular conversations around the science of reading (see Hanford, 2019; Spear-Swerling, 2019; Wexler, 2018, 2019; Will, 2019), building on classic research papers (e.g., Adams, Treiman, & Pressley, 1998; Foorman, Francis, Shaywitz, Shaywitz, & Fletcher, 1997), have focused heavily on the need to explicitly teach code-related skills (e.g., sound awareness, phonics), so that children can navigate the orthographically opaque language of English (Harris & Perfetti, 2017).

Yet the scientific literature has also shown

that the development of language, and particularly vocabulary, plays a profoundly important, direct role in reading by allowing children to make sense of decoded text and, ultimately, to comprehend it (Lervåg, Hulme, & Melby-Lervåg, 2018; Marchman et al., 2018; McCutchen, Northey, Herrera, & Clark, 2022). In addition, indirectly, knowing more words helps children decode more quickly by reducing cognitive load (Byrnes, 2021). Moreover, expansive vocabulary knowledge can support phonological awareness (Walley, Metsala, & Garlock, 2003), presumably as a larger catalog of words invites more comparisons among the universe of phonemes. Finally, language is heavily implicated in interpersonal competence (Jahng, 2020) and self-regulation (Winsler, 2009), both of which contribute to success in reading and, broadly, learning.

The Science of Language Development

Because, in our view, language skills have received relatively less attention than code-focused skills in both popular discussion of the science of reading (Hanford, 2019; Spear-Swerling, 2019; Wexler, 2019) and in many classrooms (Neuman & Dwyer, 2010; Wright & Neuman, 2013), we briefly review the science of language development (see also Rowe, Romeo, & Leech, Chapter 2, this volume). In the first months of life, most children become familiar with the specific sounds that comprise their native language(s) (Newman, Ratner, Jusczyk, Jusczyk, & Dow, 2006), and by the end of their first year, acquire their first receptive and, frequently, expressive vocabulary words (Wagner & Hoff, 2013). Over the next 2 years, they collect other linguistic skills, including knowledge of syntax and other features of grammar that clarify how individual words fit together (Farrow, Wasik, & Hindman, 2020; Vasilyeva, Waterfall & Huttenlocher, 2008). While most children master the phonology and syntax of their native language(s) well before adolescence, the unconstrained skills of receptive and expressive vocabulary grow throughout the lifespan (Perfetti & Stafura, 2014).

Components of Conversation That Promote Language

The process of language learning is driven largely by frequent, back-and-forth interactions with linguistically engaged adults at home (Donnelly & Kidd, 2021; Leech & Rowe, 2021) and in early education settings (La Paro et al., 2009; Weiland & Yoshikawa, 2013; Cabell & Hwang, Chapter 15, this volume). Classroom-based conversations may be especially important for young children whose households include fewer of the specific vocabulary words and syntactic structures that they will encounter in the conversations and texts of formal schooling (Golinkoff, Hoff, Rowe, Tamis-LeMonda, & Hirsh-Pasek, 2019). Seminal projects such as Hart and Risley's (1995) study of families (not without limitations; please see Kuchirko, 2017, or Sperry, Sperry, & Miller, 2018) and Snow and colleagues' Harvard Home–School Study (Dickinson & Tabors, 2001) revealed that a key predictor of language learning in these interactions was adults' use of *sophisticated and varied vocabulary* with and around children. In general, children who heard more words in early childhood knew more words later on and were stronger readers. More recent work (Rowe & Snow, 2020) has taken a finer-grained look at this problem, and one major discovery is that children generally need *multiple, meaningful exposures* to the vocabulary words that schools and families aim to teach (Dobinson & Dockrell, 2021). In fact, "knowing" a word can be thought of as a continuum ranging from no familiarity to vague receptive understanding, to conceptual mastery and expressive fluency (Samuelson, 2021). This increasing understanding typically accumulates gradually over time, augmented by each individual exposure to the word (Coyne, McCoach, Loftus, Zipoli, & Kapp, 2009).

But adult talk alone is not enough. Justice, Jiang, and Strasser (2018) found that teachers' *open-ended questions*, which invite young children to use language, uniquely predict children's vocabulary development above and beyond the effects of other classroom characteristics. Moreover, when adults provide *feedback* on children's talk, extending their language and conceptual understanding, vocabulary and other language outcomes increase (Barnes, Dickinson, & Grifenhagen, 2017; Cabell, Justice, McGinty, DeCoster, & Forston, 2015; Zucker, Cabell, Justice, Pentimonti, & Kaderavek, 2013). Finally, when parents or teachers use more *complex syntax*, children make greater gains in language and vocabulary (Farrow et al., 2020; Huttenlocher, Waterfall, Vasilyeva, Vevea, & Hedges, 2010).

In summary, the language (and particularly

vocabulary) skills that children learn through linguistic interactions with adults are a driving force behind reading acquisition.

Challenges of Building Language and Vocabulary in Classrooms

Unfortunately, many early childhood classrooms provide relatively little exposure to rich, varied, and extended language exchanges, particularly about new words (Neuman & Dwyer, 2010; Wright & Neuman, 2013). For example, Neuman and Dwyer (2010) concluded that vocabulary instruction is virtually nonexistent in preschool curricula, and current What Works Clearinghouse (WWC; 2019) reviews echo this finding. Furthermore, classroom observations show very little time (approximately 5 minutes/day) spent in conversations or explicit vocabulary activities (Cunningham, Zibulsky, Stanovich, & Stanovich, 2009; La Paro et al., 2009; Wright, 2012), even during book reading (Deshmukh et al., 2019). Implicit opportunities to learn vocabulary through give-and-take conversations are also infrequent, with teachers providing fully 93% of the talk (Dickinson & Caswell, 2007), often of a managerial nature (e.g., "Clean up," "Put X over by Y") rather than open-ended, response-inviting remarks (Barnes et al., 2017).

Language development opportunities in early childhood classrooms may be limited by logistical realities. One teacher generally serves nine (in preschool) to 25 or 30 (in kindergarten and beyond) children, making lengthy conversations with one or two children difficult. In addition, early grade teachers typically cover all content areas (math, science, social studies, and reading), each with a separate curriculum, which complicates the identification and consistent reinforcement throughout the day of a single set of target vocabulary words. Not surprisingly, empirical data (Morrison, Kim, Connor, & Grammer, 2019; U.S. Department of Health and Human Services, 2010) show that vocabulary learning in the first years of school is often minimal.

Effective PD for Improving Language Instruction and Outcomes

PD can improve early childhood educators' literacy and language instruction and, as a result, help children lay the foundation for reading success (Hamre, Partee, & Mulcahy, 2017; Piasta et al., 2022). PD in early childhood typically includes training through workshops or coursework (e.g., Cunningham, Etter, Platas, Wheeler, & Campbell, 2015; Hamre et al., 2012). An additional coaching component may offer teachers expert, individualized guidance, typically through cycles of direct observation of teachers using new practices in their own classrooms, feedback on that instruction, and opportunities to try the strategies again (e.g., Buysse, Castro, & Peisner-Feinberg, 2010; Garet et al., 2008). Below, we summarize the literature on the effectiveness of PD for early language and literacy (see also Cunningham, Firestone, & Zegers, Chapter 18, this volume).

Overall Effectiveness of PD

With or without coaching, PD can raise educators' knowledge and practice in many areas, but the degree of effectiveness varies across (Schachter, 2015) and even within (Landry, Swank, Anthony, & Assel, 2011) studies. Several recent reviews and meta-analyses, most focused on preschool, show that teachers' knowledge, practice, and/or skills moderately increased following PD participation, at least in the short term (Egert, Fukkink, & Eckhardt, 2018; Kraft, Blazar, & Hogan, 2018; Markussen-Brown et al., 2017).

However, many PD interventions do not examine child outcomes at all, particularly vocabulary (Egert et al., 2018). Among those that do, many show null effects on child outcomes (Kraft et al., 2018; Piasta et al., 2022). Very few show effects on both taught words (i.e., the words specifically targeted by the intervention) and standardized assessments (i.e., widely used measures including a broad array of different words) (Wasik, Hindman, & Snell, 2016). Including standardized measures is important, because these tools elucidate whether children are building generalized word knowledge and, in the case of children from less advantaged backgrounds, beginning to close the vocabulary gap that separates them from more affluent peers as early as 18 months of age (Golinkoff et al., 2019). Taken together, the extant literature raises questions about how to most effectively support teachers so as to engender meaningful change in their skills and child outcomes.

What Makes PD Most Effective

Syntheses of the literature and meta-analyses reveal several key principles about what works for building teacher and child outcomes in early language and literacy. First, ample evidence indicates that PD is most effectively delivered through a *combination of training and coaching* (Kraft et al., 2018; Markussen-Brown et al., 2017; Schacter, 2015). However, one important recent review (Kennedy, 2016) highlights that some kinds of coaching are better than others; specifically, this work emphasizes the value of helping teachers translate new ideas into effective practice, and providing individualized feedback to teachers' own situations and perspectives. Second, *longer duration* (e.g., one school year or more) and higher intensity (e.g., meetings monthly or more) PD typically results in greater impact on teachers and children, with "one and done" workshops rarely sufficient to help teachers master new techniques (Yoon, Duncan, Lee, Scarloss, & Shapley, 2007). Here, again, Kennedy (2016) notes that longer is not always more productive; teachers need to use the time to deepen their conceptual and procedural understanding of strategies and apply them in real-world settings.

Third, teachers are advantaged by PD that includes clear evidence of successful use of the target techniques, including through *exemplary classroom videos*, even in short snippets (Van Es, Tunney, Goldsmith, & Seago, 2014; Mathers, 2021). This evidence may be particularly persuasive or helpful to teachers when videos demographically match their own student population and feature familiar, relatable problems of practice (e.g., curriculum issues, behavior management challenges) (Kennedy, 2016). Finally, opportunities for teachers to *view videos of their own practices* and reflect on them with the coach may be powerful (Van Es et al., 2014).

Taken together, there is clear evidence that PD is needed around early literacy and language (especially vocabulary), but that effective PD may be quite complex to deliver.

Specific Lines of Our Research

As the field of early language and literacy PD has matured, identifying the key components

and best practices detailed earlier, many models have transitioned toward serving larger teams of teachers, requiring efficient and scalable approaches. Our own model represents a microcosm of this larger trend, evolving from largely face-to-face PD into a hybrid, partly distance-mediated approach. The central challenge in this evolution has been streamlining without stripping away the "active ingredients" that underlie teacher and child outcome gains.

Intensive Coaching and Materials

The earliest iteration of our PD model, the Johns Hopkins Language and Literacy Project (JHLLP), was grounded in the idea that teachers (and, ultimately, children) benefit if all aspects of language and literacy instruction (vocabulary, phonological sensitivity, alphabet knowledge, and writing) center around a core set of vocabulary words, with extensive face-to-face guidance on teaching these words. Over a full academic year, teachers attended eight (monthly) interactive, face-to-face group trainings led by a coach. Each 2- to 3-hour training focused on a specific topic (e.g., modeling rich language in the classroom) and provided teachers with explicit instructional strategies (e.g., use adjectives to describe the world, narrate children's activities for them, articulate your own thinking/actions).

In addition, the day after the training, the coach visited each teacher's classroom to model the new strategies for about 30 minutes. This powerful experience allowed teachers to see, firsthand, (1) how the strategy should be implemented, (2) that it could be implemented successfully with their children, and (3) that children could learn the words (obviating common concerns that the words were too difficult for young children). Teachers used a fidelity tool to observe the coach, and the coach used the same fidelity measure to observe the teacher several weeks later, establishing a sense of transparency and partnership. After the modeling, teachers practiced the strategies for 1–2 weeks, and then the coach returned to observe for about 45–60 minutes and conferenced with the teacher for 45 minutes, offering feedback on the observation. If needed, the coach would reobserve the following week. Finally, JHLLP provided enough materials to cover all book readings and related center activities throughout the academic year. Teachers received 10 trade books per month, featuring a total of 15 selected target words, one lesson plan per book showing how to teach the target words, and one prop representing each target word.

The pilot study (Wasik & Bond, 2001) and evaluation (Wasik, Bond, & Hindman, 2006) showed significant effects of the intervention on the quality of the teacher talk during book reading, as well as on child outcomes, including hard-to-change standardized vocabulary (Peabody Picture Vocabulary Test [PPVT]) scores ($d = 0.40$ for expressive language and 0.73 for receptive language). In addition, anecdotal data revealed that teachers were highly satisfied with the supports, and particularly with the materials. One surprising discovery was that many children in the preschool classroom did not know even very straightforward, commonplace words (i.e., Tier One words) such as *sandwich* or *bowl*, which helped to shape our target word selection going forward.

This model was subsequently expanded with Early Reading First grants to include progress monitoring on taught words at least three times per year. Teachers used these and other data to identify three to five children in the classroom with low target-word knowledge to receive weekly small-group review activities. Results (Wasik & Hindman, 2011) showed that classroom quality improved substantially ($d = 0.75$ on the Early Language and Literacy Classroom Observation [ELLCO] and $d = 0.50$ on the Classroom Assessment Scoring System [CLASS]). In addition, children learned 70–85% of target words (Wasik, Hindman, & Jusczyk, 2009). Finally, standardized receptive vocabulary outcomes increased ($d = 0.25$), especially among those with lower skills (Wasik & Hindman, 2011), as did phonological awareness ($d = 0.44$).

Distance-Mediated Supports

The JHLLP model, while effective, was time-intensive, with one coach serving a maximum of eight teachers per year. To scale up, we experimented with using technology to improve the coach:teacher ratio, supported by the U.S. Department of Education Investing in Innovation (i3) fund. In the Exceptional Coaching for Early Language and Literacy (ExCELL) project, we streamlined the content of the PD to just language skills (vocabulary and phonological sensitivity), excluding writing and alphabet knowledge. At the same time, we added information

to help teachers support English learners (ELs), in light of their growing representation around the nation (Vespa, Medina, & Armstrong, 2018).

We also explored how technology could offset the need for intensive face-to-face interaction. We replaced the monthly face-to-face workshops with monthly online, self-paced modules written in teacher-friendly language. Instead of having coaches model in classrooms, we embedded into the online modules a series of videos (about 1–2 minutes each) of teachers using the modules' strategies effectively. Videos were recorded in school districts serving primarily children of color with high levels of family poverty, the same population with whom our target teachers worked. To replace the informal, coach-led conversations during trainings that gauged teacher understanding, multiple-choice quizzes were placed throughout the modules. Quiz results were shared with coaches, who followed up with teachers if their quiz scores were low. After watching a module and taking the quiz, teachers practiced on their own; then, at the end of the month, rather than having a coach visit, they video-recorded themselves using the module strategies in their own classrooms. They uploaded their videos to our website, where their coach viewed it and offered written feedback and a real-time, 30-minute conference via Skype or Zoom.

Yet another aspect of streamlining involved materials. ExCELL teachers received only two or three books per month, for which lesson plans and other materials were made available online. They were expected to primarily teach from their own curriculum, and to select target words and appropriate activities on their own. No props were provided.

Analysis of data from a small, randomized controlled trial (Limlingan, Hammer, Hindman, & Wasik, 2020) showed that the ExCELL intervention substantially increased the quality of teachers' classroom practices, as measured by the Instructional Support domain of the CLASS ($d = 1.42$). However, there were no main effects of ExCELL training on children's language and literacy skills, and no effects on key subgroups (e.g., those with low or high initial skills, English language learners). Given the multiple differences between ExCELL and JHLLP, it is difficult to empirically determine the reason for these disparate results. However, given our anecdotal evidence, one of our chief hypotheses is that the reduction of coaching time from weekly (about

4 hours/month) to monthly (about 30 minutes/month, by video) did not allow teachers enough in person coach guidance. In addition, the online environment may not have offered enough opportunity for coaches to build relationships with teachers and their classrooms, which may have reduced (1) the coach's understanding of teachers' strengths and weaknesses and/or (2) teachers' willingness to take and use coach advice.

We are currently refining ExCELL, along with our colleague Carol Hammer, to target teachers of ELs, funded by the Office of English Language Acquisition. To enhance model effectiveness, we have integrated new techniques for ELs (e.g., using visual aids, bringing the home language into the classroom). At the same time, we are working to strengthen the coach–teacher relationship to enhance teacher uptake of PD strategies.

Using Materials to Offset In-Person Coaching Needs

On the heels of the challenges of translating the heavily face-to-face JHLLP into the distance-mediated ExCELL, we sought funding from the Institute of Education Sciences to develop a different approach to streamlining. In the Story Talk model, we aimed to offload some of the face-to-face coach teacher scaffolding of JHLLP into materials, while maintaining a close coach–teacher relationship.

First, we again narrowed our content focus, this time specifically to vocabulary for native speakers of English. Second, we not only reintegrated elements of the distance-based ExCELL approach but also reintroduced some aspects of the intensive, in-person JHLLP project. Story Talk included monthly, in-person workshops by the coach (similar to JHLLP), but because of the more discrete content focus, only four workshops were given (September, October, November, and January) rather than the JHLLP's eight. We also included exemplary videos in the workshops to replace coach in-classroom modeling. The coach visited each classroom every other week and, 4 weeks after the workshop, videotaped the teacher's classroom instruction. The coach offered written feedback and compiled clips of the teacher's video to watch at a face-to-face conference. Third, as in JHLLP, we provided materials for all classroom book readings and center activities for the year. We provided trade books, lesson plans with a soft script for three readings of each book, and directions and questions for all book-related center-based activities. Props were replaced by picture cards of the target vocabulary because of the challenges of scale-up using props. In this way, some of the JHLLP coach support was embedded in classroom materials, and workshops focused on training teachers in understanding and using the materials.

A small, randomized controlled trial of Story Talk revealed that this model was highly effective for improving the quality of teachers' instruction ($d = 1.51$ for CLASS instructional support and .77 for classroom organization), as well as for raising children's knowledge of taught words ($d = 0.88$) and of standardized vocabulary ($d = 0.19$ for receptive vocabulary and $d = 0.14$ for expressive vocabulary) (Wasik & Hindman, 2020).

Here, again, strict comparison between models is impossible, but our observations indicate that mechanisms undergirding teacher success included (1) increasing the coaching dosage to every other week, while (2) reducing the total number of strategies we presented to teachers, creating a better match between content and instruction than we had in ExCELL. In addition, (3) the trade books and soft scripts helped teachers ask questions about target words throughout the classroom day, so that children had extended, repeated opportunities to use those words (Bleses et al., 2018). Conversely, in ExCELL, teachers chose their target words and developed their own instruction around those words, leaving opportunities for slippage.

Reaching Teachers of Toddlers and Kindergartners

At this stage in the model's evolution, Story Talk appears to have an appropriate balance of active ingredients and feasibility. A recent project, in collaboration with Dr. Patricia Snyder, extends features of Story Talk to 2- and 3-year-olds in Early Head Start and the first year of Head Start who are at risk for specific language impairment. Although only preliminary data have been collected (Hindman, Farrow, Anderson, Wasik, & Snyder, 2021), our evidence suggests that this revised Story Talk approach has promise to raise the quality of teachers' instruction and the frequency of children's use of target words. At the same time, we are beginning work on extending Story Talk into general education kindergarten.

Essential Implications for This and Other Projects

The trajectory of our model's development offers several implications for the field.

Changing the Way Teachers Talk Is Very Challenging

As is the case with experts in any field (Ericsson & Pool, 2016), many of the choices that teachers make and the strategies they deploy in classrooms are automatized, so that cognitive load is reduced in these demanding settings (Byrnes, 2021). Among these routine processes are many aspects of how they talk to and with children, including their use of question stems (e.g., "Why . . . ?" vs. "What is that?") and feedback strategies ("Tell me more . . . " vs. "Great job!"). Consequently, changing the way teachers talk with children is, at least for us, a multiphase endeavor that begins with guiding them to attend to and reflect on their current practices; offering new, effective strategies and convincing teachers of their benefits; helping teachers perfect the use of the new strategies; and finally, supporting teachers in integrating new strategies into their permanent instructional repertoires. Moreover, we have frequently found that teachers' success in incorporating new practices around child talk rests partly on adjusting their classroom management routines to foster more child talk (e.g., we train teachers in a song to guide children in good listening), adding another layer to PD. For this reason, PD around early vocabulary tends to be complex and costly. As the field approaches larger-scale PD interventions, policymakers and practitioners must understand the magnitude and nuance of classroom changes required, so that PD can be deployed with adequate resources to support its success.

Teachers Need Specific, Concrete Guidance on Using New Behaviors

Our team has observed that because changing teachers' linguistic interaction patterns can be very difficult, they fare best when provided with very specific guidance on what to do. Our most successful PD endeavors (in terms of teacher and child effects) have provided teachers with comprehensive classroom materials that show them how to use the strategies they are trained on (e.g., defining vocabulary words, asking open-ended questions) via soft scripts. In the field of education, there has been some long-standing concern that scripts of any kind may limit teacher autonomy and responsiveness (Ball & Cohen, 1996; Schulman, 1983), making them infeasible in real-world classrooms. Our experience, however, points in the opposite direction; highly structured materials that model the target strategies have reduced the amount of training necessary and have been well-received by teachers.

Teachers Benefit from Reflecting on Videos of Their Own Instruction

In the earliest versions of our model (e.g., 1995–2000), videotaping teachers in classrooms was an expensive and technologically cumbersome practice, and it was particularly challenging to show teachers their own videos soon after the recordings had taken place (aside from rewinding a tape and replaying pieces of it for the teacher on the small video camera screen). The advent of digitized recording has facilitated the coach intentionally selecting a snippet of the teacher's video, which they watch together to foster discussion and reflection. Along with other scholars (Mathers, 2021), we see this as an incredibly helpful development. First, the coach can watch with the teacher, stopping the video to discuss particular points and then rewinding if needed, offering direct evidence to support suggestions. Second, teachers may not accurately recall exactly what they said, and videos can be very illuminating regarding their specific questions and comments. Third, teachers benefit from seeing how all children were engaged (or not) in the instruction, including those who did not offer verbal responses and those who were distracted by stimuli that teachers did not initially notice. Fourth, teachers can repeatedly rewatch their videos (even alternating a focus on the teacher and the children) to gain a deeper understanding of the lesson. Finally, teachers can—if desired—share their videos with peers in a learning community and view others' instruction, disrupting some of the professional isolation that early childhood teachers often experience. This approach may be particularly productive for teachers of minoritized populations with fewer widely available video exemplars of strong instruction with their particular population(s) of students. Seeing strategies being used successfully by peers with children from backgrounds similar to those of their own students' can be affirming and motivating.

Teachers Need Individualized Coaching

In recent years, the PreK–12 field has widely embraced individualized classroom instruction as an important ingredient in successful learning; however, PD has remained relatively one-size-fits-all, featuring large-group workshops or premade online modules, or massive open online courses. Certainly, these can be efficient forums through which to offer information that all teachers need to know, but they offer little flexibility to help teachers explore what they are most interested in or address their personally weaker areas. There is widespread agreement that a strong coach–teacher relationship is a fertile context for providing teachers with new ideas (Sailors & Shanklin, 2010). However, our work has suggested that one particularly important facet of coaching, and indeed of the coach–teacher relationship, is the coach's willingness and capacity to help teachers understand when their practice is not congruent with research and could be improved, and to gently but firmly push the teacher to try new things.

Perhaps because our target strategies (e.g., using open-ended prompts, modeling rich language) are typically familiar to our audience, teachers often report at trainings that "I already ask open-ended questions" or that "My children talk all the time!" even as initial observations reveal considerable room for improvement. Aligned with the idea of "academic press" for students, effective coaches in our model have been able to gracefully and supportively show teachers evidence (videos, transcripts) of missed opportunities in their own classrooms, then encourage and ultimately empower them to try new approaches. Aligned with Kennedy's (2016) observations about coaching alone not ensuring success, we have found that coach focus and persistence is an important ingredient in the model's success.

Future Research

Future research around PD supporting teachers' language and literacy instruction, and children's outcomes, is needed on many fronts; we offer several that are particularly pressing.

Active Ingredients of Effective PD

Despite considerable recent progress, many questions remain regarding what, specifically, are the most important "active ingredients" in effective PD for teachers and for children. For example, what makes video exemplars particularly persuasive, and to what degree are nonexemplars (i.e., teachers inconsistent with best practices) valuable? Furthermore, although much has been written about the coach–teacher relationship, there are relatively few analyses of the precise nature of productive coach–teacher interactions. We wonder: Are there any specific considerations (i.e., personality, temperament, experience level) to matching coaches and teachers to set up a thriving relationship? And how can coach–teacher interactions best be monitored over time to ensure continued productivity together? There is also a need for well-defined protocols that guide coaches in leading teachers through reflection, including around challenging points. Taken together, more clarity on these and other logistical points would help the field, particularly as we look toward increasing the scale of our PD.

Preservice Teacher Instruction

Many of the same ideas that support successful inservice PD can be translated to preservice settings, which could considerably improve the quality of teaching that children receive (Hindman, Morrison, Connor, & Connor, 2020). Although much of the science of reading discourse about preservice teachers has focused on changing the reading strategies in which they are trained, evidence from the inservice PD literature suggests that *how* preservice teachers are trained, and especially the field experiences and coaching they receive, is very important. Future research should experiment with bringing effective inservice PD techniques to preservice PD, ultimately reducing the need for inservice support.

Child Assessment Tools

In light of the pressing need to accurately assess children's language and literacy skills on standardized measures, it is important to address limitations in the measurement tools available to the field. In the area of vocabulary, for example, widely used assessments such as the Peabody Picture Vocabulary Test–4 (PPVT-4; Dunn & Dunn, 2007), the Expressive One-Word Picture Vocabulary Test (EOWPVT-4; Martin & Brownell, 2011), and the vocabulary measures in the Woodcock–Johnson III tools (WJ-III; Woodcock, McGrew, & Mather, 2001) have improved significantly over time in their cultural responsiveness but still offer normed versions primarily in English and Spanish. As the nation's EL population rises, addressing this gap is important. In addition, continued attention to fairness and accuracy across different subpopulations is needed.

Conclusion

Ultimately, the science of reading points to the importance of early language skills, and the science of language in turn points to the value of linguistic exchanges with adults. Burgeoning evidence shows that teachers can scaffold children's language (and thus their later reading) by offering models of rich language, inviting children to share their own ideas, and providing feedback on what children have said. Yet many classrooms lack these high-quality experiences. As we and others have documented in our research, there is strong potential for strategic PD to close this gap and improve outcomes for children in early childhood and beyond. Our model offers one avenue for reaching these goals, and its evolution over time offers insight into how the field has changed and what challenges lie ahead.

References

Adams, M. J., Treiman, R., & Pressley, M., (1998). Reading, writing, and literacy. In W. Damon, I. E. Sigle, & A. K. Renninger (Eds.), *Handbook of child psychology: Child psychology in practice* (pp. 275–355). Wiley.

Anthony, J. L., Chen, Y. I., Williams, J. M., Cen, W., & Erazo, N. A. (2021). U.S. children's understanding of the English alphabet: Its acquisition, conceptualization, and measurement. *Journal of Educational Psychology, 113*(6), 1073–1087.

Ball, D. L., & Cohen, D. K. (1996). Reform by the book: What is or might be the role of curriculum materials in teacher learning and instructional reform. *Educational Research, 25*(9), 6–14.

Barnes, E. M., Dickinson, D. K., & Grifenhagen, J. F. (2017). The role of teachers' comments during book reading in children's vocabulary growth. *Journal of Educational Research, 110*(5), 515–527.

Bleses, D., Hojen, A., Justice, L. M., Dale, P. S., Dybdal, L., Piasta, S. B., . . . Haghish, E. F. (2018). The effectiveness of a large-scale language and preliteracy intervention: The SPELL randomized controlled trial in Denmark. *Child Development, 89*(4), e42–e63.

Buysse, V., Castro, D. C., & Peisner-Feinberg, E. (2010). Effects of a professional development program on classroom practices and outcomes for Latino dual language learners. *Early Childhood Research Quarterly, 25*(2), 194–206.

Byrnes, J. P. (2021). *Cognitive development for academic achievement: Building skills and motivation.* Guilford Press.

Cabell, S., Justice, L., McGinty, A., DeCoster, J., & Forston, L. D. (2015). Teacher–child conversations in preschool classrooms: Contributions to children's vocabulary development. *Early Childhood Research Quarterly, 30*, 80–92.

Cain, K., Compton, D. L., & Parrila, R. K. (Eds.). (2017). *Theories of reading development.* John Benjamins.

Connor, C. M., (2016). A lattice model of the development of reading comprehension. *Child Development Perspectives, 10*(4), 269–274.

Coyne, M. D., McCoach, D. B., Loftus, S., Zipoli, R., Jr., & Kapp, S. (2009). Direct vocabulary instruction in kindergarten: Teaching for breadth versus depth. *Elementary School Journal, 110*, 1–18.

Cunningham, A. E., Etter, K., Platas, L., Wheeler, S., & Campbell, K. (2015). Professional development in emergent literacy: A design experiment of Teacher Study Groups. *Early Childhood Research Quarterly, 31*, 62–77.

Cunningham, A. E., Zibulsky, J., Stanovich, K. E., & Stanovich, P. J. (2009). How teachers would spend their time teaching language arts: The mismatch between self-reported and best practices. *Journal of Learning Disabilities, 42*(5), 418–430.

Deshmukh, R. S., Zucker, T. A., Tambyraja, S. R., Pentimonti, J., Bowles, R. P., & Justice, L. M. (2019). Teachers' use of questions during shared book reading: Relations to child responses. *Early Childhood Research Quarterly, 49*, 59–68.

Dickinson, D. K., & Caswell, L. (2007). Building support for language and early literacy in preschool classrooms through in-service professional development: Effects of the Literacy Environment Enrichment Program (LEEP). *Early Childhood Research Quarterly, 22*(2), 243–260.

Dickinson, D. K., Golinkoff, R. M., & Hirsh-Pasek, K. (2010). Speaking out for language: Why language is central to reading development. *Educational Researcher, 39*(4), 305–310.

Dickinson, D. K., & Tabors, P. O. (2001). *Young children learning at home and school: Beginning literacy with language.* Brookes.

Dobinson, K. L., & Dockrell, J. E. (2021). Universal strategies for the improvement of expressive language skills in the primary classroom: A systematic review. *First Language, 41*(5), 527–554.

Donnelly, S., & Kidd, E. (2021). The longitudinal relationship between conversational turn-taking and vocabulary growth in early language development. *Child Development, 92*(2), 609–625.

Duke, N. K., & Cartwright, K. B. (2021). The science of reading progresses: Communicating advances beyond the simple view of reading. *Reading Research Quarterly, 56*(Suppl. 1), S25–S44.

Dunn, D. M., & Dunn, L. M. (2007). *Peabody Picture Vocabulary Test: Fourth Edition*. Pearson.

Egert, F., Fukkink, R. G., & Eckhardt, A. G. (2018). Impact of in-service professional development programs for early childhood teachers on quality ratings and child outcomes: A meta-analysis. *Review of Educational Research, 88*(3), 401–433.

Ericsson, A., & Pool, R. (2016). *Peak: Secrets from the new science of expertise*. Mariner Books.

Farrow, J., Wasik, B. A., & Hindman, A. H. (2020). Exploring the unique contributions of teachers' syntax to preschoolers' and kindergarteners' vocabulary learning. *Early Childhood Research Quarterly, 51*, 178–190.

Foorman, B. R., Francis, D. J., Shaywitz, S. E., Shaywitz, B. A., & Fletcher, J. M. (1997). The case for early reading intervention. In B. A. Blachman (Ed.), *Foundations of reading acquisition and dyslexia: Implications for early intervention* (pp. 243–264). Erlbaum.

Garet, M. S., Cronen, S., Eaton, M., Kurki, A., Ludwig, M., Jones, W., . . . Silverberg, M. (2008). *The impact of two professional development interventions on early reading instruction and achievement* (NCEE 2008–4030). U.S. Department of Education.

Golinkoff, R. M., Hoff, E., Rowe, M. L., Tamis-LeMonda, C. S., & Hirsh-Pasek, K. (2019). Language matters: Denying the existence of the 30-million-word gap has serious consequences. *Child Development, 90*(3), 985–992.

Hamre, B. K., Partee, A., & Mulcahy, C. (2017). Enhancing the impact of professional development in the context of preschool expansion. *AERA Open, 3*(4), 1–16.

Hamre, B. K., Pianta, R. C., Burchinal, M., Field, S., LoCasale-Crouch, J., Downer, J. T., . . . Scott-Little, C. (2012). A course on effective teacher–child interactions: Effects on teacher beliefs, knowledge, and observed practice. *American Education Research Journal, 49*, 88–123.

Hanford, E. (2019). At a loss for words: What's wrong with how schools teach reading. Retrieved from *www.apmreports.org/story/2019/08/22/whats-wrong-how-schools-teach-reading*.

Harris, L. N., & Perfetti, C. (2017). Individual differences in phonological feedback effects: Evidence for the orthographic recoding hypothesis of orthographic learning. *Scientific Studies of Reading, 21*, 31–45.

Hart, B., & Risley, T. R. (1995). *Meaningful differences in the everyday experience of young American children*. Brookes.

Hindman, A. H., Farrow, J. M., Anderson, K. A., Wasik, B. A., & Snyder, P. (2021). Understanding child-directed speech around book reading in toddler classrooms: Evidence from Early Head Start programs. *Frontiers in Psychology: Developmental Psychology, 12*, 1–17.

Hindman, A. H., Morrison, F. J., Connor, C. M., & Connor, J. A. (2020). Bringing the science of reading to preservice elementary teachers: Tools that bridge research and practice. *Reading Research Quarterly, 55*(1), 197–206.

Huttenlocher, J., Waterfall, H., Vasilyeva, M., Vevea, J., & Hedges, L. V. (2010). Sources of variability in children's language growth. *Cognitive Psychology, 61*(4), 343–365.

Jahng, K. E. (2020). The moderating effect of children's language abilities on the relation between their shyness and play behavior during peer play. *Early Child Development and Care, 190*(13), 2106–2118.

Justice, L., Jiang, H., & Strasser, K. (2018). Linguistic environment of preschool classrooms: What dimensions support children's language growth? *Early Childhood Research Quarterly, 42*, 79–92.

Kennedy, M. M. (2016). How does professional development improve teaching? *Review of Educational Research, 86*(4), 945–980.

Kraft, M., Blazar, D., & Hogan, D. (2018). The effect of teacher coaching on instruction and achievement: A meta-analysis of the causal evidence. *Review of Educational Research, 88*(4), 547–588.

Kuchirko, Y. (2017). On differences and deficits: A critique of the theoretical and methodological underpinnings of the word gap. *Journal of Early Childhood Literacy, 19*(4), 533–562.

Landry, S. H., Swank, P. R., Anthony, J. L., & Assel, M. (2011). An experimental study evaluating professional development activities within a state funded pre-kindergarten program. *Reading and Writing, 24*(8), 971–1010.

La Paro, K. M., Hamre, B. K., Locasale-Crouch, J., Pianta, R. C., Bryant, D., Early, D., . . . Burchinal, M. (2009). Quality in kindergarten classrooms: Observational evidence for the need to increase children's learning opportunities in early education classrooms. *Early Education and Development, 20*, 657–692.

Leech, K. A., & Rowe, M. L. (2021). An intervention to increase conversational turns between parents and young children. *Journal of Child Language, 48*(2), 399–412.

Lervåg, A., Hulme, C., & Melby-Lervåg, M. (2018). Unpicking the developmental relationship between oral language skills and reading comprehension: It's simple, but complex. *Child Development, 89*(5), 1821–1838.

Limlingan, M. C., Hammer, C. S., Hindman, A. H., Wasik, B. A. (2020, June). *Developing from a distance: Web-mediated coaching.* Paper presented at the biannual meeting of the National Research Conference on Early Childhood, Washington, DC.

Marchman, V. A., Loi, E. C., Adams, K. A., Ashland, M., Fernald, A., & Feldman, H. M. (2018). Speed of language comprehension at 18 months old predicts school-relevant outcomes at 54 months old in children born preterm. *Journal of Developmental and Behavioral Pediatrics, 39*(3), 246–253.

Markussen-Brown, J., Juhl, C. B., Piasta, S. B., Bleses, D., Højen, A., & Justice, L. M. (2017). The effects of language- and literacy-focused professional development on early educators and children: A best-evidence meta-analysis. *Early Childhood Research Quarterly, 38,* 97–115.

Martin, N. A., & Brownell, R. (2011). *Expressive One-Word Picture Vocabulary Test, Fourth Edition.* PRO-ED.

Mathers, S. (2021). Using video to assess preschool teachers' pedagogical knowledge: Explicit and higher-order knowledge predicts quality. *Early Childhood Research Quarterly, 55,* 64–78.

McCutchen, D., Northey, M., Herrera, B. L., & Clark, T. (2022). What's in a word?: Effects of morphologically rich vocabulary instruction on writing outcomes among elementary students. *Reading and Writing, 35,* 325–351.

Morrison, F. J., Kim, M. H., Connor, C. M., & Grammer, J. K. (2019). The causal impact of schooling on children's development: Lessons for developmental science. *Current Directions in Psychological Science, 28*(5), 441–449.

Neuman, S. B., & Dwyer, J. (2010). Missing in action: Vocabulary instruction in Pre-K. *Reading Teacher, 62*(5), 384–392.

Newman, R., Ratner, N. B., Jusczyk, A. M., Jusczyk, P. W., & Dow, K. A. (2006). Infants' early ability to segment the conversational speech signal predicts later language development: A retrospective analysis. *Developmental Psychology, 42*(4), 643–655.

Perfetti, C., & Stafura, J. (2014). Word knowledge in a theory of reading comprehension. *Scientific Studies of Reading, 18*(1), 22–37.

Piasta, S. B., Logan, J. A. R., Farley, K. S., Strang, T. M., & Justice, L. M. (2022). Profiles and predictors of children's growth in alphabet knowledge. *Journal of Education for Students Placed at Risk, 27*(1), 1–26.

Rowe, M. L., & Snow, C. E. (2020). Analyzing input quality along three dimensions: Interactive, linguistic, and conceptual. *Journal of Child Language, 47*(1), 5–21.

Sailors, M., & Shanklin, N. L. (2010). Introduction: Growing evidence to support coaching in literacy and mathematics. *Elementary School Journal, 111*(1), 1–6.

Samuelson, L. K. (2021). Toward a precision science of word learning: Understanding individual vocabulary pathways. *Child Development Perspectives, 15*(2), 117–124.

Schachter, R. E. (2015). An analytic study of the professional development research in early childhood education. *Early Education and Development, 26*(8), 1057–1085.

Shulman, L. S. (1983). Autonomy and obligation: The remote control of teaching. In L. Shulman & G. Sykes (Eds.), *Handbook of teaching and policy* (pp. 484–504). Longman.

Spear-Swerling, L. (2019). Structured literacy and typical literacy practices: Understanding differences to create instructional opportunities. *Teaching Exceptional Children, 51,* 201–211.

Sperry, D. E., Sperry, L. L., & Miller, P. J. (2018). Reexamining the verbal environments of children from different socioeconomic backgrounds. *Child Development, 90*(4), 1303–1318.

U.S. Department of Health and Human Services, Administration for Children and Families. (2010). *Head Start Impact Study: Final Report.* Author.

Van Es, E. A., Tunney, J., Goldsmith, L. T., & Seago, N. (2014). A framework for the facilitation of teachers' analysis of video. *Journal of Teacher Education, 65*(4), 340–356.

Vasilyeva, M., Waterfall, H., & Huttenlocher, J. (2008). Emergence of syntax: Commonalities and differences across children. *Developmental Science, 11*(1), 84–97.

Vespa, J., Medina, L., Armstrong, D. M. (2018). *Demographic turning points for the United States: Population projections for 2020–2060: Current population reports.* U.S. Census Bureau.

Wagner, L., & Hoff, E. (2013). Language development. In R. M. Lerner, M. A. Easterbrooks, J. Mistry, & I. B. Weiner (Eds.), *Handbook of psychology: Developmental psychology* (pp. 173–196). Wiley.

Walley, A. C., Metsala, J. L., & Garlock, V. M. (2003). Spoken vocabulary growth: Its role in the development of phoneme awareness &early reading ability. *Reading and Writing, 16,* 5–20.

Wasik, B. A., & Bond, M. A. (2001). Beyond the pages of a book: Interactive book reading and language development in preschool classrooms. *Journal of Educational Psychology, 93*(2), 243–250.

Wasik, B. A., Bond, M. A., & Hindman, A. (2006). The effects of a language and literacy intervention on Head Start children and teachers. *Journal of Educational Psychology, 98*(1), 63–74.

Wasik, B. A., & Hindman, A. H. (2011). Improving vocabulary and pre-literacy skills of at-risk preschoolers through teacher professional development. *Journal of Educational Psychology, 103*(2), 455–469.

Wasik, B. A., & Hindman, A. H. (2020). Increasing preschoolers' vocabulary development through a streamlined teacher professional development intervention. *Early Childhood Research Quarterly, 50,* 101–113.

Wasik, B. A., Hindman, A. H., & Jusczyk, A. M. (2009). Using curriculum specific progress monitoring to determine Head Start children's vocabulary learning. *National Head Start Association: Dialog Journal, 12,* 257–275.

Wasik, B. A., Hindman, A. H., & Snell, E. K. (2016). Book reading and vocabulary development: A systematic review. *Early Childhood Research Quarterly, 37,* 39–57.

Weiland, C., & Yoshikawa, H. (2013). Impacts of a prekindergarten program on children's mathematics, language, literacy, executive function, and emotional skills. *Child Development, 84*(6), 2112–2130.

Wexler, N. (2018). Why American students haven't gotten better at reading in 20 years. Retrieved from *www.theatlantic.com/education/archive/2018/04/-american-students-reading/557915/?utm_source=share&utm_campaign=share.*

Wexler, N. (2019). Elementary education has gone terribly wrong. Retrieved from *www.theatlantic.com/magazine/archive/2019/08/the-radical-case-for-teaching-kids-stuff/592765/?utm_source=share&utm_campaign=share.*

What Works Clearinghouse. (2019). Find what works based on the evidence: Literacy. Retrieved from *https://ies.ed.gov/ncee/wwc/fww/results?filters =literacy.*

Will, M. (2019, December 3). Will the science of reading catch on in teacher prep? Retrieved from *www.edweek.org/ew/articles/2019/12/04/most-ed-professors-favor-balanced-literacy.html.*

Winsler, A. (2009). Still talking to ourselves after all these years: A review of current research on private speech. In A. Winsler, C. Fernyhough, & I. Montero (Eds.), *Private speech, executive functioning, and the development of verbal self-regulation* (pp. 3–41). Cambridge University Press.

Woodcock, R. W., McGrew, K. S., & Mather, N. (2001). *Woodcock–Johnson III Tests of Achievement.* Riverside.

Wright, T. S., (2012). What classroom observations reveal about oral vocabulary instruction in kindergarten. *Reading Research Quarterly, 113*(3), 353–355.

Wright, T. S., & Neuman, S. B. (2013). Vocabulary instruction in commonly used kindergarten core reading curricula. *Elementary School Journal, 113*(3), 386–408.

Yoon, K. S., Duncan, T., Lee, S. W.-Y., Scarloss, B., & Shapley, K. (2007). Reviewing the evidence on how teacher professional development affects student achievement (Issues & Answers Report, REL 2007-No. 033). Retrieved from *http://ies.ed.gov/ncee/edlabs.*

Zucker, T. A., Cabell, S. Q., Justice, L. M., Pentimonti, J. M., & Kaderavek, J. N. (2013). The role of frequent, interactive prekindergarten shared reading in the longitudinal development of language and literacy skills. *Developmental Psychology, 49*(8), 1425–1439.

CHAPTER 20

Using the Science of Early Literacy to Design Professional Development for Writing

Hope K. Gerde and Gary E. Bingham

Teachers of young children make many decisions about the types of early writing experiences they provide children in their classroom and the nature of instructional strategies they use. Because writing is a complex task that integrates children's skills in idea generation/composing, handwriting, spelling, and their understanding of print concepts (Kaderavek, Cabell, & Justice, 2009; Puranik & Lonigan, 2014), teachers must make decisions about how they guide children through the writing process or how they respond "in the moment" to children's writing ideas or actions. Children's early writing begins with the generation of an idea or multiple ideas that they want to communicate to others. They then must leverage their oral language skills as they share their ideas with others verbally, which will be "translated" into written language through making marks on a page (Quinn, Bingham, & Gerde, 2021; Rowe & Wilson, 2015). These early marks may take the form of scribbles, drawings, or letter-like forms, that eventually become more conventional (i.e., letter-like shapes become letters) and organized as their understanding of letter forms and their orthographic representations become more complex (i.e., knowledge of letter–sound correspondence). During this process, early writing attempts are heavily constrained by children's fine motor skills and self-regulation (Chandler et al., 2021), which are also developing during preschool.

To provide successful supports for writing, teachers need a deep knowledge of what early writing is, including the complex integration of multiple skills across developmental domains (Gerde, Skibbe, Bowles, & Martoccio, 2012), how it develops, and how to prepare the environment and enact supports that promote children's development of this essential literacy skill. Fortunately, the science of early writing provides guidance! Our team integrated that science to create a fully online professional learning (PL) program designed to promote early language and literacy skills through high-quality writing opportunities. In this chapter, we examine what the science reveals about promoting early writing development, then describe how the science of writing was used to design PL, and the outcomes of engagement in the PL, for teachers and children.

Designing Rich Writing Environments

Studies of early childhood classrooms offer important glimpses into the writing environments that preschool teachers provide children, as well as instructional interactions available to support children's early writing development. In order to create effective PL experiences for teachers of young children, it is essential to have a rich understanding of these environments and of typical practice, as teachers are more likely to improve their instructional practices when they align with, and are embedded into, existing classroom routines (Zhang & Bingham, 2019). Foundational to literacy instructional approaches is the need for varying materials and environments dedicated toward supporting both intentional daily writing experiences and capitalizing on children's natural interest in writing when it is intentionally situated in early childhood classrooms. Children as young as 2 years of age show interest in writing-related interactions as long as writing is approached in a manner that is supportive of children's developmental skill and connected to their play (Rowe & Nietzel, 2010).

Strong beliefs that children learn through play-based interactions within classroom-based settings have guided professional recommendations of how to establish rich environmental supports for young children's early writing development (Bingham, Quinn, McRoy, Zhang, & Gerde, 2018; Neuman, Copple, & Bredekamp, 2000). Although the need for rich writing environments with varied materials is positioned in the professional literature, with recommendations focusing on the need for a dedicated learning center for writing and multiple writing materials throughout the classroom and during classroom routines (Gerde, Bingham, & Wasik, 2012; Copple & Bredekamp, 2009), limited empirical research directly ties such supports to children's early writing or reading development. Using the Early Language and Literacy Classroom Observation (Smith & Dickinson, 2001), Diamond, Gerde, and Powell (2008) show no discernable impacts from simply having materials in the classroom. After designing a more robust and sensitive environmental rating assessment, Gerde, Bingham, and Pendergast (2015) document a significant and meaningful association among (1) the presence of a dedicated writing center, (2) writing materials throughout the learning centers, and (3) meaningful environmental print that can be referenced by teachers, and children's early writing development across the preschool year. Findings from this study, however, reveal wide variation in preschool children's access to writing materials and the nature of these materials, representing a disconnect between everyday learning opportunities and professional recommendations (Gerde, Bingham, et al., 2012; Copple & Bredekamp, 2009).

Encouragingly, research documents that most early childhood classrooms provide children with access to early writing materials for almost an hour a day (Gerde, Wright, & Bingham, 2019; Quinn, Gerde, & Bingham, 2022); however, a sizable percentage (24%) do not contain dedicated early writing centers. Access to writing implements and tools that can possibly support children's writing development is also uneven, with nearly all classrooms providing varied writing materials (pencils, markers, or crayons) and types of paper (white, colored, craft), but fewer containing materials that might create additional interest around the writing process (whiteboards, index cards, Post-it Notes, letter stencils) or demonstrate varied purposes for writing (envelopes, stationery, list paper). Interviews with teachers reinforced the perspective that tools are important for supporting children's interest in early writing experiences, but few teachers addressed how materials are intentionally used to promote children's writing beyond strengthening fine motor skills necessary for writing (i.e., supporting handwriting) (Gerde, Wright, et al., 2019). Furthermore, only 22% of teachers spoke about the importance of placing writing materials throughout the classroom to support play-based writing interactions, and these were observed to be primarily provided in the dramatic play area of the classroom (31% of observed classrooms). Few writing materials or interactions were observed to take place in other learning centers, such as science or construction/block areas. Exposure to print in meaningful contexts, such as during dramatic play (e.g., veterinary clinic, hospital, post office), with appropriate adult mediation of materials is documented to have a significant impact on young children's print awareness skills (Neuman & Roskos, 1993; Vulkelich, 1994). However, teachers need support in learning to engage in print-related mediation in a manner that supports early writing (Gerde et al., 2015) or reading (e.g., Zucker, Ward, & Justice, 2009) outcomes.

An additional concerning result is a recent study documenting that writing materials are not frequently refreshed in a manner that maintains children's interests and correlates with ongoing curriculum experiences (i.e., limited environmental print to accompany a study of insects or a transportation unit). Rather, findings illustrate that teachers are intentional about establishing these environments early in the school year, but that a large percentage of teachers tend to "set and forget" these environmental supports rather than "refresh and retool" as curricular experiences evolve and children's early writing skills develop (Bingham, Rohloff, & Gerde, 2018). Young children show interest in writing activities, particularly those that are meaningful (Zhang & Quinn, 2020), and even toddlers spent time in writing centers that are established by teachers to support early writing skills (Rowe, 2008). Interestingly, the manner in which young children experience writing centers can vary based on the child's approach to early writing (Rowe & Nietzel, 2010) and teachers' didactic interactions that often focus on how writing is defined and supported within a particular context (Rowe, 2008).

Taken together, findings point to the importance of early environments in supporting children's writing development but also highlight key challenges that early childhood teachers face in fully stocking and refreshing the materials in a manner that can enrich children's play and learning daily (Gerde, Bingham, Bowles, Meier, & Zhang, 2019). Unlike resources needed to support other early literacy areas (i.e., books, letters, word cards, phonological awareness activities), writing materials are highly consumable, which presents obstacles for early childhood teachers in settings with fewer physical resources. Furthermore, although early writing environments are essential to promoting children's early writing development, having a dedicated writing center in an early childhood classroom and sufficient materials for writing does not guarantee use. In a recent observational study of 71 early childhood classrooms across varied program types (Head Start, state PreK, community child care), Quinn, Gerde, et al. (2022) document that only 51% of writing centers were used by teachers or children, suggesting that many teachers likely need support in how to make the writing center engaging for young children and how to best maximize the presence of such materials within their curriculum. In another study, materials were cited as barriers to teacher's engagement in writing practices with children (Gerde, Bingham, et al., 2019).

Although well-supplied early writing environments don't guarantee use, they do set the tone for where and how writing instructional interactions take place in classrooms. Instances of independent, or child-initiated, writing are more likely to be observed in the writing center than in other parts of the room (Gerde et al., 2015), likely because of the concentrated presence of materials. However, teachers are more likely to engage children in writing interactions in the art area

than in the writing center, suggesting the importance of this learning center for opportunities to practice writing (e.g., writing name on artwork, dictating ideas about an art product that are then documented by the teacher). The focus of writing interactions also varied by instructional context. Art-based writing interactions that were largely driven by teachers tended to focus on transcription skills, which involved helping children write their names on artwork, form a letter to add to their art, or sound out a word. In contrast, writing interactions that occurred in the dramatic play area were more likely to be focused on composing, meaningfully linked to purposes of writing and play setting (e.g., making a shopping list or taking an order in a restaurant), and occur between a teacher and an individual child (Quinn, Gerde, et al., 2022). Large-group interactions tended to focus on both composing and transcription skills, with a frequent pattern observed with teachers talking about the curricular theme or focus of the day, then writing it down in a manner that draws attention to how to form letters or listen to sounds in words (i.e., transcription). The interplay between environments and instructional interactions establishes the importance of attending to how writing occurs in early learning spaces and provides insight into how to best support teacher practice.

What We Know about Instructional Practices for Early Writing

Detailed observational studies highlight wide variability in the frequency and nature of early writing instructional experiences in preschool settings. Although varied methodologies lead to a slightly different picture about the frequency of writing in preschool classrooms, studies suggest that writing instruction or interactions occur for only a few minutes a day, with some classrooms offering no writing instructional supports (Pelatti, Piasta, Justice, & O'Connell, 2014; Zhang, Hur, Diamond, & Powell, 2015). For example, Quinn, Gerde, et al. (2022) observed an average of six writing interactions during a full morning of preschool instruction, with nine classrooms (12.6%) offering no writing instructional opportunities. Similarly, Zhang et al. (2015) document a low frequency of teacher writing facilitation with fall and spring observations of teachers, revealing that more than 50% of teachers do not engage in modeling writing or supporting young children through adult mediation. In a separate study of 54 Head Start teachers across two states, Bingham, Gerde, and Zhang (2020) used an expanded video coding system to document the presence of writing events. *Writing events* were defined as instructional experiences that contained opportunities for teachers and children to engage in writing-focused conversations or activities that occurred in whole-group, small-group, teacher-led, or child-initiated writing interactions. A total of 143 writing events were observed across the classrooms ($M = 2.65$, $SD = 2.00$), with events lasting 5 minutes on average ($SD = 3.50$). As the relatively large standard deviations demonstrate, however, wide variation exists across classrooms in the number of minutes children were engaged in writing-related tasks and the nature of these interactions.

Although writing interactions occur infrequently in early childhood settings, particularly in relation to other early literacy activities (Pelatti et al., 2014; Zhang et al., 2015), teachers enact a variety of practices designed to support children's early writing skills. *Writing mediation behaviors* (i.e., the strategies that teachers engage in to support children's writing) take many forms and serve different functions. In our own research, we document that teachers' behaviors can be organized into general categories such as providing instructions, modeling, and teacher scaffolding, which contain a host of supportive behaviors that we loosely suggest that teachers engage in to support children's writing attempts and experiences (see Gerde et al., 2015; Bingham, Quinn, & Gerde, 2017). In a recent study examining how teacher–child dyads engage in writing during a picture description writing task, Gabas, Wood, and Cabell (2022) found that teachers enacted the following mediation behaviors during one-on-one interactions: directives, modeling, providing choices, closed-ended requests, open-ended requests, explanations or elaborations, and review. Teachers engaged in three additional strategies during handwriting-focused interactions, namely, tracing, child dictation, and task structuring. Although teachers enacted varying adult mediation strategies during this task, employing on average eight of the 10 strategies, they were twice as likely to offer directives than the next two most commonly used writing-mediated behaviors (i.e., modeling and closed-ended requests). Adult strategy use varied by writing component (handwriting, spelling, and composing), with teachers provid-

ing directions most frequently when focusing on spelling-related skills and modeling when focusing on handwriting skills. We explore teacher modeling and scaffolding in additional detail in the next few paragraphs.

Observational studies of typical teacher practice note that preschool teachers frequently engage in teacher modeling, with modeling behaviors serving a variety of purposes, including (1) illustrating for young children how to write letters or words ("I am going to write *M* by going up and down, up and down with straight and slanted lines"), (2) drawing attention to how one connects oral and written language ("I am going to write *Happy Birthday* on this large card that we can all sign for Ms. May"), and (3) providing examples using writing tools for various purposes ("I am going to use a dry erase marker to write down our favorite foods in case we change our minds"). Early childhood teachers primarily engage in modeling-related behaviors in whole-group contexts (Quinn, Gerde, et al., 2022) and primarily draw attention to transcription skills that support children's handwriting development (Bingham et al., 2017). For example, in a study of teachers' instructional practices, Gabas et al. (2022) found that modeling, on average, accounted for 39% of teachers' handwriting-based interactions. Although supporting children's ability to form letters and write their names is an important instructional focus, as it has been shown to promote children's writing development (Zhang & Bingham, 2019), an overemphasis on such skills is not documented to be related to children's writing development (Bingham et al., 2017).

In addition to teacher modeling, teachers engage in a variety of instructional strategies or adult mediation behaviors that seek to support young children's writing efforts. For the sake of this chapter, we position the nature of these writing interactions within a broad category of teacher scaffolds. Sociocultural perspectives emphasize that teachers scaffold children in a variety of ways and provide individualized support to children that helps them complete a task they cannot complete independently (Van de Pol, Volman, & Beishuzen, 2010). The *zone of proximal development* (ZPD; Vygotsky, 1978), the gap between what the child can do independently and with support, provides parameters for the scaffolding process and how teachers might engage young children in activities that support their transcription skills, composing skills, or understanding of print works. We organize teachers' early writing scaffolding strategies into two broad categories: (1) breaking down a task into various steps to make it easier for the child and (2) cognitively or physically challenging children in a manner that expands their involvement. Teachers may engage in multiple strategies within each broad category; however, teachers are almost twice as likely to break down a task during writing interactions than to offer expansions (Bingham, Gerde, Rohloff, Zhang, & Bowles, 2021). Quality also varies substantially within each category, a finding we explore in more detail below.

Breaking down the task can take many forms, such as the context of the interaction, the teacher's instructional goal, or the writing component that is being emphasized. For example, to support a child's ability to hear sounds in a word he or she wants to write, a teacher might stretch an initial sound to make it easier for a child to hear the /d/ as he or she writes the word *dad*. Similarly, a teacher may support children's handwriting skills as they attempt to write their names by pointing out the shape of the letter, drawing children's attention to the straight or slanted lines in the letter (e.g., "Remember, Max, the *x* in your name has two slanted lines"). For composing, a teacher might engage a child in a conversation to help him or her focus on the main idea of what he or she wants to communicate in the message in order to make the task more manageable ("Oh, so you've made a pizza shop. I wonder what we can write to help our friends know that it is a pizza restaurant. Yes, that's right, we can write the word *pizza* or draw a picture of a pizza to communicate to our friends what type of restaurant this is"). Because strategies that make the task easier are designed to offer children sufficient support to complete a task that may be too demanding, the teacher may break the task up into various steps focused on different early writing skills (Bingham et al., 2017). Although teachers engage in scaffolding-related behaviors to make writing easier for children, these instructional supports heavily emphasize handwriting skills (85%) and typically involve the process of the teacher providing hints about letters and how to write them (Bingham et al., 2022).

A second set of scaffolding strategies engage children to expand their thinking or promote involvement with a writing task. Writing-based expansions (Bingham et al., 2022) challenge children's thinking or deepen involvement by (1) asking children open-ended questions about their writing process, (2) asking them to make a connection with other curricular or personal experiences, or (3) encouraging them to assess their writing process or product in a manner that deepens understanding or engagement (e.g., "How is your letter different from the one in the book? What else do you need?"). Rather than breaking down the task into smaller components, expansions serve the function of broadening knowledge or participation in a manner that is cognitively or physically challenging to children. At their most simple form, expansions may involve open-ended questions designed to engage children in the composing or writing process, prompting them to extend or connect the ideas that they generate (Quinn, Gerde, & Bingham, 2016). Another expansion strategy is to encourage children to elaborate on information in order to deepen or extend their understanding of writing-related processes. Although an additional strategy involves encouraging children to assess their writing process or product to review what they wrote, or intended to write, in order to deepen the child's understanding of writing (Gabas et al., 2022). This strategy challenges children cognitively to evaluate their writing in a manner that leads to some form of addition to, or revisions of, their written product. At their core, expansion strategies cognitively or physically engage children in the writing task in a manner that enriches involvement. Of course, if a teacher is out of sync with a child's ZPD, expansions can be too cognitively or physically demanding for a child to complete, even with adult assistance. We find that teachers who engage in expansions during the writing process also spend considerable time breaking down the task to support the child's ability to fully engage in the writing process (Bingham et al., 2021). In other words, teachers rarely engage in writing mediation strategies in isolation. Rather, they tend to move and shift their instructional focus and the strategies that they employ across writing events in a manner that supports student learning and engagement (Gabas et al., 2022; Rowe, Shimizu, & Davis, 2021).

Summary of Teachers' Instructional Practices

Taken together, research on typical classroom practice illustrates that most early childhood teachers engage children in writing experiences daily and use a variety of instructional strategies to support children's engagement in writing-related tasks. Although variation exists across studies, suggesting that some teachers have wide repertoires on which to draw when supporting children's writing, most interactions are centered on completing writing tasks in a manner that is primarily directive, emphasizing conventionality (product) over process, and requiring low to moderate cognitive demands for children to complete. Furthermore, teachers spend an inordinate amount of these writing interactions supporting procedural skills related to handwriting over composing and spelling. Because a large percentage of these scaffolds are of low quality, they often involve activities focused on letter formation, such as copying, and are not rich meaning-based experiences that focus on writing as communication. Teacher supports that are of more limited quality unnecessarily constrain the cognitive or physical demand placed on children, as teachers tend to take over the cognitive or physical act of writing in ways that undermine children's ability to learn from the few minutes a day that are devoted to writing. Furthermore, because many early writing opportunities that children experience are not meaningfully or richly connected to curricular experiences, children experience limited explicit and intentional guidance around how to connect oral and written language in a developmentally sensitive way (be it a picture, a mark, or a letter). Recent studies of early childhood teachers' early writing practices demonstrate that varying instructional contexts lend themselves to different types of writing experiences. Although some writing-based research has capitalized on the nature of these instructional contexts (Zhang & Bingham, 2019) much more research is needed to explore best approaches for supporting how teachers enact writing-based supports in a manner that promotes children's development of handwriting, spelling, *and* composing skills (McMaster, Birinci, Shanahan, & Lembke, Chapter 10, this volume).

Where Do Teachers' Practices Originate?

Teachers' practices are not produced in isolation. Knowledge, beliefs, histories, and contextual/professional factors influence how teachers engage in writing interactions with children and what skills they focus on during these interactions. PL approaches to support teachers' practices must approach adult learning in a manner that not only supports content and pedagogical

content knowledge but also works to ensure that teachers' beliefs about children's early writing development (Gerde, Wright, et al., 2019) and their personal literacy histories (Hall, 2016; Hall & Grisham-Brown, 2011) don't impede such efforts. Understanding the source of teachers' practices can guide PL approaches to be better attuned to varying knowledge, beliefs, and skills levels. Although a detailed review of the varied factors that should be considered when designing a PL system for preschool teachers' early writing practices is beyond the scope of this chapter, we briefly illustrate how professional (standards and curriculum) and personal (beliefs and knowledge) factors support or undermine these efforts.

U.S. state early learning standards, including the Head Start Outcomes Framework and early childhood curriculum provide early educators with guidance on which early writing skills should be taught, how to teach these skills, and how teachers might assess children's progress toward these learning targets. Overwhelmingly, U.S. standards emphasize children's transcription skills (54%), with far fewer standards articulating the development of composing (38%) and writing concept (26%; note that because 22% of standards included more than one writing component, the totals add up to more than 100%) skills (Torterelli, Gerde, Rohloff, & Bingham, 2021). A detailed look at the transcription standards reveals that most (95.4%) focused on handwriting skills, while far fewer (12.3%) addressed spelling. Gerde, Skibbe, et al. (2019) document similar unevenness in early childhood curriculum with their coding of the most widely used curricula in Head Start, revealing that although curriculum varied considerably in writing focus (i.e., two more heavily emphasizing transcription skills, two writing materials, one composing), no curriculum provided guidance on how to promote writing holistically (i.e., focused on the multidimensional nature of transcription and composing skills). Furthermore, although writing-focused objectives and strategies were noted in each curriculum, three of the five did not provide explicit guidance for how to support these skills. The few examples of explicit guidance for supporting writing skills focused on handwriting skills (i.e., letter formation). The focus of standards and curriculum likely shape early educators' writing beliefs, knowledge, and practices.

Early educators' early writing beliefs and knowledge are an important source of influence on how they engage young children in writing opportunities (Bingham et al., 2022). Researchers note wide variability in teachers' beliefs about early writing development (Gerde, Wright, et al., 2019; Hindman & Wasik, 2008), document their connection to personal experiences with writing as K–12 students (Hall, 2016; Hall & Grisham-Brown, 2011), and illustrate distinctive patterns that relate to their perceptions about children's needs in their classrooms (Lynch, 2009). Beliefs, knowledge, and practices intersect in predictable ways. For example, Bingham et al. (2020) found that preschool teachers could be organized into three profiles: wholistic writers, transcribers, and "drawing isn't writing." The wholistic writer group (39% of the total sample) articulated beliefs and knowledge perspectives that valued multiple early writing skills (transcription, composing, and print concepts) and were more likely than the other teachers to emphasize composing in written responses and daily practice. The transcriber group's (43% of teachers) beliefs and knowledge heavily emphasized transcription skills, and their classroom practices focused on supporting children in forming letters, learning letter shapes, and letter–sound associations. In contrast, the "drawing isn't writing" group (19% of teachers) articulated beliefs that failed to recognize developmental processes of early writers (i.e., scribbling, scribble writing, drawing as communication, marks intended to have meaning). This group of teachers was less knowledgeable about early writing development and offered fewer and lower-quality writing interactions with children than the other two groups. Because existing knowledge and belief systems act as a lens through which new information is experienced (Brandsford, Brown, & Cocking, 2000), PL approaches need to be differentiated in a manner that meets the varying knowledge, beliefs, and skills of early educators.

How Do We Apply This Knowledge?

Understanding the nature of environments and instructional opportunities early educators provide in their classrooms is key to designing PL experiences that have deep relevance to teachers and ultimately promote change in their practice. The studies reviewed earlier contribute to the burgeoning literature on the science of teaching early writing and demonstrate the current state of our understanding of teachers' knowledge, beliefs, and practices for supporting early writ-

ing and how these are impacted by the learning standards and curricula available to them. We designed the iWRITE PL program to capitalize on what teachers are doing already, to reinforce and increase knowledge that expands teachers' current understanding, to introduce practices that are familiar but can be used specifically for writing, and to connect and interpret how teachers can use learning standards, curricula, and assessments to their favor. In addition, we leveraged high-quality PL approaches informed by adult learning theory to create engaging learning opportunities for early educators.

The iWRITE PL Program

The iWRITE PL represents the most fully developed, remotely delivered intervention for early writing to date. Capable of being integrated into any early childhood curriculum, iWRITE was designed to support Head Start teachers to (1) develop knowledge of what early writing is and how it develops, (2) prepare high-quality writing environments, and (3) engage in teacher–child interactions that promote children's writing development directly and their language and literacy development indirectly. This occurs as teachers, with individualized guidance from their expert coach, work through a series of eight online learning modules (OLMs) and engage in two virtual coaching sessions monthly. In alignment with adult learning theory (Bransford et al., 1999; Putnam & Borko, 2000) and key criteria of effective PL and coaching (Egert, Fukkink, & Eckhardt, 2018; Kraft, Blazar, & Hogan, 2018), modules offer extensive and repeated opportunities for teachers to observe high-quality instructional practices and learn about how these practices support young writers (Powell, Diamond, Burchinal, & Koehler, 2010; Wasik & Hindman, 2020), receive ongoing and individualized feedback framed on a shared set of criteria or data (Crawford, Zucker, Van Horne, & Landry, 2017; Desimone & Garet, 2015; Wasik & Hindman, 2011), and participate in supervised self-reflection of their own practice through differentiated coaching (Desimone, 2009; Downer, Locasale-Crouch, Hamre, & Pianta, 2009; Elek & Page, 2019). OLMs include the following educative resources:

1. Content text focusing on children's writing, language, and literacy development.
2. Video exemplars with commentary about how the video illustrates best-practice.

3. Practice-based learning experiences that offer assignments, tailored to OLM content, in which teachers execute new skills, submit a product of their work (e.g., video of implementing modeling for spelling), and receive individual feedback from their coach, based on an assessment of classroom writing.
4. A coaching platform in which coaches, who are experts in early childhood language and literacy development and practice, offer ongoing, individualized feedback to teachers that highlight, using the iWRITE framework, where (a) teachers are using quality practices and (b) enhancements are needed, features of effective coaching (Dudek, Reddy, Lekwa, Hua, & Fabiano, 2019; Fabiano, Reddy, & Dudek, 2018).
5. Space for engaging teachers in self-reflection on their own teaching, with scaffolded guidance and supporting critique by their coach.

To learn more about iWRITE, watch our introductory video (*www.youtube.com/watch?v=ero ijpnletc*).

Technology Innovations and Virtual Learning

The iWRITE PL program was developed to be a fully virtual program to leverage the benefits associated with distance learning models of PL. Such approaches are essential for early childhood teachers given time and staffing constraints of educators currently in service (Whitebook & Sakai, 2003) and have grown in importance particularly during the COVID-19 pandemic. The iWRITE PL program capitalized on the following benefits of online PL delivery: reduced time out of the classroom; reduced disruption during class time to deliver PL; reduced travel time for teachers and coaches; and opportunities for teachers to revisit PL topics, exercises, or exemplar videos because they are available online (Douglas, Nordquist, Kammes, & Gerde, 2017; Moon, Passmore, Reiser, & Michaels, 2014; Powell, Diamond, & Koehler, 2010). Also, distance delivery permits teachers to work through PL materials/assignments at their own pace, which is essential for a teaching staff who enter the field with a wide range of educational and experiential backgrounds (Early et al., 2010; Zigler & Styfco, 2010), have variations in their teaching schedules, and are offered very little paid time for planning or PL (Powell & Dia-

mond, 2013). Distance learning approaches are particularly relevant for early childhood programs in the United States that range in size and cover urban, rural, and remote areas. Distance learning approaches can break down geographic barriers to high-quality PL and reach teachers in remote and isolated locations to promote equity for teachers who are often marginalized from quality PL opportunities.

Building Knowledge and Skills

The iWRITE PL program utilizes a comprehensive definition of early writing that places communication at the center of writing instruction *and* captures both the multidimensional nature of early writing and the wide range of writing-like practices that children employ in early childhood. In alignment with multiple theories of early writing (Berninger & Chanquoy, 2012; Berninger & Winn, 2006; Kaderavak et al., 2009; Kim, 2020), iWRITE conceptualizes early writing as containing text generation, often called *composing and transcription*, which includes mechanics (fine motor/handwriting) and orthography (spelling). Both handwriting (Graham, Harris, & Fink, 2000) and spelling (Hooper, Roberts, Nelson, Zeisel, & Kasambira Fannin, 2010; Kim, Al Otaiba, & Wanzek, 2015) are related to later writing achievement. Composing captures how children generate ideas for what to write and the translation of thought into language (Quinn, Bingham, et al., 2021; Rowe & Wilson, 2015). Young children demonstrate their composition skills in a variety of ways that are influenced by their sociocultural context and motivations for writing (Dyson, 2013). When writing is characterized in this way, early educators see writing as a developmentally appropriate and achievable experience for preschool-age children, because children can participate in writing experiences even when skills across all components are not mastered (e.g., fine motor [mechanics], letter–sound correspondence [orthography]).

Using the science of literacy, we integrated throughout the iWRITE OLMs a knowledge of what writing is, how it develops, and how it is supported using clear and meaningful definitions of composing, spelling, and handwriting. The use of consistent terminology gave teachers and coaches a shared language to use as they progressed through the modules to build knowledge and skills and made connections to their curriculum, learning standards, and assessments, which do not have unified definitions or terminology. In fact, each module included research-based content of writing development and practices, as well as direct quotes from Head Start and National Association for the Education of Young Children (NAEYC) standards supporting the recommended practices. This knowledge building was essential for multiple reasons. Teacher preparation programs provide limited coursework in early writing development and instruction (Zimmerman, Morgan, & Kidder-Brown, 2014), which means they must rely on their own, often negative experiences with writing or guidance from learning standards and curricula. Recall that our work identified curriculum supports for writing to be uneven and incomplete (Gerde, Skibbe, et al., 2019), as not all curricula cover all components of writing or offer explicit guidance to support writing in ways that promote children's development. Moreover, there is a misalignment of standards across early childhood in both the language used and the writing skills targeted (Tortorelli et al., 2021), leaving teachers with more questions than guidance about how to successfully support early writing development. Perhaps most challenging is the lack of integration for supporting early reading and writing skills together, which can result in teachers feeling that they do not have time to teach writing, too.

Creating Space to See High-Quality Practice

To accompany the content knowledge provided in text, our team curated a video and picture library of high-quality practices for supporting writing. The use of video exemplars in online PL is the "gold standard," because it allows teachers to view quality practice and learn why the practice is valuable (e.g., Crawford et al., 2021; Powell, Diamond, & Koehler, 2010; Moon et al., 2014; Wasik & Hindman, 2020). Based on our work recognizing that writing opportunities were rare in preschool classrooms (Gerde et al., 2015; Zhang et al., 2015) and that teachers' supports for writing were overwhelmingly low level and focused on handwriting (Bingham et al., 2017; Gerde, Wright, et al., 2019), we knew it was essential to show and not just tell teachers how to engage in high-quality supports for early writing. Within this context, it was very unlikely for a teacher to be able to walk down

the hall and see another teacher engaging in the types of practices the iWRITE PL was asking of teachers. While video exemplars have the power to enhance learning by showing real-life scenarios, explaining challenging concepts, and acting as triggers for discussions to inspire learning (Oliver, Osa, & Walker, 2012), they must be carefully designed to effectively wield this power. Following guidance from experts in the design of effective educative videos, we adopted a set of criteria necessary for each video exemplar integrated into the iWRITE modules:

- *Show, don't just tell, about quality practices.* Adult learners better understand new practices when they are able to watch videos in which target teaching practices occur (Yadav, Bouck, Da Fonte, & Patton, 2009); videos of lecturing about the topic, on the other hand, reduce adult viewership (Koehler, Yadav, Phillips, & Cavazos-Kottke, 2005).
- *Couple the knowledge of quality practice with videos of actual practice.* Inclusion of a guiding narrative targeting particular practices or skills prompts teachers to apply what they have learned from the video (Powell, Diamond, & Koehler, 2010). Videos that combine a demonstration of the target practice and a narrative describing the practice yield enhanced content retention and skills development (Mayer & Moreno, 2002).
- *Include subtitles.* Subtitles are a key feature of quality videos of any type, as they enhance the viewer capacity to understand the video in the first viewing, including participants who are English language learners (Powell, Diamond, & Koehler, 2010). This practice aligns with the regulations set forth by the Americans with Disabilities Act (ADA, Section 508, 1998).
- *Time is a factor; shorter is better.* The average viewing time for educative videos is 4 minutes in length (Hibbert, 2014). Even for 4-minute videos, students watch just 73.4% of the video (i.e., about 3 minutes; Lei et al., 2016), which suggests that even shorter is better. In general, iWRITE videos last 1–2 minutes.
- *Show real teachers in real classrooms.* Teachers are more likely to adopt new practices when they can visualize the practice in their own classroom. Thus, our videos captured real Head Start classrooms, teachers, and children engaging in authentic, high-quality writing practices. The inclusion of children's

actual behaviors and teachers' enjoyment of interacting with children creates meaningful videos that are salient to participants due to the emotion elicited by the real-life situations, which increases retention of ideas and practices presented in educative videos (Koehler et al., 2005).

The iWRITE PD modules include 308 brief but targeted videos of real teachers and children demonstrating high-quality writing practices, with voiceovers explaining why the practice is quality, and subtitles to support a diverse group of teachers to successfully engage.

To enhance engagement within the virtual learning modules, teachers completed two practice-based lessons in each module and posted a video of their practice to the iWRITE website for review by their coach. In alignment with a body of evidence identifying coaching as an effective approach to improve teaching practices (e.g., Egert et al., 2018; Kraft et al., 2018; Markussen-Brown et al., 2017), teachers received individualized feedback on their practice-based video posts twice per month from coaches expert in early literacy practice. iWRITE uses an interactive coaching approach in which the practice-based assignments are broken into steps, with drop-down options for responding to questions about preparation, implementation, and guided reflection, vital parts of effective PL (Durst, Aggestam, & Ferenhof, 2015), and coaching (Desimone & Garet, 2015). This process initiates communication from the coach at each step, thus increasing coach–teacher interaction and supporting the teachers' efficacy in demonstrating key skills. The more interactive drop-down boxes minimize task demands, which enhance engagement (Van Merriënboer, Kirschner, & Kester, 2003). Also, we leveraged the affordances of online PL by offering options to post and receive from the coach video/audio responses rather than written ones, which allowed us to retain the open-ended questions essential for reflection (Elek & Page, 2019).

Collaborating with Teachers to Design iWRITE

To create PL that would function within the lives of real teachers, iWRITE was codeveloped in partnership with diverse early educators from several Head Start programs. Using an itera- tive process, we engaged teachers in reviewing the content of each module, which yielded additional content and areas where clarification was needed. Next, teachers critically reviewed video exemplars and the practice-based learning experiences. Overwhelmingly, teachers reported in their survey feedback that the videos were "the most important part of the learning modules," and 100% of teachers strongly agreed that the videos "helped teachers to learn the strategies in the module and included practices that would benefit the children in their classrooms." Moreover, 100% of reviewing teachers agreed or strongly agreed that the teaching practices included in the practice-based learning experiences reflected practices they would use in their own classroom. Finally, a group of teachers worked through full OLMs to help us identify the appropriate pacing for OLMs and the feasibility of engaging with the OLMs in real schools within the course of real work weeks. While the iWRITE permits maximum flexibility due to its portable online platform, the teachers identified guidelines for how typical teachers approach the OLMs within the context of their real lives and noted where navigability could be enhanced. Making adjustments to the OLMs, assignments, navigation, and pacing were based on the feedback received from teachers throughout our iterative codevelopment process.

Impact of iWRITE for Teachers and Children

To evaluate the impact of participation in iWRITE on teachers' writing and literacy practices and children's writing outcomes, our team conducted a randomized controlled trial of iWRITE, funded by the U.S. Department of Education, Institute of Education Sciences (R305A150210). Our participants included 54 lead Head Start teachers (Treatment Group = 34) and 497 diverse 4-year-old children in their classrooms. Teachers/classrooms were observed for the full morning session (~2.5 hours) preintervention and again 7 months after intervention commencement by observers trained to reliability in the observational measures used. Observers live-coded the ELLCO (Smith, Brady, & Anastasopoulos, 2008) and the writing materials subsection of the Writing Resources in Teaching Environments (WRITE; Gerde et al., 2015). Children were assessed individually at the beginning and end of the school year on their writing, including their skill for letter writing (i.e., writing 10 dictated letters) and invented spelling (i.e., writing 5 dictated consonant–vowel–consonant [CVC] words). Children's writing was coded by researchers trained to reliability (kappa = .91) using a coding system that accounts for early writing-like behaviors (e.g., scribbles/drawing, letter-like forms) as well as letters, developing sound awareness, and conventional writing (Gerde et al., 2015; Thomas et al., 2020).

Linear latent growth curve analysis identified that treatment teachers who participated in iWRITE demonstrated significant increases in teachers' preparation of quality writing environments (i.e., faster growth, 2.3 times faster, p = .002) and higher final scores (6.4 points higher, d = 0.9, p < .001) and faster growth (3.0 times faster, p < .001) and higher posttest scores (d = 1.4, p = .001) on the ELLCO writing subscale measuring writing materials and teacher–child interactions to support early writing (Gerde, Bingham, et al., 2019). Treatment teachers exhibited higher ELLCO total scores (d = 0.8, p = .05) compared to control teachers. Analysis of covariance revealed that children in classrooms of teachers who optimally engaged in iWRITE (i.e., completed five or more OLMs) had higher writing outcomes (e.g., letter writing F = 7.92, p = .005, spelling CVC words F = 12.73, p = .0005) than children in classrooms of teachers who did not optimally engage. While these findings are positive, similar to so many PL (e.g., Downer et al., 2009; Powell, Diamond, Burchinal, et al., 2010), many teachers (46%) did not participate in iWRITE as planned, that is, without significant ad hoc supports (e.g., in-person coaching to reengage) from the project team. During the pilot, the study team added supports as needed, but not in an a priori, protocolized manner.

Given that iWRITE works for Head Start teachers who fully engage, it is a valuable PL to promote quality writing and literacy practices and can enhance children's writing development. These findings also provide evidence that designing and evaluating an enhanced and adaptive iWRITE PL may be advantageous for creating PL that is effective for a broad range of teachers, which is essential for scaled-up delivery. Future work should focus on protocolization of supports for engaging all teachers, which will promote replicability of effects and scale-up.

Designing Strength-Based PL for Diverse Educators

The design and evaluation of a PL such as iWRITE has much to offer in terms of lessons learned and guidance for future PL development. First, it is important to acknowledge that teachers' implementation of new instructional approaches is difficult, even when they fully intend to participate and enact the new practices introduced. iWRITE PL is an example of a PL approach that changed the practices of teachers, and ultimately children's outcomes, for *some* teachers, but not all. Although the PL was intentionally designed to alleviate a range of barriers teachers faced, teachers evidenced varying levels of engagement that likely attenuated the impact of the PL on teacher practice and child outcomes. Our program of research into teachers' early writing practices illustrates that teachers are impacted by a multitude of personal, professional, and environmental barriers keeping them from full engagement in and implementation of content learned in PL. These factors also act as a lens through which new information is filtered and how it is taken up and enacted in practice.

One clear pattern that emerged from this work was the need to better identify the personal experiences and strengths that teachers bring with them to new learning opportunities. Personal factors related to teachers' early writing knowledge and beliefs, literacy histories, and self-efficacy play a role in the daily literacy practices they provide to children and the early strategies they use to support early writing specifically. We recently developed an innovative assessment of teachers' early writing knowledge and beliefs to accomplish this task. The Early Writing Knowledge Assessment (EWKA; Bingham et al., 2022) uses authentic writing scenarios and children's writing samples to elicit teachers' knowledge of writing development and beliefs about supportive practices within the context of their everyday classroom experiences. This assessment provides insight into which writing components teachers are most knowledgeable about and insight into their belief systems for the best way to support children's writing development. Teacher's knowledge and beliefs are an important asset that should be built upon as they are guided to deepen and enrich existing understandings with evidence-based knowledge about how to best support young children's writing.

Strengths also include existing practices teachers are already employing that can be leveraged for greater impact, and the resources they currently have in their programs and classrooms. For example, based on our observational work, teachers appear to vary their instructional focus somewhat based on the age of children in their classroom, which is a proxy of early writing skills level; that is, teachers of younger preschool children focused more on composing related supports, while teachers of older preschool children focused more on spelling supports (Bingham et al., 2022). This variation in practices may relate to the general early writing skills of the child with whom they were interacting (Gabas et al., 2022). PL design must accommodate teachers' own background knowledge and experiences by considering how new knowledge and practices can build on teachers' strengths and be embedded into the classroom routines teachers already have in place.

Moving forward, researchers evaluating PL must continue to break down barriers by identifying approaches to maximize engagement, so that all teachers can reap the benefits of high-quality PL offerings such as iWRITE. This requires that evaluation studies include details about the teachers themselves (e.g., knowledge, beliefs, skills) and explain PL processes and dosage data that provide insight into how the intervention is and isn't working (see Zucker, Jacbos, & Cabell, 2021). In addition, researchers should use a range of methods—survey, interview, focus group—to carefully identify the barriers facing teachers and programs within the context of the PL implementation. It is important that researchers are open and honest about these processes, as pressures to show impact or effects can often counteract efforts for transparent scholarship. Understanding and identifying barriers are key to designing PL that is better aligned to the professional goals and capacities of diverse early childhood educators. It is also key to providing high-quality learning environments that provide young children a culturally and linguistically sustaining curriculum.

One barrier that we have identified and worked toward resolving is the need to understand early educators' classroom practices more deeply. We developed the WRITE observational assessment (Gerde et al., 2015) as one way to identify writing environmental and pedagogical features that best support early writing development. This assessment allowed us to identify how teachers approach writing and what types of strategies they use to promote children's writing develop-

ment. We are currently developing a system that would be more diagnostic for teachers and children by gathering formative data that would help to identify both teachers' strengths and specific areas to target in PL. Such data will highlight teachers' personal growth and inform the design of a strengths-based early writing PL system.

It is important to remember that resources are different for individual participants, and individual teachers are differentially impacted by barriers. The theoretical domains framework identifies multiple categories of barriers, and resources within each category can influence teachers' participation in PL or implementation of a new practice (Cane et al., 2012). Although patterns of teacher background characteristics (e.g., degree level, years of experience) did not emerge from our data, future work should examine how individuals and whole groups of teachers are impacted by particular barriers as a way to better engage participants who are marginalized. A valuable resource moving forward would be the development of a survey to identify individual- or program-level resources that could be used as research–practice partnerships develop and co-create PL that is most effective for the teachers and program.

Early childhood educators are a diverse group of professionals who need equally diverse options for continuing education. Having multiple pathways to access the early childhood profession is beneficial for creating a diverse workforce that not only reflects the children the teachers serve but also means that PL cannot be "one size fits all." What is clear is that PL that promotes knowledge and skills is essential. Many early childhood degree programs do not offer supervised practicum experiences with young children, so support, including video exemplars of real teachers implementing new practices in real classrooms, are necessary for facilitating teachers' use of new practices with children in their own classrooms. For example, one core challenge with supporting teachers is that early childhood teachers are very directive with young children's writing (Bingham et al., 2022; Gerde et al., 2015). Although teachers might see providing directions or directives as needed instructional supports for helping children to complete writing-related tasks, the directive nature of teacher communication limits the cognitive complexity of the interaction and children's ability to fully represent their knowledge and skills. Furthermore, such teachers may see writing as an area of focus that is more product-than process-driven. Providing video exemplars that help teachers to see how writing supports can be conversational in ways that give children opportunities to use oral language to compose ideas, consider words and messages they want to write, and think about purposes for their writing is necessary for revising teachers' directive approaches to writing instruction.

Another successful feature of iWRITE PL was the need for PL that is digestible in smaller dosages and supports teachers to use a range of practices. The use of multiple, short learning modules focused on one topic with two specific skills aligning with two opportunities to practice those skills offered teachers easily manageable amounts of content to consume and try out. As global curricular approaches for supporting children are generally unsuccessful (e.g., Preschool Curriculum Evaluation Research Consortium, 2008), we need content-rich approaches, such as iWRITE, that teachers can take up and that connect to existing practices in meaningful and additive ways rather than trying to shift too many practices at once. As another example, opportunities for individualization were integrated across modules as a repeating theme. The individualization strategies were reintroduced across modules within different contexts, including during play, routines and transitions, and group experiences. In this way, teachers could use skills they had already learned but apply them to a new context.

Finally, it is important that PL developers keep innovating about remote delivery of PL because of the numerous benefits distance learning provides to teachers, particularly those who are geographically isolated and have few resources for investing in PL. Within the context of the current COVID-19 pandemic, distance learning approaches are essential now and in the future. In fact, within the climate of COVID-19, teachers may be more receptive to online learning than we have experienced in the past. From our own experiences engaging teachers in remote PL prior to the pandemic, teachers now have spent significantly more time using technology for both teaching and learning opportunities. Thus, their willingness and skills to engage in technology for continuing educational opportunities have increased.

Conclusion

While research continues to identify a notable need for high-quality teacher PL in the area of early writing, it is important to design PL that is founded in the scientific evidence base of early writing development and instruction. We urge the research community to continue to investigate writing development and effective writing practices and assessment to expand on this growing knowledge base. Importantly, successful PL should build on teachers' strengths, including their background knowledge, skills, and experience, and leverage what is known about effective PL and engagement of adult learners.

Acknowledgments

We thank our early childhood program partners, teachers, families, and children who participated in our research. Some of the research reported here was supported by the Institute of Education Sciences, U.S. Department of Education, through Grant R305A150210 to Michigan State University. The opinions expressed are those of the authors and do not represent views of the Institute or the U.S. Department of Education.

References

Berninger, V. W., & Chanquoy, L. (2012). What writing is and how it changes across early and middle childhood development. In E. L. Grigorenko, E. Mambrino, & D. D. Preiss (Eds.), *Writing: A mosaic of new perspectives* (pp. 65–84). Psychology Press.

Berninger, V. W., & Winn, W. (2006). Implications of advancements in brain research and technology for writing development, writing instruction, and educational evolution. In C. A. MacArthur, S. Graham, & J. Fitzgerald (Eds.), *Handbook of writing research* (pp. 96–114). Guilford Press.

Bingham, G. E., Gerde, H. K., Pikus, A. E., Rohloff, R., Quinn, M. F., Bowles, R. P., & Zhang, X. Y. (2022). Examining teachers' early writing knowledge and practices. *Reading and Writing, 35,* 2201–2227.

Bingham, G. E., Gerde, H. K., Rohloff, R. Zhang, X. Y., & Bowles, R. P. (2021, December). Are they in sync?: Examining associations between teachers' early writing practices and children's early writing development. In G. Bingham (Chair) *How, What, and Why?: Examining early writing instructional and assessment practices.* A symposium presented for the Literacy Research Association's 71st Annual Conference, Atlanta, GA.

Bingham, G. E., Gerde, H. K., & Zhang, X. Y. (2020, December). Patterns of Interactions: Profiles of teacher supports for emergent writing. In D. Rowe (Chair), *Improving early writing instruc-*

tion: *Insights about instructional materials and teachers' pedagogical interactions*. A symposium presented at the annual conference of the Literacy Research Association (virtual conference).

Bingham, G. E., Quinn, M. F., & Gerde, H. K. (2017). Examining early childhood teachers' writing practices: Associations between pedagogical supports and children's writing skills. *Early Childhood Research Quarterly, 39*, 35–46.

Bingham, G. E., Quinn, M. F., McRoy, K., Zhang, X., & Gerde, H. K. (2018). Integrating writing into the early childhood curriculum: A frame for intentional and meaningful writing experiences. *Early Childhood Education Journal, 46*(6), 601–611.

Bingham, G. E., Rohloff, R., & Gerde, H. K. (2018, November). Examining the nature of early writing supports in preschool classrooms. In D. Rowe (Chair), *Adult support of emergent writers*. A symposium presented at the Literacy Research Association's 68th Annual Conference, Indian Wells, CA.

Bransford, J. D., Brown, A. L., & Cocking, R. R. (1999). *How people learn: Brain, mind, experience, school*. National Academy Press.

Cane, J., O'Connor, D., & Michie, S. (2012). Validation of the theoretical domains framework for use in behaviour change and implementation research. *Implementation Science, 7*, Article 37.

Chandler, M., Gerde, H. K., Bowles, R. P., McRoy, K. Z., Pontifex, M. B., & Bingham, G. E. (2021). Self-regulation moderates the relationship between fine motor skills and writing in early childhood. *Early Childhood Research Quarterly, 57*, 239–250.

Copple, C., & Bredekamp, S. (2009). *Developmentally appropriate practice in early childhood programs serving children from birth through age 8* (3rd ed.). National Association for the Education of Young Children.

Crawford, A., Varghese, C., Hsu, H.-Y., Zucker, T., Landry, S., Assel, M., . . . Bhavsar, V. (2021). A comparative analysis of instructional coaching approaches: Face-to-face versus remote coaching in preschool classrooms. *Journal of Educational Psychology, 113*(8), 1609–1627.

Crawford, A., Zucker, T., Van Horne, B., & Landry, S. (2017). Integrating professional development content and formative assessment with the coaching process: The Texas school ready model. *Theory Into Practice, 56*(1), 56–65.

Desimone, L. M. (2009). Improving impact studies of teachers' professional development: Toward better conceptualizations and measures. *Educational Researcher, 38*, 181–199.

Desimone, L. M., & Garet, M. S. (2015). Best practices in teachers' professional development in the United States. *Psychology, Society, and Education, 7*, 252–263.

Diamond, K. E., Gerde, H. K., & Powell, D. R. (2008). Development in early literacy skills during the pre-kindergarten year in Head Start: Relations between growth in children's writing and understanding of letters. *Early Childhood Research Quarterly, 23*(4), 467–478.

Douglas, S. N., Nordquist, E., Kammes, R., & Gerde, H. (2017). Online parent training to support children with complex communication needs. *Infants and Young Children, 30*(4), 288–303.

Downer, J. T., Locasale-Crouch, J., Hamre, B., & Pianta, R. (2009). Teacher characteristics associated with responsiveness and exposure to consultation and online professional development resources. *Early Education and Development, 20*(3), 431–455.

Dudek, C. M., Reddy, L. A., Lekwa, A., Hua, A. N., & Fabiano, G. A. (2019). Improving universal classroom practices through teacher formative assessment and coaching. *Assessment for Effective Intervention, 44*, 81–94.

Durst, S., Aggestam, L., & Ferenhof, H. A. (2015). *Understanding knowledge leakage: A review of previous studies*. Vine.

Dyson, A. H. (2013). The case of the missing childhoods: Methodological notes for composing children in writing studies. *Written Communication, 30*(4), 399–427.

Early, D. M., Iruka, I. U., Ritchie, S., Barbarin, O. A., Winn, D.-M. C., Crawford, G. M., . . . Pianta, R. C. (2010). How do pre-kindergarteners spend their time?: Gender, ethnicity, and income as predictors of experiences in pre-kindergarten classrooms. *Early Childhood Research Quarterly, 25*(2), 177–193.

Egert, F., Fukkink, R.G., & Eckhardt, A.G. (2018). Impact of in-service professional development programs for early childhood teachers on quality ratings and child outcomes: A meta-analysis. *Review of Educational Research, 88*(3), 401–433.

Electronic and Information Technology Accessibility Standards, 36 CF.R. $ 1194 (1998), available at *www. hhs.gov/sites/default/files/Intro%20 to%20Accessibility%20and%20508.pdf*

Elek, C., & Page, J. (2019). Critical features of effective coaching for early childhood educators: A review of empirical research literature. *Professional Development in Education, 45*(4), 567–585.

Fabiano, G. A., Reddy, L. A., & Dudek, C. M. (2018). Teacher coaching supported by formative assessment for improving classroom practice. *School Psychology Quarterly, 33*, 293–304.

Gabas, C., Wood, C., & Cabell, S. Q. (2022). Write this way: Examining teachers' supportive strategies to facilitate children's early writing in preschool. *Reading and Writing, 35*, 479–507.

Gerde, H. K., Bingham, G. E., Bowles, R. P., Meier, A., & Zhang, X. (2019, July). Teacher and child-level outcomes of the iWRITE professional development intervention. In H. Gerde (Chair), *Writing development: Predictors, profiles, and intervention*. A symposium presented at the annual conference of the Society for the Scientific Study of Reading, Toronto, Ontario, Canada.

Gerde, H. K., Bingham, G. E., & Pendergast, M. L. (2015). Reliability and validity of the Writing Resources and Interactions in Teaching Environments (WRITE) for preschool classrooms. *Early Childhood Research Quarterly, 31*, 34–46.

Gerde, H. K., Bingham, G. E., & Wasik, B. A. (2012). Writing in early childhood classrooms: Guidance for best practices. *Early Childhood Education Journal, 40*(6), 351–359.

Gerde, H. K., Skibbe, L. E., Bowles, R. P., & Martoccio, T. L. (2012). Child and home predictors of children's name writing. *Child Development Research, 12*, 1–12.

Gerde, H. K., Skibbe, L. E., Wright, T. S., & Douglas, S. N. (2019). Evaluation of Head Start curricula for standards-based writing instruction. *Early Childhood Education Journal, 47*, 97–105.

Gerde, H. K., Wright, T. S., & Bingham, G. E. (2019). Preschool teachers' beliefs about and instruction for writing. *Journal of Early Childhood Teacher Education, 40*(4), 326–351.

Graham, S., Harris, K. R., & Fink, B. (2000). Extra handwriting instruction: Prevent writing difficulties right from the start. *Teaching Exceptional Children, 33*(2), 88–91.

Hall, A., & Grisham-Brown, J. (2011) Writing development over time: Examining preservice teachers' attitudes and beliefs about writing. *Journal of Early Childhood Teacher Education, 32*(2), 148–158.

Hall, A. H. (2016). Examining shifts in preservice teachers' beliefs and attitudes toward writing instruction. *Journal of Early Childhood Teacher Education, 37*(2), 142–156.

Hibbert, M. C. (2014). What makes an online instructional video compelling? Retrieved from *https://er.educause.edu/articles/2014/4/what-makes-an-online-instructional-video-compelling*.

Hindman, A. H., & Wasik, B. A. (2008). Head Start teachers' beliefs about language and literacy instruction. *Early Childhood Research Quarterly, 23*(4), 479–492.

Hooper, S. R., Roberts, J. E., Nelson, L., Zeisel, S., & Kasambira Fannin, D. (2010). Preschool predictors of narrative writing skills in elementary school children. *School Psychology Quarterly, 25*(1), 1–12.

Kaderavek, J. N., Cabell, S. Q., & Justice, L. M. (2009). Early writing and spelling development. In P. M. Rhyner (Ed.), *Emergent literacy and*

language development: Promoting learning in early childhood (pp. 104–152). Guilford Press.

Kim, Y.-S. (2020). Interactive dynamic literacy model: An integrative theoretical framework for reading–writing relations. In R. Alves, T. Limpo, & M. Joshi (Eds.), *Reading–writing connections: Towards integrative literacy science* (pp. 11–34). Springer.

Kim, Y.-S., Al Otaiba, S., & Wanzek, J. (2015). Kindergarten predictors of third grade writing. *Learning and Individual Differences, 37*, 27–37.

Koehler, M. J., Yadav, A., Phillips, M., & Cavazos-Kottke, S. (2005). What is video good for?: Examining how media and story genre interact. *Journal of Educational Multimedia and Hypermedia, 14*(3), 249–272.

Kraft, M. A., Blazar, D., & Hogan, D. (2018). The effect of teacher coaching on instruction and achievement: A meta-analysis of the causal evidence. *Review of Educational Research, 88*, 547–588.

Lei, C. U., Oh, E., Leung, E., Gonda, D., Qi, X., Leung, R., & Lau, R. (2016, December). Scale out teaching, scale up learning: Professional development for e-teaching/learning. In *Teaching, assessment, and learning for engineering (TALE)* (pp. 265–270). IEEE.

Lynch, J. (2009). Preschool teachers' beliefs about children's print literacy development. *Early Years, 29*, 191–203.

Markussen-Brown, J., Juhl, C. B., Piasta, S. B., Bleses, D., Hojen, A., & Justice, L. M. (2017). The effects of language- and literacy-focused professional development on early educators and children: A best-evidence meta-analysis. *Early Childhood Research Quarterly, 38*, 97–115.

Mayer, R. E., & Moreno, R. (2002). Animation as an aid to multimedia learning. *Educational Psychology Review, 14*(1), 87–99.

Moon, J., Passmore, C., Reiser, B. J., & Michaels, S. (2014). Comparing the impact of online and face-to-face professional development in the context of curriculum implementation. *Journal of Teacher Education, 65*(2), 172–176.

Neuman, S. B., Copple, C., & Bredekamp, S. (2000). *Learning to read and write: Developmentally appropriate practices for young children*. National Association for the Education of Young Children.

Neuman, S. B., & Roskos, K. (1993). Access to print for children of poverty: Differential effects of adult mediation and literacy-enriched play settings on environmental and functional print tasks. *American Educational Research Journal, 30*(1), 95–122.

Oliver, A., Osa, J., O., & Walker, T. M. (2012). Using instructional technologies to enhance teaching and learning for the 21st century preK–12 students: The case of a professional education programs unit. *International Journal of Instructional Media, 39*, 283–295.

Pelatti, C. Y., Piasta, S. B., Justice, L. M., & O'Connell, A. (2014). Language- and literacy-learning opportunities in early childhood classrooms: Children's typical experiences and within-classroom variability. *Early Childhood Research Quarterly, 29*(4), 445–456.

Powell, D. R., & Diamond, K. E. (2013). Implementation fidelity of a coaching-based professional development program for improving head start teachers' literacy and language instruction. *Journal of Early Intervention, 35*(2), 102–128.

Powell, D. R., Diamond, K. E., Burchinal, M. R., & Koehler, M. J. (2010). Effects of an early literacy professional development intervention on Head Start teachers and children. *Journal of Educational Psychology, 102*(2), 299–312.

Powell, D. R., Diamond, K. E., & Koehler, M. J. (2010). Use of case-based hypermedia resource in an early literacy coaching intervention with pre-kindergarten teachers. *Topics in Early Childhood Special Education, 29*, 239–249.

Preschool Curriculum Evaluation Research Consortium. (2008). *Effects of Preschool Curriculum Programs on School Readiness* (NCER 2008–2009). National Center for Education Research, Institute of Education Sciences, U.S. Department of Education.

Puranik, C. S., & Lonigan, C. J. (2014). Emergent writing in preschoolers: Preliminary evidence for a theoretical framework. *Reading Research Quarterly, 49*(4), 453–467.

Putnam, R. T., & Borko, H. (2000). What do new views of knowledge and thinking have to say about research on teacher learning? *Educational Researcher, 29*(1), 4–15.

Quinn, M. F., Bingham, G. E., & Gerde, H. K. (2021). Who writes what when?: Examining children's early composing. *Reading and Writing: An Interdisciplinary Journal, 34*, 79–107.

Quinn, M. F., Gerde, H. K., & Bingham, G. E. (2016). Help me where I am: Scaffolding writing in preschool classrooms. *Reading Teacher, 70*(3), 353–357.

Quinn, M. K., Gerde, H. K., & Bingham, G. E. (2022). Who, what, & where: Classroom contexts for preschool writing experiences. *Early Education and Development, 33*, 1439–1460.

Rowe, D. W. (2008). Social contracts for writing: Negotiating shared understandings about text in the preschool years. *Reading Research Quarterly, 43*, 66–95.

Rowe, D. W., & Neitzel, C. (2010). Interest and agency in 2- and 3-year-olds' participation in emergent writing. *Reading Research Quarterly, 45*(2), 169–195.

Rowe, D. W., Shimizu, A. Y., & Davis, Z. G. (2021). Essential practices for engaging young children as writers: Lessons from expert early writing teachers. *Reading Teacher, 75*(4), 485–494.

Rowe, D. W., & Wilson, S. J. (2015). The development of a descriptive measure of early childhood writing: Results from the Write Start! writing assessment. *Journal of Literacy Research, 47*(2), 245–292.

Smith, M. W., Brady, J. P., & Anastasopoulos, L. (2008). *Early Language and Literacy Classroom Observation Tool, Pre-K (ELLCO Pre-K)*. Brookes.

Smith, M. W., & Dickinson, D. K. (2001). *Early Language and Literacy Classroom Observation (ELLCO) research edition*. Brookes.

Thomas, L. J., Gerde, H. K., Piasta, S. B., Logan, J. A. R., Bailet, L., & Zettler-Greeley, C. (2020). The early writing skills of children identified as at risk for literacy difficulty. *Early Childhood Research Quarterly, 51*, 392–402.

Tortorelli, L., Gerde, H. K., Rohloff, R., & Bingham, G. E. (2021). Ready, set, write: Early learning standards for writing in the Common Core era. *Reading Research Quarterly, 57*(3), 729–752.

Van de Pol, J., Volman, M., & Beishuizen, J. (2010). Scaffolding in teacher–student interaction: A decade of research. *Educational Psychology Review, 22*(3), 271–296.

Van Merriënboer, J. J., Kirschner, P. A., & Kester, L. (2003). Taking the load off a learner's mind: Instructional design for complex learning. *Educational Psychologist, 38*(1), 5–13.

Vukelich, C. (1994). Effects of play interventions on young children's reading of environmental print. *Early Childhood Research Quarterly, 9*(2), 153–170.

Vygotsky, L. S. (1978). Socio-cultural theory. *Mind in Society, 6*, 52–58.

Wasik, B. A., & Hindman, A. H. (2011). Improving vocabulary and pre-literacy skills of at-risk preschoolers through teacher professional development. *Journal of Educational Psychology, 103*(2), 455–469.

Wasik, B. A., & Hindman, A. H. (2020). Increasing preschoolers' vocabulary development through a streamlined teacher professional development intervention. *Early Childhood Research Quarterly, 50*, 101–113.

Whitebook, M., & Sakai, L. (2003). Turnover begets turnover: An examination of job and occupational instability among child care center staff. *Early Childhood Research Quarterly, 18*(3), 273–293.

Yadav, A., Bouck, E., Da Fonte, A., & Patton, S. (2009). Instructing special education pre-service teachers through literacy video cases. *Teaching Education, 20*(2), 149–162.

Zhang, C., & Bingham, G. E. (2019). Promoting high-leverage writing instruction through an early childhood classroom daily routine (WPI):

A professional development model of early writing skills. *Early Childhood Research Quarterly, 49,* 138–151.

Zhang, C., Hur, J., Diamond, K. E., & Powell, D. (2015). Classroom writing environments and children's early writing skills: An observational study in Head Start classrooms. *Early Childhood Education Journal, 43,* 307–315.

Zhang, C., & Quinn, M. F. (2020). Preschool children's interest in early writing activities and perceptions of writing experience. *Elementary School Journal, 121*(1), 52–74.

Zigler, E., & Styfco, S. J. (2010). *Development at risk series. The hidden history of Head Start.* Oxford University Press.

Zimmerman, B. S., Morgan, D. N., & Kidder-Brown, M. K. (2014). The use of conceptual and pedagogical tools as mediators of preservice teachers' perceptions of self as writers and future teachers of writing. *Action in Teacher Education, 36*(2), 141–156.

Zucker, T. A., Jacbos, E., & Cabell, S. Q. (2021). Exploring barriers to early childhood teachers' implementation of a supplemental academic language curriculum. *Early Education and Development, 32,* 1194–1219.

Zucker, T. A., Ward, A. E., Justice, L. M. (2009). Print referencing during read-alouds: A technique for increasing emergent readers' print knowledge. *Reading Teacher, 63*(1), 62–72.

CHAPTER 21

Structuring Adaptations for Scaling Up Evidence-Based Literacy Interventions

James S. Kim and Douglas M. Mosher

Our purpose in this chapter is to tackle a vexing question confronting literacy researchers and practitioners. In short, why is it so difficult to scale up evidence-based literacy interventions that can accelerate and equalize student literacy outcomes? And more critically, how can researchers, practitioners, and program developers work together to solve this problem? In response to these questions, the field has focused attention on building professional learning that enables teachers to faithfully implement evidence-based curricula, programs, and practices that have been subjected to systematic programs of research (Debarger, Choppin, Beauvineau, & Moorthy, 2013; Durlak & DuPre, 2008; Polikoff, Porter, & Smithson, 2011; Remillard, 2005). Indeed, recent research suggests that teachers' implementation fidelity is a critical lever for improving students' literacy outcomes. At the broadest level, *implementation fidelity* refers to the "degree to which teachers and other program providers implement programs *as intended by the program developers*" (Dusenbury, Brannigan, Falco, & Hansen, 2003, p. 240). A recent review of 76 classroom intervention studies revealed that poor implementation fidelity resulted in lower student outcomes (Hill & Erickson, 2019). The implication from this study seems clear-cut: Stronger implementation fidelity is a precondition for stronger program outcomes. As a result, the elusive goal of understanding how to maintain implementation fidelity at scale continues to be a central concern among researchers (Garet et al., 2008; Hulleman & Cordray, 2009; Lareau, 2009).

We argue in this chapter that the concept of structured adaptations should play a more central role in models for scaling up evidence-based literacy interventions. By *structured adaptations,* we mean that teachers receive guidance on how to make productive adaptations that maintain implementation fidelity and enhance teacher and student engagement, and, ultimately, improve student literacy outcomes (Durlak & DuPre, 2008; Kim et al., 2017; Sailors et al., 2014). Structured adaptations emphasize the need for both generalizable knowledge about what works on average and the specific local knowledge needed to make interventions "work reliably over diverse contexts and populations" (Bryk, 2015, p. 469).

This chapter is organized into three sections. First, we define what it means to successfully scale up a literacy intervention. Second, we introduce and expand on the concept of structured adaptations as an approach to bridging the research–practice divide at scale. Finally, we use four case studies as a proof of concept that structuring teacher adaptations is a feasible and effective approach across literacy interventions with diverse aims and theories of change. Thus, the lessons from the cases yield principles that are likely to generalize across a variety of literacy interventions.

What Does It Mean to Scale Up a Literacy Intervention?

The concept of scale means different things to different scholars. Therefore, it is critical to define key terms in the research literature, particularly as it pertains to scaling up literacy interventions, including researcher-initiated curricula, programs, and practices. For example, *scale* has most commonly been defined in strictly quantitative terms—that is, by the breadth of impact as captured by the numbers of districts, schools, teachers, and students served by a new intervention (Deiglmeier, & Greco, 2018; Quint, Zhu, Balu, Rappaport, & DeLaurentis, 2015). Other scholars, however, have argued that the concept of scale should go beyond numbers and attend to qualitative indicators such as depth—that is, the extent to which practitioners understand the deeper foundational principles underpinning a new curriculum, program, or practice (Coburn, 2003). Building on conceptualizations of scale that emphasize both breadth and depth, we argue that literacy interventions have successfully scaled up when their impact matches the level of need in society and schools (Deiglmeier & Greco, 2018).

Scaling What Works Advances Systemic Equity in Literacy

In the 21st century, the level of need in literacy is unprecedented. Stated simply, gaps in reading comprehension between low- and high-performing children are large and have expanded over the past 5 years, underscoring a need for scalable solutions for reducing inequality in student achievement in general and literacy achievement in particular during elementary grades (U.S. Department of Education, 2019). For example, from 2015 to 2019, fourth graders' reading comprehension declined modestly on the National Assessment of Educational Progress (NAEP). However, the drop in performance was greater among students at the 25th percentile (a 4-point drop) and greatest for students at the 10th percentile (a 6-point drop). There is growing evidence that the COVID-19 pandemic has only exacerbated inequality. For example, from 2020

to 2022, the drop in the long-term NAEP reading scores for 9-year-olds was five times larger for students at the 10th percentile, whose scores decreased by 10 points, than for students at the 90th percentile, whose scores decreased by only 2 points (U.S. Department of Education, 2022). Furthermore, emerging evidence from state and local literacy assessment data suggests that the achievement gaps between lower- and higher-performing students has grown wider since the school closures triggered by the COVID-19 pandemic (Kuhfeld et al., 2020).

Few Evidence-Based Literacy Interventions Achieve Impact at Scale

Despite this need, few literacy interventions have produced more equitable outcomes at scale. Figure 21.1 highlights the challenge of bridging the research–practice divide as researchers conduct long-term programs of research that reach more teachers, students, and schools. Note that along the horizontal axis, researchers aim to implement long-term and systematic research programs in what we call "fidelity-focused research." In this phase of work, researchers focus on exploring and identifying core components of curriculum and instruction, developing and testing interventions, and evaluating and replicating impact. In the field of literacy, a surprisingly large number of interventions have demonstrated success in early-stage efficacy studies—that is, randomized controlled trials of interventions tested under optimal conditions (Kim, 2019). By *optimal conditions,* we mean that researchers are able to tightly control implementation fidelity by selecting sites with unusually motivated practitioners in a smaller number of settings.

Unfortunately, these same interventions fail to work effectively at scale, as shown by the divide in Figure 21.1. To bridge this divide, teachers need to go the extra mile to apply both research knowledge of content and instruction and their local knowledge to integrate the intervention into their particular school and classroom contexts. What are the potential barriers to scaling what works? Put simply, when there are more teachers and sites involved in scale-up, there is also more variability in practitioners' skill and will to implement an intervention. Furthermore, the work of implementation occurs in noisy, real-world contexts in which practitioners must coordinate multiple competing demands (Lareau, 2009; Tipton et al., 2016).

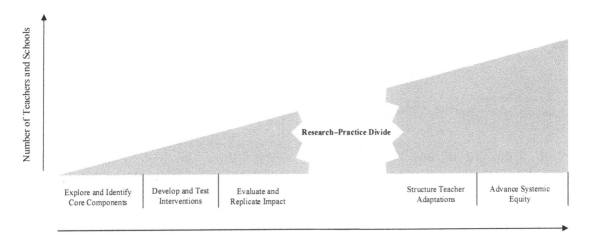

FIGURE 21.1. The challenge of bridging the research–practice divide at scale.

These factors are often cited as the reason for failed implementations and poor outcomes in several literacy program scale-ups. Indeed, the field has witnessed the proliferation of large-scale studies reporting null effects on student reading outcomes when using highly scripted curricula focused on developing foundational word reading skills (Quint et al., 2015; Vaden-Kleinan et al., 2018), as well as intensive professional development curricula focused on the science of early literacy instruction (Garet et al., 2008). More recently, early elementary interventions from the Reading for Understanding initiative (Connor et al., 2018; Language and Reading Research Consortium, Jiang, & Logan, 2019), a national research program intended to improve students' reading comprehension, have shown few significant positive impacts on students' standardized reading comprehension outcomes.

How Might Structuring Teacher Adaptations Bridge the Research–Practice Divide?

The failure of large-scale literacy projects to move the needle on student reading outcomes is disappointing. In the following section, we discuss in greater detail the challenge of taking current research studies to scale and the potential of structuring adaptations to bridge the research–practice divide.

Is Structural Fidelity Enough?

As literacy interventions are brought to scale, researchers and program developers are confronted with the daunting task of measuring and promoting implementation fidelity. Indeed, implementation fidelity and teacher take-up of new curricula are routinely viewed as the causal pathway for improving student outcomes. Implementation fidelity, moreover, has been conceptualized as *structural fidelity*, which usually assesses treatment group teachers' adherence to core program components or the intended curriculum. *Process fidelity*, however, captures dimensions such as program differentiation and measures aspects of implementation in both treatment and control teachers (Hill & Erickson, 2019). Implementation fidelity has been theorized to mediate the effects of new interventions on student outcomes (Rimm-Kauffman et al., 2014; Vaughn et al., 2015), and professional development has emphasized teachers' acquisition of the procedures needed to faithfully implement evidence-based interventions.

To date, researchers have largely focused on building an infrastructure to support structural fidelity—that is, teachers' adherence to program specific elements. Focusing on the needed infrastructure to maintain structural fidelity has led researchers to undertake translational research or "use-inspired basic research" (Stokes, 1997, p. 37) whereby program-specific elements validated in applied research studies are turned into "manualized" scripts, routines, and tools that are easy to transport to more and more sites. This, in turn, has led researchers and professional development providers to develop an infrastructure for measuring and monitoring implementation fidelity at scale (Cohen & Bhatt, 2012). Although implementation fidelity is a multidimensional construct, researchers have largely focused on structural fidelity measures that do not adequately measure the quality of program delivery, program differentiation, and participant engagement (Dane & Schneider, 1998). Importantly, structural fidelity only captures surface-level indicators of implementation and teachers' compliance with procedures and routines specific to an intervention. We argue that to successfully bridge the research–practice divide at scale, researchers will need to consider new ways to maintain implementation fidelity while also building teachers' motivation, resulting engagement, and underlying knowledge of content and instruction.

Can Experimental and Improvement Scientists Help Bridge the Research–Practice Divide?

In recent years, improvement scientists have argued that implementation fidelity alone is insufficient to ensure that evidence-based literacy interventions will reliably improve student learning across a large number of diverse school contexts. For example, improvement scientists have proposed new ways of building usable knowledge to scale what works. More specifically, Bryk (2015) has argued that results from randomized trials that emphasize implementation fidelity "are not principally designed to tell us how to make interventions work reliably for different subgroups of students and teachers working under varying contextual conditions. Improvement science, in contrast, places primacy on variability in outcomes as the central problem to address" (p. 473). Moreover, some scholars have noted that emphasizing rigid adherence to research-based programs and practices may contribute to lower implementation fidelity and greater resistance and animosity among practitioners (Dane & Schneider, 1998; Meyer, Miller, & Herman, 1993).

When thinking about how best to reframe the challenge of scaling evidence-based interventions, it is useful to consider how the field might capitalize on the affordances of both experimental and improvement paradigms. For example, in Figure 21.2, we emphasize that fidelity and adaptation are two dimensions of program implementation. We have intentionally drawn the axes for fidelity and adaptation to be orthogonal to emphasize key differences between the two paradigms (Lewis, 2015). The experimental science paradigm emphasizes fidelity over adaptation. In this paradigm, researchers and program developers aim to implement proven programs with fidelity at scale, monitor implementation, approve adaptations as needed, and use incentives to promote practitioners' adherence to core principles. Experimental science, with its emphasis on fidelity, is a top-down approach for scale. It assumes that knowledge is in tools such as curricula, and educational improvement occurs through faithful implementation of validated programs and practices.

In contrast to experimental science, improvement science privileges adaptation over fidelity to address the problem of variability in the impact of evidence-based interventions brought to scale. In other words, improvement scientists emphasize that practitioners must have a deep knowledge of their local contexts to make an externally developed intervention work reliably and consistently across a range of classroom and school settings. More specifically, efforts to scale evidence-based practices require integration and adaptation to fit local contexts, to build buy-in to enact innovations, and to understand how to get better at getting better (Berwick, 2008). Improvement science, with its emphasis on adaptation, is a bottom-up approach to scale. It assumes that knowledge is in people and systems that use innovative curricula and programs, improvement depends primarily on building knowledge among practitioners in systems, and finding adaptations to improve the fit between programs and local contexts are critical to success at scale.

There is ostensibly an unbridgeable divide between two dominant approaches for scaling up what works. Each approach to scale seems to rest on competing epistemologies about knowledge, assumptions about the nature of scale, and the pathway to large-scale literacy improvement.

Fidelity and Adaptation Can Co-Occur

In many ways, however, fidelity and adaptation inevitably co-occur in the context of an evidence-based intervention that is brought to scale in a

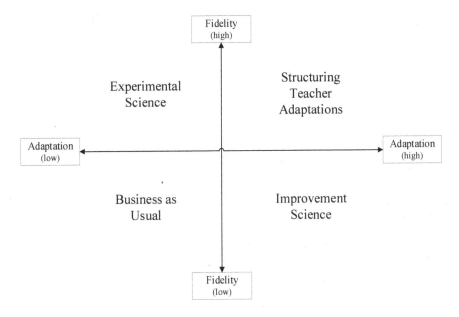

FIGURE 21.2. How structuring teacher adaptations can bridge the research–practice divide.

wider range of local contexts. This is because large-scale literacy improvement depends on teachers who can use both generalizable research knowledge and their professional knowledge of their local contexts to adapt instruction for their particular students. Rather than asking whether experimental science or improvement science represents a superior path to achieving impact at scale, the question we should ask is—*How might we rethink the intersecting roles of fidelity and adaptation as researchers and practitioners draw upon prior experimental evidence and local knowledge to improve student outcomes?* Doing so might help reconceptualize the nature of scale by emphasizing the role of structured adaptations as two sides of the implementation coin.

In Figure 21.2, we provide a heuristic to help visualize how we conceptualize scale-up of program implementation. This scaffolded sequence of program implementation (Quinn & Kim, 2017) begins with experimental research in the top-left quadrant, which emphasizes the concept of fidelity over adaptation. At this stage, experimental research seeks to identify core components that need to be implemented with fidelity. As research projects then progress to the top-right quadrant, emphasis shifts to the concept of structuring teacher adaptations, that is, giving teachers time to learn how an intervention works

and how to adapt and customize the program to make it work better locally. It also capitalizes on ideas from improvement science by emphasizing continuous improvement efforts and strategies for adaptively integrating externally developed interventions into larger numbers of school districts, schools, and classrooms.

We have drawn the bottom-left quadrant to emphasize that business-as-usual practice for teachers is focused on neither fidelity nor adaptation of an evidence-based program. We would argue that business-as-usual practices are not sufficient to address the literacy demands of the 21st century. Thus, our goal here is to illustrate how structuring teacher adaptations to an evidence-based intervention is an integrative solution for scaling what works. It encourages researchers and practitioners to apply solutions from both the experimental and improvement science paradigms as evidence-based literacy interventions are brought to scale.

Structured Adaptations and Adaptive Expertise

How, then, might the concept of structured teacher adaptations, particularly in the context of teachers' professional learning opportunities, help to bridge the research–practice divide? First, the notion of structured adaptations recognizes the need for professional development to support teachers' adaptive expertise (Hatano & Inagaki, 1986; Koellner & Jacobs, 2015; Murnane & Nelson, 2007). Classroom-based intervention studies inevitably emphasize teacher learning and subsequent improvement in practice as the critical levers of change. In experimental research, professional development begins with an emphasis on routine expertise, where teachers acquire procedural knowledge to adhere closely to curriculum scripts and to be faithful to foundational principles. The structure of scripts and professional development training is necessary but not sufficient to help teachers become adaptive experts. In other words, adaptive experts perform procedural skills efficiently and have deeper conceptual knowledge of the theory and principles underlying a new program or curriculum in order to invent novel solutions for their local context. Thus, teachers' adaptations that hew closely to foundational principles and emerge from teachers' own knowledge of their context may improve rather than impede scale-up.

Bridging the last mile from research to practice requires teachers to become adaptive experts who can transfer what they learn in specialized programs—for example, a randomized controlled trial of a researcher-developed intervention—to their normal, everyday routines. An insistence on fidelity may develop routine experts with the procedural knowledge to adhere superficially to core components. However, beyond a surface understanding of a theory of change and adherence to program specific elements, adaptive experts must also recognize the deeper theoretical principles for a curriculum or practice and local knowledge needed to improve, modify, and enhance both implementation and student outcomes at scale.

Structured Adaptations and Teachers' Intrinsic Motivation

Second, structured adaptations bridge the research–practice divide by attending to practitioners' intrinsic motivation to understand the *what* and *why* behind a newly acquired procedural skill or theory of change. Successful scale-up requires teachers and systems to sustain an innovation that worked then and there here and now, to have depth of understanding, to own an external reform, and to interleave new practices into the fabric of their daily professional work (Coburn, 2003). Therefore, intrinsic motivation

is a critical precursor to scale. Motivation theorists (Ryan & Deci, 2000) have long argued that autonomy-supportive workplaces that build professional competence and relatedness foster professionals' intrinsic motivation. Accordingly, structured adaptations emphasize teachers' autonomy, build their professional capacity and competence, emphasize peer learning and connections, and push on levers that build intrinsic motivation. Adaptive experts have the intrinsic motivation to understand what works, why it works, and can judge whether adaptations are appropriate, helpful, and consistent with foundational principles (Greeno, 1980).

Structured Adaptations and Situated Learning

Third, structured adaptations recognize that any successful program implementation may require situated learning. Situated learning views teacher learning as the acquisition and use of knowledge in socially organized activities (Borko, 2004; Cobb, 1994; Greeno, 2003). From a situated learning perspective, teacher learning is understood as a "process of increasing participation in the practice of teaching, and through this participation, a process of becoming knowledgeable in and about teaching" (Adler, 2000, p. 37). Thus, teacher learning can occur in many contexts, including formal professional development programs, school professional learning communities, classrooms, and in hallway conversations with colleagues. Thus, a situative perspective recognizes that professional development is only one of many contexts in which teachers learn, and it widens the lens for studying how teachers acquire and use knowledge to improve their practice. Furthermore, a situative perspective suggests that individual teachers can acquire research-based knowledge in professional development programs connected to externally developed interventions and in their broader professional contexts—that is, their classrooms, their professional learning communities, and their informal interactions with peers (Borko, 2004; Quinn & Kim, 2017).

Are There Emerging Evidence-Based Principles for Designing Structured Adaptations?

Our search through the literature yielded very few systematic research programs that used structuring teacher adaptations to bridge the research–practice divide. Given the nascent research in this area, we highlight three evidence-based principles using four literacy projects as an existence proof, as shown in Table 21.1. Each project, moreover, is working toward, or has achieved, impact at scale. To date, researchers have reported findings from initial tests of program effectiveness and follow-up replication research, as well as more recent efforts to structure adaptations for teachers in scaling what works across more diverse district, school, and classroom contexts. Finally, we purposefully selected literacy interventions with very different aims and theories of change. Despite their diverse aims and theories of change, each project has the shared goal of advancing systemic equity through large-scale implementation of evidence-based Tier 1 whole-class interventions focused on students at risk of falling behind in reading comprehension.

Principle 1: Fidelity First, Adaptation Second

When researchers and program developers initiate a long-term program of research to understand what works, for whom, and under what conditions, the first aim is to answer the question: What core components do practitioners need to implement with fidelity to replicate positive impact at scale and advance systemic equity? In essence, the chief aim of exploring mechanisms, developing innovations, and testing and replicating impact is to build a structure to support faithful replication of an evidence-based intervention at scale—for example, robust professional learning activities to build teachers' knowledge and motivation, clear curriculum scripts to enable teachers to improve the quality of classroom instruction, and sound measures to monitor and promote fidelity and engagement. In essence, it is the bridge that enables more and more teachers, policymakers, and education leaders who did not participate in the original research and development studies to sustain and implement practices in their local contexts, ultimately with the end goal of advancing systemic equity.

Case 1: Adapting Reading Enhances Achievement During Summer

Is there an existence proof that the fidelity first, adaptation second principle to scale-up is feasible and effective? We illustrate how this principle operates using research on literacy inter-

ventions with quite different goals, starting with Reading Enhances Achievement During Summer (READS), a low-cost, large-scale summer reading intervention for elementary grade children. READS was designed to improve reading comprehension outcomes for elementary grade children, particularly in high-poverty school and neighborhood contexts. In the fidelity first phase of research, we drew on descriptive and correlational research (Alexander, Entwisle, & Olson, 2001; Heyns, 1978; Stanovich, 2000) and intervention research (National Reading Panel, 2000) to develop an initial theory of change with two critical components. The READS theory of change highlighted the importance of (1) providing books matched to each student's reading level and interest and (2) implementing teacher scaffolding for summer reading in the form of end-of-year reading comprehension lessons and materials sent to children's homes during summer vacation. Early-stage randomized controlled trials indicated that professional learning that emphasized faithfully implementing the procedures for providing children with matched books and scaffolding summer reading through end-of-year reading comprehension lessons improved student reading comprehension outcomes (Kim, 2007; Kim & White, 2008). When teachers omitted either core component—that is, the matched books or the teacher scaffolded lessons—there was no impact on students' reading comprehension outcomes (Kim & Guryan, 2010; Wilkins et al., 2012). Collectively, findings from the fidelity-focused experimental studies and smaller studies in a single school district indicated that READS had larger effects with students in higher-poverty schools and neighborhoods (White, Kim, Kingston, & Foster, 2014). In short, the fidelity first stage of exploring and identifying core components, developing and testing the intervention, and evaluating and replicating effects provided a foundation for scaling up READS to more high-poverty schools and districts.

But could these results be replicated across more than one school system and advance equity at a state level? More specifically, how could we shift the focus from a fidelity-first research agenda to one that focused on the role of structured adaptations? We grappled with new questions. For example, how could we promote and monitor fidelity to core program components while providing guidance to teachers to adapt READS in acceptable ways? How could we document adaptations and whether they helped

TABLE 21.1. Guiding Principles and Questions for Bridging the Research-Practice Divide

Principles and questions	Adaptive READS	Customized KPALS	Soft-scripted WOW
Principle 1: Fidelity first, adaptation second			
1. As you conduct fidelity-focused research in early stages of research and development, how well do you identify core and noncore components in the intervention theory of change?	×	×	×
2. As you build structures to support teachers to faithfully implement your evidence-based intervention, how well do you measure *structural fidelity* indicators to assess treatment group teachers' adherence to intervention-specific components (e.g., professional development activities, lesson scripts, student materials), and how well do you also measure *process fidelity* indicators such as the quality of classroom discussions and task complexity in both treatment and control group teachers' classrooms?	×	×	×
3. As you explore mechanisms, develop literacy interventions, and conduct randomized controlled trials to test and replicate their impact on student literacy outcomes, is there evidence that teachers' faithful implementation of core components is a precursor to improving targeted student outcomes? Conversely, is there evidence that omission or modification of these core components contribute to weaker effects on student outcomes?	×		×
4. As you design structured adaptations to bridge the research–practice divide, how do you plan to foster teachers' motivation and knowledge? In particular, what is the theory underlying professional learning?	×		
Principle 2: Structured adaptations promote teacher and student engagement			
5. How well do structured teacher adaptations promote teacher engagement?	×	×	×
6. How well do structured teacher adaptations promote student engagement?	×	×	×
7. How well does your study design support inferences that structuring teacher adaptations caused the improvement in teacher engagement and student engagement?	×		×
Principle 3: Structured teacher adaptations are penultimate; systemic equity is ultimate			
8. How well are you monitoring the impact on systems-level indicators of improvement (e.g., end-of-year standardized reading comprehension tests required by state law)?	×		
9. How does scaling up your evidence-based intervention accelerate and equalize literacy outcomes across systems—entire districts, states, and nations?			

fidelity and outcomes? And most importantly, what impact would structured teacher adaptations have on students' reading comprehension?

To address these questions at scale, we designed two studies in North Carolina that were carried out in a majority of high-poverty schools and districts. In the Year 1 study, we tested the impact of READS when fidelity of implementation to the core components was emphasized in a large randomized controlled trial involving second- and third-grade students

in 59 schools across seven district sites (Kim et al., 2016). One year later, students in the treatment group outperformed control group students in an end-of-grade reading comprehension test, and effects were larger in high-poverty schools than in moderate-poverty schools. In the Year 2 study, we continued to implement READS in 27 of the same high-poverty schools from the previous year's study. Here, we tested two approaches to scaling up what worked. The schools were randomly assigned to either the Core READS condition that emphasized faithfully replicating implementation procedures in the previous study or the Adaptive READS condition that emphasized fidelity to core components, while also giving teachers autonomy to implement structured adaptations they felt would make the program work better in their local contexts.

Using self-determination theory to guide professional learning, our chief aim for Adaptive READS schools was to build both teachers' knowledge and intrinsic motivation through an emphasis on autonomy, competence, and belongingness supports (Ryan & Deci, 2000). Accordingly, Adaptive READS teachers were organized into grade-level teams (belongingness supports), where they worked with their peers to learn about the program theory (competence supports) and used local data to adapt READS (autonomy supports) to tackle a practical improvement goal: "How can we, as a school, foster student engagement with books over the summer?" Over the course of program implementation, teachers in Adaptive READS were given structured opportunities to use research knowledge, their local knowledge, and school data to extend, modify and improve READS for their local settings. Results indicated that students in Adaptive READS schools outperformed core READS students by 0.12 standard deviations on a standardized reading comprehension test, and teachers' fidelity of implementation of core components was high in both conditions. Importantly, teachers in Adaptive READS schools made acceptable adaptations that improved student and family engagement with summer books (Kim et al., 2017) and also reported acquiring more knowledge about the core components (Quinn & Kim, 2017).

Case 2: Customizing Kindergarten Peer-Assisted Learning Strategies

How generalizable is the principle of fidelity first and adaptation second? In other words, are there other existence proofs beyond Adaptive READS? To address this question, we highlight this principle in action with two early literacy programs with quite different theories of change. Kindergarten Peer-Assisted Learning Strategies (KPALS) is a supplemental, peer-mediated early literacy program intervention focused on improving children's foundational word-reading skills (e.g., phonological awareness, decoding, word identification, fluency), particularly

for children at risk of later reading difficulties. Across a 9-year program of research in a single district (Nashville, Tennessee), researchers found strong evidence of success and impact on targeted student outcomes. In this fidelity-first stage of research, the program developers identified core components, which teachers were asked to faithfully implement "by the book." However, subsequent effective trials that examined the impact of KPALS at scale in three state contexts showed much weaker effects on student outcomes.

As KPALS was brought to scale (Lemons, Fuchs, Gilbert, & Fuchs, 2014), researchers allowed teachers to continue implementing KPALS "by the book" with fidelity or to customize KPALS by adapting and modifying noncore components to better meet the needs of their students. Although teachers could modify or replace noncore components, they could not omit or change core components in any way. Thus, in contrast to Adaptive READS, the instantiation of structured adaptations in KPALS was focused more on distinctions between acceptable and unacceptable changes, allowing individual teachers rather than teams to make structured adaptations (McMaster et al., 2014). Customized KPALS teachers used both research knowledge from previous studies and their local knowledge to make the program work better in new contexts that were fundamentally different from the original research studies (Goldenberg & Gallimore, 1991; Kim, 2019).

Case 3: Soft Scripting the World of Words Lessons

A fidelity first, adaption second model for bridging the research practice can also work when teachers are implementing whole-class vocabulary interventions. The World of Words (WOW) curriculum is designed to improve preschoolers' vocabulary and conceptual knowledge through taxonomic organization of science vocabulary and embedded multimedia (Neuman, Newman, & Dwyer, 2011). In the fidelity first stage of research, Neuman and colleagues conducted early efficacy studies to examine the implementation of core program components, to monitor teachers' adherence to core components, and to test effectiveness under optimal conditions with strong organizational supports that strengthened implementation of WOW. Importantly, teachers' average fidelity to core components was 90% and laid the foundation for moving to the adaptation phase of research and scaling up what worked in earlier studies. The first stage of efficacy testing suggested that the core, non-negotiable components that were essential included introducing new target words, engaging learners with child-friendly definitions, and connecting words to broader concepts during interactive and shared reading. These non-negotiables were critical to supporting immediate and long-term positive impacts on children's vocabulary and categorical knowledge.

The question of how best to bridge the research–practice divide and promote systemic equity at scale led to the development of structured adaptations to the WOW lesson scripts. Thus, professional learning emphasized the theory behind the WOW curriculum, the core non-negotiables, and the structured scripts to guide vocabulary instruction. Much like the grade-level teams in Adaptive READS, teachers worked with their peers to understand how the curriculum was aligned to foster conceptual knowledge in science and to follow a "soft-scripting" approach to implementing WOW. Soft-scripting was designed to enhance teachers' knowledge and motivation by providing "teachers with greater autonomy to adjust the scripted language to meet their children's needs while maintaining the core elements of the programs" (Neuman, Samudra, & Danielson, 2021, p. 404). Compared to children in the control group, children taught by teachers using the soft-scripting approach performed better on curriculum-based vocabulary and concept knowledge measures, while teachers' fidelity to core components was comparable (81%) to the fidelity-focused efficacy study of WOW. This soft-scripting approach helped teachers enact language extensions and back-and-forth discussions that supported the acquisition of vocabulary and conceptual knowledge (Neugebauer et al., 2017). As noted by Neuman et al. (2021), the results indicated that "adapting an explicit and scripted program to allow for teachers' modifications, within specific parameters, holds promising for scaling an intervention" (p. 405).

Principle 2: Structured Adaptations Promote Teacher and Student Engagement

Collectively, the eclectic group of literacy interventions that followed a fidelity first, adaptation second model of program implementation shared an immediate goal of improving teacher and student engagement. Engagement is a multidimensional construct (Fredricks, Blumenfeld, & Paris, 2004). It includes behavioral indicators such as time on task, cognitive indicators such as accuracy and quality of performance on challenging tasks, and affective indicators such as task values and self-competence beliefs (Guthrie, Wigfield, & You, 2012). As such, the second principle emphasizes that structured teacher adaptations should enhance both teacher and student engagement, and that researchers should employ designs and measures to assess the impact of these adaptations on both teacher and student engagement.

More specifically, Debarger and colleagues (2013) have argued that productive teacher adaptations should lead to better student engagement. As a result, teachers should move away from traditional initiate–response–evaluate forms of discourse to more dialogic forms of talk that spark rich classroom discussions and high student engagement (Correnti et al., 2021; Hatano & Inagaki, 1986; Zook-Howell, Matsumura, Walsh, Correnti, & Bickel, 2020). And perhaps most critically, a productive teacher adaptation should maintain task complexity, whereby teachers encourage students to pursue challenging academic goals. In short, a critical criterion for determining the productivity of an adaption is whether it enhances student engagement during literacy instruction and maintains task complexity.

There are specific examples from our cases to illustrate how structured adaptations promoted greater teacher and student engagement. For example, the final study of Adaptive READS indicated that teachers were able to maintain implementation fidelity while also going the extra mile to engage students and families. Evidence for stronger engagement emerged on multiple measures, including observations of classrooms and interviews with teachers. For example, Adaptive READS teachers taught longer lessons and were less likely to read from lesson scripts during end-of-year comprehension instruction. In addition, Adaptive READS teachers reported using more locally developed strategies to engage students and families, including sending home teacher-generated documents and personalized phone messages to inform parents about the program. In the WOW intervention, the soft-scripting approach helped teachers adjust lesson scripts to improve their students' engagement while helping teachers maintain adherence to curricular non-negotiables. Importantly, this soft-scripting approach facilitated teachers' ability to foster language extensions and back-and-forth discussions that supported their children's acquisition of vocabulary and conceptual knowledge. The added flexibility provided by soft scripts appeared to spark impromptu language interactions that reflected teachers' greater motivation to make the intervention work better in their classrooms.

More generally, structured adaptations are critical catalysts for helping teachers enhance the lexical environments of children's classrooms. One example is evidenced in a study of teachers' language extensions during the implementation Elements of Reading: Vocabulary (McKeown & Beck, 2004). This schoolwide vocabulary program requires teachers to explicitly teach students five Tier Two vocabulary words (i.e., words with high utility across content areas) per week for 24 weeks. Words are introduced during a read-aloud, and children are given multiple exposures with the target vocabulary through picture cards, graphic organizers, and semantic maps. While the program provides recommended language, it also gives teachers autonomy to include additional child-friendly definitions and connections to related words, with an eye toward promoting student engagement. Neugebauer, Coyne, McCoach, and Ware (2017) found that teachers who went beyond adherence to surface features of the intervention were able to support extended language practices. Such practices included providing amended definitions of words, connecting target vocabulary with semantically related words, and encouraging more classroom discussion. Teachers' structured adaptations to lesson scripts provided additional learning opportunities for students to engage with target vocabulary and were positively associated with standardized vocabulary scores.

In whole-class vocabulary programs, teachers' structured adaptations to researcher-developed lesson scripts may reduce the word-learning burden by helping children internalize word meanings through meaningful encounters that reveal information about the target word and words with semantic overlap (McKeown, Deane, Scott, Krovetz, & Lawless, 2017). An implication of these studies is that teachers must go beyond intervention prescriptions by enacting productive adaptations that enhance the quality of classroom instruction and improve word-learning opportunities in the early grades. Most importantly, high-quality discourse cannot be scripted.

When teachers develop the skill to enact adaptive interactions that are sensitive to students' needs and discourse, they help foster greater student engagement during vocabulary instruction (Neugebauer, Coyne, McCoach, & Ware, 2021; Neuman et al., 2021).

Principle 3: Structured Teacher Adaptations Are Penultimate; Systemic Equity Is Ultimate

Virtually every program of research reviewed in this chapter aims to support the literacy learning of vulnerable children—children from high-poverty schools and communities, children growing up in language-poor environments, and children who begin their schooling careers with weaker language and literacy skills. Indeed, reading the scientific research underpinning programs like READS, WOW, KPALS, and Elements of Reading: Vocabulary, it is clear that researchers and practitioners are focused on intervening in contexts where business-as-usual practice is not advancing systemic equity. In many ways, structured teacher adaptations are penultimate, not ultimate.

The third principle emphasizes the notion that structuring teacher adaptations is a bridge to an ultimate goal—advancing systemic equity. As interventions are scaled up and expand their reach and impact, the critical question becomes: Is there evidence that gaps between lower- and higher-performing students are closing? When implemented at scale, how well do our evidence-based interventions accelerate and equalize literacy outcomes across entire systems, including school districts, states, and nations? Of course, it is difficult to connect the expansion of an evidence-based intervention to improvement at the systems level, because there are no treatment and control groups—by definition, scale and diffusion efforts aim to target whole districts and states. At minimum, however, researchers might consider using systems-level indicators to measure implementation and impact. For example, as the KPALS intervention was scaled up in Nashville schools over a decade, researchers used systems-level indicators to monitor implementation across schools, which led to overall improvements on students' early word reading and fluency skills (Lemons et al., 2014; Stein et al., 2008). Thus, the story of KPALS highlights the successful transition from using researcher-developed measures to assess program effectiveness to systems-level indicators used to monitor literacy performance at the district and state level (Table 21.1: Principle 3, Criterion 8).

Indeed, the past decade has witnessed an unprecedented research and development effort to scale up a range of literacy interventions, including whole-classroom literacy curricula (Vaden-Kiernan et al., 2018), comprehensive schoolwide literacy programs (Quint et al., 2015), response-to-intervention models to prevent early reading failure (Balu et al., 2015), and a national Reading for Understanding initiative involving kindergarten to grade 3 aligned programs (Pearson, Palincsar, Biancarosa, & Berman, 2020). As these projects continue to expand their reach over the next decade, it will be critical to understand whether embedding structured teacher adaptations in future implementations can advance systemic equity.

Implications

Taken together, the evidence-based principles for designing and studying the effectiveness of structured adaptations surfaces several implications for literacy researchers. Perhaps the most direct implication of our work is that society depends on researchers to take a long-term view of literacy problems and solutions. Notably, we have highlighted an existence proof that structuring adaptations to several evidence-based literacy interventions supported both fidelity and local adaptations that helped teams of researchers and practitioners bridge the research–practice divide. Going one step further, we acknowledge that research on structured adaptations is nascent, requiring more systematic inquiry. In Table 21.1, we describe key evidence-based principles and illustrate how they might be applied to current and future intervention research.

The principle of fidelity first, adaptation second suggests that practitioners need time to learn the foundational principles of an intervention theory of change before they enact adaptations. In a scaffolded sequence of program implementation, teachers would develop proficiency implementing intervention-specific components with fidelity before implementing adaptations (Quinn & Kim, 2017). We have provided an example of a 2-year scaffolded sequence for implementing Core READS and then Adaptive READS to illustrate the effectiveness of such an approach. In other programs of research, even teachers who are new to a program such as soft-

scripted WOW may still benefit from the opportunity to make structured adaptations that support student learning (Neuman et al., 2021).

However, across many of the studies we have reviewed in this chapter, discussion of professional learning for teachers was notably underspecified and undertheorized in the fidelity and adaptation phase of research. In most cases, teacher professional development activities largely focused on helping teachers develop routine expertise to enhance structural fidelity—adherence to intervention-specific elements. There was limited discussion of the pathways through which teachers become adaptive experts—professionals who flexibly apply interventions in their local contexts, have the intrinsic motivation to sustain intervention activities, and have the organizational supports to make productive changes that enhance rather than undermine student outcomes (Hatano & Inagaki, 1986). Thus, future research needs to attend to a number of questions: What is the theory underlying professional learning? How well does professional learning foster teachers' adaptive expertise to flexibly implement validated interventions, programs, and practices in their classrooms? To what extent does professional learning promote teacher autonomy by creating the conditions to support competence building and belongingness for teachers? Efforts to bridge the research–practice divide will require more robust theories of professional learning that emphasize teacher learning across multiple contexts over time.

The second principle underscores that effective structured adaptations should have their most immediate impact on stronger teacher and student engagement. In the literacy case studies we reviewed, there was consistent attention by all researcher teams to provide autonomy to teachers to make changes that would maintain the cognitive challenge of classroom discussions, including time-on-task behaviors and performance on targeted student outcomes. Importantly, the use of experimental designs suggests that it is possible to identify the causal effects of providing opportunities for teachers to make structured adaptations to an evidence-based intervention. Many of the case illustrations of structured adaptations were based on rigorous experimental designs in which whole schools were randomly assigned to implement either a fidelity only version of the program or fidelity with structured adaptations. Some studies also used multiple measures to assess the nature and consequences of the adaptations on teacher and student engagement. In the case of Adaptive READS, the researchers undertook content analyses of grade-level adaptation plans, observed lessons to assess teacher and student engagement, and interviewed teachers to better understand how intervention-specific components were conceived and modified. Because structured adaptations to programs or curricula look different for every teacher, researchers also need to engage in deeper analyses of the quality of discourse and impromptu interactions that support students' engagement in classrooms (Neugebauer et al., 2021).

Finally, structured adaptations are a means to the ultimate goal of advancing systemic equity. For example, the KPALS project provides an important illustration of how researchers began to use systemic indicators of children's literacy outcomes across a whole district to monitor scale-up and diffusion efforts. As evidence-based interventions continue to expand their reach across entire school districts, states, and nations, there will be more opportunities for researchers, program developers, and practitioners to measure progress toward equity. Some progress toward that goal has been made in large-scale research focused on early literacy tutoring (D'Agostino & Rodgers, 2017), whole-school comprehensive reforms (Quint et al., 2015), and aligned preschool to grade 3 curricula (Stipek, Franke, Clements, Farran, & Coburn, 2017). To some extent, then, our cases are part of a broader story of researchers' ongoing efforts to bridge the research–practice divide and to expand the impact of large-scale interventions that improve young children's literacy performance.

Conclusion

This chapter was motivated by a persistent challenge facing literacy researchers and practitioners: Why do so many literacy interventions fail to scale up, and what can we do about it? Our hopeful and optimistic conclusion is that structured adaptations may help the field accelerate and equalize students' literacy outcomes at scale. Ultimately, we believe the use of structured adaptations can strengthen the bridge between research and practice and build teachers' skill and will to co-create knowledge of what works, for whom, and under what local conditions.

References

Adler, J. (2000). Social practice theory and mathematics teacher education: A conversation between theory and practice. *Nordic Mathematics Education Journal, 8*(3), 31–53.

Alexander, K. L., Entwisle, D. R., & Olson, L. S. (2001). Schools, achievement, and inequality: A seasonal perspective. *Educational Evaluation and Policy Analysis, 23*(2), 171–191.

Balu, R., Zhu, P., Doolittle, F., Schiller, E., Jenkins, J., & Gersten, R. (2015). *Evaluation of response to intervention practices for elementary school reading* (NCEE 2016-4000). National Center for Education Evaluation and Regional Assistance, Institute of Education Sciences, U.S. Department of Education.

Berwick, D. M. (2008). The science of improvement. *Journal of the American Medical Association, 299*(10), 1182–1184.

Borko, H. (2004). Professional development and teacher learning: Mapping the terrain. *Educational Researcher, 33*(8), 3–15.

Bryk, A. S. (2015). 2014 AERA distinguished lecture: Accelerating how we learn to improve. *Educational Researcher, 44*(9), 467–477.

Cobb, P. (1994). Where is the mind?: Constructivist and sociocultural perspectives on mathematical development. *Educational Researcher, 23*(7), 13–20.

Coburn, C. E. (2003). Rethinking scale: Moving beyond numbers to deep and lasting change. *Educational Researcher, 32*(6), 3–12.

Cohen, D. K., & Bhatt, M. P. (2012). The importance of infrastructure development to high-quality literacy instruction. Retrieved from *https://futureofchildren.princeton.edu/sites/futureofchildren/files/media/literacy_challenges_for_the_twenty-first_century_22_02_fulljournal.pdf*

Connor, C. M., Phillips, B. M., Kim, Y. G., Lonigan, C. J., Kaschak, M. P., Crowe, . . . Al Otaiba, S. (2018). Examining the efficacy of targeted component interventions on language and literacy for third and fourth graders who are at risk of comprehension difficulties. *Scientific Studies of Reading, 22*(6), 462–484.

Correnti, R., Matsumura, L. C., Walsh, M., Zook-Howell, D., Bickel, D. D., & Yu, B. (2021). Effects of online content-focused coaching on discussion quality and reading achievement: Building theory for how coaching develops teachers' adaptive expertise. *Reading Research Quarterly, 56*(3), 519–558.

D'Agostino, J. V., & Rodgers, E. (2017). Literacy achievement trends at entry to First Grade. *Educational Researcher, 46*(2), 78–89.

Dane, A. V., & Schneider, B. H. (1998). Program integrity in primary and early secondary prevention: Are implementation effects out of control? *Clinical Psychology Review, 18*(1), 23–45.

Debarger, A. H., Choppin, J., Beauvineau, Y., & Moorthy, S. (2013). Designing for productive adaptations of curriculum interventions. *Yearbook of the National Society for the Study of Education, 112*(2), 298–319.

Deiglmeier, K., & Greco, A. (2018). Why proven solutions struggle to scale up. Stanford Social Innovation Review. Retrieved from *https://ssir.org/articles/entry/why_proven_solutions_struggle_to_scale_up#*

Durlak, J. A., & DuPre, E. P. (2008). Implementation matters: A review of research on the influence of implementation on program outcomes and the factors affecting implementation. *American Journal of Community Psychology, 41*(3–4), 327–350.

Dusenbury, L., Brannigan, R., Falco, M., & Hansen, W. B. (2003). A review of research on fidelity of implementation: Implications for drug abuse prevention in school settings. *Health Education Research, 18*(2), 237–256.

Fredricks, J. A., Blumenfeld, P. C., & Paris, A. H. (2004). School engagement: Potential of the concept, state of the evidence. *Review of Educational Research, 74,* 59–109.

Garet, M. S., Cronen, S., Eaton, M., Kurki, A., Ludwig, M., Jones, W., . . . Silverberg, M. (2008). *The impact of two professional development interventions on early reading instruction and achievement.* Institute of Education Sciences, U.S. Department of Education.

Goldenberg, C., & Gallimore, R. (1991). Local knowledge, research knowledge, and educational change: A case study of early Spanish reading improvement. *Educational Researcher, 20*(8), 2–14.

Greeno, J. G. (1980, July). *Forms of understanding in mathematical problem solving.* Paper presented at the 22nd International Congress of Psychology, Leipzig, Germany.

Greeno, J. G. (2003). Situative research relevant to standards for school mathematics. In J. Kilpatrick, W. G. Martin, & D. Schifter (Eds.), *A research companion to principles and standards for school mathematics* (pp. 304–332). National Council of Teachers of Mathematics.

Guthrie, J. T., Wigfield, A., & You, W. (2012). Instructional contexts for engagement and achievement in reading. In S. L. Christenson, A. L. Reschly, & C. Wylie (Eds.), *Handbook of research on student engagement* (pp. 601–634). Springer.

Hatano, G., & Inagaki, K. (1986). Two courses of expertise. In H. Stevenson, H. Azuma, & K. Hakuta (Eds.), *Child development and education in Japan* (pp. 262–272). Freeman.

Heyns, B. (1978). *Summer learning and the effects of schooling.* Academic Press.

Hill, H. C., & Erickson, A. (2019). Using implementation fidelity to aid in interpreting program impacts: A brief review. *Educational Researcher, 48*(9), 590–598.

Hulleman, C. S., & Cordray, D. S. (2009). Moving from the lab to the field: The role of fidelity and achieved relative intervention strength. *Journal of Research on Educational Effectiveness, 2*(1), 88–110.

Kim, J. S. (2007). The effects of a voluntary summer reading intervention on reading activities and reading achievement. *Journal of Educational Psychology, 99*(3), 505–515.

Kim, J. S. (2019). Making every study count: Learning from replication failure to improve intervention research. *Educational Researcher, 48*(9), 599–607.

Kim, J. S., Burkhauser, M. A., Quinn, D. M., Guryan, J., Kingston, H. C., & Aleman, K. (2017). Effectiveness of structured teacher adaptations to an evidence-based summer literacy program. *Reading Research Quarterly, 52*(4), 443–467.

Kim, J. S., & Guryan, J. (2010). The efficacy of a voluntary summer book reading intervention for low-income Latino children from language minority families. *Journal of Educational Psychology, 102*(1), 20–31.

Kim, J. S., Guryan, J., White, T. G., Quinn, D. M., Capotosto, L., & Kingston, H. C. (2016). Delayed effects of a low-cost and large-scale summer reading intervention on elementary school children's reading comprehension. *Journal of Research on Educational Effectiveness, 9*(Suppl. 1), 1–22.

Kim, J. S., & White, T. G. (2008). Scaffolding voluntary summer reading for children in grades 3 to 5: An experimental study. *Scientific Studies of Reading, 12*(1), 1–23.

Koellner, K., & Jacobs, J. (2015). Distinguishing models of professional development: The case of an adaptive model's impact on teachers' knowledge, instruction, and student achievement. *Journal of Teacher Education, 66*(1), 51–67.

Kuhfeld, M., Soland, J., Tarasawa, B., Johnson, A., Ruzek, E., & Liu, J. (2020). Projecting the potential impact of COVID-19 school closures on academic achievement. *Educational Researcher, 49*(8), 549–565.

Language and Reading Research Consortium, Jiang, H., & Logan, J. (2019). Improving reading comprehension in the primary grades: Mediated effects of a language-focused classroom intervention. *Journal of Speech, Language, and Hearing Research, 62*(8), 2812–2828.

Lareau, A. (2009). Narrow questions, narrow

answers: The limited value of randomized controlled trials for education research. In P. Walters, A. Lareau, & S. H. Ranis (Eds.), *Education research on trial: Policy reform and the call for scientific rigor* (pp. 145–161). Routledge.

Lemons, C. J., Fuchs, D., Gilbert, J. K., & Fuchs, L. S. (2014). Evidence-based practices in a changing world: Reconsidering the counterfactual in education research. *Educational Researcher, 43*(5), 242–252.

Lewis, C. (2015). What is improvement science?: Do we need it in education? *Educational Researcher, 44*(1), 54–61.

McKeown, M. G., & Beck, I. L. (2004). Direct and rich vocabulary instruction. In J. F. Baumann & E. J. Kame'enui (Eds.), *Vocabulary Instruction* (pp. 13–27). Guilford Press.

McKeown, M. G., Deane, P. D., Scott, J. D., Krovetz, R., & Lawless, R. R. (2017). *Vocabulary assessment to support instruction: Building rich word-learning experiences.* Guilford Press.

McMaster, K. L., Jung, P. G., Brandes, D., Pinto, V., Fuchs, D., Kearns, D., . . . Yen, L. (2014). Customizing a research-based reading practice. *Reading Teacher, 68*(3), 173–183.

Meyer, A., Miller, S., & Herman, M. (1993). Balancing the priorities of evaluation with the priorities of the setting: A focus on positive youth development programs in school settings. *Journal of Primary Prevention, 14*(2), 95–113.

Murnane, R., & Nelson, R. (2007). Improving the performance of the education sector: The valuable, challenging, and limited role of random assignment evaluations. *Economics of Innovation and New Technology, 16*(5), 307–322.

National Reading Panel. (2000). *Teaching children to read: An evidence-based assessment of the scientific research literature on reading and its implications for reading instruction.* National Institute of Child Health and Human Development.

Neugebauer, S., Coyne, M., McCoach, B., & Ware, S. (2017). Teaching beyond the intervention: The contribution of teacher language extensions to vocabulary learning in urban kindergarten classrooms. *Reading and Writing, 30*(3), 543–567.

Neugebauer, S., Coyne, M., McCoach, B., & Ware, S. (2021). Reframing adherence: Active ingredients and impromptu interactions that support vocabulary implementation effectiveness. *Early Childhood Research Quarterly, 56*, 52–64.

Neuman, S. B., Newman, E. H., & Dwyer, J. (2011). Educational effects of a vocabulary intervention on preschoolers' word knowledge and conceptual development: A cluster-randomized trial. *Reading Research Quarterly, 46*(3), 249–272.

Neuman, S. B., Samudra, P., & Danielson, K. (2021). Effectiveness of scaling up a vocabulary intervention for low-income children, pre-k through first grade. *Elementary School Journal, 121*(3), 385–409.

Pearson, P. D., Palincsar, A. S., Biancarosa, G., & Berman, A. I. (Eds.). (2020). *Reaping the rewards of the Reading for Understanding Initiative.* National Academy of Education.

Polikoff, M. S., Porter, A. C., & Smithson, J. (2011). How well aligned are state assessments of student achievement with state content standards? *American Educational Research Journal, 48*(4), 965–995.

Quinn, D. M., & Kim, J. S. (2017). Scaffolding fidelity and adaptation in educational program implementation: Experimental evidence from a literacy intervention. *American Educational Research Journal, 54*(6), 1187–1220.

Quint, J., Zhu, P., Balu, R., Rappaport, S., & DeLaurentis, M. (2015). Scaling up the success for all model of school reform: Final report from the investing in innovation (i3) evaluation. Manpower Demonstration Research Corporation. Available at *www.mdrc.org/sites/default/files/SFA_2015_FR.pdf.*

Remillard, J. T. (2005). Examining key concepts in research on teachers' use of mathematics curricula. *Review of Educational Research, 75*(2), 211–246.

Rimm-Kaufman, S. E., Larsen, R. A. A., Baroody, A. E., Curby, T. W., Ko, M., Thomas, J. B., . . . DeCoster, J. (2014). Efficacy of the responsive classroom approach: Results from a 3-year, longitudinal randomized controlled trial. *American Educational Research Journal, 51*(3), 567–603.

Ryan, R. M., & Deci, E. L. (2000). Self-determination theory and the facilitation of intrinsic motivation, social development, and well-being. *American Psychologist, 55*(1), 68–78.

Sailors, M., Hoffman, J. V., Pearson, P. D., McClung, N., Shin, J., Phiri, L. M., & Saka, T. (2014). Supporting change in literacy instruction in Malawi. *Reading Research Quarterly, 49*(2), 209–231.

Stanovich, K. E. (2000). *Progress in understanding reading: Scientific foundations and new frontiers.* Guilford Press.

Stein, M. L., Berends, M., Fuchs, D., McMaster, K., Saenz, L., Yen, L., . . . Compton, D. L. (2008). Scaling up an early reading program: Relationships among teacher support, fidelity of implementation, and student performance across different sites and years. *Educational Evaluation and Policy Analysis, 30*(4), 368–388.

Stipek, D., Franke, M., Clements, D., Farran, D., & Coburn, C. (2017). PK–3: What does it mean for instruction? *Social Policy Report, 30*(2), 1–21.

Stokes, D. (1997). *Pasteur's Quadrant: Basic sci-*

ence and technological innovation. Brookings Institution Press.

Tipton, E., Fellers, L., Caverly, S., Vaden-Kiernan, M., Borman, G. D., Sullivan, S., & Ruiz de Castilla, V. (2016). Site selection in experiments: An assessment of site recruitment and generalizability in two scale-up studies. *Journal of Research on Educational Effectiveness, 9*(Suppl. 1), 209–228.

U.S. Department of Education, Institute of Education Sciences, National Center for Education Statistics, National Assessment of Educational Progress (NAEP). (2019). 2015 and 2019 Reading Assessments. Retrieved from *www.nationsreportcard.gov/reading/nation/scores/?grade=4.*

U. S. Department of Education, Institute of Education Sciences, National Center for Education Statistics. (2022). National Assessment of Educational Progress (NAEP Long-Term Trend Assessment Results: Reading and Mathematics. Retrieved October 3, 2022 from *www.nationsreportcard.gov/highlights/ltt/2022.*

Vaden-Kiernan, M., Borman, G., Caverly, S., Bell, N., Sullivan, K., Ruiz de Castilla, V., . . . Hughes Jones, D. (2018). Findings from a multiyear scale-up effectiveness trial of open court reading.

Journal of Research on Educational Effectiveness, 11(1), 109–132.

Vaughn, S., Roberts, G., Swanson, E. A., Wanzek, J., Fall, A.-M., & Stillman-Spisak, S. J. (2015). Improving middle-school students' knowledge and comprehension in social studies: A replication. *Educational Psychology Review, 27*(1), 31–50.

White, T. G., Kim, J. S., Kingston, H. C., & Foster, L. (2014). Replicating the effects of a teacher-scaffolded voluntary summer reading program: The role of poverty. *Reading Research Quarterly, 49*(1), 5–30.

Wilkins, C., Gersten, R., Decker, L. E., Grunden, L., Brasiel, S., Brunnert, K., & Jayanthi, M. (2012). *Does a summer reading program based on Lexiles affect reading comprehension?* (NCEE 2012-4006). National Center for Education Evaluation and Regional Assistance, Institute of Education Sciences, U.S. Department of Education.

Zook-Howell, D., Matsumura, L. C., Walsh, M. W., Correnti, R., & Bickel, D. D. (2020). Developing adaptive expertise at facilitating dialogic text discussions. *Reading Teacher, 74*(2), 179–189.

CHAPTER 22

Together We Can Do So Much

Aligned School and Home Efforts Using a Multi-Tiered Systems of Support Framework

Tricia A. Zucker, Gloria Yeomans-Maldonado, Sarah Surrain, and Susan H. Landry

Increasingly, researchers and school leaders are using multi-tiered systems of support (MTSS) structures to design school–family partnerships that enact evidence-based approaches to early preventive support (McIntyre & Phaneuf, 2008; Weingarten, Zumeta Edmonds, & Arden, 2020). We argue in this chapter that school–family partnerships in MTSS frameworks provide (1) opportunities for collaboration and problem solving between parents and teachers with the shared goal of improving students' language, literacy, and academic outcomes; (2) a logical and equitable structure for organizing family engagement efforts with a rationale for decisions to increase family support for students who need it; and (3) a proactive approach to planning services for culturally and linguistically diverse caregivers that is manageable for schools to deliver. We use the terms *parents, caregivers,* and *family* interchangeably, acknowledging that there are diverse family structures. We first describe a framework for early childhood school–home MTSS including the unique affordances of this over traditional family engagement approaches. Then we explain our initial tests of this model that demonstrate the promise of doing more with teachers and parents together, rather than with interventions in the school or the home alone. We close with a call for other researchers to examine school–home MTSS that will help educators understand the potential of this approach.

Key Components and Opportunities within an Aligned School-Home MTSS

A school–home MTSS leverages two key caregivers—teachers and parents—in the shared goal of improving students' language and literacy outcomes. Many MTSS models include both social–behavioral and academic supports (e.g., Weist, Garbacz, Lane, & Kincaid, 2017), but we concentrate specifically on academic outcomes related to language and literacy. Our research has focused on the first two tiers of MTSS within early childhood grades; other models include three levels of support starting in elementary grades (Balu et al., 2015). The three levels of intervention include primary, secondary, and tertiary supports, which become increasingly individualized and intensive. *Tier 1* is universal support for all students, with a focus on preventing language and literacy difficulties both at school and at home. *Tier 2* is targeted support, with a focus on responsive adult behaviors to keep linguistically rich conversations going and to guide literacy learning with scaffolding. *Tier 3* is intensive support in language and literacy; this tier may require support for social–behavioral difficulties that often co-occur with academic difficulties. Table 22.1 outlines these three tiers of aligned strategies across the school and home environments.

A large body of research exists on MTSS in the school setting alone (for reviews, see Buysse et al., 2016; Gersten et al., 2008; Carta & Greenwood, Chapter 28, this volume); this model aligns with these school-based approaches, which are also referred to as response to intervention (RTI) (Freudenthal, Zaru, & Al Otaiba, Chapter 4, this volume). Over 94% of states are using school-based MTSS frameworks to deliver evidence-based core Tier 1 instruction, preventive Tier 2 support, and intensive Tier 3 intervention (Berkeley, Scanlon, Bailey, Sutton, & Sacco, 2020). Indeed, classroom MTSS that focuses on Tiers 1 and 2 are useful for improving language and literacy skills of young students demonstrating language and literacy difficulties (e.g., Pullen, Tuckwiller, Konold, Maynard, & Coyne, 2010; Solari, Denton, Petscher, & Haring, 2018; Zucker, Solari, Landry, & Swank, 2013). Lonigan and Phillips (2016) demonstrated that Tier 2 PreK classroom supports need to be closely matched to students' assessed language and literacy needs. However, we argue that it is unlikely that even well-implemented school MTSS will be of sufficient intensity to close long-standing achievement gaps between children experiencing poverty and their peers, particularly for language gaps that require ongoing intensive support across many years (Wasik & Hindman, 2015). Therefore, enlisting parents in efforts to support learning provides important opportunities to close gaps and strengthen school–family rapport.

Schools have long recognized the importance of engaging families in their child's learning. But adopting a school–home MTSS provides opportunities to invest in school capacity building and ensure that family engagement approaches are sustainable for educators to manage. Making data-informed decisions about which children need increased levels of support can help schools overcome barriers such as educators' time constraints and lack of funding for family engagement (Christenson, 2004). Rather than a one-size-fits-all approach, tiered parent interventions are acceptable to families and allow families with greatest need to be routed to more specialized supports (cf. Nowak & Heinrichs, 2008; Kamiyama & Noro, 2020; Mendelsohn et al.,

2011). Moreover, school–home MTSS provide opportunities to invest in educator training that addresses negative stereotypes or narrow conceptualizations of how diverse families and families experiencing poverty can support learning. Most educators have little to no formal training on family–school partnerships and would benefit from professional learning communities or other contexts that allow teachers to work through complex scenarios on how to partner with families in ways that do not threaten parents' position or culture (Edwards et al., 2019). Additionally, schools that use classroom MTSS are accustomed to screening to identify students who need support (Fletcher, Francis, Foorman, & Schatschneider, 2021), so there are already set points in the school year to invite families to take part in more intensive tiers of family support.

School–Home MTSS: A Better Structure for Family Engagement Efforts

What is unique about school–home MTSS is that they provide schools with a logical and equitable framework for organizing aligned family engagement efforts. The logic for aligned MTSS comes from several theories. First, ecological theories of development emphasize that consistency and alignment across settings in which young children spend a great deal of time (school and home) are essential for optimal learning (Bronfenbrenner & Morris, 2006). Second, development frameworks emphasize that both teachers and parents can utilize key strategies to support early learning, including (1) *responsiveness* to the child's literacy interests, questions, or bids for attention; (2) *guided learning* that scaffolds children's understanding of literacy tasks or language; and (3) *organized routines* such as shared book reading and predictable opportunities for multiple-turn conversations (e.g., Ainsworth, 1979; Grusec & Davidov, 2010; Vygotsky, 2012). Within a context of ensuring equity, some reframe families as "essential" learning partners rather than "desirable extras"; therefore, the goal is to remove barriers, so that *all* families are supported (Christenson, 2004). To help families from nondominant cultures find their "place" in schools and their child's learning (Barajas-López & Ishimaru, 2020), MTSS can tailor support to families' unique strengths and needs, while promoting equity in access to school services (Garbacz, Vatland, & Kern, 2020).

TABLE 22.1. Components of a School–Home MTSS

All students: Universal support for all students to prevent academic difficulties

Focus on awareness and importance of early language and literacy support from responsive caregivers	Tier 1: School
	• Implement evidence-based *core curriculum* and instructional approaches
	• Implement *universal screening* and progress monitoring measures
	• Analyze data and use *benchmarks* to route students to increasing tiers of support
	• Support teachers to meet needs of *English learners* (ELs) in classroom
	• Provide *family engagement training* and professional learning communities that work through scenarios for building relationships with culturally diverse families
	
	Tier 1: Family
	• Early in the school year, *get to know families* and explain how families can communicate with different staff within the school to address questions/concerns
	  ♦ Ask families their preferred language(s) for school communications
	  ♦ Provide families with the MTSS framework to ensure transparency
	• Coordinate *home–school communication* channels (newsletters, text messages)
	• Discuss screening data with family at *parent–teacher conferences*/video conferences
	• Offer *events* to share information and resources on informal learning for grade/class
	• Encourage predictable *home routines* for learning and to prevent behavior problems

Some students: Targeted support in core academic subjects with responsive caregivers

Focus on problem solving using individual student screening data and goal setting	Tier 2: School • Evidence-based supplemental *small-group intervention* (four to six students) • Support teachers to implement interventions with *adequate fidelity and quality* • *Set goals* for student learning and track progress • Analyze student *response to instruction* based on progress monitoring data • Support teachers *to make connections with ELs* home language and literacy • Provide professional learning communities with scenarios for explaining students' need for support and for *handling complex conversations* with families Tier 2: Family • Provide *written notice* to family that student is receiving intervention • Explain the intervention approach and *progress monitoring plan* • Offer information and *aligned activities* to extend learning at home • *Set goals* for parent involvement in home language and literacy activities • Address common *misconceptions* for ELs and maintain rich home language supports • Share *progress monitoring reports* and discuss with family at least *quarterly*

Few students: Intensive support in core academic subjects, as well as social–behavioral needs

Focus on two-way communication around IDEA rights, problem-solving using progress monitoring data, and family member concerns	Tier 3: School • Evidence-based *individualized interventions* (two to three students per group) • Support specialists to implement interventions with *adequate fidelity and quality* • Analyze *response to instruction* and adjust using progress monitoring data • Provide professional learning communities with scenarios for *explaining neurodiversity* and developmental disabilities with families Tier 3: Family • Collaborate with school psychologists for *comprehensive evaluations* • Explain the *students' rights* under IEP or 504, if appropriate • Invite families to *problem-solving meetings* and data review meetings • Share *progress monitoring reports* and discuss with family *monthly* • Consult with school counselors/social workers to provide *social–emotional support* • Provide resources on *parent advocacy and support* networks for families of children with developmental disabilities and neurodevelopmental diversity

Note. IDEA, Individuals with Disabilities Education Act; IEP, individualized education plan.

A goal of school–home MTSS in early childhood is for families to be seen (by self and educators) as their child's first and most important teacher. We refer to *family engagement* as a process in which educators and families develop a relationship focused on supporting children's success via two-way communications and approaches that are strengths-based and culturally affirming (National Academies of Sciences, Engineering, and Medicine [NASEM], 2017). An outcome of school–home MTSS can be increased *parent involvement* in their child's learning outside of school time. Although there are many dimensions of parent involvement, such as school events, committees, or communications (Fantuzzo, McWayne, Perry, & Childs, 2004), we focus on learning at home because parent–child learning activities (e.g., sharing books, mealtime conversations, exploring science or engineering) are more consistently related to child outcomes than other types of involvement (e.g., Haring-Biel et al., 2019; Jeynes, 2012; McWayne, Hampton, Fantuzzo, Cohen, & Sekino, 2004; Sénéchal & Young, 2008).

Most schools already use various family engagement strategies that range in intensity, but without an MTSS structure. About 33% of U.S. parents experience more intensive, individualized consultation with educators at their child's school, whereas most parents (75–89%) experience only low-intensity approaches such as school communications/newsletters, class events, or parent-teacher conferences (Hanson & Pugliese, 2020). However, a meta-analysis of early childhood family engagement interventions found small to no effects of these low-intensity approaches on child outcomes (Grindal et al., 2016); only higher-intensity parent coaching approaches were effective for children's academic outcomes (effect sizes [ES] = 0.30 to 0.42). Yet due to limited funding or time constraints, most schools do not have the capacity to provide individualized coaching or consultation to all families. Thus, family–school MTSS models are a cost-effective method of directing more costly and intensive tiers of coaching support to families with greatest need (Eagle, Dowd-Eagle, Snyder, & Holtzman, 2015). Early demonstration programs such as the Perry Preschool Project included weekly home visits from teachers, yet this intensity of program would have cost over $13,000 per child, per school year in 2017 dollars (Arnold Ventures, 2021). In more recent studies, the cost the of intensive home visiting programs ranges from $2,500 per student (up to 16 sessions; Jones, Bierman, Crowley, Welsh,

& Gest, 2019) to $3,000 per student (up to 19 sessions; Knight et al., 2019). But if this is support directed to only some students (e.g., Tier 2 or Tier 3), then the costs become feasible for schools. In contrast, Tier 1 family engagement supports are lower cost, such as $250 for materials to host a group family education event or $100 for a text messaging service to communicate with all early childhood parents (Zucker et al., 2021). Therefore, modern schools could use school–home MTSS to make equitable and cost-effective decisions about which families require intensive support such as ongoing home visits or remote coaching.

Designing School-Home MTSS for Culturally and Linguistically Diverse Families

School–home MTSS models may be particularly important for cultivating partnerships with culturally and linguistically diverse families, provided they are designed to recognize and build on families' existing cultural values and language practices. Children whose families speak a language other than English at home or whose cultural practices differ from those of middle-class, English-speaking, White families are a large and growing segment of school-age children in the United States (Romo, Thomas, & García, 2018). For these children, continuing to develop their home languages and cultural identities alongside learning the language and cultural norms of the school environment is foundational to their long-term well-being and academic outcomes (Müller, Howard, Wilson, Gibson, & Katsos, 2020; Rivas-Drake et al., 2014; Winsler, Kim, & Richard, 2014). Therefore, school–home MTSS must be intentional about how families' existing language and cultural practices are valued and sustained through home- and school-based systems of supports.

While this presents a challenge to scaling up school–home MTSS given the vast diversity of linguistic and cultural backgrounds represented in many early childhood programs (Baker & Páez, 2018), it also presents opportunities to improve educator–family relationships and support children's development in both their home and school languages during the critical first years of school. School–home interventions that have incorporated the languages and cultural practices of participating families have been particularly effective for engaging parents and promoting positive child outcomes (Caesar &

Nelson, 2014; Grøver, Rydland, Gustafsson, & Snow, 2020; Leyva & Skorb, 2017; for a review, see Melzi, Schick, & Scarola, 2019). The success of such programs may be due to several factors. First, they leverage and build on parents' existing linguistic and cultural practices rather than seeking to replace them with practices that may feel unnatural or uncomfortable (Reese, Leyva, Sparks, & Grolnick, 2010). Second, they hold the potential to strengthen relationships between educators and families through developing mutual respect, understanding, and trust. And finally, school–home aligned programs that support children's development in each of their languages may facilitate metalinguistic awareness and cross-linguistic transfer of language and literacy skills (for a recent review, see Gottardo, Chen, & Huo, 2021).

Based on the previous literature and our initial efforts to develop and test strengths-based and culturally affirming school–home MTSS, we outline a few key ingredients that future work should consider.

1. Providing resources and coaching in families' preferred languages is an essential first step, but alone it is insufficient.
2. Educators and coaches delivering the program components need to adopt a stance that recognizes the complexity and value of all languages and dialects, and recognizes the diverse linguistic and cultural strengths of all families.
3. Program activities should be enjoyable for families and children, and build on the cultural knowledge and practices of families.
4. Program expectations should also be sensitive to the constraints and stressors that families face. In addition to the limited time that working parents may have to support their child's learning in the home, activities need to be accessible for parents with different levels of literacy in their home languages.
5. Finally, a strengths-based school–home approach is bidirectional. Not only are parents introduced to new ways to build on existing practices to support their child's success in school, but school-based components should recognize, celebrate, and incorporate the linguistic and cultural practices of families in the classroom.

In the next sections, we describe key findings from school–home research studies our team has conducted in Texas over the last decade with culturally and linguistically diverse families. These studies reveal the importance of intensive family support for students experiencing poverty and/or academic difficulties.

Multicomponent School–Home Interventions

Although most of what we describe in this chapter stems from our own work around family and school interventions, there are many examples of studies that have implemented multicomponent interventions with various levels of school–home component intensity. For example, the Head Start Research-Based, Developmentally Informed (REDI) program (Bierman et al., 2008; Bierman, Heinrichs, Welsh, Nix, & Gest, 2017) was designed as a Tier 1 type of intervention delivered by classroom teachers, with a focus on language and emergent literacy, and social–emotional skills. REDI also included a family component where "take-home" packets were mailed to families. These packets included parenting tips and learning activities to reinforce both language/emergent literacy and social–emotional skills. At the end of preschool, the REDI program had positive and significant effects on children's vocabulary (ES = 0.15), emergent literacy skills (ES ranging from 0.35 to 0.39), and social cognition (ES ranging from 0.21 to 0.35). Sustained, long-term effects were reported for the social-emotional domain (ES ranging from 0.12 to 0.34) 6 years after participation in the REDI program (Welsh et al., 2020). These sustained effects also included parent involvement, as reported by teachers (ES = 0.24). Another example of an intervention with both a school and family component is NURTURES (Paprzycki et al., 2017), a program designed to increase PreK–grade 2 teachers' science content knowledge through a 2-week summer institute and a series of year-round professional learning communities. In Networking Urban Resources with Teachers and University to Enrich Early Childhood Science (NURTURES), the family component includes family packs that are sent home and family community science events. Based on quasi-experimental evidence, NURTURES found effect sizes of 0.07 for literacy, 0.25 for reading, and 0.14 for math; sustained, long-term effects in fifth-grade science have been reported (ES = 0.16; Kaderavek et al., 2020).

To our knowledge, most of the experimental work around family and school interventions has relied on randomized controlled trial

(RCT) designs with a multicomponent program in which the treatment group gets both the family and school intervention. Although rigorous, these designs are not intended to inform the efficacy of specific components of the intervention (i.e., school or family) responsible for any observed effects. One exception to this is a recent study by Kim, Asher, Burkhauser, Mesite, and Leyva (2019), in which the authors used a Sequential Multiple Assignment Randomized Trial (SMART) design to develop an adaptive K–2 literacy summer intervention with personalized texts accompanied by app-based digital content. Specifically, this intervention included (1) pretraining in-school lessons delivered by teachers, and (2) a family component in which parents attend an afterschool family literacy event and receive printed texts and app-based digital content to support formal and informal home literacy activities. One of the novelties of this intervention is the adaptive nature of the design. Specifically, based on families' different levels of responsiveness, some families receive a gamified version of the app meant to motivate the student to complete literacy activities *or* a gamified version of the app plus text messages to parents. Authors found evidence suggesting that adding the text messages to the gamified app had a significant and positive impact on students' reading comprehension (ES = 0.27). This study highlights the importance of using a flexible design that allows for the examination of the effectiveness of particular school or home intervention components or varying levels of intensities of a single component. In the next sections, we describe a series of studies designed to answer questions about the additive value of a family component and about the optimal conditions that best support students' language and literacy skills.

Examining School-Home MTSS with Factorial Designs

Across the past 10 years, our team has conducted multiple studies that examined aspects of Tier 1 and Tier 2 levels of support across school and home environments. The first set of studies used factorial, experimental designs to examine classroom or home interventions alone and in combination to determine whether the combined approach was better than either single intervention alone. The second set of studies used additive experimental designs to evaluate optimal conditions of combined school plus home interventions that best supported outcomes for families experiencing poverty. These studies all occurred in Texas with families experiencing poverty; we enrolled samples in which one-third to two-thirds of families spoke languages other than English at home. Most of these families spoke Spanish at home, but there was considerable linguistic diversity (e.g., Urdu, Creole). We discuss studies based on theories of change similar to Figure 22.1, which shows how key inputs and tiered intervention activities seek to improve three domains of adult behaviors that are mechanisms for improved child outcomes.

The key hypothesis we tested using the factorial design was that the combined, theoretically aligned interventions would produce a synergistic effect on child outcomes. Study 1 (Landry et al., 2017) and a remotely delivered replication in Study 2 (Landry et al., 2021) tested the benefits of a classroom intervention called Texas School Ready (TSR; Crawford, Zucker, Van Horne, & Landry, 2017; Landry, Swank, Smith, Assel, & Gunnewig, 2006), a parent intervention called Play and Learning Strategies (PALS; Landry, Smith, Swank, & Guttentag, 2008), or a combined approach featuring TSR plus PALS delivered concurrently (although participants were blind to whether students were receiving single or concurrent interventions). These interventions occurred in Head Start centers and trained both adults—teachers and parents—to use strategies across three areas: (1) responsiveness: sensitivity attending to children's signals; (2) guided learning: matching teaching to children's level and scaffolding; and (3) organization: establishing predictable routines to help children feel secure. The TSR program provides Tier 1 and Tier 2 professional development and supplemental curricula across multiple domains (e.g., language, literacy and social–emotional instruction); Tier 2 is teacher-delivered to a small group using leveled activities to match students' assessed language and literacy skills on a PreK screening measure (Center for Improving the Readiness of Children for Learning and Education [CIRCLE] Progress Monitoring; Landry et al., 2014). The PALS program is a Tier 2 type of support with a series of individualized coaching sessions in which parents review strategies and modeling videos before they practice the strategy with their child during play, informal learning, or other family activities. The PALS coach provides feedback and support to the parent in reflecting on their videotaped parent–child interaction; then they set goals for using the focal strategies in the next week.

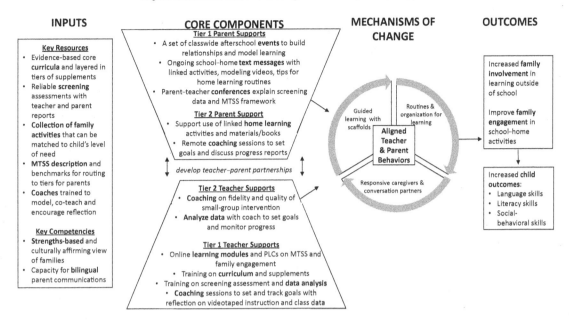

FIGURE 22.1. Theory of change guiding a series of studies.

The first study delivered the teacher and parent coaching interventions using in-person coaching (Landry et al., 2017), but the second study replicated this design using remote delivery (Landry et al., 2021). Both of these studies used teacher training (14 hours) and coaching (14 sessions) to improve the quality of Tier 1 and 2 classroom instruction and Tier 2 type of parent coaching (20 hours). Although there were some promising synergistic results for the combined school plus home approach for children's engagement during book reading (Study 1: $d = 0.54$, $p < .05$), vocabulary (Study 2: $g = 0.30$, $p < .10$) as well as other domains such as self-regulation (Study 2: $g = 0.21$, $p < 0.05$), there were many nonsignificant differences. Figure 22.2 shows the factorial designs of the original and replication study, with effect sizes for each group on children's language and literacy outcomes. We show these outcomes in this chapter focused on language and literacy; however, the treatments were heavily focused on social–behavioral outcomes that are detailed in other impact reports (Landry et al., 2017, 2021).

The pattern of language and literacy results across the two studies suggested slightly greater language benefits when the parent coaching was included; there were many null findings for literacy outcomes, with the exception of an unexpected positive effect for in-person parent

coaching on print knowledge ($d = 0.14$) and a negative effect of the combined in-person interventions on phonological awareness ($d = −0.33$, Landry et al., 2017). There were only two trends (book-reading engagement, expressive vocabulary) supporting the hypothesis that there is a greater effect of combined interventions at both school and home. Nonetheless, improving parent behaviors was key to many of the positive outcomes for children, somewhat more than teacher impacts. Given mediation analyses that demonstrate changes in both TSR teachers and PALS parents behaviors are the mechanisms by which child outcomes are impacted (Crawford et al., 2021; Landry et al., 2012, 2021), we are continuing to pursue additional questions around how to cost-effectively improve these adult behaviors and how to optimize aligned school–home interventions for diverse populations.

For example, we are currently conducting a new study in this line of research that replicates the factorial design with a bilingual population (Landry & Zucker, 2020). The purpose of the new study is to evaluate a dual language approach that maintains and builds on the home language skills of dual language learners (DLLs) who speak mostly Spanish in their homes. The factorial design will contrast the PALS Spanish program alone, a classroom shared book-reading program alone, or a combined approach that

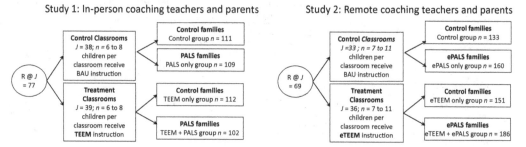

Select Child Outcomes	Main Effect of PALS (d)	Main Effect of TEEM (d)	Interaction of PALS and TEEM (d)	> ES if school + home		Main Effect of ePALS (g)	Main Effect of eTEEM (g)	Interaction of ePALS and eTEEM (g)	> ES if school + home
Book reading engagement	0.27*	0.18	0.54*	Yes		0.51**	0.07	−0.02	No (> parent)
Book reading language use	0.28*	0.20	0.24	No (> parent)		0.50**	−0.08	0.08	No (> parent)
Print knowledge	0.14*	0.10	0.03	No (> parent)		−0.15	−0.04	−0.05	Null
Phonological awareness	−0.04	0.10	−0.33*	No (< school)		−0.01	0.08	−0.13	Null
Expressive vocabulary	−0.04	0.05	−0.01	Null		0.02	−0.03	0.30†	Yes

FIGURE 22.2. Factorial study design replicated across in-person and remote delivery. The effect sizes test the hypothesis that aligned interventions at school and home would produce a synergistic effect on child outcomes.

simultaneously coaches parents to maintain the home language and coaches teachers to use an explicit cross-language transfer approach. The classroom program, called *Hablemos Juntos/ Developing Talkers*, introduces sophisticated vocabulary and concepts in Spanish shared reading before learning the same concepts in English texts. The expected outcome of this project is increased understanding of effective classroom instruction and family engagement approaches for DLLs who are screened and meet criteria for Tier 2 support based on limited Spanish vocabulary at the beginning of PreK. We also are more closely aligning the bilingual shared-reading components across school and home settings, which is expected to have benefits in not only the home language but also English (Grøver et al., 2020; Roberts, 2008).

Examining School–Home MTSS with Additive Experimental Designs

In a second line of research, we explored what types of supports at each tier are most effective for increasing parent involvement and child out-comes. In these studies, we did not use the factorial design to isolate the effects of school versus home but instead explored research questions around the optimal components within family engagement services. The key hypothesis we were testing using additive, experimental designs was that families of children experiencing poverty needed access to increasingly tailored supports to increase parent involvement in their child's learning that would, in turn, have an effect on child outcomes. These increasing layers of supports were akin to moving to higher tiers of MTSS support and were designed to address potential barriers to supporting learning at home. For example, we experimentally manipulated additional supports such as provision of home learning materials or parent coaching, above and beyond the universal family engagement approaches.

In Study 3, we developed a school–home MTSS supplemental PreK program called Teaching Together (Zucker et al., 2021). The Tier 1 and Tier 2 interventions included aligned, supplemental classroom curricular and family engagement activities to support language and literacy skills of students who scored below predetermined screening benchmarks. Specifically, we screened all students in Head Start PreK classrooms to identify students who scored below the benchmarks for 4-year-old rapid vocabulary naming and/or rapid letter naming screening criteria (CIRCLE Progress Monitoring; Landry et al., 2014). We supported teachers to use Tier 1 whole-group shared-reading approaches that addressed code-related skills via print referencing and meaning-related skills via direct vocabulary instruction and comprehension questions. Teachers also implemented small-group Tier 2 lessons to review and extend taught literacy and language concepts. Research staff members facilitated a series of Tier 1 after-school family engagement events and sent families text messages about what their child was learning at school and tips to extend learning at home (Cabell, Zucker, DeCoster, Copp, & Landry, 2019). For Tier 2 students and families, we randomly assigned two types of Tier 2 family supports featuring either (1) take-home kits with family learning activities and shared reading books, or (2) kits plus four parent-coaching sessions that were a derivative of the PALS approach but were less intensive, with just four modules and coaching calls (3.5 to 4 hours total) to discuss each topic and reflect on videotaped parent–child interactions for goal setting.

The findings of Study 3 showed that the enhanced Tier 2 with individualized parent coaching was the only condition that significantly improved children's proximal academic vocabulary learning ($g = 0.46$). Yet there were promising, albeit nonsignificant, findings, that the Tier 1 only school–home intervention improved children's standardized vocabulary on the Peabody Picture Vocabulary Test (PPVT; $g = 0.39$). There seemed to be no benefit of sending materials alone (without extra support or coaching) to the Tier 2 families for children's language outcomes. Unexpectedly, all intervention groups showed negative results on literacy outcomes ($g = -0.09$ to -0.39); therefore, we have removed these literacy components from the intervention for future studies, as they seemed to be not sufficiently intensive and/or aligned with the core program. In terms of parent behavior change, this study's additive design supported the hypothesis that adding more intensive components to each tier of a closely aligned school–home MTSS best supported parent involvement in their child's language and literacy learning. As summarized in Figure 22.3, the most intensive condition with kits and coaching produced larger effect sizes for parent involvement, using a parent report measure (Zill et al., 2000). We measured home-based parent involvement in language and literacy learning with items from other national studies (cf. Graves & Brown Wright, 2011). This most intensive tier of support also best supported the academic vocabulary development of children considered at risk at the beginning of PreK. Thus, the Tier 2 classroom instruction was more effective when paired with family coaching on language support strategies, which have been extensively demonstrated as effective, such as responsively facilitating conversations, explaining words, and sharing books at home (Greenwood, Schnitz, Carta, Wallisch, & Irvine, 2019).

We have initial findings for one cohort of Study 4 (Zucker et al., 2022), the next in this line of Teaching Together research exploring additive designs. The larger study is still in progress, recruiting additional cohorts; moreover, this study was impacted by COVID-related school closures, such that no child outcomes could be measured at posttest. Nonetheless, the initial findings on parent involvement changes warrant consideration, because they, too, suggest that the more intensive tiers of support produced larger change in parent behaviors (Zucker et al., 2022). The instructional foci of this study target academic language but do so by engaging parents and PreK children in science, technology, engineering, and math (STEM) activities that are known to elicit more sophisticated causal reasoning and academic discourse (e.g., Peterson & French, 2008). We evaluated an afterschool STEM family engagement program that was delivered in schools by museum-based informal learning experts who facilitated a series of family events aimed at getting PreK parents and children to inquire about their world and discuss math and science within everyday routines. We again used text messages to provide parents with tips on how to get involved in their child's learning and experimentally manipulated other components that could be added onto the core Teaching Together treatment (group Tx A) of family events and text messages. The added enhancements included take-home STEM activity kits in the second treatment group (Tx B) and in a third treatment group (Tx C), we added monetary rewards. Parents in this final condition could receive $2.50 when they texted a photo or explanation of a learning activity they did with their child.

These added Teaching Together components in Study 4 were designed to address potential

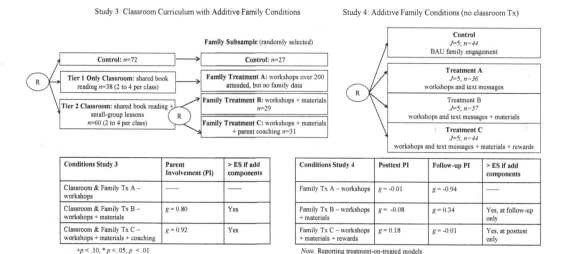

FIGURE 22.3. The additive design experiments that layer additional supports onto various tiers of school–home MTSS models. The tables at the bottom of the figure show effect sizes for parent involvement outcomes.

barriers faced by families experiencing poverty, including limited *access* to learning materials/books (e.g., Neuman, 2017) and limited *time* to devote to home learning given demanding work schedules or other parent responsibilities (e.g., Justice, Chen, Tambyraja, & Logan, 2018). This study included 181 families in schools where 92% of students received free/reduced lunch and 50% of children were English learners. Although there were no significant impacts of any treatment group compared to the control group on parent involvement in STEM, the more intensive treatments, which included take-home activity kits and rewards. These conditions produced larger effect sizes (Zucker et al., 2022) compared to the control group (see Figure 22.3). However, the effects of rewards faded over time and the effect of providing family kits increased at the delayed follow-up timepoint, perhaps because families had more time to utilize these STEM kits. The combination of rewards and kits may have scaffolded home-based parent involvement in STEM, because they provided photos and bilingual, step-by-step instructions to use a set of inquiry activities that were designed to elicit rich conversations, such as how balloon-powered cars work or how to build a boat that can hold as much weight as possible.

We will soon begin another study in this line of research, again using an additive design to explore school–home MTSS for students experiencing language difficulties (Zucker et al., 2021). In early childhood classrooms serving low-income students, up to 50% of children may exhibit language difficulties (Lonigan & Phillips, 2016), yet early intervention featuring evidence-based language support strategies can ameliorate many of these difficulties (Greenwood et al., 2019). This Teaching Together efficacy study will focus on the benefits and costs of increasingly tailored, tiered interventions in school only or at school plus home, with important findings on cost-effectiveness of each tier of school–home MTSS.

Future Directions

The overall evidence from our series of studies, as well as the larger literature, suggests that school-based interventions with low-intensity family engagement are not of sufficient intensity to narrow large vocabulary and achievement gaps for children eligible for Tier 2 and at risk for later language and reading difficulties (Chatterji, 2006; Wasik & Hindman, 2015). In contrast, the tailored Tier 2 family engagement supports were more promising, likely because the materials scaffolded parent involvement in home learning activities, and coaching provided individualized opportunities for feedback, as well as problem solving with realistic goal setting. The pattern of results does not fully demonstrate the hypothesized synergistic effect of aligned school–home interventions, yet there is enough evidence of promise, as well as theoretical rationale, to warrant further investigation.

We encourage other researchers and educators to consider how MTSS can support tiers of school-to-family partnerships. To further tease apart potential synergies with school–home MTSS, we encourage other researchers to use causal impact studies to evaluate the impacts of early school intervention, home intervention, or the combination of school and home across diverse academic and social–behavioral outcomes. Factorial designs as well as sequential, multiple assignment randomized trials are well suited to these research questions. To further unpack which intervention components are most effective within school–home MTSS, we encourage other researchers to use causal impact studies of different early, tiered intervention components, so we can begin to understand what conditions and dosage of interventions close achievement gaps for students demonstrating risk on early screeners. Perhaps some families need more basic support to address health care, food insecurities, and healthy sleep habits alongside support for learning at home. Future questions should consider the optimal intensity of interventions, families' uptake of offered supports, longitudinal family treatments across grade levels, and how well aligned the school and home environments need to be for different learner profiles. We hope that future studies can help educators understand how the level of personalization or tailoring of components should be matched to individual family needs to expand on the school–home MTSS outlined in this chapter.

Disclosures

Gloria Yeomans-Maldonado and Sarah Surrain have no conflicts of interest. Tricia Zucker has received research grants from Scholastic Inc. and the University of Texas Health Science Center at Houston, royalties for the Developing Talkers/*Hablemos Juntos* products discussed in this chapter.

Acknowledgments

Research reported in this publication was supported by the Institute of Education Sciences under award number R305A210157 and the Advancing Informal STEM Learning division of the National Science Foundation under award number 1811356.

We are particularly grateful to the many staff members who helped us execute these studies. To name a few, Cara Price, Ivet Hirlas, Cathy Caldwell, Cindy Elias, Heather Mui, and Erin Jacobs are some of the research coordinators who worked carefully to organize the day-to-day activities in the studies described in this chapter. Our thanks to them for their hard work.

References

Ainsworth, M. S. (1979). Infant–mother attachment. *American Psychologist, 34*(10), 932–937.

Arnold Ventures. (2021, October). Social programs that work: Perry Preschool Project. Retrieved from *https://evidencebasedprograms.org/document/perry-preschool-project-evidence-summary.*

Baker, M., & Páez, M. (2018). *The language of the classroom: Dual language learners in Head Start, public pre-k, and private preschool programs.* Migration Policy Institute.

Balu, R., Zhu, P., Doolittle, F., Schiller, E., Jenkins, J., & Gersten, R. (2015). *Evaluation of Response to Intervention Practices for Elementary School Reading* (NCEE 2016–4000). National Center for Education Evaluation and Regional Assistance.

Barajas-López, F., & Ishimaru, A. M. (2020). "Darles el lugar": A place for nondominant family knowing in educational equity. *Urban Education, 55*(1), 38–65.

Berkeley, S., Scanlon, D., Bailey, T. R., Sutton, J. C., & Sacco, D. M. (2020). A snapshot of RTI implementation a decade later: New picture, same story. *Journal of Learning Disabilities, 53,* 332–342.

Bierman, K. L., Domitrovich, C. E., Nix, R. L., Gest, S. D., Welsh, J. A., Greenberg, M. T., . . . Gill, S. (2008). Promoting academic and social-emotional school readiness: The Head Start REDI Program. *Child Development, 79*(6), 1802–1817.

Bierman, K. L., Heinrichs, B. S., Welsh, J. A., Nix, R. L., & Gest, S. D. (2017). Enriching preschool classrooms and home visits with evidence-based programming: Sustained benefits for low-income children. *Journal of Child Psychology and Psychiatry, 58*(2), 129–137.

Bronfenbrenner, U., & Morris, P. A. (2006). The bioecological model of human development. In R. M. Lerner & W. Damon (Eds.), *Handbook of child psychology: Theoretical models of human development* (pp. 793–828). Wiley.

Buysse, V., Peisner-Feinberg, E., Soukakou, E., Fettig, A., Schaaf, J., & Burchinal, M. (2016). Using Recognition & Response (R&R) to improve children's language and literacy skills: Findings from two studies. *Early Childhood Research Quarterly, 36,* 11–20.

Cabell, S. Q., Zucker, T. A., DeCoster, J., Copp, S. B., & Landry, S. (2019). Impact of a parent text messaging program on pre-kindergarteners' literacy development. *AERA Open, 5.*

Caesar, L. G., & Nelson, N. W. (2014). Parental involvement in language and literacy acquisition: A bilingual journaling approach. *Child Language Teaching and Therapy, 30*(3), 317–336.

Chatterji, M. (2006). Reading achievement gaps, correlates, and moderators of early reading achievement: Evidence from the Early Childhood Longitudinal Study (ECLS) kindergarten to first grade sample. *Journal of Educational Psychology, 98,* 488–507.

Christenson, S. L. (2004). The family–school partnership: An opportunity to promote the learning competence of all students. *School Psychology Review, 33*(1), 83–104.

Crawford, A., Varghese, C., Hsu, H. Y., Zucker, T., Landry, S., Assel, M., . . . Bhavsar, V. (2021). A comparative analysis of instructional coaching approaches: Face-to-face versus remote coaching in preschool classrooms. *Journal of Educational Psychology, 113,* 1609–1627.

Crawford, A., Zucker, T., Van Horne, B., & Landry, S. (2017). Integrating professional development content and formative assessment with the coaching process: The Texas School Ready model. *Theory Into Practice, 56*(1), 56–65.

Eagle, J. W., Dowd-Eagle, S. E., Snyder, A., & Holtzman, E. G. (2015). Implementing a multi-tiered system of support (MTSS): Collaboration between school psychologists and administrators to promote systems-level change. *Journal of Educational and Psychological Consultation, 25*(2–3), 160–177.

Edwards, P. A., Spiro, R. J., Domke, L. M., Castle, A. M., White, K. L., Peltier, M. R., & Donohue, T. H. (2019). *Partnering with families for student success: 24 scenarios for problem solving with parents.* Teachers College Press.

Fantuzzo, J., McWayne, C., Perry, M. A., & Childs, S. (2004). Multiple dimensions of family involvement and their relations to behavioral and learning competencies for urban, low-income children. *School Psychology Review, 33*(4), 467–480.

Fletcher, J. M., Francis, D. J., Foorman, B. R., & Schatschneider, C. (2021). Early detection of dyslexia risk: Development of brief, teacher-administered screens. *Learning Disability Quarterly, 44*(3), 145–157.

Garbacz, S. A., Vatland, C. H., & Kern, L. (2020). Family–school partnerships within tiered systems of support to increase access, improve equity, and promote positive outcomes for all children and families. In C. S. Clauss-Ehlers, A. B. Sood, & M. D. Weist (Eds.), *Social justice for children and young people: International perspectives* (pp. 194–210). Cambridge University Press.

Gersten, R., Compton, D., Connor, C. M., Dimino, J., Santoro, L., Linan-Thompson, S., & Tilly, W. D. (2008). Assisting students struggling with reading: Response to intervention and multi-tier intervention for reading in the primary grades: A practice guide (NCEE 2009–4045). Retrieved from *http://ies. ed.gov/ncee/wwc/publications/practiceguides.*

Gottardo, A., Chen, X., & Huo, M. R. Y. (2021). Understanding within- and cross-language relations among language, preliteracy skills, and word reading in bilingual learners: Evidence from the science of reading. *Reading Research Quarterly, 56*(Suppl. 1), S371–S390.

Graves, S. L., Jr., & Brown Wright, L. (2011). Parent involvement at school entry: A national examination of group differences and achievement. *School Psychology International, 32*(1), 35–48.

Greenwood, C. R., Schnitz, A. G., Carta, J. J. Wallisch, A., & Irvine, D. W. (2019). A systematic review of language intervention research with low-income families: A word gap prevention perspective. *Early Childhood Research Quarterly, 50,* 230–245.

Grindal, T., Bowne, J. B., Yoshikawa, H., Schindler, H. S., Duncan, G. J., Magnuson, K., & Shonkoff, J. P. (2016). The added impact of parenting education in early childhood education programs: A meta-analysis. *Children and Youth Services Review, 70,* 238–249.

Grøver, V., Rydland, V., Gustafsson, J.-E., & Snow, C. E. (2020). Shared book reading in preschool supports bilingual children's second-language learning: A cluster-randomized trial. *Child Development, 91*(6), 2192–2210.

Grusec, J. E., & Davidov, M. (2010). Integrating different perspectives on socialization theory and research: A domain-specific approach. *Child Development, 81*(3), 687–709.

Hanson, R., & Pugliese, C. (2020). *Parent and family involvement in education: 2019: First Look—Summary* (NCES 2020–076). National Center for Education Statistics.

Haring Biel, C. H., Buzhardt, J., Brown, J. A., Romano, M. K., Lorio, C. M., Windsor, K. S., . . . Goldstein, H. (2019). Language interventions taught to caregivers in homes and classrooms: A review of intervention and implementation fidelity. *Early Childhood Research Quarterly, 50,* 140–156.

Jeynes, W. (2012). A meta-analysis of the efficacy of different types of parental involvement programs for urban students. *Urban Education, 47*(4), 706–742.

Jones, D. E., Bierman, K. L., Crowley, D. M., Welsh, J. A., & Gest, J. (2019). Important issues in estimating costs of early childhood educational interventions: An example from the REDI program. *Children and Youth Services Review, 107,* Article 104498.

Justice, L. M., Chen, J., Tambyraja, S., & Logan, J. (2018). Increasing caregivers' adherence to an early-literacy intervention improves the print knowledge of children with language impairment. *Journal of Autism and Developmental Disorders, 48*(12), 4179–4192.

Kaderavek, J. N., Paprzycki, P., Czerniak, C. M., Hapgood, S., Mentzer, G., Molitor, S., & Mendenhall, R. (2020). Longitudinal impact of early childhood science instruction on 5th grade science achievement. *International Journal of Science Education, 42*(7), 1124–1143.

Kamiyama, T., & Noro, F. (2020). Effectiveness of a tiered model of a family-centered parent training for the families of children with autism spectrum disorder. *Journal of Special Education Research, 8*(2), 41–52.

Kim, J. S., Asher, C. A., Burkhauser, M., Mesite, L., & Leyva, D. (2019). Using a Sequential Multiple Assignment Randomized Trial (SMART) to develop an adaptive K–2 literacy intervention with personalized print texts and app-based digital activities. *AERA Open, 5*(3), 1–18.

Knight, D. S., Landry, S., Zucker, T. A., Merz, E. C., Guttentag, C. L., & Taylor, H. B. (2019). Cost-effectiveness of early childhood interventions to enhance preschool: Evidence from a randomized experiment in Head Start Centers enrolling historically underserved populations. *Journal of Policy Analysis and Management, 38*(4), 891–917.

Landry, S. H., Assel, M., Williams, J., Zucker, T. A., Swank, P. R., Gunnewig, S., & Crawford, A. (2014). *The CIRCLE Progress Monitoring System technical manual.* University of Texas Health Science Center at Houston.

Landry, S. H., Smith, K. E., Swank, P. R., & Guttentag, C. (2008). A responsive parenting intervention: the optimal timing across early childhood for impacting maternal behaviors and child outcomes. *Developmental Psychology, 44*(5), 1335–1353.

Landry, S. H., Smith, K. E., Swank, P. R., Zucker, T., Crawford, A. D., & Solari, E. F. (2012). The effects of a responsive parenting intervention on parent–child interactions during shared book reading. *Developmental Psychology, 48*(4), 969–986.

Landry, S. H., Swank, P. R., Smith, K. E., Assel, M. A., & Gunnewig, S. B. (2006). Enhancing early literacy skills for preschool children: Bringing a professional development model to scale. *Journal of Learning Disabilities, 39*(4), 306–324.

Landry, S. H., & Zucker, T. (2020). Effects of home and classroom practices on language, cognitive, and social development of young Spanish-speaking English learners. Retrieved from *https://ies.ed.gov/funding/grantsearch/details.asp?id=4501.*

Landry, S. H., Zucker, T. A., Montroy, J. J., Hsu, H. Y., Assel, M. A., Varghese, C., . . . Feil, E. G. (2021). Replication of combined school readiness interventions for teachers and parents of Head Start pre-kindergarteners using remote delivery. *Early Childhood Research Quarterly, 56,* 149–166.

Landry, S. H., Zucker, T. A., Williams, J. M., Merz, E. C., Guttentag, C. L., & Taylor, H. B. (2017). Improving school readiness of high-risk preschoolers: Combining high quality instructional strategies with responsive training for teachers and parents. *Early Childhood Research Quarterly, 40,* 38–51.

Leyva, D., & Skorb, L. (2017). Food for thought: Family food routines and literacy in Latino kindergarteners. *Journal of Applied Developmental Psychology, 52,* 80–90.

Lonigan, C. J., & Phillips, B. M. (2016). Response to instruction in preschool: Results of two randomized studies with children at significant risk of reading difficulties. *Journal of Educational Psychology, 108*(1), 114–129.

McIntyre, L. L., & Phaneuf, L. K. (2008). A three-tier model of parent education in early childhood: Applying a problem-solving model. *Topics in Early Childhood Special Education, 27*(4), 214–222.

McWayne, C., Hampton, V., Fantuzzo, J., Cohen, H. L., & Sekino, Y. (2004). A multivariate examination of parent involvement and the social and academic competencies of urban kindergarten children. *Psychology in the Schools, 41*(3), 363–377.

Melai, G., Schick, A. R., & Scarola, L. (2019). Literacy interventions that promote home to-school links for ethnoculturally diverse families of young children. In C. M. McWayne, F. Doucet, & S. M. Sheridan (Eds.), *Ethnocultural diversity and the home-to-school link* (pp. 123–143). Springer International.

Mendelsohn, A. L., Huberman, H. S., Berkule, S. B., Brockmeyer, C. A., Morrow, L. M., & Dreyer, B. P. (2011). Primary care strategies for promoting parent–child interactions and school readiness in at-risk families: The Bellevue Project for Early Language, Literacy, and Education Success. *Archives of Pediatrics and Adolescent Medicine, 165*(1), 33–41.

Müller, L.-M., Howard, K., Wilson, E., Gibson, J., & Katsos, N. (2020). Bilingualism in the family and child well-being: A scoping review. *International Journal of Bilingualism, 24,* 1049–1070.

National Academies of Sciences, Engineering, and Medicine. (2017). *Promoting the educational success of children and youth learning English: Promising futures.* National Academies Press.

Neuman, S. B. (2017). The information book flood: Is additional exposure enough to support early literacy development? *Elementary School Journal, 118*(1), 1–27.

Nowak, C., & Heinrichs, N. (2008). A comprehensive meta-analysis of Triple P-Positive Parenting Program using hierarchical linear modeling: Effectiveness and moderating variables. *Clinical Child and Family Psychology Review, 11*(3), 114–144.

Paprzycki, P., Tuttle, N., Czerniak, C. M., Molitor, S., Kadervaek, J., & Mendenhall, R. (2017). The impact of a framework-aligned science professional development program on literacy and mathematics achievement of K–3 students. *Journal of Research in Science Teaching, 54*(9), 1174–1196.

Peterson, S. M., & French, L. (2008). Supporting young children's explanations through inquiry science in preschool. *Early Childhood Research Quarterly, 23*(3), 395–408.

Pullen, P. C., Tuckwiller, E. D., Konold, T. R., Maynard, K. L., & Coyne, M. D. (2010). A tiered intervention model for early vocabulary instruction: The effects of tiered instruction for young students at risk for reading disability. *Learning Disabilities Research and Practice, 25*(3), 110–123.

Reese, E., Leyva, D., Sparks, A., & Grolnick, W. (2010). Maternal elaborative reminiscing increases low-income children's narrative skills relative to dialogic reading. *Early Education and Development, 21*(3), 318–342.

Rivas-Drake, D., Seaton, E. K., Markstrom, C., Quintana, S., Syed, M., Lee, R. M., . . . Yip, T. (2014). Ethnic and racial identity in adolescence: Implications for psychosocial, academic, and health outcomes. *Child Development, 85*(1), 40–57.

Roberts, T. A. (2008). Home storybook reading in primary or second language with preschool children: Evidence of equal effectiveness for second-language vocabulary acquisition. *Reading Research Quarterly, 43*(2), 103–130.

Romo, H. D., Thomas, K. J. A., & García, E. E. (2018). Changing demographics of dual language learners and English learners: Implications for school success. *Social Policy Report, 31*(2), 1–35.

Sénéchal, M., & Young, L. (2008). The effect of family literacy interventions on children's acquisition of reading from kindergarten to grade 3: A meta-analytic review. *Review of Educational Research, 78*(4), 880–907.

Solari, E. J., Denton, C. A., Petscher, Y., & Haring, C. (2018). Examining the effects and feasibility of a teacher-implemented Tier 1 and Tier 2 intervention in word reading, fluency, and comprehension. *Journal of Research on Educational Effectiveness, 11*(2), 163–191.

Vygotsky, L. S. (2012). *Thought and language.* MIT Press.

Wasik, B. A., & Hindman, A. H. (2015). Talk alone won't close the 30-million word gap. *Phi Delta Kappan, 96,* 50–54.

Weingarten, Z., Zumeta Edmonds, R., & Arden, S. (2020). Better together: Using MTSS as a structure for building school–family partnerships. *TEACHING Exceptional Children, 53*(2), 122–130.

Weist, M. D., Garbacz, S. A., Lane, K. L., & Kincaid, D. (2017). *Aligning and integrating family engagement in Positive Behavioral Interventions and Supports (PBIS): Concepts and strategies for families and schools in key contexts* (Center for Positive Behavioral Interventions and Supports, funded by the Office of Special Education Programs, U.S. Department of Education). University of Oregon Press.

Welsh, J. A., Bierman, K. L., Nix, R. L., & Heinrichs, B. N. (2020). Sustained effects of a school readiness intervention: 5th grade outcomes of the Head Start REDI program. *Early Childhood Research Quarterly, 53,* 151–160.

Winsler, A., Kim, Y. K., & Richard, E. R. (2014). Socio-emotional skills, behavior problems, and Spanish competence predict the acquisition of English among English language learners in poverty. *Developmental Psychology, 50*(9), 2242–2254.

Zill, N., Resnick, G., Kim, K., O'Donnell, K., Sorongon, A., Ziv, Y., & Alva, S. (2000). Head Start Performance Measures Center, Family and Child Experiences Survey (FACES): Technical report. Retrieved from *www.acf.hhs.gov/opre/report/head-start-performance-measures-center-family-and-child-experiences-survey-faces-2000.*

Zucker, T. A., Cabell, S. Q., Petscher, Y., Mui, H., Landry, S. H., & Tock, J. (2021). Teaching Together: Pilot study of a tiered language and literacy intervention with Head Start teachers and linguistically diverse families. *Early Childhood Research Quarterly, 54,* 136–152.

Zucker, T. A., Maldonado, G. Y., Assel, M., McCallum, C., Elias, C., Swint, J. M., & Lal, L. (2022). Informal science, technology, engineering, and math learning conditions to increase parent involvement with young children experiencing poverty. *Frontiers in Psychology, 13.*

Zucker, T. A., Solari, E. J., Landry, S. H., & Swank, P. R. (2013). Effects of a brief tiered language intervention for pre-kindergartners at risk. *Early Education and Development, 24*(3), 366–392.

CHAPTER 23

Family Engagement for Early Literacy

Interventions That Promote Family-School Partnerships

Karalynn E. Brown and Susan M. Sheridan

Young children's language and literacy skills are foundational for academic achievement in elementary school and beyond, setting the stage for successful outcomes later in life. It is now generally understood that young children's development, including the development of language and early literacy skills, does not occur in isolation. Rather, myriad experiences in their immediate home and preschool environments, and interactions between them, are influential in supporting children's acquisition and use of early language and literacy skills. Partnerships established among adults across environments create a unique system of support that positions children for positive developmental trajectories (Christenson & Sheridan, 2001). A family–school partnership approach invites families to collaborate equally with school personnel in meeting children's needs (Kim & Sheridan, 2015). Among a number of programs, two empirically supported interventions that utilize a family–school partnership approach to enhance children's outcomes include conjoint behavioral consultation (CBC; Sheridan & Kratochwill, 2007) and Getting Ready (Sheridan, Marvin, Knoche, & Edwards, 2008). This chapter reviews the links between family engagement and early literacy, describes and situates CBC and Getting Ready in the literature, and presents several research directions that will enhance the current understanding of family–school partnerships for early literacy.

Family Engagement

Benefits of Family Engagement

Family engagement in children's education is a multifaceted construct (Fantuzzo, McWayne, Perry, & Childs, 2004). It generally involves actions taken by parents to support their child's learning, including actions at home, at school, and in collaboration with their children's educators. The literature on family engagement in children's education is replete with examples and evidence of its importance in establishing conditions for children's academic success (cf. Brotman et al., 2013; Bierman, Welsh, Heinrichs, Nix, & Mathis, 2015). One meta-synthesis, integrating the results of nine meta-analyses, found positive relationships between parental engagement and children's academic achievement across studies (Wilder, 2014). More nuanced research has uncovered aspects of engagement that are most robustly linked to student academic achievement. In a meta-analysis synthesizing outcomes across 117 intervention studies and 592 total effect sizes, Smith, Sheridan, Kim, Park, and Beretvas (2020) found those that utilized home-based activities (e.g., interactive book reading), communication with parents, and collaboration between parents and teachers led to significant improvements in children's academic outcomes. Similarly, Jeynes (2012) found that children had better academic outcomes when their parents participated in engagement programs that included shared reading activities, partnerships between parents and teachers, checking homework, and parent–teacher communication.

Early Family Engagement

Family engagement in early childhood can set the stage for children's positive development later on in life. Indeed, early parental engagement has been found to predict children's readiness for kindergarten (Barnett, Paschall, Mastergeorge, Cutshaw, & Warren, 2020), academic success in subsequent grades (Froiland, Peterson, & Davison, 2013), later motivation (Hayakawa, Englund, Warner-Richter, & Reynolds, 2013), and educational attainment (Gottfried, Schlackman, Gottfried, & Boutin-Martinez, 2015). As young children prepare to enter formal learning environments, they may experience varying levels of cognitive and social–emotional readiness for the challenges that await them. However, readiness also encompasses the degree to which significant systems (e.g., schools, homes) are prepared for children's transition to school (Sheridan et al., 2008). Sheridan and colleagues define readiness as "the capabilities of children, families, and practicing professionals that promote positive and adaptive student outcomes in formal and informal educational settings" (Sheridan, Knoche, Edwards, Bovaird, & Kupzyk, 2010, p. 126). These many influential actors—and the relationships among them—are crucial in establishing young children's readiness for formal education.

Family engagement practices that promote literacy readiness may vary according to children's developmental level. In early childhood, parents engage with their child by interacting in warm, sensitive, and responsive ways; supporting their child's emerging autonomy in a developmentally appropriate manner; and participating actively and meaningfully in their child's learning (Edwards, Sheridan, & Knoche, 2010; Sheridan et al., 2008). Participating in learning, in particular, encompasses the myriad things parents do to intentionally support their child's acquisition of knowledge and skills that are important in becoming an independent learner (e.g., engaging in conversation, encouraging problem solving). Opportunities provided in children's natural environments, including language-rich interactions between parents and their young child (Moody, Baker, & Blacher, 2018), shared and dyadic experiences around print (Mol, Bus, de Jong, & Smeets, 2008), and warm and responsive parenting practices (Knoche, Boise, Sheridan, & Cheng, in press; Sheridan et al., 2008) contribute to children's language and literacy readiness.

Family–School Partnerships

Myriad terms have been used interchangeably in the educational literature to capture the construct of family engagement in children's learning. However, conceptual and practical distinctions between engagement approaches are apparent (Kim & Sheridan, 2015). Discussions of parent *involvement* emphasize the form or structure of activities demonstrated by parents to provide support for their child's education (i.e., "what parents do"; Fischel & Ramirez, 2005). Some activities may occur at school (e.g., attending parent–teacher conferences or school events, volunteering in the classroom, or becoming involved in the parent–teacher association) whereas others occur at home (e.g., talking with the child about school, reading with the child, or taking the child to the library) (Fantuzzo et al., 2004). Oftentimes, parent involvement activities are directed by educators and intended to instruct parents in particular practices that support school-determined goals.

An alternative approach for engaging with families is through *partnership*. Family–school partnerships represent a particular form of engagement wherein parents and educators "cooperate, coordinate, and collaborate to enhance opportunities and success for children and adolescents across social, emotional, behavioral, and academic domains" (Kim & Sheridan, 2015, p. 5). Distinct from an involvement paradigm that focuses on the structural features of parents' roles (e.g., strategies they use or activities they attend), family–school partnerships emphasize the interpersonal relationships between parents and early childhood educators who are jointly responsible for children's development. Partnership approaches are often grounded in ecological systems theory (Bronfenbrenner, 1977), which posits that children develop dynamically within a series of overlapping and interactional spheres of influence. The *mesosystem,* or connections between home and school, provides a context that supports learning when there is continuity and coordination among them.

From a partnership perspective, optimal

learning occurs when the roles of family members and educators are clear, and when goals and outcomes are seen as the joint responsibility shared by parents and teachers (Christenson & Sheridan, 2001). Whereas parent involvement is concerned primarily with distinct and separate (albeit important) actions for parents and teachers, family–school partnerships are characterized by reciprocal relationships, bidirectional communication, constructive connections, and complementary roles among home and school systems to promote positive outcomes for children and youth (Christenson & Sheridan, 2001). Partnering with families implies that school personnel reach out to families by inviting them into the partnership and supporting them in ways that enhance their child's learning. Thus, parents are engaged as partners in educational programming and support services (McKay & Bannon, 2004).

Characteristics of effective partnerships include active and mutual participation and cooperation among participants, sensitivity and responsiveness toward one another, and acknowledgment and reinforcement of participants' skills and competencies (Jeynes, 2012; Sheridan, Rispoli, & Holmes, 2014). Garbacz, Swanger-Gagné, and Sheridan (2015) offered a multidimensional framework in an attempt to operationalize the elements most salient in family–school partnerships programs. The five main components specify that in partnerships (1) the roles of educators and family members reflect their shared responsibility for promoting the child's learning and development, (2) family members and educators engage in joint work, (3) the nature of interactions between educators and family members is collaborative, (4) both home and school are potential contexts for intervention activities, and (5) there is open communication allowing for bidirectional flow of information.

Why Family-School Partnerships for Early Literacy?

Family engagement has value in promoting positive outcomes and literacy readiness in young children; however, approaches to engagement vary. While a family involvement paradigm involves early childhood educators directing parents' engagement with their child, a partnership approach emphasizes co-creation of educational environments and cross-systemic interactions that promote readiness (Kim & Sheridan, 2015).

The Division for Early Childhood (2014) of the Council for Expectational Children and the Office of Head Start (U.S. Department of Health and Human Services, 2018) recognize families as essential partners in the education of young children. However, family–school partnerships may be difficult to construct, especially when children present with significant difficulties (Sheridan et al., 2012). The following sections present two examples of empirically supported family–school partnership interventions that have implications for early childhood settings.

Family-School Partnership Interventions

Conjoint Behavioral Consultation

CBC (also known as Teachers and Parents as Partners [TAPP]; Sheridan & Kratochwill, 2007) is a family–school partnership intervention that engages parents and teachers in a collaborative problem-solving process to address a student's behavioral, academic, or social–emotional difficulties. CBC/TAPP's aims include enhancing the student's functioning, promoting meaningful parent engagement, and strengthening relationships between home and school contexts (Sheridan & Kratochwill, 2007). TAPP/CBC is an indirect service delivery model whereby a trained consultant works with participating teachers and parents who share responsibility for a student with an identified concern (Sheridan & Kratochwill, 2007).

As part of the intervention process, a CBC/TAPP consultant leads a teacher and parent(s) through an 8-week intervention process that comprises a series of three structured meetings across four distinct stages. These stages are identifying student needs, analyzing needs and developing an intervention plan, implementing the plan, and evaluating the plan's effectiveness (Sheridan & Kratochwill, 2007). Specific outcome objectives are accomplished at each stage of the CBC/TAPP intervention; Table 23.1 lists these objectives. In addition to the meetings, the consultant facilitates semistructured contacts with teacher and parent participants to maintain their collaboration between meetings (Sheridan & Kratochwill, 2007). CBC/TAPP's focus on encouraging meaningful parent engagement, and increasing partnerships between home and school necessitates a relationship-building approach that is woven into all stages of the process (Sheridan & Kratochwill, 2007). In order to meet these goals, TAPP/CBC includes several essential relationship-building objectives, listed in Table 23.1. These relationship objectives help the TAPP/CBC consultant model and foster positive, strengths-based interactions between parents and teachers throughout the process.

Effects and Mechanisms of CBC

A preponderance of evidence indicates that CBC/TAPP has the potential to enhance the outcomes of young children. Two randomized controlled trials (RCTs) have examined the effects of participating in CBC/TAPP on young children and their parents and teachers. The first study, involving children in grades K–3 with disruptive behaviors, found that children who participated in the intervention experienced decreases in problem behaviors (Sheridan, Ryoo, Garbacz, Kunz, & Chumney, 2013) and increases in adaptive and social skills

(Sheridan et al., 2012). For these children, level of family socioeconomic risk moderated intervention efficacy, such that children with more risk factors experienced greater decreases in problem behaviors than children with less risk (Sheridan et al., 2013). Another RCT examined the effects of participating in CBC/TAPP on children in grades K–3 living in rural communities. Compared to peers not in the CBC/TAPP group, children who were part of the CBC/TAPP intervention demonstrated greater decreases in teacher-reported school problems and observed off-task behaviors, and more substantial increases in parent-reported and observed adaptive behaviors (Sheridan, Witte, Holmes, Coutts, et al., 2017; Sheridan, Witte, Holmes, Wu, et al., 2017). Some of these gains were maintained 1 year after the intervention ended (Sheridan, Witte, Wheeler, et al., 2019).

As an indirect intervention delivery model, CBC/TAPP involves parents and teachers assum-

TABLE 23.1. CBC/TAPP Stages and Objectives

Outcome Objectives	
Stage	Objectives
Conjoint Needs Identification ("Building on Strengths")	• Clarify the strengths and goals of the student, family, and teacher. • Specifically define the child's identified concern or need in behavioral terms. • Establish a method for collecting baseline data about the identified concern across settings.
Conjoint Needs Analysis/ Plan Development ("Planning for Success")	• Analyze the baseline data collected at home and school, including exploring trends. • Discuss the function, conditions, and skill needs that may be contributing to the identified concern. • Develop intervention procedures at home and school based on the information discussed. • Provide training and materials as needed to carry out the intervention.
Plan Implementation	• Implement the intervention plan in the home and school settings. • Assess the degree to which parents and teachers are able to implement the intervention as intended. • Continue monitoring the student's behavior.
Conjoint Plan Evaluation ("Checking and Reconnecting")	• Establish whether the intervention was successful and joint goals were met. • Decide whether to continue, modify, or terminate the intervention plan. • Discuss whether further meetings are needed and how to continue the parent-teacher partnership.
Relationship objectives	
	• Enhance communication and understanding among parents and teachers. • Encourage shared responsibility for the child's education and the intervention process. • Facilitate perspective taking on the part of all participants. • Focus on positive aspects of the intervention process. • Highlight connections and consistencies between the home and school settings. • Increase shared commitment to the education of the child. • Model openness to other parties' unique strengths and experiences.

Note. Objectives based on Sheridan and Kratochwill (2007). Copyright © 2007 Springer Science+Business Media, LLC.

ing the responsibility for implementing the behavioral intervention plan. Therefore, several studies have examined the intervention's effects on participating teachers and parents. Reports from both RCTs indicated that participating in CBC/TAPP led to increases in parents' and teachers' reports of their relationship quality and communication compared to those who did not participate (Sheridan et al., 2012, 2013; Sheridan, Witte, Holmes, Coutts, et al., 2017; Sheridan, Witte, Holmes, Wu, et al., 2017). Additionally, multiple studies indicate that participating parents and teachers had greater competence for solving problems after the intervention period than their counterparts (Sheridan et al., 2013, 2018; Sheridan, Witte, Holmes, Wu, et al., 2017). Finally, CBC/TAPP can impact the strategies teachers and parents use to respond to the children in their care. Participating teachers self-reported and demonstrated increased appropriate classroom strategy use (Sheridan et al., 2018), and participating parents reported using more effective parenting strategies after intervention (Sheridan, Witte, Holmes, Wu, et al., 2017), relative to nonparticipating teachers.

Enhanced parent–teacher relationships and problem-solving skills represent key mechanisms for explaining the change that occurs as part of the CBC/TAPP intervention process. Through CBC/TAPP, teachers establish stronger relationships with parents, which leads to improvements in children's behavioral outcomes (Sheridan et al., 2012; Sheridan, Witte, Holmes, Coutts, et al., 2017; Sheridan, Witte, Holmes, Wu, et al., 2017). Teachers also learn to be more effective problem solvers as part of the TAPP/CBC process, which is partially responsible for their improved strategy use; that is, increased problem-solving competence partially explains improvements in classroom practices that occurred as a function of the intervention (Sheridan et al., 2018). Taken together, these mechanisms echo the key aims of the CBC/TAPP, which include improving the outcomes of children, enhancing parent engagement, and building home–school partnerships (Sheridan & Kratochwill, 2007).

Implications for Early Literacy

CBC/TAPP is applicable to a variety of presenting concerns within home and school environments (Sheridan & Kratochwill, 2007). It has been shown to enhance the social–behavioral functioning of young children, which can facili-

tate learning both immediately (Schmitt, Pratt, & McClelland., 2014) and over time (Breslau et al., 2009). Indeed, the CBC/TAPP process may lay the foundation for academic and literacy success. One study examined how CBC/TAPP impacted the academic behaviors of a small number of students with symptoms of attention deficit/hyperactivity disorder. Relative to controls, CBC/TAPP students demonstrated significant increases in their teacher-rated academic skills and productivity (Murray, Rabiner, Schulte, & Newitt, 2008).

Additionally, CBC/TAPP has been shown to enrich the quality of the parent–teacher relationship, an aspect of parental engagement that has been linked to improved academic achievement for young children (Jeynes, 2012; Smith et al., 2020). Participating in CBC/TAPP has been found to enhance the skills of teachers and parents for responding to children in a positive manner. If parents and teachers respond appropriately to young children, they may be more likely to engage them in the types of interactions (e.g., Cabell, Justice, McGinty, DeCoster, & Forston, 2015; Moody et al., 2018) that set the stage for literacy development. Therefore, family–school partnership interventions such as CBC/TAPP have much to offer in facilitating contexts and cross-context interactions that promote early literacy.

Getting Ready

Another intervention the leverages the power of family–school partnerships is Getting Ready (Sheridan et al., 2008), designed for use in early childhood settings. Getting Ready has its foundations in conjoint consultation models (Sheridan & Kratochwill, 2007), as well as triadic consultation—a model that supports the competencies of parents for responding appropriately to their young child through consultation with professionals (McCollum & Yates, 1994). The purpose of Getting Ready is to promote the readiness of children from birth through age 5 and their caregivers through relationships with early childhood educators (Sheridan et al., 2008). In order to accomplish this, early childhood educators (1) guide parents to engage in interactions with their child that are marked by warmth, support for autonomy, and engagement in learning, and (2) build collaborative, strengths-based relationships with parents around enhancing children's outcomes (Sheridan et al., 2008). Getting Ready offers early childhood professionals a flexible set of strategies that can be adapted to a variety of scenarios in which they serve young children and their families, such as parent–teacher conferences or home visits (Marvin, Moen, Knoche, & Sheridan, 2020). Table 23.2 lists these strategies and their definitions.

Effects of Getting Ready

One RCT has examined the effects of participating in Getting Ready over 2 years on children experiencing low income and economic marginalization (LIEM) and participating in Head Start or Early Head Start preschool programs. Teachers of children and families assigned to the treatment condition received professional development and coaching in implementing Getting Ready when engaging in home visits with families; those in the control condition received professional development that was child-focused (Sheridan, Knoche, Kupzyk, Edwards, & Mar-

vin, 2011). Results of this study indicated that Getting Ready was associated with a variety of positive outcomes among the participating children over time. These included greater increases in teacher ratings of their oral language, reading, and writing skills over the study period (Sheridan et al., 2011), as well as teacher ratings of social–emotional skills (Sheridan, Knoche, Edwards, Bovaird, & Kupzyk, 2010).

Moderation analyses revealed that children participating in Getting Ready who experienced developmental delays, and who did not speak English, demonstrated more language growth than their peers through the study period (Sheridan et al., 2011). Additionally, children who had more than one parent in the home, whose parent had at least a general equivalency degree (GED), and whose parent did not have personal health stressors benefited more in terms of language and literacy development (Sheridan et al., 2011). A second RCT examined how Getting Ready functions in a sample of preschool-age children with delays in one or more areas. Within this

TABLE 23.2. Getting Ready Strategies

Strategy	Definition
1. Communicate openly and clearly	• Engage in conversations and discussions rather than reporting information. • Use open-ended questions and active listening to encourage parent input.
2. Encourage parent–child interactions	• Encourage the parent to interact with the child for shared observation, reflection, and/or practice.
3. Affirm parent competencies	• Reinforce the parent's ideas, actions, and insights on their child's needs and development.
4. Make mutual joint decisions	• Set goals and priorities, and decide on approaches, based on shared values and perspectives.
5. Focus parent's attention	• Highlight the child's strengths, needs, or the effects of parent's actions.
6. Use observation and data to explain child's development	• Observe the child at play or when engaged in daily routines, and discuss the meaning of these observations with parents. • Use recent data and observations to guide planning and reporting.
7. Share developmental information and resources	• Label, interpret, and explain the child's behaviors developmentally. • Provide guides to developmentally appropriate expectations and activities.
8. Model, suggest, and practice	• If necessary, demonstrate an action or wording. • Suggest minor adjustments in parent's actions or ideas. • Invite the parent to practice these ideas in the moment, while providing useful feedback to ensure understanding.

Note. Adapted from Marvin, Knoche, and Sheridan (2020, p. 41). Copyright ©2019 Division for Early Childhood.

sample, participating in the intervention led to increases in children's expressive language skills over 2 years, but only for families that reported low stress and low initial levels of home-based involvement (Knoche et al., in press). Therefore, Getting Ready may be maximally effective at enhancing the literacy readiness of children with developmental delays when parents engage little with their child at home and experience few contextual stressors.

Consistent with Getting Ready's goal of enhancing parent–child interactions, parents who participate in Getting Ready have demonstrated parenting behaviors that are associated with positive child development. For parents of children enrolled in Early Head Start home programming, those who received the Getting Ready intervention demonstrated more quality interactions with their children (marked by warmth and autonomy support) than control parents (Knoche et al., 2012). Early childhood educators who participate in the interventions have also demonstrated behavioral changes. Teachers receiving the intervention discussed goals and plans with parents at a higher rate than did their peers, a behavior that was associated with parent engagement in visits (Knoche, Marvin, & Sheridan, 2015). Participating educators who received Getting Ready training and coaching demonstrated more use of the intervention strategies than their counterparts and were typically able to implement strategies with fidelity (Knoche, Sheridan, Edwards, & Osborn, 2010).

Implications for Early Literacy

Getting Ready has clear implications for young children's early literacy and language development. It has been shown to enhance early childhood educators' partnership-building skills with families, as well as families' improved abilities to engage with their children in ways that facilitate positive development. The intervention's significant effects on children's social–emotional and literacy readiness demonstrate the benefits of early childhood educators engaging in partnerships with their students' families. For children who experience developmental delays, these strategies may be especially impactful. Getting Ready's documented impacts on children, families, and teachers demonstrate the immense potential for family–school partnership interventions to build literacy readiness in early childhood.

Future Research Directions

There is now ample evidence that parent engagement and family–school partnership intervention programs are efficacious at enhancing language and literacy outcomes for young children. Beyond determining effects on children's development, a number of emerging research directions are in need of attention. These include a need for deeper understandings of how (1) family voice and perspective, especially the perspectives of minoritized family members, can be fully integrated into partnership programs; (2) programs tested in controlled research settings (e.g., using RCTs) can be integrated naturally into settings such as families' homes and educational programs; and (3) partnership practices and effects vary over time.

Ensuring Family Voice and Perspective

The basic tenets of partnerships, such as shared responsibility, collaboration, mutuality, and responsivity, can only be realized if there is co-equality among participants. Co-equal rights and status in the parent–teacher partnership may be achievable for some, but it remains highly aspirational for minoritized families who remain oppressed in schools and other societal systems (Sheridan & Garbacz, 2021). Indeed, schools in the United States reflect White, middle-class values and expectations (Doucet, 2011). They are part of a larger racialized society wherein socioeconomic, health and health care, housing, and education inequities exist (Delgado, 1995; Iruka et al., Chapter 29, this volume). Thus, as long as macro-level racist oppressions continue to impinge on the experiences of families who are Black, Indigenous, and people of color (BIPOC), true partnerships may be unachievable. In short, because "the macrosystem of the United States is racialized, so [too must be] the conversation about family–school partnerships . . . necessitat[ing] acknowledgment of social stratification mechanisms (e.g., racism, discrimination) that are part of a racialized society" (Sanders & Molgaard, 2019, p. 20).

Research investigating the implementation and effects of family–school partnerships may be at a crossroads. Whereas a growing literature is now honing definitions of family engagement to differentiate between involvement and partnership orientations (e.g., Kim & Sheridan, 2015), much less attention has been given to the parents (and their race, culture, values, and experiences) who have an essential role in the partnership. It is critical that partnership researchers adopt a social justice orientation and approach their work in ways that are genuine and accessible to minoritized families (Miranda & Radliff, 2016; Powell & Coles, 2021), centering their voices and understanding their perspectives as primary foci of research agendas (Sheridan & Garbacz, 2021). Unless and until this is made a priority in partnership research, findings and conclusions will be irrelevant for a significant percentage of families and schools.

Translation from Research to Practice

Aligned with understanding families' perspectives is the need to discern methods for translating what we have learned from empirical studies into structures and practices that support real-world challenges. Indeed, one of the goals of partnership intervention research is to impact practice, so that efficacious programs, interventions, and strategies are accessible in natural settings (e.g., homes, schools). Research such as that summarized in this chapter relies on highly controlled experimental settings but often fails to account for the complexities that arise when implementation moves to naturalistic settings. Contextual factors such as daily structures and routines, available resources (e.g., human, financial, material), local policies, historical precedent, and myriad other considerations may facilitate or impede the capacity for implementation (i.e., uptake) of family–school partnership interventions in unknown ways. Because *efficacy* (evidence of desired effects) and *implementation* (uptake of intervention in desired practice settings) "set a ceiling for real-world impact" (Cook & Odom, 2013, p. 139), simultaneous documentation of efficacy and attention to implementation is critical in our understanding of what works. Fundamentally, this means that the effects derived in studies like those summarized herein may or may not be realized when removed from the experimental context and transported into practice sites.

To address the gap between evidence-based programs and practices in early childhood settings, researchers should aim to build "real-world" evidence by focusing from the outset on the unique structural, contextual, cultural, and interpersonal realities of early childhood educational programs (Sheridan et al., 2020). Building

real-world evidence requires an approach characterized by a reciprocal and dynamic relationship between research and practice (Kratochwill et al., 2012). Involving key parties in the research process can help researchers examine factors that influence capacity for implementation (e.g., structural or organizational variables) and decisions to commit to the various principles of partnerships (e.g., collaborating, two-way information sharing, mutual decision making). Modifying partnership programs can be based on the information gathered to ensure programs align with the needs of specific families and educators. A practice-based evidence framework (Kratochwill et al., 2012) involves practitioners providing information during intervention implementation to complement traditional experimental research methods, uncovering strategies that may need revision, and elucidating the effects of natural variations in partnership programs on targeted outcomes.

Temporal Aspects of Family–School Partnership Research

One finding from the research summarized herein is that partnership-based interventions effectively strengthen relationships between parents and educators at a point in time. Given the myriad studies pointing to the benefits of partnerships, it seems particularly important to understand processes or factors that may promote the maintenance of partnerships over time, for example, from one program or grade level to the next. By design, family–school partnerships are transient; the partners, and thus the relationships, change as children progress through the schooling process. It is generally understood that family involvement practices (e.g., school-based involvement) decrease from preschool to kindergarten and into the elementary years (Sheridan, Koziol, Witte, Iruka, & Knoche, 2019). However, family–school partnership approaches, focusing on relationships versus activities, may assume different patterns and produce unique benefits over time. As children develop, different approaches, strategies, and practices may produce differential effects. There is a need to elucidate personal and contextual factors that support the generalization and maintenance of family–school partnerships over development, grade level, and changing parent–teacher relationships. A related question concerns not only the effects of partnerships on children's learning at one point in time but also the effect of cumulative partnerships on children's development over multiple years. Statistical analyses and methods that model temporal and contextual variation of partnership practices within the natural schooling sequence, and their cumulative effects, are necessary.

Conclusion

Decades of research attest to the value of families in promoting children's academic skills, including skills in literacy and language. Indeed, engagement is pivotal to the academic outcomes of children at all stages of development. In the early years, families set the stage for early literacy development by promoting children's autonomy, showing warmth and sensitivity, and participating in their learning (Edwards et al., 2010). Family engagement is conceptually broad, but several specific approaches exist. Educators who take a family–school partnership approach collaborate and build relationships with families rather than prescribing how they should engage with their child (Christenson & Sheridan, 2001). Two interventions that use a family–school partnership approach include conjoint behavioral consultation (Sheridan & Kratochwill, 2007) and Getting Ready (Sheridan et al., 2008). Both interventions have solid empirical foundations to enhance the functioning of young children, while also boosting the capacity of their parents and teachers to respond to them in ways that facilitate the development of early literacy skills. Much is known about the power of family–school partnerships for early literacy, but more understanding is needed in several key areas. These include attending to questions of social justice when engaging BIPOC families in partnership, translating family–school partnership research to authentic practice settings, and understanding the trajectories of family–school partnerships over time.

Acknowledgments

The research reported herein was supported by the Institute of Education Sciences, U.S. Department of Education, Grant Nos. R324A160017 and R324A120153 (Susan M. Sheridan, Principal Investigator). The opinions expressed are those of the authors and do not represent views of the Institute or the U.S. Department of Education.

References

Barnett, M. A., Paschall, K. W., Mastergeorge, A. M., Cutshaw, C. A., & Warren, S. M. (2020). Influences of parent engagement in early childhood education centers and the home on kindergarten school readiness. *Early Childhood Research Quarterly, 53,* 260–273.

Bierman, K. L., Welsh, J., Heinrichs, B. S., Nix, R. L., & Mathis, E. T. (2015). Helping Head Start parents promote their children's kindergarten adjustment: The REDI parent program. *Child Development, 86,* 177–189.

Breslau, J., Miller, E., Breslau, N., Bohnert, K., Lucia, V., & Schweitzer, J. (2009). The impact of early behavior disturbances on academic achievement in high school. *Pediatrics, 123*(6), 1472–1476.

Bronfenbrenner, U. (1977). Toward an experimental ecology of human development. *American Psychologist, 32*(7), 513–531.

Brotman, L., Dawson-McClure, S., Calzada, E., Huang, K., Kamboukos, D., Palamar, J., & Petkova, E. (2013). Cluster (school) RCT of ParentCorps: Impact on kindergarten academic achievement. *Pediatrics, 131*(5), e1521–e1529.

Cabell, S. Q., Justice, L. M., McGinty, A. S., DeCoster, J., & Forston, L. D. (2015). Teacher-child conversations in preschool classrooms: Contributions to children's vocabulary development. *Early Childhood Research Quarterly, 30,* 80–92.

Christenson, S. L., & Sheridan, S. M. (2001). *Schools and families: Creating essential connections for learning.* Guilford Press.

Cook, B. G., & Odom, S. L. (2013). Evidence-based practices and implementation science in special education. *Exceptional Child, 79*(3), 135–144.

Delgado, R. (1995). *Critical race theory: The cutting edge.* Temple University Press.

Division for Early Childhood. (2014). DEC recommended practices in early intervention/early childhood special education 2014. Retrieved from *www.dec-sped.org/dec-recommended-practices.*

Doucet, F. (2011). Parent involvement as ritualized practice. *Anthropology and Education Quarterly, 42*(4), 404–421.

Edwards, C. P., Sheridan, S. M., & Knoche, L. (2010). Parent–child relationships in early learning. In E. Baker, P. Peterson, & B. McGaw (Eds.), *International Encyclopedia of Education,* (Vol. 5, pp. 438–443). Elsevier.

Fantuzzo, J., McWayne, C., Perry, M. A., & Childs, S. (2004). Multiple dimensions of family involvement and their relations to behavioral and learning competencies for urban, low-income children. *School Psychology Review, 33,* 467–480.

Fishel, M., & Ramirez, L. (2005). Evidence-based

parent involvement interventions with schoolaged children. *School Psychology Quarterly, 20,* 371–402.

Froiland, J. M., Peterson, A., & Davison, M. L. (2013). The long-term effects of early parent involvement and parent expectation in the USA. *School Psychology International, 34*(1), 33–50.

Garbacz, S. A., Swanger-Gagné, M. S., & Sheridan, S. M. (2015). The role of school–family partnership programs for promoting student SEL. In J. A. Durlak, C. E. Domitrovich, R. P. Weissberg, & T. P. Gullotta (Eds.), *Handbook of social and emotional learning* (pp. 244–260). Guilford Press.

Gottfried, A. W., Schlackman, J., Gottfried, A. E., & Boutin-Martinez, A. S. (2015). Parental provision of early literacy environment as related to reading and educational outcomes across the academic lifespan. *Parenting, 15*(1), 24–38.

Hayakawa, M., Englund, M. M., Warner-Richter, M. N., & Reynolds, A. J. (2013). The longitudinal process of early parent involvement on student achievement: A path analysis. *NHSA Dialog, 16*(1), 103–126.

Jeynes, W. (2012). A meta-analysis of the efficacy of different types of parental involvement programs for urban students. *Urban Education, 47*(4), 706–742.

Kim, E. M., & Sheridan, S. M. (2015). Foundational aspects of family–school connections: Definitions, conceptual frameworks, and research needs. In S. M. Sheridan & E. M. Kim (Eds.), *Research on family–school partnerships: An interdisciplinary examination of state of the science and critical needs* (Vol. 1, pp. 1–14). Springer.

Knoche, L. L., Boise, C. E., Sheridan, S. M., & Cheng, K. (in press). Promoting expressive language skills for preschool children with developmental concerns: Effects of a parent–educator partnership intervention. *Elementary School Journal.*

Knoche, L. L., Edwards, C. P., Sheridan, S. M., Kupzyk, K. A., Marvin, C. A., Cline, K. D., & Clarke, B. L. (2012). Getting ready: Results of a randomized trial of a relationship-focused intervention on the parent–infant relationship in rural early Head Start. *Infant Mental Health Journal, 33*(5), 439–458.

Knoche, L. L., Marvin, C. A., & Sheridan, S. M. (2015). Strategies to support parent engagement during home visits in Early Head Start and Head Start. *Dialog, 18*(1), 19–42.

Knoche, L. L., Sheridan, S. M., Edwards, C. P., & Osborn, A. Q. (2010). Implementation of a relationship-based school readiness intervention: A multidimensional approach to fidelity measurement for early childhood. *Early Childhood Research Quarterly, 25,* 299–313.

Kratochwill, T. R., Hoagwood, K. E., Kazak, A. E.,

Weisz, J. R., Hood, K., Vargas, L. A., & Banez, G. A. (2012). Practice-based evidence for children and adolescents: Advancing the research agenda in schools. *School Psychology Review, 41,* 215–235.

Marvin, C. A., Moen, A. L., Knoche, L. L., & Sheridan, S. M. (2020). Getting Ready strategies for promoting parent–professional relationships and parent–child interactions. *Young Exceptional Children, 23*(1), 36–51.

McCollum, J. A., & Yates, T. J. (1994). Dyad as focus, triad as means: A family-centered approach to supporting parent–child interactions. *Infants and Young Children, 6*(4), 54–63.

McKay, M. M., & Bannon, W. M., Jr. (2004). Engaging families in child mental health services. *Child and Adolescent Psychiatric Clinics of North America, 13,* 905–921.

Miranda, A. H., & Radliff, K. M. (2016). Consulting with a social justice mind-set. In A. H. Miranda (Ed.), *Consultation across cultural contexts: Consultee-centered case studies* (pp. 13–22). Routledge.

Mol, W. E., Bus, A. G., de Jong, M. T., & Smeets, D. J. H. (2008). Added value of dialogic parent–child book readings: A meta-analysis. *Early Education and Development, 19*(1), 7–26.

Moody, C. T., Baker, B. L., & Blacher, J. (2018). Contribution of parenting to complex syntax development in preschool children with developmental delays or typical development. *Journal of Intellectual Disability Research, 62*(7), 604–616.

Murray, D. W., Rabiner, D., Schulte, A., & Newitt, K. (2008). Feasibility and integrity of a parent–teacher consultation intervention for ADHD students. *Child and Youth Care Forum, 37*(3), 111–126.

Powell, T., & Coles, J. A. (2021). "We still here": Black mothers' personal narratives of sense making and resisting antiblackness and the suspensions of their Black children. *Race, Ethnicity and Education, 24*(1), 76–95.

Sanders, K., & Molgaard, M. (2019). Considering race within early childhood education: A misunderstood and underexplored element of family–school partnerships in child care. In C. M. McWayne, F. Doucet, & S. M. Sheridan (Eds.), *Ethnocultural diversity and the home-to-school link* (pp. 19–36). Springer.

Schmitt, S. A., Pratt, M. E., & McClelland, M. M. (2014). Examining the validity of behavioral self-regulation tools in predicting preschoolers' academic achievement. *Early Education and Development, 25*(5), 641–660.

Sheridan, S. M., Bovaird, J. A., Glover, T. A., Garbacz, S. A., Witte, A., & Kwon, K. (2012). A randomized trial examining the effects of conjoint behavioral consultation and the mediating role of the parent–teacher relationship. *School Psychology Review, 41*(1), 23–46.

Sheridan, S. M., Fernandez, V. A., Knoche, L., Stacks, A. M., Van Horne, B. S., Bouza, J., . . . EHS Parent–Teacher Intervention Consortium. (2020). Building a real-world evidence base for improving child and family outcomes. *Journal of Applied Research on Children, 11*(1), Article 11.

Sheridan, S. M., & Garbacz, S. A. (2021, August). Centering families: Advancing a new paradigm for school psychology. *School Psychology Review.*

Sheridan, S. M., Knoche, L. L., Edwards, C. P., Bovaird, J. A., & Kupzyk, K. A. (2010). Parent engagement and school readiness: Effects of the Getting Ready intervention on preschool children's social–emotional competencies. *Early Education and Development, 21*(1), 125–156.

Sheridan, S. M., Knoche, L. L., Kupzyk, K. A., Edwards, C. P., & Marvin, C. A. (2011). A randomized trial examining the effects of parent engagement on early language and literacy: The Getting Ready intervention. *Journal of School Psychology, 49*(3), 361–383.

Sheridan, S. M., Koziol, N., Witte, A. L., Iruka, I., & Knoche, L. L. (2019). Longitudinal and geographic trends in family engagement during the pre-kindergarten to kindergarten transition. *Early Childhood Education Journal, 48*, 365–377.

Sheridan, S. M., & Kratochwill, T. R. (2007). *Conjoint behavioral consultation: Promoting family–school connections and interventions* (2nd ed.). Springer Science + Business Media.

Sheridan, S. M., Marvin, C. A., Knoche, L. L., & Edwards, C. P. (2008). Getting Ready: Promoting school readiness through a relationship-based partnership model. *Early Childhood Services, 2*, 149–172.

Sheridan, S. M., Rispoli, K., & Holmes, S. (2014). Treatment integrity in conjoint behavioral consultation: Active ingredients and potential pathways of influence. In L. Sanetti & T. Kratochwill (Eds.), *Treatment integrity: A foundation for evidence-based practice in applied psychology* (pp. 255–278). American Psychological Association.

Sheridan, S. M., Ryoo, J. H., Garbacz, S. A., Kunz, G. M., & Chumney, F. L. (2013). The efficacy of conjoint behavioral consultation on parents and children in the home setting: Results of a randomized controlled trial. *Journal of School Psychology, 51*(6), 717–733.

Sheridan, S. M., Witte, A. L., Holmes, S. R., Coutts, M. J., Dent, A. L., Kunz, G. M., & Wu, C. (2017). A randomized trial examining the effects of conjoint behavioral consultation in rural schools: Student outcomes and the mediating role of the teacher–parent relationship. *Journal of School Psychology, 61*, 33–53.

Sheridan, S. M., Witte, A. L., Holmes, S. R., Wu, C., Bhatia, S. A., & Angell, S. R. (2017). The efficacy of conjoint behavioral consultation in the home setting: Outcomes and mechanisms in rural communities. *Journal of School Psychology, 62*, 81–101.

Sheridan, S. M., Witte, A. L., Kunz, G. M., Wheeler, L. A., Angell, S. R., & Lester, H. F. (2018). Rural teacher practices and partnerships to address behavioral challenges: The efficacy and mechanisms of conjoint behavioral consultation. *Elementary School Journal, 119*(1), 99–121.

Sheridan, S. M., Witte, A. L., Wheeler, L. A., Eastberg, S. R., Dizona, P. J., & Gormley, M. J. (2019). Conjoint behavioral consultation in rural schools: Do student effects maintain after 1 year? *School Psychology, 34*(4), 410–420.

Smith, T. E., Sheridan, S. M., Kim, E. M., Park, S., & Beretvas, S. N. (2020). The effects of family–school partnership interventions on academic and social–emotional functioning: A meta-analysis exploring what works for whom. *Educational Psychology Review, 32*(2), 511–544.

U.S. Department of Health and Human Services, Administration for Children and Families, Office of Head Start, National Center on Parent, Family, and Community Engagement. (2018). Head Start parent, family, and community engagement framework. Retrieved from *https://eclkc.ohs.acf.hhs.gov/sites/default/files/pdf/pfce-framework.pdf.*

Wilder, S. (2014). Effects of parental involvement on academic achievement: A meta-synthesis. *Educational Review, 66*(3), 377–397.

PART V

USING THE SCIENCE OF EARLY LITERACY TO SUPPORT EQUITY

CHAPTER 24

Literacy Architectures

Making the Case for Systems of Learning and Teaching to Cultivate Readers and Writers in Linguistically Diverse Schools

Emily Phillips Galloway and Nonie K. Lesaux

Multilingual children bring tremendous resources to the task of becoming readers and writers. Outside the United States, speaking two or more languages is often associated with faster development of early literacy skills such as phonemic and metalinguistic awareness, as well as related academic achievement (Durgunoğlu, Nagy, & Hancin-Bhatt, 1993; Gottardo, Yan, Siegel, & Wade-Woolley, 2001). Yet the U.S. education system, which is still dominated by English-only instruction and an often underdeveloped conception of literacy for instructional purposes, struggles to capitalize on these linguistic resources: Even after years of U.S. schooling, multilingual learners (MLLs), on average, do not attain grade-level English literacy skills (August & Shanahan, 2008; Kieffer, 2011; Mancilla-Martinez & Lesaux, 2011). For example, children who begin to learn English in kindergarten, on average, are reading 2 years below grade level by second grade (Kieffer, 2011).

However, this evidence has often been misinterpreted, leading to reforms that frame multilingualism as a risk factor for reading difficulty (Mancilla-Martinez, Chapter 3, this volume). Such strategies neglect a systemic issue that compromises education for all students: limited exposure to sustained, intensive, research-rooted literacy learning opportunities. The "at risk" framing also disregards broader inequities that MLLs face, such as limited access to material resources and social supports. Furthermore, MLLs often lack opportunities to receive instruction that capitalizes on their linguistic and cultural resources, despite research suggesting that bilingual programs can produce stronger long-term English proficiency and boost reading and English/language arts achievement relative to English-only instructional models (National Academies of Sciences, Engineering, and Medicine, 2017).

However, instruction in U.S. schools has evolved in recent decades to better meet the needs of learners from diverse linguistic backgrounds. Studies using National Assessment of Educational Progress (NAEP) data and examining the achievement of various groups of MLLs, including students from multilingual homes who were designated as English learners (ELs), others who were never designated as ELs, and others who were formerly EL-designated, show differences between multilingual and monolingual students on average. But they also show that between 2003 and 2015, differences in fourth-grade reading performance narrowed by 24%, and multilingual students' reading scores improved nearly two times as much as those of their monolingual peers (Kieffer & Thompson, 2018). Though studies have yet to pinpoint the mechanisms underlying these increases, this positive progress likely reflects an educational landscape better aligned to MLLs' needs. At the same time, much remains to be done, and we know that many English-only monolingual students—MLLs' classroom peers—also need a boost in literacy skills. Today, only 35% of U.S. fourth-graders are considered proficient readers (NAEP, 2019).

For educators, school leaders, policymakers, and those like us, who work at the nexus of research and practice, the landscape of achievement raises the central question that motivates this chapter: *How can we design literacy instruction that centers multilingual children, who represent the largest and fastest-growing segment of the school-age population in the United States (and in other industrialized nations), as a foundation for creating excellent and equitable literacy instruction for all?* Here, we review the research on MLLs' literacy development and their contexts of literacy learning and teaching as it relates to multilingualism and to their peers. Based on that review, we derive instructional principles that are crucial to serving today's linguistically diverse population—and we bring those principles to life by describing our *advanced literacies leadership (ALL) framework*, implemented in several large, urban school districts in the United States. The ALL framework is our response to the need for *literacy architectures* in today's schools—action plans that create systems of learning and teaching that propel MLLs' literacy development—rather than continually adding programs and practices haphazardly. Ultimately, applying the research on MLLs, together with the principles of universal design for learning, is a matter of social justice. For too long, instruction for MLLs has been conceptualized as intervention and/or a stand-alone, segregated, brief set of learning experiences occurring around the margins of an instructional model designed for monolingual children.

We focus on a literacy architecture that centers the needs of MLLs in the context of English-medium instruction—not because it is preferable, but because it is the most common instructional setting in which MLLs become readers and writers. Though research shows that opportunities to learn bilingually are beneficial to multilingual learners and to their monolingual peers (Collier & Thomas, 2017), we know that English remains the dominant language of instruction in U.S. schools and that the vast majority of learners (estimates range from 80–94%) have no access to dual language instruction (Gándara & Escamilla, 2017). Thus, we offer principles for the design of language and literacy instruction at a level that is generalizable both to settings that provide instruction solely in English and to those using bilingual models.

The Multilingual Population and Their Schooling Contexts

Multilingual Learners

MLLs are students who are exposed to and/or given opportunities to learn two or more languages in home and community settings (Paradis, Genesee, & Crago, 2011). Over 350 languages other than English (LOTEs) are spoken in the United States, but most multilingual children here are Spanish speakers (76.44%; Office of English Language Acquisition, 2020). By 2030, about 40% of school-age children will speak a LOTE at home (U.S. Census Bureau, 2003), and growth among Spanish speakers will continue through the next decade (Lopez, Gonzalez-Barrera, & Patten, 2013). Therefore, in our review, we emphasize studies that focus on language and literacy development for children acquiring both Spanish and English.

Most multilingual ELs immigrated before kindergarten or were born in the United States (Hernandez, Denton, & Macartney, 2008). Not all students share this profile, however, and students who are just beginning to acquire English literacy skills as adolescents have experiences that are vastly different from those of young children (see Lesaux & Geva, 2006, on English literacy development in older bilingual learners).

Geographic patterns of immigration shape a school's population of multilingual children. For example, between 2000 and 2019, the Latine population increased more rapidly in the Southeastern United States than in any other region (Noe-Bustamante, Lopes, & Krogstad, 2020). Demography scholars now call Alabama, Arkansas, Georgia, Kentucky, Mississippi, Missouri, North Carolina, South Carolina, and Tennessee the "New Latino South," the "New Latinx South," or the "Nuevo South/Sur" (Salas & Portes, 2017). In these new destination states—compared to, for example, Texas, California, or Arizona, which have long received high numbers of immigrants—a higher proportion of MLLs are born outside of the United States. These students are also more likely to have experienced trauma in their home countries or during border crossing (Filindra, Blanding, & Garcia Coll, 2011; Rodriguez, Monreal, & Howard, 2020).

Schooling Contexts

Because schools in different locations experience different sociohistorical, demographic, economic, political, and educational systems and norms, they are differentially prepared to support MLLs. Some educators in new destination states create welcoming environments for immigrant students (and serve as advocates) (Rodriguez & McCorkle, 2020), but many schools lack infrastructure and systems-level strategies to meet the population's needs. Educators in these regions are overwhelmingly monolingual English speakers; they receive little preparation or on-the-job training to teach multilingual children (Straubhaar, Vasquez, Mellom, & Portes, 2021), and they often report feeling "unprepared" or "less prepared" to do so (Lee & Hawkins, 2015). At the same time, policies rooted in historical racism that limit access to schooling (and to other social services) are more prevalent in regions serving high percentages of first-generation immigrant children (Browne & Odem, 2012; Filindra et al., 2011).

Beyond differences in infrastructure and systems-level strategies, schools classify MLLs in different ways. On the basis of home language reports or English language proficiency assessments, some students are designated as ELs (sometimes referred to as MLLs or ELLs [English language learners]) and given specialized instruction. Others are never designated as such and receive no additional support for English learning. And from kindergarten to fourth grade, many students initially designated as ELs are redesignated as "English proficient," often on the basis of an English language proficiency assessment, though thresholds for redesignation vary widely (Linquanti, Cook, Bailey, & MacDonald, 2016). This makes it harder to design instruction that supports all MLLs and also underscores the need for learning and teaching architectures that center linguistic diversity and variation in student experiences to optimize learning. The ALL framework we describe here aims to design instruction in relation to the literacy profiles of the learner population.

A Research- and Practice-Informed Set of Design Principles

In what follows, we outline three salient findings from research with MLLs that function as principles for designing literacy architectures in settings serving linguistically diverse populations (Figure 24.1). These principles informed our implementation of a literacy architecture in one of the largest U.S. urban districts serving large numbers of MLLs; this architecture since been adopted by other large urban districts. To support our review and synthesis, we focus on two broad sets of competencies in the literacy construct. One set encompasses the skills needed to read and spell words accurately and efficiently ("code-based skills") and the other set encompasses the skills needed to make meaning when reading and to convey meaning when writing ("meaning-based skills"). These skills are at play whether students are learning to read in a first or an additional language (Verhoeven, Perfetti, & Pugh, 2019).

Research Finding 1. Language knowledge, whether acquired in a first or an additional language, plays a substantial role in text comprehension and production processes for MLLs, and requires more sustained opportunities for development.

To extract and construct meaning from print, students need meaning-based skills, including knowledge of academic language and strategic processes. *Academic language* is the knowledge predominantly found in print and often used to express abstract concepts; *strategic processes* are actions, such as synthesizing or rereading, that promote deep comprehension. Studies in U.S. schools suggest that MLLs, on average, rapidly develop meaning-based skills: For example, Mancilla-Martinez and Lesaux (2011) found that from age 4½ through middle school entry, the rate of English vocabulary growth experienced by Spanish–English MLLs exceeded that of their monolingual classmates. However, despite this promising developmental trend, instruction in meaning-based skills was not intensive enough to ensure that the MLLs achieve levels of English vocabulary commensurate with those of their monolingual English peers. Similar patterns are observed in studies of MLLs developing academic language skills (Phillips Galloway & Uccelli, 2020).

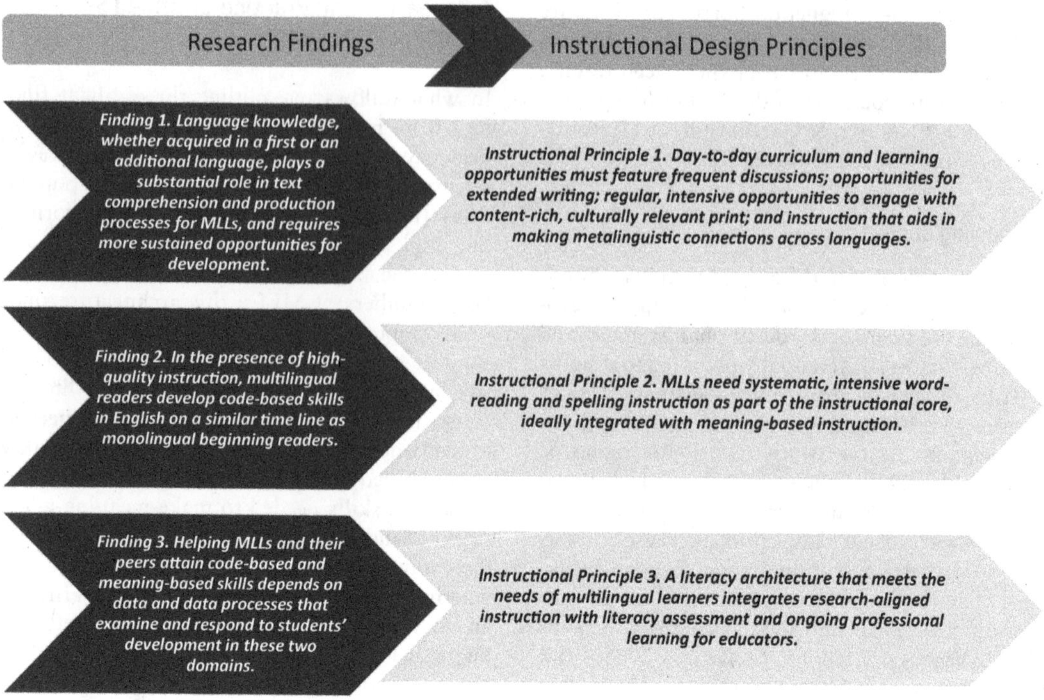

Research Findings → **Instructional Design Principles**

Finding 1. Language knowledge, whether acquired in a first or an additional language, plays a substantial role in text comprehension and production processes for MLLs, and requires more sustained opportunities for development.

Instructional Principle 1. Day-to-day curriculum and learning opportunities must feature frequent discussions; opportunities for extended writing; regular, intensive opportunities to engage with content-rich, culturally relevant print; and instruction that aids in making metalinguistic connections across languages.

Finding 2. In the presence of high-quality instruction, multilingual readers develop code-based skills in English on a similar time line as monolingual beginning readers.

Instructional Principle 2. MLLs need systematic, intensive word-reading and spelling instruction as part of the instructional core, ideally integrated with meaning-based instruction.

Finding 3. Helping MLLs and their peers attain code-based and meaning-based skills depends on data and data processes that examine and respond to students' development in these two domains.

Instructional Principle 3. A literacy architecture that meets the needs of multilingual learners integrates research-aligned instruction with literacy assessment and ongoing professional learning for educators.

FIGURE 24.1. Three key research findings and corresponding instructional design principles to inform systems of learning and teaching.

Researchers have also recently asked whether MLLs' meaning-based skills development and reading achievement might simply be nonlinear, occurring on a different time line than that of monolingual readers; these studies have been conducted in part to address widespread deficit narratives that arise when benchmarks for determining reading progress that were developed with monolinguals are applied to multilinguals (Hopewell & Escamilla, 2014). This line of research suggests that time in the English-medium school setting, as well as initial levels of proficiency in English and LOTEs, may mediate the development of English text comprehension skills. For example, in one study, students speaking Spanish at home who were EL-designated in kindergarten, on average, required 3 to 4 years to attain grade-level English proficiency skills (Arellano, Liu, Stoker, & Slama, 2018). However, of those who were reclassified as English proficient, only a small percentage demonstrated grade-level reading performance at grades 4 and 5. Importantly, students with higher initial levels of proficiency in Spanish were more likely to demonstrate grade-level readiness in English by

grades 4 and 5 than were students with lower levels of Spanish proficiency in kindergarten (Arellano et al., 2018). Thus, Arellano et al. concluded that educators should pay greater attention to students' skills in LOTEs when considering criteria for early literacy intervention—and, we would add, when designing the instructional core. This, of course, makes sense if we imagine that meaning-based skills, often operationalized as vocabulary or academic language skills, are largely proxies for conceptual knowledge (O'Reilly, Wang, & Sabatini, 2019). In summary, meaning-based skills development in MLL learners—and associated text comprehension skills—are best conceptualized as the sum of linguistic knowledge across all languages rather than just English.

Finally, MLLs' metalinguistic skills, or awareness that language can be analyzed to identify similarities in form and communicative function, play a role in text comprehension (Oxley & De Cat, 2021). For example, common Spanish and English morphology knowledge—a component of metalinguistic skill—supports comprehension of cognates (i.e., Spanish and English words that share a common origin, such as *estructura* and *structure*) common in academic texts (Crosson & Moore, 2017). Similarly, Spanish–English bilinguals in dual language classrooms show strong associations between their academic language resources developed in school in English and Spanish, with both Spanish and English academic language resources making unique contributions to English reading comprehension (Aguilar, Uccelli, & Phillips Galloway, 2020; Phillips Galloway, Uccelli, Aguilar, & Barr, 2020). Yet these multilingual skills are rarely cultivated in schools or used as resources for meaning-based skills development.

Instructional Principle 1: *Day-to-day curriculum and learning opportunities must feature frequent discussions; opportunities for extended writing; regular, intensive opportunities to engage with content-rich, culturally relevant print; and instruction that aids in making metalinguistic connections across languages.*

Literacy research reveals a systematic lack of intensive opportunities for MLLs and their classmates to develop English academic language, which, as is well documented, is best accomplished through reading a multitude of rich, engaging texts on culturally relevant topics. Nor do students have many opportunities to use such language in meaningful ways when speaking or writing throughout the day, as opposed to specific, isolated instances of instruction (Callahan, 2005; Olson, 2007). Yet in schools where MLLs are the majority, we often see a misguided focus on literacy interventions instead of on the core. This is costly on a number of fronts—the lost instructional time, the resources needed for interventions and interventionists, and the persistent associated underachievement of our students.

Ultimately, day-to-day instruction needs to offer more rich opportunities for language learning, for talk, and for writing. Literacy architectures can enable much more intensive and sustained opportunities to learn and use language for reading, writing, and speaking in classrooms where knowledge building about complex, engaging topics is the goal. We are not talking about a shallow concentration on mastering "facts," but rather a dynamic focus—with connections across reading, writing, and discussion—on issues and concepts that facilitate understanding of abstract ideas and rich content (see Lesaux & Russ Harris, 2015; Wright & Gotwals, Chapter 14, this volume). Adopting a more expansive view of MLLs' language resources is crucial for instructional design; knowledge of students' capabilities across languages at school entry can help identify learners with the meaning-based skills—in English and other languages—that will serve them as they become readers.

For all students, this instruction should feature culturally relevant topics. But MLLs in particular need instruction that includes chances to learn in ways that are culturally sustaining and that make visible and capitalize on the language, literacy, and conceptual knowledge they acquire at home and in the community (de Jong & Harper, 2005; Gonzalez, Moll, & Amanti, 2005; Noguerón-Liu, 2020). We have each designed curricula that foster metalinguistic attention to language and the use of LOTEs as resources for text comprehension, and we have shown that these approaches can be used successfully by educators who are not themselves bilingual (TRANSLATE curriculum; Phillips Galloway, Jimenez, White, Khanna, & McFadden, 2019; see also Bauer, Presiado, & Colomer, 2017; Daniel, Jiménez, Pray, & Pacheco, 2019). Our curricular design work has also made use of fiction and nonfiction print and digital text sets focused on children's immigration experiences (Phillips Galloway et al., 2019). Lessons featuring extended writing tasks, as well as discussion in English and LOTEs, are supported through translingual strategies that draw on skills such as translation and transliteration. And explicit instruction in high-utility vocabulary and academic language elements helps students new to English engage with ideas and concepts at an appropriate developmental level.

To be equitable, high-quality instruction must also support MLLs at different levels of English language development, requiring varied pedagogical strategies. Working with 1,138 Latine youth and their classmates across one academic year in 60 U.S. classrooms (ages 10–14; grades 4–7), we discovered that practices such as allowing students choices, acknowledging students' perspectives and existing knowledge, and providing opportunities for peer collaboration and leadership were particularly beneficial for developing the academic language skills of Latine students whose language skills were initially greater than those of their peers. Yet the same strategies did not support academic language development among students whose language skills were initially less developed, possibly because they afforded fewer opportunities for the teacher-scaffolded learning those students need (Phillips Galloway et al., 2021). Similarly, for young MLLs just becoming readers, and especially for those just acquiring English, teacher scaffolds that leverage all language resources appear to be most equitable; for example, a recent study linked regular Spanish use and text exposure to English language and reading outcomes for children who speak Spanish at home (Wagley, Marks, Bedore, & Kovelman, 2022). We know that additional teacher-provided and peer-supported scaffolding opportunities are needed in many classrooms across the United States, especially for MLLs. As part of additional focus on scaffolding, teachers in English-only classes who are not proficient in MLLs' native language can nevertheless promote language development by supporting students' own connections to their home language (Phillips Galloway et al., 2019).

Research Finding 2. In the presence of high-quality instruction, multilingual readers develop code-based skills in English on a similar timeline as monolingual beginning readers.

For all children, code-based skills such as phonological processing support development of accurate and efficient word reading, as well as spelling in alphabetic orthographies (i.e., English, German, Spanish) (August & Shanahan, 2008; Gottardo & Mueller, 2009; Lipka & Siegel, 2007, 2012). Fluent word reading and spelling draw on knowledge of both sight words—or words that through multiple exposures in print have come to reside in memory (as orthographic representation) (Ehri, 2014)—and letter-to-sound relationships that support decoding and encoding in the target language (August & Shanahan, 2008; Treiman, 2017). Indeed, studies reveal that for MLLs, spelling performance is related to lexicon size, while performance in spelling non-words (which mirrors the task of spelling words not in the writer's lexicon) depends heavily on phonological awareness (Czapka, Klassert, & Festman, 2019).

Given adequate English phonological awareness and phonics instruction (about 20 minutes daily through grade 2), MLLs who are developing typically, on average, demonstrate similar levels of English phonological processing skills as their monolingual peers (Lesaux, Crosson, Kieffer, & Pierce, 2010). In the early stages of reading development, they may even outperform monolinguals on measures of rapid naming speed and phonological awareness (August & Shanahan, 2008; Lesaux & Siegel, 2003). In elementary and middle school, which focus more on word-reading accuracy and efficiency, similar patterns are seen: Given sufficient opportunities to learn, MLLs and monolingual ELs demonstrate similar levels of English word-reading accuracy and efficiency (August & Shanahan, 2008; Mancilla-Martinez & Lesaux, 2011; Melby-Lervåg & Lervåg, 2014; Raudszus, Segers, & Verhoeven, 2019).

As a final note, the demarcation between code-based and meaning-based skills often seen in research and instruction is a false binary. Vocabulary skills are related to code-based skills. For example, Pendergast, Bingham, and Patton-Terry (2015) found that among Spanish-speaking 4-year-olds educated in an English-only PreK program, children's English vocabulary skills and growth in Spanish code skills were both related to English invented spelling at the end of the school year. Similarly, Peng, Orosco, Wang, Swanson, and Reed (2021) found that for third- to fifth-grade multilingual students, phonological awareness in English and in Spanish positively predicted students' English writing performance. These findings reinforce the need to support meaning-based skills, as well as Spanish and English code-based skills in early literacy development.

> Instructional Principle 2: *MLLs need systematic, intensive word-reading and spelling instruction as part of the instructional core, ideally integrated with meaning-based instruction.*

Despite its promise, explicit code-based teaching for all is rare (Duke & Mesmer, 2019; Mesmer & Griffith, 2005). For this reason, we help schools where we work implement curricular approaches that explicitly build knowledge of sound and letter links through not only teaching grapheme–phoneme correspondence but also studying morphology and etymology (Foorman, Chapter 6, this volume). This instruction need not be solely in English; there appears to be no detriment to multilingual phonics instruction that focuses on closely related languages. However, schools often struggle to implement such instruction given a monolingual English-speaking teaching force and a scarcity of bilingual phonics approaches. But it is often possible to adopt broader guidelines for examining MLLs' oral reading performance, as Briceño and Klein (2019) and Kabuto (2016) suggest. This involves careful analyzing miscues to understand how students' might be drawing on knowledge of grapheme–phoneme correspondence in LOTEs, as well probing questions to help understand whether a miscue is related to a student's lack of knowledge of a word or concept, or simply lack of familiarity with the English label.

For designing literacy architectures, it is important to remember that word-reading and spelling skills fall on a developmental time line distinct from that of the meaning-making skills needed to comprehend grade-level texts or convey concepts in writing (Crosson & Lesaux, 2010; Mancilla-Martinez & Lesaux, 2011; Verhoeven, Voeten, & Vermeer, 2019). Code-based skills can and should be taught to mastery in a relatively short time—generally 3 years, from school entry through the end of second grade, for both MLLs and their English-only peers (Fletcher, Savage, & Vaughn, 2021). Thus, as we discuss in Research Finding 3, schools need assessment practices to monitor developing code-based skills among MLLs and their peers and to ensure support and timely interventions for all learners, irrespective of language background, whose code-based skills are not developing as expected.

Finally, research shows that instruction should ideally focus on mastering these skills with texts that are both aligned with the phonics instructional sequence and on topics currently under study. Using texts on a series of topics not connected to a plan for knowledge building means a missed opportunity for MLLs and many of their peers given the crucial role that language and knowledge play in successful reading and the need for sustained learning opportunities across the school years in these domains (Snow & Uccelli, 2009; Cabell & Hwang, Chapter 15, this volume).

Research Finding 3. Helping MLLs and their peers attain code-based and meaning-based skills depends on data and data processes that examine and respond to students' development in these two domains.

Effective instructional practice begins with effective assessment. Studies on reader subtypes have confirmed that there are specific reader profiles, and that sources of difficulty vary among MLLs at different developmental stages (e.g., Grimm, Solari, Gerber, Nylund-Gibson, & Swanson, 2019; Lesaux et al., 2010)—just as research has shown for decades with monolinguals (Dinsmore, Fox, Parkinson, & Bilgili, 2019). In this light, approaches that are common in today's schools, such as using assessment data to derive a single "reading level" or to classify students as "reading at grade level" or "proficient," offer little information about how students are developing specific code- and meaning-based skills. Instead, the research we reviewed earlier suggests the need for a developmental assessment system that identifies MLL students' code- and meaning-based skills, monitors progress, and identifies breakdowns.

Importantly, these data and data processes speak to not only the needs of individuals but also the needs of the student population: Patterns and trends at the collective level can and should guide instructional design. For example, as discussed earlier, data from population-level studies, and in many schools, show that MLLs and their peers generally need an intensive, systematic approach to instruction and intervention with specific content features, including, for example, a focus on vocabulary knowledge, explicit word-reading instruction, and text-based reading comprehension instruction. For example, a meta-analysis examining reading component skills development in monolingual students and MLLs found very small differences in phonological awareness and decoding skills between the two groups over time, but persistent large differences in meaning-based skills, including vocabulary and language comprehension (Melby-Lervåg & Lervåg, 2014; Raudszus et al., 2019).

Instructional Principle 3: *A literacy architecture that meets the needs of multilingual learners integrates research-aligned instruction with literacy assessment and ongoing professional learning for educators.*

In practice, a coordinated blueprint for literacy instruction uses literacy assessment data to accomplishes two objectives: (1) identifying the needs and strengths of the learner population to inform the curriculum and pedagogical elements of the instructional core, and (2) identifying individual learners who need more intensive code- and/or meaning-based instruction than their classmates as part of designing supplemental instruction. Crucially, when data show that most students are struggling in one area—say, vocabulary development—this suggests a need to address this through the instructional core rather than jumping right to a more costly and inefficient intervention.

Compounding the problem of insufficient data at the level of readers' skills is whether and how schools use data for improvement. Unequivocal evidence shows that knowledgeable educators are instrumental in nurturing strong readers and writers. Developing this workforce begins with a strong culture of adult learning: educators who have the greatest impact on student learning generally operate in collaborative contexts in which student data are at the core of daily work experience. In other words, ongoing, high-quality professional development focused on students' literacy needs is instrumental to educators' performance and on-the-job learning (Boyle, August, Tabaku, Cole, & Simpson-Baird, 2015; Cheung & Slavin, 2012; National Academies of Sciences, Engineering, and Medicine, 2017). However, schools rarely have data processes in place; thus, it's also rare that instructional priorities and practices to support MLLs reflect needs surfaced through data. It's also rare for educators' professional learning opportunities to be continuous, data-based, and collaborative (Bryk, Gomez, & Grunow, 2010).

Helping educators design instructional opportunities and learning environments requires 21st-century adult learning opportunities and conditions. Research clearly shows that effective professional learning opportunities have these characteristics:

- They are continuous, involving site-based work guided and refined by data.
- They are supported by site-based teams of educators and instructional leaders with decision-making authority.
- They are linked to opportunities for feedback on teaching and guided reflection on practice (via professional learning communities, coaching, etc.).

In turn, these characteristics form the basis for the cycle of continuous, site-level improvement that is at the core of adult learning and transformation in practice. Circling back to the content itself, goals for implementation and practice should focus on a limited set of pedagogical strategies and approaches designed to build student skills as surfaced by data (rather than general interest topics or fads), and anchored in a knowledge-building plan for learners and educators.

Supporting MLLs at Scale: The ALL Framework

Readers may wonder: *Taking the research findings and corresponding instructional design principles outlined earlier under consideration, what does the responsive approach to supporting learning and teaching in large, urban districts with a linguistically diverse population look like?*

Our ALL framework was developed through a long-term partnership with the largest district in the United States (Figure 24.2). Refined over multiple years and with feedback from district partners, the ALL framework has two key design features.

Gap Analysis Methodology

Rather than immediately encouraging specific instructional programs, practices, or interventions, we designed a systematic, efficient process for district- and school-based teams to first map and analyze their landscape of learning and teaching against proven practices and their readers' needs. Many other sectors have a long, successful history of "gap analysis" to drive improvement. Gap analysis is not to be confused with strategic planning, which is widespread in districts and schools, and not typically an actionable process that supports continuous improvement; where strategic plans are to identify and articulate broad goals, gap analysis is a systematic methodology for teams and organizations to examine the status of any domain against effective practices, structures, and supports in the context of their needs and goals. The analysis itself drives data-based action. Described in more detail below, in this case, following the gap analysis, teams work on their "literacy architecture," to create more a more coordinated, higher-impact system of learning and teaching.

A Focus on Universal Design

Following decades of work on universal design in education and its benefits for population-

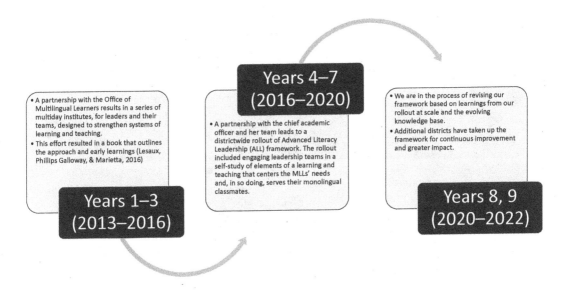

FIGURE 24.2. A research–practice partnership timeline leading to the ALL framework.

based work, we were motivated to create an approach that centers the multilingual population's needs and resources, while also supporting their monolingual peers. It's important to note some of the overlap between the two populations with respect to opportunity gaps; while MLLs in the United States face economic precarity that influences their literacy-learning opportunities, many English-only peers from homes with low material resources are in the same position; that is, studies document that when monolingual ELs and their multilingual peers come from homes with low material resources, their reading performance does not differ significantly (Kieffer, 2011; Lesaux & Kieffer, 2010). Schools can address these opportunity gaps for both populations.

In putting forth an architecture that focuses on universal design, we are not arguing for instruction that neglects or overlooks the MLL population's unique needs and competencies; rather, educators, school leaders, and policymakers should design daily instruction that (1) aligns with research that illuminates the developmental processes through which children acquire two (or more) languages and how these experiences impact multilingual learners' early literacy development, and (2) supports the overlap in literacy development needs between multilingual learners and their monolingual classmates—arguably the greatest point of leverage in most settings where multilingual and monolingual students are learning side by side.

The ALL Framework in Action

The ALL framework is a self-study process for examining a district's or school's architecture against what is known about effective practices, structures, and supports, with an explicit focus on serving MLLs (Lesaux, Phillips Galloway, & Marietta, 2016). The framework comprises four elements: assessment, curricular design and materials, pedagogy, and professional learning. Gap analyses are conducted in teams, bringing together various members of the school community—administrators, educators, and specialists—who collaborate using a set of inventories designed by our team (Lesaux et al., 2016). We provide one inventory for each of the four elements of the literacy architecture, and each inventory includes a series of indicators that teams use to analyze and evaluate their work (Figure 24.3). Given the nature of the self-study process, the inventories become a springboard for dialogue about areas of strength, growth areas and priorities, and issues that relate to the local context. The indicators serve as a set of things to look for and, over time, help teams align their shared vision for literacy instruction (Bryk et al., 2010).

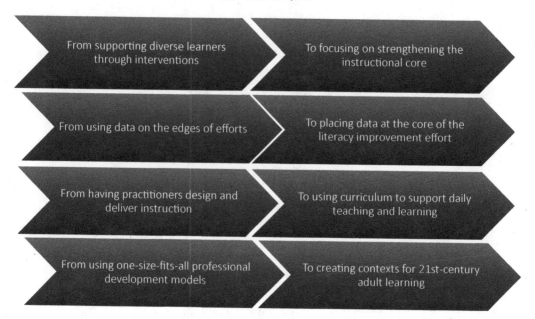

FIGURE 24.3. Process for the design of a literacy architecture informed by extant research findings.

With each of the four inventories complete, we suggest that teams select one or two of the four elements to begin with, because it is not feasible to adjust assessments, curricula, pedagogy, and professional learning all at once. There is no set starting place; the initial focus could be the element or elements where the school or district has the most room to grow or where some relatively straightforward tweaks would make material differences. Ultimately, teams make their decisions based on a number of factors, including student needs, shifting demographics, current approaches to continuous improvement and professional learning, educators' interests and priorities, and available time and resources (Figure 24.4). During this decision-making process, also using tools we designed (Lesaux et al., 2016), teams reach consensus on short- and long-term priorities and begin to craft an action plan.

Over 2 to 3 years, teams address all aspects of the literacy architecture at their sites. When teams elect to begin with a focus on curriculum and instruction, an inventory of their current instructional practices, texts, and materials leads to adjustments in the curriculum and instruction offered daily. In some schools, the gap analysis leads to greater emphasis on code-based skills

instruction, and in nearly all sites it leads to more of a focus on immersive knowledge building that prioritizes meaningful opportunities for thinking as a vehicle for teaching students to become readers and writers. This focus on the instructional core is often a significant shift: Many schools bet on interventions that sit outside the instructional core to bolster literacy achievement, especially for MLL students.

When responding to student needs, schools have tended to keep adding programs, practices, and supplemental supports, often in the form of interventions or add-ons to standard practice. Over time, this additive approach produces a patchwork of activity, inadvertently favoring tinkering on the edges and trying to find additional minutes here and there for specific programs rather than carefully analyzing and strengthening the instructional core. For many schools that serve large MLL populations, gap analysis leads to adopting a shared curricular platform and instructional practices better aligned with these learners' strengths and needs, as well as reducing in the number of supplemental programs. Other schools, after carefully examining instructional practices, may identify an area—for example, the use of dialogic talk practices or explicit academic

Leader's Tool: Evaluating the Quality of Curricular Plans and Materials

Purpose: Use this tool to evaluate curriculum, plans, and materials for the hallmarks.

The Hallmarks of Advanced Literacies are present in all lessons and across units	
Hallmark # 1: Work with a variety of texts that feature "big" ideas and rich content *Curricular Indicators*	
• Texts are closely tied to the unit, they include essential knowledge that students need to answer the 'big' questions or idea that guides the **unit's** assignments and learning tasks.	
• Texts tackle the **unit's** topics from many perspectives and angles, reflect a range of cultures, groups and experiences in ways that are accurate, dynamic, and validating.	
• Multiple texts of many genres or text types, including visual texts, are used throughout the unit.	
• Texts at a range of reading levels (below-grade level, at-grade level, above-grade level) on topics that comprise the instructional focus are provided.	
• Rich, authentic literature on topics that comprise the instructional focus and are of high interest to students.	
• Texts use language like that used in the discipline—the same language students need to produce during their classroom and academic work.	
• Guiding questions accompany the reading of each text (i.e., text-focused questions)—these help students to identify ideas and information central to comprehend the text.	
Hallmark # 2: Talk/discuss to build language and knowledge *Curricular Indicators*	
• Materials that support oral language activities (sentence stems for discussing texts, organizers/reproducibles to support preparation for debates) are provided.	
• Students are asked to use the target words and other academic language when speaking as part of each lesson in the unit.	

FIGURE 24.4. Example of indicators from our curriculum inventory. Adapted from Lesaux, Phillips Galloway, and Marietta (2016). Copyright © 2016 The Guilford Press. Reprinted by permission.

language teaching—that might be bolstered to support learners.

Yet other schools might elect to focus on different elements of the literacy architecture. For example, gap analyses of assessment practices

often lead schools to identify a common trend: Learners are overassessed using assessments that fail to isolate code- and meaning-based development. The result is often a poor alignment between students' needs and the instructional core. A gap analysis may lead schools to redesign assessment systems with the aim of optimizing efficiency and information specificity—often administering fewer assessments and moving to a screening approach to monitor code- and meaning-based skills in the overall population. In other instances, a focus on professional learning has led schools to redesign their approach to support for educators, aligning it with what is known about adult learning and centering it on students' needs surfaced through data. Some schools may elect to design professional learning that aims to bolster knowledge of how to build meaning-based skills in MLLs, while others may focus on professional learning that increases educators' skill in delivering code-based instruction that builds on MLLs' LOTEs.

The ALL framework is therefore not a top-down model; it is a structured self-study process that gives teams an opportunity to systematically examine their own landscape on four key elements of any system of learning and teaching against best practices and in light of their priorities. In turn, given the self-study nature of the process, schools often focus on addressing gaps in different orders, then take different tacks to continuous improvement. Through a process of realignment, leaders work in close collaboration with teams to determine adjustments, changes, and/or new approaches, and enhance their coordination and shared vision for success to best support both learners and educators.

Conclusion

Learning what to notice about literacy instruction is, in the long run, a central outcome of gap analysis. In school communities where it is practiced consistently, leaders and educators continuously examine the literacy architecture and adjust it to meet MLLs' needs. We have shared a process that schools might use to create literacy architectures that both respond to the needs of MLL students and support their monolingual peers. This approach offers a way to achieve high-quality literacy instruction at scale in varied contexts where MLLs are educated across the United States, bringing together what we know from research on MLLs' literacy development—as a set of understandings that is continually evolving—and implementation science, which suggests schools need processes to bring research-informed practice to scale.

Acknowledgments

We thank our school district partners who have been instrumental in our efforts to link research and practice, especially Stela Radovanovic and Linda Chen. We also thank the dozens of school leadership teams that engaged deeply with this work and shared their learning, their triumphs, and their challenges—and whose experiences reflect the complexity of serving an increasingly diverse population within a shifting educational landscape. Finally, we thank Sky Marietta, a long-time collaborator and thought partner, for her crucial contributions to the early stages of this work.

References

Aguilar, G., Uccelli, P., & Phillips Galloway, E. (2020). Toward biliteracy: Unpacking the contribution of mid-adolescent dual language learners' Spanish and English academic language skills to English reading comprehension. *TESOL Quarterly, 54*(4), 1010–1036.

Arellano, B., Liu, F., Stoker, G., & Slama, R. (2018). *Initial Spanish proficiency and English language development among Spanish-speaking English learner students in New Mexico* (REL 2018–286). Regional Educational Laboratory Southwest.

August, D., & Shanahan, T. (Eds.). (2008). *Developing reading and writing in second-language learners: Lessons from the report of the National Literacy Panel on Language-Minority Children and Youth*. Taylor & Francis.

Bauer, E. B., Presiado, V., & Colomer, S. (2017). Writing through partnership: Fostering translanguaging in children who are emergent bilinguals. *Journal of Literacy Research, 49*(1), 10–37.

Boyle, A., August, D., Tabaku, L., Cole, S., & Simpson-Baird, A. (2015). *Dual language education programs: Current state policies and practices*. Office of English Language Acquisition, U.S. Department of Education.

Briceño, A., & Klein, A. F. (2019). A second lens on formative reading assessment with multilingual students. *Reading Teacher, 72*(5), 611–621.

Browne, I., & Odem, M. (2012). "Juan Crow" in the Nuevo South?: Racialization of Guatemalan and Dominican immigrants in the Atlanta metro area. *Du Bois Review, 9*(2), 321–337.

Bryk, A. S., Gomez, L. M., & Grunow, A. (2010). *Getting ideas into action: Building networked improvement communities in education*. Carnegie Foundation for the Advancement of Teaching.

Callahan, R. M. (2005). Tracking and high school English learners: Limiting opportunity to learn. *American Educational Research Journal, 42*(2), 305–328.

Cheung, A. C., & Slavin, R. E. (2012). Effective reading programs for Spanish-dominant English language learners (ELLs) in the elementary grades: A synthesis of research. *Review of Educational Research, 82*(4), 351–395.

Collier, V., & Thomas, W. (2017). Validating the power of bilingual schooling: Thirty-two years of large-scale, longitudinal research. *Annual Review of Applied Linguistics, 37*, 203–217.

Crosson, A. C., & Lesaux, N. K. (2010). Revisiting assumptions about the relationship of fluent reading to comprehension: Spanish-speakers' text-reading fluency in English. *Reading and Writing, 23*(5), 475–494.

Crosson, A. C., & Moore, D. (2017). When to take up roots: The effects of morphology instruction for middle school and high school English learners. *Reading Psychology, 38*(3), 262–288.

Czapka, S., Klassert, A., & Festman, J. (2019). Executive functions and language: Their differential influence on mono- vs. multilingual spelling in primary school. *Frontiers in Psychology, 10*, Article 97.

Daniel, S. M., Jiménez, R. T., Pray, L., & Pacheco, M. B. (2019). Scaffolding to make translanguaging a classroom norm. *TESOL Journal, 10*(1), Article e00361.

De Jong, E. J., & Harper, C. A. (2005). Preparing mainstream teachers for English-language learners: Is being a good teacher good enough? *Teacher Education Quarterly, 32*(2), 101–124.

Dinsmore, D. L., Fox, E., Parkinson, M. M., & Bilgili, D. (2019). Using reader profiles as snapshots to investigate students' reading performance. *Journal of Experimental Education, 87*(3), 470–495.

Duke, N. K., & Mesmer, H. A. E. (2019). Phonics faux pas: Avoiding instructional missteps in teaching letter–sound relationships. *American Educator, 42*(4), 12–16.

Durgunoğlu, A. Y., Nagy, W. E., & Hancin-Bhatt, B. J. (1993). Cross-language transfer of phonological awareness. *Journal of Educational Psychology, 85*(3), 453–465.

Ehri, L. C. (2014). Orthographic mapping in the acquisition of sight word reading, spelling memory, and vocabulary learning. *Scientific Studies of Reading, 18*(1), 5–21.

Filindra, A., Blanding, D., & Garcia Coll, C. (2011). The power of context: State-level policies and politics and the educational performance of the children of immigrants in the United States. *Harvard Educational Review, 81*(3), 407–437.

Fletcher, J. M., Savage, R., & Vaughn, S. (2021). A commentary on Bowers (2020) and the role of phonics instruction in reading. *Educational Psychology Review, 33*(3), 1249–1274.

Gándara, P., & Escamilla, K. (2017). Bilingual education in the United States. In O. García, A. Lin, & S. May (Eds.), *Bilingual and Multilingual Education (Encyclopedia of Language and Education)* (3rd ed.). Springer International.

Gonzalez, N., Moll, L. C., & Amanti, C. (Eds.). (2005). *Funds of knowledge: Theorizing practices in households, communities, and classrooms*. Routledge.

Gottardo, A., & Mueller, J. (2009). Are first-and second-language factors related in predicting second-language reading comprehension?: A study of Spanish-speaking children acquiring English as a second language from first to second grade. *Journal of Educational Psychology, 101*(2), 330–344.

Gottardo, A., Yan, B., Siegel, L. S., & Wade-Woolley, L. (2001). Factors related to English reading performance in children with Chinese as a first language: More evidence of cross-language transfer of phonological processing. *Journal of Educational Psychology, 93*(3), 530–542.

Grimm, R., Solari, E. J., Gerber, M. M., Nylund-Gibson, K., & Swanson, H. L. (2019). A cross-linguistic examination of heterogeneous reading profiles of Spanish-speaking bilingual students. *Elementary School Journal, 120*(1), 109–131.

Hernandez, D. J., Denton, N. A., & Macartney, S. E. (2008). Children in immigrant families: Looking to America's future. *Social Policy Report, 22*(3), 1–24.

Hopewell, S., & Escamilla, K. (2014). Biliteracy development in immersion contexts. *Journal of Immersion and Content-Based Language Education, 2*(2), 181–195.

Kabuto, B. (2016). The social construction of a reading (dis) ability. *Reading Research Quarterly, 51*(3), 289–304.

Kieffer, M. J. (2011). Converging trajectories: Reading growth in language minority learners and their classmates, kindergarten to grade 8. *American Educational Research Journal, 48*(5), 1187–1225.

Kieffer, M. J., & Thompson, K. D. (2018). Hidden progress of multilingual students on NAEP. *Educational Researcher, 47*(6), 391–398.

Lee, S. J., & Hawkins, M. R. (2015). Policy, context and schooling: The education of English learners in rural new destinations. *Global Education Review, 2*(4), 40–59.

Lesaux, N. K., Crosson, A. C., Kieffer, M. J., & Pierce, M. (2010). Uneven profiles: Language minority learners' word reading, vocabulary, and reading comprehension skills. *Journal of Applied Developmental Psychology, 31*(6), 475–483.

Lesaux, N. K., & Geva, E. (2006). *Synthesis: Development of literacy in language-minority students*. Routledge.

Lesaux, N. K., & Kieffer, M. J. (2010). Exploring sources of reading comprehension difficulties among language minority learners and their classmates in early adolescence. *American Educational Research Journal, 47*(3), 596–632.

Lesaux, N. K., Phillips Galloway, E., & Marietta, S. H. (2016). *Teaching advanced literacy skills: A guide for leaders in linguistically diverse schools.* Guilford Press.

Lesaux, N. K., & Russ Harris, J. (2015). *Cultivating knowledge, building language: Literacy Instruction for English Learners in elementary school.* Heinemann.

Lesaux, N. K., & Siegel, L. S. (2003). The development of reading in children who speak English as a second language. *Developmental Psychology, 39*(6), 1005–1019.

Linquanti, R., Cook, H. G., Bailey, A. L., & MacDonald, R. (2016). *Moving toward a more common definition of English learner: Collected guidance for states and multi-state assessment consortia.* Council of Chief State School Officers.

Lipka, O., & Siegel, L. S. (2007). The development of reading skills in children with English as a second language. *Scientific Studies of Reading, 11*(2), 105–131.

Lipka, O., & Siegel, L. S. (2012). The development of reading comprehension skills in children learning English as a second language. *Reading and Writing, 25*(8), 1873–1898.

Lopez, M. H., Gonzalez-Barrera, A., & Patten, E. (2013). *Closing the digital divide: Latinos and technology adoption.* Pew Hispanic Center.

Mancilla-Martinez, J., & Lesaux, N. K. (2011). The gap between Spanish speakers' word reading and word knowledge: A longitudinal study. *Child Development, 82*(5), 1544–1560.

Melby-Lervåg, M., & Lervåg, A. (2014). Reading comprehension and its underlying components in second-language learners: A meta-analysis of studies comparing first-and second-language learners. *Psychological Bulletin, 140*(2), 409–433.

Mesmer, H. A. E., & Griffith, P. L. (2005). Everybody's selling it—but just what is explicit, systematic phonics instruction? *Reading Teacher, 59*(4), 366–376.

National Academies of Sciences, Engineering, and Medicine. (2017). *Promoting the educational success of children and youth learning English: Promising futures.* National Academies Press.

National Assessment of Educational Progress. (2019). *NAEP Report Card: 2019 NAEP Reading Assessment.* National Center for Education Statistics.

Noe-Bustamante, L., Lopez, M. H., & Krogstad, J. M. (2020, July 7). US Hispanic population surpassed 60 million in 2019, but growth has slowed. Retrieved from *www.pewresearch.org/fact-tank/2020/07/07/u-s-hispanic-population-surpassed-60-million-in-2019-but-growth-has-slowed.*

Noguerón-Liu, S. (2020). Expanding the knowledge base in literacy instruction and assessment: Biliteracy and translanguaging perspectives from families, communities, and classrooms. *Reading Research Quarterly, 55,* S307–S318.

Office of English Language Acquisition. (2020). *Our nation's English learners.* U.S. Department of Education.

Olson, K. (2007). Lost opportunities to learn: The effects of education policy on primary language instruction for English learners. *Linguistics and Education, 18*(2), 121–141.

O'Reilly, T., Wang, Z., & Sabatini, J. (2019). How much knowledge is too little?: When a lack of knowledge becomes a barrier to comprehension. *Psychological Science, 30*(9), 1344–1351.

Oxley, E., & De Cat, C. (2021). A systematic review of language and literacy interventions in children and adolescents with English as an additional language (EAL). *Language Learning Journal, 49*(3), 265–287.

Paradis, J., Genesee, F., & Crago, M. (2011). *Dual language development and disorders: A handbook on bilingualism and second language learning* (2nd ed.). Brookes.

Pendergast, M., Bingham, G., & Patton-Terry, N. (2015). Examining the relationship between emergent literacy skills and invented spelling in prekindergarten Spanish-speaking dual language learners. *Early Education and Development, 26*(2), 264–285.

Peng, A., Orosco, M. J., Wang, H., Swanson, H. L., & Reed, D. K. (2022). Cognition and writing development in early adolescent English learners. *Journal of Educational Psychology, 114,* 1136–1155.

Phillips Galloway, E., Hsin, L. B., Jensen, B., LaRusso, M. D., Hong, M. K., & Mankowski, K. (2021). Examining the role of learner and classroom characteristics in the later language learning of Latinx youth and their classmates. *Journal of Applied Developmental Psychology, 77,* Article 101353.

Phillips Galloway, E., Jimenez, R., White, H., Khanna, M., & McFadden, S. (2019). *Teaching reading and new strategic language approaches to emergent bilinguals* [Curriculum]. Vanderbilt University.

Phillips Galloway, E., McClain, J. B., & Uccelli, P. (2020). Broadening the lens on the science of reading: A multifaceted perspective on the role of academic language in text understanding. *Reading Research Quarterly, 55,* S331–S345.

Phillips Galloway, E., & Uccelli, P. (2019). Examining developmental relations between core academic language skills and reading comprehension for English learners and their peers. *Journal of Educational Psychology, 111*(1), 15–31.

Phillips Galloway, E., Uccelli, P., Aguilar, G., & Barr, C. D. (2020). Exploring the cross-linguistic contribution of Spanish and English academic language skills to English text comprehension for middle-grade dual language learners. *AERA Open, 6*(1), 2332858419892575.

Raudszus, H., Segers, E., & Verhoeven, L. (2019). Situation model building ability uniquely predicts first and second language reading comprehension. *Journal of Neurolinguistics, 50,* 106–119.

Rodriguez, S., & McCorkle, W. (2020). On the educational rights of undocumented students: A call to expand teachers' awareness of policies impacting undocumented students and strategic empathy. *Teachers College Record, 122*(12), 1–34.

Rodriguez, S., Monreal, T., & Howard, J. (2020). It's about hearing and understanding their stories": Teacher empathy and socio-political awareness toward newcomer undocumented students in the new Latino South. *Journal of Latinos and Education, 19*(2), 181–198.

Salas, S., & Portes, P. R. (Eds.). (2017). *US Latinization: Education and the New Latino South.* SUNY Press.

Snow, C. E., & Uccelli, P (2009). The challenge of academic language. In D. R. Olson & N. Torrance (Eds.), *The Cambridge handbook of literacy* (pp. 112–133). Cambridge University Press.

Straubhaar, R., Vasquez, M., Mellom, P. J., & Portes, P. (2021). "They wouldn't go to our school": Unpacking the racialization of Latinx children through a civil rights lesson in a New South classroom. *Journal of Latinos and Education, 20*(4), 363–375.

Treiman, R. (2017). Learning to spell words: Findings, theories, and issues. *Scientific Studies of Reading, 21*(4), 265–276.

U.S. Census Bureau. (2003). *U.S. Census Bureau American Housing Survey.* Author.

Verhoeven, L., Perfetti, C., & Pugh, K. (2019). Cross-linguistic perspectives on second language reading. *Journal of Neurolinguistics, 50,* 1–6.

Verhoeven, L., Voeten, M., & Vermeer, A. (2019). Beyond the simple view of early first and second language reading: The impact of lexical quality. *Journal of Neurolinguistics, 50,* 28–36.

Wagley, N., Marks, R. A., Bedore, L. M., & Kovelman, I. (2022). Contributions of bilingual home environment and language proficiency on children's Spanish–English reading outcomes. *Child Development, 93,* 881–899.

CHAPTER 25

The Development of Early Orthographic Representations in Children

The Lexical Asymmetry Hypothesis and Its Implications for Children with Dyslexia

**Donald L. Compton, Laura M. Steacy, Nuria Gutiérrez,
Valeria M. Rigobon, Ashley A. Edwards, and Nancy C. Marencin**

Dyslexia is a developmental word-reading and spelling disorder affecting anywhere from 6 to 17% of school-age children, with variability in prevalence estimates depending largely on the severity of the cutoff point adopted for diagnosis (Fletcher, Lyon, Fuchs, & Barnes, 2018). While definitions vary (see Fletcher, 2009), the vast majority contain a common set of key elements, including that (1) dyslexia is neurobiological in origin; (2) the dominant characteristics or symptoms are persistent and severe difficulties in the development of accurate and/or fluent word recognition, decoding, and spelling skills; and (3) the neurocognitive influences are multifactorial, primarily involving phonological processing deficits, as well as weaknesses in other oral language skills and processing speed (Pennington, 2009; Peterson & Pennington, 2015). Developmentally, *phonological processing deficits*—impaired representation of, or access to, the abstract units of spoken language—have been implicated as the principal source of reading difficulties in children with dyslexia by disrupting the ability to establish various levels of spelling-to-sound correspondence knowledge (Brady & Schankweiler, 1991; Bruck, 1992; Juel, Griffith, & Gough, 1986; Shankweiler et al., 1999; Sie-

gel, 1989; Stanovich & Siegel, 1994; Torgesen, 2000; Vellutino et al., 1996). This knowledge underlies accurate and fluent word recognition development through the process of phonological decoding (see Vellutino, Fletcher, Snowling, & Scanlon, 2004), supporting self-teaching (Share, 1995), and/or orthographic learning (see Castles & Nation, 2006; Nation & Castles, 2017). As such, deficits in individuals with dyslexia are more likely to be observed when the phonological demands of the word-reading task are greater (e.g., decoding of pronounceable non-words), giving rise to the well-documented non-word reading deficit in children with developmental dyslexia (e.g., Harm & Seidenberg, 1999; Metsala, Stanovich, & Brown, 1998; Rack, Snowling, & Olson, 1992).

For children with dyslexia, lack of spelling-to-sound routines profoundly affects the growth of the orthographic lexicon by limiting the development of high-quality representations and resulting in what we have referred to as *lexical asymmetry* (see Compton, 2002; Steacy, Petscher, Rueckl, Edwards, & Compton, 2021). As described in detail below, lexical asymmetry refers to an uneven pattern of growth in the subsystems that make up the orthographic lexicon, disrupting the development of the orthographic lexicon and limiting word-reading and spelling skills development. Within the computational modeling literature (see Harm & Seidenberg, 1999) this has been referred to as *overfitting,* in which representations between orthographic and phonological units are overfit at the level of the whole word at the expense of smaller sublexical orthographic to phonological (O → P) connections that are needed for orthographic learning (see Castles, Rastle & Nation, 2018; Ziegler & Goswami, 2005). This significantly hinders the process of item-based orthographic learning by starving the lexicon of the rich sublexical O → P connections needed to learn to read unfamiliar words.

In summary, we hypothesize that the developmental consequence of lexical asymmetry is a significant reduction of successful self-teaching opportunities in children with dyslexia as a result of limited sublexical O → P knowledge necessary for phonological decoding. In this chapter, we seek to flesh out and expand on the notion of lexical asymmetry as it relates to developmental dyslexia by providing an overview of orthographic learning; reviewing the knowledge sources that have been proposed to support the development of high-quality orthographic representations in typically developing readers; examining how difficulties in phonological processing can differentially limit the growth of important knowledge sources that support development of the orthographic lexicon and lead to lexical asymmetry in children with dyslexia; considering how lexical asymmetry can negatively affect the normal process of statistical learning that is critical to advanced word-reading and decoding skills in English; and reviewing the convergence of data from behavioral studies and computational models supporting the asymmetry hypothesis of dyslexia.

Orthographic Learning: Mechanism for Word-Reading Development

Orthographic learning (see Nation & Castles, 2017; Perfetti, 1992) explains the transition from novice to skilled word reading through the continuous addition of high-quality and fully specified word-specific representations to the orthographic lexicon (Foorman, Chapter 6, this volume). High lexical quality includes well-specified and redundant representations of

form (orthography and phonology) and flexible representations of meaning, allowing for rapid and reliable meaning retrieval (Perfetti, 2007). *Orthographic learning* is an item-based acquisition process that relies heavily on the application of phonological decoding skills to novel printed words via self-teaching (see Share, 1995, 2011), which results in the formation of stable item-specific orthographic representations that permit an orthographic input to sufficiently and uniquely identify the word to be read (Castles et al., 2018). Studies of early reading development have reported that relatively few successful exposures to a word are required for the acquisition of word-specific representations in typically developing readers (e.g., Brooks, 1977; Ehri & Saltmarsh, 1995; Reitsma, 1983), implying that word-specific representations form relatively rapidly as children develop reading skills. Furthermore, item-based acquisition theories acknowledge that at any point in time a child may be reading some words slowly and with great effort, while reading other words automatically (Castles & Nation, 2006; Share, 1995). This item-level variation likely depends on individual differences in the frequency and richness of reading (Cunningham & Stanovich, 1998), phonological decoding skill (de Jong, Bitter, Van Setten, & Marinus, 2009; Nation & Castles, 2017), and semantic knowledge (Ouellette & Fraser, 2009; Perfetti & Stafura, 2014).

Quasi-regular orthographies, such as English, contain substantial ambiguities between orthography and phonology that place added demands on developing readers (see Seymour, Aro, & Erskine, 2003) and an increased level of complexity to the process of orthographic learning. At the level of the item (e.g., the specific word to be learned), there are word features and child characteristics that either promote or inhibit orthographic learning. For developing readers, attempting to decode an unfamiliar letter string can result in either full or partial decoding (see Castles & Nation, 2006; Elbro, de Jong, Houter, & Nielsen, 2012; Keenan & Betjemann, 2008; Tunmer & Chapman, 2012; Venezky, 1999). Full decoding occurs when a reader has sufficient phonological decoding skills to sound out words containing regular (or decodable) relationships between orthography and phonology. Partial decoding, on the other hand, occurs when the reader does not have sufficient phonological decoding skills to sound out the word, or the word is irregular and cannot be pronounced correctly by applying common decoding rules (e.g., *was, have, come, said, shoe, wasp, stomach, soup*; Wang, Nickels, Nation, & Castles, 2013). During full or partial decoding, the role of the reader is to match the assembled phonology from phonological decoding with the lexical representation of the word (see Share, 2008; Venezky, 1999). Thus, the decodability of a word depends on both the decoding knowledge of the child and the relative regularity of the O → P relationships of the word (Seidenberg, Waters, Barnes, & Tanenhaus, 1984). Furthermore, the availability of top-down support, either through activation of the stored phonological form (e.g., Duff & Hulme, 2012; Wang et al., 2013) or meaning (Ouellette & Fraser, 2009), help a child to determine the exact pronunciation of a novel letter string based on a partial decoding attempt. This suggests lexical support in orthographic learning under conditions of decoding ambiguity (see Wang, Castles, & Nickels, 2012; Wang et al., 2013). As such, orthographic learning is relevant to the learning of all words, with differences in a child's ability to acquire a reliable orthographic representation being influenced by a combination of child characteristics (e.g., phonological awareness and phonological decoding skill and ability, and availability of semantic and phonological form) and word characteristics (e.g., the word's regularity, orthographic complexity, and frequency), and the overall number of word exposures the child experiences (see Cunningham & Stanovich, 1998; Reitsma, 1983). Our work suggests that there are substantial individual differences in developing readers' ability to form high-quality orthographic representations (Compton, 2002; Edwards et al., 2022; Gilbert, Compton, & Kearns, 2011; Kearns et al., 2016; Siegelman et al., 2020; Steacy & Compton, 2019; Steacy et al., 2017; Steacy, Petscher, Elliott, et al., 2021; Steacy, Compton, et al., 2019; Steacy, Petscher, Rueckl, et al., 2021; Steacy, Wade-Woolley, et al., 2019), which has motivated us to explore the various knowledge sources associated with the orthographic lexicon that support orthographic learning in children.

Evolution of the Knowledge Sources Supporting Development of the Orthographic Lexicon

A typically developing reader's orthographic lexicon contains approximately 10,000 word-specific representations (excluding inflectional forms) by eighth grade (Ehri, 2005; Harris & Jacobson, 1982). This requires a lexical system that can quickly establish and reliably retrieve word-specific spellings that activate pronunciation, meaning, and syntax. The orthographic lexicon comprises four major components (i.e., knowledge sources): word-specific representations, orthographic units, phonological units, and sublexical O → P connections (see Compton, Miller, Elleman, & Steacy, 2014). As children learn to read, the orthographic lexicon changes in two important ways (Compton, 2002; Ehri, 2014; Perfetti, 1992). First, there is a continuous increase in the absolute number of orthographically addressable entries, referred to as *word-specific representations,* which are considered less dependent on phonological processes because they have been supplanted by specific connections linking spelling directly to pronunciations (Harm & Seidenberg, 2004; Perfetti, 1992; Share, 1995) and as such are relatively impenetrable to factors such as knowledge and expectation (Perfetti, 1992; Perfetti & Hart, 2002; Stanovich, 1991).

The second change in the orthographic lexicon associated with reading development is an increase in the overall quantity and quality of sublexical O → P connections (Perfetti, 1992). Sublexical connections between orthographic and phonological codes exist at multiple levels: for instance, individual letter-phonemes, letter cluster-phonemes, letter cluster-rimes, letter cluster-syllables, and letter cluster-morphemes (see Berninger, 1994; Ziegler & Goswami, 2005). Early O → P connections are initially based on simple one-to-one correspondences that are relatively insensitive to orthographic context (see Share, 1995). With reading development, initially incomplete and oversimplified representations become sophisticated context-dependent connections (Steacy, Compton, et al., 2019; Treiman, Kessler, & Bick, 2003; Treiman, Kessler, Zevin, Bick, & Davis, 2006; Kemp & Treiman, Chapter 9, this volume). These sublexical connections between O → P units form what Gough, Juel, and Griffith (1992) referred to as the *cipher.* The cipher is best conceptualized as a set of abstract, context-dependent relationships between orthography and phonology that are *"implicit, very numerous, and very fast"* (Gough et al., 1992, p. 38). We maintain that disruptions in the formation of both basic and sophisticated sublexical O → P knowledge compromise the development of context-dependent decoding rules and result in asymmetrical growth between word-specific representations and context-sensitive decoding rules. We continue by expanding on the behavioral consequences of lexical asymmetry in children with dyslexia.

Lexical Asymmetry and Word Processing in Developmental Dyslexia

The two lexical acquisition systems simultaneously develop and are mutually facilitative as a child learns to read, with Perfetti (1992, pp. 161–162) stating that "the more powerful the context-sensitive decoding rules (or analogic capabilities), the more entries the learner can acquire. And the more entries, the more powerful the decoding rules." As mentioned previously, deficits in phonemic awareness skills limit the growth of important sublexical O → P associations in children with dyslexia (see Harm & Seidenberg, 2004). As a result, children with dyslexia exhibit a general tendency to process only partial information about words and to rely on sources of information other than sublexical O → P associations that are considerably less efficient to facilitate word recognition (see Stanovich, 1988). This is consistent with the view that children with dyslexia may be overreliant on a global processing strategy, which results in insufficient attention to individual letters or groupings of letters (Ehri & Saltmarsh, 1995; Frith, 1985; Siegel, Share, & Geva, 1995) and the corresponding phonological representations. The result is that children with dyslexia tend to add word-specific representations to the lexicon without associated growth in sublexical O → P associations (i.e., the behavioral equivalent of overfitting).

From a grain size perspective (see Ziegler & Goswami, 2005), attention to the coarser whole-word phonological grain prevents the development of finer O → P associations that support the development and expansion of important context-dependent sublexical O → P associations (see also Harm, McCandliss, & Seidenberg, 2003; Steacy, Compton, et al., 2019). We (Compton, 2002; Compton et al., 2014; Steacy, Petscher, Rueckl, et al., 2021) have conceptualized this as *asymmetrical* development of the lexical system in which children with dyslexia add word-specific representations (i.e., whole word → phonological grain) to their orthographic lexicons without the corresponding development of

sublexical associations (i.e., fine grained O → P associations) seen in typically developing readers. The asymmetry explanation is consistent with the behavioral observation of the non-word reading deficit in children with developmental dyslexia (e.g., Metsala, 1999; Metsala et al., 1998; Rack et al., 1992). The lack of sublexical O → P associations in children with dyslexia has important implications for learning to read quasi-regular orthographies such as English.

Development of Context-Dependent Decoding Rules through Statistical Learning

Compared to other alphabetic scripts, English is considered particularly difficult for developing readers (see Seymour, 2005) because of inconsistencies with respect to smaller orthography-to-phonology (O → P) units (i.e., letters or letter clusters corresponding to single phonemes), along with inconsistencies with respect to larger reading units, such as rimes or syllables (Treiman, Mullennix, Bijeljac-Babic, & Richmond-Welty, 1995). Much of the variation in English O → P connections is associated with vowels and vowel combinations (see Venezky, 1999). This requires children learning to read English to develop decoding strategies at multiple grain sizes, with flexible appreciation of context-dependent variation. For instance, to decode the most frequent 3,000 monosyllabic English words, a child needs to know mappings between approximately 600 different orthographic patterns and 400 phonological rimes—far more than would be needed if the child could simply learn how to map 26 letters onto 26 phonemes (see Ziegler & Goswami, 2005).

In "deep" orthographies such as English, phonological decoding skills are necessary to support orthographic learning; however, these skills are not sufficient to guarantee the formation of a particular word-specific representation (see Nation & Castles, 2017; Share, 2008). In contrast to a transparent orthography (e.g., Spanish), in which there is a nearly one-to-one mapping between letters and phonemes, English phonemes can be represented by either letters or letter clusters (e.g., -ph in *graph*), and most graphemes can be pronounced in more than one way (cf. *find* vs. *hint*, *bead* vs. *head*). Inconsistency in the O → P mapping poses significant challenges to the beginning reader. For example, Seymour et al. (2003) observed that by the middle of first grade, the word and non-word reading achievement of English-speaking children lagged far behind that of readers of transparent orthographies. Readers of transparent orthographies could learn to decode by acquiring a set of rules linking each grapheme with a particular phoneme, then applying these rules (grapheme–phoneme conversion [GPC] rules) in a left-to-right fashion, thus assembling the pronunciation of a written word (or non-word). Quasi-regular orthographies such as English are problematic for a reader relying on rules of this sort, because not all words can be correctly pronounced using GPC rules (e.g., words such as *head* and *pint*).

As Venezky (1999) and others have noted, much of the ambiguity associated with the pronunciation of a particular grapheme can be resolved by considering the context in which that grapheme occurs. For instance, *ea* is pronounced as /i/ in *beat*, /ɛ/ in *head*, and /eɪ/ in *steak*. However, /i/ is the most frequent pronunciation of *ea* in –*eat*, but /ɛ/ is the most frequent pronunciation in –*ead*. In a corpus analysis, Kessler and Treiman (2001) found that the consistency of vowel pronunciation increases significantly when the syllable coda is considered. Thus, a decoding process based on multi-grapheme units could successfully decode both *beat* and *head*. There is substantial evidence that both children and adult readers make use of knowledge of regularities involving units larger than individual graphemes and phonemes. For example, Treiman et al. (2003, 2006) observed that how readers pronounce a non-word containing an ambiguous vowel (e.g., *ea*) depends on the context in which it occurs. Thus, whereas *cheam* is almost always read as rhyming with *beam*, *chead* is sometimes read as rhyming with *bead* and other times as rhyming with *head*, suggesting that the decoding process is sensitive to the context in which a grapheme appears. The Treiman et al. (2003, 2006) studies demonstrate that in typically developing readers, sensitivity to grapheme context develops early (i.e., first grade) and continues through elementary school (i.e., fifth grade) and is most pronounced in adults. In addition, the ability of children to use "consonantal context" correlated highly with standardized word-reading performance across a large grade range, indicating a strong relationship between inductive learning of orthographic–phonological statistical relationships and general word-reading ability.

During reading development, context-dependent sublexical connections evolve to represent the probabilistic co-occurrences and constraints that exist between orthographic and phonological units that resemble rule-like behavior (Perfetti, 1992; Seidenberg, 2005; Steacy, Compton, et al., 2019; Treiman & Kessler, 2006; Treiman et al., 2003). As a result, skilled readers come to realize that position within a word and surrounding letters affect correspondence between orthography and phonology. Although skilled readers process words rapidly without conscious employment of these context-dependent correspondences, they are knowledgeable about such relations upon reflection and can call on them when confronted with the task of pronouncing unfamiliar words (Perfetti, 1992). Our work suggests that children are more likely to use an alternative vowel pronunciation that is context-dependent as they become more proficient readers and as the occurrence of the alternative vowel pronunciation is increasingly supported by the corpus of words. As would be expected in such a model of word-reading development, child and corpus attributes work to tune variant vowel pronunciations across individual children and non-words, with important variance associated with both factors (Steacy, Compton, et al., 2019). Children with dyslexia, on the other hand, appear to benefit far less from corpus feedback and therefore are less likely to develop context-dependent sublexical O → P associations (Steacy, Petscher, Elliott, et al., 2021). These results again support the hypothesis that children with dyslexia process only partial information from words by placing insufficient attention on individual letters or groupings of letters (Ehri & Saltmarsh, 1995; Frith, 1985; Siegel et al., 1995) and the corresponding phonological representations.

The evolution of the orthographic lexicon to include context-dependent O → P relations in developing readers arises from complex interactions between experiential and child-specific factors related to word-reading development (see Steacy, Compton, et al., 2019). As such, we hypothesize that sensitivity to, and knowledge of, the statistical regularities and co-occurrences between orthography and phonology represented in the lexicons of children varies as a function of the strength of a child's underlying phonological skills that facilitate item-level learning, the ability to generalize statistical regularities across a set of learned items, the corpus of words to which that child has been exposed, the level of subword processing employed while processing words, and instructional history (e.g., experience with explicit and systematic phonics instruction). We have previously characterized statistical learning as the primary inductive learning mechanism by which children derive abstract probabilistic knowledge of O → P relationships (Steacy, Elleman, & Compton, 2017). Knowledge of the probabilistic relationships governing O → P mappings appear particularly important in quasi-regular orthographies such as English. Further, we maintain that skilled readers develop and rely on complex context-dependent decoding rules based on statistical learning to build fully specified lexical representations. Whereas measurable deficits in child-specific skills (e.g., phonological processing skill) likely limit the growth of important sublexical O → P connections that support the development of context-dependent decoding skills (Ehri & Saltmarsh, 1995). This has led us to hypothesize that skilled and less skilled word readers differ in their ability to learn and exploit probabilistic constraints that define the relationships between orthographic and phonological units (Compton et al., 2014; Elleman, Steacy, & Compton, 2019; Steacy, Elleman, & Compton, 2017). Thus, we maintain that skilled readers develop and rely on complex "context-dependent" O → P relations to build fully specified lexical representations (particularly as words become longer and more complex), whereas children with dyslexia tend to develop and rely on simplistic "context-independent" decoding rules that fail to promote fully specified lexical representations. Results from connectionist models (Harm et al., 2003; Harm & Seidenberg, 1999) mirrored differences in statistical learning between typically developing readers and children with phonological dyslexia. These results support a model of dyslexia in which a lack of phonological knowledge disrupts the normal statistical learning of the probabilistic co-occurrences and constraints that exist between orthographic and phonological units and further interrupts the transfer of sublexical knowledge to new letter strings. In the next section we expand on the convergence of computational modeling and behavioral studies supporting the lexical asymmetry hypothesis of dyslexia.

Convergence of Behavioral and Computational Models

The research on the mechanisms of reading has given rise to a number of sophisticated compu-

tational models (e.g., Coltheart, Rastle, Perry, Langdon, & Ziegler, 2001). Here we adopt the triangle model of reading (see Figure 25.1) based on principles of the connectionist or parallel distributed processing framework (Harm & Seidenberg, 1999, 2004; Seidenberg & McClelland, 1989). In the triangle model, the reading system is instantiated in a network of neuron-like processing units that communicate by sending excitatory and inhibitory signals to one another. The network is organized into distinct "layers" (sets of nodes), including layers responsible for representing the various linguistic properties (orthographic, phonological, and semantic) of a word, as well as layers of "hidden units" that function to mediate the associative mappings between the orthographic, phonological, and semantic layers. Like neural synapses, the connections in a network are plastic, and a learning algorithm is used to adjust their strengths (or weights) based on the interaction of the network and its task environment. Seeing a word causes a pattern of activation over the orthographic–phonological–semantic layers specific to that word. This results in a cascading flow of excitatory and inhibitory signals throughout the network, and over time, the network settles into a stable pattern of activation that serves as the representation of that word. The hidden units increase the computational power of the network by extending the range and complexity of problems the model can solve (Rumelhart, Hinton, & Williams, 1986) These hidden units have an interesting theoretical interpretation: they are the model's basis for developing underlying representations that abstract away from surface features of the input and output codes. Thus, learning in such systems is not merely the creation of associations between patterns. Instead, the hidden units allow generalizations to be learned by permitting the patterns of activation over the hidden units to represent the intermediate code formed by this abstraction process. The existence of these intermediate units gives the networks a different character than older approaches, in which behavior was construed as simple stimulus–response associations or associative chains. As such, hidden units allow the model to abstract important context-dependent relations between orthography and phonology that represent the probabilistic co-occurrences and constraints that exist between orthographic and phonological units (Seidenberg, 2005).

Because the connectionist architecture is by

design distributed, it is not wholly appropriate to describe separate "word-specific" and "subword" O → P associations as in the behavior models. Instead, distributed models allow O → P associations of all sizes to be represented in the connections between layers, and these connections over time represent the natural co-occurrence of O → P associations in the reading system. Connectionist models that incorporate moderate to severe phonological impairments have demonstrated a type of asymmetry in how O → P associations are represented in the model (for details see Harm & Seidenberg, 1999, 2004; Harm et al., 2003). All phonologically impaired models demonstrate impairments in non-word reading, with non-word reading performance being inversely correlated with the degree of phonological impairment. Mild phonological impairment only affects non-word reading while "sparing" word reading, whereas more severe phonological impairments affect word reading as well. In an unimpaired model, the phonological system contributes to decoding by "cleaning up" noisy or incomplete phonological representations. This allows the hidden units to provide the phonological system with somewhat incomplete input that captures the regularities in the mapping from orthography to phonology but can be easily overridden by the cleanup process in the case of exception words (e.g., *said*). In the impaired phonological system, more work must be done by the hidden units, because the phonological system is less able to repair degraded or incomplete phonological representations that result from the decoding process. This increased workload on the hidden units causes them to "memorize" word forms

and form "item-specific" representations. Harm and Seidenberg (1999, 2004) hypothesize that the effect of requiring the hidden units to perform a more exact computation results in overfitting of the training data, which interferes with generalization (i.e., O → P overfitting hypothesis). As such, the impaired network treats words differently from each other, representing them more like unanalyzed, individual wholes with less overlapping structure. The impaired model cannot take advantage of the similarity between words when reading the non-word, even though it can correctly pronounce real words. The model provides a computational account of why poor phonological representations lead to poor reading, and in particular poor generalization of fine-grained O → P associations needed to read non-words. Instead of forming representations sensitive to subword O → P units, the hidden units in the impaired simulations tend to learn item-specific representations. The formation of these item-specific representations is what directly impairs non-word reading.

Connectionist models have eloquently modeled this asynchrony between word-specific representations and sublexical O → P units in children with dyslexia. Harm and Seidenberg (1999) simulated phonological dyslexia by impairing the representations of phonological information before training the model to read words. Results showed that in the normal reading system, neighbor words such as *meat*, *treat*, and *eat* showed only small differences in their activation patterns, indicating that the rime pattern represented by *eat* is represented in hidden units of close proximity in the model. However, the phonologically

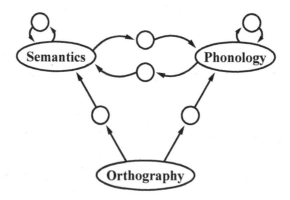

FIGURE 25.1. The triangle model of reading. From Compton et al. (2019). Copyright © 2019 John Wiley & Sons, Inc. Reprinted by permission.

impaired reading system formed divergent representations in which words sharing the same rime were represented in hidden units distributed across a larger space of hidden units. The difference in the distribution of hidden units across the two models also resulted in qualitatively different performance on non-word reading, with only the typical model correctly pronouncing the non-word *geat*. In the case of the impaired model, the representations developed for the words containing the rime *eat* did not overlap enough to allow for the correct pronunciation of *geat*.

The model provides a computational account of why poor phonological representations lead to poor reading, and in particular poor non-word generalization. The crucial insight from these simulations is that a phonological impairment leads to poor learning in the O → P component. Instead of forming representations sensitive to subword units such as onsets and rimes, the hidden units in the impaired simulations learn item-specific representations. The formation of these item-specific representations is what directly impairs non-word reading. The poor non-word reading in the model is not due to the phonological system's impaired ability to assemble phonemes produced by the reading system, but rather the phonological impairment causes poor O → P representations at multiple grain sizes to be formed during learning.

We see a convergence between the hypothesized time course of non-word and word-reading development according to computational and behavioral theories of dyslexia. Namely, initially weak phonological representations lead to a global processing strategy in word learning, resulting in asymmetrical development of the lexical system in children with dyslexia such that word-specific representations are added to the orthographic lexicon without the corresponding development of sublexical O → P associations that allow the decoding of non-words. In a recent developmental study (see Steacy, Petscher, Rueckl, et al., 2021), we tested this hypothesis behaviorally by modeling parallel growth of word-reading and non-word-reading factor scores across the entire distribution of reading skills (N = 588 children) using a growth curve of factors approach, focusing especially on those children with low levels of initial reading skill in first grade (i.e., children at risk for developing dyslexia). Vector plots (see Figure 25.2) were used to visualize the codevelopment between individual word-reading–non-word-reading factor trajectories across grades 1–4 as a function of

initial word-reading and non-word-reading skill in first grade. This was the first study to model, and display visually, the relations between word-reading and non-word-reading growth trajectories in a large sample of developing readers, thus allowing the "asymmetry/overfitting" hypotheses of dyslexia to be appraised.

Vector visualization indicates that children with low initial word-reading and non-word-reading skills tend to exhibit relatively flat word-reading–non-word-reading codevelopment (i.e., word-reading growth without concomitant non-word-reading growth), again supporting the well-documented non-word-reading deficit in children with developmental dyslexia (see Rack et al., 1992). Additionally, results indicate that while word-reading and non-word-reading growth factors are highly related in the sample, the relation between word-reading and non-word-reading trajectories changes in a nonlinear fashion as a function of initial word-reading and non-word-reading skill. Specifically, the angle of word-reading–non-word-reading vectors moves from nearly 45° in children with average and high initial word-reading skill to much more horizontal in children with low initial word reading. Flat vectors indicate word-reading growth without concomitant growth in non-word reading. In addition, children with low initial word-reading skills also had lower phonological awareness skills compared to children with average and high initial word-reading skills.

From both a connectionist modeling and behavioral asymmetry perspective, this failure to generalize word-reading skills to reading novel non-words suggests that children with dyslexia may be overreliant on a global processing strategy that affords insufficient attention to individual letters or groupings of letters (Ehri & Saltmarsh, 1995; Frith, 1985; Siegel et al., 1995) and the corresponding phonological representations (Harm & Seidenberg, 1999, 2004). Thus, the observed nonlinear relation between initial word reading and the word-reading–non-word-reading codevelopment vectors are consistent with explanations offered by both the lexical asymmetry models of developmental dyslexia and the triangle model. From a lexical asymmetry standpoint, Ehri and Saltmarsh (1995) have hypothesized that children with dyslexia lack sufficient "grapho-phonic" knowledge to fully analyze matches between orthographic and phonological units in order to store high-quality representations that include complete sublexical O → P associations. This is consistent with

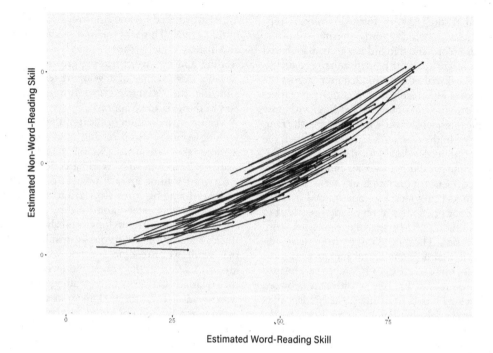

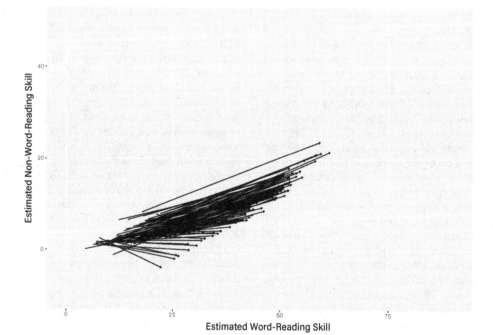

FIGURE 25.2. Vector plots illustrating estimated growth trajectories of word reading (*x*-axis) versus non-word (*y*-axis) reading (grades 1–4) as a function of estimated initial word-reading and non-word-reading skill in first grade in a random sampling of 25% of the subjects (top panel); and total sample of subjects with low initial word-reading skill (bottom panel). Shiny App depicting vectors as a function of first-grade phonological awareness skill for the entire sample: *https://wordreadinggrowth.shinyapps.io/vector_plot.*

the view that phonological processing deficits in children with dyslexia lead to a processing strategy that affords insufficient attention to sublexical O → P relations. In terms of the triangle model's overfitting hypothesis, poor non-word reading is caused by the formation of what are known as "noncomponential" O → P associations that are more holistic mappings (i.e., overfitting results in exact O → P associations that limit generalization). Componential representations, on the other hand, share structure with other items; hence, pronunciation can be aided through this overlapping structure (see Harm et al., 2003; Harm & Seidenberg, 1999). In the triangle model, such noncomponential representations are themselves caused by poor phonological representations at the beginning of the acquisition of reading. Given that learning is dependent on existing representations, once poor representations have been formed, subsequent learning exploits the (poor) characteristics of these existing representations (Harm et al., 2003). It is important to emphasize that both the lexical asymmetry and the overfitting hypotheses view this dependence on more global orthographic structure in dyslexia not as a strategy but as a consequence of how O → P mappings are learned.

Conclusion

In this chapter we have introduced the asymmetry hypothesis of dyslexia. The hypothesis refers to an unbalanced pattern of growth in the subsystems that make up the orthographic lexicon, disrupting the development of the orthographic lexicon and consequently limiting word reading and spelling skills development. Specifically, because underlying phonological processing difficulties tend to limit the growth of important sublexical O → P associations, children with dyslexia exhibit a general tendency to process only partial information about words and further rely on sources of information other than sublexical O → P associations that are considerably less efficient to facilitate word recognition. This is consistent with the view that children with dyslexia may be overreliant on a global processing strategy that results in insufficient attention to individual letters or groupings of letters and the corresponding phonological representations. Furthermore, we have highlighted results from both behavioral and computational modeling that support the lexical asymmetry hypotheses in children with dyslexia. Importantly, we have stressed that chil-

dren with dyslexia depend on more global orthographic processing as a consequence of how O → P mappings are learned, not as an effective strategy for word reading. Finally, our evidence that poor readers form word-specific representations that do promote the growth of important sublexical O → P associations provides insights into diagnostic tests that determine the locus of word-reading problems and suggests interventions tuned to the specific source of the impairment. Certainly, our results suggest that contrasting early word-reading and non-word-reading skills growth across time in struggling readers could help to quickly identify those children with characteristic flat word–non-word reading trajectories that indicate elevated risk for poor word-level reading outcomes. Furthermore, the instruction to which children are exposed plays a role in how they learn to read words, and how this affects the decoding of novel words (and non-words), particularly in children struggling to learn to read. Instructional routines that focus students' attention on connections at the sublexical level in a systematic way have an impact on the pattern of results observed regarding word reading versus decoding. Thompson, Connelly, Fletcher-Flinn, and Hodson (2009) observed differences in adult decoding patterns depending on whether participants had received phonics or no phonics in childhood reading instruction. They found that adults who had received phonics instruction read words that had alternative acceptable pronunciations using more regular, context-free grapheme–phoneme correspondences than adults who had not received phonics instruction as children, suggesting an apparent "cognitive footprint" of childhood phonics instruction.

Acknowledgments

This research was supported in part by Grant No. P20HD091013 from the Eunice Kennedy Shriver National Institute of Child Health and Human Development (NICHD). Statements do not reflect the position or policy of these agencies, and no official endorsement by them should be inferred.

References

Berninger, V. W. (1994). *The varieties of orthographic knowledge I: Theoretical and developmental issues*. Kluwer Academic Press.

Brady, S. A., & Shankweiler, D. P. (Eds.). (1991).

Phonological processes in literacy: A tribute to Isabelle Y. Liberman. Erlbaum.

Brooks, L. (1977). Visual pattern in fluent word identification. In A. S. Reber & D. L. Scarborough (Eds.), *Towards a psychology of reading* (pp. 95–110). Erlbaum.

Bruck, M. (1992). Persistence of dyslexics' phonological awareness deficits. *Developmental Psychology, 28*, 874–886.

Castles, A., & Nation, K. (2006). How does orthographic learning happen? In S. Andrews (Ed.), *From inkmarks to ideas: Current issues in lexical processing* (pp. 151–179). Psychology Press.

Castles, A., Rastle, K., & Nation, K. (2018). Ending the reading wars: Reading acquisition from novice to expert. *Psychological Science in the Public Interest, 19*(1), 5–51.

Coltheart, M., Rastle, K., Perry, C., Langdon, R., & Ziegler, J. (2001). DRC: A dual route cascaded model of visual word recognition and reading aloud. *Psychological Review, 108*, 204–256.

Compton, D. L. (2002). The relationship between phonological processing, orthographic processing, and lexical development in reading-disabled children. *Journal of Special Education, 35*, 201–210.

Compton, D. L., Miller, A. C., Elleman, A. M., & Steacy, L. M. (2014). Have we forsaken reading theory in the name of "quick fix" interventions for children with reading disability? *Scientific Studies of Reading, 18*(1), 55–73.

Compton, D. L., Steacy, L. M., Petscher, Y., Rueckl, J. G., Landi, N., & Pugh, K. R. (2019). Linking behavioral and computational approaches to better understand variant vowel pronunciations in developing readers. *New Directions for Child and Adolescent Development, 2019*(165), 55–71.

Cunningham, A. E., & Stanovich, K. E. (1998). What reading does for the mind. *American Educator, 22*, 8–17.

de Jong, P. F., Bitter, D. J., Van Setten, M., & Marinus, E. (2009). Does phonological recoding occur during silent reading, and is it necessary for orthographic learning? *Journal of Experimental Child Psychology, 104*(3), 267–282.

Duff, F. J., & Hulme, C. (2012). The role of children's phonological and semantic knowledge in learning to read words. *Scientific Studies of Reading, 16*(6), 504–525.

Edwards, A., Steacy, L. M., Seigelman, N., Rigobon, V. M., Kearns, D. K., Rueckl, J. R., & Compton, D. L. (2022). Unpacking the unique relationship between set for variability and word reading development: Examining word- and child-level predictors of performance. *Journal of Educational Psychology, 114*, 1242–1256.

Ehri, L. C. (2005). Learning to read words: Theory, findings, and issues. *Scientific Studies of Reading, 9*, 167–188.

Ehri, L. C. (2014). Orthographic mapping in the acquisition of sight word reading, spelling memory, and vocabulary learning. *Scientific Studies of Reading, 18*(1), 5–21.

Ehri, L. C., & Saltmarsh, J. (1995). Beginning readers outperform older disabled readers in learning to read words by sight. *Reading and Writing, 7*, 295–326.

Elbro, C., de Jong, P. F., Houter, D., & Nielsen, A. M. (2012). From spelling pronunciation to lexical access: A second step in word decoding? *Scientific Studies of Reading, 16*(4), 341–359.

Elleman, A. M., Steacy, L. M., & Compton, D. L. (2019). The role of statistical learning in word reading and spelling development: More questions than answers. *Scientific Studies of Reading, 23*, 1–7.

Fletcher, J. M. (2009). Dyslexia: The evolution of a scientific concept. *Journal of the International Neuropsychological Society, 15*, 501–508.

Fletcher, J. M., Lyon, G. R., Fuchs, L. S., & Barnes, M. A. (2018). *Learning disabilities: From identification to intervention*. Guilford Press.

Frith, U. (1985). Beneath the surface of developmental dyslexia. In K. Patterson, J. Marshall, & M. Coltheart (Eds.), *Surface dyslexia* (pp. 301–330). Erlbaum.

Gilbert, J. K., Compton, D. L., & Kearns, D. K. (2011). Word and person effects on decoding accuracy: A new look at an old question. *Journal of Educational Psychology, 103*, 489–507.

Gough, P. B., Juel, C., & Griffith, P. L. (1992). Reading, spelling, and the orthographic cipher. In P. B. Gough, L. C. Ehri, & R. Treiman (Eds.), *Reading acquisition* (pp. 35–48). Erlbaum.

Harm, M. W., McCandliss, B. D., & Seidenberg, M. S. (2003). Modeling the successes and failures of interventions for disabled readers. *Scientific Studies of Reading, 7*(2), 155–182.

Harm, M. W., & Seidenberg, M. S. (1999). Phonology, reading acquisition, and dyslexia: Insights from connectionist models. *Psychological Review, 106*, 491–528.

Harm, M. W., & Seidenberg, M. S. (2004). Computing the meanings of words in reading: Cooperative division of labor between visual and phonological processes. *Psychological Review, 111*(3), 662–720.

Harris, A., & Jacobson, M. (1982). *Basic reading vocabulary*. Macmillan.

Juel, C., Griffith, P. L., & Gough, P. B. (1986). Acquisition of literacy: A longitudinal study of children in first and second grade. *Journal of Educational Psychology, 78*(4), 243–255.

Kearns, D. K., Steacy, L. M., Compton, D. L., Gilbert, J. K., Goodwin, A. P., Cho, E., . . . Collins, A. A. (2016). Modeling polymorphemic word recognition: Exploring differences among children with early-emerging and late-emerging word reading difficulty. *Journal of Learning Disabilities, 49,* 368–394.

Keenan, J. M., & Betjemann, R. S. (2008). Comprehension of single words: The role of semantics in word identification and reading disability. In E. Grigorenko (Ed.), *Single-word reading: Behavioral and biological perspectives* (pp. 191–209). Erlbaum.

Kessler, B., & Treiman, R. (2001). Relationship between sounds and letters in English monosyllables. *Journal of Memory and Language, 44*(4), 592–617.

Metsala, J. L. (1999). The development of phonemic awareness in reading-disabled children. *Applied Psycholinguistics, 20*(1), 149–158.

Metsala, J. L., Stanovich, K. E., & Brown, G. D. (1998). Regularity effects and the phonological deficit model of reading disabilities: A meta-analytic review. *Journal of Educational Psychology, 90*(2), 279–293.

Nation, K., & Castles, A. (2017). Putting the learning in orthographic learning. In K. Cain, D. Compton, & R. Parrila (Eds.), *Theories of reading development* (pp. 147–168). John Benjamins.

Ouellette, G., & Fraser, J. R. (2009). What exactly is a yait anyway: The role of semantics in orthographic learning. *Journal of Experimental Child Psychology, 104,* 239–251.

Pennington, B. F. (2009). *Diagnosing learning disorders: A neuropsychological framework* (2nd ed.). Guilford Press.

Perfetti, C. A. (1992). The representation problems in reading acquisition. In P. B. Gough, L. C. Ehri, & R. Treiman (Eds.), *Reading acquisition* (pp. 145–174). Erlbaum.

Perfetti, C. (2007). Reading ability: Lexical quality to comprehension. *Scientific Studies of Reading, 11*(4), 357–383.

Perfetti, C. A., & Hart, L. (2002). The lexical quality hypothesis. *Precursors of Functional Literacy, 11,* 67–86.

Perfetti, C., & Stafura, J. (2014). Word knowledge in a theory of reading comprehension. *Scientific Studies of Reading, 18*(1), 22–37.

Peterson, R. L., & Pennington, B. F. (2015). Developmental dyslexia. *Annual Review of Clinical Psychology, 11,* 283–307.

Rack, J. P., Snowling, M. J., & Olson, R. K. (1992). The nonword reading deficit in developmental dyslexia: A review. *Reading Research Quarterly, 27*(1), 29–53.

Reitsma, P. (1983). Printed word learning in beginning readers. *Journal of Experimental Child Psychology, 36*(2), 321–339.

Rumelhart, D. E., Hinton, G. E., & Williams, R. J. (1986). Learning internal representations by error propagation. In D. E. Rumelhart & J. L. McClelland (Eds.), *Parallel distributed processing: Explorations in the microstructure of cognition* (Vol. 1, pp. 318–362). MIT Press.

Seidenberg, M. S. (2005). Connectionist models of word reading. *Current Directions in Psychological Science, 14,* 238–242.

Seidenberg, M. S., & McClelland, J. L. (1989). A distributed, developmental model of word recognition and naming. *Psychological Review, 96,* 523–568.

Seidenberg, M. S., Waters, G. S., Barnes, M. A., & Tanenhaus, M. K. (1984). When does irregular spelling or pronunciation influence word recognition? *Journal of Verbal Learning and Verbal Behavior, 23*(3), 383–404.

Seymour, P. H. K. (2005). Early reading development in European orthographies. In M. J. Snowling & C. Hulme (Eds.), *The science of reading: A handbook* (pp. 296–315). Blackwell.

Seymour, P. H. K., Aro, M., & Erskine, J. M. (2003). Foundation literacy acquisition in European orthographies. *British Journal of Psychology, 94*(Pt. 2), 143–174.

Shankweiler, D., Lundquist, E., Katz, L., Stuebing, K. K., Fletcher, J. M., Brady, S., . . . Shaywitz, B. A. (1999). Comprehension and decoding: Patterns of association in children with reading difficulties. *Scientific Studies of Reading, 3*(1), 69–94.

Share, D. L. (1995). Phonological recoding and self-teaching: Sine qua non of reading acquisition. *Cognition, 55,* 151–218.

Share, D. L. (2008). Orthographic learning, phonological recoding, and self-teaching. *Advances in Child Development and Behavior, 36,* 31–82.

Share, D. L. (2011). On the role of phonology in reading acquisition: The self teaching hypothesis. In S. A. Brady, D. Braze, & C. A. Fowler (Eds.), *Explaining individual differences in reading: Theory and evidence* (pp. 45–68). Psychology Press.

Siegel, L. S. (1989). IQ is irrelevant to the definition of learning disabilities. *Journal of Learning Disabilities, 22*(8), 469–478.

Siegel, L. S., Share, D., & Geva, E. (1995). Evidence for superior orthographic skills in dyslexics. *Psychological Science, 6*(4), 250–254.

Siegelman, N., Rueckl, J. G., Steacy, L. M., Frost, S. J., van den Bunt, M., Zevin, J. D., . . . Morris, R. D. (2020). Individual differences in learning the regularities between orthography, phonology, and semantics predict early reading skills. *Journal of Memory and Language, 114,* Article 104145.

Stanovich, K. E. (1988). Explaining the differences between the dyslexic and the garden-variety poor reader: The phonological-core variable-difference model. *Journal of Learning Disabilities, 21,* 590–604.

Stanovich, K. E. (1991). Word recognition: Changing perspectives. In P. D. Pearson, R. Barr, M. L. Kamil, & P. Mosenthal (Eds.), *Handbook of reading research* (Vol. II, pp. 418–452). Erlbaum.

Stanovich, K. E., & Siegel, L. S. (1994). Phenotypic performance profile of children with reading disabilities: A regression-based test of the phonological-core variable difference model. *Journal of Educational Psychology, 86*(1), 24–53.

Steacy, L. M., & Compton, D. L. (2019). Examining the role of imageability and regularity in word reading accuracy and learning efficiency among first and second graders at-risk for reading disabilities. *Journal of Experimental and Child Psychology, 178,* 226–250.

Steacy, L. M., Compton, D. L., Petscher, Y., Elliott, J. D., Smith, K., Rueckl, J., . . . Pugh, K. (2019). Development and prediction of context-dependent vowel pronunciation in elementary readers. *Scientific Studies of Reading, 23,* 49–63.

Steacy, L. M., Elleman, A. M., & Compton D. L. (2017). Opening the "black box" of learning to read: Inductive learning mechanisms supporting word-learning development with a focus on interventions for children who struggle to read. In K. Cain, D. L. Compton, & R. K. Parilla, R. (Eds.), *Theories of reading development,* (pp. 99–121). John Benjamins.

Steacy, L. M., Kearns, D. N., Gilbert, J. K., Compton, D. L., Cho, E., Lindstrom, E. R., & Collins, A. A. (2017). Exploring individual differences in irregular word recognition among children with early-emerging and late-emerging word reading difficulty. *Journal of Educational Psychology, 109,* 51–69.

Steacy, L. M., Petscher, Y., Elliott, J. D., Smith, K., Rigobon, V. M., Abes, D., . . . Compton, D. L. (2021). The effect of facilitative vs. inhibitory word training corpora on word reading accuracy growth in children with dyslexia. *Learning Disability Quarterly, 44*(3), 158–169.

Steacy, L. M., Petscher, Y., Rueckl, J. G., Edwards, A., & Compton, D. L. (2021). Modeling and visualizing the co-development of word and nonword reading in children from first through fourth grade: Informing developmental trajectories of children with dyslexia. *Child Development, 92*(3), e252–e269.

Steacy, L. M., Wade-Woolley, L., Rueckl, J. G., Pugh, K. R., Elliott, J. D., & Compton, D. L. (2019). The role of set for variability in irregular word reading: Word- and child-predictors in typically developing readers and students at-risk for reading disabilities. *Scientific Studies of Reading, 23,* 523–532.

Thompson, G. B., Connelly, V., Fletcher-Flinn, C. M., & Hodson, S. J. (2009). The nature of skilled adult reading varies with type of instruction in childhood. *Memory and Cognition, 37,* 223–234.

Torgesen, J. K. (2000). Individual differences in response to early interventions in reading: The lingering problem of treatment resisters. *Learning Disabilities Research and Practice, 15*(1), 55–64.

Treiman, R., & Kessler, B. (2006). Spelling as statistical learning: Using consonantal context to spell vowels. *Journal of Educational Psychology, 98*(3), 642–652.

Treiman, R., Kessler, B., & Bick, S. (2003). Influence of consonantal context on the pronunciation of vowels: A comparison of human readers and computational models. *Cognition, 88*(1), 49–78.

Treiman, R., Kessler, B., Zevin, J. D., Bick, S., & Davis, M. (2006). Influence of consonantal context on the reading of vowels: Evidence from children. *Journal of Experimental Child Psychology, 93*(1), 1–24.

Treiman, R., Mullennix, J., Bijeljac-Babic, R., & Richmond-Welty, E. D. (1995). The special role of rimes in the description, use, and acquisition of English orthography. *Journal of Experimental Psychology: General, 124*(2), 107–136.

Tunmer, W. E., & Chapman, J. W. (2012). Does set for variability mediate the influence of vocabulary knowledge on the development of word recognition skills? *Scientific Studies of Reading, 16,* 122–140.

Vellutino, F. R., Fletcher, J. M., Snowling, M. J., & Scanlon, D. M. (2004). Specific reading disability (dyslexia): What have we learned in the past four decades? *Journal of Child Psychology and Psychiatry, 45*(1), 2–40.

Vellutino, F. R., Scanlon, D. M., Sipay, E. R., Small, S. G., Pratt, A., Chen, R., & Denckla, M. B. (1996). Cognitive profiles of difficult-to-remediate and readily remediated poor readers: Early intervention as a vehicle for distinguishing between cognitive and experiential deficits as basic causes of specific reading disability. *Journal of Educational Psychology, 88*(4), 601–638.

Venezky, R. L. (1999). *The American way of spelling: The structure and origins of American English orthography.* Guilford Press.

Wang, H., Castles, A., & Nickels, L. (2012). Word regularity affects orthographic learning. *Quarterly Journal of Experimental Psychology, 65,* 856–864.

Wang, H., Nickels, L., Nation, K., & Castles, A. (2013). Predictors of orthographic learning of regular and irregular words. *Scientific Studies of Reading, 17*(5), 369–384.

Ziegler, J. C., & Goswami, U. (2005). Reading acquisition, developmental dyslexia, and skilled reading across languages: A psycholinguistic grain size theory. *Psychological Bulletin, 131*(1), 3–29.

CHAPTER 26

Developmental Language Disorder

What It Is and Why It Matters

Maura Curran and Tiffany Hogan

What Is Developmental Language Disorder?

Children with developmental language disorder (DLD) exhibit difficulties understanding or producing language compared to same-age peers, difficulties that are significant and persistent enough to result in functional challenges affecting communication and education (Bishop, Snowling, Thompson, Greenhalgh, & Catalise-2 Consortium, 2017). In essence, DLD is a learning disability that results in difficulties in learning language. DLD that is not associated with a biomedical condition is not the result of another disorder; rather, children with DLD present with language difficulties that are not explained by another diagnosis or their medical history. In this chapter, we discuss the definition of DLD and outline the early childhood and long-term impact of DLD on children's academic and life outcomes. We also discuss disparities in identification and support across demographic groups (e.g., boys vs. girls) and how teachers and other professionals can best support children with DLD in the early years.

Population

Even though many professionals have never heard of DLD, it is in fact a very common learning disability—approximately 7% of children have DLD (Tomblin et al., 1997), making it far more common than more well-known disorders such as autism spectrum disorder (Xu, Strathearn, Liu, & Bao, 2018). In a program with 30 children, you can expect to enroll two children with DLD simply by chance. A DLD diagnosis can be firmly established as early as around 5 years of age, and younger children may be identified as exhibiting significant, persistent language difficulties and risk factors known to be associated with a heightened risk of DLD (Bishop et al., 2017). Children with DLD at ages 5–7 are likely to exhibit persistent language learning difficulties and do not typically close the gap between their skills and those of peers over time (Law, Tomblin, & Zhang, 2008; Rice & Hoffman, 2015).

Characteristics

Compared to typically developing (TD) children, preschool and early school-age children with DLD present with smaller vocabularies, poor grammatical skills, and difficulties with oral narratives (Leonard, 2014). They are also at risk for poor phonological awareness. Children with DLD have a higher rate of speech-sound disorders than TD children, but many children with DLD exhibit clear articulation and are not difficult for adults to understand (Tomblin et al., 1997). Children with DLD in the preschool and early school years *are* verbal: These children are able to hold a conversation with an adult or peer. However, they typically use shorter sentences and more general vocabulary (e.g., *that thing*) than peers and may not respond to questions or verbal directions accurately. Children with DLD especially struggle with complex language skills such as abstract vocabulary or comprehension of lengthy and complex verbal information. Children with DLD may be perceived as immature or speaking like younger children by parents or others.

The History of DLD

Although the terms we use to talk about children with unexplained language difficulties are relatively new, children with language difficulties existed prior to the use of terms such as DLD. Children who were slow to talk were observed prior to the existence of a formal field of research investigating child development as we know it today. In the modern era, researchers examined the characteristics and course of development of children with language difficulties and began to investigate the differences between these children and other children. A brief overview of the modern study of language disorders provides insight into how we currently understand DLD and some of the recent gains in the field.

Developmental Aphasia

Aphasia is the disorder exhibited by an adult with language production or comprehension disorders following a stroke or other neurological injury. During the 1960s and 1970s, it was common for researchers to refer to children with unexplained language difficulties as children with *developmental aphasia* or *developmental dysphasia* (Leonard, 2020). The use of these terms in reference to children faded as researchers came to understand the extent to which developmental difficulties differed from adult disorders exhibited after injury. During this period, researchers investigated the perceptual skills of children with language difficulties, the specific aspects of language that posed difficulty for these children, and the course of their development over time. They also began to better determine how to diagnose and treat children with language disorders.

Specific Language Impairment

The term *specific language impairment* (SLI) emerged in an attempt to better characterize the group of children of interest to researchers and to address the methodological weaknesses of earlier research (e.g., Leonard, 1989). Children with SLI were proposed to exhibit an impairment in language despite entirely preserved nonverbal IQ—thus, a disability *specific* to language (e.g., Bishop, 1992). Children with nonverbal IQ scores outside of the average range were not included in this group, even when they did not have intellectual impairment. Research continued to outline the difficulties and skills of children with SLI, and great advances in diagnosis and treatment occurred. However, over the years, increasing debate surrounded both the term SLI and the strict boundaries regarding which children exhibited true SLI as compared to a more general learning difficulty. For example, children with SLI tend to score lower than TD children on nonverbal IQ measures as a group and exhibit subtle difficulties in areas other than language, indicating that their impairment is not quite so specific to language alone as once thought (Gallinat & Spaulding, 2014). The clinical population of children with poor language skills did not reflect a strict cutoff between children with SLI and children with poor language who also had below-average IQ scores, and the use of strict criteria in diagnosing SLI impaired advocacy and outreach efforts (Reilly et al., 2014).

Developmental Language Disorder

Both the term *developmental language disorder* and the specific definition of DLD were developed by a multinational panel of English-speaking experts on language impairments in children. Based on the recommendations of this panel, DLD was defined as a profile that comprises difficulties in language associated with functional impairment in a poor prognosis for recovery (Bishop et al., 2017). According to the guidelines of the panel, DLD could be reliably identified by age 5 years, but younger children could exhibit early warning signs prior to this point. Currently, children with DLD are understood to exhibit a range of nonverbal skills and to exhibit difficulties in terms of function, not just on specific language skills tested by researchers. The work around DLD brings a new focus to the functional impacts of language difficulties on individuals. This, in turn, makes it clear that researchers, families, educators, and clinicians should focus on not only isolated skills that may be impaired but also how individuals with DLD may require support and accommodations to be successful in key life settings and skills. Literacy, of course, is a skill essential to successful participation in a modern society, and, as we outline in this chapter, it is one area in which children with DLD exhibit a need for targeted supports.

Comorbidities

As noted earlier, the focus of this chapter is DLD that is not associated with a biomedical cause. Thus, children with DLD do not have additional diagnoses known to result in language difficulties such as autism, intellectual disability, hearing impairment, or cerebral palsy. However, there are a number of conditions that are observed at a higher rate in children with DLD than in TD children. These can be referred to as *comorbid conditions*. Here, we focus on a subset of common comorbid conditions that may be observed in early childhood. However, note that this is not an exhaustive list.

Attention-Deficit/Hyperactivity Disorder

Children with attention-deficit/hyperactivity disorder (ADHD) present with difficulties in attention, distractibility, and hyperactivity that are pronounced enough to result in impairments in functioning across social and academic settings (Centers for Disease Control and Prevention, n.d.). Children with DLD exhibit a higher rate of ADHD than do TD children (Redmond, Ash, & Hogan, 2015). Most studies of children with language disorder and ADHD rely on the SLI approach; all children with nonverbal IQ below the typical range were excluded, even if they did not fall in the range of intellectual disability. Studies have revealed that co-occurrence of ADHD and DLD is *not* associated with more severe symptoms of DLD (Redmond et al., 2015). In fact, children with both ADHD and DLD perform slightly better than children with DLD alone on some language tasks, possibly because children with ADHD may be more likely to receive in-school intervention than do children with DLD alone.

Dyslexia

Dyslexia is a learning disability characterized by difficulty reading printed words despite sufficient instruction and absence of intellectual disability (Compton et al., Chapter 25, this volume). Whereas children with DLD struggle with oral language, including vocabulary, grammar, and narrative skills, children with dyslexia exhibit difficulties in learning to decode written words due to phonological processing challenges. Children with DLD exhibit higher rates of dyslexia than do TD children, though different researchers have found varied degrees of comorbidity across these populations (Snowling, Hayiou-Thomas, Nash, & Hulme, 2020; Alonzo, McIlraith, Catts, & Hogan, 2020). In other words, dyslexia and DLD are distinct disorders, but they co-occur more often than would be expected by chance in children (Catts, Adlof, Hogan, & Weismer, 2005). Young children who have DLD but not dyslexia may appear to have intact reading abilities as they begin decoding words. However, these children typically struggle with reading comprehension in later years as the language involved in reading and writing grows more complex. Young children with dyslexia exhibit difficulty in acquiring prereading and reading skills, including letter names, early decoding, and early spelling; as they grow older, these children exhibit reading comprehension difficulties associated with their inaccurate, slow, and laborious decoding. Children who have both DLD and dyslexia exhibit poorer alphabetic knowledge in kindergarten than children with DLD alone (Alonzo, McIlraith, Catts, & Hogan, 2020). As they grow older, this group exhibits poorer reading comprehension skills than children with dyslexia alone or children with DLD alone, and require interventions to support both their decoding and their oral language skills. Professionals working with young children who have DLD should be aware that these children have a heightened risk of dyslexia and should monitor reading progress closely.

Underserved Populations

While DLD is underidentified in general, a number of factors that affect which children receive intervention in the early years are not related to actual need for language support. For example, DLD presents at a highly similar rate in boys and girls, and there are no notable differences in severity across the sexes (cf. Tomblin et al., 1997). However, in both Australia and the United States, boys are more likely to receive preschool speech–language services (Morgan et al., 2017; Skeat et al., 2014). Similarly, preschool-age Black children are less likely than non-Hispanic White peers to receive school-based services with a primary diagnostic category of speech and language needs in the United States (Morgan et al., 2017). Children who speak more than one language are at particular risk of being misidentified in terms of DLD. Bilingual children may be over- or underidentified, depending on the screening and assessment procedures in use (Bedore & Peña, 2008). In some studies, parental concern is one of the strongest predictors of intervention receipt (e.g., Skeat et al., 2014). This seems to indicate that one highly engaged, invested adult can make a difference in terms of whether a child is identified or not during the early years, which could be of particular importance for children from underserved populations.

Impact of DLD in Early Childhood

The diagnosis of DLD explicitly requires that children exhibit significant enough difficulties in communication that these difficulties affect their functioning on a persistent basis. When we discuss children with DLD during the early childhood years, there are consistent patterns that emerge in terms of the functional impact of DLD in academic and other settings. Note that there is a great deal of within-group variation—no single child with DLD is exactly like another child with DLD. Despite this, there are commonly occurring areas of need and relative strength for children.

Preliteracy and Early Literacy

As noted earlier, children with DLD are more likely than TD children to have dyslexia and may exhibit early signs of dyslexia during the first stages of literacy instruction. Children with DLD frequently exhibit difficulty in phonological awareness (Alonzo et al., 2020) and benefit from preschool interventions targeting phonological awareness skills (e.g., Gillon, 2002). Children with DLD who do not have dyslexia may appear to have typical reading skills during the early stages of learning to read; decod-

ing may appear fairly typical for these children. However, members of this population cannot be regarded as "typical readers" even during early school years. The underlying language disorder is still present; it simply may not be detected in the context of written language when assessment focuses on decoding. Although the reading comprehension difficulties exhibited by children with DLD may not be detected until later grades, they reflect ongoing difficulties with the oral language skills that make up the basis for reading comprehension and written expression that can be detected during the early education years. An educator working with a young child with DLD may note that the child does not comprehend new vocabulary words taught during a read-aloud in the classroom or takes longer than peers to learn these new words. This child may not respond to questions about a narrative or expository text accurately and may exhibit difficulties with "story grammar" and share narratives that are confusing, brief, or incomplete. Children may struggle to express themselves verbally and in writing, and may become frustrated with their difficulties.

Social-Emotional Skills and Friendships

Although children with DLD do not exhibit the severe and pervasive difficulties with social–emotional reciprocity that characterize the profile of children with autism, they do struggle with social–emotional skills compared to TD children. During the preschool years, children with DLD have smaller social networks within a classroom and are more likely to be isolated within a classroom than TD peers (Chen, Justice, Rhoad-Drogalis, Lin, & Sawyer, 2020). The isolation a child with DLD may face within a preschool classroom does not arise solely from the actions of the child with DLD. Rather, TD peers are more likely to seek out and interact with other TD peers and are relatively less likely to spend time with DLD peers—just as children with DLD are more likely to spend time with peers who also have DLD than with TD peers. As children grow older, the nature of their difficulties may shift. For example, children with DLD exhibit more withdrawn and passive behaviors and lower levels of prosocial behavior than peers (Fujiki, Brinton, Morgan, & Hart, 1999), and these differences can be reliably identified through the use of teacher observational scales (Fujiki, Brinton, Hart, Olsen, & Coombs, 2019). Along these lines, 7- to 9-year-old children with DLD are more likely to exhibit difficulties with peer relationships and inattention than TD peers (Redmond & Ash, 2014). In addition, children with DLD from ages 5 to 8 are also at an increased risk of being bullied by other children, and/or of bullying other children (Øksendal et al., 2021). Overall, children with DLD enter the preschool years with social–emotional vulnerabilities, and these continue as they grow older, though the exact manifestation of these needs evolves over development. Children with DLD do not live in a vacuum: They are affected by their peers, their school experiences, and their interactions with others over time. Thus, if we wish to support the social–emotional health of children with DLD, we must consider children's functioning within the greater system of their environments and past experiences.

Behavioral Challenges

Children with DLD may struggle with externalizing behavior (behavior directed outward, e.g., tantrums) or internalizing behavior (behavior directed inward, e.g., social withdrawal) to a greater degree than their TD peers (Curtis et al., 2018). Children with DLD often struggle more with emotional regulation compared to TD peers and may exhibit executive functioning difficulties as well. Some research indicates that changes in externalizing behavior over time are related to changes in children's language abilities over time. Note that children with DLD exhibit less widespread and severe difficulties with behavior and executive function than children with ADHD. In fact, when analyses control for the effect of language and academics, attention and behavioral ratings for 7- to 9-year-old children with DLD and TD children may no longer appear significantly different (Redmond & Ash, 2014).

Impact of DLD Beyond Early Childhood

School-Age Years

Children with DLD exhibit difficulty in understanding grade-level text, even when they can decode that text. Thus, as academic and literacy demands move from "learning to read" to "reading to learn," children with DLD typically exhibit increasing difficulties as compared to peers—including children with DLD who

do not have dyslexia. Reading comprehension relies on understanding of the written language on the page. Compared to oral language, written language includes more frequent use of rare and abstract vocabulary words, a higher rate of complex sentence structure, and other characteristics that are more challenging for people with poor language skills to comprehend. This is true even in children's books, though the language demands inherent in written language increase as children grow older and are expected to read and understand increasingly complex material (e.g., Curran, 2020).

Although literacy is the most well-studied and obvious area in which older children with DLD are at risk for difficulty, other academic areas may be challenging as well. This may be due, in part, to their underlying language needs; children must engage their language skills to learn new concepts presented verbally (i.e., teacher talking to the class) or in textbooks (i.e., reading assigned texts). It may also be due, in part, to their general difficulties in learning more broadly. Children with DLD tend to exhibit greater difficulty in areas of study that require a great deal of language, but they may also perform below peers in areas such as math (Cross, Joanisse, & Archibald, 2019) and science (Matson & Cline, 2012).

Adolescent and Adult Outcomes

Children with DLD exhibit highly variable outcomes as adults. They graduate high school at a lower rate than TD peers (Conti-Ramsden, Durkin, Mok, Toseeb, & Botting, 2016) With that said, there are individuals with DLD who do successfully complete college degree programs. Data are mixed regarding whether adults with DLD are more likely to experience low income or unemployment than TD peers (Conti-Ramsden et al., 2016). Women with speech or language disabilities are more likely to experience sexual assault by age 25 than TD peers (Brownlie, Jabbar, Beitchman, Vida, & Atkinson, 2007). Young men with DLD are more likely to have contact with the police and to be incarcerated than TD peers, and young offenders with DLD exhibit a higher recidivism rate than other young offenders (Winstanley, Webb, & Conti-Ramsden, 2021). Although individuals with DLD are at heightened risk, this does not indicate that any one individual with DLD will experience some or all of the negative adult outcomes reported here.

For example, in contrast to the overall pattern of findings indicating elevated risk of committing criminal offenses, a U.K. study found that young adults with DLD who received targeted intervention as children were less likely to report police contact than TD peers (Winstanley, Webb, & Conti-Ramsden, 2018). Researchers have found that some of the emotional difficulties observed in children and adolescents with DLD are associated with peer relationships, which indicates that supportive peer relationships may mitigate the risk of these challenges (Forrest, Gibson, Halligan, & St Clair, 2018).

DLD in the Classroom

A common phrase used in education is "If you know better, you do better." In this chapter, we have described a common childhood condition, developmental language disorder. Epidemiological studies show that approximately two children in each classroom have DLD. Even so, teacher training programs and professional development include little to no information about DLD. A recent survey confirmed that teachers have very little knowledge about DLD (Peltier, Washburn, Heddy, & Binks-Cantrell, 2022). If educators know more about DLD, they can support these children in their classrooms.

Nation, Clarke, Marshall, and Durand (2004) called DLD "a hidden disorder," because unless you assess language skills explicitly using a comprehensive language assessment, these children often blend in with their peers. For many decades, study after study has shown that only approximately one-third of children with DLD are identified for school support (Tomblin et al., 1997; Hendricks, Adlof, Alonzo, Fox, & Hogan, 2019; Wittke & Spaulding, 2018). Of those identified, teachers and parents often did not know the child with DLD was struggling (Hendricks et al., 2019). Those identified for services don't show the most severe language deficits either (Tomblin et al., 1997). Instead, they are children who have an educated mother or those who have co-occurring ADHD (Wittke & Spaulding, 2018). The 70% who go unidentified struggle to comprehend and express their thoughts, but their deficits aren't revealed until the later grades, when texts become more complex (Catts, Hogan, & Adlof, 2005).

In our clinical experience, parents and teachers label children with DLD as not academically inclined, lazy, low intelligence, or inattentive. Educators we encounter have blamed parents for not talking to their children enough or letting them spend too much time on electronics. These negative labels impact the child's self-perception and place needless blame on parents.

Future Directions

As we have reviewed in this chapter, DLD is a neurobiological variation in which a child is born having difficulty understanding and using language. In this section, we provide a "call to action" for both educators and researchers to positively impact the lives of children with DLD. We encourage researchers and educators to consider accomplishing these goals together, and, when appropriate, by using *implementation science,* which is an approach to research that considers contextual influences on implementation with a team of researchers and stakeholders (e.g., educators, administrators, parents; Petscher et al., 2020). In our laboratory, we have used implementation science as a roadmap to establish sustainable school partnerships (Alonzo et al., 2022) and to determine barriers and facilitators to implementation of assessment and intervention for children with dyslexia and DLD (Komesidou et al., 2022). Implementation science is at its core a methodology that aims to reduce the research-to-practice gap (Solari et al., 2020), accelerating sustained positive impacts on clinical practice and, in turn, child outcomes. It seeks to achieve the following:

1. *Improve identification of DLD.* Research into how best to identify children with DLD in school settings is badly needed. School-based universal screenings are common practice. The goal of universal screening in schools is to accurately identify students at risk for failing academically. It includes screening for hearing loss, vision impairment, and, most recently, dyslexia (Ward-Lonergan & Duthie, 2018). However, current screenings, such as Dynamic Indicators of Basic Early Literacy Skills (DIBELS; Good & Kaminski, 2002), miss children with DLD (Adlof & Hogan, 2019; Weiler, Schuele, Feldman, & Krimm, 2018). Not screening for DLD has dire consequences, because children with DLD are at high risk for failing academically (Duff, Hendricks, Fitton, & Adlof, 2022). We have been working with schools to implement

screenings for DLD and, as a result, we recently reviewed the availability of screening tests for DLD (Bao, Komesidou, & Hogan, 2022). A link to our most recent version of this list can be found in this open-access document: *https://tinyurl.com/screen4dld*. We will update it as new screening tests are published. Our laboratory's goal is to work with school partners to identify those at risk for DLD, establish infrastructure and training to provide those who are at risk a comprehensive assessment of language abilities, and establish evidence-based Tier 1, 2, and 3 language stimulation to improve educational achievement and social–emotional skills in children with DLD. If we don't assess language in every child, we won't know who is at risk. As noted earlier, these children's weak language skills are often hidden in plain sight until much later in their academic careers, when negative self-image and poor achievement are well established. The earlier these children are identified, the earlier they can begin receiving the support they need to mitigate failure. Research should focus on adding more time-efficient yet psychometrically sound screening measures for DLD and progress monitoring tools to assess language skills over time, with a focus on culturally appropriate and sensitive measures that use the "disorder within diversity" framework (Oetting, 2018). The CUBED assessment is an example of such a measure that has been developed and refined in the past decade (Petersen & Spencer, 2016) for use with children who are monolingual and bilingual Spanish–English speakers.

2. *Advocate for DLD.* Teachers have limited knowledge about DLD (Peltier et al., 2022). This is through no fault of their own; teacher education programs rarely focus on DLD. In the past, it has been the exclusive purview of speech–language pathologists (SLPs). The focus has been on children that have individualized education plans (IEPs) for speech and/or language impairment. In most education models, these children are taken from the classroom with an SLP to work on speech and language skills in the "speech room." In some models, the SLP works with a child with DLD in the classroom. Recently, advocacy and awareness efforts have increased, led by persons with DLD, their parents, researchers, and SLPs who work with persons with DLD. These efforts have resulted in informational websites (*www.radld.org*; *www.dldandme.org*) and advocacy/awareness days. International DLD Awareness Day was observed for the fourth time on October 14, 2022. To bring awareness, monuments all over the world were lit last year. Information and pictures can be found at *https://radld.org/dld-awareness-day/light-up-events*. The goal of these events is to get people talking about DLD. Researchers and educators have an important role in increasing awareness about DLD by incorporating language measures and including DLD in literacy studies and sharing information about DLD widely with students and their families and colleagues. Additionally, research and practice should consider the effects of verbiage and views of disability on children with DLD. Studies of mental health show that stigma around conditions can be reduced by talking about the condition (Volkow, Gordon, & Koob, 2021); the same likely holds for disabilities such as DLD. Efforts around neurodiversity also highlight the importance of destigmatizing individual differences. *Neurodiversity,* a term coined in the late 1990s (Blume, 1997; Singer, 1999), describes variation in cognitive–linguistic social skills in a nonpathological sense, challenging the view that disorders are inherently bad. Neurodiversity adopts the social model of disability in which societal expectations are the lens through which disability is viewed. Persons with autism report that neurodiversity awareness has created more positive feelings about their self-perception (Kapp, Gillespie-Lynch, Sherman, & Hutman, 2013). Within the context of our partnerships with schools and teachers, our team has studied educator training on DLD in a neurodiversity framework as a part of the whole child's strengths and weaknesses. It is our goal to improve a child with DLD's self-perception by creating and refining training modules for educators to confidently discuss neurodiversity in classrooms, which in turn we believe will positively impact academic achievement and social–emotional well-being for all children, but especially those with DLD and other learning disabilities.

3. *Increase quality language input in the classroom.* Classroom educators serve a key role for children who receive SLP services, as well as for children who are not eligible for IEPs or other SLP services. Children with DLD benefit from high-quality language input in the classroom: Children's language growth over the course of a year is related to teachers' language usage. Educators frequently adjust their own language based on the language skills of individual chil-

dren during interactions. Even for children who receive SLP services, the SLP alone cannot provide sufficient exposure to new words and concepts for children to make adequate progress; children with DLD require engagement from others as well (McGregor, Van Horne, Curran, Cook, & Cole, 2021). We know that children's language growth is related to teacher's language use, and that different children may benefit from different types of language input and scaffolding strategies (Justice, McGinty, Zucker, Cabell, & Piasta, 2013; Pentimonti et al., 2017). Researchers can investigate specific characteristics of classroom talk that support children with DLD. Researchers who focus specifically on issues around language disabilities and intervention can collaborate with researchers who focus on classroom and literacy outcomes for a broader population to enrich the evidence base. We need to know how children with DLD respond to typical classroom support strategies, and how best to provide the type of language input these children need in their classroom settings. For educators, a clear action step would be to work closely with SLPs and determine how best to increase quality language input in the classroom. Research and applied efforts can focus on the effect of techniques used in-the-moment in the classroom (e.g., use of a prompt to help a child respond to an educator's question) and learning over time (e.g., providing enough exposure to new words to acquire target vocabulary).

There are specific interventions and resources that may be of use for educators or educator–SLP teams in supporting children with DLD in the early childhood classroom. As part of a grant from the department of education, a team of researchers developed a supplementary Tier 1 (full classroom) reading comprehension curriculum for children from PreK to third grade and tested its efficacy (Language and Reading Research Consortium [LARRC], 2019). This curriculum is available for free at *https://larrc.ehe.osu.edu/curriculum*. Educators and SLPs may also need to adapt interventions and strategies to fit the needs of their specific settings and populations. A checklist and guide to this process in Curran, Komesidou, and Hogan (2022) is based on adaptations made to the LARRC curriculum during virtual teaching during the COVID-19 school shutdowns in 2020. Please note that interventions designed to target decoding do not automatically result in gains in oral language; evidence-based interventions for oral language and comprehension are required to support gains in these areas. Future studies should determine how to adapt, implement, and study the efficacy of language comprehension lessons across the grades for Tiers 1, 2, and 3.

4. *Support peer relationships and social engagement.* Children with DLD may need support from educators to build friendships and other positive relationships with peers, and peers may need support to engage with children with DLD. Researchers are still building the evidence base regarding the social profile of children with DLD, and how best to intervene to support peer relationships and social engagement. Given the importance of these factors for long-term outcomes such as quality-of-life ratings, additional research in this area would be welcome. For educators and clinicians, one key step is to monitor the interactions of children with DLD and TD peers to ensure that children with DLD are not isolated. Educators can model and scaffold social communication with additional supports for children who may be struggling. Consulting with the SLP where possible and necessary to ensure success for all children.

Educational researchers have the potential to significantly advance the field of research into DLD, thus supporting strong outcomes for children with DLD. Research into how children with DLD respond to classroom-level or other interventions, how to support peer relationships, and other areas could have huge impacts on the quality of life of children with DLD.

Educators have a strong influence on their students' academic success, self-perception, and emotional well-being (Jimerson & Haddock, 2015). Learning about DLD and using strategies in the classroom can mitigate failure in children with DLD and have a lifelong positive influence. Although children with DLD show clear vulnerabilities in terms of literacy skills and other essential life outcomes, educators can support positive growth and outcomes for these children.

References

Adlof, S. M., & Hogan, T. P. (2019). If we don't look, we won't see: Measuring language development to inform literacy instruction. *Policy Insights from the Behavioral and Brain Sciences, 6*, 210–217.

Alonzo, C. N., McIlraith, A. L., Catts, H. W.,

& Hogan, T. P. (2020). Predicting dyslexia in children with developmental language disorder. *Journal of Speech, Language, and Hearing Research, 63*(1), 151–162.

Bao, X., Komesidou, R., & Hogan, T. P. (2022). *A review of screening tests to identify risk of developmental language disorder.* Manuscript in preparation.

Bedore, L. M., & Peña, E. D. (2008). Assessment of bilingual children for identification of language impairment: Current findings and implications for practice. *International Journal of Bilingual Education and Bilingualism, 11*(1), 1–29.

Bishop, D. V. (1992). The underlying nature of specific language impairment. *Journal of Child Psychology and Psychiatry, 33*(1), 3–66.

Bishop, D. V., Snowling, M. J., Thompson, P. A., Greenhalgh, T., & the Catalise-2 Consortium. (2017). Phase 2 of CATALISE: A multinational and multidisciplinary Delphi consensus study of problems with language development: Terminology. *Journal of Child Psychology and Psychiatry, 58*(10), 1068–1080.

Blume, H. (1997). "Autism and the Internet" or "It's the wiring, stupid." Retrieved July 2021 from *http://web.mit.edu/comm-forum/legacy/papers/blume.html.*

Brownlie, E. B., Jabbar, A., Beitchman, J., Vida, R., & Atkinson, L. (2007). Language impairment and sexual assault of girls and women: Findings from a community sample. *Journal of Abnormal Child Psychology, 35*(4), 618–626.

Catts, H. W., Adlof, S. M., Hogan, T. P., & Weismer, S. E. (2005). Are specific language impairment and dyslexia distinct disorders? *Journal of Speech, Language, and Hearing Research, 48*(6), 1378–1396.

Catts, H. W., Hogan, T. P., & Adlof, S. M. (2005). Developmental changes in reading and reading disabilities. In H. W. Catts & A. G. Kamhi (Eds.), *The connections between language and reading disabilities* (pp. 38–51). Psychology Press.

Centers for Disease Control and Prevention. (n.d.). *What Is ADHD?* Author. Available at *www.cdc.gov/ncbdd/adhd/facts.html.*

Chen, J., Justice, L. M., Rhoad-Drogalis, A., Lin, T. J., & Sawyer, B. (2020). Social networks of children with developmental language disorder in inclusive preschool programs. *Child Development, 91*(2), 471–487.

Conti-Ramsden, G., Durkin, K., Mok, P. L., Toseeb, U., & Botting, N. (2016). Health, employment and relationships: Correlates of personal wellbeing in young adults with and without a history of childhood language impairment. *Social Science and Medicine, 160,* 20–28.

Cross, A. M., Joanisse, M. F., & Archibald, L. M. (2019). Mathematical abilities in children with developmental language disorder. *Language,*

Speech, and Hearing Services in Schools, 50*(1), 150–163.

Curran, M. (2020). Complex sentences in an elementary science curriculum: A research note. *Language, Speech, and Hearing Services in Schools, 51*(2), 329–335.

Curran, M., Komesidou, R., & Hogan, T. P. (2022). Less is more: Implementing the minimal intervention needed for change approach to increase contextual fit of speech–language interventions. *Language, Speech, and Hearing Services in Schools, 53,* 317–328.

Curtis, P. R., Frey, J. R., Watson, C. D., Hampton, L. H., & Roberts, M. Y. (2018). Language disorders and problem behaviors: A meta-analysis. *Pediatrics, 142*(2), Article e20173551.

Duff, D., Hendricks, A. E., Fitton, L., & Adlof, S. (2022, June 22). Reading and math achievement in children with dyslexia, developmental language disorder, or typical development: Achievement gaps persist from second through fourth grades. *Learning Disabilities.* [Epub ahead of print] doi: 10.1177/00222194221105515

Forrest, C. L., Gibson, J. L., Halligan, S. L., & St Clair, M. C. (2018). A longitudinal analysis of early language difficulty and peer problems on later emotional difficulties in adolescence: Evidence from the Millennium Cohort Study. *Autism and Developmental Language Impairments, 3,* 239.

Fujiki, M., Brinton, B., Hart, C. H., Olsen, J., & Coombs, M. (2019). Using measurement invariance to study social withdrawal in children with developmental language disorders. *Language, Speech, and Hearing Services in Schools, 50*(2), 253–266.

Fujiki, M., Brinton, B., Morgan, M., & Hart, C. H. (1999). Withdrawn and sociable behavior of children with language impairment. *Language, Speech, and Hearing Services in Schools, 30*(2), 183–195.

Gallinat, E., & Spaulding, T. J. (2014). Differences in the performance of children with specific language impairment and their typically developing peers on nonverbal cognitive tests: A meta-analysis. *Journal of Speech, Language, and Hearing Research, 57*(4), 1363–1382.

Gillon, G. T. (2002). Follow-up study investigating the benefits of phonological awareness intervention for children with spoken language impairment. *International Journal of Language and Communication Disorders, 37*(4), 381–400.

Good, R. H., & Kaminski, R. A. (Eds.). (2002). *Dynamic indicators of basic early literacy skills* (6th ed.). Institute for the Development of Educational Achievement.

Hendricks, A. E., Adlof, S. M., Alonzo, C. N., Fox, A. B., & Hogan, T. P. (2019). Identifying children at risk for developmental language disorder using a brief, whole-classroom screen. *Journal of Speech, Language, and Hearing Research, 62*(4), 896–908.

Jimerson, S. R., & Haddock, A. D. (2015). Understanding the importance of teachers in facilitating student success: Contemporary science, practice, and policy. *School Psychology Quarterly, 30*(4), 488–493.

Justice, L. M., McGinty, A. S., Zucker, T., Cabell, S. Q., & Piasta, S. B. (2013). Bi-directional dynamics underlie the complexity of talk in teacher–child play-based conversations in classrooms serving at-risk pupils. *Early Childhood Research Quarterly, 28*(3), 496–508.

Kapp, S. K., Gillespie-Lynch, K., Sherman, L. E., & Hutman, T. (2013). Deficit, difference, or both?: Autism and neurodiversity. *Developmental Psychology, 49*(1), 59–71.

Komesidou, R., Feller, M. J., Wolter, J. A., Ricketts, J., Rasner, M. G., Putman, C. A., & Hogan, T. P. (2022). Educators' perceptions of barriers and facilitators to the implementation of screeners for developmental language disorder and dyslexia. *Journal of Research in Reading, 45,* 277–298.

Language and Reading Research Consortium, Jiang, H., & Logan, J. (2019). Improving reading comprehension in the primary grades: Mediated effects of a language-focused classroom intervention. *Journal of Speech, Language, and Hearing Research, 62*(8), 2812–2828.

Law, J., Tomblin, J. B., & Zhang, X. (2008). Characterizing the growth trajectories of language impaired children between 7 and 11 years of age. *Journal of Speech, Language, and Hearing Research, 51,* 739–749.

Leonard, L. B. (1989). Language learnability and specific language impairment in children. *Applied Psycholinguistics, 10*(2), 179–202.

Leonard, L. B. (2014). *Children with specific language impairment.* MIT Press.

Leonard, L. B. (2020). A 200-year history of the study of childhood language disorders of unknown origin: Changes in terminology. *Perspectives of the ASHA Special Interest Groups, 5*(1), 6–11.

Matson, G., & Cline, T. (2012). The impact of specific language impairment on performance in science and suggested implications for pedagogy. *Child Language Teaching and Therapy, 28*(1), 25–37.

McGregor, K. K., Van Horne, A. O., Curran, M., Cook, S. W., & Cole, R. (2021). The challenge of rich vocabulary instruction for children with developmental language disorder. *Language, Speech, and Hearing Services in Schools, 52*(2), 467–484.

Morgan, P. L., Farkas, G., Hillemeier, M. M., Li, H., Pun, W. H., & Cook, M. (2017). Cross-cohort evidence of disparities in service receipt for speech or language impairments. *Exceptional Children, 84*(1), 27–41.

Nation, K., Clarke, P., Marshall, C. M., & Durand, M. (2004). Hidden language impairments in children: Parallels between poor reading comprehension and specific language impairments? *Journal of Speech, Language, and Hearing Research, 47,* 199–211.

Oetting, J. B. (2018). Prologue: Toward accurate identification of developmental language disorder within linguistically diverse schools. *Language, Speech, and Hearing Services in Schools, 49*(2), 213–217.

Øksendal, E., Brandlistuen, R. E., Wolke, D., Helland, S. S., Holte, A., & Wang, M. V. (2021). Associations between language difficulties, peer victimization, and bully perpetration from 3 through 8 years of age: Results from a population-based study. *Journal of Speech, Language, and Hearing Research, 64,* 2698–2714.

Peltier, T. K., Washburn, E. K., Heddy, B. C., & Binks-Cantrell, E. (2022). What do teachers know about dyslexia? It's complicated! *Reading and Writing, 35*(1), 1–31.

Pentimonti, J. M., Justice, L. M., Yeomans-Maldonado, G., McGinty, A. S., Slocum, L., & O'Connell, A. (2017). Teachers' use of high-and low-support scaffolding strategies to differentiate language instruction in high-risk/economically disadvantaged settings. *Journal of Early Intervention, 39*(2), 125–146.

Petersen, D. B., & Spencer, T. D. (2016). *CUBED.* Language Dynamics Group.

Petscher, Y., Cabell, S. Q., Catts, H. W., Compton, D. L., Foorman, B. R., Hart, S. A., . . . Wagner, R. K. (2020). How the science of reading informs 21st century education. *Reading Research Quarterly, 55*(Suppl. 1), S267–S282.

Redmond, S. M., & Ash, A. C. (2014). A cross-etiology comparison of the socio-emotional behavioral profiles associated with attention-deficit/hyperactivity disorder and specific language impairment. *Clinical Linguistics and Phonetics, 28*(5), 346–365.

Redmond, S. M., Ash, A. C., & Hogan, T. P. (2015). Consequences of co-occurring attention deficit/hyperactivity disorder on children's language impairments. *Language, Speech, and Hearing Services in Schools, 46*(2), 68–80.

Reilly, S., Tomblin, B., Law, J., McKean, C., Mensah, F. K., Morgan, A., . . . Wake, M. (2014). Specific language impairment: a convenient label for whom? *International Journal of Language and Communication Disorders, 49*(4), 416–451.

Rice, M. L., & Hoffman, L. (2015). Predicting vocabulary growth in children with and without specific language impairment: A longitudinal study from 2; 6 to 21 years of age. *Journal of*

Speech, Language, and Hearing Research, 58(2), 345–359.

Singer, J. (1999). Why can't you be normal for once in your life?: From a "problem with no name" to the emergence of a new category of difference. In M. Corker & S. French (Eds.), *Disability discourse* (pp. 59–67). Open University Press.

Skeat, J., Wake, M., Ukoumunne, O. C., Eadie, P., Bretherton, L., & Reilly, S. (2014). Who gets help for pre-school communication problems?: Data from a prospective community study. *Child: Care, Health and Development, 40*(2), 215–222.

Snowling, M. J., Hayiou-Thomas, M. E., Nash, H. M., & Hulme, C. (2020). Dyslexia and developmental language disorder: Comorbid disorders with distinct effects on reading comprehension. *Journal of Child Psychology and Psychiatry, 61*(6), 672–680.

Solari, E. J., Terry, N. P., Gaab, N., Hogan, T. P., Nelson, N. J., Pentimonti, J. M., . . . Sayko, S. (2020). Translational science: A road map for the science of reading. *Reading Research Quarterly, 55*, S347–S360.

Tomblin, J. B., Records, N. L., Buckwalter, P., Zhang, X., Smith, E., & O'Brien, M. (1997). Prevalence of specific language impairment in kindergarten children. *Journal of Speech, Language, and Hearing Research, 40*(6), 1245–1260.

Volkow, N. D., Gordon, J. A., & Koob, G. F. (2021). Choosing appropriate language to reduce the stigma around mental illness and substance use disorders. *Neuropsychopharmacology, 26*, 2230–2232.

Ward-Lonergan, J. M., & Duthie, J. K. (2018). The state of dyslexia: Recent legislation and guidelines for serving school-age children and adolescents with dyslexia. *Language, Speech, and Hearing Services in Schools, 49*(4), 810–816.

Weiler, B., Schuele, C. M., Feldman, J. I., & Krimm, H. (2018). A multiyear population-based study of kindergarten language screening failure rates using the Rice Wexler Test of Early Grammatical Impairment. *Language, Speech, And Hearing Services in Schools, 49*(2), 248–259.

Winstanley, M., Webb, R. T., & Conti-Ramsden, G. (2018). More or less likely to offend?: Young adults with a history of identified developmental language disorders. *International Journal of Language and Communication Disorders, 53*(2), 256–270.

Winstanley, M., Webb, R. T., & Conti-Ramsden, G. (2021). Developmental language disorders and risk of recidivism among young offenders. *Journal of Child Psychology and Psychiatry, 62*(4), 396–403.

Wittke, K., & Spaulding, T. J. (2018). Which preschool children with specific language impairment receive language intervention? *Language, Speech, and Hearing Services in Schools, 49*(1), 59–71.

Xu, G., Strathearn, L., Liu, B., & Bao, W. (2018). Prevalence of autism spectrum disorder among US children and adolescents, 2014–2016. *Journal of the American Medical Association, 319*(1), 81–82.

CHAPTER 27

Autism and Early Literacy

The State of the Science

Kelly Whalon and Veronica P. Fleury

The purpose of reading is to gain meaning from print or to comprehend text (Rayner, Foorman, Perfetti, Pesetsky, & Seidenberg, 2001). The simple view of reading (SVR) is a well-supported and useful framework (e.g., Nation, 2019) that characterizes reading comprehension (RC) as the product of two discrete, independent capacities: decoding (D) and listening comprehension (LC), or RC = D × LC (Gough & Tunmer, 1986). Although distinct, these skills are applied reciprocally as good readers effortlessly and fluently decode while simultaneously constructing meaning to form a coherent mental model of text. Language is essential to these capacities, as reading is the integration of written and spoken language (Nation, 2019). For example, the ability to distinguish between speech sounds (*phonology*) helps children map sounds to letters, or *graphemes*. A well-developed vocabulary (*semantics*) facilitates understanding of text and also supports a child's decoding when encountering a familiar word while reading. Knowledge of grammar (*syntax*) is necessary to gain meaning from sentences, and the ability to link multiple sentences to interpret discourse (*pragmatics*) builds comprehension of stories and passages (Tunmer & Hoover, 2019).

This intricate relationship between reading and language presents challenges to children who experience delays or difficulties developing language (Adolf & Hogan, 2019). For children with autism spectrum disorder (ASD), communica-tion deficits are inherent and often interfere with reading development (e.g., Davidson, 2021). The communication characteristics associated with ASD begin impacting literacy development as early as preschool (e.g., Fleury & Lease, 2018), and these challenges tend to persist (Grimm, Solari, & Gerber, 2018), with some children with ASD experiencing a decline in reading achievement over time (e.g., Wei, Blackorby, & Schiller, 2011). This is alarming, as learning to read is essential to postschool success, and an inability to read is costly to an individual's quality of life and society (World Literacy Foundation, 2012). Many of the skills known to influence reading development emerge in preschool. Consequently, early childhood presents a unique opportunity to build foundational early language and literacy skills that may prevent future reading failure (National Early Literacy Panel [NELP], 2008).

This chapter explores the implications of our work over the past several years addressing the early language and literacy skills of young children with ASD. We discuss the impetus of and trajectory for our work. It is important to note that this literature base is still in its infancy, and although we are primarily focusing on our work, there are several others who are also exploring how young children with ASD develop early language and literacy skills (e.g., Davidson, Kaushanskaya, & Weismer, 2018; Dynia, Lawton, Logan, & Justice, 2014) and methods to support their early language and literacy learning (e.g., Westerveld, Paynter, & Wicks, 2020).

ASD Defined

ASD is a neurological disorder defined by the *Diagnostic and Statistical Manual of Mental Disorders* (DSM-5-TR) as a consistent difficulty with social communication and the presence of restricted or repetitive patterns of behavior, interests, or activities (American Psychiatric Association, 2022). Although all children diagnosed with ASD share these foundational characteristics, autism is a spectrum disorder representing a highly diverse group of learners. For example, approximately one-third of children with ASD also have an identified intellectual disability (Centers for Disease Control and Prevention [CDC], 2020). There is also marked variability in the language acquisition of children with ASD, with an estimated one-third developing minimal verbal speech, others acquiring speech late, and some demonstrating effective mechanics of language while having trouble using and understanding language in conversations (Paul & Simmons, 2019).

A Growing Need for Language and Literacy Research to Support Children with ASD

Historically, research has largely focused on understanding and improving the defining features associated with ASD, including social communication, language development, and behavior. In the early 2000s, the passage of the No Child Left Behind Act and the Individuals with Disabilities Education Improvement Act of 2004 mandated that all teachers provide reading instruction consistent with scientifically based reading research. State efforts to comply referred to seminal reports, including the National Institute of Child Health and Development (NICHD)-funded meta-analysis conducted by the National Reading Panel (NRP, 2000; Foorman & Nixon, 2006). The NRP emphasized the importance of comprehensive reading instruction that systematically targets five areas of reading: phonemic awareness, phonics, fluency, vocabulary, and reading comprehension (NRP & NICHD, 2000). The recommendations by the NRP are based on studies designed to prevent or remediate the reading difficulties of a range of learners,

but these studies did not include children with ASD. Following the NRP report, we conducted a review of reading intervention studies including learners with ASD. Using the simple view of reading as a framework, we identified only 11 intervention studies specifically teaching one or more of the five areas of reading (Whalon, Al Otaiba, & Delano, 2009). This small research base included no comprehensive reading intervention studies but revealed that many children and youth with ASD develop a variety of reading skills following instruction consistent with NRP recommendations.

Following these policy changes, the literacy development of children with ASD received greater attention. There was an increase in studies focusing on the reading achievement of learners with ASD that largely described a discrepant reading profile with the majority achieving average or above scores on measures of word recognition paired with poor performance on reading comprehension assessments (e.g., Mayes & Calhoun, 2003). In a seminal study, Nation, Clarke, Wright, and Williams (2006) included a sample of 41 children with ASD with a range of language abilities. Performance varied widely, with nine children unable to read and the remaining 32 scoring from floor to ceiling levels on various subtests. Similarly, the majority of participants (65%) scored at least 1 standard deviation (*SD*) below the mean on reading comprehension measures, and a substantial portion (38%) scored more than 2 *SD*s below the mean. This profile of poor reading comprehension despite average or better word recognition became a familiar pattern in the literature, and poor scores on measures of reading comprehension were also associated with low scores on measures of vocabulary, syntax, and higher-order language skills including inference making (e.g., Brown, Oram-Cardy, & Johnson, 2013; Nation et al., 2006; Norbury & Nation, 2011). Davidson and Weismer (2014) investigated the early literacy profiles of young children with ASD and found that challenges with meaning-focused skills emerged before formal reading instruction began. The majority of young children with ASD in their sample (62%) performed well on measures of alphabet knowledge and scored poorly on measures of conventions of print and meaning (i.e., comprehension of words, sentences, and passages). This accumulation of evidence indicated that most children with ASD experience difficulty reading for meaning, and interventions designed to build meaning focused skills need to begin in early childhood.

The Impetus for Shared Reading Interventions

Although our two research teams were working separately but simultaneously across the country, we came to the same conclusion: *Young children with ASD require quality early language and literacy interventions that may offset future reading comprehension difficulties.* Our research teams read several reports highlighting the notable impact of shared reading interventions on foundational skills known to influence later reading comprehension (e.g., definitional vocabulary; listening comprehension; NELP, 2008). At this time, meta-analyses consistently reported compelling findings following shared reading interventions, including moderate to large effects on the language, vocabulary, and listening comprehension of young children. These studies included a range of learners suggesting that most young children are likely to benefit from shared reading interventions (e.g., NELP, 2008; Swanson et al., 2011). Further evidence from meta-analyses demonstrated that the way adults read aloud to children matters. Instead of the adult reading aloud as the child passively listens, in quality shared reading, the adult encourages participation by asking questions, making comments, and expanding on child responses while also adjusting his or her communication level to meet the needs of the learner. This process creates a social routine as the adult and child engage in an interactive dialogue around a common stimulus (i.e., a book; Cunningham & Zibulsky, 2011).

Our research teams recognized that the social nature of interactive shared reading interventions may evoke questions or even apprehensiveness about the appropriateness of shared reading for children with ASD (Fleury, Miramontez, Hudson, & Schwartz, 2014); that is, these quality shared reading interactions capitalize on joint attention (i.e., coordinating the attention between people and objects; Pentimonti, Justice, & Piasta, 2013) and social reciprocity (Cunningham & Zbiulsky, 2011), and both are considered core challenges for young children with ASD (American Psychiatric Association, 2013). More specifically, in shared reading, joint attention occurs when the child and adult shift their gaze between each other and the book, or the child and adult share affect in response to story events. Adults also establish joint attention when pointing to and labeling items, objects, events, or emotions depicted in pictures. In addition, the reciprocal interactions generated during shared reading by questioning and commenting are created for the purpose of sharing information or enjoyment. Children with ASD often use language to request and protest but rarely to socially share (Paul & Simmons, 2019). Instead of viewing these social (i.e., joint attention, reciprocal interactions) aspects of shared reading as barriers to or prerequisites for learning, our teams identified these features as opportunities for learning. More specifically, shared reading establishes a predictable, joint routine (Pentimonti et al., 2013) that results in natural opportunities to elicit joint attention and social interaction. After participating in joint routines, children with ASD have learned a number of developmental skills, as such routines establish a shared frame of reference between the adult and child, and encourage verbal and nonverbal responses (Vivanti, 2020). Our teams perceived the predictable structure of shared reading as a way to enhance the early language and literacy skills of young children with ASD.

Dialogic Reading

One interactive shared reading routine accumulated substantial evidence: dialogic reading (DR; Phillips, Chapter 12, this volume). The What Works Clearinghouse (2007, 2010) identified DR as an effective practice for young children and a promising practice for young children with language delays. Moreover, Swanson and colleagues (2011) found that DR provides more causal evidence than other shared reading interventions, with moderate to large effects on a number of skills, including vocabulary and comprehension. In DR, books are repeatedly read over a series of days (3–5) as the adult scaffolds language to encourage the child to increasingly say more while intentionally fading his or her role as the child becomes increasingly active in sharing the story (Zevenbergen & Whitehurst, 2003). The DR instructional sequence, PEER, begins with a questioning *prompt*. After the child responds, the adult *evaluates* the response and *expands* by rephrasing and adding additional information. The child is then asked to *repeat* the expansion (Zevenbergen & Whitehurst, 2003). The acronym CROWD reminds the adult of five different questioning prompts used to initiate the PEER sequence. *Completion* prompts ask the child to fill in a blank at the end of a sentence ("Little Blue _____."). *Recall* prompts include questions about events or the main idea (e.g., "Oh no! What happened to the truck?"). *Open-ended* prompts ask the child to describe what is depicted in an illustration ("Tell me about this picture"; "What's happening?"; "What do you see?"). *Wh- questions* ask the child to label and identify the function of vocabulary in the book ("What is this?"; "What is this part called?"). *Distancing questions* require children to connect events from the story to their own experiences ("Where do you see cows?").

DR and Young Children with ASD

Fleury and colleagues (2014) were the first to apply DR with three preschool children with ASD (ages 3–5) in a single-case research design study. They compared child on-task behavior and verbal participation in a baseline condition (i.e., an adult reading aloud while responding to child comments) to a DR condition (i.e., the addition of DR prompts and instructional sequence). Compared to baseline, all three children increased their verbal participation in the DR condition. Participants with ASD exhibited high levels of engagement in baseline, and after DR, high levels of engagement continued despite the addition of DR prompts and strategies that increased the duration of shared reading. Although participants engaged during DR, their responses to CROWD question prompts were inconsistent.

Adaptations to DR for Young Children with ASD

The data from Fleury and colleagues (2014) informed our future work. It was clear from this initial data that the social nature of shared reading contexts is not an impediment to learning, as children with ASD readily engaged in baseline and intervention conditions. This is also consistent with our later work. For example, in a study comparing shared reading interactions between caregivers and their children with ASD and caregivers and their typically developing children, Fleury and Ford (2021) found no difference between the number of initiations and responses of children with ASD and their typically developing peers. Shared reading routines appear to

naturally create opportunities for adult–child interactions. This study also highlighted the importance of teaching adults interactive shared reading techniques. Although caregivers asked questions and made comments, they encouraged a limited range of responses (e.g., labeling instead of open-ended or distancing questions), suggesting that to promote and maintain reciprocal interactions, adults may need to learn additional strategies.

Our teams also learned from Fleury and colleagues (2014) that some children with ASD benefit from DR alone, while others require additional supports. Subsequently, we developed adaptations to DR that included instructional procedures consistent with naturalistic developmental behavioral interventions (NDBIs). NDBIs are considered evidence-based interventions for young children with ASD (e.g., Schreibman et al., 2015) and share several common features; that is, NDBIs (1) target a developmental domain (e.g., language, literacy); (2) are delivered in a routine context (e.g., shared reading); (3) incorporate strategies to support attention, encourage initiations, and promote joint attention; (4) create a balance of adult- and child-initiated interactions; and (5) embed an antecedent, response, consequence instructional sequence (i.e., a three-term contingency such as starting with a question, evaluating a response, and expanding on the response). The adaptations we developed were designed to (1) improve child responding to question prompts, (2) increase initiations, and (3) build vocabulary knowledge.

Supporting Responses

In NDBIs, prompts are used to promote new skills development (Schreibman et al., 2015). Our teams added least-to-most prompting hierarchies to support the responding of children with ASD, as there is strong evidence that prompting hierarchies can enhance the early learning of children with ASD (e.g., Steinbrenner et al., 2020). This technique begins by providing the learner an opportunity to respond independently and is followed by a series of prompts beginning with the least supportive and ending with the prompt that results in the child completing the task accurately (i.e., a controlling prompt). In our DR adaptations, least-to-most prompting hierarchies are included in the evaluate step of the PEER sequence; that is, after asking a question using one of the CROWD question types, if a child did not respond or responded incorrectly, the adult issued a series of prompts beginning with the least and ending with the most intrusive. Table 27.1 provides two different examples used in our adaptations of DR. Studies using prompting hierarchies have increased the independent verbal responding of young children with ASD (Fleury & Schwartz, 2017; Whalon, Hanline, & Davis, 2016; Whalon, Martinez, Shannon, Butcher, & Hanline, 2015). Whalon and colleagues (2015) noted that over time, the use of visual supports applied in the prompting hierarchy decreased as use of spontaneous correct responding to question prompts increased.

Fact- and Inference-Based Responses

The ability to make inferences is associated with reading comprehension (e.g., Oakhill & Cain, 2018) and is linked to the comprehension of children with ASD (e.g., Grimm et al., 2018; Norbury & Nation, 2011). One adaptation to DR, reading to engage children with autism in language and learning (RECALL), adds *wh-* question prompts that require prediction (e.g., "What will happen next?"), as well as emotion identification (e.g., "How do you think he feels?") and understanding ("Why is he mad?"). After RECALL, participants with ASD have increased their correct responding to fact- and inference-based questions (Whalon et al., 2015, 2016). These findings are encouraging, as inference making is a challenging skill for children with ASD (Lucas & Norbury, 2015; McIntyre et al., 2017). Although children improved their responding to inference-based questions, one child demonstrated more modest improvements (Whalon et al., 2016), which suggests that some children with ASD may require more time to learn to generate inferences or need more explicit instruction on drawing inferences from text (Whalon et al., 2016).

Encouraging Initiations

Fleury and Schwartz (2017) found that after implementing adapted DR, young children with ASD improved their responses to questions, but their initiations did not increase. One of the goals of shared reading is active participation as the child increasingly begins to take on the role of storyteller (Zevenbergen & Whitehurst, 2003). Fleury and Schwartz (2017) noted that paraprofessionals learned to implement the interactive PEER sequence with fidelity, but may have over emphasized the questioning prompts, thereby limiting opportunities for children to spontaneously initiate. Because children with ASD are less likely to initiate for the purpose of socially sharing, they may require additional prompts or supports.

To encourage initiations, RECALL embeds secure attention prompts and intentional pauses to DR. Secure attention prompts are designed to promote joint attention by directing the child's attention to something of interest or an action in the story by pointing and exclaiming (e.g., "Wow!" while pointing to a picture). Intentional pauses are used to interrupt the reading at an important part of the story or just before or after turning the page to elicit an initiation; that is, the adult pauses and looks expectantly at the child for 3–5 seconds. Following participation in RECALL, three of four children increased their spontaneous initiations, although gradually, throughout the intervention. The fourth participant showed a slight increase with RECALL, as

TABLE 27.1. Example Least to Most Prompting Hierarchies

Prompting level	Fleury & Schwartz (2017)	Whalon et al. (2015)
1	Binary choice • "Is it a car or a truck?"	Three visual response options • "Is it a car, a truck or a motorcycle?" while pointing to three visual response options.
2	Asking a yes–no question • "Is it a truck?"	Binary choice • "Is it a car or a truck?" while pointing to two visual options
3	Asking child to repeat the target word • "Say *truck*."	Direct modeling and asking child to repeat • "This is a truck [pointing]. Say *truck*."
4	Physically guiding hand of the child to a picture of the target word	Physically guiding hand of the child to a picture of the target word

he initiated at high levels in baseline (Whalon et al., 2015). Because children with ASD represent a highly heterogeneous group, what will be required to increase commenting and questioning during shared reading is likely to differ. For example, some children may require more explicit prompting or a greater frequency of secure attention prompts and intentional pauses.

Building Vocabulary Knowledge

Castles, Rastle, and Nation (2018) referred to vocabulary as fundamental to reading comprehension. The vocabulary knowledge of children with ASD predicts reading comprehension (e.g., Brown et al., 2013; Davidson et al., 2018; Davidson, 2021; Nation et al., 2006), including the ability to make inferences about text (Lucas & Norbury, 2015). Moreover, young children with ASD score more poorly on measures of vocabulary knowledge that require depth of knowledge or the ability to not only label but also provide the function of the word (e.g., Davidson & Weismer, 2014; Dynia et al., 2014; Dynia, Brock, Justice, & Kaderavek, 2017; Fleury & Lease, 2018). DR provides several opportunities to identify words and discuss their meanings. In DR, initial questions often involve teaching the label and functions of words (e.g., "What is this?"; "What is it for?"). After children begin using the target vocabulary, questions become increasingly sophisticated and require children to use the word in context (e.g., open-ended questions) or use knowledge of the word to make inferences that relate the story to their experiences (e.g., distancing questions). Following adapted DR, Fleury and Schwartz (2017) found that all nine participants with ASD improved their ability to expressively label book-specific vocabulary.

Nunes and colleagues (2021) used RECALL to teach young children with ASD (ages 4–5) to label ("What is he doing?") and identify the function (e.g., "Why do you do that?") of nouns and verbs depicted in storybooks. RECALL conditions were compared to repeated reading alone conditions. Conditions were alternated after children read the same book for 4 consecutive days. Three of the five children improved their ability to expressively identify the label and function of target nouns and verbs in the RECALL condition, and two children only increased their ability to receptively identify target words. To encourage expressive identification of words and their corresponding functions, we further adapted the intervention by reversing the prompting hierarchy. Specifically, on the first 2 days of reading, after asking a question (e.g., "What is this?"; "What is it for?"), we modeled the correct response and asked the child to repeat our model. On the third day, we added a binary choice of two visual response options, and on the fourth day, we provided three visual response options. This adaptation resulted in greater gains, but gains were more modest for one participant. This study also included a peer comparison. Typically developing peers improved their ability to label and identify the function of target vocabulary following 4 days of reading in the repeated reading and RECALL conditions; however, gains in the RECALL condition were higher. Although all children with ASD improved their ability to label and identify the function of words in the RECALL condition, only one child with ASD reached near peer levels. It is also unclear whether children with ASD began to use the words or generalized their word learning to other contexts or measures.

Extensions and Replications of Adapted DR

Additional research teams have replicated adaptations to DR and extended findings to other language and literacy skills. For example, Hudson and colleagues (2017) replicated an adapted version of DR (Fleury & Schwartz, 2017) in a randomized controlled trial comparing effects of adapted interactive shared reading to a code-focused intervention. Children in the interactive shared reading condition outperformed the comparison group on standardized measures of expressive and receptive vocabulary and listening comprehension. Two international teams (Lo & Shum, 2021; Walter & de Paula Nunes, 2020) taught caregivers to implement RECALL. In a small randomized controlled trial in China, parent–child dyads were randomly assigned to RECALL or to a control group (i.e., parents read aloud to their child using the same books as in the RECALL condition). The parent–child dyads assigned to RECALL showed more improvement than the control group on a number of measures, including a standardized assessment of emotion understanding and researcher-developed measures of story comprehension and engagement. Both the intervention and control groups made gains on a standardized receptive vocabulary measure (Lo & Shum, 2021). Walter and de Paula Nunes (2020) also found increased engagement as child initiations and responses improved during interactive shared reading.

Extending Interactive Shared Reading to Classroom Settings

Findings from our initial work suggested that interactive shared book reading can improve early language and literacy skills of young children with ASD. We have also found that natural intervention agents including caregivers (e.g., Whalon et al., 2016) and paraeducators (Fleury & Schwartz, 2017) can implement these procedures with fidelity. These studies also reaffirm that young children with ASD are a heterogeneous group, with some children responding to DR without adaptations (e.g., Fleury et al., 2014) and others responding variably even with supports (e.g., Nunes et al., 2021). Together, these studies suggest a need to better understand what adaptations are needed for whom and when (Fleury & Towson, 2021).

Adaptive interventions provide empirical guidelines for when and how to change interventions depending on learners' responses. Researchers assign learners to intervention adaptations at predetermined points depending on their response to intervention (Fleury & Towson, 2021). In an underpowered pilot sequential multiple-assignment randomized trial (SMART design), Fleury and Towson explored questions related to how and when to adapt DR. Several decision points were required, including (1) How long should young children with ASD participate in DR before making determinations about progress?; (2) What outcome variable should be used to determine if a child requires additional adaptations?; and (3) What adaptations are likely to support the learning of young children with ASD? In this study, 10 children with ASD (ages 4–5) and four teachers participated. Participants were randomized to two small group DR conditions groups: early decision small-group DR (i.e., 4 weeks) or late decision small-group DR (i.e., 8 weeks). Participants remained in the DR small-group condition if their performance on a researcher-developed expressive vocabulary measure (i.e., verbally labeling pictures illustrating book-specific vocabulary) met a set criterion (i.e., >80% correct or growth rate of 1.8 words per book). Children who did not reach the defined level of responding were randomly assigned to one of two intensified instructional conditions:

one-to-one DR or modified DR. One-to-one instruction provided greater intensity and more opportunities to respond. Modified DR included the addition of (1) visual supports representing target vocabulary, (2) questions used to elicit responses related to target vocabulary, and (3) a least-to-most prompting hierarchy beginning with a yes–no question and ending with a request to point.

No student assigned to the early response (Week 4) condition was classified as a "responder" based on identified criteria on the expressive vocabulary measure. All students were randomly assigned to an intensified instructional condition. Only one child assigned to the late-decision condition (Week 8) showed an early response and continued with the small-group DR sessions. Although there were notable differences in engagement between stages of the intervention (i.e., a decrease of 48 to 28% of time disengaged), these results were not statistically significant. Children with ASD also learned some new words, but their rate of improvement was slow, and there were no differences across conditions. Despite participating in an initial 2-hour workshop and receiving follow-up coaching, teacher implementation fidelity was low, making it difficult to determine the effects of DR or DR with adaptations (Fleury & Towson, 2021); that is, teachers did not consistently complete the PEER instructional sequence of DR including evaluating the child's response, expanding the child's response, and asking children to repeat expansions. These findings suggest that future studies will require a larger sample, and a greater emphasis on coaching and coaching dosage. In addition, more time may be required to learn target vocabulary, which would suggest prolonging decision-making time points.

Future Directions

In this chapter, we have argued that children with ASD are at high risk for reading failure due to social–communication and language difficulties inherent to the disorder (e.g., Brown et al., 2013; McIntyre et al., 2017; Nation et al., 2006). Indications of reading difficulties for many children with ASD are evident during the early childhood years. Though there has been growth in early literacy research for young children with ASD over the past decade, additional research is needed both to guide early childhood providers in their instruction and reconcile conflicting evidence (e.g., Dynia, Bean, Justice, & Kaderavek, 2019; Westerveld, Paynter, & Wicks, 2020; Westerveld et al., 2017). We conclude with our ideas for future avenues for research needed to inform the creation and implementation of early literacy interventions for young children with ASD.

First, creating quality interventions requires an understanding of how literacy develops for this heterogeneous population. In contemporary behavioral research, there is a growing tradition of using carefully crafted descriptive studies not only to inform generally, but also to identify specific variables that, if manipulated, will change an important outcome. Descriptive studies that include measures of language, literacy, and autism symptomatology over the early childhood years are needed to understand how skills related to successful reading develop in young children with ASD (Norbury & Nation, 2011). The identification of malleable factors can serve as targets in designing intervention studies. Addressing these factors early may offset challenges children with ASD will experience learning to read. Simply stated, interventions should be designed to target meaningful skills that, if improved, will lead to better learning outcomes for learners with ASD.

A second direction of future research involves identifying, and evaluating, critical elements of effective shared reading interventions. There is a lack of consensus regarding specific nuances of shared reading interventions in the literature. Studies vary considerably in both length of intervention and instructional arrangements (Towson, Fettig, Fleury, & Abarca, 2017). Specifically, we can anticipate that a proportion of children with ASD will require curricular modifications or instructional intensification to reap the full benefits of shared reading activities. A number of research groups explored various instructional adaptations to shared story reading for young children with ASD (e.g., Coogle, Floyd, & Rahn, 2018; Hudson et al., 2017), yet we lack consensus as to what adaptations are necessary for a given group of individuals. In practice, this means that educators lack empirically derived guidelines to direct their instructional practice. The uncertainty around many specifics of the intervention, including recommended modifications and strategies to intensify instruction, may prevent educators from implementing a potentially efficacious intervention in their classrooms.

A third future direction of research is broadening research samples. ASD is marked by great heterogeneity in symptom severity and demonstration of language skills. Approximately one-third of young children with ASD have difficulty developing verbal speech (Paul & Simmons, 2019), and these children often benefit from alternative modes of communication to augment or replace speech. The majority of intervention studies, however, include learners with ASD who are able to communicate using verbal language. To date, there are no studies investigating the impact of interactive shared reading strategies on the language and literacy skills of young children with ASD and complex communication needs (CCNs). Interactive shared reading may inherently provide a number of opportunities for young children with ASD and CCNs to communicate and build vocabulary knowledge when provided with a way to actively engage/participate throughout the reading. The extent to which children with CCNs can access, and benefit from, shared reading activities is an area that is ripe for research.

Shared book reading interventions vary in terms of both procedures used and how implementation is measured. It will be important to determine the critical elements of shared book reading interventions and align our fidelity measurements with those variables, so as not to inflate estimates by including measures that are not essential to improving outcomes. In addition to knowing *what* to teach, we will need to know *how to teach* others to use the intervention. The potential impact of an intervention to improve children's learning outcomes relies heavily on the extent to which it is implemented in natural settings (Fixsen, Blase, Metz, & Van Dyke, 2013). Another area of much needed focus is training educational stakeholders to implement shared reading interventions in their homes and classrooms with fidelity. Implementation science literature provides guidance to researchers in approaches to training practitioners. There is a particular emphasis in combining professional development (i.e., inservice training) and ongoing coaching as a means of improving educational programming for children at risk of school failure in early childhood education (e.g., Snyder, Hemmeter, & Fox, 2015). Shared book reading intervention researchers do not consistently report the strategies used to train interventions in their publications (Towson et al., 2017). Describing training procedures with sufficient technicality will allow researchers and professionals to replicate trainings for professional development.

In conclusion, many of the skills known to influence reading development emerge in the preschool years. Education is our best hope for improving outcomes for learners with ASD, as schools are their primary source of intervention (Suhrheinrich, Hall, Reed, Stahmer, & Schreibman, 2014). We need effective and sustainable interventions to promote literacy proficiency in preschool and beyond. This begins with the development of foundational early literacy skills that will set children up for reading success as they enter formal school. In doing so, we assume a preventive approach toward reading difficulties rather than waiting to remediate once difficulties emerge.

References

Adolf, S. M., & Hogan, T. P. (2019). If we don't look, we won't see: Measuring language development to inform literacy instruction. *Policy Insights from the Behavioral to the Brain Sciences, 6,* 210–217.

American Psychiatric Association. (2022). *Diagnostic and statistical manual of mental disorders* (5th ed., text rev.). Author.

Brown, H. M., Oram-Cardy, J., & Johnson, A. (2013). A meta-analysis of the reading comprehension skills of individuals on the autism spectrum. *Journal of Autism and Developmental Disorders, 43,* 932–955.

Castles, A., Rastle, K., & Nation, K. (2018). Ending the reading wars: Reading acquisition from novice to expert. *Psychological Science in the Public Interest, 19,* 5–51.

Centers for Disease Control and Prevention. (2020). Prevalence of autism spectrum disorder among children aged 8 years—Autism and Developmental Disabilities Monitoring Network, 11 sites, United States, 2016. Retrieved from *www.cdc. gov/mmwr/volumes/69/ss/ss6904a1.htm?s_ cid=ss6904a1_w.*

Coogle, C. G., Floyd, K. K., & Rahn, N. L. (2018). Dialogic reading and adapted dialogic reading with preschoolers with autism spectrum disorder. *Journal of Early Intervention, 40*(4), 363–379.

Cunningham, A., & Zibulsky, A. (2011). Tell me a story: Examining the benefits of shared reading. In S. Neuman & D. Dickinson (Eds.), *Handbook of early literacy research* (Vol. 3, pp. 396–411). Guilford Press.

Davidson, M. (2021). Reading comprehension in school-age children with autism spectrum disorder: Examining the many components that may contribute. *Language, Speech and Hearing Services in Schools, 52,* 181–196.

Davidson, M. M., Kaushanskaya, M., & Weismer, S. E. (2018). Reading comprehension in children with and without ASD: The role of word reading, oral language, and working memory. *Journal of Autism and Developmental Disorders, 48,* 3524–3541.

Davidson, M. M., & Weismer, S. E. (2014). Characterization and prediction of early reading abilities in children on the autism spectrum. *Journal of Autism and Developmental Disorders, 44,* 828–845.

Dynia, J. M., Bean, A., Justice, L.M., & Kaderavek, J. N. (2019). Phonological awareness emergence in preschool children with autism spectrum disorder. *Autism and Developmental Language Impairments, 4,* 1–15.

Dynia, J. M., Brock, M. E., Justice, L. M., & Kaderavek, J. N. (2017). Predictors of decoding for children with autism spectrum disorder in comparison to their peers. *Research in Autism Spectrum Disorders, 37,* 41–48.

Dynia, J. M., Lawton, K., Logan, J. A. R., & Justice, L. M. (2014). Comparing emergent-literacy skills and home-literacy environment of children with autism and their peers. *Topics in Early Childhood Special Education, 34,* 142–153.

Fixsen, D., Blase, K., Metz, A., & Van Dyke, M. (2013). Statewide implementation of evidence-based programs. *Exceptional Children, 79*(2), 213–230.

Fleury, V. P., & Ford, A. (2021). Shared reading extratextual talk with children with autism who have spontaneous speech. *Journal of Special Education, 55,* 23–33.

Fleury, V. P., & Lease, E. M. (2018). Early indication of reading difficulty?: A descriptive analysis of emergent literacy skills in children with autism spectrum disorder. *Topics in Early Childhood Special Education, 38*(2), 82–93.

Fleury, V. P., Miramontez, S. H., Hudson, R. F., & Schwartz, I. S. (2014). Promoting active participation in book reading for preschoolers with autism spectrum disorder: A preliminary study. *Child Language Teaching and Therapy, 30,* 273–288.

Fleury, V. P., & Schwartz, I. S. (2017). A modified dialogic reading intervention for preschool children with autism spectrum disorder. *Topics in Early Childhood Special Education, 37,* 16–28.

Fleury, V. P., & Towson, J. A. (2021). Early lessons learned in designing an adaptive shared reading intervention for preschoolers with autism. *Exceptional Children, 88*(1), 45–64.

Foorman, B. R., & Nixon, S. M. (2006). The influence of public policy on reading research and practice. *Topics in Language Disorders, 26,* 157–171.

Gough, P., & Tunmer, W. (1986). Decoding, reading, and reading disability. *Remedial and Special Education, 7,* 6–10.

Grimm, R. P., Solari, E. J., & Gerber, M. M. (2018). A longitudinal investigation of reading development from kindergarten to grade eight in a Spanish-speaking bilingual population. *Reading and Writing, 31,* 559–581.

Hudson, R. F., Sanders, E. A., Greenway, R., Xie, S., Smith, M., Gasamis, C., . . . Hackett, J. (2017). Effects of emergent literacy interventions for preschoolers with autism spectrum disorder. *Exceptional Children, 84,* 55–75.

Lo, J. Y. T., & Shum, K. (2021). Brief report: A randomized controlled trial of the effects of RECALL (Reading to Engage Children with Autism in Language and Learning) for preschoolers with autism spectrum disorder. *Journal of Autism and Developmental Disorders, 51,* 2146–2154.

Lucas, R., & Norbury, C. (2015). Making inferences from text: It's vocabulary that matters. *Journal of Speech, Language, and Hearing Research, 58,* 1224–1232.

Mayes, S. D., & Calhoun, S. L. (2003). Ability profiles in children with autism: Influence of age and IQ. *Autism, 6,* 65–80.

McIntyre, N. S., Solari, E. J., Grimm, R. P., Lerro, L. E., Gonzales, J. E., & Mundy, P. C. (2017). A comprehensive examination of reading heterogeneity in students with high functioning autism: Distinct reading profiles and their relation to autism symptom severity. *Journal of Autism and Developmental Disorders, 47,* 1086–1101.

Nation, K. (2019). Children's reading difficulties, language, and reflections on the simple view of reading. *Australian Journal of Learning Difficulties, 24,* 47–73.

Nation, K., Clarke, P., Wright, B., & Williams, D. (2006). Patterns of reading ability in children with autism spectrum disorder. *Journal of Autism and Developmental Disorders, 36,* 911–919.

National Early Literacy Panel. (2008). *Developing early literacy: Report of the National Early Literacy Panel.* National Institute for Literacy.

National Reading Panel (U.S.) & National Institute of Child Health and Human Development (U.S.). (2000). *Report of the National Reading Panel: Teaching children to read: An evidence-based assessment of the scientific research literature on reading and its implications for reading instruction.* U.S. Department of Health and Human Services, Public Health Service, National Institutes of Health, National Institute of Child Health and Human Development.

Norbury, C., & Nation, K. (2011). Understanding variability in reading comprehension in adolescents with autism spectrum disorder: Interactions with language status and decoding skill. *Scientific Studies of Reading, 15,* 191–210.

Nunes, D., Whalon, K., Jackson, E., Intepe-Tingir, S., & Garris, G. (2021). Effects of dialogic reading on the vocabulary knowledge of preschoolers with autism spectrum disorder. *International Journal of Disability, Development and Education, 69,* 282–301.

Oakhill, J., & Cain, K. (2018). Children with specific text comprehension problems. In K. Cain, D. L. Compton, & R. K. Parrila (Eds.), *Theories of reading development* (pp. 359–378). John Benjamins.

Paul, R., & Simmons, E. S. (2019). Communication and its development in autism spectrum disorders. In F. R. Volkmar (Ed.), *Autism and pervasive developmental disorders* (3rd ed., pp. 89–111). Cambridge University Press.

Pentimonti, J. M., Justice, L. M., & Piasta, S. B. (2013). Sharing books with children. In T. Shanahan & C. J. Lonigan (Eds.), *Early childhood literacy: The National Early Literacy Panel and beyond* (pp. 117–134). Brookes.

Rayner, K., Foorman, B. R., Perfetti, C. A., Pestesky, D., & Seidenberg, M. S. (2002). How should reading be taught? *Scientific American, 286,* 84–91.

Schreibman, L., Dawson, G., Stahmer, A. C., Landa, R., Rogers, S. J., McGee, G. G., . . . Halladay, A. (2015). Naturalistic developmental behavioral interventions: Empirically validated treatments for autism spectrum disorder. *Journal of Autism and Developmental Disorders, 45,* 2411–2428.

Snyder, P. A., Hemmeter, M. L., & Fox, L. (2015). Supporting implementation of evidence-based practices through practice-based coaching. *Topics in Early Childhood Special Education, 35,* 133–143.

Steinbrenner, J. R., Hume, K., Odom, S. L., Morin, K. L., Nowell, S. W., Tomaszewski, B., . . . Savage, M. N. (2020). *Evidence-based practices for children, youth, and young adults with autism.* University of North Carolina at Chapel Hill, Frank Porter Graham Child Development Institute, National Clearinghouse on Autism Evidence and Practice Review Team.

Suhrheinrich, J., Hall, L. J., Reed, S. R., Stahmer, A. C., & Schreibman, L. (2014). Evidence-based interventions in the classroom. In L. E. Wilkinson (Ed.), *Autism spectrum disorder in children and adolescents: Evidence-based assessment and intervention in schools* (pp. 151–172). American Psychological Association.

Swanson, E., Vaughn, S., Wanzek, J., Petscher, Y., Heckert, J., Cavanaugh, C., . . . Tackett, K. (2011). A synthesis of read-aloud interventions on early reading outcomes among preschool through third graders at risk for reading difficulties. *Journal of Learning Disabilities, 44,* 258–275.

Towson, J., Fettig, A., Fleury, V. P., & Abarca, D. (2017). Dialogic reading in early childhood settings: A summary of the evidence base. *Topics in Early Childhood Special Education, 37,* 132–146.

Tunmer, W. E., & Hoover, W. A. (2019). The cognitive foundations of learning to read: A framework for preventing and remediating reading difficulties. *Australian Journal of Learning Difficulties, 24,* 75–93.

Vivanti, G. (2020). Autism and autism treatment: Evolution of concepts and practices from Kanner to contemporary approaches. In G. Vivanti, K. Bottema-Beutel, & L. Turner-Brown (Eds.), *Clinical guide to early interventions for children with autism: Best practices in child and adolescent behavioral health care* (pp. 1–24). Springer International.

Walter, E. C., & de Paula Nunes, D. R. (2020). Avaliação da eficácia de um programa de compreensão da leitura oral dialógica por criança com autism [Evaluation of the effectiveness of an oral reading comprehension program by a child with autism]. *ETD—Educação Temática Digital, 22*(1), 27–49.

Wei, X., Blackorby, J., & Schiller, E. (2011). Growth in reading achievement of students with disabilities, ages 7 to 17. *Exceptional Children, 78,* 89–106.

Westerveld, M. F., Paynter, J., Brignell, A., & Reilly, S. (2020). No differences in code-related emergent literacy skills in well-matched 4-year-old with and without ASD. *Journal of Autism and Developmental Disorders, 50,* 3060–3065.

Westerveld, M. F., Paynter, J., Trembath, D., Webster, A. A., Hodge, A. M., & Roberts, J. (2017). The emergent literacy skills of preschool children with autism spectrum disorder. *Journal of Autism and Developmental Disorders, 47,* 424–438.

Westerveld, M. F., Paynter, J., & Wicks, R. (2020). Shared book reading behaviors of parents and their verbal preschoolers on the autism spectrum. *Journal of Autism and Developmental Disorders, 50,* 3005–3017.

Whalon, K. J., Al Otaiba, S., & Delano, M. (2009). Evidence based reading instruction for individuals with autism spectrum disorder. *Focus on Autism and Developmental Disabilities, 24,* 3–16.

Whalon, K., Hanline, M. F., & Davis, J. (2016). Parent implementation of RECALL: A systematic case study. *Education and Training.in Autism and Developmental Disabilities, 51*(2), 211–220.

Whalon, K., Martinez, J. R., Shannon, D., Butcher, C., & Hanline, M. F. (2015). The impact of reading to engage children with autism in language and learning (RECALL). *Topics in Early Childhood Special Education, 35,* 102–115.

What Works Clearinghouse. (2007). What Works Clearinghouse Intervention Report: Early Childhood Education Interventions: Literacy Express. Retrieved from *http://ies.ed.gov/ncee/wwc/InterventionReport/135.*

What Works Clearinghouse. (2010). What Works Clearinghouse Intervention Report: Early Childhood Education Interventions for Children with Disabilities: Literacy Express. Retrieved from *http://ies.ed.gov/ncee/wwc/InterventionReport/136.*

World Literacy Foundation. (2012). *The economic and social cost of illiteracy: A snapshot of illiteracy in a global context.* Author.

Zevenbergen, A., & Whitehurst, G. J. (2003). Dialogic reading: A shared picture book reading intervention for preschoolers. In A. van Kleeck, S. Stahl, & E. Bauer (Eds.), *On reading books to children* (pp. 170–191). Erlbaum.

CHAPTER 28

Multi-Tiered Systems of Support

*An Approach for Reducing Disparities in School
Readiness and Increasing Equity in Early Literacy
and Learning Opportunities for Young Children*

Judith J. Carta and Charles R. Greenwood

Even before children enter through the kindergarten classroom door, they have had unequal early literacy learning opportunities. What children experience in the years before formal schooling greatly affects their readiness to learn to read (National Early Literacy Panel, 2008; Whitehurst & Lonigan, 1998). Many factors related to children's early learning environments increase their risk of becoming struggling learners. Some children may have had limited language and literacy experiences in the home (Whitehurst & Lonigan, 1998). Others may not have had access to high-quality preschool or to the type of early literacy and language instruction essential for becoming successful readers (Bassok & Galdo, 2016). As a result, many children from low socioeconomic backgrounds enter school already at a disadvantage for experiencing school success.

Early education programs are increasingly aware that many children in their care may be at risk for later literacy problems and are seeking ways to provide these children with the timely support they need to promote their early literacy skills and prevent them from becoming struggling readers. While programs face growing challenges of addressing these children's individual needs and strengths, a variety of evidence-based practices are now available that can reduce the school readiness gap while children are still in early education (Goldstein et al., 2016, 2017; Greenwood, et al., 2015, 2016; Greenwood, Abbott, Beecher, Atwater, & Peterson, 2017). Early multi-tiered systems of support (early MTSS) offers a framework for using these practices to address these disparities by identifying children showing the first signs of delay and attending to these delays with individualized supports, therefore preventing problems and improving the likelihood that these children will be ready for success in kindergarten. (Carta, 2019).

What Is MTSS and How Does It Differ from Current Approaches?

MTSS is a dynamic, early intervening approach to providing instruction based on the principles that children are variable in how quickly they acquire new skills, and that some children learn best with greater levels of focus, support, or intensity (Gersten et al., 2009; Greenwood et al., 2015). An additional guiding principle of MTSS is that instruction should be based on the individual child's measurable success (or failure) in learning what is being taught (Fuchs & Deno,

1991). This framework is derived from prevention science wherein tiered models of support across an entire population differentiate treatment to individuals depending on their level of risk (Lembke, McMaster, & Stecker, 2010).

MTSS is based on an earlier instructional framework, response to intervention (RTI), and both approaches share the goal of identifying and addressing children's learning needs at the earliest possible time (Carta, 2019; for a review of K–3 approaches, see Freudenthal, Zaru, & Al Otaiba, Chapter 4, this volume). Fundamental to both approaches is a data-based decision-making process that guides individualization or differentiation based on a child's demonstrated need (Batsche et al., 2005; Hojnoski & Polignano, 2019). Both are evidence-based practices using performance data in making intervention decisions. While RTI focuses primarily on ways to identify and provide support that is differentiated for struggling learners in academic areas (e.g., reading, math), MTSS expands that concept by creating a continuum of systemwide strategies and structures for addressing barriers to student learning in both academic and behavioral areas (e.g., early literacy and social–emotional). The focus in MTSS is on systemwide support for instruction that will benefit all students, with alignment occurring for all practices, programs, and policies at the classroom, school, and district levels. This often means that teachers, administrators, and instructional support personnel change the way they work together as they shift into a more collaborative culture needed to provide individualized supports as early as indicated.

How Can MTSS Be Employed to Promote Equity in Early Education?

MTSS offers a framework that departs from the traditional early educational model of delivering "one size fits all" instruction and holding off on providing struggling learners with additional support until they exhibit enough delay to qualify for special education. Oftentimes, in the traditional model, children must show significant delay on standardized assessments before they qualify for additional support that is provided through special education. As a result, many children from underserved groups fail to get the level of instructional support they need prior to kindergarten, so they enter without the early lit-

eracy skills to become successful readers. In contrast, the early MTSS approach aims to intervene as quickly as possible by identifying children who need additional support through regular universal screenings. Then this additional support is provided in the general education setting through personnel who are trained to implement more intensified or focused instruction (Tier 2) or individualized support (Tier 3). One benefit of this early identification/earlier intervention approach includes less frequent "overidentification" of Black and Brown children into special education (Greenwood et al., 2011).

For early MTSS to work as intended, a program must have the following core components in place:

1. A system of ongoing universal screening to identify children who are not meeting expected benchmarks on critical skills needed for success.

2. Multiple tiers of evidence-based instructional supports arranged in a continuum of intensity.

3. A system of progress monitoring on a frequent basis to determine whether a child's additional instructional support is working to accelerate the child's learning trajectory.

4. A decision-making framework or problem-solving process in which the instructional team and parents engage that uses universal screening data to help determine the appropriate levels or tiers of instructional support, then uses progress monitoring to make adjustments when necessary (Hojnoski & Polignano, 2019; Tilly, 2008).

5. Leadership teams at the district and school levels to ensure sustained high fidelity of implementation of all of the components across the multiple levels of the educational system. When data-based decision-making processes occur, instructional data are examined frequently across system levels to identify where more system support may be needed, how best to allocate available resources, and where to enhance professional development (see Young, 2019).

6. Family involvement strategies for obtaining family members' input and involvement in each of the tiers of instructional support and especially for promoting engagement of families from diverse cultural and linguistic backgrounds (see Knoche & Sheridan, 2019).

Essential Questions Regarding Preparedness for Promoting Equity

Will early education programs be able to deliver on their potential for reducing the achievement gap by promoting equity using an MTSS framework? While MTSS might provide a structure for delivering more equitable instructional support to children who vary in their early literacy/language skills, the effectiveness of this framework for narrowing the school readiness gap depends on how well the framework is operationalized and whether the program has the tools, staff, and resources to reach the end goal of promoting children's growth on key skills necessary for school success. Critical to achieving that outcome is answering the following questions:

1. Do all children have access to high quality Tier 1 instruction?
2. Are culturally responsive measures available for identifying children who need additional support in early literacy and language and for monitoring children's progress?
3. Are evidence-based, culturally sustaining interventions available for children needing additional support in early literacy and language?

Question 1. Do all children have access to high-quality Tier 1 instruction?

A fundamental principle of early MTSS is that it begins with a strong curricular foundation experienced by all children (Tier 1). Critical steps in implementing an effective Tier 1 include (a) starting out with an evidence-based curriculum and instructional practices; (b) monitoring whether the curriculum and instructional practices are implemented with fidelity, and (c) ensuring that children receive adequate instructional opportunities (or dosage) of Tier 1 intervention and that they maintain adequate levels of active engagement in instruction (Carta, 2019; Greenwood et al., 2018).

A substantial research literature indicates that Tier 1 early literacy and language instruction provided to children in early education programs is often in the low to moderate range of quality (Guo, Sawyer, Justice, & Kaderavek, 2013). Researchers examining quality of core instruction have focused on what teachers do to support learning in general, and how well teachers promote early literacy and language more specifically, and how instruction has affected children's active engagement. Many studies using the CLASS observational measure (Pianta, La Paro, & Hamre, 2008) have reported that instructional support is generally low (e.g., Cabell, Justice, Konold, & McGinty, 2011; Hamre, 2014) and in programs aimed at underserved children, instructional quality is even lower (Bassok & Galdo, 2016).

In 2012, our Center for Response to Intervention in Early Childhood (CRTIEC) conducted a multisite investigation of the quality of Tier 1 in 65 preschool classrooms from four different types of programs (i.e., state-funded PreK, Title 1, Head Start, and tuition-based programs) across four states as experienced by 659 children in their year prior to kindergarten (Greenwood et al., 2013). Specifically, we sought to answer the questions: "What exactly is 'business as usual' in preschool Tier 1 early literacy and language instruction?" and "How do children grow in early literacy/language in response to the quality of Tier 1 instruction they receive?" (Carta et al., 2015).

At the beginning of the year, a sizable percentage of children (30%) within our sample scored in the "weak" or "very weak" range based on the Get Ready to Read! Revised Screener (GRTR; Lonigan & Wilson, 2008). In programs serving children from low-income backgrounds, up to 40% of children demonstrated either weak or very weak early literacy and language scores on the GRTR screener compared to only 10% of children in programs serving more advantaged students (i.e., the tuition-based preschools). Observations using the Classroom Assessment Scoring System (CLASS; Pianta et al., 2008) in these classrooms indicated that the mean level of instructional support was low, rated only 2.5 out of a possible 7. Also, when we conducted observations in these same classrooms of how teachers spent their time during those activities most likely to support literacy (i.e., story reading, dramatic play, and centers), we found the percentage of time teachers focused on literacy was very low (16.5% of the observation) (Greenwood et al., 2013).

This finding of low levels of literacy focus was concerning, because research has clearly demonstrated that the amount of classroom time devoted to quality language and literacy instruction is highly related to children's growth on the critically important skills of phonological awareness, comprehension, and alphabet knowledge (Phillips, Zhao, & Weekley, 2018; van Kleek, Vander Woude, & Hammett, 2006). Indeed, in this study, our assessment of children across the school year indicated that while children across the entire sample generally made positive gains in early literacy, in nearly all cases, those who began the school year with weak or very weak skills levels did not close the early literacy gap with their peers during the year and would probably enter kindergarten still significantly below their typically developing peers.

Another critical indicator of quality in Tier 1 is the level of children's active engagement in response to instruction. Literacy engagement is participation in literacy-related activities by engaging in literacy behaviors such as reading letters or words aloud, looking at books or the teacher reading a story, asking questions/providing answers, and saying letter sounds (Greenwood et al., 2018; Greenwood, Carta, Irvin, & Schnitz, 2021). Research documents that children who spent more time actively engaged in literacy-focused activities such as shared book reading realized better academic outcomes compared to children who spent more time engaging in free play (Powell & Diamond, 2011). Our behavioral observations using the Classroom Code for Interactive Recording of Children's Learning Environments (Classroom CIRCLE) observation system (Atwater et al., 2015) in classrooms indicated a clear relationship between the amount of teacher literacy focus across the classroom day and children's rates of active academic engagement (Greenwood et al., 2017).

Unfortunately, our research shows that teachers have often failed to arrange classroom activities in ways that promote active engagement. For example, in our study of four types of preschool programs across the United States, we observed that, on average, the activities that took up the largest proportion of time during the classroom day (e.g., center time) were often least likely to be those that promote children's active engagement (i.e., story time). However, when teachers received professional development on evidence-based practices for promoting early literacy focus, children's active engagement in those literacy-focused activities increased and over time, so did their early literacy outcomes (Greenwood et al., 2018).

Thus, programs aiming to ensure that Tier 1 leads to greater equity in all children's growth in early literacy and language can do the following:

1. *Begin with an evidence-based curriculum.* Excellent resources are available to programs to guide them through considerations in helping to select a curriculum. Among these resources are the What Works Clearinghouse website (Institute of Education Sciences, n.d.) and the Preschool Curriculum Evaluation Research Consortium (2008), and the Preschool Curriculum Consumer Report put out by the National Center on Quality Teaching and Learning (2015). Each of these guides provides comprehensive information that allows programs to make informed decisions when making curriculum choices.

2. *Implement evidence-based instructional practices.* While an evidence-based curriculum is a starting point for a strong Tier 1, it is not a guarantee to produce positive literacy outcomes in children unless it is accompanied by intentional teaching designed as frequent, brief, planned opportunities to practice the foundational skills of phonological awareness, print concepts, and knowledge about letters in developmentally appropriate ways. Instruction focused on these critical elements of early literacy is necessary for establishing a firm foundation for children to become successful readers. Children are unlikely to learn these skills without these experiences.

3. *Ensure that critical instructional practices are implemented with fidelity.* The quality of Tier 1 for promoting early literacy and language is dependent on high-fidelity implementation of instructional practices that are systematic, explicit, and purposeful. A necessary component for high-fidelity implementation of instructional practices is professional development guided by observational tools that can be used to document the occurrence of the critical elements of high-quality early literacy and language instruction. These PD efforts themselves must be evidence-based, sustained over time, and focused on knowledge and skills needed by teachers to provide high-quality instruction to young children.

Question 2. Are tools available for identifying children who need additional support in early literacy and for monitoring children's progress?

Universal Screening

Even with a high-quality foundation for early literacy and language delivered to all children (Tier 1), we know that some children will not make progress acquiring the key skills needed for success in kindergarten and beyond. Regular universal screening of all children in a program helps identify which children are not meeting benchmarks and may benefit from additional supports. In aggregate, universal screening of the core early literacy and language skills also provides program-level information on the proportion of children who are meeting benchmark. These data provide good evidence of whether Tier 1 is providing an adequate foundation. In RTI/MTSS models with three tiers, the approximate expected percentages of children in Tier 1, Tier 2, and Tier 3 are 80, 15, and 5%, respectively (Albritton, Stuckey, & Terry, 2021; Fuchs, Fuchs, & Compton, 2012; Stoiber & Gettinger, 2016). If programwide or classwide data on universal screeners indicate that fewer than 80% of children are meeting the benchmark expectations, programs may want to evaluate their Tier 1 with an intent on improvement. Relevant questions are the strength of evidence behind the curriculum being used and whether the intended instructional practices are actually being implemented with fidelity and with adequate dosage. If only a small percentage of children are not meeting benchmarks, the improvement focus might be on providing additional instructional support to those individual children through Tier 2 or Tier 3 interventions.

Universal screeners should allow a program to evaluate its focus on the specific types of skills on which children need more intensified instruction. Clearly, during the year prior to kindergarten, children at risk for later reading disabilities vary in their early literacy and language profiles (see Cabell et al., 2011). Some children may be struggling to learn code-focused skills (e.g., phonological awareness, alphabet knowledge, print awareness) but have strong oral language skills. Others may have strong code-focused skills but may be struggling with oral language skills. A third group may be struggling in both areas.

Conducting universal screenings for multiple outcomes a year will allow a program to develop or select interventions targeted to the areas in which children need additional instructional support. Universal screening data will also allow a program to see how children change in response to added intervention over time. For example, a child who begins the year with delays in code-focused skills may acquire these skills quickly once the program begins engaging the child with instruction targeted at phonological awareness, alphabet knowledge, or print knowledge (Olsze-

wski, Haring, Soto, Peters-Sanders, & Goldstein, 2019).

Progress Monitoring

While universal screenings support decisions regarding changing interventions for individual children, progress monitoring addresses the question: "Is it working for this child going forward?" Progress monitoring assessment is used to determine whether children are benefiting from the additional level of support. For example, if a child were identified for Tier 2 targeting her phonological awareness, the teacher could use a progress monitoring measure for determining whether the child shows an increase in the key skill of identifying the first sound or the first part of words. Using weekly progress monitoring data to track this skill might help a teacher know whether the child is narrowing the gap with typically developing peers with regard to phonological awareness and may show that Tier 2 supports are no longer necessary. Alternatively, program-monitoring data might reveal that the child is still struggling with learning sounds and might need more intensive, individualized Tier 3 instruction.

A few currently available tools that are specifically validated for MTSS universal screening and progress monitoring of preschoolers are brief, repeatable, and assess the desired outcome content of instruction. The Preschool Early Literacy Indicator (PELI; Kaminski, Abbott, Bravo-Aguayo, & Good, 2018), Individual Growth and Development Indicators—Early Literacy (IGDI-EL; McConnell, Bradfield, Wackerle-Hollman, & Rodriguez, 2012), and CIRCLE progress monitoring (Assel, Landry, Swank, & Gunnewig, 2008) focus on measuring child progress relative to normative benchmarks on key skills known to be predictive of later reading skills (e.g., phonological awareness, alphabet knowledge, vocabulary, and oral language, and comprehension). Each also has a Spanish version available (e.g., Spanish Individual Growth and Development Indicators (S-IGDI)/*Primeros Sonidos*; Wackerle-Hollman et al., 2018). For example, each of the measures is designed to be implemented in fall, winter, and spring universally to identify those children who are not meeting benchmarks and may need Tier 2 or Tier 3 supports. The measures can then also be used to monitor progress for children receiving individualized support. Progress monitoring data should help practitioners identify whether the additional support is resulting in change in children's rate of growth and whether they are closing the gap relative to benchmarks. Changes in a child's growth after a period of additional support can then be used by an instructional team to determine whether and how to adjust the level of support needed.

Instructional Decision Making

When universal screening indicates that a child is not reaching established benchmarks in key skills known to be important for later reading success, the instructional team engages in a decision-making process to determine how best to provide the child with additional support. The problem-solving model (Deno & Mirkin, 1977) was designed to help practitioners match individual students' skills to the intensity of support needed, then monitor the effectiveness of an intervention. This problem-solving or instructional decision-making model has been applied to RTI (Batsche et al., 2005; Tilly, 2008); MTSS (Pluymert, 2014), and multi-tiered models for supporting young children (Hojnoski & Polignano, 2019). The following steps define the problem-solving model:

1. *Problem identification* (determining whether there is a difference between a child(ren's) current performance and desired performance).
2. *Problem analysis* (determining the factors contributing to the problem that can be addressed through an intervention).
3. *Intervention implementation* (determining what can be done to address the problem and reduce the difference between current and expected performance).
4. *Plan evaluation* (examining how well children are responding—whether the difference between current and expected performance has been reduced to a satisfactory level and determining next steps; Batsche et al., 2005).

Question 3. Are interventions available for children needing additional support in early literacy and language?

When differences occur between current and expected performance in MTSS, instructional teams can select from two different types of instructional approaches to supplement Tier 1: the *problem-solving approach* or *standard treatment protocol* (Fuchs & Fuchs, 2006). The problem-solving approach is one in which the members of the instructional team (and the family) work together to identify strategies that could be used to supplement the instruction and promote the child's learning. These might include providing additional learning opportunities for specific skills that are embedded throughout the classroom day or it may involve providing more explicit instruction focused on a set of skills (Olszewski et al., 2019).

The other approach to providing Tier 2 intervention is the use of standard treatment protocols (STPs) that target specific skills. STPs are often used in classrooms when several children demonstrate delays in the same skill area. The STPs can be used to address those skills to small groups of children using lessons that are scripted or highly specified. Examples of STPs in early literacy and language include Story Friends (Goldstein & Kelley, 2016), PAth to Literacy (Goldstein, 2016), Story Champs (Spencer & Petersen, 2012), Read It Again! Pre-K (Justice & McGinty, 2009), Developing Talkers (Zucker, Solari, Landry, & Swank, 2013), and others (Kong, Carta, & Greenwood, 2019; Soto, Crucet-Choi, & Goldstein, 2020; Zucker et al., 2021; Phillips, Chapter 12, and Zucker, Yeomans-Maldonado, Surrain, & Landry, Chapter 22, this volume). Each of these Tier 2 interventions was designed specifically to address a skills area known to be important for later reading success (e.g., phonological awareness, oral language/vocabulary, comprehension or print knowledge), all have been documented as effective in peer-reviewed studies, and many are available in English and Spanish. The first two curricula were developed by the CRTIEC (Greenwood et al., 2015). PAth to Literacy was designed for children demonstrating delays in the emergent literacy skills of phonological awareness and alphabet knowledge in their prekindergarten year. The curriculum uses scripted lessons that introduce small groups of children to phonological awareness skills in 12 units. Children are given feedback and multiple opportunities to respond. In a randomized trial, Goldstein and CRTIEC collaborators (Goldstein et al., 2017) reported that children who participated in this intervention for 12 weeks were significantly more likely to meet benchmarks in phonological awareness compared to children in a control group.

While there is common understanding of how Tier 3 intervention should be designed (i.e., more intensive than Tiers 1 and 2, with more frequent progress monitoring and structured problem solving and individualization (Barnett, VanDer-Heyden, & Witt, 2007), few standardized Tier 3 interventions have been developed and validated. Effective Tier 3 interventions are different from those used for Tier 2 in that they are typically more systematic, more explicit, more focused on prioritized content, include more opportunities to respond, and are more individualized (Connor, Alberto, Compton, & O'Connor, 2014; Simmons, 2015). In a small, multiple-baseline study, Kaminski and Powell-Smith (2017) demonstrated the efficacy of a Tier 3 standard protocol intervention focused on improving phonemic awareness skills in preschoolers and found that it was effective in improving that targeted skill area. Nonetheless, the authors noted that the variability in children's performance suggest that Tier 3 interventions must be structured but allow flexibility and use ongoing assessment to inform adjustments to improve effectiveness for individual children.

Moving Early MTSS into the Reality of Preschool Programs

While assessment and intervention tools have been developed and validated, the widescale adoption of MTSS/RTI in early literacy/language by early education programs is still a long way off. While some states are developing the infrastructure to support statewide implementation of MTSS in preschool (e.g., Vermont, Iowa), there has been comparatively less uptake of MTSS in early education than in K–12 programs. Interestingly, even when publicly funded prekindergarten programs are located within elementary schools, the PreK programs are not often invited to participate in schoolwide MTSS initiatives (Wackerle-Hollman et al., 2022). Among the challenges that have been offered for the difficulty in scaling up MTSS/RTI in early education settings are (1) the lack of a unified early childhood system; (2) an early education workforce that often lacks the training and expertise to implement evidence-based practice and the lack of high-quality professional development to address this concern; and (3) the scarcity of evidence-based Tier 1 curricula in early literacy (Carta, 2019).

Addressing the Lack of Early Education Systems

The fact that there are no unified early education systems creates numerous challenges to mounting any initiative as complex as MTSS. Programs for preschool children are varied and range from state-funded PreK programs to community-based child care programs, and programs such as Head Start, targeted to children from low-income families. Because each of them has a different approach to service delivery, administrative structure, funding mechanisms, and professional development and certification, trying to develop a unified structure to support MTSS presents a daunting challenge.

Professional Development Needs

One barrier to quality implementation of MTSS is the level of training and expertise of the workforce in many early education settings. When early childhood education (ECE) program personnel across the nation were surveyed about their perceptions of the biggest challenges to implementing tiered models such as RTI or MTSS in ECE programs, the most significant challenge reported was the lack of a trained workforce (Greenwood et al., 2011). Almost 40% of the early childhood workforce have no degree or professional credential (Schleiber, Austin, & Valencia López, 2020). Moreover, even credentialed ECE professionals with degrees have reported feeling unprepared for the types of complex practices required in implementing tiered models such as data-based decision making or implementing evidence-based small-group interventions (Muccio, Kidd, White, & Burns, 2014). Therefore, if states seek widescale implementation of MTSS across their programs, they must develop an infrastructure to provide sustained professional development (PD) to support each of the MTSS components: the curricula that forms the foundation for the entire MTSS framework; targeted interventions that can supplement the Tier 1 core curriculum; and sensitive, valid, and culturally appropriate assessments.

To support high-fidelity implementation of each of these steps, PD must also be evidence-based. In the last decade, a variety of approaches to PD in early childhood programs, such as practice-based coaching (PBC; Snyder, Hemmeter, & Fox, 2015), have been validated and have been used successfully across tiered models of intervention (Barton, Velez, Pokorski, & Domingo,

2019; Fettig & Artman-Meeker, 2016; Fox, Hemmeter, Snyder, Binder, & Clarke, 2011; Hemmeter, Hardy, Schnitz, Adams, & Kinder. 2015; Sutherland, Conroy, Vo, & Ladwig, 2015).

While coaching has been recognized as fundamental for high fidelity implementation of tiered models, it typically requires intensive amounts of time and resources to be carried out well. Some alternative cost-effective approaches to coaching include tiered models that target intensive coaching only to those practitioners who need greater levels of support (Fettig, Artman-Meeker, Jeon, & Chang, 2022), or providing "just-in-time" individualized coaching supports in response to a learner's immediate concern or need. Whatever approach to PD is used, programs should strive to offer PD that includes characteristics known to enhance its effectiveness: (1) It is intensive and ongoing; (2) it is delivered in ways that allow educators to observe quality practice, enact practices, receive feedback, and engage in self-reflection (Hemmeter, Snyder, Kinder, & Artman, (2011); (3) it is focused on content and skills known to improve children's outcomes (Schacter, Gerde, & Hatton-Bowers, 2019).

Areas of Growth Potential in Early MTSS

While we have outlined the core components and basic process in early MTSS, we have had limited space to describe recent developments and future directions in early MTSS. One growing need is for an integrated early MTSS model that combines separate multi-tiered systems and merges assessment and instruction across a whole range of domains (i.e., language/early literacy, social–emotional, and math) (Lane, Oakes, & Menzies, 2014; McIntosh & Goodman, 2016). Current MTSS approaches for use in early education are most often domain-specific and force programs to implement separate approaches for each targeted domain. So, for example, a program would carry out universal screening, data-based decision making, tiered interventions, and progress monitoring separately in the early literacy/language and the social–emotional/behavioral domains; and each of these steps would be carried out by separate problem-solving teams. A truly integrated reconceptualized early MTSS model would address multiple domains simultaneously and create resources that could address multiple domains simultaneously, thereby reducing the number of tools that practitioners would

need to learn and implement. While the creation of an integrated system will require the creation of new measures and interventions, such a system would increase efficiency, potentially improve effectiveness, and be more cost-effective (Lane et al., 2014).

Addressing the Needs of Dual Language Learners

Another critical need in early MTSS models is the development of interventions that are linguistically and culturally responsive, with accompanying assessments that measure outcomes and monitor progress in children's home language and English. Almost half of Latinx preschoolers enter kindergarten with delays in their literacy skills in Spanish and English (Fuller, 2011). Unless they receive effective supplemental intervention, these children may be at risk of persistent reading difficulty (Soto et al., 2020). While MTSS is a promising approach for meeting these children's needs, research and development in this area is still in its infancy. While some interventions have begun to be developed in MTSS for children who are dual language learners (Soto et al., 2020; Spencer, Petersen, Restrepo, Thompson, & Gutierrez Arvizu, 2019; Zucker et al., 2021; Zucker et al., Chapter 22, this volume), these resources are still relatively scarce. Similarly, screening and progress monitoring measures are needed to measure children's language and early literacy in their home language, as well as English. Examples of these measures that have been developed for Spanish speakers are the IGDI-Español suite for measuring early literacy and another suite for measuring language skills (Wackerle-Hollman et al., 2016, 2018). With interventions and measures available, a greater focus must be placed on developing effective approaches for accelerating early literacy and language in Spanish-speaking children as a means of improving equity in reading achievement and ultimately their long-term outcomes.

Addressing Equity

Equity is at the heart of MTSS. From their inception, tiered models of instruction such as MTSS and RTI were developed to provide instruction and intervention at varying levels of intensity based on individual student needs. These models recognize the role of individual differences in learning from instruction. They were initially developed out of necessity for more objective ways to identify students with delays or disabilities in learning and have since evolved into a more holistic practice that aims to better meet the needs of all students through a streamlined, data-driven approach to instructional differentiation (McMaster, Birinci, Shanahan, & Lembke, Chapter 10, this volume). The essential features of the framework should provide a more equitable approach to meeting the needs of all students. First, a *culturally responsive, evidence-based Tier 1 core instruction* should provide students from diverse backgrounds with opportunities to have meaningful learning experiences that will lead to improved outcomes for all. Second, the *periodic use of sensitive, valid culturally responsive universal screening measures* should allow instructional teams to objectively identify students in need of additional support in one or more desired outcomes. Third, the *use of progress monitoring assessment* should allow instructional teams to have an objective way of measuring student growth and determining whether greater levels of instructional support help to narrow the gap for children receiving additional tiers of instruction.

Conclusion

Are we making progress in reducing inequities in early education through MTSS? Many people look to early education and early intervention as the panacea to reduce the achievement gap. But are early education programs able to deliver on that promise? We are still far from providing the level of instructional quality and support that each child needs to benefit from early education. But we are beginning to compile the tools needed to build the system to reduce disparities and increase equity. MTSS, like other tiered approaches, is based on the principle of "targeted universalism" (Powell, Menendian, & Ake, 2019). Targeted universalism rejects the notion that equivalent or equitable outcomes can be produced by providing functionally equivalent resources for individuals (or groups) who differ in their support needs. Rather, the principle of targeted universalism posits that to produce results that are similar across individuals or groups with different needs, resources must be allocated differently based on those needs.

In early education, MTSS can be a means of operationalizing targeted universalism, so, for children at risk for later academic achievement problems, MTSS provides the framework and the tools for providing additional levels of instruction or support as soon as possible. Early MTSS does this through procedures that identify children who would likely benefit from supplemental instruction, interventions that increase in intensity based on evidence of need, and protocols to assess progress frequently to continuously refine the nature and intensity of intervention.

Thus, early MTSS offers the potential to improve equity and reduce the achievement gap that has persisted for so long (Barton & Coley, 2010). Achievement of this promise will require ongoing collaboration of parents, teachers, program directors, policymakers, researchers, higher education faculty and others. It will require a new infrastructure to support high-fidelity implementation and a clear commitment to conduct continuous review and ascertain improvement over time. While we have begun to see demonstrations of the promise in early MTSS, the time has come to turn that potential into reality and bring the practice of early MTSS to scale.

References

Albritton, K., Stuckey, A., & Terry, N. P. (2021). Multitiered early literacy identification in 3-year-old children in Head Start settings. *Journal of Early Intervention, 44*, 23–29.

Assel, M., Landry S., Swank P., & Gunnewig, S. (2008). *CIRCLE: Phonological awareness, language, and literacy system*. Ridgway.

Atwater, J. B., Reynolds, L. H., Schiefelbusch, J., Peterson, S., Lee, Y., Montagna, D., & Tapia, Y. (2015). *Classroom CIRCLE: Classroom Code for Interactive Recording of Children's Learning Environments (2.0): Android Version*. Juniper Gardens Children's Project, University of Kansas.

Barnett, D. W., VanDerHeyden, A. M., & Witt, J. C. (2007). Achieving science-based practice through response to intervention: What it might look like in preschools. *Journal of Educational and Psychological Consultation, 17*, 31–54.

Barton, E. E., Velez, M., Pokorski, E. A., & Domingo, M. (2019). The effects of email performance-based feedback delivered to teaching teams: A systematic replication. *Journal of Early Intervention, 42*, 143–162.

Barton, P. E., & Coley, R. J. (2010). *The black–*

white achievement gap: When progress stopped. Educational Testing Service.

Bassok, D., & Galdo, E. (2016). Inequality in preschool quality?: Community-level disparities in access to high-quality learning environments. *Early Education and Development, 27,* 128–144.

Batsche, G., Elliott, J., Graden, J. L., Grimes, J., Kovaleski, J. F., Prasse, D., . . . Tilly, W. D. (2005). *Response to intervention: Policy considerations and implementation.* National Association of State Directors of Special Education.

Cabell, S. Q., Justice, L. M., Konold, T. R., & McGinty, A. S. (2011). Profiles of emergent literacy skills among preschool children who are at risk for academic difficulties. *Early Childhood Research Quarterly, 26*(1), 1–14.

Carta, J. J. (2019). Introduction to multi-tiered systems of support. In J. J. Carta & R. M. Young (Eds.), *Multi-tiered systems of support for young children: Driving change in early education* (pp. 1–14). Brookes.

Carta, J. J., Greenwood, C. R., Atwater, J., McConnell, S. R., Goldstein, H., & Kaminski, R. A. (2015). Identifying preschool children for higher tiers of language and early literacy instruction within a response to intervention framework. *Journal of Early Intervention, 36*(4), 281–291.

Connor, C., Alberto, P. A., Compton, D. L., & O'Connor, R. E. (2014, February). *Improving reading outcomes for students with or at risk for reading disabilities: A synthesis of the contributions from the Institute of Education Sciences Research Centers.* U.S. Department of Education, Institute of Education Sciences, National Center for Special Education Research.

Deno, S. L., & Mirkin, P. K. (1977). *Data-based program modification: A manual.* Council for Exceptional Children.

Fettig, A., & Artman-Meeker, K. (2016). Group coaching on preschool teachers' implementation of Pyramid Model strategies: A program description. *Topics in Early Childhood Special Education, 36*(3), 147–158.

Fettig, A., Artman-Meeker, K., Jeon, L., & Chang, H. C. (2022). Promoting a person-centered approach to strengthening early childhood practices that support social–emotional development. *Early Education and Development, 33,* 75–91.

Fox, L., Hemmeter, M. L., Snyder, P., Binder, D. P., & Clarke, S. (2011). Coaching early childhood special educators to implement a comprehensive model for promoting young children's social competence. *Topics in Early Childhood Special Education, 3*(3), 178–192.

Fuchs, D., & Fuchs, L. S. (2006). Introduction to response to intervention: What, why, and how valid is it? *Reading Research Quarterly, 41*(1), 93–99.

Fuchs, D., Fuchs, L. S., Compton, D. L. (2012).

Smart RTI: A next-generation approach to multilevel prevention. *Exceptional Children, 78*(3), 263–279.

Fuchs, L. S., & Deno, S. L. (1991). Paradigmatic distinctions between instructionally relevant measurement models. *Exceptional Children, 57,* 488–500.

Fuller, L. (2011). The "silent crisis" of the Latino dropout rate. Retrieved from *http://neatoday. org/2011/06/the-silent-crisis-of-thelatino-dropout-rate-2.*

Gersten, R., Compton, D., Connor, C. M., Dimino, J., Santoro, L., Linan-Thompson, S., & Tilly, W. D. (2009). *Assisting students struggling with reading: Response to Intervention (RtI) and multi-tier intervention in the primary grades* (NCEE 2009-4045). National Center for Education Evaluation and Regional Assistance, Institute of Education Sciences, U.S. Department of Education.

Goldstein, H. (2016). *PAth to Literacy: A phonological awareness intervention for young children.* Brookes.

Goldstein, H., & Kelley, E. S. (2016). *Story Friends Teacher Guide: An early literacy intervention for improving oral language.* Brookes.

Goldstein, H., Kelley, E. S., Greenwood, C. R., McCune, L., Carta, J. J., Atwater, J., . . . Spencer T. (2016). Embedded instruction improved vocabulary learning using automated storybook reading among high-risk preschoolers. *Journal of Speech, Language, and Hearing Research, 59,* 484–500.

Goldstein, H., Olszewski, A., Haring, C., Greenwood, C. R., McCune, L., Carta, J., . . . Kelley, E. S. (2017). Efficacy of a supplemental phonemic awareness curriculum to instruct preschoolers with delays in early literacy development. *Journal of Speech, Language and Hearing Research, 60*(1), 89–103.

Greenwood, C. R., Abbott, M., Beecher, C., Atwater, J., & Petersen, S. (2017). Development, validation, and evaluation of Literacy 3D: A package supporting Tier 1 preschool literacy instruction implementation and intervention. *Topics in Early Childhood Special Education, 37*(1), 29–41.

Greenwood, C. R., Beecher, C., Atwater, J., Petersen, S., Schiefelbusch, J., & Irvin, D. (2018). An eco-behavioral analysis of child academic engagement: Implications for preschool children not responding to instructional intervention. *Topics in Early Childhood Special Education, 37*(4), 219–233.

Greenwood, C. R., Bradfield, T., Kaminski, R. A., Linas, M., Carta, J. J., & Nylander, D. (2011). The response to intervention (RTI) approach in early childhood. *Focus on Exceptional Children, 43,* 1–22.

Greenwood, C. R., Carta, J. J., Atwater, J., Goldstein, H., Kaminski, R., & McConnell, S. (2013).

Is a response to intervention (RTI) approach to preschool language and early literacy instruction needed? *Topics in Early Childhood Special Education, 33(1)*, 48–64.

Greenwood, C. R., Carta, J. J., Goldstein, H., Kaminski, R., McConnell, S. R., & Atwater, J. (2015). The Center on Response to Intervention in Early Childhood (CRTIEC): Developing evidence-based tools for a multi-tier approach to preschool language and early literacy instruction. *Journal of Early Intervention, 36(4)*, 246–262.

Greenwood, C. R., Carta, J. J., Irvin, D., & Schnitz, A. G. (2021). Advancing children's learning through innovations in the measurement of literacy engagement. *Topics in Early Childhood Special Education, 41(3)*, 191–206.

Greenwood, C. R., Carta, J. J., Spencer, E., Guerrero, G., Kong, N. Y., Atwater, J., & Goldstein, H. (2016). The effects of a Tier 2 vocabulary and comprehension storybook intervention on preschool children's early learning: A replication. *Elementary School Journal, 116(4)*, 574–599.

Guo, Y., Sawyer, B. E., Justice, L. M., & Kaderavek, J. N. (2013). Quality of the literacy environment in inclusive early childhood special education classrooms. *Journal of Early Intervention, 35(1)*, 40–60.

Hamre, B. K. (2014). Teachers' daily interactions with children: An essential ingredient in effective early childhood programs. *Child Development Perspectives, 8(4)*, 223–230.

Hemmeter, M. L., Hardy, J. K., Schnitz, A. G., Adams, J. M., & Kinder, K. A. (2015). Effects of training and coaching with performance feedback on teachers' use of Pyramid Model practices. *Topics in Early Childhood Special Education, 35(3)*, 144–156.

Hemmeter, M. L., Snyder, P., Kinder, K., & Artman, K. (2011). Impact of performance feedback delivered via electronic mail on preschool teachers' use of descriptive praise. *Early Childhood Research Quarterly, 26*, 96–106.

Hojnoski, R. L., & Polignano, J. C. (2019). Using data-based decision making to improve learning outcomes for all children. In J. J. Carta & R. M. Young (Eds.), *Multi-tiered systems of support for young children: Driving change in early education* (pp. 73–95). Brookes.

Institute of Education Sciences. (n.d.). Retrieved from *http://ies.ed.gov/ncee/wwc/default.aspx*.

Justice, L. M., & McGinty, A. S. (2009). *Read It Again Pre-K: A preschool curriculum supplement to promote language and literacy foundations.* Children's Learning Research Collaborative.

Kaminski, R. A., Abbott, M., Bravo-Aguayo, K., & Good, R. H. (2018). *Preschool early literacy indicators.* Dynamic Measurement Group.

Kaminski, R. A., & Powell-Smith, K. A. (2017). Early literacy intervention for preschoolers who need Tier 3 support. *Topics in Early Childhood Special Education, 36(4)*, 205–217.

Knoche, L., & Sheridan, S. (2019). Engaging families in multitiered systems of support. In J. J. Carta & R. M. Young (Eds.), *Multi-tiered systems of support for young children: Driving change in early education* (pp. 235–251). Brookes.

Kong, N. Y., Carta, J., & Greenwood, C. (2019). Studies in MTSS problem solving: Improving response to a pre-kindergarten supplemental vocabulary intervention. *Topics in Early Childhood Special Education, 41(2)*, 86–99.

Lane, K. L., Oakes, W. P., & Menzies, H. M. (2014). Comprehensive, integrated, three-tiered (CI3T) models of prevention: Why does my school—and district—need an integrated approach to meet students' academic, behavioral, and social needs? *Preventing School Failure: Alternative Education for Children and Youth, 58*, 121–128.

Lembke, E. S., McMaster, K. L., & Stecker, P. M. (2010). The prevention science of reading research within a response-to-intervention model. *Psychology in the Schools, 47(1)*, 22–35.

Lonigan, C., & Wilson, S. B. (2008). *Report on the revised Get Ready to Read! screening tool: Psychometrics and normative information* [Technical report]. National Center for Learning Disabilities.

McConnell, S., Bradfield, T., Wackerle-Hollman, A., & Rodriquez, M. (2012). *Individual Growth and Development Indicators of Early Literacy (IGDIs EL).* Early Learning Labs.

McIntosh, K., & Goodman, S. (2016). *Integrated multi-tiered systems of support: Blending RTI and PBIS.* Guilford Press.

Muccio, L. S., Kidd, J. K., White, C. S., & Burns, M. S. (2014). Head Start instructional professionals' inclusion perceptions and practices. *Topics in Early Childhood Special Education, 34(1)*, 40–48.

National Center on Quality Teaching and Learning. (2015). Preschool Curriculum Consumer Report. Retrieved from: *https://eclkc.ohs.acf.hhs.gov/sites/default/files/pdf/curriculum-consumer-report.pdf*.

National Early Literacy Panel. (2008). *Developing Early Literacy: Report of the National Early Literacy Panel.* National Institute for Literacy.

Olszewski, A., Haring, C., Soto, X. T., Peters-Sanders, L., & Goldstein, H. (2019). Designing and implementing Tier 2 instructional support in early literacy and language. In J. J. Carta & R. M. Young (Eds.), *Multi-tiered systems of support for young children: Driving change in early education* (pp. 113–130). Brookes.

Phillips, B., Zhao, Y., & Weekley, M. K. (2018). Teacher language in the preschool classroom:

Initial validation of a classroom environment observation tool. *Early Education and Development, 29*(3), 379–397.

Pianta, R. C., La Paro, K. M., & Hamre, B. K. (2008). *Classroom Assessment Scoring System™ Manual K–3.* Brookes.

Pluymert, K. (2014). Problem-solving foundations for school psychological services. In P. L. Harrison & A. Thomas (Eds.), *Best practices in school psychology: Data-based and collaborative decision making* (pp. 25–40). National Association of School Psychologists.

Powell, D. R., & Diamond, K. E. (2011). Improving the outcomes of coaching-based professional development interventions. In S. B. Neuman & D. K. Dickinson (Eds.), *Handbook of early literacy research* (Vol. 3, pp. 295–307). Guilford Press.

Powell, J., Menendian, S., & Ake, W. (2019). Targeted universalism: Policy and practice. Retrieved from *https://escholarship.org/uc/item/9sm8b0q8.*

Preschool Curriculum Evaluation Research Consortium. (2008, July). Effects of preschool curriculum programs on school readiness. Retrieved from *https://digital.library.unt.edu/ark:/67531/metadc950252.*

Schachter, R. E., Gerde, H. K., & Hatton-Bowers, H. (2019). Guidelines for selecting professional development for early childhood teachers. *Early Childhood Education Journal, 47*(2), 395–408.

Schleiber, M., Austin, L. J. E., & Valencia López, E. (2020). *Marin County Center-Based Early Care & Education Workforce Study.* Center for the Study of Child Care Employment, University of California, Berkeley.

Simmons, D. (2015). Instructional engineering principles to frame the future of reading intervention research and practice. *Remedial and Special Education, 36*(1), 45–50.

Snyder, P. A., Hemmeter, M. L., & Fox, L. (2015). Supporting implementation of evidence-based practices through practice-based coaching. *Topics in Early Childhood Special Education, 35*(3), 133–143.

Soto, X., Crucet-Choi, A., & Goldstein, H. (2020). Effects of a supplemental Spanish phonological awareness intervention on Latino preschoolers' dual language emergent literacy skills. *American Journal of Speech–Language Pathology, 29*(3), 1283–1300.

Spencer, T. D., & Petersen, D. B. (2012). *Story Champs: A multi-tiered language intervention program.* Language Dynamics Group.

Spencer, T. D., Petersen, D. B., Restrepo, M. A., Thompson, M., & Gutierrez Arvizu, M. N. (2019). The effect of Spanish and English narrative intervention on the language skills of young dual language learners. *Topics in Early Childhood Special Education, 38*(4), 204–219.

Stoiber, K. C., & Gettinger, M. (2016). Multi-tiered systems of support and evidence-based practices. In S. R. Jimerson, M. K. Burns, & A. M. VanDerHeyden (Eds.), *Handbook of response to intervention: The science and practice of multi-tiered systems of support* (pp. 121–141). Springer Science + Business Media.

Sutherland, K. S., Conroy, M. A., Vo, A., & Ladwig, C. (2015). Implementation integrity of practice-based coaching: Preliminary results from the BEST in CLASS efficacy trial. *School Mental Health, 7,* 21–33.

Tilly, W. D. (2008). The evolution of school psychology to a science-based practice: Problem solving and the three-tiered model. In A. Thomas & J. Grimes (Eds.), *Best practices in school psychology* (Vol. 1, pp. 17–36). National Association of School Psychologists.

van Kleek, A., Vander Woude, J., & Hammett, L. (2006). Fostering literal and inferential language skills in Head Start preschoolers with language impairment using scripted book-sharing discussions. *American Journal of Speech and Language Pathology, 15*(1), 85–95.

Wackerle-Hollman, A., Durán, L., Brunner, S., Palma, J., Kohlmeier, T., Callard, C., & Rodriguez, M. (2018). *Technical manual for IGDIs Español.* University of Minnesota.

Wackerle-Hollman, A., Durán, L., Miranda, A., Chávez, C., Rodriguez, M., & Medina Morales, N. (2022). Understanding how language of instruction impacts early literacy growth for Spanish-speaking children. *School Psychology Review, 51,* 406–426.

Wackerle-Hollman, A., Durán, L., Rodriguez, M., Brunner, S., Palma, J., Kohlmeier, T., & Callard, C. (2016). *Spanish Individual Growth and Development Indicators technical manual.* University of Minnesota.

Whitehurst, G. J., & Lonigan, C. J. (1998). Child development and emergent literacy. *Child Development, 69,* 848–872.

Young, R. M. (2019). Leadership practices to design and operationalize MTSS frameworks for young children. In J. J. Carta & R. M. Young (Eds.), *Multi-tiered systems of support for young children: Driving change in early education* (pp. 15–39). Brookes.

Zucker, T. A., Cabell, S. Q., Petscher, Y., Mui, H., Landry, S. H., & Tock, J. (2021) Teaching Together: Pilot study of a tiered language and literacy intervention with Head Start teachers and linguistically diverse families. *Early Childhood Research Quarterly, 54,* 136–152.

Zucker, T. A., Solari, E. J., Landry, S. H., & Swank, P. R. (2013). Effects of a brief tiered language intervention for prekindergartners at risk. *Early Education and Development, 24*(3), 366–392.

CHAPTER 29

Factors Associated with Black Children's Early Development and Learning

Iheoma U. Iruka, Amber B. Sansbury, Nicole A. Telfer,
Nneka Ibekwe-Okafor, Nicole Gardner-Neblett, and Tonia R. Durden

School readiness is a multidimensional construct that, arguably, is a marker for children's preparedness for formal schooling (i.e., kindergarten), which subsequently leads to school achievement and life success (National Academies of Sciences, Engineering, and Medicine [NASEM], 2019). Some of the life successes include postsecondary enrollment and attainment, stable employment and a livable wage, optimal health, and a stable family. The National Education Goals Panel (NEGP, 1999) proposed a set of standards for school readiness to monitor and improve America's overall educational performance.

NEGP was charged with reporting national and state progress toward educational goals, identifying promising practices for improving education and helping to build a national, bipartisan consensus to achieve the goals. The five dimensions of school readiness conceived by NEGP included (1) physical well-being and motor development; (2) social and emotional development; (3) approaches to learning; (4) language development (including early literacy); and (5) cognition and general knowledge. These school readiness goals are evident in local and national early childhood education (ECE) programs, such as Head Start and in the most used child assessments, including Teaching Strategies GOLD®,

Work Sampling System®, and HighScope's Child Observation Record (Lambert, Kim, & Burts, 2015).

At this critical moment in our nation's history, amid a global pandemic and mass activism demanding racial justice due to the murder of George Floyd, Breonna Taylor, and other unarmed Black people in the summer of 2020, America's eyes have been opened. We see more clearly the structural racism and White privilege that have always existed throughout our society and, specifically, in ECE. Arguably, a White-normative lens has been part of how school readiness has been conceived in standards, assessments, and evidence of what promotes these established school readiness outcomes.

Conceptual Framework

Using the integrative model for the study of developmental competencies for minority children (integrative model; García Coll et al., 1996) and critical race theory (CRT; Bell, 1992; Delgado & Stefancic, 2001), we expand on what constitutes school readiness and what factors are likely to promote school readiness for Black children. The integrative model notes that beyond the White normative standards of cognitive, social, emotional, and linguistic competencies, there is a need to identify "alternative competencies in children of color" (García Coll et al., 1996, p. 1908), such as coping with racism and bicultural adaptation. Beyond the identification of non-dominant standards, García Coll and colleagues highlight factors that likely impact developmental competencies (i.e., school readiness and achievement) of minoritized children, including Black children. Social position variables such as race, ethnicity, gender, and social class create stratification that influences families' functioning and practices and opportunities. Specifically, one's race, gender, social class, and related social categories are likely to impact their experiences with racism, discrimination, and oppression.

When the integrative model is overlaid with CRT, the salience and normality of racism and White supremacy in U.S. life, law, and culture are made visible. Emerged from the field of critical legal studies, CRT explores the salience and normality of racism and White supremacy (Bell, 1992). The purpose of CRT is to describe and critically analyze how racism is and has always been embedded in life, law, and culture. Additionally, CRT examines the meaning of White privilege in the United States, and challenges ideas such as fairness and equity in a society that perpetuates racial discrimination and oppression (Crenshaw, Gotanda, Peller, & Thomas, 1995). CRT in education has been used as an analytic tool to offer critical perspectives on how racism, inequity, and oppression manifest in school and within our educational system (Taylor, Gillborn, & Ladson-Billings, 2009). For example, Black children, especially those living in low-income households, are likely to live in economically disadvantaged communities, where there are high rates of poverty that limit their access to health care, early education, schools, employment, green/open spaces, and so much more (Jargowsky, 2015). There is evidence, however, that Black majority communities and environments are likely to provide protective and buffering spaces for children and their families that center their cultural heritage, language, and way of being and promote positive racial and cultural identity (Smithsimon, 2018). Even with the potential for positive outcomes in Black majority enclaves, it is essential to recognize how racism likely shapes the living conditions that produce the racial disparities experienced by Black children and their families in almost all sectors of life.

Black Children's Current Achievement

Based on the U.S. Department of Education, National Center for Education Statistics, and Early Childhood Longitudinal Study—Kindergarten 2010–11 data (ECLS-K:2011), gaps exist between Black children and their peers—specifically, White and Asian children—from kindergarten entry and extending even through postsecondary education. ECLS-K:2011 data show Black children have significantly lower reading scores than White and Asian children in the fall of kindergarten (Bernstein, West, Newsham, & Reid, 2014; see Table 29.1). These racial gaps are also evident in math scores. In addition, Black children score lower than Asian and White children on working memory (i.e., children asked to hold a span of numbers in their memory while performing a math operation) and cognitive flexibility (i.e., children asked to sort cards one way, switch, and then sort the same cards a new way). Racial disparities also are evident in the risks experienced by children, such as living in a household below the poverty level. Bernstein and colleagues (2014) found that 76% of White children have zero risk factors compared to only 33% of Black children.

These racial gaps continue to persist over time. Little (2017) found that the racial gaps in reading, math, and executive function persisted at least through second grade, above and beyond socioeconomic status (SES; see Figure 29.1). Black students enter kindergarten performing 0.08 standard deviation lower, on average, in reading compared to White children. These gaps increase threefold to 0.24 standard deviation[1] by spring of second grade. For math, the gaps are even starker. Black students enter kindergarten performing 0.30 standard deviation lower, on average, in math compared to White children. These gaps double to 0.60 standard deviation by spring of second grade. Executive function skills tell the same story, with the Black–White gap in working memory, on average, remaining the same from fall of kindergarten through spring of second grade. For cognitive flexibility, Black children, on average, enter kindergarten 0.31 standard deviation lower than their White peers; this gap increases to 0.42 standard deviation by the spring of second grade.

Beyond these academic and executive skills in the early years, data from the U.S. Department of Education, Office for Civil Rights, indicate racial differences in school experiences. Black children represent 18% of preschool enrollment but 48%

TABLE 29.1. Racial Differences in Academic and Executive Function in the Fall of Kindergarten, ECLS-K:2011

	Reading	Math	Working memory	Cognitive flexibility
All children	34.70	29.30	94.04	8.45
Black	32.93	25.80	88.89	7.68
Asian	40.48	34.55	99.96	8.42
White	36.61	31.75	96.96	8.98

Note. From U.S. Department of Education, National Center for Education Statistics, Early Childhood Longitudinal Study, Kindergarten Class of 2010-11 (ECLS-K:2011) Restricted-use kindergarten data file. From Little (2017). Copyright © 2017 SAGE Publishing. Reprinted by permission.

of preschool children receiving more than one out-of-school suspension. In comparison, White students represent 43% of preschool enrollment but 26% of preschool children receiving more than one out of school suspension (Office for Civil Rights, 2014; see Figure 29.2). Black students are suspended and expelled at a rate three times greater than White students. On average, 5% of White students are suspended, compared to 16% of Black students. Through an intersectionality lens of race and disability, the Office for Civil Rights data also show that more than 1 out of 4, primarily Black and Latino boys with disabilities (served by the Individuals with Disabilities Education Act), and nearly 1 in 5, primarily Black and Latina girls with disabilities, receives an out-of-school suspension.

While most national data often show White children doing better than Black children, there are emerging data showing where Black children score higher compared to White children. For example, in their analyses of the Early Childhood Longitudinal Study—Birth Cohort (ECLS-B) examining the social–emotional health, developmental, and educational outcomes of young Black boys, Aratani, Wight, and Cooper (2011) found that whereas White boys were performing higher than Black boys as early as 9 months of age in many areas, when analyses accounted for SES, financial resources, and other demographic characteristics,[2] the gaps disappeared and, in some instances, Black boys were performing at a higher level. For example, the 9-month gap in cognitive development disappeared, as did the gap in preschool reading, kindergarten math, and preschool language.

Some studies show that Black children excel in various areas, including oral language and

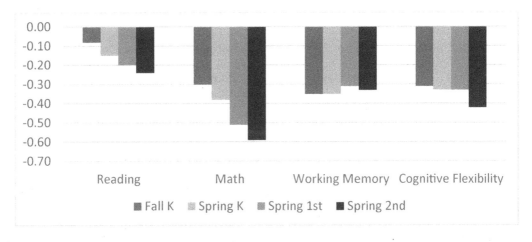

FIGURE 29.1. Coefficients of the Black gap in achievement outcomes and executive function, holding constant SES. From U.S. Department of Education, National Center for Education Statistics, Early Childhood Longitudinal Study—Kindergarten Class of 2010–11 (ECLS-K:2011) restricted-use kindergarten data file. The reference category is White. From Bernstein, West, Newsham, and Reid (2014). Copyright © 2014 Mathematica Policy Research. Reprinted by permission.

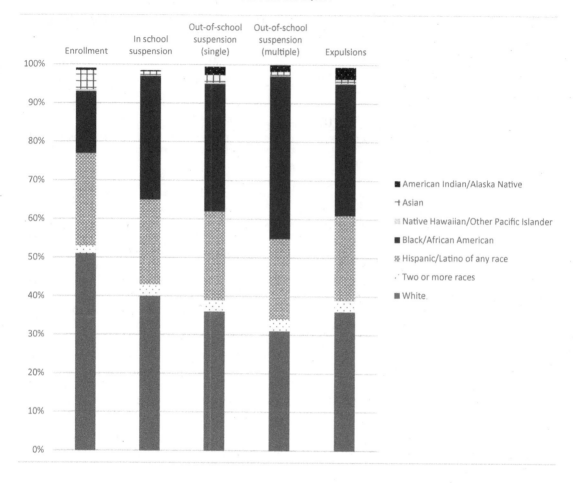

FIGURE 29.2. Students receiving suspension and expulsions, by race and ethnicity. Detail may not sum to 100% due to rounding. Totals: Enrollment is 49 million students, in-school suspension is 3.5 million students, single out-of-school suspension is 1.9 million students, multiple out-of-school suspension is 1.55 million students, and expulsion is 130,000 students. Data reported in this figure represent 99% of responding schools. From U.S. Department of Education, Office for Civil Rights, Civil Rights Data Collection, 2011–12.

storytelling, social–emotional competence, and coping with racism and bias (Gardner-Neblett, Iruka, & Humphries, 2022). Research shows that Black children have strong oral language, especially in storytelling (Gardner-Neblett & Iruka, 2015), and grammatical language features in their narratives aligned with literacy skills and cognitive reasoning (Curenton, Craig, & Flanigan, 2008). There is also an indication that Black children are excelling in their social–emotional skills, especially related to self-regulation and attention (Humphries & Iruka, 2017). Barbarin and colleagues (2013) found that most Black boys were rated as having

high self-regulation of emotions and attention, and that Black preschoolers were observed with moderate to high levels of positive coping strategies in their classrooms. This finding is notable, as Black children are likely to be in learning environments where they experience low expectations and biased interactions with teachers (Kunesh & Noltemeyer, 2019).

Factors That Promote Early Learning

Based on the integrative model and CRT, there are critical areas of influence for Black children's readiness; we highlight critical, not exhaustive, factors found to promote the early learning of Black children. We seek to identify key malleable factors consistently noted as benefiting Black children's learning, while highlighting areas that require more attention. The key factors identified by extant literature include family SES, parenting practices, health promotion, and early childhood experiences.

Family SES

SES directly affects Black children's learning and learning opportunities but primarily operates through the environments where children live and learn (i.e., homes, schools, communities). According to the family investment model (FIM), families' SES provides them with the knowledge and financial ability to purchase goods, materials, health-promoting supports (e.g., nutritious foods), experiences (e.g., early care education, museums), and services (e.g., early intervention, tutors, extracurricular activities) that then promote children's development (Mistry, Biesanz, Chien, Howes, & Benner, 2008). The median household income is much lower for Black families than other families (i.e., $45,438 for Black households in 2019 vs. $76,057 for Whites, $98,174 for Asians, $56,113 for Latines). These economic differences are even more staggering when wealth is examined: Black families' median wealth is less than 15% of that of White families, at $24,100 compared to $188,200 (Bhutta, Chang, Dettling, & Hsu, 2020). This wealth gap is concerning, because children born into poverty or who grow up in poverty are less prepared for school and have worse health and social outcomes (Roos, Wall-Wieler, & Boram Lee, 2019); this is even more dire when dealing with a global pandemic and other unexpected challenges (e.g., loss of job, medical condition, natural disaster).

Parenting Practices

The family stress model (FSM) indicates that the psychological stress associated with economic instability and material hardship (i.e., inability to pay for food, shelter, and health) disrupts parents' ability to be sensitive and nurturing to children, potentially limiting children's access to language-rich and emotionally supportive interactions and cognitively stimulating opportunities that build their cognitive, emotional, and linguistic competencies (Nievar, Moske, Johnson, & Chen, 2014).

In their examination using the nationally representative data, ECLS-B, to examine the extent to which the FIM and FSM explained the link between SES and outcomes for Black and White children, Iruka, LaForett, and Odom (2012) found that the FIM was a salient explanatory model linking SES to outcomes for White children but not Black children. On the other hand, FSM was a salient explanatory model for Black and White children. Specifically, sensitive parent–child interactions mediated the link between maternal education and household income and Black children's early language and emergent numeracy skills. The authors postulate that the lack of relevance for FIM for Black children (and other children of color) may be due to the lack of culturally grounded indicators that constitute investment activities and that "parent–child activities and interactions may focus more on preparing children to cope with bias based on historical (i.e., in the United States) and personal experiences with discrimination and prejudice" (p. 366).

One culturally grounded indicator that is particularly salient for Black children's development and learning is ethnic–racial socialization (ERS), which is multidimensional and encompasses many behaviors, including parental teaching of racial history, culture, and traditions; group differences; discrimination; and diversity to support children in dealing with the biased experiences that are likely in children's daily lives outside the home (i.e., early education settings, schools, community) (Hughes, Watford, & Del Toro, 2016). Extensive evidence shows that ERS practices are necessary to develop a positive racial identity and mitigate the psychological harm from continuous negative messages about one's race (Hughes, 2003; Huguley, Wang, Vasquez, & Guo, 2019; Murry, Smith, & Hill, 2001). There are links between positive beliefs about one's racial group (i.e., positive racial identity) and Black children's achievement and social–emotional development (Butler-Barnes, Williams, & Chavous, 2012). Children's receipt of messages that promote their positive self-identity balanced with messages about racial inequalities also contributes to positive school grades (Sanders, 1997), academic curiosity, and persistence (Neblett, Philip, Cogburn, & Sellers, 2006).

Health Promotion

Good health is instrumental for Black children's development and learning (Shonkoff & Phillips,

2000). Early adversity can change the timing of critical periods of brain development, impacting the "plasticity" of developmental processes driven by experiences in the life of the young child and the family. A child's healthy development begins in the preconception period and depends on a solid foundation built prenatally. Access to basic resources that support nutrition, and psychosocial and healthy development for both children and the household is critical for optimal development and may be instrumental in closing racial and SES disparities (NASEM, 2019).

Unfortunately, Black children, compared to their peers, are more likely to experience health vulnerabilities in the first few years of life. Being born preterm or low birthweight (LBW, i.e., less than 5.5 pounds at birth) puts a child at risk for several health and developmental problems early in life and over the long term (Pabayo et al., 2019). Black women are more likely to have preterm births compared to White women; in 2019, the rate was 14.4 and 9.3%, respectively (Centers for Disease Control and Prevention [CDC], 2021). Babies born preterm are likely to have breathing problems, developmental delay, and vision and hearing problems, which can impact their optimal development, as well as higher rates of death and disability (CDC, 2021). Similarly, there are racial disparities for LBW. In 2018, the LBW rate was 14.07% for Black infants compared to 6.91% for Whites (Martin, Hamilton, Osterman, & Driscoll, 2019). While there is some indication that low-income status is one of the primary drivers for LBW (Cutland et al., 2017), along with low parental education, maternal stress, domestic violence, and other abuse (CDC, 2016), these are not necessarily the only factors for Black mothers, as some have identified the impact of racism and racialized experiences (Mustillo et al., 2004).

Black children also experience inequities in access to basic resources and supports, such as adequate and nutritious food, and safe and healthy housing,which is critical for healthy development and learning. *Food insecurity* is the inability to obtain adequate nutritious food (Nitschke, 2017). Over 20% of Black households experienced food insecurity compared to 10 percent of White households. Historical racism that leads to poverty, food deserts, and inequitable access to nutritious foods have been implicated in food insecurity (Coleman-Jensen, Rabbitt, Gregory, & Singh, 2017).

Early Childhood Experiences

The first few years are critical for setting up children for school and life. Early childhood is a sensitive period for promoting children's cognitive, emotional, social, and cultural competencies. Early childhood experiences that are nurturing and sensitive, enriching, language-rich, and that meet individual needs and leverage children's assets set children up for school and life (Williams & Lerner, 2019). These experiences can occur in diverse settings, including children's homes or out of their homes, such as informal or formal ECE settings, such as home-, center-, or school-based experiences. Sixty-three percent of Black children are in at least one weekly nonparental care arrangement from birth through age 5, according to the U.S. Department of Education (Cui & Natzke, 2021). The majority of Black children (59%) were likely to be in center-based care, 45% in relative care, and 13% in relative care (Cui & Natzke, 2021).

Although most Black children are likely to be in nonparental arrangements, they are least likely to be in high-quality ECE settings (Barnett, Carolan, & Johns, 2013; Iruka, Curenton, Durden, & Escayg, 2020). Based on national data (ECLS-B), 75% of Black 4-year-olds in center-based care are in low-to-moderate quality care (Barnett et al., 2013) and 100% of Black 4-year-olds in home-based care are in low-to-moderate quality programs. Seminal early childhood intervention programs, like the Carolina Abecedarian Study (Campbell, Ramey, Pungello, Sparling, & Miller-Johnson, 2002) and HighScope Perry Preschool Program (Schweinhart et al., 2005) indicate that when children from low-income households (the majority of whom were Black) experienced high-quality early child care and education, there were long-term positive and intergenerational benefits for children's academic and life outcomes (Heckman & Karapakula, 2019).

There is also a need to examine access and experiences of early intervention (EI) and special education programs, which help support children who are developmentally delayed. Unfortunately, there is evidence of disproportionality in access to and quality of services as early as 24 months, as well as overidentification in certain categories (e.g., learning and intellectual disability) and underidentification in others (e.g., autism) (Boyd, Iruka, & Pierce, 2018). For instance, using the ECLS-B, Feinberg, Silverstein, Donahue, and Bliss (2011) found that at 9 months of age, there were not Black–White differences in receipt of services among the 1,000 children eligible for EI services. By 24 months of age, however, Black children were five times less likely to receive services than White children among the 1,000 children eligible for EI services. These racial differences were especially pronounced based on developmental delay alone versus established medical conditions. Racial disparities are also seen in receipt of therapy services (Boyd et al., 2018). Khetani, Richardson, and McManus (2017) found that Black children have nearly 75% lower odds of receiving physical therapy (PT) than their White peers and receive an hour less per month of physical therapy than their White peers.

Advancing the Science on Black Children's Early Development and Learning

There are multiple implications for future scholarship that examines root causes and mechanisms that lead to racial inequities while incorporating the strengths of various methods (e.g., casual, quasi-experimental, mixed-methods, qualitative). Advocacy and research from this stance have been led by Black developmentalists and practitioners, recognized throughout our chapter, but too often unheralded by mainstream, peer-reviewed publications or untapped by funding institutions. In this chapter, we call explicitly for increased actionable research about young Black children, their families, and communities conducted with an anti-racist, culturally grounded lens to understand their experiences and leverage their cultural assets in the early years with the following components:

1. *Race-conscious, strengths-based theoretical frameworks.* Historically, developmental research and programs targeting Black families have centered on deficit views through biased, Westernized lenses of cultural deprivation based on White and middle-class norms (García Coll et al., 1996; James & Iruka, 2018). Conventional theories are operationalized to tell the dominant story of deprivation, pathology, and criminality related to the context of Black homes and neighborhoods. We call for more child development research that promotes ongoing investment, responsive intervention, and aligned research–family partnerships that recognize assets and funds of knowledge of Black families (Moll,

Amanti, Neff, & Gonzalez, 1992; Yosso, 2005). To achieve this goal, we must build on, create, and validate reimagined theories that respond to the nuanced lived experiences and within-group differences for Black children in America. We must also consider how Black families adapt and cultivate promotive factors (e.g., healthy relationships, learning, prosocial behavior, emotional well-being) in the face of racism.

2. *Construct validity.* To understand the effects of racism on young Black children, measures are needed that capture the mechanisms and manifestations of racism during the earliest stages of life. For example, very few studies consider the "extent to which structural and historical racial discrimination in policies across sectors might contribute to disparities in access to high-quality [ECE] across racial and ethnic groups" (Banghart et al., 2020, p. 48). Similarly, meaningful scholarship on the role of racism in influencing disproportionate adverse birth and health outcomes for Black children is limited, because few existing instruments and methodologies are appropriate to examine the racialized processes related to pregnancy such as LBW, depressive symptoms during prenatal care, infant mortality, preterm birth, and other pregnancy-related health outcomes (Nuru-Jeter et al., 2009). With more attuned instruments and research methods, decision-makers will learn more about the effects and links between racism and pregnancy stress, the delivery of prenatal care, and ultimately adverse birth outcomes. Greater knowledge of Black parents and families' racial trauma in and out of health care settings will contribute to systems-level thinking about critical supports before, during, and after pregnancy.

3. *Responsive research designs.* Throughout extant literature, researchers contend with recurring limitations of cross-sectional designs and a lack of funding support for longitudinal experimental and quasi-experimental studies focused on young Black children and their families and communities, and other issues of relevance for Black communities (Ginther et al., 2011, 2018; Hoppe et al., 2019). Child advocates and elected officials subsequently grapple with pinpointing the impacts of racism across a wide range of variables (e.g., specific incidents of racist violence, daily experiences with racism, chronic race-related stressors over time) and factors during the first 3 years for Black children (Caughy, O'Campo, & Muntaner, 2011). This priority also would foster meaning-

ful but understudied local qualitative research on critical matters of relevance for young Black children, including, but not limited to, disabilities and early intervention; rural and isolated areas; immigrant, mixed-status or transnational families; and families with same-sex partnerships or underrepresented family structures.

Conclusion

In a recent report, *Black Parent Voices: Resilience in the Face of the Two Pandemics—COVID-19 and Racism*, Iruka and colleagues (2021) note that Black people and communities are under siege due to the two pandemics: COVID-19 and racism. Their report unearths the realities of systemic barriers in the lives of Black families and their young children, such as economic instability, health challenges, and experiences with discrimination, pushing elected officials and human service agencies to examine the trajectories of young Black children and their families with renewed commitment. Without intentional efforts to center an anti-racist and equity lens, developmental scholarship may uphold White supremacy implicitly (and explicitly) and remain misaligned to the needs, conditions, and full range of lived experiences of Black children and their families. Furthermore, science will continue to see racial disparities as a child and family problem and seek to "fix" Black children and their families rather than fixing the racist systems and institutions that continue to oppress and deny equitable opportunities that promote and support Black children's development and learning.

Notes

1. Standard deviation is the amount of deviation from the average. For most standard measures, such as reading or math, the average is 100 and the standard deviation is 15. So, if a child scores 115, he or she is 1 standard deviation above the average; if the child scores 85, then he or she is 1 standard deviation below the average. A score of 107.5 is 0.50 standard deviation, representing a half of a standard deviation above the mean.
2. The child and family characteristics examined include children born with low birthweight, child age, mother's educational attainment, having two parents, receiving WIC, teen mother, family income, having a checking/savings account, providing toys to children, parental warmth, and mother not being depressed.

References

Aratani, Y., Wight, V. R., & Cooper, J. L. (2011). *Racial gaps in early childhood: Socio-emotional health, developmental and education outcomes among african american boys.* Columbia University, Teachers' College, National Center for Children in Poverty.

Banghart, P., Halle, T., Bamdad, T., Cook, M., Redd, Z., Cox, A., & Carlson, J. (2020). A review of the literature on access to high-quality care for infants and toddlers. Retrieved May 31, 2021, from *www.childtrends.org/wp-content/uploads/2020/05/highqualitycarelitreview_childtrends_may2020.pdf*.

Barbarin, O., Iruka, I. U., Harradine, C., Winn, D.-M. C., McKinney, M. K., & Taylor, L. C. (2013). Development of social–emotional competence in boys of color: A cross-sectional cohort analysis from pre-K to second grade. *American Journal of Orthopsychiatry, 83(2–3),* 145–155.

Barnett, W. S., Carolan, M., & Johns, D. (2013). *Equity and excellence: African-American children's access to quality preschool.* Rutgers University, National Institute for Early Education and Research, Center on Enhancing Early Learning Outcomes.

Bell, D. A. (1992). *Faces at the bottom of the well: The permanence of racism.* Basic Books.

Bernstein, S., West, J., Newsham, R., & Reid, M. (2014). *Kindergartners' skills at school entry: An analysis of the ECLS-K.* Mathematica.

Bhutta, N., Chang, A. C., Dettling, L. J., & Hsu, J. W. (2020). Disparities in wealth by race and ethnicity in the 2019 Survey of Consumer Finances. Retrieved May 31, 2021 from *www.federalreserve.gov/econres/notes/feds-notes/disparities-in-wealth-by-race-and-ethnicity-in-the-2019-survey-of-consumer-finances-20200928.htm*.

Boyd, B. A., Iruka, I. U., & Pierce, N. P. (2018). Strengthening service access for children of color with autism spectrum disorders: A proposed conceptual framework. In M. M. Burke (Ed.), *International Review of Research in Developmental Disabilities: Service delivery systems for individuals with intellectual and developmental disabilities and their families across the lifespan* (pp. 1–33). Elsevier.

Butler-Barnes, S. T., Williams, T. T., & Chavous, T. M. (2012). Racial pride and religiosity among African American boys: Implications for academic motivation and achievement. *Journal of Youth and Adolescence, 41(4),* 486–498.

Campbell, F. A., Ramey, C. T., Pungello, E., Sparling, J., & Miller-Johnson, S. (2002). Early childhood education: Young adult outcomes from the Abecedarian Project. *Applied Developmental Science, 6(1),* 42–57.

Caughy, M., O'Campo, P., & Muntaner, C. (2011).

Experiences of racism among African American parents and the mental health of their preschool-aged children. *American Journal of Public Health, 94*(12), 2118–2124.

Centers for Disease Control and Prevention. (2016). Reproductive and birth outcomes. Retrieved April 17, 2019, from *https://ephtracking.cdc.gov/showrblbwgrowthretardationenv.action.*

Centers for Disease Control and Prevention. (2021). Preterm birth. Retrieved from *www.cdc.gov/reproductivehealth/maternalinfanthealth/pretermbirth.htm.*

Coleman-Jensen, A., Rabbitt, A. P., Gregory, C. A., & Singh, A. (2017). *Household food security in the United States in 2016, ERR-237.* U.S. Department of Agriculture, Economic Research Service.

Crenshaw, K., Gotanda, N., Peller, G., & Thomas, K. (Eds.). (1995). *Critical race theory: The key writing that formed the movement.* New Press.

Cui, J., & Natzke, L. (2021). Early childhood program participation: 2019 (NCES 2020–075REV). Retrieved May 31, 2021, from *http://nces.ed.gov/pubsearch/pubsinfo.asp?pubid=2020075rev.*

Curenton, S. M., Craig, M. J., & Flanigan, N. (2008). Use of decontextualized talk across story contexts: How oral storytelling and emergent reading can scaffold children's development. *Early Education and Development, 19*(1), 161–187.

Cutland, C. L., Lackritz, E. M., Mallett-Moore, T., Bardají, A., Chandrasekaran, R., Lahariya, C., . . . Muñoz, F. M. (2017). Low birth weight: Case definition and guidelines for data collection, analysis, and presentation of maternal immunization safety data. *Vaccine, 35*(48, Part A), 6492–6500.

Delgado, R., & Stefancic, J. (2001). *Critical race theory. An introduction.* New York University Press.

Feinberg, E., Silverstein, M., Donahue, S., & Bliss, R. (2011). The impact of race on participation in Part C early intervention services. *Journal of Developmental and Behavioral Pediatrics, 32*(4), 284–291.

García Coll, C., Lamberty, G., Jenkins, R., McAdoo, H. P., Crnic, K., Wasik, B. H., & Garcia, H.V. (1996). An integrative model for the study of developmental competencies in minority children. *Child Development, 67*(5), 1891–1914.

Gardner-Neblett, N., & Iruka, I. U. (2015). Oral narrative skills: Explaining the language-emergent literacy link by race/ethnicity and SES. *Developmental Psychology, 51*(7), 889–904.

Gardner-Neblett, N., Iruka, I. U., & Humphries, M. (2022, August 10). Dismantling the Black–White achievement gap paradigm: Why and how we need to focus instead on systemic change. *Journal of Education.* [Epub ahead of print] *doi:10.1177/00220574211031958.*

Ginther, D. K., Basner, J., Jensen, U., Schnell, J.,

Kington, R., & Schaffer, W. T. (2018). Publications as predictors of racial and ethnic differences in NIH research awards. *PLOS ONE, 13*(11), Article e0205929.

Ginther, D. K., Schaffer, W. T., Schnell, J., Masimore, B., Liu, F., Haak, L. L., & Kington, R. (2011). Race, ethnicity, and NIH research awards. *Science, 333*(6045), 1015–1019.

Heckman, J. H., & Karapakula, G. (2019). *The Perry Preschoolers at late midlife: A study in design-specific inference.* University of Chicago.

Hoppe, T. A., Litovitz, A., Willis, K. A., Meseroll, R. A., Perkins, M. J., Hutchins, B. I., . . . Santangelo, G. M. (2019). Topic choice contributes to the lower rate of NIH awards to African-American/black scientists. *Science Advances, 5*(10), Article eaaw7238.

Hughes, D. (2003). Correlates of African American and Latino parents' messages to children about ethnicity and race: A comparative study of racial socialization. *American Journal of Community Psychology, 31*(1), 15–33.

Hughes, D. L., Watford, J. A., & Del Toro, J. (2016). A transactional/ecological perspective on ethnic-racial identity, socialization, and discrimination. *Advances in Child Development and Behavior, 51*, 1–41.

Huguley, J. P., Wang, M.-T., Vasquez, A. C., & Guo, J. (2019). Parental ethnic–racial socialization practices and the construction of children of color's ethnic–racial identity: A research synthesis and meta-analysis. *Psychological Bulletin, 145*(5), 437–458.

Humphries, M., & Iruka, I. U. (2017). Ring the alarm: Moving from educational gaps to educational opportunities for Black students. In I. U. Iruka, S. M. Curenton, & T. Durden (Eds.), *African American children in early childhood education* (Vol. 5, pp. 15–34). Emerald Group.

Iruka, I. U., Curenton, S. M., Durden, T. R., & Escayg, K. A. (2020). *Don't look away: Embracing anti-bias classrooms.* Gryphon House.

Iruka, I. U., Curenton, S. M., Sims, J., Escayg, K. A., Ibekwe-Okafor, N., & RAPID-EC. (2021). *Black parent voices: Resilience in the face of the two pandemics—COVID-19 and racism.* Researchers Investigating Sociocultural Equity and Race (RISER) Network.

Iruka, I. U., LaForett, D. R., & Odom, E. C. (2012). Examining the validity of the family investment and stress models and relationship to children's school readiness across five cultural groups. *Journal of Family Psychology, 26*(3), 359–370.

James, C., & Iruka, I. U. (2018). Delivering on the promise of effective early childhood education. Retrieved May 31, 2021, from *www.nbcdi.org/nbcdi-releases-delivering-promise-effective-early-childhood-education-white-paper-examines-policy.*

Jargowsky, P. A. (2015). *The architecture of segre-*

gation: *Civil unrest, the concentration of poverty, and public policy*. Century Foundation.

Khetani, M. A., Richardson, Z., & McManus, B. M. (2017). Social disparities in early intervention service use and provider-reported outcomes. *Journal of Developmental and Behavioral Pediatrics, 38*(7), 501–509.

Kunesh, C. E., & Noltemeyer, A. (2019). Understanding disciplinary disproportionality: Stereotypes shape pre-service teachers' beliefs about black boys' behavior. *Urban Education, 54*(4), 471–498.

Lambert, R. G., Kim, D.-H., & Burts, D. C. (2015). The measurement properties of the Teaching Strategies GOLD® assessment system. *Early Childhood Research Quarterly, 33*, 49–63.

Little, M. (2017). Racial and socioeconomic gaps in executive function skills in early elementary school: Nationally representative evidence from the ECLS-K:2011. *Educational Researcher, 46*(2), 103–109.

Martin, J. A., Hamilton, B. E., Osterman, M. J. K., & Driscoll, A. K. (2019). Births: Final data for 2018. *National Vital Statistics Reports, 68*(13), 1–47. National Center for Health Statistics.

Mistry, R. S., Biesanz, J. C., Chien, N., Howes, C., & Benner, A. D. (2008). Socioeconomic status, parental investments, and the cognitive and behavioral outcomes of low-income children from immigrant and native households. *Early Childhood Research Quarterly, 23*, 193–212.

Moll, L. C., Amanti, C., Neff, D., & Gonzalez, N. (1992). Funds of knowledge for teaching: Using a qualitative approach to connect homes and classrooms. *Theory Into Practice, 31*(2), 132–141.

Murry, V. M., Smith, E. P., & Hill, N. E. (2001). Introduction to the Special Section: Race, ethnicity, and culture in studies of families in context. *Journal of Marriage and Family, 63*(4), 911–914.

Mustillo, S., Krieger, N., Gunderson, E. P., Sidney, S., McCreath, H., & Kiefe, C. I. (2004). Self-reported experiences of racial discrimination and Black-White differences in preterm and low-birth-weight deliveries: The CARDIA Study. *American Journal of Public Health, 94*(12), 2125–2131.

National Academies of Sciences, Engineering, and Medicine. (2019). *Vibrant and healthy kids: Aligning science, practice, and policy to advance health equity*. National Academies Press.

National Education Goals Panel. (1999). The National Education Goals Report: Building a Nation of Learners, 1999. Retrieved from *https://govinfo.library.unt.edu/negp/page1-7.htm*.

National Kids Data Count. (2019). Children who live in unsafe communities by race and ethnicity in the United States, 2017–18. Retrieved from *https://datacenter.kidscount.org*.

Neblett, E. W., Jr., Philip, C. L., Cogburn, C. D., &

Sellers, R. M. (2006). African American adolescents' discrimination experiences and academic achievement: Racial socialization as a cultural compensatory and protective factor. *Journal of Black Psychology, 32*(2), 199–218.

Nievar, M. A., Moske, A. K., Johnson, D. J., & Chen, Q. (2014). Parenting practices in preschool leading to later cognitive competence: A family stress model. *Early Education and Development, 25*(3), 318–337.

Nitschke, M. (2017). Hunger is a racial equity issue. Retrieved from *https://alliancetoendhunger.org/wp-content/uploads/2017/07/hill-advocacy-fact-sheet_hunger-is-a-racial-equity-issue_alliance-to-end-hunger.pdf*.

Nuru-Jeter, A., Dominguez, T. P., Hammond, W. P., Leu, J., Skaff, M., Egerter, S., . . . Braveman, P. (2009). "It's the skin you're in": African-American women talk about their experiences of racism: An exploratory study to develop measures of racism for birth outcome studies. *Maternal and Child Health Journal, 13*(1), 29–39.

Office for Civil Rights. (2014). *Data Snapshot: School Discipline, Issue Brief No. 1*. U.S. Department of Education, Office for Civil Rights.

Pabayo, R., Ehntholt, A., Davis, K., Liu, S. Y., Muennig, P., & Cook, D. M. (2019). Structural racism and odds for infant mortality among infants born in the United States 2010. *Journal of Racial and Ethnic Health Disparities, 6*(6), 1095–1106.

Roos, L. L., Wall-Wieler, E., & Boram Lee, J. (2019). Poverty and early childhood outcomes. *Pediatrics, 143*(6), Article e20183426.

Sanders, M. G. (1997). Overcoming obstacles: Academic achievement as a response to racism and discrimination. *Journal of Negro Education, 66*, 83–93.

Schweinhart, L. J., Montie, J., Xiang, Z., Barnett, W. S., Belfield, C. R., & Nores, M. (2005). *Lifetime effects: The High/Scope Perry Preschool study through age 40*. High/Scope Press.

Shonkoff, J. P., & Phillips, D. (2000). *From neurons to neighborhoods: The science of early childhood development*. National Academies Press.

Smithsimon, G. (2018). Are African American families more vulnerable in a largely white neighborhood? Retrieved May 31, 2021, from *www.theguardian.com/books/2018/feb/21/racial-segregation-in-america-causes*.

Taylor, E., Gillborn, D., & Ladson-Billings, G. (2009). *Foundations of critical race theory in education*. Routledge.

Williams, P. G., & Lerner, M. A. (2019). School readiness. *Pediatrics, 144*(2), Article e20191766.

Yosso, T. J. (2005). Whose culture has capital?: A critical race theory discussion of community cultural wealth. *Race Ethnicity and Education, 8*(1), 69–91.

PART VI

USING THE SCIENCE OF EARLY LITERACY TO LEARN ACROSS BOUNDARIES

CHAPTER 30

Early Literacy in Everyday Spaces

Creating Opportunities for Learning

Susan B. Neuman

Young children have an inordinate curiosity about their world. From visits to their local bodegas to neighborhood playgrounds and laundromats, every place holds the potential to be a place of wonder and a context for early learning. In these settings, children are likely to pick up words, some say as many as nine new words per day, without explicit word-by-word instruction (Golinkoff & Hirsh-Pasek, 1999). Instead, they seem to absorb new meanings almost effortlessly as they encounter them in conversational interactions. Although the mechanisms for doing so are not fully understood, it seems that children may rely on situations in which a single unfamiliar word is surrounded by known linguistic contexts, and the situation provides a clear meaning for the word (Bloom, 2000). In some unspecified manner, the child infers the matchup between word and meaning.

Most often the context for learning words in the language acquisition literature is that of a dyadic interchange between an adult and a child. Yet less frequently mentioned is the situation or the spaces in which these exchanges take place. In these contexts, children are likely to be exposed to vocabulary specific to the context. A conversation about a trip to the zoo or to the grocery store, for example, is likely to present young learners with different sets of words, and different repetitions of these words close in time

within the context (Montag, Jones, & Smith, 2015). Therefore, across these different spaces, children in interactions with their parents and other adults are likely to be exposed to small sets of conversations that include and repeat unique words in that context.

Most recently, a number of scholars have begun to recognize the potential of these common "everyday spaces" for enhancing children's language and early literacy development (Hassinger-Das, Palti, Golinkoff, & Hirsh-Pasek, 2020). This work comes largely in recognition of the striking disparities in school readiness for children who come from underresourced communities compared to their well-resourced peers. Recent evidence, for example, shows a wealth gap between America's richest and poorest families that has more than doubled in recent years, with the richest 5% of families having 248 times as much wealth as poorest families (Pew Research Center, 2015). Too often, children from these poor communities are likely at the "starting gate" (Lee & Burkam, 2002) to enter school lagging far behind their peers in alphabetic skills, vocabulary, and early numeracy, setting a cycle of low motivation and achievement throughout their school years.

To address these striking disparities, policymakers have largely turned to early schooling including 3K (prekindergarten for 3-year-olds) and preschool programs to engage children in learning resources to close the gap (Friedman-Krauss et al., 2021). Although these efforts have been laudatory, the question remains whether early schooling alone is sufficiently powerful to change the trajectory of low achievement, considering that often only 20% of children's waking hours are often spent in the school context, with the other 80% of time is spent in home and community settings (Meltzoff, Kuhl, Movellan, & Sejnowski, 2009). In addition, by focusing our attention primarily on formal learning, we may miss the opportunity to investigate learning in the contexts that may matter most to young children with their families, neighborhood, and friends, when learning may flow across time and settings. It allows us to consider the broader life spheres of a young child and the possible interdependencies between settings.

This chapter first focuses on the learning ecology framework that shapes our work in these informal, day-to-day settings. It then provides several examples of how modest transformations in public spaces can shape novel learning opportunities for young children. It emphasizes how "hybrid spaces" (Moje et al., 2004) can foster a breadth of language and content-rich learning in contextualized settings in everyday interactions that are meaningful to young children. It also highlights how literacy learning can be distributed across time and resources in these multiple settings, contributing to a young child's overall learning ecology.

Our Theoretical Framework

Our work draws on ecological perspectives, as well as constructs developed from sociocultural and activity theory (Rogoff, 1990; Tharp & Gallimore, 1988). These perspectives highlight the interdependencies between children and their environment, and the intertwining of people and context. Bronfenbrenner's (1979) formalization of this approach, for example, was of a set of nested, overlapping but isomorphic systems involving microsystems (i.e., parent and child interactions) to macrosystems (cultural group or nation–state). The environment—its affordances or possibilities and its purposes affect what activity settings are likely to be possible, the task demands, the scripts, the purposes or motives of the participants, and the cultural meaning of the interactions. These activity settings come to shape children's first literacy experiences.

These environmental factors are known to affect both the physical and the psychological aspects of caregiving (e.g., the parent belief systems, parenting styles, and maternal guidance for educating young children) (Owens, Reardon, & Jencks, 2016; Rowe, 2018). For example, studies have shown that having books in close proximity creates an "environmental press" (Gump, 1989), a tendency to enact an activity associated with print. However, how these materials and the symbolic tools they represent are used may only be meaningful when located in the larger sphere of cultural practices and values (Kruger & Tomasello, 2000). Literacy is a profoundly social process, embedded in social relationships with caregivers who assist and help to frame an activity as important, useful and enjoyable (McLane & McNamee, 1990). Therefore, the environment includes not only the physical materials but also the psychological supports, the human relationships, that determine when, how often, and in what situations children are given opportunities to engage with print.

This learning ecology perspective foregrounds the fact that young children are actively engaged and participate in learning in many different settings. Within these settings, they are likely to experience different clusters of language interactions particular to the setting: for example, talk about foods in the grocery, personal care and hygiene in the barbershop, patterns and cycles in the laundromat, creating additive exchanges that can promote language and content knowledge. This perspective recognizes the variety of language practices and forms of knowledge that are developed *outside* of more formal learning and institutional settings. It suggests that boundaries of learning are far more permeable and subject to influence in more ways than previously acknowledged.

Recognizing the potential of "hybrid" spaces as spheres for learning in early childhood raises a number of interesting questions related to the possible interdependencies between settings. For example, how does learning in everyday spaces contribute to children's language and literacy development? In what ways might learning in context influence decontextualized language? And finally, is it possible to nurture informal learning by providing additional resources that help support family engagement early on in children's development?

Learning in Everyday Spaces

Studies of family interactions in homes attest to the influence of everyday spaces and their contributions to children's language development and early literacy. For example, in an effort to capture the rich details of everyday life, Snow, Baines, Chandler, Goodman, and Hemphill (1991), in a groundbreaking study of home and school for 74 Head Start children, found that mealtimes seemed an especially rich context to support language-rich interactions. In a follow-up study, researchers found that during this informal time, caregivers used techniques such as definitions, synonyms, inference and comparison, and the child's prior experience in the social or physical context to help understand what the new words meant (Snow & Beals, 2006). On average, these highly contextualized conversations appeared to influence children's "language of schooling"; furthermore, children who heard more new words within the family and understood more words had stronger decontextualized early literacy skills later in kindergarten.

Research suggests that the socioeconomic disparities in children's school readiness skills arise, at least in part, from disparities in these informal experiences during their infant, toddler, and preschool years. Numerous social scientists (Fiorini & Keane, 2014; Phillips, 2011) have theorized that how young children spend their time influences their academic success, and that particular contexts such as novel environments may generate conversations with their caregivers that are especially educatively productive. Much of the research in the time-use literature has centered on the importance of reading to young children and its positive association with children's verbal skills. Using time-use diaries to record how young children spent their time (Phillips, 2011), for example, the Panel Study of Income Dynamics Child Development Supplement estimates that by the time they enter school, higher-income children will have spent over 400 more hours in literacy activities than their lower-income peers. Less recognized, however, but possibly just as critical, is that these children from higher-income families will have spent more than 900 hours in these nonroutine contexts (e.g., outside of the home) than children from low-income families. For example, young children from higher-income families spend about 4.5 hours per week in indoor or outdoor recreation places, church, business, or other institutions compared

to lower-income families. It seems probable that these activities may stimulate adult–child conversations, encourage analytic thinking, or result in problem-solving opportunities that supports more extended discourse. In short, the everyday family experiences of young children from different socioeconomic backgrounds may differ in ways that most likely contribute to disparities in school readiness.

Family literacy programs and home-based interventions for lower-income families have attempted to enhance language and literacy practices with only modest success in the long term (Kornrich & Furstenberg, 2013). Families may be sensitive to influences and incentives such as book giveaway programs, but more often than not, these policies or programs cannot help to offset, overcome, or compensate for huge preexisting differences created by social position, family culture, and practices. Added to these impediments is the problem of resources (Duncan & Murnane, 2014) that may affect the capacity of lower-income families to implement their educational goals, owing in part to insufficient social capital, among other issues.

Families, of course, comprise more than a parent and a child. They include siblings, extended kin living nearby, and close friends who may take an active part in child care and childrearing. In addition, a learning ecology perspective recognizes the interdependencies between child-level and environmental variables, and the intertwining of person and context in producing developmental change. These cross-context linkages, such as relationships with people and institutions in the community other than one's immediate family, may have a powerful influence on children's development.

Rethinking Everyday Spaces to Promote Early Literacy

This section highlights a number of projects that transform places into hybrid spaces for literacy learning. These projects build on the notion of improving opportunities to learn by enhancing a more deliberate print presence in the community. Previous studies (Hanner, Braham, Elliott, & Libertus, 2019; Ridge, Weisberg, Ilgaz, Hirsh-Pasek, & Golinkoff, 2015), for example, have shown initial evidence for the addition of attractive signage designed to include open-ended questions in supermarket spaces (e.g., "Where does milk come from?"), and how these signs can serve as springboards for caregiver–child conversations and interactions. Researchers (Ridge et al., 2015) found that posting the signage seemed to support a 33% increase in the frequency and quality of caregiver–child interactions compared to when the signs were taken down.

These initial findings suggested that modest transformations to the environment could potentially support greater social interaction and become a conduit for promoting literacy-related activities and behaviors for children and their families. Working with Foundations and Corporate Social Responsibility offices, along with my partners, I began a more targeted effort to bring the science of early literacy into community settings.

Reaching Families Where They Are: Vending Machines in the Community

Children in poor neighborhoods often live in *book deserts,* communities in which there is limited to no access to children's books and other resources. In one study, for example, 833 children in a district in Washington, DC, would have to share *one* book over the summer to be able to read (Neuman & Moland, 2019). Obviously, this is likely to contribute to the *summer slide,* the associated declines in achievement particularly for those living in low-income neighborhoods (Alexander & Entwisle, 1988; Burke, Greene, & McKenna, 2016). Even branch libraries, the only existing safety net in some of these neighborhoods, may have reduced hours and limited funding for replenishing and updating their collections. Together, this research draws attention to the structural inequalities in neighborhoods rather than the individual or family characteristics that result in academic gaps between communities.

Working with our corporate partners (e.g., JetBlue Airlines; Random House and Simon & Schuster book sellers), we devised an innovative book distribution program designed to reach families "where they are" in four under-resourced neighborhoods: three in Detroit and one in DC (Neuman & Knapczyk, 2020). Each of these neighborhoods had strong community associations and churches, all with local leadership ties to their constituents. Pastor Maurice, a church leader in Anacostia, DC, for example, was passionate about reading and helping students get ahead. He, along with a gaggle of teens who seemed ever-present in the community, were

among our greatest champions. Church leaders, Directors of park and recreation centers, local child care organizations, excited about the potential, all came on board for the project.

Supported by these neighborhood champions, JetBlue placed a number of bright blue vending machines in neighborhoods over the summer months, only instead of dispensing candy or soda pop, these machines carried carefully wrapped books designated by age-ranges (birth through teen) that were available for free. Similar to a snack machine, the notion was that an individual could review the selections (see Figures 30.1a and 30.1b), press a button, and out would come the product—in this case, a book.

Machines were placed in high-traffic areas such as the local church, Safeway, the health center, and the parks and recreation center. Anyone could come and use them. Our role as the evaluation team was to understand how greater access to books might affect behaviors about reading, as well as whether it could potentially stem summer reading loss. We used a variety of measures, including observations, analyses of traffic patterns, title recognition measures, and a simple pre- and posttest measure known as "Get Ready to Read" to examine children's school readiness skills. We wanted to construct a knowledge base with the explicit intention of making it useful to policymakers and scholars involved in community-based research.

And here's what we found: nothing short of an overwhelming response. In 8-weeks' time, over 64,000 books were distributed through these machines: 26,200 to unique, one-time users, and 38,325 to return users. At the same time, three other sources of data provided more details on their use. The first came from traffic patterns. Placing books in close proximity to where people are likely to traffic clearly mattered. Product placement managers, for example, have known this for years. Put an impulse item near the checkout stand, and it's likely to be picked up. Similarly, we found that placing the machine close to the checkout line in the grocery store resulted in greater frequency of use (e.g., it had to be refilled every hour on weekdays). The second insight was that those who were most attracted to the machine were already interested in reading. For those who were not, the "environmental press" of greater access to books was not sufficiently compelling to encourage changes in their negative views of reading. And the third insight was that despite recommendations from librar-

FIGURE 30.1a. The book vending machine. Photo by Susan B. Neuman. Used by permission.

FIGURE 30.1b. Making a book selection. Photo by Susan B. Neuman. Used by permission.

ians and literature specialists on the book selections, those that were most popular were either nonfiction (e.g., biography of Barack Obama), or screen-related titles like *The Maze Runner,* a current movie of the time.

In addition, we found that most children's readiness scores remained stable over the summer. However, when we cross-referenced those children who visited the machine in their child care program with families that also used the machines weekly, we found an interesting pattern. In this case, instead of stalling, or showing declines, children's readiness scores grew over the summer, in fact, for some, almost approaching a ceiling effect (e.g., average 18.3 out of 24 items; see Figures 30.2 and 30.3).

Our analysis has provided a useful lens for our further work on everyday space. First, it suggests that the collective socialization of having books in close proximity to where one lives in a neighborhood surrounded by parents, grandparents, friends and young children, may exert an influence on children's interest and engagement in reading. It also further validated the impor-

tance of environment, and how changes in one's proximal settings may support certain behaviors such as reading.

Creating Play and Learning Environments

Since then, we have learned that many public spaces can be contexts for children's early literacy development, even the public playground. In collaboration with Shane's Inspiration in Los Angeles, known for their work on creating inclusive playgrounds for children with (dis)abilities, Too Small to Fail and Landscape Structures developed signage throughout three of these playgrounds to spark language and literacy development. Posted in English and Spanish, the signs were placed along the periphery of the playground, as well as within structures to encourage interactive and creative play among the children and their caregivers. Some of the signs, as shown below, included didactic messages, such as "Talking is teaching" and "Let's talk about play." Other signs focused on the specific theme of the park and included informational messages, such as what caused

Percent of VM Books Children Recognized

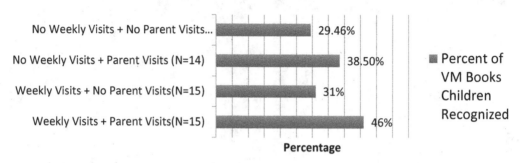

FIGURE 30.2. Percent of vending machine books children recognized.

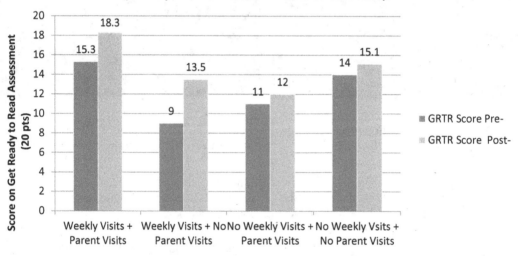

FIGURE 30.3. School readiness scores by adult support.

weather changes. Still others were designed to encourage play themes like "I spy with my little eye." Altogether, about 20 new signs could be seen throughout the playground environment. In addition, three inclusive playgrounds in contiguous low-income neighborhoods were designated the "control playgrounds." These playgrounds included the same inclusive structures, swings, and sandboxes but without the addition of signage. Following the project, they too would be outfitted for signage at some later point.

Our role was to examine the ways the signage might represent an added feature for learning in these and other playgrounds (see Figures 30.4a and 30.4b). Using multiple methods over a 6-month period, we conducted 46 observations that included 769 parent–child dyads, 100 interviews, and 235 surveys, making sure that these were equally distributed across treatment and control sites (Neuman & Karbachinskiy, 2022). Our results showed that in playgrounds with signage, there was a 30% difference in the frequency of talk between caregivers and children. Similarly, the signage seemed to spark a 20% increase in child-to-child interactions.

However, equally important were parents' responses to the signage. The signage seemed to facilitate a shift in parents' views of the play-

FIGURE 30.4a. Thematic signage in playgrounds in Spanish and English. Used by permission.

FIGURE 30.4b. Thematic signage in playgrounds in Spanish and English. Photo by Susan B. Neuman. Used by permission.

grounds themselves. More than a physical play space devoted to physical development, the signs contributed to the perception of the playground as a "play *and* learning environment."

One caregiver indicated that she appreciated that the playground "now integrates both reading and thinking while children play in the structure." A father suggested that the signs "inadvertently teach children basic reading and comprehension skills," which is why he enjoys taking his son to that particular playground. Another parent stated that "it's a useful way for children to learn as they play." Still another parent enjoyed the thematic signs (along the train structure), since she believed it helped her child practice his numbers and shapes, and the pictures made it fun to look at: "They don't even realize they're learning. To them it's just play."

The signage appeared to remind parents of the importance of talking and reading, and how brain development in these early years is crucial for their children's learning. Parents frequently described how they supported children's developing knowledge, and social–emotional development through talk. Furthermore, having the signs in English and Spanish further supported the inclusiveness of these playgrounds.

It is yet another example that everyday spaces, like the public playground in a neighborhood, can become part of the literacy learning ecology in the early years for caregivers and children. Attractive signage in these public settings appeared to promote conversations between parents and children, and between groups of children. They served as effective tools to promote talking, singing, and reading, and served as an important source of information for parents. Caregivers viewed these additions to the playground as a positive development for the neighborhood, making the already existing attractions of these inclusive playgrounds even more enticing for children and their families.

Literacy in the Laundromat

Among all of these everyday spaces, however, laundromats might be the most unconventional "hybrid space" for early literacy learning. Laundromats often conjure up a picture of a rather sterile environment with limited seating, rows and rows of machines, blaring TV, and a few gumball machines. Nevertheless, they are a fixture of the urban experience, especially in predominantly renter-occupied, densely populated areas such as New York City (67% households occupied by renters) or Chicago (37% renters) (United States Census Bureau, 2017). Mostly mom and pop operations, these communal spaces bring people in neighborhoods together for an estimate of 2–3 hours weekly (*https://laundrycares.org*), often with their young children in tow.

The laundry industry, along with its trade organization, knew their reputation as a family-friendly setting was at risk in neighborhoods across the country. Convinced that "doing good was good for business," they established a Foundation and a subsequent collaboration with Too Small to Fail, the Clinton Foundation. Taking on an asset-based approach to neighborhoods, this team went into action. First on a pilot basis in New York City (Neuman, Portillo, & Celano, 2020), then in a much larger trial in Chicago (Neuman & Knapczyk, 2022), they created small, attractive nooks in 10 laundromats that included an open-faced bookshelf filled with children's paperback books, a small couch for parent–child reading, child-size table and chairs, a whiteboard, magnetic letters, puppets, paper and markers, a pint-size washer–dryer, and a puppet stage in three laundromats. These materials were designed to support talking, singing, reading, writing, and play, essential activities for early literacy development in the targeted laundromats in the study. The open-faced bookshelves included an evolving set of children's books for parent–child reading and pretend reading, activities to promote parent–child talk, puppets to encourage abstract language, and magnetic letters and drawing tools to encourage written expression. In addition, attractive signs with ideas for family engagement dotted the landscape, offering parents helpful ideas for home-based activities (see Figures 30.5a and 30.5b).

With our research team, we examined these laundromats for evidence of literacy-related activity, comparing them with others nearby, which served as control sites or "business as usual." In 6 weeks' time, we recorded 30 times more literacy-related activities among the young children than in these control sites. The literacy-related play centers appeared to create a "social infrastructure" where families could gather, network, and engage with others around early reading activities. Children met new friends, engaged in literacy play together, and wrote notes and drew pictures that enlivened the laundromats, making it a more personal space. For example:

> Young girl (7 years) walks over to literacy corner where two boys (African American, age 6 years) are sitting. Girl asks, "What's your name, do you go to school? I go to school over there. Do you want to play?" One of the boys responds and says, "My name is Osbourne." They end up reading the papers posted on the wall and use the plastic alphabetic letters.

And another example:

FIGURE 30.5a. Librarian reading to a child in the laundromat. Photo by Susan B. Neuman. Used by permission.

FIGURE 30.5b. Creating an early literacy environment in the laundromat. Photo by Susan B. Neuman. Used by permission.

A girl and a boy come to literacy corner (7 and 5 years old, respectively). The two children play together with letter board and puppets. The older child begins to ask the younger child about letters, slowly teaching him. Then she tells him to find a book. The boy begins to run around. When he settles, the girl picks up a book and begins to read to him.

In both cases, these literacy-related activities were generated by the children themselves. The environment helped to spark their play in ways that naturally involved reading and talking. These types of activities were common in these centers, giving children time to play with older children who might use more complex and diversified language models.

Importantly, the responses from the community were strikingly similar to the reaction to our work in playgrounds. These changes and additions were universally appreciated. Over 60% of the families we interviewed, for example, had limited resources in their home to support children's early reading; some had fewer than 10 books in their home. Consequently, we were not surprised that the responses to these literacy-related centers were positive. These families believed that their local institution was taking them seriously, and that the owners cared deeply about members in their community. Families reported greater loyalty to the laundromat as a result. Examples from the brief interviews are below:

"There are no other places in the community where children have access to books so the literacy corner has been really good for my kid." —Mother, Lavanderia (Bronx, Treatment)

"This is my fourth time coming to this laundromat. We started coming here because of the literacy corner. I like the laundromat a lot because instead of giving my kid the phone, we can read together. Compared to other laundromats in the area, this one is big and gives access of books to children."—Father and Mother, Lavanderia (Queens, Treatment)

"I started bringing my youngest daughter to this laundromat because of the literacy corner. She loves playing with the puppets. Aside from the library, this is the only place in the community that offers access to books."—Mother, Lavanderia (Queens, Treatment)

In contrast, families at the control laundromats wished they had such literacy-related resources. For example, one parent found that it was "difficult to amuse my child" when she spent time at the laundromat. Another parent suggested that it was "hard to educate her young child, with so few resources in the community." Together, these comments indicated the need for books and other resources for families who come from low-income communities.

Our analysis revealed that infusing these everyday spaces in laundromats with literacy-rich materials and activities provided children and their families with valuable learning opportunities. In a space once dominated by heavy machinery and dull noises, we heard laughter and singing as children met new friends and enlivened their spaces with reading, writing, and artwork. Parents observed models of active literacy activities, watching their children engage with others in a community of literacy practice, seeing the joys that such practices might bring to their young ones.

Conclusion

Taken together, these case studies highlight how everyday spaces may contribute to early literacy in early childhood. It shows some of the ways in which learning may occur across the boundaries of time and space, with people, places, and contexts that matter most to young children.

The effort to create such hybrid spaces comes at an important moment. In recent years, for example, studies have documented a striking rise in income inequality, and opportunity gaps for children (Bischoff & Reardon, 2014). As others have shown before us, there are striking enrichment gaps in children's access to print, classes and clubs, and spaces for learning that enable rich modes of participation and interaction. These gaps appear to be disproportionately experienced by children in lower-income families. Coley, Kruzik, and Votruba-Drzal (2020), for example, found that higher-income families were able to spend over 60% more time on enriching materials and opportunities for their children, such as educational programs, literacy materials, and extracurricular activities than their lower-income peers. With the growing income inequality, this gap in resources and time has only increased between high- and low-income families (Kornrich & Furstenberg, 2013).

Realistically then, schools alone are ill-equipped to address the myriad challenges that are associated with poverty. Rather, it suggests that we need to create hybrid spaces that build connections across homes, schools, and communities to strengthen children's learning opportunities. In these spaces, literacy learning may be distributed across settings—whether its laundromats, hair salons, or grocery stores for extended time periods, with young learners and their partners in the community playing important roles in assembling resources, establishing connections, and being involved in learning that is contextualized within settings. This broader conceptualization recognizes that literacy learning occurs in an ecological and sociocultural context, and encourages us to consider the interdependencies between children and their environment (Bronfenbrenner, 1979). It also builds on an asset-based cultural perspective that recognizes the enormous talents and funds of knowledge that nondominant communities may bring to these social and ecological settings.

New collaborations like these are beginning to build synergies across school and community. For example, strategies to catalyze cross-setting learning are occurring across women, infant, and children (WIC) centers, doctor's offices, and grocery stores, to name just a few. Organizations such as the Education Redesign Lab (e.g., edredesignlab.org) for example, have launched a network of communities to create collaborative, cross-setting solutions to establish systems of support and opportunity for children, birth through schooling. These innovations support network improvement communities (Bryk, Gomez, Grunow, & LeMahieu, 2015), a system of continuous support, with groups of stakeholders solving problems together that has begun to take hold and has the potential to scale in under-resourced communities. It can help bridge and leverage the expertise from community partners to create social and ecological niches that can become important sites of opportunity that connect children's everyday experiences to literacy learning.

References

Alexander, K., & Entwisle, D. (1988). Achievement in the first 2 years of school: Patterns and processes. *Monographs of the Society for Research in Child Development, 53*(2, Serial No. 218), 1–157.

Bischoff, K., & Reardon, S. (2014). Residential segregation by income, 1970–2009. In J. Logan (Ed.), *Diversity and disparities: America enters a new century* (pp. 208–233). Russell Sage Foundation.

Bloom, P. (2000). *How children learn the meanings of words*. MIT Press.

Bronfenbrenner, U. (1979). *The ecology of human development*. Harvard University Press.

Bryk, A., Gomez, L., & Grunow, A. (2010). *Getting ideas into action: Building networked improvement communities in education*. Carnegie Foundation for the Advancement of Teaching.

Bryk, A., Gomez, L., Grunow, A., & LeMahieu, P. (2015). *Learning to improve: How America's schools can get better at getting better*. Harvard Education Press.

Burke, K., Greene, S., & McKenna, M. (2016). A critical geographic approach to youth civic engagement: Reframing educational opportunity zones and the use of public spaces. *Urban Education, 5*, 143–169.

Coley, R., Kruzik, C., & Votruba-Drzal, E. (2020). Do family investments explain growing socioeconomic disparities in children's reading, math, and science achievement during school versus summer months? *Journal of Educational Psychology, 112*, 1183–1196.

Duncan, G., & Murnane, R. (2014). *Restoring opportunity: The crisis of inequality and the challenge for American education*. Harvard Education Press.

Fiorini, M., & Keane, M. (2014). How the allocation of children's time affects cognitive and noncognitive development. *Journal of Labor Economics, 32*, 787–836.

Friedman-Krauss, A., Barnett, W. S., Garver, K., Hodges, K., Weisenfeld, G., & Gardiner, B. (2021). *The state of preschool 2020: State preschool yearbook*. National Institute for Early Education Research, Rutgers University.

Golinkoff, R., & Hirsh-Pasek, K. (1999). *How babies talk: The magic and mystery of language in the first three years of life*. Dutton.

Gump, P. (1989). Ecological psychology and issues of play. In M. Bloch & A. D. Pellegrini (Eds.), *The ecological context of children's play* (pp. 35–56). Ablex.

Hanner, E., Braham, E., Elliott, L., & Libertus, M. (2019). Promoting math talk in adult–child interactions through grocery store signs. *Mind, Brain and Education, 13*, 110–118.

Hassinger-Das, B., Palti, J., Golinkoff, R., & Hirsh-Pasek, K. (2020). Urban thinkscape: Infusing public spaces with STEM conversation and interaction opportunities. *Journal of Cognition and Development, 21*, 125–147.

Kornrich, S., & Furstenberg, F. (2013). Investing in children: Changes in parental spending on children, 1972–2007. *Demography, 50*, 1–23.

Kruger, A., & Tomasello, M. (2000). Cultural learning and learning culture. In D. Olson & N. Torrance (Eds.), *Handbook of education and human development: New models of learning, teaching, and schooling* (pp. 355–371). Blackwell.

Lee, V., & Burkam, D. (2002). *Inequality at the starting gate*. Economic Policy Institute.

McLane, J. B., & McNamee, G. (1990). *Early literacy*. Harvard University Press.

Meltzoff, A., Kuhl, P., Movellan, J., & Sejnowski, T. (2009). Foundations for a new science of learning. *Science, 325*(5938), 284–288.

Moje, E., Ciechanowski, K., Kramer, K., Ellis, L., Carrillo, R., & Collazo, T. (2004). Working toward third space in content area literacy: An examination of everyday funds of knowledge and discourse. *Reading Research Quarterly, 39,* 38–70.

Montag, J., Jones, M., & Smith, L. (2015). The words children hear: Picture books and the statistics for language learning. *Psychological Science, 26,* 1489–1496.

Neuman, S. B., & Karbachinskiy, S. (2022). *The effects of signage in inclusive playgrounds.* New York University.

Neuman, S. B., & Knapczyk, J. (2020). Reaching families where they are: Examining an Innovative Book Distribution Program. *Urban Education, 55,* 542–569.

Neuman, S. B., & Knapczyk, J. (2022, April). Early literacy in everyday settings: Creating an opportunity to learn for low-income young children. *Reading Research Quarterly.* [Epub ahead of print] *doi: 10.1002/rrq.468*

Neuman, S. B., & Moland, N. (2020). Book deserts: The consequences of income segregation on children's access to books. *Urban Education, 54,* 126–147.

Neuman, S. B., Portillo, M., & Celano, D. (2020). Looking for literacy in all the right spaces: The laundromat. *Reading Teacher, 74,* 29–38.

Owens, A., Reardon, S., & Jencks, C. (2016). Income segregation between schools and school districts. *American Educational Research Journal, 53*(4), 1159–1197.

Pew Research Center. (2015). Parenting in America: Outlook, worries, aspirations are strongly linked to financial situation. Retrieved from *www.pewresearch.org/social-trends/2015/12/17/parenting-in-america.*

Phillips, M. (2011). Parenting, time use, and disparities in academic outcomes. In G. Duncan & R. Murnane (Eds.), *Whither opportunity?* (pp. 207–228). Russell Sage Foundation.

Ridge, K., Weisberg, D., Ilgaz, H., Hirsh-Pasek, K., & Golinkoff, R. (2015). Supermarket speak: Increasing talk among low-socioeconomic status families. *Mind, Brain, and Education, 9*(3), 127–135.

Rogoff, B. (1990). *Apprenticeship in thinking: Cognitive development in social context.* Oxford University Press.

Rowe, M. (2018). Understanding socioeconomic differences in parents' speech to children. *Child Development Perspectives, 12*(2), 122–127.

Snow, C., Baines, W., Chandler, J., Goodman, I., & Hemphill, L. (1991). *Unfulfilled expectations: Home and school influences on literacy.* Harvard University Press.

Snow, C., & Beals, D. (2006). Mealtime talk that supports literacy development. *New Directions for Child and Adolescent Development, 111,* 51–66.

Tharp, R., & Gallimore, R. (1988). *Rousing minds to life.* Cambridge University Press.

United States Census Bureau. (2017). New York City Housing and Vacancy Survey. Available at *www.census.gov/programs-surveys/nychvs.html.* Author.

CHAPTER 31

Digital Picture Books

Opportunities and Utilities

Adriana G. Bus and Trude Hoel

Book reading with children is one of the activities that has demonstrated significant correlational and causal influences on children's concurrent and long-term language outcomes. Books have proven to be a much richer resource for language within the family than any other activity that involves verbal interaction (for a review, see Dickinson & Morse, 2019) However, it is vital that book reading occurs regularly from an early age (e.g., DeBaryshe, 1993; De Bondt & Bus, 2022). When children read many books during preschool, it significantly increases context-rich language exposure and stimulates language skills. It makes a massive difference for language input whether children hear five books read aloud daily or one or two books a few times a week. Logan, Justice, Yumus, and Chaparro-Moreno (2019) calculated that the difference could be as high as a million words over 4 years.

Traditionally, print books have been the primary source for joint book reading experiences. However, we now have other opportunities to mediate narratives, increasingly in downloadables on mobile phones and tablets with new digital technologies. Digital books seem very promising because they are comparatively cheap for users and are more easily accessible than books in a print format when families are not regular visitors of book stores or libraries. We discuss in this chapter why digital picture books could be a promising way to narrow the gap between families that differ in young children's book reading experiences.

Even when parents acknowledge the importance of book reading, parent–child book sharing may not be a daily activity due to time pressures or other parental challenges: Think of reading difficulties, discomfort with reading children's books, unfamiliarity with the language, or lack of awareness of its benefits in early childhood (Justice, Logan, & Damschroder, 2015). Digital books enable children to read unassisted, making book reading less dependent on parents' ability or willingness to engage in joint reading with young children. In addition to illustrations and written text, digital books can include an oral narration, and digital enhancements may mediate a literary text in a way reminiscent of an adult pointing and commenting. Moreover, digital books can be made available with a choice of languages, thus making picture books available to families speaking less widely used local languages or immigrants' languages.

To make the arguments, we first review what we know about enhancements in digital books and which ones benefit children's story comprehension and the narrative language (book language) that is often hard to understand due to a complex vocabulary and grammar (Montag, 2019). After an in-depth analysis of the enhancements in digital books, we present evidence-based insights into which digital enhancements are beneficial for meaning making and incidental word learning. We then discuss the research regarding digital books' potential impact on book reading routines in families, with a particular focus on multilingual families. We end with a set of recommendations for enhancing and investigating the utility of digital books in the early years.

Enhancements in Digital Books

Digital Picture Books Differ from Animations

Our focus is on digital picture books with a literary narrative conveyed through the interplay between text and illustrations (Sipe, 2008). To clarify this focus, we first discuss the difference between an excellent award-winning picture book and an animation of the same story. The book meets all the criteria of quality literature (vander Pol, 2010). It has a coherent narrative concerning a character with personality, in more advanced language than everyday language. Furthermore, it elicits tension in the reader to hear about the problem and subsequent attempts to solve it On YouTube, we find many examples of well-known picture books turned into animations. From the perspective of language input, looking at such animations is a learning experience that is very different from reading a picture book. The story is the same, yet the premises of the picture book differ from the premises of the animation. Turning a picture book into animation, still images become moving images, and spreads and motifs become (shorter and longer) scenes. Some motifs may become more central or more marginal, and the filmmaker may add new motifs. Furthermore, the soundtrack becomes different, with natural sound and music. The verbal text changes as well, often into more direct speech and dialogue (Mjør, 2013). In this adaptation of the book's verbal text, the amount of verbal language is reduced, and complex sentences and sophisticated vocabulary (book language) are simplified, in line with the premises of the film medium.

The verbal text can overlap, and, as Neuman, Preeti, and Wong (2021) found, both hearing words through a print book or film promotes children's word learning. In general, however, the language input via picture books is much richer than via watching animations on YouTube or programs on popular platforms such as Disney. Book reading is therefore a much stronger incentive for language acquisition than watching animations. For example, take the first four pages of *Frog in Winter* by Max Velthuijs, presented for the picture book and the story's animation found on YouTube in Figure 31.1. First, the book's text is much lengthier than the animation, as also applies to the rest of the story. The first four pages include 74 words, while the spoken words in the animation are limited to 19 words.

Second, the language in the picture book involves greater statistical diversity of words and linguistic contexts than the language in the animation. For example, the book's written text includes words less often used in daily communication (e.g., *immediately, slippery, slid, bank* [meaning: border]), and among those words for mental states (e.g., *notice, surprise, astonished*). Likewise, picture books contain more rare and complex sentence types—passive sentences and sentences containing relative clauses—than the animation, as the examples in Figure 31.1 illustrate (Montag, 2019). Only the picture book includes sentences such as "*Astonished, he ran outside,*" or "*before he knew it, he slid off the bank into the water.*" In other words, the animation offers much less opportunity for familiarizing with new words and grammar, thereby preparing children for understanding literary and academic reading in later years. Many studies suggest that greater statistical diversity of words and linguistic contexts is associated with better language outcomes (e.g., Mol & Bus, 2011).

Another difference between a picture book and animation is related to the time dimension. The animation is a continuous and defined time structure that lasts the same amount of time for everyone who watches—and every time someone watches. Both image and sound are constants. The picture book's dramaturgy uses stills and spreads, which motivates use of dense expressions. The illustrations and spreads in the picture book are constant factors, yet the readers control how much time they spend on each spread during reading. Both ways, reading a picture book and watching an animation, invite the children to actively use their own experiences to create meaning. Yet the book reader can construct the text and the time axis to a greater extent.

Digital Enhancements Making Picture Books Interactive

The first generations of digital picture books primarily included possibilities for interaction. It could be games mostly related to the narrative

Picture book	Animation
"One morning when Frog woke up, he immediately noticed that something had changed in the world." [The picture shows Frog sitting on the bedside.] *"He jumped out of bed and went to the window."* [The following picture shows Frog looking out of the window.] *"To his surprise, he saw that everything was white."* [Next picture shows Frog running to the water.] *"Astonished, he ran outside. There was snow everywhere."* [The following illustration shows him lying on the ice.] *"It was very slippery, and before he knew it, he slid off the bank into the water. But the water was frozen, and there lay Frog on the hard cold ice."*	In the animation, we first see Frog asleep and waking up. He says, *"Something is wrong with the world this morning."* Next, we see him jump out of bed, and he repeats, *"Something has changed."* Next, he walks to the window, opens the curtains to look outside, and says, *"Everything is white. Everything is completely white."* Then we see him open the door of his house and glide into the water. He tumbles down, and, laying on his back on the ice, we hear Frog say: *"Ice."*

FIGURE 31.1. Differences between the picture book *Frog in Winter* and the animation of this story to be found on YouTube (*www.youtube.com/watch?v=-gVnBxZBuJE*).

but only marginally (e.g., when the story refers to a balloon, children can choose to do a game with balloons). Other familiar additions to the primarily skeuomorphic designs are story-congruent animations or sounds when a user touches a specific spot on the screen (Christ, Wang, Chiu, & Strekaleva-Hughes, 2019; Korat & Falk, 2017; Unsworth, 2014). For example, the Israeli digital book *The Beat Monsters* (Rubinger, 2010) is about a green monster who plays the contrabass. When the child clicks on the green monster, it starts to play the instrument. These interactive enhancements, first analyzed in 2003, are still present 10 years after, but unlike the first generation of digital books, they are better embedded in the storyline (Korat & Falk, 2017).

However, we doubt their contribution to meaning making. And what is worse, even though the child may receive information about the meaning of a not-so-familiar word, *contrabass*, such additions may distract children's attention from the storyline, thereby interfering with meaning making, as is confirmed in a recent meta-analysis (Furenes, Kucirkova, & Bus, 2021). A dictionary explaining words in between readings of the story appears to interfere with comprehension. Fisch's (2000) distance model helps distinguish more helpful from distracting enhancements. As working memory capacity is limited, comprehension of digital books depends on not only the cognitive demands of the narrative and the features embedded in the narrative but also the degree to which the enhancements are integral or tangential to the narrative. When the embedded enhancements are woven tightly into the narrative, processing becomes complementary, and comprehension is likely to be strengthened.

Toward an Embodied Interactivity

Interactivity is an expression of the digital medium's intention to promote children's involvement (Richter & Courage, 2017). Humans benefit from conditions that allow them to be active processors who seek to make sense of further details. Meaningful learning happens when the learner is actively engaged and in control of the pace at which new information is presented (Mayer, 2014). In the new generation of digital books, we see attempts to delineate beneficial interactivity more integrated with the storyline. To that end, some proposed to afford gestures and embodied actions that may simulate empathy with story characters and their activities (cf. Bus, Roskos, & Burnstein, 2021; Sargeant, 2015; Zhao & Unsworth, 2017). For instance, Sargeant's (2014) app *How Far Is Up?* allows users to move a toy rocket around a scene by tilting the hardware device or dragging a finger across the screen. This playful activity aims to help users experience the bodily feeling of moving an object in a fictional space. In the digital picture book app *Looking for Lightning* (Coenraads & de Wijs, 2017), the story character searches for the correct button on a dashboard (Figure 31.2). At this point, the story stops, and the button selected by the story character lights up. The reader needs to press (touch) this same button, just as the story character did to forward the story. Thus, interaction is part of the natural flow of the enhanced story version. Such digital designs may promote perspective taking, affording the experience of perceiving the world from another person's perspective (Kucirkova, 2019). Embodiment theory predicts that virtually experiencing, *as if* another person, might be superior to just imagining experience (Mangen & Pirhonen, 2022; Robbins & Aydede, 2009). The reader carrying out similar actions as the main characters may feel *as if* or "complicit" in the experience of the story character and events. We hypothesize that embodied actions realized with the help of digital affordances can increase the empathy-building potential of narratives. Some evidence for this assumption comes from research showing that students remember a text better if they can physically manipulate toy objects referred to in the text (Glenburg, Gutierrez, Levin, Japuntich, & Kaschak, 2004).

Other Promising Digital Storytelling Techniques

Apart from interactive elements, digital books may include automatic visual and auditory enhancements to promote better comprehension. It can be a virtual camera moving through the illustration or details of illustrations in motion, thereby guiding the reader's visual attention in sync with the narrative. Such visual enhancements must be added carefully to ensure the interaction between illustrations and written text in the picture book. Even more common

enhancements in digital books are auditory effects that may include soft or loud music and environmental sounds, such as in *A Frog Thing* by Eric Drachman (2006). At several places, auditory enhancements emphasize events. For instance, Frog Frank is loudly laughed at when he tries to fly, and when one of his attempts to fly fails, we hear a loud splash. In well-designed digital books, the enhancements may promote children's literary engagement and help them make sense of the narrative.

Visual Enhancements

Visual enhancements, including zooming in on details and setting details in motion, are designed not just to synchronize text with pictures but are added more or less intuitively to facilitate the reader's processing of a literary text. In picture books, words and pictures work together on an equal footing to produce a total effect (Sipe, 2008). The digital enhancements may aim to improve this coordination: They help synchronize illustrations with referential expressions in the text, aid in understanding essential story elements such as who the storyteller is, or make the reader aware of contradictions between the written text and pictures as a manifestation of irony. Visual enhancements can also focus the reader's attention on the story characters' typical way of responding or reinforce the tension elicited by the story problem and successive attempts to solve it (Van der Pol, 2012). To illustrate such enhancements in digital books, we describe examples

FIGURE 31.2. After the reader presses the button selected by the story character in the second screenshot, the story advances, thus making the reader "complicit" in the experience of the story character. From the interactive picture book *Looking for Lightning*. Copyright © 2017 Het Woeste Woud, Groningen, Netherlands. Written by Christiaan Coenraads, Illustrated by Leo de Wijs. Used by permission.

without pretending to be all-inclusive. We took the illustrations from the digital version of *Little Kangaroo* (*Het Woeste Woud*) (Van Genechten, 2005):

1. The first spread shows Mama Kangaroo jumping cumbersomely with a large and heavy stomach while the narrator explains, "Mommy Kangaroo has a problem. . . . " This combination of picture and narrative may make children curious about her problem. As a result, they may more attentively and actively search for the cause of Mama Kangaroo's sufferings. By contrast, in the print book version by Guido van Genechten, the illustration betrays that Mama Kangaroo suffers from the heavy weight of baby Kangaroo, visible in the book's first spread (Genechten, 2005).

2. The next spread explains how comfortable Mama Kangaroo's pouch is to Little Kangaroo. The still image in the picture book shows how Little Kangaroo gets a wash, one of the comforts (Figure 31.3, top row). The digital version also visualizes other comforts, such as getting milk and no need to walk, in addition to the explanations in the narrative (Figure 31.3, bottom row).

3. Some enhancements attract the reader's attention to Little Kangaroo's character by emphasizing the ambivalence in her behavior, for instance, in the spread where Mama Kangaroo focuses her attention on the birds' singing. Little Kangaroo fervently denies liking the singing of the birds. The picture depicts her demonstratively putting her fingers in her ears. However, simultaneously, the narrative indicates that she is tapping her foot to the beat of the music. In the digital version, Little Kangaroo's foot in motion attracts children's attention while the narrator in the narrative says that she dislikes the sound but taps her foot. This ambivalence in Little Kangaroo's behavior aligns with the deeper level of the story: Little Kangaroo's unwillingness to leave the comforts of her mom's pouch despite the numerous attractions in the outside world (Sipe, 2008).

4. One of the last spreads shows Mama Kangaroo and Little Kangaroo looking at a herd of giraffes running across a wide plain. Again, the narrative emphasizes that the scenery is intimidating, which the digital version highlights by zooming in on the fast-running giraffes and emphasizing how fast they move, thus making the tension—the plain's overwhelming effect with the running giraffes—more tangible.

5. The print version of the same spread shows Little Kangaroo cheering in Mama Kangaroo's pouch while she looks at the giraffes running fast across the plain. Yet the still image does not draw attention to her ambivalence and finally liking the pouch better than the outside world as the narrator's voice says, "In mama's pouch she knew every little corner." In the digital version, we see Little Kangaroo disappear in the pouch, thus emphasizing that she prefers the pouch.

In other words, all these subtle visual enhancements signify to readers which parts of the often richly illustrated spreads they should attend to for optimal story understanding, and they thus promote comprehension of the story character, the problem, and the attempts to solve it (e.g., Bus & Anstadt, 2021; Flack & Horst, 2017; Godwin, Eng, Murray, & Fisher, 2019; Verhallen & Bus, 2010). By reducing extraneous perceptual information and not forcing young children to continually switch between exploring the entertaining visuals in the picture book and processing the story narrative, children may be more successful in meaning making (cf. Sweller, 1988). Recent eye-tracking research supports the hypothesis that visual enhancements influence children's visual attention (Sun, Roberts, & Bus, 2022). It contrasted visually and auditorily enhanced books with static books or only auditorily enhanced books. The digital books with visual enhancements maintained greater visual attention from children than did the other two conditions across four repetitive readings. The visual enhancements help explain the contrasts in the story (Little Kangaroo balancing between excitement and security) or make readers reflect more on suggestions in the narrative. The literary engagement is strengthened by conveying critical information about the plot's trajectory in ways that cannot be easily achieved by the narrative combined with still images. However, the enhancements are not added so that the story does not appeal anymore to children's imagination and creativity in interpreting the events as literature should (Van der Pol, 2010). Not all story events are made transparent and explicit. The enhancements benefit story comprehension by drawing readers' attention to subtle aspects and more profound layers that they can easily miss as long as they have problems understanding the story language.

> But Little Kangaroo didn't want to hop. Her Mommy's pouch was nice and soft. And every day, Little Kangaroo got milk and a wash. And....the pouch was handy, she didn't have to jump everywhere herself.

> But Little Kangaroo didn't want to hop. Her Mommy's pouch was nice and soft. And every day, Little Kangaroo got milk

> And a wash. And....the pouch was handy . . .

> She didn't have to jump everywhere herself.

FIGURE 31.3. Screenshots from *Little Kangaroo*. From the top left, the first image is used by permission of Clavis Books. Copyright © 2005 Clavis Uitgeverij Hasselt–Alkmaar–New York. Images from *Little Kangaroo* by Guido Van Genechten. The second, third, and fourth images are used by permission of Het Woeste Woud from the animated picture book *Little Kangaroo*. Animation based on the picture book *Little Kangaroo* by Guido van Genechten, published by Clavis Publishing, EAN 9789044802856. All English text is used by permission of Het Woeste Woud.

Auditory Enhancements

Likewise, the app designer added music and environmental sounds to highlight the characters' emotions and feelings as outcomes or motives, as the following enhancements in *Little Kangaroo* illustrate:

1. In the first spread, the noise every hop makes emphasizes how exhausted Mama Kangaroo is. The sound accompanying the hops enhances the visual information.
2. After a few hops, we see her stop for a moment while we simultaneously hear her sigh.
3. Soft, pleasant music starts to play when Little Kangaroo emerges from the pouch, empha-

sizing that she makes her mom happy despite how large and heavy she is.

4. The next scene explains how comfortable Mama's pouch is to Little Kangaroo. In the digital version, we hear the sound of licking while we see Mama Kangaroo's tongue, thus clarifying what she is doing (Figure 31.3, bottom row, middle picture).
5. The enhancements in the same scene also highlight that Little Kangaroo gets milk; only her ears are visible, while we simultaneously hear the sound of someone drinking (Figure 31.3, bottom row, left picture).
6. When the herd of giraffes runs by, we hear a loud, intrusive noise, making the visual

impression of the large animals running by even more overwhelming.

Music in the digital book may help children apprehend the mood and feelings of the story characters, such as happiness or excitement (Bus, Takacs, & Kegel, 2015). For example, when Mama Kangaroo says, "Look how beautifully the butterflies flutter from flower to flower," the peaceful and soft background music arises at the same time to highlight the beauty of the scenery. In addition, each time Little Kangaroo disappears in her mama's pouch, soft, pleasant music is audible. The music highlights how lovely the pouch is to her, and it makes her preference understandable despite Mama Kangaroo's persistent efforts to make her explore the outside world. Moreover, sounds can help children better understand what Little Kangaroo finds unpleasant in some situations. For example, the sharp chirping birds may help explain why Little Kangaroo is annoyed by the birds and wants to stay in her mama's pouch.

Basic Learning Principles

Using technology in digital picture books, designers take into account learning principles highlighted by multimedia theory from which especially the following bear relevance for digital picture books (Mayer, 2014):

1. The coherence principle (people learn better when extraneous material is excluded rather than included).
2. The temporal contiguity principle (people learn better when words and pictures are temporally integrated).
3. The self-explanation principle (people learn better when they are encouraged to generate self-explanations).
4. The embodiment principle (gestures and embodied actions increase empathy).
5. The redundancy principle (people learn better when the information is not present in more than one format).

Impact of Digital Picture Books

If enhancements in digital books are well designed, we may expect that children's understanding of these enhanced books will outperform their understanding of books without the enhancements, especially when children do not share the books with an adult but read them alone. In addition, we expect that digitally enhanced books promote learning unknown words. If the enhancements facilitate story comprehension, children's incidental word learning may improve due to the enhanced verbal and visual context.

Impact of the Medium

As a first step, we look at the medium (print vs. digital) effect. In a meta-analysis, Furenes and colleagues (2021) established whether the medium influences children's story comprehension and vocabulary learning. They compared studies where the print and digital versions of the same story were practically the same. The two versions only differed in a voiceover or highlighted print as additional features in the digital book. A set of 10 studies meeting this criterion shows that comprehension of the print book outperformed that of the digital book ($g = -0.22$, 95% confidence interval [-0.36, -0.08]). The negative effect of the digital version on meaning making aligns with the coherence principle in multimedia learning (Mayer, 2014), positing that each information processing channel (audio or visual) has a limited capacity (Kahneman, 1973), and information overload quickly interferes with learning. The finding that print outperforms digital versions despite the similarity between the two versions suggests the device is attracting young children's attention at the expense of attention paid to the story. The resources available for processing the primary information in picture books—the central narrative—may have been misallocated due to the means of achieving it (e.g., point, click, and swipe), thus hampering meaning making. Another source of interference could be that children expect interactivity, because they are accustomed to game-like activities on devices and actively search for such possibilities, which distracts their attention from the story. Thus, the increased demand placed on cognitive resources when children read digital books might explain the performance disadvantage found in the meta-analysis (Furenes et al., 2021).

Impact of Visual and Auditory Enhancements

Professionally created automatic digital storytelling techniques are extensively tested and proved to stimulate children's comprehension and word learning. Research has been carried out in various languages (Dutch, English, Turkish, and Mandarin), all using similarly enhanced digital books, aligning multimedia learning principles (e.g., Bus & Anstadt, 2021; Sarı, Asûde Başal, Takacs, & Bus, 2019; Sun, Loh, & Roberts, 2019; Verhallen & Bus, 2010). However, the target books in most studies framed the visual enhancements in a smooth, film-like presentation that may be engaging by itself. According to the arousal theory, a film-like format may attract children's attention and help them stay attentive, thereby comprehending the story better, as several researchers claim (e.g., Richter & Courage, 2017). Consequently, not the digital enhancements but increased attention due to the smooth, film-like presentation often enriched with music might explain the enhanced books' effect on story comprehension. In a recent study, Bus and Anstadt (2021) sought support for the hypothesis that deliberately added visual enhancements, not framed in a film-like format, help convey the critical information about the character and the plot's trajectory more effectively than can be achieved with illustrational sequence and verbal text alone. One key finding was that this relatively small but purposive accessory technology—one or two virtual camera movements within an illustration highlighting the characters' responses or the plot's trajectory in sync with the narration—was beneficial. However, these effects were only present in the 50% of children (4- and 5-year-olds) who were least proficient in language and literacy skills. The impact in this group amounted to a partial eta squared of 0.163, equivalent to slightly less than one standard deviation (Cohen's $d = 0.88$). So, still images combined with virtual camera movements reveal substantially higher story comprehension scores than still images alone.

Multiple Information Sources: Risky for the Youngest Group

The main focus in Li's dissertation (2020) is the impact of visual and auditory enhancements in the youngest group of children compared to older children. She focused on three age groups: 3-, 4-, and 5-year-olds. Her findings show that combining visual enhancements (virtual camera movements and motion) with auditory enhancements (music and environmental sounds) in the youngest sample is less effective than one source, use of either visual or auditory enhancements. The 3-year-olds' comprehension benefited more

from one enhancement than from both, while 4- and 5-year-olds benefited as much from single as from combined enhancements. The finding that both enhancements are less helpful than one source of additional information aligns with the redundancy principle, one of the multimedia learning principles. Too much additional information may hinder children from interpreting the story details, making inferences, and figuring out word meanings (Calvert, Huston, Watkins, & Wright, 1982). It may quickly lead to cognitive overload, especially for young learners (Kalyuga & Sweller, 2014). Children need to coordinate multiple information sources, which adds cognitive load to their memory and may interfere with apprehending the information. Mayer's (2014) redundancy principle predicts that children, trying to attune the auditory and visual information, experience unnecessary extra load to working memory. Cognitive overload may explain that two different sources simultaneously are at the expense of story comprehension and word learning.

Digital Book-Reading Routines

A not so widely researched question is the impact digital books have on book reading routines in families and classrooms. We first discuss whether digital storytelling techniques outweigh adult guidance. Do digital book reading routines depend on adults just as with print books, or can children successfully read digital books independently?

Are Our Digital Features Comparable with Adult Guidance?

If digital books are well designed, we expect that enhancements in digital books can compensate for no or inadequate guidance by adults (High et al., 2014). In line with a meta-analysis by Takacs, Swart, and Bus (2014), we expected that the adults' mediation during reading of print books would be as effective as the enhancements in digital books read by children independently. Just as adults help children understand a story by pointing to details in illustrations or commenting (e.g., Krcmar & Cingel, 2014), well-designed enhancements guide children's visual attention and support their literary engagement. There were no significant differences between the learning outcomes of stories enhanced with animated illustrations, background music, or sound effects and sharing traditional print-like stories with an adult. The researchers concluded that multimedia features provide similar scaffolding of story comprehension and word learning. However, the more recent meta-analysis by Furenes and colleagues (2021) does not replicate this finding for another set of studies. Instead, it suggests that adult guidance outperforms the effects of enhanced digital books. Unlike the 2015 meta-analysis, this meta-analysis excluded all studies targeting film and television shows. It thus provides a more valid comparison between digital book enhancements and adult mediation. In a small subset of seven studies, the print condition outperformed the digital condition, meaning that the enhancements available in the target digital books in this set of studies did not outweigh the adult support only available while sharing a print book ($g = -0.22$, 95% confidence interval [-0.38, -0.06]). However, note that the digital books tested in the seven studies were far from optimally enhanced: Only three books had enhancements that targeted the story content (e.g., providing background knowledge or additional explanations). The rest included a dictionary, alone or in addition to content-related enhancements. In other words, the enhancements in the digital books in this small subsample of seven studies were often rather low-quality, not enabling a fair comparison of adult guidance with enhanced digital books. We need further research into this question because we suspect that young children often read digital books alone.

New Book-Reading Routines in Families?

So far, we know very little about the impact that packages of digital books, as nowadays advertised in many countries (main arguments: cheap and no effort needed to make the books available), have on reading routines and finally on language and literacy development. For example, does access to a platform or package giving access to digital books change the frequency of book reading, the number of books children read per week, and how often they reread books? It may also affect the process quality and result in more independent readings than shared readings. Hereafter, we report a pilot study in a small group mainly composed of immigrant families, exploring some of these questions (Bus & Anstadt, 2020). The authors compared the effects of 1 month of access to a platform with digital picture books with 1 month of print books on language learning. Each month, families had access to six similar books in Dutch, the environmental language used at centers and school, and were instructed to share them with their 2- to 3-year-old children. Using a two-period crossover design, we could observe the same families while accessing books in print or a digital format. When the families had access to the digital books, the program automatically registered logins, including the day, the time, and book titles accessed per session. Our observations suggest that digital books can substantially contribute to how much Dutch children hear.

It was most common for the children to visit the picture book platform two to three times a week, reading a relatively large number of books at a time. On average, this sample of 28 children read six books per session—usually not six different books but two or three books several times in a row. For example, a child may read *The Very Hungry Caterpillar* twice, then *A New House for Mouse*, and finally *Saar Becomes a Big Sister* three times. It is not possible to deduce the exact duration of the sessions from the analytics, because it is unclear whether children were sitting in front of the screen the whole period or took a break in between without interrupting the program. However, based on the number of books read in full, we estimate that sessions could last from half an hour to an hour.

Further research is needed to test the effect a digital book package has on the routines. In this case, children had the same six books for 4 weeks. They may even read more books if we expand the set with new books after a particular period or when children have read all available books or more. On average, the children read 37 digital books during 1 month. The number of books ranged from 21 to 89, indicating that young children enjoy hearing the same book repeatedly. Most children had favorites, which they frequently reread, while they read other books not at all or only a few times. By contrast, based on a questionnaire completed by parents after the period in which they read print books, we concluded that they read fewer print books in 1 month (range: 8–24). Children may reread digital books more often because repetition does not depend on the willingness of a parent to reread the same book again and again. The increasing amount of time spent on solitary use of smartphones and tablets (e.g., Barr & Linebarger,

2017) seems to add this new dimension to book reading. We had the impression that most children mainly read digital books independently. However, we do not exclude the possibility that children replayed the same stories independently after sharing a book a few times (Kucirkova & Littleton, 2016). We need replications comparing the reading habits with digital and print books to estimate the extra language input when children regularly visit a digital book platform. Reading an average of 37 digital books with an average length of 300 words in a month implies an estimated increase of 11,100 words. If the family reads one print book daily, as 19% of parents in this study reported, the input from reading is 8,400 words. So even when parents would read one book daily, as was more the exception than the rule, the language input in traditional reading lags far behind the average input through digital books. Note that we focused on bilingual children reading stories in the environmental language. Considering that many parents had low proficiency in Dutch, the voice-over in Dutch may have made digital books particularly appealing. Whether findings would be similar in Dutch families remains to be proved.

New Book-Reading Routines in Classrooms

Hoel and Tønnessen's (2019) findings show that teachers, sharing an enhanced digital book, struggle to define their role. In Norwegian kindergartens, book reading occurs in small groups of five to six 4- and 5-year-olds, led by one adult reader—a pattern that they continue with digital books. Hoel and Tønnessen's findings confirm that children are keen to take part in the hands-on exploration of digital books: tapping hot spots to initiate sounds, simple animations, and dialogue/sounds from the characters. Consequently, children are often distracted from the storyline. Even in sessions where teachers strictly control children's responses, taking turns tapping hot spots interrupted the reading, resulting in lacking coherence.

Multilingual Books

Digital books can include a narrative in various languages and make it possible to switch from one language to another. This possibility might open up new opportunities for bilingual learners—a worldwide, growing group. It may motivate parents to read books with their children if digital books enable reading in the heritage language. A voiceover in the environmental language might be another incentive for book reading. It allows bilingual learners to listen to stories in the environmental language even though their parents do not speak it fluently and find it hard to read to their children in this language. Unfortunately, digital picture books that include less widely used languages in addition to English and other main languages are relatively rare as a content analysis targeting Dutch, Catalan, Ifrit, Maltese, and Norwegian shows (Bus et al., 2020).

In two recent tryouts with 4- to 5-year-olds (Bus, Broekhof, Vaessen, & Coenraads, 2021) and 2- to 3-year-olds, families had access to 10 digital books. In both groups, half had only access to the environmental language (Dutch), and the other half had a choice between the environmental and the heritage language. All participants were from families where parents (one or both) have a heritage language other than Dutch. To our surprise, it appeared that if children had a choice between the environmental and heritage language, they hardly read books in the heritage language. Instead, the users almost uniformly preferred the environmental language. In both groups, only one of 12 or 13 children with a choice mainly read books in the heritage language. An explanation could be that children's proficiency in the heritage language lags behind the environmental language. Activities such as book reading may mainly or exclusively occur in the child center or at school, allowing children to familiarize themselves with a richer vocabulary and grammar in the environmental language than in the heritage language. Also, we cannot exclude that parents prefer the environmental language because school success depends on it, and they stimulate the selection of that language.

When children are more proficient in the heritage language, their learning of the environmental language might benefit from listening to stories in the heritage language preceding hearing the same stories in the environmental language (e.g., Eisenworth, Asian, Yesilyurt, Till, & Klier, 2018). So far, tests of this tantalizing hypothesis are mixed. In the Roberts study (2008), children were randomized to heritage or environmental language (here English) home picture book reading treatment. Home picture book reading in the heritage language was, in one experiment, more effective than home picture book reading in English for English vocabulary learning.

However, they could not replicate this finding in a second experiment. A Norwegian study tested a researcher-developed intervention organized around loosely scripted, content-rich shared reading in school and at home (Grøver, Rydland, Gustfsson, & Snow, 2020). Some books parents shared with their children in the heritage language were used for classroom shared reading in Norwegian. The researchers detected a small and marginally significant indirect effect of reading books at home in a heritage language on a Norwegian vocabulary test.

Recently, we tested the hypothesis that reading the story in the heritage language (in this sample: Polish) before reading it in Norwegian, the environmental language, would help in learning Norwegian (Tunkiel & Bus, 2022). The findings did not align with the advantage of first reading the story in Polish. Instead, it was more beneficial if they heard the story only in Norwegian. Note, however, that the conditions in this study may not have been optimal for testing the hypothesis. All participants were quite advanced in the environmental language (Norwegian), and all parents explained story events in Polish. In a new project supported by the Norwegian Research Council, we explore the long-term effect of reading books in the heritage language at home. We might expect that it is a stimulus for book-reading routines in the family and, via an increase in book-reading experiences, on environmental language learning.

Future Directions

Further Research into Digital Book Enhancements

Picture book reading is a powerful tool to promote children's early language and literacy skills. Without having a chance to familiarize themselves with literary texts, children are at risk for school failure. We have argued that there is a difference between book reading and watching YouTube animations. Of course, children can benefit from delightful stories on YouTube, just as in books, but watching stories on YouTube is not the same as reading a quality picture book. Digital books are like book reading but include technology that may guide children's processing of a literary text and support meaning making provided enhancements are implemented in a knowledge-based way. Due to many experiments with digital books carried out over the last two decennia, it is becoming evident which

enhancements to digital books are beneficial for meaning making. Dominant in first-generation digital books were possibilities that allowed the children to interact with the illustration but often had little or no relevance to the story. The research helped us fine-tune more promising enhancements: small auditory and visual additions that support children's literary engagement and stimulate them to reflect on story events. Techniques such as zooming in, setting details of illustrations in motion, or adding music or background sounds, can make children connect nonverbal information sources with the narrative, reflect on story events, and enhance the tension that the problem and subsequent actions elicit. Adding interactive enhancements might promote empathic responses to the story characters in digital picture books, thus improving meaning making. Further meta-analytic and experimental research seems warranted to disentangle the effects of various kinds of interactivity built into digital books. To create and author high-quality interactive books for further experimentation, we need to unite app developers, computer specialists, literacy educators, and specialists in digital learning.

Digital Books for All Children

New media may create a critical safety net for young children who do not regularly benefit from a caregiver reading to them (cf. Neuman, 2009). We found support for the hypothesis that regular visits to a digital book platform could have significant consequences for language and literacy development, particularly in groups where a daily reading routine for young children is missing. We hypothesize that an open-access platform with multilingual picture books guarantees book reading in a much wider group of young children than promoting traditional print book reading. Not all parents welcome a shift from print to digital books and prefer to use print for children's learning, relaxation, entertainment, and parent–child bonding (Strouse, Newland, & Mourlam, 2019). We are particularly interested in how digital books are gauged when parents are less able or unwilling to read to their young children. Governmental support is sometimes provided to produce digital books in less widely used languages, thus protecting those languages (Bus et al., 2020). Still, the funding is limited and does not enable large-scale, high-quality production in less widely used languages.

Recently, we started in collaboration with German, Maltese, and Turkish colleagues an Erasmus+ project, Stimulating Adventures for Young Learners (SAYL). It aims to build a large-scale, high-quality book platform in various more or less widely used languages across Europe. We invite the international community to join and contribute multilingual books that will allow experimental research and advance what we know about the role of digital materials in early literacy education.

References

Barr, R., & Linebarger, D. N. (Eds.). (2017). *Media exposure during infancy and early childhood: The effect of content and context on learning and development.* Springer.

Bus, A. G., & Anstadt, R. (2020). *Thuis Voorlezen met Digitale Prentenboeken.* [*Reading digital picture books at home.*] Kohnstamm Instituut.

Bus, A. G., & Anstadt, R. (2021). Towards digital picture books for a new generation of emergent readers. *AERA Open,7*(1), 1–15.

Bus, A. G., Broekhof, K., Vaessen, K., & Coenraads, C. (2021). *Strengthening the educational home environment using multilingual digital picture books.* Sardes.

Bus, A. G., Hoel, T., Aliagas, C., Jernes, M., Korat, O., Mifsud, C. L., & Van Coillie, J. (2020). Availability and quality of storybook apps across five less widely used languages. In O. Erstad, R. Flewitt, B. Kümmerling-Meibauer, & I. S. Pires Pereira (Eds.), *The Routledge handbook of digital literacies in early childhood* (pp. 308–321). Routledge.

Bus, A. G., Roskos, K., & Burstein, K. (2021). Promising interactive functions in digital storybooks for young children. In: K. J. Rohlfing & C. Müller-Brauers (Eds.), *International perspectives on digital media and early literacy. The impact of digital devices on learning, language acquisition and social interaction* (pp. 7–26). Routledge.

Bus, A. G., Takacs, Z. K., & Kegel, C. A. T. (2015). Affordances and limitations of electronic storybooks for young children's emergent literacy. *Developmental Review, 35*, 79–97.

Calvert, S. L., Huston, A. C., Watkins, B. A., & Wright, J. C. (1982). The relation between selective attention to television forms and children's comprehension of content. *Child Development, 53*, 601–610.

Carle, E. (1997). *Rupsje nooitgenoeg* [The very hungry caterpillar]. Gottmer (Animated by Bereslim).

Christ, T., Wang, C., Chiu, M. M., & Strekaleva-

Hughes, E. (2019). How app books' affordances are related to young children's reading behaviors and outcomes. *AERA Open, 5*, 1 –18.

Coenraads, C., & de Wijs, L. (2017). *Bliksem!* [Looking for Lightning]. Het Woeste Woud.

DeBaryshe, B. D. (1993). Joint picture-book reading correlates of early oral language skill. *Journal of Child Language, 20*, 455–461.

DeBondt, M. G., & Bus, A. G. (2022). Tracking the long-term effects of the Bookstart intervention: Associations with temperance and book-reading habits. *Learning and Individual Differences, 98*, 102199.

Dickinson, D. K., & Morse, A. B. (2019). *Connecting through talk: Nurturing children's development with language.* Brookes.

Drachman, E. (2006). *A frog thing* [with CD]. Kidwick Books.

Eisenworth, B., Asian, H., Yesilyurt, S., Till, B., & Klier, C. (2018). Language development in children with migration background and parental reading to children. *Zeitschrift für Kinder- und Jugendpsychiatrie und Psychotherapie, 46*(2), 99–106.

Fisch, S. M. (2000). A capacity model of children's comprehension of educational content on television. *Media Psychology, 2*, 63–92.

Flack, Z. M., & Horst, J. S. (2017). Two sides to every story: Children learn words better from one storybook page at a time. *Infant and Child Development, 27*, Article e2047.

Furenes, M. I., Kucirkova, N., & Bus, A. G. (2021). A comparison of children's reading on paper versus screen: A meta-analysis. *Review of Educational Research, 20*, 1–35.

Glenberg, A. M., Gutierrez, T., Levin, J. R., Japuntich, S., & Kaschak, M. P. (2004). Activity and imagined activity can enhance young children's reading comprehension. *Journal of Educational Psychology, 96*, 424–436.

Godwin, K., Eng, C., Murray, G., & Fisher, A. (2019). Book design, attention, and reading performance: Current practices and opportunities for optimization. *Proceedings of the Annual Meeting of the Cognitive Science Society, 41*, 1851–1857.

Grøver, V., Rydland, V., Gustafsson, J. E., & Snow, C. E. (2020). Shared book reading in preschool supports bilingual children's second-language learning: A cluster-randomized trial. *Child Development, 91*, 2192–2210.

High, P. C., Klass, P., Donoghue, E., Glassy, D., DelConte, B., Earls, M., . . . Williams, P. G. (2014). Literacy promotion: An essential component of primary care pediatric practice. *Pediatrics, 134*, 404–409.

Hoel, T., & Tønnessen, E. S. (2019). Organizing shared digital reading in groups: Optimizing the affordances of text and medium. *AERA Open,* *5*(4), 1–14.

Horáček, P. (2006). *Kleine muis zoekt een huis* [A New House for Mouse]. Gottmer (Animated by Bereslim).

Justice, L. M., Logan, J. R., & Damschroder, L. (2015). Designing caregiver-implemented shared-reading interventions to overcome implementation barriers. *Journal of Speech, Language, and Hearing Research, 58,* 1851–1863.

Kahneman, D. (1973). *Attention and effort.* Prentice Hall.

Kalyuga, S., & Sweller, J. (2014). The redundancy principle in multimedia learning. In R. Mayer (Ed.), *The Cambridge handbook of situated cognition* (2nd ed., pp. 247–262). Cambridge University Press.

Korat, O., & Falk, Y. (2017). Ten years after: Revisiting the question of e-book quality as early language and literacy support. *Journal of Early Childhood Literacy, 19,* 206–223.

Krcmar, M., & Cingel, D. P. (2014). Parent–child joint reading in traditional and electronic formats. *Media Psychology, 17,* 262–281.

Kucirkova, N. (2019). How could children's storybooks promote empathy?: A conceptual framework based on developmental psychology and literary theory. *Frontiers in Psychology, 10,* Article 121.

Kucirkova, N., & Littleton, K. (2016). The digital reading habits of children: A national survey of parents' perceptions of and practices in relation to children's reading for pleasure with print and digital books. Retrieved from *www.booktrust. org.uk/globalassets/resources/research/digital_ reading_survey-final-report-8.2.16.pdf.*

Li, X. (2020). *The effect of enhanced e-books on young children's story comprehension and vocabulary learning.* Unpublished doctoral dissertation, University of Houston.

Logan, J. A. R., Justice, L. M., Yumus, M., & Chaparro-Moreno, L. J. (2019). When children are not read to at home: The million word gap. *Journal of Developmental and Behavioral Pediatrics, 40,* 383–386.

Mangen, A., & Pirhonen, A. (2022). Reading, writing, technology, and embodiment. In S. L. Macrine & J. M. B. Fugate (Eds.), *Movement matters. How embodied cognition informs teaching and learning* (pp. 103–117). The MIT Press.

Mayer, R. E. (2014). Cognitive theory of multimedia learning. In *The Cambridge handbook of multimedia learning* (2nd ed., pp. 43–71). Cambridge University Press.

Mjør, I. (2013). Frå Apan fin (1999) til Hej då, lilla apa! (2008). Bildebok og animasjonsfilm—resepsjon og medieestetikk [From Apan fin (1999) to Hej då, lilla apa! (2008). Picture book and

animated film—reception and media aesthetics]. *Nordic Journal of ChildLit Aesthetics, 4*(1), 1–10.

Mol, S. E., & Bus, A. G. (2011). To read or not to read: A meta-analysis of print exposure from infancy to early adulthood. *Psychological Bulletin, 137*(2), 267–296.

Montag, J. L. (2019). Differences in sentence complexity in the text of children's picture books and child-directed speech. *First Language, 39,* 527–546.

Neuman, S. B. (2009). The case for multimedia presentations in learning. In A. G. Bus & S. B. Neuman (Eds.), *Multimedia and literacy development: Improving achievement for young learners* (pp. 44–56). Routledge.

Neuman, S. B., Preeti, S., & Wong, K. M. (2021). Two may be better than one: Promoting incidental word learning through multiple media. *Journal of Applied Developmental Psychology, 73,* Article 101252.

Oud, P. (2012). *Saar wordt grote zus* [Saar becomes a big sister]. Clavis (Animated by Bereslim).

Richter, A., & Courage, M. L. (2017). Comparing electronic and paper storybooks for preschoolers: Attention, engagement and recall. *Journal of Applied Developmental Psychology, 48,* 92–102.

Robbins, P., & Aydede, M. (2009). A short primer on situated cognition. In P. Robbins & M. Aydede (Eds.), *The Cambridge handbook of situated cognition* (pp. 3–10). Cambridge University Press.

Roberts, T. A. (2008). Home storybook reading in primary or second language with preschool children: Evidence of equal effectiveness for second-language vocabulary acquisition. *Reading Research Quarterly, 43,* 103–130.

Rubinger, A. (2010). *The beat monsters* [Tizmort Miflazot Haketsv]. Evrit Liladeim.

Sargeant, B. (2014). How far is up? (Version 1.2). Retrieved October 20, 2014 from *https://itunes.apple.com/app/how-far-is-up/ id860628627?mt=8*

Sargeant, B. (2015). What is an ebook? What is a book app? And why should we care? An analysis of contemporary digital picture books. *Children's Literature in Education, 46,* 454–466.

Sarı, B., Asûde Başal, H., Takacs, Z. K., & Bus, A. G. (2019). A randomized controlled trial to test efficacy of digital enhancements of storybooks in support of narrative comprehension and word learning. *Journal of Experimental Child Psychology, 179,* 212–226.

Sipe, L. R. (2008). *Storytime: Young children's literary understanding in the classroom.* Teachers College Press.

Strouse, G. A., Newland, L. A., & Mourlam, D. J. (2019). Educational and fun? Parent versus preschooler perceptions and co-use of digital and print media. *AERA Open, 5*(3), 1–14.

Sun, H., Loh, J., & Roberts, A. C. (2019). Motion and sound in animated storybooks for preschoolers' visual attention and Mandarin language learning: An eye-tracking study with bilingual children. *AERA Open, 5*, 1–19.

Sun, H., Roberts, A. C., & Bus, A. G. (2022). Bilingual children's visual attention while reading digital picture books and story retelling. *Journal of Experimental Child Psychology, 215*, Article 105327.

Sweller, J. (1988). Cognitive load during problem solving: Effects on learning. *Cognitive Science, 12*(2), 257–285.

Takacs, Z. K., Swart, E. K., & Bus, A. G. (2014). Can the computer replace the adult for storybook reading?: A meta-analysis on the effects of multimedia stories as compared to sharing print stories with an adult. *Frontiers in Psychology, 5*, Article 1366.

Tunkiel, K. A., & Bus, A. G. (2022). Digital picture books for young dual language learners: Effects of reading in the second language. *Frontiers in Education, 7*, Article 901060.

Unsworth, L. (2014). Interfacing visual and verbal narrative art in paper and digital media: Recontextualising literature and literacies. In G. Barton (Ed.), *Literacy in the arts* (pp. 55–76). Springer International.

Van der Pol, C. (2010). *Prentenboeken lezen als literatuur. Een structuralistische benadering van het concept "literaire competentie" voor kleuters* [Reading picture books as literature. A structuralist approach to the concept of "literary competence" for preschoolers]. Stichting Lezen.

Van Genechten, G. (2005). *De kleine kangoeroe* [Little kangaroo]. Clavis (Animated by Het Woeste Woud).

Velthuijs, M. (2015). *Kikker in de kou* [Frog in winter]. Leopold.

Verhallen, M. J. A. J., & Bus, A. G. (2010). Low-income immigrant pupils learning vocabulary through digital picture storybooks. *Journal of Educational Psychology, 102*, 54–61.

Zhao, S., & Unsworth, L. (2017). Touch design and narrative interpretation: A socio-semiotic approach to picture book apps. In N. Kucirkova & G. Falloon (Eds.), *Apps, technology and younger learners, international evidence for teaching* (pp. 87–98). Routledge.

CHAPTER 32

e-Books with a Digital Dictionary as a Support for Word Learning

Ofra Korat and Ora Segal-Drori

A rich vocabulary is vital for word-level reading and reading comprehension, which have a long-term effect on academic achievements (Bleses, Makransky, Dale, Højen, & Ari, 2016; Côté, Rouleau, & Macoir, 2014). Studies showed large differences in the volume of young children's vocabulary before school age (Hart & Risley, 1995), which can endanger the reading comprehension and academic achievements of those who lag behind (Snow, Burns, & Griffin, 1998). Shared storybook reading with young children is regarded as a successful context for vocabulary development in the family context and the education system, especially for children from a low socioeconomic status (SES) (e.g., Whitehurst & Lonigan 2001; Shahaeian et al., 2018).

In our technological era, digital technology has become an integral part of people's lives, including young children (Marsh, Lahmar, & Plowman, 2021; Neumann, 2015). This has led to the availability of different software with oral and literacy products, including electronic books (e-books), to many homes and education systems. These e-books may offer different multimedia effects beyond the traditional printed form, including story content expansions and a computerized dictionary, which can support children's story comprehension and vocabulary enrichment (Furenes, Kucirkova, & Bus, 2021; Rohlfing & Muller-Brausers, 2021; Bus & Hoel, Chapter 31, this volume). In this chapter we present studies performed

to date that have examined the ability and efficacy of e-books with a dictionary in different multimedia designs and executed in different contexts, to enhance young children's vocabulary.

Studies performed over the last decades related to vocabulary knowledge as a key factor in reading and reading comprehension (Stanovich, 1986). The idea is that a good vocabulary level establishes a good source for supporting word decoding for beginning readers, which in turn sustains reading comprehension (Carlisle & Rice, 2002). Today, it is better understood that formal reading instruction is not sufficient for enabling children with a limited vocabulary to develop a good reading level. The process of learning the meaning of words is independent of a code-based skill, which is usually learned in school. Vocabulary learning can be well supported independently before school age (Loftus & Coyne, 2013) and later serves as a good foundation for more successful reading. Taking this notion into account, researchers and educators have been asking how young children expand their vocabulary, and what context is efficient for supporting this important learning.

Book Reading and Vocabulary Support

The adult–child storybook reading activity is considered a suitable context for enriching young children's vocabulary (Dickinson & Morse, 2019; Whitehurst & Lonigan, 2001), with adults "providing" the meaning of difficult words (Korat & Shamir, 2012; Kotaman, 2020; Toub et al., 2018). Intervention studies showed that when adults explain unknown words to young children (Kotaman, 2020; Toub et al., 2018), the children learn them efficiently. Following conversations with adults through shared book reading, they are exposed to novel words that they may not hear in everyday typical discourse. It is therefore an ideal activity for explicit vocabulary instruction (Lorio & Woods, 2020).

Interestingly, some studies showed that parents tend to relate to the meaning of only one or two words' meanings from the story in a "natural," everyday, shared book-reading activity without any external intervention (Evans, Reynolds, Shaw, & Pursoo, 2011; Korat, Segal-Drori, & Spielberg, 2018). One explanation offered by researchers for this behavior was that parents may fear interfering with their child's story attention and the storyline flow. However, no research is available on this point to support this assumption. This can be seen as a missed opportunity given that books include nonfamiliar words that can be explained and discussed with young children and enrich their vocabulary. The evidence that word explanations provided by adults to children during shared reading may promote word learning (Mol, Bus, De Jong, & Smeets, 2008) and the low frequency of this activity (Evans et al., 2011) led several researchers to the thought that parents and educators need support in order to improve their shared reading and enrich children's vocabulary (Resetar, Noell, & Pellegrin, 2006). We assume that suggesting word explanations as part of storybook reading in a suitable dosage (e.g., six to eight words out of a 30-page children's book) could be a successful way to enrich young children's vocabulary without interfering with the storyline and comprehension.

e-Books for Young Children

Young children today may be exposed to storybooks in different languages (e.g., English, Dutch, Hebrew, Arabic) not only as hard-copy books when an adult reads to them, but also by independently using e-books. This format of story reading can expand adult–child storybook reading opportunities on different occa-

sions, including war or conflict, health issues, lockdowns and pandemics (Furenes et al., 2021; Gaudreau et al., 2020). For example, a recent study that examined family digital activities during the COVID-19 pandemic found that middle-SES Israeli parents reported increased use of digital tools, including e-books, among their 2- to 6-year-old children. During the lockdown period, children were engaged about 60 minutes a day with e-books compared to 30 minutes prior to this period. Similar results were reported among Hebrew- and Arabic-speaking young children (Korat, Amer, Mahameed, & Gnaiem Kabha, 2021).

Many e-books include multimedia effects, such as written text, oral reading, oral discourse, music, sound effects, and static or dynamic visual presentation (animation) that might serve as potential tools for supporting story comprehension and vocabulary enrichment. A character or object on the screen can automatically or by clicking on it say things that do not appear in the original text. If this text expansion is related to the storyline and supports its language, it may help children better understand the content and expand their language level, including their vocabulary. In some e-books, the meaning of infrequent words, which are less familiar to young children, is stated by the narrator automatically or when clicking on hot spots, with an oral explanation and pictorial presentation.

Based on the dual-coding theory, visual and auditory multimedia stimulation can complement each other and support comprehension better than the use of either one alone (Mayer & Moreno, 1999). According to Paivio (1990), by presenting the illustration at the same time as hearing the spoken word that represents it, the learner constructs the visual and the verbal representations of the object, thus forming a connection between the two. Furthermore, based on the theory of synergy, animation makes learning more effective and allows for better implementation of information (Neuman, 1995), since it includes an active ingredient that connects the illustration and the spoken text. It can help focus children's attention (movement attracts children's attention more than a static illustration) and can demonstrate processes that might otherwise be difficult to understand (e.g., Mayer & Moreno, 1999). For example, children may understand the word *blooming* better if they see a flower slowly opening and turning from a bud into a flower, than when looking at a static image (Korat,

Levin, Atishkin, & Turgeman, 2014). In this chapter we examine the effectiveness of "reading" electronic storybooks by young children (ages 3 to 8) to support learning the meaning of target words from the story. In our chapter, the term *reading* also refers to listening/looking at the digital books, since at this age, most children are not formal readers. Multimedia effects in children's e-books can provide the user with a lively picture of the story meaning, including both linguistic and paralinguistic features such as body language, gestures, prosody, and so forth (Fidelman, 1997). Oral reading of the text by a narrator is sometimes accompanied by highlighted text, which may provide insights into the nature of the written text by allowing children to carefully follow the written words or phrases being read to them. Activating e-books that incorporate a built-in dictionary and highlighted text may offer young children the opportunity to learn not only the meaning of new words but also accurate word reading and spelling, and consequently better story comprehension.

The e-Book as a Tool for Vocabulary Enrichment

Over the last 20 years, a new body of research has focused on the efficacy of e-books in promoting children's language and literacy (e.g., Chera & Wood, 2003; Segers, Nooijen, & de Moor, 2006), including vocabulary enrichment (Verhallen, Bus, & de Jong, 2006; Korat, Atishkin, & Segal-Drori, 2021; Smeets & Bus, 2014; Zhou & Yadav, 2017; Zipke, 2016). The option of using a dictionary that explains difficult words within the authentic storybook context in e-books was suggested by several researchers as a possibly efficient way to directly enrich young children's vocabulary. Some of these e-books were selected from the commercial market, while others were developed by researchers.

In this chapter, we refer to e-books with a dictionary that provides audio word labels (saying a word separately from the narrator's book reading) with or without its pictorial presentation, and with or without providing the word's explanation. The visual representation can be dynamic or static, with or without the need to click on the word. All e-books we describe are read by a narrator. In some, the written text appears along with the narrator's reading, with or without highlighting the text. In most cases, learning

the words referred to receptive knowledge and sometimes related to expressive learning (usually providing the word's meaning).

The available research literature on e-books with a dictionary is described in this chapter under four leading issues: (1) dictionary design; (2) children's independent e-book reading compared to adult–child printed book reading; (3) e-book reading with a dictionary together with an adult; (4) using the e-book with a dictionary by children with learning difficulties. Since some overlap between issues can be found, we decided that research will be ascribed to a specific issue based on the main research goals. These four issues are elaborated below.

Dictionary Design

Several studies have examined the effect of dictionary design on young children's word learning. These studies focused mainly on dynamic visual (DV) compared to static visual (SV) presentations of new words, with some variations. The main idea is that DVs in e-books have a better potential for supporting young children's language learning than static presentations. Animations are regarded as requiring a less effortful process. They may present temporal changes and process durations more explicitly than a static presentation. The viewer must only perceive the change and does not need to infer it from the image (Hegarty, Kriz, & Cate, 2003). This may work well for learning the meaning of a new word. Several studies found support for this assumption, demonstrating that video stories are more effective in stimulating word learning than the same stories with static pictures among both typically developing (TD) (Smeets & Bus, 2012) and language-delayed children (Silverman & Hines, 2009; Verhallen & Bus, 2010; Verhallen et al., 2006).

For example, Verhallen et al. (2006) compared the effects of two versions of an e-book, one with SVs and the other with DVs, on language skills. Both versions had identical text, were told in the same voice, and were presented on a computer screen. The only difference was that in one version, the oral text was accompanied by static pictures, while in the other it was accompanied by dynamic pictures with music and sounds. The video and sounds related mainly to the main aspects of the story, such as characters, location, time, problem, goal, story events, resolution, and theme (Labbo & Kuhn, 2000). They found that kindergartners (from low-income immigrant families in the Netherlands) who were exposed to DVs demonstrated greater progress in language skills than those who were exposed to SVs. They concluded that multimedia storybooks could be an efficient vehicle for promoting linguistic information, especially for children who lag behind their cohorts in language and literacy skills. In all these studies, word meaning support was provided by animated representations that appeared on the screen, while the text was read by a narrator (e.g., Verhallen & Bus, 2010). In both versions, the printed text was not shown on the screen.

Similar results appeared in a study with Israeli Hebrew-speaking children. In this research, word-meaning support appeared automatically at the end of the reading of a screen by the narrator (Korat, Levin, Atishkin, et al., 2014). The e-book had two versions of word support: DV or SV presentation. For example, the explanation of the word *blossomed* in the static dictionary is as follows: At the end of the narrator's reading of the screen, a large bubble appears with the target written form of the word and a figurative static presentation of a flower, with the narrator concomitantly saying a short explanation of the word. In the DV dictionary, the explanation for the word is presented in exactly the same way, except that a large bubble that appears on the screen shows an animation of a bud slowly turning into a flower. Word-meaning support also included two options, with and without the printed word that was explained. The children were 7 years old (second graders) from low-income families. The children who benefited most from the intervention were those who read the e-book with DVs with the printed word. This was followed by reading the e-book with SVs with the printed word. These findings show that when the pictorial presentation is dynamic (animated), it attracts children's attention more than the static presentation, which may further support the contiguity between the oral presentation and the illustrations (e.g., Mayer, 2009). Furthermore, the printed format of the words had another important value for word meaning. This supports Rosenthal and Ehri's (2008) assumption that a printed word incorporated with an oral explanation will be learned better compared to a word explanation without its printed form. These results were also congruent with Mayer's (2009) redundancy principle, which aims at minimizing cognitive load by using short printed words next to the pictorial presentation and simultaneously presenting the oral narration that corresponds to the two graphical presentations.

DVs and SVs were also compared to an adult's word-meaning support in book reading (Korat, Levin, Ben-Shabat, Shneor, & Bokovza, 2014). In one group, the kindergarten teacher read an e-book (without a built-in dictionary) with the children after she was instructed by the researcher to explain focal words from the story. In the second group, the children read the same e-book with a built-in dictionary and SVs independently, and in a third group the children read the same e-book with a built-in dictionary with DVs. The fourth group read the same e-book without a dictionary (control). It was found that reading with an adult's vocabulary support was the most efficient way to learn the meaning of the words. This was followed by reading the e-book independently with DVs, then reading it with SVs. Children in all groups outperformed the control. These results show that adult mediation of word meaning works best for children's learning when an explanation is provided. It also supports the idea that DVs are more efficient than SVs, and all these options work much better than when no word meaning is provided.

Another recent study used an e-book with DVs or SVs, including either asking or not asking the child to say the difficult focal word (Korat, Mahamid, Hassunah-Arafat, & Altman, 2022). Kindergartners were randomly divided into five groups. The experimental groups read the e-book with a dictionary (1) with a dynamic illustration and a request to vocalize the word, (2) with a dynamic illustration without a request to vocalize the word, (3) with a static illustration and a request to vocalize the word, and (4) with a static illustration without a request for vocalization. The control group read the book without a dictionary. The greatest progress was achieved following word vocalization. This was followed by DV presentation of target words, and the smallest progress was found in the control group, which was not exposed to the dictionary at all.

The assumption is that children's repetition of the target words supported the phonological representation of the word, thus strengthening its meaning in memory, and apparently also helped its later lexical representation. These findings are in line with previous studies showing that vocal repetition of a word serves as a strategy for the internalization of meanings of new words and their recognition (Alt & Spaulding, 2011; Ellis & Sinclair, 1996). These processes apparently supported the ability to allocate the suitable representation of word meaning in the receptive and expressive word test, more than in a situation where children were exposed to the visual representation of the word in the dictionary either dynamically or statically, without any vocalization. Furthermore, previous results regarding the efficiency of word meaning following a dynamic compared to a static presentation were consistent. In conclusion, dynamic visual presentation of a word, together with its written printed form, is efficient for promoting vocabulary learning. Saying the word in the process of learning with dynamic and static visual presentation is another valuable way of word learning. This is followed by dynamic visuals, followed by static visuals with potential moderate support for word learning.

Children's Independent e-Book Reading with a Dictionary Compared to Adult–Child Printed-Book Reading

Following the social-cognitive theory (Vygotsky, 1978), shared storybook reading events are used as cultural tools that serve the mediation of adults to their children to expand knowledge. Children's independent learning ability is realized more effectively through a mediator who knows how to promote the children's understanding. With this help, children might reach higher levels of cognitive function, especially those who lag behind (e.g., low SES children) and need the instruction of an adult. The question is whether reading an e-book by young children who are not independent readers can serve as good mediation in supporting children's learning, similar to the "traditional" adult–child printed book reading. More specifically, the question is whether reading an e-book with a dictionary by young children without any support can serve as good support for children's word learning (similarly, more efficiently or less efficiently) than "traditional" adult–child printed book reading.

We found only one study that focused on this exact question. Korat and Shamir (2007) examined the effect of adult–child storybook reading compared to independent book reading with a dictionary on young children's receptive word learning. They used a built-in dictionary in the e-book they developed. This e-book

offered oral reading of the text. In addition, the explanation of one difficult word appeared automatically on each screen after the entire page was read by the narrator. Difficult words were pronounced clearly by the narrator. This was stimulating, as it was associated with pictures supporting the word meaning. The participants included 128 Hebrew-speaking kindergartners from low- and middle-SES families. The two intervention groups included three book-reading sessions each. In one group, the children read the e-book, which included dictionary support independently. In another group, the children were read the same printed book by the experimenter (education graduate student) individually. Reading sessions were executed in a strictly prescribed manner based on a pilot study provided by kindergarten teachers on how they read stories to children. The experimenters were given a list of the dictionary words with the same explanation that was given in the e-book, and were asked to explain these words to the children within the book-reading context (e.g., telling the children *greased* [in Hebrew *garaze*] means to put oil on a tool or a machine and a *container* [in Hebrew, *meihal*] is a big bottle). A third group, which served as a control, received the regular kindergarten program. The children's receptive vocabulary scores in both intervention groups improved to a similar extent following the reading activity compared to the control group. Thus, children who read the e-book with the dictionary support by themselves learned new words to the same extent as those who were read the printed book by adults who provided them with word explanations during the reading.

Reading an e-Book with a Dictionary Together with Adults

Several studies examined e-book reading with a dictionary support in adult–child joint reading (Korat, Atishkin, et al., 2022; Korat, Shamir, & Heibal, 2013; Korat & Shneor, 2019; Leacox & Jackson, 2014; Zhou & Yadav, 2017). Some compared children's reading this type of e-book without any help to reading the same e-book together with adults. In two studies, researchers (Korat, Atishkin, et al., 2022; Leacox & Jackson, 2014) found that children learned the new words better when they read them with adults, compared to reading them by themselves. In one study, children were encouraged to click on all the words' animations to learn the new words

(Leacox & Jackson, 2014). In the other one, the adults repeated and elaborated the meaning of focal words with the children (Korat, Atishkin, et al., 2022). A study (Zhou & Yadav, 2017) with a similar research design showed no advantage for adults reading an e-book with a dictionary together with children compared to children reading the same e-book by themselves. In this research, adult support was given by asking the children questions about the story content, including word labels in the story. These results may relate to cognitive load (Kirschner, 2002) when focusing simultaneously on story content and word labeling.

Furthermore, when low-SES parents received a short coaching on how to support children's vocabulary while reading a printed story focusing on target vocabulary, or when using the same story in an e-book with a dictionary, children learned the words better than the control group that did not receive any coaching (Korat et al., 2013). Interestingly, in one study (Korat & Shneor, 2019), low-SES mothers, who used an e-book with a dictionary without any coaching in their shared book reading with their kindergarten children, supported their children's vocabulary learning better than a group that used the e-book with their children without a dictionary. A comparison between mother–child interactions of both groups showed better support for children's learning by mothers who were provided coaching for using this tool. In conclusion, reading an e-book that includes a dictionary together with adults seems, in general, to be a good support for vocabulary learning, more than children's independent reading with a dictionary. In addition, a dictionary in the e-book might help adults to better mediate vocabulary learning to their young children.

Using e-Books with Dictionaries by Children with Learning Difficulties

The efficacy of e-books with a dictionary to promote the vocabulary of children with learning difficulties indicated gains in learning receptive (Shamir, 2017; Shamir & Baruch, 2012; Shamir, Korat, & Fellah, 2012; Shamir, Korat, & Shlafer, 2011; Shamir, Segal-Drori, & Goren, 2018) and expressive words (Korat, Graister, & Altman, 2019; Segers et al., 2006). In most of these studies, the participants were children at risk for learning disabilities (ALD). This relates to diverse disorders thought to be neuro-logical in origin and developmental in character (National Joint Committee on Learning Disabilities [NJCLD], 2006). As such, their manifestations begin to appear before or during preschool (Hutinger, Bell, Daytner, & Johanson, 2005) and continue into adulthood. The disorders in question interfere with basic cognitive functioning as a result of children's impaired perception and memory capacities (Breznitz, 1997), as well as with their acquisition of basic reading and writing skills, including vocabulary acquisition (NJCLD, 2006). These conditions necessitate the incorporation of multisensory events (visual, auditory, and sensory) within any learning program (Hetzroni, 2004; Lipka, Lesaux, & Siegel, 2006). Early childhood educators thus pay special attention to young children who exhibit developmental delay in language (including vocabulary) and early literacy, placing them at risk for learning disabilities.

The previously mentioned results indicate that reading an e-book with a dictionary may be a good avenue for promoting the learning of new words for children at risk. For example, Shamir and Baruch (2012) tested 52 ALD preschoolers and found that children who read an e-book with a built-in dictionary six times improved receptive word learning more than the control group that continued with their regular preschool activities. The built-in dictionary in the e-book included a picture presenting the focal word, including explanations for 10 difficult words that appeared automatically on the screen. This appeared after the entire page was read by the narrator, and children could click on hot spots of the dictionary at will. Similar results appeared in a follow-up study, and progress was maintained even 7 weeks after the intervention (Shamir et al., 2018).

Few studies compared the efficacy of learning new words after reading an e-book with a dictionary between children with learning difficulties and TD children (Korat et al., 2019; Shamir et al., 2011). Shamir et al. examined the effect of an activity with the e-book with a dictionary on receptive learning of new words of ALD children compared to TD children. The research sample consisted of 136 kindergartners. Of these, 77 ALD children and 60 TD children were randomly assigned to one of two groups: an experimental group, which was exposed to the e-book activity (6 times), and a control group, which continued with the standard kindergarten program. Their findings indicated significant improvement in the experimental groups of TD and ALD children.

Korat et al. (2019) examined the efficacy of e-book reading for promoting word learning among kindergarteners with specific language impairment (SLI) compared to those with typical language development (TLD). Three types of dictionary support were tested. All dictionary words were given a pictorial and auditory support, while one-third of them were given a short definition, one-third were defined using the story content, and one-third were given a combined definition. Twenty kindergartners with SLI and 20 with TLD were read the e-book with dictionary support five times. Each child was exposed to the three types of dictionary support in each e-book reading. A significant improvement in new word learning in the children's receptive knowledge, word definitions, and use of target words was observed in both groups following the e-book reading. The two groups progressed to a greater extent in explaining new words following the provision of a dictionary definition and following story context definition. Children with SLI progressed in word use after receiving the dictionary definition. The combined definition was especially efficient for children in the two groups that had a low initial level of using new words.

Two of the studies compared the ability of children with special needs to learn new words after reading an e-book with a dictionary to adult reading of the printed version of the same book (reading as usual) (Segers et al., 2006; Shamir et al., 2012). Both studies showed that after reading an e-book with a dictionary, children with special needs progressed in word learning more than when listening to the reading by an adult, or without exposure to reading the books at all. In conclusion, an e-book with a dictionary was found to be a good avenue for promoting the learning of new words for ALD children in different research contexts.

e-Book Reading with a Dictionary and Story Comprehension

The question of whether multimedia additions in e-books support or distract children from story comprehension is very important. We agree that storybooks for young children "tell" stories, and their main purpose and benefit should be that children understand the storyline (the problem and solution) that is part of the story structure, the main characters' feelings and thoughts, and more. At the same time, as is well known, most children's books are written in a "written register" that has a rich language, including a vocabulary that is used less in everyday oral discourse (e.g., Dickinson & Morse, 2019). Thus, storybook reading, including e-books, may include this option of language support. We are aware that embedded dictionaries in e-books, with their added multimedia effects, may distract young children's attention from the storyline focus, which consequently can harm children's story comprehension.

According to the cognitive load theory (Kirschner, 2002), instructional formats that impose high demands on working memory capacity may result in ineffective transfer of information to the long-term memory store, due to unavailable cognitive resources. As for narrative comprehension, human information processing systems have a limited capacity for distributing cognitive resources while being exposed to a story narrative, and this may have negative effects on children's comprehension (Mayer, 2009). As a result of this limitation, instruction should be designed such that working memory is capable of processing the information.

The importance of e-book design for children's story comprehension was addressed by several researchers (Christ, Wang, Chiu, & Strekalova-Hughes, 2019), including a recent meta-analysis (Furenes et al., 2021) that focused on dictionary use in e-books as a possible hindrance to story comprehension. Thirty-nine e-books in different languages (Arabic, English, Dutch, Hebrew, and Spanish) were tested. The results showed that an embedded dictionary in e-books had no effect or a negative effect on children's story comprehension, but a positive effect on vocabulary learning. More specifically, only 10 studies focused on digital books that included a dictionary and no other enhancements. No preference was found for a dictionary when reading a digital compared to a paper book. Only three studies included a combined focus on story content expansion and dictionary. In these cases, digital e-books tend to do worse than the printed books in supporting word learning. When digital books had only content support without a dictionary, children understood the story better than when these two options appeared together. The studies that included e-books with a dictionary showed a positive effect on word learning, especially when they did not include any other enhancement (i.e., story content expansions). These results are important for researchers who focus on optimal e-book design to support children's story comprehension, as well as vocabulary learning. Although the sample of e-books in this study is limited and conclusions should be drawn with care, this result should be taken into account by book developers, researchers, parents, and educators.

By doing so, we suggest that e-books should include different channels of learning (as found in Korat and her colleagues' studies), one with a dictionary that supports children's vocabulary, and one that extends children's story comprehension. This type of design may enable children to enjoy the benefits of books, including e-books, for language enrichment, as well as story comprehension. This will enable young children (and their parents and educators), and especially those from low-SES families, to enjoy the advantages offered by well-designed e-books.

Conclusion

The design of a dictionary in e-books is a crucial factor in supporting young children's learning of new words. The effect of dynamic visuals as a good potential for supporting word learning was tested when e-books began to be examined by researchers (Verhallen et al., 2006; Verhallen & Bus, 2010). The dynamic effect in e-books that include a dictionary was expanded to test other effects, such as printed words (Korat, Levin, Ben-Shabat, et al., 2014) and saying the words by the children when presented the meaning of new words together with pictorial dynamic presentations (Korat, Atishkin, et al., 2022). In these two contexts, children learned the new words better than when exposed only to animation. Being aware of the danger of cognitive load (Kirschner, 2002; Mayer, 2009), only one word was explained in each screen, explanations for words were short, and oral explanations appeared together with the pictorial dynamic presentation. Furthermore, and very importantly, the dictionary in all these studies appeared in a different channel from story content expansion, in order to avoid a negative impact on the learning process. It seems that very careful design worked well for the children's word learning. We also know from the available literature that children who read the e-book with the dictionary by themselves

learned new words to a similar extent as children who were read the printed book by adults who provided them with word explanations during the reading (Korat et al., 2013). However, if the adults read to them "as usual," without any coaching, they progressed less than when reading an e-book with a dictionary independently (Korat & Shneor, 2019). Thus, an e-book that has a well-designed dictionary can be very efficient for enriching the vocabulary of many young children who lag behind.

Furthermore, when e-books with a dictionary were read in joint reading with adults (without any coaching), they supported children's vocabulary learning more than when children read the same e-book with a dictionary independently. The adult in this joint reading was encouraged to mediate new words to the children by the built-in dictionary, and this may be the cause for the children's new vocabulary learning (Korat & Shneor, 2019). In general, the efficient learning of new words using e-books appeared with not only TD children but also ALD children. It is important to note that most of the children who participated in these studies were from low-income families. The results show that the poorer the children's initial vocabulary, the greater their improvement following reading with a dictionary. Multimedia effects that include pictures, motions, print, listening to explanations, and using your own voice to utter the words with optimal load (not overloaded) worked well for children's learning. These results seem to be a good start for learning about the efficacy of direct word teaching by using multimedia additions such as a dictionary on children's vocabulary learning. However, more studies are needed to better understand the effects of multimedia on children's vocabulary learning when they include direct word teaching. Only a few longitudinal studies were carried out to test the long-term effect of this learning. Furthermore, no studies tested how children's general vocabulary knowledge can be advanced beyond focal words following the reading of an e-book with a dictionary. Only a few studies tested the implementation of such e-books by families and schools. The last issue, but not the least, is the question of whether and to what extent storybook comprehension is distracted when e-books include story content expansion and dictionary support in the same channel (Furenes et al., 2021). If so, how should we design e-books so they can support both story comprehension and a rich vocabulary?

References

Alt, M., & Spaulding, T. (2011). The effect of time on word learning: An examination of decay of the memory trace and vocal rehearsal in children with and without specific language impairment. *Journal of Communication Disorders, 44*(6), 640–654.

Bleses, D., Makransky, G., Dale, P. S., Højen, A., & Ari, B. A. (2016). Early productive vocabulary predicts academic achievement 10 years later. *Applied Psycholinguistics, 37*(6), 1461–1476.

Breznitz, Z. (1997). Effects of accelerated reading rate on memory for text among dyslexic readers. *Journal of Educational Psychology, 89*(2), 289–297.

Carlisle, J., & Rice, M. S. (2002). *Improving reading comprehension: Research-based principles and practices.* York Press.

Chera, P., & Wood, C. (2003). Animated multimedia "talking books" can promote phonological awareness in children beginning to read. *Learning and Instruction, 13*(1), 33–52.

Christ, T., Wang, X. C., Chiu, M. M., & Strekalova-Hughes, E. (2019). How app books' affordances are related to young children's reading behaviors and outcomes. *AERA Open, 5*(2), 1–18.

Côté, I., Rouleau, N., & Macoir, J. (2014). New word acquisition in children: Examining the contribution of verbal short-term memory to lexical and semantic levels of learning. *Applied Cognitive Psychology, 28*(1), 104–114.

Dickinson, D., & Morse, A. B. (2019). *Connecting through talk: Instructing children's development with language.* Brookes.

Ellis, N. C., & Sinclair, S. G. (1996). Working memory in the acquisition of vocabulary and syntax: Putting language in good order. *Quarterly Journal of Experimental Psychology A, 49*(1), 234–250.

Evans, M. A., Reynolds, K., Shaw, D., & Pursoo, T. (2011). Parental explanations of vocabulary during shared book reading: A missed opportunity. *First Language, 31*(2), 195–213.

Fidelman, C. G. (1997). Extending the language curriculum with enabling technologies: Nonverbal communication and interactive video. In K. A. Murphy-Judy (Ed.), *NEXUS: The convergence of language teaching and research using technology* (pp. 28–41). CALICO.

Furenes, M. I., Kucirkova, N., & Bus, A. G. (2021). A comparison of children's reading on paper versus screen: A meta-analysis. *Review of Educational Research, 91*, 483–517.

Gaudreau, C., King, Y. A., Dore, R. A., Puttre, H., Nichols, D., Hirsh-Pasek, K., & Golinkoff, R. M. (2020). Preschoolers benefit equally from video chat, pseudo-contingent video, and live book reading: Implications for story time during the Coronavirus pandemic and beyond. *Frontiers in Psychology, 11*, Article 2158.

Hart, B., & Risley, T. R. (1995). *Meaningful differences in the everyday experience of young American children.* Brookes.

Hegarty, M., Kriz, S., & Cate, C. (2003). The roles of mental animations and external animations in understanding mechanical systems. *Cognition and Instruction, 21*(4), 209–249.

Hetzroni, O. E. (2004). Literacy and assistive technology for children with special needs. *Script, 7–8*, 195–218. (Hebrew)

Hutinger, P., Bell, C., Daytner, G., & Johanson, J. (2005). *Disseminating and replicating an effective emerging literacy technology curriculum: A final report.* Office of Special Education and Rehabilitation Services. (ERIC Document Reproduction Service No. ED 489575)

Kirschner, P. A. (2002). Cognitive load theory: Implication of cognitive load theory on design of learning. *Learning and Instruction, 12*(1), 1–10.

Korat, O., Amer, K., Mahameed, W., & Gnaiem Kabha, H. (2021). Use of screens in early childhood during the COVID-19 outbreak: Comparison between Israeli children in Jewish and Arab sectors. *Researching the Early Childhood, 13*, 1–30. (Hebrew)

Korat, O., Atishkin, S., & Segal-Drori, O. (2022). Vocabulary enrichment using an E-book with and without kindergarten teacher's support among LSES children. *Early Child Development and Care, 192*, 1384–1401.

Korat, O., Graister, T., & Altman, C. (2019). Contribution of reading an e-book with a dictionary to word learning. Comparison between kindergarteners with and without SLI. *Journal of Communication Disorders, 79*, 90–102.

Korat, O., Levin, I., Atishkin, S., & Turgeman, M. (2014). E-book as facilitator of vocabulary acquisition: Support of adults, dynamic dictionary and static dictionary. *Reading and Writing, 27*(4), 613–629.

Korat, O., Levin, I., Ben-Shabat, A., Shneor, D., & Bokovza, L. (2014). Dynamic compared to static dictionary with and without printed focal words in e-book reading as facilitator for word learning. *Reading Research Quarterly, 49*(4), 371–386.

Korat, O., Mahamid, N. Hassunah-Arafat, S., & Altman, C. (2022). What contributes to word learning and story retelling of Arabic-speaking children?: Investigation of an e-book reading intervention. *Journal of Literacy and Instruction, 61*, 158–176.

Korat, O., Segal-Drori, O., & Spielberg, L. (2018). Word explanation and content expansion during storybook reading: Relation to SES and children's language. *Early Child Development and Care, 188*(6), 691–708.

Korat, O., & Shamir, A. (2007). Electronic books

versus adult readers: effects on children's emergent literacy as a function social class. *Journal of Computer Assisted Learning, 23*(3), 248–259.

Korat, O., & Shamir, A. (2012). Direct and indirect teaching: Using e-books for supporting vocabulary, word reading and story comprehension. *Journal of Education Computing Research, 46*(2), 135–152.

Korat, O., Shamir, A., & Heibal, S. (2013). Expanding the boundaries of shared book reading: E-books and printed books in parent–child reading as support for children's language. *First Language, 33*(5), 504–523.

Korat, O., & Shneor, D. (2019). Can e-books support low SES parental mediation to enrich children's vocabulary? *First Language, 39*(3), 344–364.

Kotaman, H. (2020). Impacts of dialogical storybook reading on young children's reading attitudes and vocabulary development. *Reading Improvement, 57*(1), 40–45.

Labbo, L. D., & Kuhn, M. R. (2000). Weaving chains of affect and cognition: A young child's understanding of CD-ROM talking books. *Journal of Literacy Research, 32*(2), 187–210.

Leacox, L., & Jackson, C. W. (2014). Spanish vocabulary-bridging technology enhanced instruction for young English language learners' word learning. *Journal of Early Childhood Literacy, 14*(2), 175–197.

Lipka, O., Lesaux, N. K., & Siegel, L. S. (2006). Retrospective analyses of the reading development of Grade 4 students with reading disabilities: Risk status and profiles over 5 years. *Journal of Learning Disabilities, 39*(4), 364–378.

Loftus, S. M., & Coyne, M. D. (2013). Vocabulary instruction within a multi-tier approach. *Reading and Writing Quarterly, 29*(1), 4–19.

Lorio, C. M., & Woods, J. J. (2020). Multi-component professional development for educators in an early head start: Explicit vocabulary instruction during interactive shared book reading. *Early Childhood Research Quarterly, 50*(1), 86–100.

Marsh, J., Lahmar, J., & Plowman, L. (2021). Under threes' play with tablets. *Journal of Early Literacy Research, 19*, 283–297.

Mayer, R. E. (2009). *Multimedia learning* (2nd ed.). Cambridge University Press.

Mayer, R. E., & Moreno, R. (1999). A split-attention effect in multimedia learning: Evidence for dual processing systems in working memory. *Journal of Educational Psychology, 90*(2), 312–320.

Mol, S. E., Bus, A. G., De Jong, M. T., & Smeets, D. J. (2008). Added value of dialogic parent–child book readings: A meta-analysis. *Early Education and Development, 19*(1), 7–26.

National Joint Committee on Learning Disabilities.

(2006). Learning disabilities and young children: Identification and intervention. Retrieved from *www.ldonline.org/about/partners/njcld#reports*.

Neuman, S. B. (1995). *Literacy in the television age: The myth of the TV effect* (2nd ed.). Ablex.

Neumann, M. M. (2015). Young children and screen time: Creating a mindful an approach to digital technology. *Australian Educational Computing, 3*(2), 1–15.

Pavio, A. (1990). *Mental representations: A dual coding approach.* Oxford University Press.

Resetar, J. L., Noell, G. H., & Pellegrin, A. L. (2006). Teaching parents to use research-supported systematic strategies to tutor their children in reading. *School Psychology Quarterly, 21*(3), 241–261.

Rohlfing, K. J., & Muller-Brausers, C. (2021). *International perspective on digital media and early literacy: The impact of digital devices on learning, language acquisition and social interaction.* Routledge/Taylor & Francis Group.

Rosenthal, J., & Ehri, L. C. (2008). The mnemonic value of orthography for vocabulary learning. *Journal of Educational Psychology, 100*(1), 175–191.

Segers, E., Nooijen, M., & de Moor, J. (2006). Computer vocabulary training in kindergarten children with special needs. *International Journal of Rehabilitation Research, 29*(4), 343–345.

Shahaeian, A., Wang, C., Tucker-Drob, E., Geiger, V., Bus, A. G., & Harrison, L. J. (2018). Early shared reading, socioeconomic status, and children's cognitive and school competencies: Six years of longitudinal evidence. *Scientific Studies of Reading, 22*(6), 485–502.

Shamir, A. (2017). Expanding the boundaries of kindergartners' e-book reading: Metacognitive guidance for e-book support among young children at risk for learning disabilities. *Teachers College Record, 119*(13), 1–14.

Shamir, A., & Baruch, D. (2012). Educational e-books: A support for vocabulary and early math for children at risk for learning disabilities. *Educational Media International, 49*(1), 33–47.

Shamir, A., Korat, O., & Fellah, R. (2012). Promoting vocabulary, phonological awareness and concept about print among children at risk for learning disability: Can e-books help? *Reading and Writing, 25*(1), 45–69.

Shamir, A., Korat, O., & Shlafer, I. (2011). The effect of activity with e-book on vocabulary and story comprehension: A comparison between kindergarteners at risk of learning disabilities and typically developing kindergarteners. *European Journal of Special Needs Education, 26*(3), 311–322.

Shamir, A., Segal-Drori, O., & Goren, I. (2018). Educational electronic book activity supports language retention among children at risk for learning disabilities. *Education and Information Technologies, 23*(3), 1231–1252.

Silverman, R., & Hines, S. (2009). The effects of multimedia-enhanced instruction on the vocabulary of English-language learners and non-English-language learners in pre-kindergarten through second grade. *Journal of Educational Psychology, 101*(2), 305–314.

Smeets, D. J., & Bus, A. G. (2012). Interactive electronic storybooks for kindergartners to promote vocabulary growth. *Journal of Experimental Child Psychology, 112*(1), 36–55.

Smeets, D. J. H., & Bus, A. G. (2014). The interactive animated e-book as a word learning device for kindergartners. *Applied Psycholinguistics, 36*(4), 899–920.

Snow, C. E., Burns, M. S., & Griffin, P. (1998). *Preventing reading difficulties in young children.* National Academy Press.

Stanovich, K. (1986). Matthew effects in reading: Some consequences of individual differences in the acquisition of literacy. *Reading Research Quarterly, 21,* 360–407.

Toub, T. S., Hassinger-Das, B., Nesbitt, K. T., Ilgaz, H., Weisberg, D. S., Hirsh-Pasek, K., & Dickinson, D. K. (2018). The language of play: Developing preschool vocabulary through play following shared book-reading. *Early Childhood Research Quarterly, 45*(4), 1–17.

Verhallen, M. J., & Bus, A. G. (2010). Low-income immigrant pupils learning vocabulary through digital picture storybooks. *Journal of Educational Psychology, 102*(1), 54–61.

Verhallen, M. J., Bus, A. G., & de Jong, M. T. (2006). The promise of multimedia stories for kindergarten children at risk. *Journal of Educational Psychology, 98*(2), 410–419.

Vygotsky, L. S. (1978). Interaction between learning and development. In M. Cole, V. John-Steiner, S. Scribner, & E. Souberman (Eds.), *Mind in society: The development of higher psychological process* (pp. 79–91). Harvard University Press.

Whitehurst, G. J., & Lonigan, C. J. (2001). Emergent literacy: Development from prereaders to readers. In S. B. Neuman & D. K. Dickinson (Eds.), *Handbook of early literacy research* (pp. 11–29). Guilford Press.

Zhou, N., & Yadav, A. (2017). Effects of multimedia story reading and questioning on preschoolers' vocabulary learning, story comprehension and reading engagement. *Educational Technology Research and Development, 65*(6), 1523–1545.

Zipke, M. (2016). The importance of flexibility of pronunciation in learning to decode: A training study in set for variability. *First Language, 36*(1), 71–86.

CHAPTER 33

Leveraging Research–Practice Partnerships to Support Evidence Use in Early Childhood

Lessons Learned from Atlanta 323

Nicole Patton Terry, Gary E. Bingham,
Anita Faust Berryman, Janelle Clay, and Kate Caton

Early childhood education (ECE) is increasingly a focus of policymakers at the federal and state levels, with efforts aimed at addressing access to high-quality early learning settings. Researchers have long argued for caution in positioning early childhood learning as a panacea for eliminating school readiness and academic achievement gaps that are present before children enter kindergarten (Burchinal et al., 2018; Lipsey, Farran, & Durkin, 2018). Early childhood is a critical time in children's development, when learning is most malleable and investments are most cost-effective for the long-term (Heckman, Moon, Pinto, Savelyev, & Yavitz, 2010). Ample empirical evidence demonstrates the positive immediate and long-term impact of high-quality ECE on cognitive, academic, behavioral, and social–emotional outcomes (Barnett, 2011; Duncan et al., 2007; Yazejian et al., 2017). Yet many children, especially children from historically and systemically marginalized communities, experience early childhood systems that are limited in scope and quality (Ewen & Herzfeldt-Kamprath, 2016; Nores & Barnett, 2014). Limited access to high-quality early learning experiences, which are available in healthy and well-connected neighborhoods, contributes to differences in the academic and social skills that children gain from later school-

ing experiences (Yoshikawa et al., 2013). Consequentially, increased access to high-quality ECE has become a critical component of strategies designed to support children's social and academic outcomes, alleviate opportunity gaps, and prevent later challenges in school (Burchinal et al., 2018; Magnuson & Waldfogel, 2005).

However, access alone is insufficient. Accumulating evidence suggests that the early childhood programs and services children and families encounter vary drastically in quantity and quality, perpetuating educational and opportunity gaps that these programs were often designed to alleviate (Friedman-Krauss, Barnett, & Nores, 2016). In addition, despite substantial investments in federal and state initiatives, many programs designed to serve children from historically and systemically marginalized communities do not always produce intended results (Lipsey et al., 2018). Recent attention highlights how deficit framing within the goals and programming of well-intentioned early childhood programs and initiatives may promote a narrative that frames the culture, history, values, assets, and needs of families and communities in a manner that fails to acknowledge both the confounds between race and poverty in the United States and the strengths that every child and family bring to the learning environment (Bruno & Iruka, 2022; Cabrera & The SRCD Ethnic and Racial Issues Committee, 2013; Iruka et al., Chapter 29, this volume).

These issues are only compounded and complicated by the fragmented implementation of early childhood services. Primary among these is access to reliable and actionable child-level and program-level data to understand, create, and sustain cohesive preschool through third-grade (P3) systems (Kagan & Kauerz, 2012) that bridge the divide between early childhood (birth to age 5 years) and elementary education (kindergarten to fifth grade). In addition, communities from state to state vary widely in the opportunities they provide young children, and differences between licensing and quality initiatives at state and local levels create confusion for researchers, educators, families, providers, and policymakers (Duncan et al., 2007; Edwards, Terry, Bingham, & Singer, 2021). The fragmented nature of the early childhood system and varied services available to children and families make it challenging to assess program reach or impact in a manner that supports decision making and program improvement.

These kinds of systemic and structural barriers are complex and often have afforded little integrated attention in research and in practice, resulting in a limited evidence base on how best to achieve intended outcomes from investments in ECE, especially for student populations that are vulnerable to experiencing difficulty in school. Both researchers and practitioners have argued that robust partnerships and engagement are the key to overcoming these kinds of systems-level obstacles (Bruner, 2012; Fantuzzo & Culhane, 2009; Farrell, Wentworth, & Nayfack, 2021). However, positioning partnership as a tool to use research and evidence to create change is not without its own challenges. It is in this context that we present Atlanta 323—a research–practice partnership (RPP) focused on creating a cohesive, citywide P3 early learning system to support equitable school readiness and early school achievement in Atlanta, Georgia. First, we discuss RPPs, reviewing defining characteristics and emerging evidence on their effectiveness in supporting educational outcomes. We then turn our attention to current early childhood RPP work, noting shared challenges and opportunities within these partnerships. Next, we discuss Atlanta 323 and share findings from descriptive research studies carried out with partners in the school district and ECE providers in the surrounding community. Finally, we propose future promising areas of research that are needed to move RPP work in ECE settings forward.

Education RPPs

RPPs refer to formal relationships and collaborations between researchers and education practitioners, created to produce and use research to improve educational outcomes and support equitable transformation of services across local or state education ecosystems (Coburn, Penuel, & Geil, 2013; Donovan, Snow, & Huyghe, 2021; Farrell, Penuel, Coburn, Daniel, & Steup, 2021). RPPs are traditionally conceptualized as a formalized connection between university-based researchers and practitioners in local- and state-education agencies. Importantly, the notion that partnerships between researchers and practitioners could improve education-related outcomes is not new (National Research Council, 1999; Snow, 2014). However, challenges with progress in translating findings from educational research into routine practice in school-based settings has led to the organization of contemporary RPPs as formalized, long-term relationships that exist beyond one specific research study or initiative. As such, RPPs are envisioned as a two-way interaction between research and practitioners, with research agendas and goals being developed jointly in ways that are mutually beneficial to all partners. More recently, RPPs are being positioned in ways that are more inclusive of practitioners' and communities' needs, both by elevating diverse forms of expertise that exist on the practice-based side of the partnership and by ensuring that all partners are vocal contributors in developing and executing a joint agenda (Chicago Beyond, 2019; Farrell et al., 2021). Framed as approaches to support equitable outcomes, processes, and systems, such practices are thought to support strong communication between researchers and practitioners about problems of practice and create more egalitarian and supportive spaces for engaging the partners who are most proximal to students the partnership is seeking to serve.

Guiding Principles for RPPs

Over the past decade, as more formal RPPs have emerged, there has been a concerted effort to better define and understand the components, mechanisms, and impact of these relationships. Building on the initial definitions proposed by Coburn et al. (2013) and informed by primary research and interviews with RPP leaders, Farrell et al. (2021) define education RPPs as a "long-term collaboration aimed at educational improvement or equitable transformation through engagement with research. These partnerships are intentionally organized to connect diverse forms of expertise and shift power relations in the research endeavor to ensure that all partners have a say in the joint work" (p. 5). While there are commonalities among RPPs, there are also notable differences in their organizational structure, research intent or purpose, and their research approaches, which are largely informed by their local context and funding sources. Nonetheless, five key RPP principles emerge from the conceptualization of RPPs as defined by Coburn et al. (2013) and Farrell et al. (2021).

First, RPPs are long-term collaborations, characterized not by time-bound engagement, but a willingness to commit and maintain a collaboration that goes beyond a single agreement or funding opportunity. Longer engagement allows partners to develop trust and work collaboratively over time, creating space for deep exploration of critical issues. Second, RPPs work toward educational improvement or equitable transformation. RPPs generally organize around policies or practices affecting educational outcomes, with the goal of influencing educational institutions to create better processes and programs. RPPs work within existing structures to leverage their strengths while also designing new systems based on identified goals and needs. In this way, RPPs are well positioned to focus on equitable transformation as researchers work in partnership with, and are held accountable by, practitioners and community members to produce research that is timely and relevant. RPPs that seek equitable transformation do so by centering the needs of those most affected by the outcomes they seek to change, lifting up or illuminating existing disparities, and moving entire systems toward greater equity.

Third, engagement with research is a leading activity in RPPs. Unlike other partnership activities that may be based in educational environments, RPPs exist to produce, disseminate, and use research evidence to inform policy and practice based on pressing issues, with the intent of research engagement characterized by knowledge-generating or problem solving (Donovan et al., 2021). RPPs that focus on knowledge generation do so to produce knowledge and information about the relevance and impact of district policies without developing specific solutions to address the issue. In contrast, RPPs that focus on problem solving conduct research with the goal of directly informing and altering educational practices. Although RPPs exist outside of these dimensions and change in approach across time, research generated from these RPPs is expected to contribute to both the field at large and the local context. Fourth, RPPs are organized intentionally to bring together a diversity of expertise to shape the research agenda. Expertise captures those with traditional institutional power such as researchers and educational leaders, as well as community members whose expertise is based on experiences in their local context. RPPs leverage these diverse perspectives through collaborating on research questions, study design, analyses, meaning making of study findings, and dissemination.

Finally, RPPs employ strategies to shift power relations in research endeavors to make sure all participants have a voice in the decision-making process. RPPs have long contended with power imbalances in how practitioners are engaged in research activities (Chicago Beyond, 2019). More recently, these challenges have been framed from an equity lens (Diamond, 2021; Wilson, 2021). Farrell et al. (2021) argue that equity should be an explicit feature of all RPPs, although approaches to achieve equity may be conceptualized and prioritized differently. For example, some RPPs may focus on achieving equitable outcomes, exploring disparities in outcomes between specific student groups, and identifying policies, practices, or interventions to address it. Others may focus on achieving equitable systems by explicitly addressing the historical, political, social, or economic systems that produce and contribute to disparities. Still others may focus on achieving equitable processes by implementing organizational structures and adopting specific practices that broaden participation in partnership activities and elevate perspectives from marginalized groups. Although RPPs strive to address their partners' needs, equity is not an explicit priority for all RPPs (Diamond, 2021; Wilson, 2021). Some do not explicitly identify reducing inequities as a goal of the partnership and others do not engage in efforts to address inequities in outcomes, processes, or systems.

RPPs in ECE

Research evidence on the nature and impact of RPPs in ECE contexts is limited compared to primary and secondary settings, in part because fewer partnerships exist. Among the multiple reasons for a lack of RPPs with ECE partners, primary among them are funding and fragmentation. The economic landscape of early childhood varies considerably across states, with ECE programs pulling resources from federal, state, and local agencies (McCabe & Sipple, 2011). Few of these sources fund ECE in a manner that allows for significant investments in research and collaboration activities across sectors (Schilder, Broadstone, & Curenton, 2017). It is important to note that although funding variation also exists across the United States for K–12 education, K–12 systems have much stronger investment models and more formalized budgetary allocations at the state and federal level for supporting school improvement. The dispersed and fragmented economic engine that drives ECE programming creates considerable distance between research on effective practice and programs that provide services for young children, contributing to the uneven distribution of high-quality early learning experiences. For example, empirical research fails to reflect how early childhood partnership activities support early childhood program quality, program decision making, or children's developmental outcomes (Hong et al., 2019; Schilder et al., 2017).

Drivers behind who funds ECE at the state and federal level have real-world implications for the physical and human resource infrastructure available for conducting RPP work with ECE practitioners and community partners (Connors, Pacchiano, Stein, & Swartz, 2021). For example, because research is a key component of RPPs, engaging in RPP initiatives requires sufficient organizational capacity and physical resources for working with data, including hardware and software; data storage and integration systems; formalized assessment protocols; valid and reliable assessments, surveys, and observation tools to collect child-, family-, classroom-, and site-level data; and staff to support data gathering, management, and reporting. Even with these resources in place, ECE partners must also have knowledgeable staff members who have sufficient time to engage in RPP program development, implementation, evaluation, and continuous improvement processes. Many K–12 school districts, let alone ECE providers, do not have these resources, limiting their ability to participate in RPPs in a manner that is both useful and equitable (Connors et al., 2021). A related tension within this work is the need to develop an RPP plan that meets the needs of the ECE partner while also addressing program requirements of various funding agencies that support ECE (Penuel, Allen, Coburn, & Farrell, 2015). Program-level requirements impact the entire cycle of program development, implementation, and evaluation as various sources of funding and oversight impact the goals of programs, the nature of standards, and what assessments are used to document children's learning and development. Program requirements often exist about how these data are collected, managed, and reported to external agencies. For example, in Georgia, all Georgia's PreK classrooms must use Work Sampling Online to examine children's developmental progress two times a year (Meisels, Marden, Jablon, & Dichtelmiller, 2011). These external requirements influence what data exist in the partner agency, how regularly these data are collected and reported, and what types of data infrastructure exist to accomplish these tasks (both at the program level and state oversight).

Despite these challenges, ECE-focused RPPs are emerging and have provided evidence that supports their partners and the field. Often, they include multiple types of research and practitioner organizations, reflecting the diverse and cross-sector array of stakeholders in the ECE ecosystem. In this way, many ECE focused RPPs adopt a P3 approach.

P3 Systems to Support Coordination and Equity

Kagan and Kauerz (2012) describe cohesive P3 systems as early childhood systems that include early care and education programs, services for children from birth to 8 years old, and comprehensive services that support child health, school readiness, and early achievement. These systems are characterized by coordination and alignment of multiple programs and services for early childhood (infant, toddler, preschool, and PreK) and primary grades (K–3). They also highlight the importance of promoting smooth transitions by linking contextual systems in both horizontal (e.g., teacher–parent) and vertical (e.g., PreK teacher–kindergarten teacher) ways (Pianta & Kraft-Sayre, 2003). Such supports are particularly important to address the needs of young learners who may require support from multiple public and community agencies to ensure healthy beginnings, including children with disabilities, children growing up in poverty, and children with complex social, emotional, learning, and behavioral needs. P3 systems recognize that school readiness is a multidimensional construct, reflecting multiple domains within the child that develop rapidly over time, and multiple environmental factors outside of the child that interact to influence development (Maxwell & Clifford, 2004). Finally, because children enter systems from different backgrounds, with different learning capacities, and with diverse early learning opportunities, P3 systems emphasize that systematic and comprehensive focus is necessary to ensure that policies and programs meet all children's needs and ensure equitable opportunity for school success (Bruner, 2012).

Empirical research demonstrates positive relations between students' participation in effective P3 systems and their school readiness and achievement. The most well-known and frequently cited examples of effective comprehensive P3 systems for children growing up in poverty include the Carolina Abecedarian Project, the Chicago Child–Parent Center and Expansion Program, and Head Start/Follow Through (for reviews of these programs and findings from evaluation studies, see Reynolds, 2003; Reynolds, Magnuson, & Ou, 2006). Findings across these studies show positive immediate and long-term effects on students' K–12 academic achievement, delinquency and suspensions, parent involvement in school, graduation rates and postsecondary attainment, employment, and many indicators of overall well-being. Mounting research evidence also supports many components of P3 systems. For example, using the Early Childhood Longitudinal Study Kindergarten Cohort, Reynolds et al. (2006) explored patterns in children's third-grade achievement by their participation in different components of P3 programs, including full-day kindergarten, preschool attendance, school stability from K–3, high parent involvement, certified teachers, and high-quality reading instruction. Findings indicated that children who experienced more components of a P3 system demonstrated stronger math and reading achievement than children who experienced some or none of the P3 components. Children who did not experience any components of a P3 system were three times more likely than their peers to be retained by third grade.

These findings notwithstanding, Bruno and Iruka (2022) remind us that many of these well-intentioned projects were developed from a deficit lens, seeking to provide intervention for children and families living in historically and systemically marginalized communities rather than to leverage their assets to address their priorities and needs. A growing body of research examining within-group variation in early language, reading, and literacy skills among children growing up in poverty and children from specific racial and ethnic groups affirms patterns of strength and needs that could be addressed positively within an RPP (Iruka, Curenton, & Gardner, 2015; Iruka, Curenton, Sims, Blitch, & Gardner, 2020). However, in the absence of sufficient evidence, the benefits of addressing inequities in ECE through RPPs remains speculative.

Examples of RPPs in ECE

Below, we briefly describe three ECE-focused RPPs that adopt P3 principles in their shared goals, organizational structure, and research and partnership activities. First, the Partnership for Early Education Research (PEER) focuses on education and well-being outcomes for children from birth through age 8 and their families in communities in Connecticut. PEER is a partnership between a single research institution (Yale University School of Medicine), multiple public school districts (Bridgeport, Norwalk, and Stamford), a nonprofit research institution, two state education agencies, and multiple early childhood education stakeholders. PEER's research and priority areas have focused on multilingual learners, family engagement, kindergarten readiness, and instructional and assessment practices.

Second, the New York City Early Childhood Research Network is a collaborative between researchers, policymakers, and funders who work to inform public policy for children from birth through age 8. The network includes researchers from multiple higher education institutions, research organizations, and early education organizations. The network is housed within the New York Early Childhood Professional Development Institute at the City University of New York, which provides infrastructure support, identifies funding resources and opportunities, and generally supports collaboration among partners. The network's research and priority areas have focused on instructional leadership, male ECE teachers, dual language learners, and students with disabilities.

Finally, the Miami–Dade IDEAS Consortium for Children is a partnership between the University of Miami, Miami–Dade County Public Schools, the Early Learning Coalition of Miami–Dade/Monroe Counties, the Miami–Dade County Community Action Agency and Human services, and the Children's Trust. The partnership has focused on developing and maintaining data-sharing capacity across partner agencies to inform practices and policies for all children from birth through age 8. Members from the founding organizations serve as the governance committee, while researchers from the university and other academic institutions serve as academic advisors, and leaders from local organizations serve as community advisors. Using administrative data collected from partner agencies, the consortium has conducted research on a variety of priority areas: preschool experiences of kindergarten children; attendance rates across preschool programs and the relationship with school readiness skills; and the relation between residential neighborhood and childhood resiliency.

Lessons from Atlanta 323

Guided by RPP principles and research evidence, researchers, school district leaders, ECE providers, and community members in the city of Atlanta envisioned a metropolitan region where data and partnerships are used in meaningful ways to ensure that all children have a seamless high-quality early learning pathway from birth to third grade. Atlanta 323 emerged from this shared vision. Highly functioning RPPs develop formalized structures and processes that leverage a host of human, fiscal, and physical resources to support strong decision making about when and how to utilize research and evidence in a manner that fosters organizations that can learn and improve (Booker, Conaway, & Schwartz, 2019; Wentworth, Mazzeo, & Connolly, 2017). Thus, below we describe early work within the Atlanta 323, organized by key components and mechanisms that undergirded its research and partnership activities.

Organizational Structure

The seeds for Atlanta 323 were codeveloped initially by leaders and researchers in the uni-

versity and the school district. Both had active relationships with local ECE providers in the community. However, the university and school district had existing infrastructure that could serve as a backbone to formalize the partnership. Specifically, the Atlanta Educational Research Board was formed in 2012 as a comprehensive research partnership between the Atlanta Public Schools and Georgia State University to develop and enact a shared research agenda to benefit the children of Atlanta. The board was formally established in 2014 and was supported by both the superintendent of the school district and the dean of the College of Education and Human Development at the university.

One of the board's first partnership projects was Atlanta 323—a research alliance between the university, the school district, early learning providers, and community organizations focused on Atlanta's P3 early learning system. Organizationally, the partnership was led equally by the university, the school district, and the largest ECE and Head Start providers in the area, with leadership in each entity securing funding and resources; setting the research agenda; attending regular meetings, sharing data, communicating findings; and using results to inform collaborative programs, initiatives, and policies. Community organizations such as the United Way of Greater Atlanta and the Georgia Early Education Alliance for Ready Students (GEEARS), provided support and direction as advisors, connectors, and champions of the partnership.

The point person for each Atlanta 323 partner was a leader and decision-maker in his or her organization and identified a designee who could step in if needed. Engaging with these practitioners regularly helped to ensure that the partnership activities remained a priority for each organization. It also facilitated partners' use of the research findings to inform their programs, practices, and policies. One challenge, however, was that these individuals were quite busy. In order to facilitate continuous focused attention to the partnership, Atlanta 323 meetings were embedded within existing committees, meetings, and other engagements that were already organized by the partners. One unintended benefit of this approach was that Atlanta 323 became a familiar agenda item for other people in the organization, thereby elevating perceptions of its importance to each partner organization.

Initially, the university took responsibility for managing and implementing partnership and research activities, because it had existing resources in place to support them, including developing data-sharing agreements, establishing compliance for research with human subjects, and software and systems to house and analyze data. These supports allowed all partners to focus first on the work of the partnership, while building capacity in all organizations for RPP work. Partnership and data-sharing agreements were developed between the university and each partner organization to formalize their engagement in Atlanta 323.

Building Infrastructure and Capacity to Generate and Use Research

In 2016, Atlanta 323 received funding from the Institute of Education Sciences and the Spencer Foundation to launch new research activities focused on one of the critical stages in the evolution of a P3 system: developing the research infrastructure to utilize data to inform programmatic, practice, and policy decisions (Kagan & Kauerz, 2012). Specifically, researchers and practitioners worked collaboratively to build an integrated longitudinal database linking school readiness data from ECE providers with K–3 student achievement data from the school district to examine student pathways from preschool through third grade. Importantly, Atlanta 323 was designed explicitly to address disparities in young children's access to and opportunities for quality of early experiences, particularly children growing up in historically and systemically marginalized schools and communities. Partners sought to create equitable processes (e.g., including leaders from ECE Head Start providers and the school district) and systems (e.g., integrated database and tools to support use) to achieve equitable student outcomes (e.g., school readiness and early school achievement).

Data-driven decision making was also central to Atlanta 323's research and partnership activities. Partners in the school district and ECE centers articulated the need to better understand children's early learning experiences before they entered kindergarten, and existing data systems were inadequate to support data utilization practices among school leaders and teachers (Guss, Norris, Horm, Monroe, & Wolfe, 2013; Hamre, LoCasale-Crouch, & Pianta, 2008). Research evidence indicates that teachers' use of both observational data on classroom instruction and student performance data encourages reflective practice that results in changes in instructional practices and improvements in student behavior and achievement (Connors et al., 2021; Crawford, Zucker, Williams, Bhavsar, & Landry, 2013). However, little empirical evidence is available on positive relations between data utilization at the P3 systems level and student readiness and education outcomes. Few P3 integrated data systems exist that would allow for these kinds of analyses and strategic actions (Fantuzzo & Culhane, 2009).

With its focus on achieving equity for children in historically and systemically marginalized communities, Atlanta 323 served as an important first step in understanding the varied pathways young children were experiencing from preK to third grade. This capacity building was equally important for all partners, because it facilitated both the infrastructure and decision-making processes necessary to engage in improvement efforts (Booker et al., 2019; Bryk, Gomez, Grunow, & LeMahieu, 2015; Farrell, Wentworth, et al., 2021). Processes, mechanisms, and tools were created to gather, manage, store, and analyze data, such as a shared codebook with information on data collected within each organization; syntax for linking and analyzing data in statistical software packages; and trainings on how to formulate research questions and design studies to answer priority questions with varying degrees of rigor and relevance. Processes, mechanisms, and tools were also created to help partners better understand the data that they collected regularly on children, classrooms, and families, and make informed decisions for improvements with and across organizations, such as shared research agendas and governance structure; standing meetings and shared events; assigned roles and responsibilities; and briefs, reports, and presentations that were used to communicate about findings and the partnership internally between partners and externally with stakeholders. By building an integrated, longitudinal P3 database, partners created a foundational resource on which to create and sustain a research agenda and partnership structures.

Developing a Research Agenda

An important "proof point" for the integrated database was its ability to provide reliable, valid descriptive information on children in Atlanta's P3 ecosystem. Although researchers often prioritize complex and rigorous analyses to answer research questions that produce generalizable knowledge, practitioners often value simple, descriptive analyses that can help them communicate with their stakeholders (Booker et al., 2019; Farley-Ripple, May, Karpyn, Tilley, & McDonough, 2018). Thus, partners requested descriptive studies that would serve as a baseline for Atlanta 323's research and practice activities moving forward.

Early studies focused on comparisons between three groups of students: those who attended Georgia's PreK in the school district, those who attended Georgia's PreK with ECE partners (who were all also Head Start providers), and those who attended neither (their PreK experiences were unknown). Therefore, we organized our research activities to answer three sets of questions: (1) PreK performance and kindergarten readiness (e.g., How ready were children when they enter PreK and kindergarten, and did it vary by PreK experience?); (2) PreK gains (e.g., What gains in specific readiness indicators are observed among students, and do they vary by PreK experience?); and (3) achievement in kindergarten and first grade (e.g., Do achievement and transition patterns of students in kindergarten and first grade vary by PreK experience?).

Getting and Using Data

To answer these questions, researchers at the university worked to link administratively available demographic, readiness, academic achievement, and behavioral data on students from PreK through first grade. All sources of information came from existing data that were housed by the school district or ECE providers. All students in Georgia's PreK and public schools are assigned Georgia Testing Identification numbers during enrollment. Therefore, partners were able to track students from the different Georgia's PreK programs to the school district. However, this process was not without challenges. For example, sometimes students were assigned different numbers when they transitioned between sites, between districts, or to kindergarten. In addition, both the ECE providers and the school district had multiple identification numbers for students that were held in multiple data management systems that were managed by different offices within the organization. Some of these identification numbers were assigned at enrollment, others corresponded to specific programs

and accountability process, and still others were assigned for different purposes.

There were also challenges associated with data quality and availability and with assessment tools. For example, many ECE providers did not have systems available to archive their PreK data. Student performance data that were available in both hard copy and in electronic formats were often purged at the end of reporting periods. In some cases, data were available but housed in disparate hard copy and electronic files. Much of the assessment data had to be entered manually into Excel spreadsheets, increasing both the opportunity for error and the time between data gathering and data reporting. Finally, although multiple assessments were used to measure student progress in PreK through first grade, there was not a singular assessment that was utilized across all partners and for each grade level. In addition, indicators for common demographic categories were often derived from different metrics. For instance, indicators for family income were captured by participation in free and reduced lunch programs in the school district, and by participation in income-based social services programs in the ECE centers.

Finally, differences in processes for program delivery and assessment complicated data quality for research. For example, services for students with disabilities were governed with individualized family service plans (IFSPs) in ECE centers and individualized education plans (IEPs) in the school district. Children often transitioned from IFSPs to IEPs at some point during the PreK year as they began to receive services from the district. This transition requires physical systems that capture these changes in real time and communicate them within and across the ECE centers and school district—a challenge for both partners to achieve. For research, the result is a large amount of missing data on students, about whom the partnership is seeking to make evidence-informed decisions.

These challenges related to data are not uncommon in ECE and require research partners to provide significant support to build research infrastructure and capacity in the partnership (Jordan, King, Banghart, & Nugent, 2018; Jordan, Schultz, & King, 2015; King et al., 2016). For Atlanta 323, supervised doctoral students at the university served as data strategists for each agency. The students interfaced with points of contact at the school district and ECE providers on a regular basis to clean and cull data into a combined dataset.

This process took place over 3 years—another threat to the partnership. Partners worked collaboratively to pose high-leverage, relevant questions. There was a clear sense of urgency to get the answers quickly, so that they could be used to advocate for significant changes within their organizations. In order to address their concerns without compromising the integrity of the database, researchers worked with partners to share results from preliminary analyses that could inform more immediate decisions. They also helped the partner agencies with their own independent data analyses, providing coaching and technical assistance as staff within the school district and the ECE centers began to explore their own data in new ways in response to activities within Atlanta 323. Partners also appreciated opportunities to provide feedback on the data, both to confirm or challenge preexisting notions about the data and to prepare to communicate about the data with external stakeholders.

Eventually, these efforts yielded a data file and codebook that contained information on students enrolled in the school district and ECE centers during the 2014–2019 academic years from PreK to third grade. However, only data from the 2017–2019 academic years were available from the partner ECE providers. Thus, initial analyses included data only for children from PreK to first grade, who represented two cohorts of Atlanta 323 students.

Initial Research Findings

In order to answer the research questions, separate sets of analyses were conducted, based on available data for the student measures. Analyses related to PreK readiness used data from the state-mandated, performance-based measure: Work Sampling Online (WSO). Scores represented teacher ratings of children's performance on seven developmental domains in the fall and spring of the PreK year, including arts, language, math, personal and social development, physical development, science, and social studies. Each item was rated on a 3-point scale: *not yet, in process,* or *proficient.* Analyses included only students for whom the assessment was completed during fall and spring.

Analyses related to achievement in kindergarten and first grade used data from STAR 360 Early Literacy, Reading, and Math Assessments

(STAR) given to elementary students across the district. Scores represented student performance on the computer adaptive, standardized assessments given to kindergarten and first-grade children three times a year. These analyses focused on the Atlanta 323 partners as a group, because partners were interested in making collaborative decisions about how to support students who matriculated from their programs into the school district. Therefore, students who completed Georgia's PreK at an Atlanta 323 site (either in the school district or in an ECE center) were included in the Atlanta 323 group in these analyses. All other kindergarten and first-grade students in the school district, whose early learning experiences were unknown, were included in the comparison group, referred to as the non-A323 group.

Partners gained important insights about areas of strength and improvement in their shared P3 ecosystem. For example, the data revealed that, collectively, Atlanta 323's partners served a largely Black student population in PreK (68% of the sample), with most students growing up in poverty or low-income households. Less than 10% of students in the sample were identified with disabilities or as emerging bilingual leaners, who primarily spoke a language other than English at home. Disaggregated data showed few to no differences between teacher's initial ratings of student proficiency on the WSO by gender or race. However, ratings differed at the end of PreK, with average teacher ratings for White students being higher than those for Black and Latinx students. Gains for emerging bilinguals were comparable to other groups; however, they did not gain enough to close achievement gaps between their performance and that of their peers. On average, across all Atlanta 323 partners, students ended PreK rated proficient on approximately 71% of WSO items.

Analyses for students in kindergarten and first grade revealed that those who attended Georgia's PreK at an Atlanta 323 partner site were more likely to be Black, to be growing up in low-income households, and to have an IEP. On average, Atlanta 323 students entered kindergarten performing below the 50th percentile on the STAR Early Literacy subtest. However, by the end of kindergarten, over 80% of students were performing at or above the 50th percentile; by the end of first grade, only about half of the students were performing at this level. Disaggregated data revealed that among Black students and students growing up in low-income households, those who attended Georgia's PreK at an Atlanta 323 partner site entered and exited kindergarten and first grade with stronger STAR Early Literacy performance than their peers who did not.

Finally, because many students in the school district transitioned to kindergarten from one of the partner ECE providers, partners were interested in developing strategies aligned to students' physical transition patterns. Four comparison groups were established by PreK provider (the school district or ECE center) and by distance. For students who attended Georgia's PreK in an elementary school in the district, groups were defined as transitioning to kindergarten in the same building or between buildings. For students who attended Georgia's PreK in one of the ECE partner sites, the two groups were defined by a distance of less than or more than 5 miles from the elementary school where the student enrolled. Within the sample, the majority of students transitioned from PreK to kindergarten in the same building, with relatively equal numbers transitioning from another school in the district or from an ECE center within 5 miles of their elementary school. Average STAR Early Literacy scores for students who transitioned within the school district (either the same school building or between school buildings) were significantly higher than those of students who transitioned from partner PreK sites.

Using the Results to Make Decisions

The analyses revealed several key findings, some that affirmed the partners' assumptions about their students and others that were unexpected. All were helpful for making decisions about next steps for the partnership and for Atlanta's emerging P3 ecosystem. The organizational, infrastructure, and capacity-building activities helped partners grow in their ability to act on the research evidence they generated collectively and collaboratively. The findings led to recommendations for partner organizations related to investments in data stewardship; addressing disparities in performance outcomes for specific subgroups; disparities between teacher ratings and student performance for specific subgroups; supporting the transition from PreK to kindergarten for students who attend Georgia's PreK outside of the school district but within feeder patterns to local elementary schools; and examining efforts to maintain achievement gains beyond kindergarten.

Some of these recommendations were acted upon immediately. For example, one ECE partner hired its first director of research. Another was encouraged to share strategies used across the organization's ECE centers to promote school readiness and strong transitions to kindergarten for Black children and families. The school district launched a common PreK enrollment process and transportation services, so that access to high-quality programming was not limited by the neighborhood in which a family lived. Finally, the school district and one of the ECE providers teamed up to focus their transition efforts in one geographic cluster of elementary schools where many students matriculated from PreK in local ECE centers.

Other recommendations were addressed over time as decisions about where to take the partnership beyond its initial launching period were informed by challenges and opportunities within the current educational context in the city. Before Atlanta 323, there were few spaces and opportunities to have these conversations between community ECE centers and the school district. Atlanta 323 gave partners the opportunity to build trusting relationships and strategize around child and family needs in planful ways. In this way, Atlanta 323 provided a proof-point that various agencies across the city could engage productively in joint research and practice activities. However, partners changed as new leaders came on board in the university, school district, community organizations, and the city. The funding landscape also changed, as local private foundations became interested in how the partnership could inform their investments in ECE. Eventually, what emerged was an RPP model that is now embedded in a citywide alliance of agencies working to support high-quality learning and education for children in Atlanta from birth to age 5, aptly named Promise that All Atlanta Children Thrive (PAACT). PAACT has scaled many of Atlanta 323's initial activities to include an array of early learning programs and initiatives, with a recent $5 million investment from the city of Atlanta and considerable philanthropic investments.

Future Directions

Many have argued that education RPPs like Atlanta 323 present a promising strategy to support research and evidence use to improve educational practices, organizational learning, and outcomes (Penuel, Riedy, et al., 2020; Tseng, Fleischman, & Quintero, 2018; Tseng & Nutley, 2014; Wentworth et al., 2017). However, the challenges and opportunities of RPPs to inform research and practice could not be more acute than in the ECE space. On the one hand, interest, expertise, data, programming, and policies are all available to examine outcomes and make decisions to support high-leverage changes for children. On the other hand, significant human, social, and fiscal investments are required to create infrastructure, build capacity, and implement research and practice processes across multiple sectors that engage in ECE. Our experiences with Atlanta 323 certainly reflect these challenges and opportunities.

However, systematic inquiry through rigorous research on the RPP, in and of itself, is limited for Atlanta 323 and many other RPPs. Evidence on education RPPs is just emerging (Coburn & Penuel, 2016; Farrell et al., 2022; Penuel, Riedy, et al., 2020). Studies have focused on the effects of interventions developed with RPPs (e.g., Booth et al., 2015; Snow, Lawrence, & White, 2009; Yarnall, Shechtman, & Penuel, 2006) and dynamics and mechanisms in the partnership structure that support access to and use of research to make decisions (Allensworth, 2015; Coburn, Toure, & Yamashita, 2009; Honig, Venkateswaran, & McNeil, 2017; Hubbard, 2010). However, much of the research on RPPs has not been grounded in theory or carried out systematically in ways that identify critical components and strategies, compare different kinds of partnerships, delineate intended and unintended outcomes, establish causal relations between these factors, or specify conditions to promote effectiveness (Coburn & Penuel, 2016; Farrell et al., 2022; Henrick, Cobb, Penuel, Jackson, & Clark, 2017; Scott et al., 2017).

Specifically, for RPPs in ECE, more empirical evidence is needed on the infrastructure and routines of research and practice partners; the beliefs, knowledge, and skills of individuals on both the practice and research sides and how they interact with partnership outcomes and dynamics; the decision-making processes and experiences around data and knowledge utilization; and the political contexts that influence funding, power differentials, competing priorities, and other external forces on partnerships. These kinds of advances will require investments in the research, as well as the partnerships. However, doing so will create a broader evidence base for whom and under what conditions early childhood education RPPs can deliver on their potential to use research to ensure that all of children have a seamless, high-quality pathway from birth to early schooling and beyond.

Acknowledgments

This work was supported in part by funding from the Spencer Foundation (201700094) and the Institute of Education Sciences (R305H170054). The opinions expressed are ours and do not represent views of the funding agencies. We would like to thank the teachers, leaders, children, and families who participated in this project, without whom this research would not have been possible.

References

Allensworth, E. (2015). The use of ninth-grade early warning indicators to improve Chicago schools. *Journal of Education for Students Placed at Risk, 18*(1/2), 68–83.

Barnett, W. S. (2011). Effectiveness of early educational intervention. *Science, 333*(6045), 975–978.

Booker, L., Conaway, C., & Schwartz, N. (2019). *Five ways RPPs can fail and how to avoid them: Applying conceptual frameworks to improve RPPs.* William T. Grant Foundation.

Booth, J. L., Cooper, L. A., Donovan, M. S., Huyghe, A., Koedinger, K., & Pare-Blagoev, E. J. (2015). Design-based research within the constraints of practice: AlgebraByExample. *Journal of Education for Students Placed at Risk, 20*(1/2), 79–100.

Bruner, C. (2012). A systems approach to young children's healthy development and readiness for school. In S. L. Kagan & K. Kauerz (Eds.), *Early childhood systems: Transforming early learning* (pp. 35–40). Teachers College Press.

Bruno, E. P., & Iruka, I. U. (2022). Reexamining the Carolina Abecedarian Project using an antiracist perspective: Implications for early care and education research. *Early Childhood Research Quarterly, 58*, 165–176.

Bryk, A. S., Gomez, L. M., Grunow, A., & LeMahieu, P. G. (2015). *Learning to improve: How America's schools can get better at getting better.* Harvard Education Press.

Burchinal, M., Carr, R. C., Vernon-Feagans, L., Blair, C., Cox, M., & Family Life Project Key Investigators. (2018). Depth, persistence, and timing of poverty and the development of school readiness skills in rural low-income regions: Results from the family life project. *Early Childhood Research Quarterly, 45*, 115–130.

Cabrera, N. J., & the SRCD Ethnic and Racial Issues Committee. (2013). Positive development of minority children. *Social Policy Report, 27*(2), 1–22.

Chicago Beyond. (2019). Why am I always being researched?: A guidebook for community organizations, researchers, and funders to help us get from insufficient understanding to more authentic truth. Retrieved from *https://chicagobeyond. org/researchequity*.

Coburn, C. E., & Penuel, W. R. (2016). Research–practice partnerships in education: Outcomes, dynamics, and open questions. *Educational Researcher, 45*(1), 48–54.

Coburn, C. E., Penuel, W. R., & Geil, K. E. (2013). *Research–practice partnerships: A strategy for leveraging research for educational improvement in school districts*. William T. Grant Foundation.

Coburn, C. E., Toure, J., & Yamashita, M. (2009). Evidence, interpretation, and persuasion: Instructional decision making at the district central office. *Teachers College Record, 111*(4), 1115–1161.

Connors, M. C., Pacchiano, D. M., Stein, A. G., & Swartz, M. I. (2021). Building capacity for research and practice: A partnership approach. *The Future of Children, 31*, 119–136.

Crawford, A. D., Zucker, T. A., Williams, J. M., Bhavsar, V., & Landry, S. H. (2013). Initial validation of the prekindergarten Classroom Observation Tool and goal setting system for data-based coaching. *School Psychology Quarterly, 28*(4), 277–300.

Diamond, J. B. (2021). *Racial Equity and Research–Practice Partnerships 2.0: A critical reflection*. William T. Grant Foundation.

Donovan, M. S., Snow, C. E., & Huyghe, A. (2021). Differentiating research–practice partnerships: Affordances, constraints, criteria, and strategies for achieving success. *Studies in Educational Evaluation, 71*, Article 101083.

Duncan, G., Dowsett, C., Classens, A., Magnuson, K., Huston, A., Klebanov, P., . . . Japel, C. (2007). School readiness and later achievement. *Developmental Psychology, 43*, 1428–1446.

Edwards, E. B., Terry, N. P., Bingham, G. E., & Singer, J. L. (2021). Perceptions of classroom quality and well-being among Black women teachers of young children. *Education Policy Analysis Archives, 29*, Article 56.

Ewen, D., & Herzfeldt-Kamprath, R. (2016). Examining quality across the preschool-to-third-grade continuum. Available at *https://cdn.americanprogress.org/wp-content/ uploads/2016/01/07110047/pre-3_accessto-quality.pdf*.

Fantuzzo, J., & Culhane, D. (2009). *Kids integrated data system*. University of Pennsylvania Graduate School of Education, School of Social Policy and Practice Bulletin.

Farley-Ripple, E., May, H., Karpyn, A., Tilley, K., & McDonough, K. (2018). Rethinking connections between research and practice in education: A conceptual framework. *Educational Researcher, 47*(4), 235–245.

Farrell, C. C., Penuel, W. R., Allen, A., Anderson, E. R., Bohannon, A. X., Coburn, C. E., & Brown, S. L. (2022). Learning at the boundaries of research and practice: A framework for understanding research–practice partnerships. *Educational Researcher, 51*(3), 197–208.

Farrell, C. C., Penuel, W. R., Coburn, C. E., Daniel, J., & Steup, L. (2021). *Research–practice partnerships in education: The state of the field*. Spencer Foundation/W.T. Grant Foundation.

Farrell, C. C., Wentworth, L., & Nayfack, M. (2021). What are the conditions under which research–practice partnerships succeed? *Phi Delta Kappan, 102*(7), 38–41.

Friedman-Krauss, A., Barnett, S., & Nores, M. (2016). How much can high-quality universal pre-K reduce achievement gaps? Available at *https://cdn.americanprogress.org/wp-content/ uploads/2016/04/01115656/nieer-achievement-gaps-report.pdf*.

Guss, S., Norris, D. J., Horm, D. M., Monroe, L. A., & Wolfe, V. (2013). Lessons learned about data utilization from classroom observations. *Early Education and Development, 24*(1), 4–18.

Hamre, B. K., LoCasale-Crouch, J., & Pianta, R. (2008). Formative assessment of classrooms: Using classroom observations to improve implementation quality. In L. M. Justice & C. Vukelich (Eds.), *Achieving excellence in preschool literacy instruction* (pp. 102–119). Guilford Press.

Heckman, J. J., Moon, S. H., Pinto, R., Savelyev, P. A., & Yavitz, A. (2010). The rate of return to the High Scope Perry Preschool Program. *Journal of Public Economics, 94*(1), 114–128.

Henrick, E. C., Cobb, P., Penuel, W. R., Jackson, K., & Clark, T. (2017). *Assessing research–practice partnerships: Five dimensions of effectiveness*. William T. Grant Foundation.

Hong, S. H., Yazejian, N., Guss, S., Stein, A., Connors, C., Horm, D., & Kainz, K. (2019). Broadening the definition of collaboration in early care and education. *Early Education and Development, 30*, 1084–1093.

Honig, M. I., Venkateswaran, N., & McNeil, P. (2017). Research use as learning: The case of fundamental change in school district central offices. *American Educational Research Journal, 54*(5), 938–971.

Hubbard, L. (2010). Research to practice: The case of Boston Public Schools, Education Matters and the Boston Plan for Excellence. In C. E. Coburn & M. K. Stein (Eds.), *Research and practice in education: Building alliances, bridging the divide* (pp. 55–72). Rowman & Littlefield.

Iruka, I. U., Curenton, S. M., & Gardner, S. (2015). How changes in home and neighborhood environment factors are related to change in Black children's academic and social development from kindergarten to third grade. *Journal of Negro Education, 84*(3), 282–297.

Iruka, I. U., Curenton, S. M., Sims, J., Blitch, K. A., & Gardner, S. (2020). Factors associated with early school readiness profiles for Black girls. *Early Childhood Research Quarterly, 51,* 215–228.

Jordan, E., King, C., Banghart, P., & Nugent, C. (2018). Improving the lives of young children through data. Retrieved from *www.childtrends. org/wp-content/uploads/2019/09/ecdc_kidscount_ecids_report.pdf.*

Jordan, E., Schultz, T., & King, C. (2015). Linking Head Start data with state early care and education coordinated data systems. Retrieved from *www.childtrends.org/wp-content/uploads/ 2015/03/ecdc-head-start-brief.pdf.*

Kagan, S. L., & Kauerz, K. (2012). Early childhood systems: Looking deep, wide, and far. In S. L. Kagan & K. Kauerz (Eds.), *Early childhood systems: Transforming early learning* (pp. 3–17). Teachers College Press.

King, C., Epstein, D., Maxwell, K. L., Lin, V. K., Abrams, J., Hutchison, L., & Burgess, K. (2016). Strength in numbers: Supporting quality improvement in early care and education programs using linked administrative data. Retrieved from *https://aspe.hhs.gov/sites/ default/files/migrated_legacy_files//153746/ strengthinnumbersfullreport.pdf.*

Lipsey, M. W., Farran, D. C., & Durkin, K. (2018). Effects of the Tennessee Prekindergarten Program on children's achievement and behavior through third grade. *Early Childhood Research Quarterly, 45,* 155–178.

Magnuson, K. A., & Waldfogel, J. (2005). Early childhood care and education: Effects on ethnic and racial gaps in school readiness. *The Future of Children, 15,* 169–196.

Maxwell, K. L., & Clifford, R. M. (2004). School readiness assessment. *Young Children, 59*(1), 42–46.

McCabe, L. A., & Sipple, J. W. (2011). Colliding worlds: Practical and political tensions of prekindergarten implementation in public schools. *Educational Policy, 25,* e1–e26.

Meisels, S. J., Marden, D. B., Jablon, J. R., & Dichtelmiller, M. (2011). *Work Sampling System* (WSS, 5th ed.). Pearson.

National Research Council. (1999). *Improving student learning: A strategic plan for education research and its utilization.* National Academies Press.

Nores, M., & Barnett, W. (2014). Access to high quality early care and education: Readiness and opportunity gaps in America. Available at *http:// ceelo.org/wp-content/uploads/2014/05/ceelo_ policy_report_access_quality_ece.pdf.*

Penuel, W. R., Allen, A., Coburn, C. E., & Farrell, C. (2015). Conceptualizing research–practice partnerships as joint work at boundaries. *JESPAR: Journal of Education for Students Placed at Risk, 20,* 182–197.

Penuel, W. R., Farrell, C. C., Anderson, E. A., Coburn, C. E., Allen, A.-R., Bohannon, A. X., . . . Brown, S. (2020). *A comparative, descriptive study of three research-practice partnerships: Goals, activities, and influence on district policy, practice, and decision making* (Technical Report No. 4). National Center for Research in Policy and Practice.

Penuel, W. R., Riedy, R., Barber, M. S., Peurach, D. J., LeBouef, W. A., & Clark, T. (2020). Principles of collaborative education research with stakeholders: Toward requirements for a new research and development infrastructure. *Review of Educational Research, 90*(5), 627–674.

Pianta, R. C., & Kraft-Sayre, M. (2003). *Successful kindergarten transition: Your guide to connecting children, families, and schools.* Brookes.

Reynolds, A. J. (2003). The added value of continuing early intervention into the primary grades. In A. J. Reynolds, M. C. Wang, & H. J. Walberg (Eds.), *Early childhood programs for a new century.* Child Welfare League of America Press.

Reynolds, A. J., Magnuson, K., & Ou, S. (2006). P-3 Education: Programs and practices that work in children's first decade. Available at *http://fcdus.org/sites/default/files/programsandpractices. pdf.*

Schilder, D. E., Broadstone, M., & Curenton, S. M. (2017). Special issue: Early care and education collaboration. *Early Education and Development, 28*(8), 1072–1074.

Scott, J., DeBray, E., Lubienski, C., La Londe, P. G., Castillo, E., & Owens, S. (2017). Urban regimes, intermediary organization networks, and research use: Patterns across three school districts. *Peabody Journal of Education, 92*(1), 16–28.

Snow C. (2014). Rigor and realism: Doing educational science in the real world. *Educational Researcher, 44*(9), 460–466.

Snow, C. E., Lawrence, J., & White, C. (2009). Generating knowledge of academic language among urban middle school students. *Journal of Research on Educational Effectiveness, 2*(4), 325–344.

Tseng, V., Fleischman, S., & Quintero, E. (2018). Democratizing evidence in education. In B. Bevan & W. R. Penuel (Eds.), *Connecting research and practice for educational improvement: Ethical and equitable approaches* (pp. 3–16). Routledge.

Tseng, V., & Nutley, S. (2014). Building infrastructure to improve the use and usefulness of research in education. In K. S. Finnigan & A. J. Daly (Eds.), *Using research evidence in education: From the schoolhouse door to Capitol Hill* (pp. 163–176). Springer.

Yarnall, L., Shechtman, N., & Penuel, W. R. (2006). Using handheld computers to support improved classroom assessment in science: Results from a field trial. *Journal of Science Education and Technology, 15*(2), 142–158.

Yazejian, N., Bryant, D. M., Hans, S., Horm, D., St. Clair, L., File, N., & Burchinal, M. (2017). Child and parenting outcomes after 1 year of Educare. *Child Development, 88*(5), 1671–1688.

Yoshikawa, H., Weiland, C., Brooks-Gunn, J., Burchinal, M. R., Espinosa, L. M., Gormley, W. T., . . . Zaslow, M. (2013). *Investing in our future: The evidence base on preschool education.* Society for Research in Child Development and Foundation for Child Development.

Wentworth, L., Mazzeo, C., & Connolly, F. (2017). Research practice partnerships: A strategy for promoting evidence-based decision-making in education. *Educational Research, 59*(2), 241–255.

Wilson, C. M. (2021). *Research–practice partnerships for racially just school communities.* William T. Grant Foundation.

Index